Lecture Notes in Artificial Intelligence   3538

Edited by J. G. Carbonell and J. Siekmann

Subseries of Lecture Notes in Computer Science

Liliana Ardissono   Paul Brna
Antonija Mitrovic (Eds.)

User Modeling
2005

10th International Conference, UM 2005
Edinburgh, Scotland, UK, July 24-29, 2005
Proceedings

 Springer

Series Editors

Jaime G. Carbonell, Carnegie Mellon University, Pittsburgh, PA, USA
Jörg Siekmann, University of Saarland, Saarbrücken, Germany

Volume Editors

Liliana Ardissono
Università di Torino
Dipartimento di Informatica
Corso Svizzera 185, 10149 Torino, Italy
E-mail: liliana@di.unito.it

Paul Brna
University of Glasgow
The SCRE Centre
St Andrew's Building, 11 Eldon Street, Glasgow G3 6NH, UK
E-mail: Paul.Brna@scre.ac.uk

Antonija Mitrovic
University of Canterbury
Dept. of Computer Science and Software Engineering
Private Bag 4800, Christchurch, New Zealand
E-mail: tanja@cosc.canterbury.ac.nz

Library of Congress Control Number: 2005928952

CR Subject Classification (1998): H.5.2, I.2, H.5, H.4, I.6, J.4, J.5, K.4, K.6

ISSN   0302-9743
ISBN-10   3-540-27885-0 Springer Berlin Heidelberg New York
ISBN-13   978-3-540-27885-6 Springer Berlin Heidelberg New York

Springer is a part of Springer Science+Business Media

springeronline.com

© Springer-Verlag Berlin Heidelberg 2005
Printed in Germany

Typesetting: Camera-ready by author, data conversion by Scientific Publishing Services, Chennai, India
Printed on acid-free paper   SPIN: 11527886   06/3142   5 4 3 2 1 0

Preface

The papers presented within this volume represent current work in the exciting area of user modeling — an area that promises much to a range of economic and socially beneficial activities. The potential is enormous, and the applications of the technologies that have been developed are increasingly ambitious and relevant to the needs of the 21st century. The editors hope you enjoy, and benefit from, reading the papers within these proceedings.

The International User Modeling Conferences represent the central forum for the discussion and presentation of research and industry results in the development of personalized systems, as well as basic research about personalization. In the last 25 years, the field of user modeling has produced significant new theories and methods to analyze and model computer users in short- and long-term interactions. Moreover, methods for personalizing human-computer interaction based on user models have been successfully developed, applied and evaluated in a number of domains, such as information filtering, e-commerce, adaptive natural language and adaptive educational systems. New user modeling topics are emerging, including adaptation to user attitudes and affective states, personalized interaction in mobile, ubiquitous and context-aware computing and in user interactions with embodied autonomous agents. User modeling research is being influenced by different fields, such as artificial intelligence, human-computer interaction, cognitive psychology, linguistics and education, as well as by newly emerging links with Customer Relationship Management and technologies for communication on the Web, such as Web Services and the Semantic Web.

The 10th International Conference on User Modeling (UM 2005), held in Edinburgh, Scotland, UK, on 24–29 July, 2005, is the latest in a conference series begun in 1986, and follows recent meetings in Johnstown (2003), Sonthofen (2001), Banff (1999), Sardinia (1997), Hawaii (1996) and Cape Cod (1994). UM 2005 included 3 invited lectures, 33 full paper presentations, 30 poster presentations, 12 Doctoral Consortium presentations, 9 workshops and 2 tutorials. The conference received 139 paper submissions and 21 poster submissions with a 23% full paper acceptance rate, which is in line with previous UM conferences and guaranteed a high-quality program. The conference had a strongly international flavor — as indicated by the distribution of accepted papers (posters): Europe 14 (16), North America 12 (11), Australia/New Zealand 3 (0), Asia 4 (0), South America 0 (3). There were also 42 Doctoral Consortium submissions.

This volume includes the abstracts of the invited lectures and the texts of the papers, posters and Doctoral Consortium articles selected for presentation in the main conference program, which was enriched by the following joint events:

Tutorials:

Creating Adaptive Web-Based Applications, by Paul De Bra, Computer Science Department, Eindhoven University of Technology

Adaptable Interfaces Through Recommender Systems, by John Riedl, University of Minnesota

Workshops:

W1: Adapting the Interaction Style to Affective Factors, organized by Sandra Carberry and Fiorella de Rosis

W2: Decentralized, Agent-Based and Social Approaches to User Modeling (DASUM), organized by Julita Vassileva and Peter Dolog

W3: Evaluation of Adaptive Systems (EAS), organized by Stephan Weibelzahl, Alexandros Paramythis and Judith Masthoff

W4: Machine Learning for User Modeling: Challenges, organized by Colin de la Higuera

W5: PROLEARN: Personalized Adaptive Technologies for Professional Training, organized by Marcus Specht

W6: Personalisation for eHealth, organized by Floriana Grasso, Silvana Quaglini, Cecile Paris, Alison Cawsey and Ross Wilkinson

W7: Personalized Information Access, organized by Peter Brusilovsky, Andreas Nuernberger and Charles Callaway

W8: Personalization on the Semantic Web (PerSWeb), organized by Lora Aroyo, Vania Dimitrova and Judy Kay

W9: Privacy-Enhanced Personalization, organized by Alfred Kobsa and Lorrie Cranor

UM 2005 was hosted by Heriot-Watt University under the auspices of User Modeling, Inc. Sponsors included Universitá di Torino, the University of Canterbury, the University of Glasgow, Heriot-Watt University, the University of Edinburgh, Leeds University, the University of Delaware, York University and Robert Gordon University. We are especially thankful for the sponsorship of Microsoft Research, Springer GmbH, which provided support for the Best Paper award, and the James Chen family for sponsoring the Best Student Paper awards.

We would like to thank all the members of the Program Committee, who supported us in the selection of papers and who provided insightful comments to help the authors improve their contributions. Many thanks to the additional reviewers, acknowledged in this volume, who supported the Program Committee members with their revision work. We would especially like to thank Alison Cawsey, Vania Dimitrova, Kathleen McCoy, Kalina Bontcheva, Jon Oberlander, Daniel Kudenko, Ayse Goker, Nicolas Van Labeke and Helen Pain. Also, many thanks to Brent Martin for his help with CyberChair, Paul Irvine for his superb graphics skills and his excellent designs for the conference, and Jon Lewin for his Acrobat skills, and all those persons, including the authors, who gave their time to make the event a success and these proceedings a reality.

May 2005   Liliana Ardissono, Università di Torino, Italy
                                              Paul Brna, University of Glasgow, UK
                                  Tanja Mitrovic, University of Canterbury, New Zealand

Organization

UM 2005 was organized by the Department of Computer Science, Heriot-Watt University in cooperation with UM, Inc.

Executive Committee

Conference Chair	Paul Brna, University of Glasgow, UK
Program Co-chairs	Liliana Ardissono, Università di Torino, Italy
	Antonija Mitrovic, University of Canterbury, New Zealand
Organizing Chair	Alison Cawsey, Heriot-Watt University, UK
Workshop and Tutorial	Kathleen McCoy, University of Delaware, USA
Co-chairs	Vania Dimitrova, Leeds University, UK
Doctoral Consortium Co-chairs	Jon Oberlander, University of Edinburgh, UK
	Kalina Bontcheva, Sheffield University, UK
Sponsorship Chair:	Daniel Kudenko, York University, UK
Publicity Co-chairs:	Ayse Goker, Robert Gordon University, UK
	Nicolas Van Labeke, University of Glasgow, UK

Program Committee

Lora Aroyo, The Netherlands
Mathias Bauer, Germany
Joseph Beck, USA
Peter Brusilovsky, USA
Susan Bull, UK
Sandra Carberry, USA
Noelle Carbonell, France
Keith Cheverst, UK
David Chin, USA
Luca Chittaro, Italy
Cristina Conati, Canada
Albert Corbett, USA
Paul De Bra, The Netherlands
Nadja De Carolis, Italy
Fiorella de Rosis, Italy
Vania Dimitrova, UK
Peter Dolog, Germany
Gerhard Fischer, USA

Elena Gaudioso, Spain
Piotr Gmytrasiewicz, USA
Brad Goodman, USA
Jim Greer, Canada
Haym Hirsh, USA
Eric Horvitz, USA
Anthony Jameson, Germany
Gal Kaminka, Israel
Judy Kay, Australia
Alfred Kobsa, USA
Joseph Konstan, USA
Antonio Krueger, Germany
Frank Linton, USA
Diane Litman, USA
Brent Martin, New Zealand
Mark Maybury, USA
Gordon McCalla, Canada
Kathleen McCoy, USA

Eva Millan, Spain
Riichiro Mizoguchi, Japan
Wolfgang Nejdl, Germany
Helen Pain, UK
George Paliouras, Greece
Cecile Paris, Australia
Daniela Petrelli, UK
Candy Sidner, USA
Barry Smyth, Ireland

Markus Specht, Germany
Carlo Tasso, Italy
Julita Vassileva, Canada
Gerhard Weber, Germany
Stephan Weibelzahl, Germany
Ross Wilkinson, Australia
Frank Wittig, Germany
Ingrid Zukerman, Australia

Additional Reviewers

Andrea Bunt
Stefano Burigat
Stefan Carmien
Demis Corvaglia
Melissa Dawe
Luca De Marco
Hal Eden
Josef Fink
Cristina Gena
Elisa Giaccardi
Andrew Gorman
Anna Goy
Daniele Gunetti
Félix Hernández

Lucio Ieronutti
Shinichi Konomi
Vitaveska Lanfranchi
Heather Maclaren
Rafael Morales
Tomohiro Oda
Dimitrios Pierrakos
Roberto Ranon
Augusto Senerchia
James Sullivan
Yunwen Ye
Daniel Wilson

Table of Contents

Invited Talks

Papers

Adaptive Hypermedia

Affective Computing

Data Mining for Personalization and Cross-Recommendation

ITS and Adaptive Advice

Modeling and Recognizing Human Activity

Multimodality and Ubiquitous Computing

Recommender Systems

Student Modeling

User Modeling and Interactive Systems

Web Site Navigation Support

Doctoral Consortium Papers

User Modeling Meets Usability Goals

Anthony Jameson*

German Research Center for Artificial Intelligence (DFKI)
and International University in Germany,
Stuhlsatzenhausweg 3, 66123 Saarbrücken,
Germany
jameson@dfki.de
http://dfki.de/~jameson

It has long been recognized that systems based on user modeling and adaptivity are associated with a number of typical usability problems—which sometimes outweigh the benefits of adaptation. This talk will show that the anticipation and prevention of usability side effects should form an essential part of the iterative design of user-adaptive systems, just as the consideration of medical side effects plays a key role in the development of new medications. This strategy requires a comprehensive understanding of the reasons for typical usability problems and of strategies for preventing them.

Figure 1 (adapted from [1]) summarizes and integrates a number of the relevant ideas and results. The generally desirable *Usability Goals* shown in the third column are often threatened by the *Typical Properties* of user-adaptive systems shown in the second column. Each of the *Preventive Measures* may be able to modify a typical property so as to reduce its negative impact on usability. The *Compensatory Measures* can increase the likelihood that the usability goals are fulfilled even if the threats created by the typical properties cannot be fully prevented.

In terms of this schema, the overall goal is to ensure an adequate fulfillment of the usability goals without eliminating the benefits of adaptivity. As the figure shows, there are also trade-offs among the usability goals themselves: A measure introduced to reduce one usability problem may aggravate another one.

Another complication is that the design solution that yields the best overall balance may differ sharply from one user or situation to the next. For this reason, the problem of finding the best balance itself often requires some form of adaptability and/or adaptivity (for example, so that different forms of user control can be realized for different users and situations).

Ways of dealing with usability challenges within this framework will be illustrated in the talk with case studies and examples from recent and current research and practice (see, e.g., [2]).

* The research of the author has been supported by the German Science Foundation (DFG) in its Collaborative Research Center on Resource-Adaptive Cognitive Processes, SFB 378, and by the German Ministry of Education and Research (BMBF).

L. Ardissono, P. Brna, and A. Mitrovic (Eds.): UM 2005, LNAI 3538, pp. 1–3, 2005.

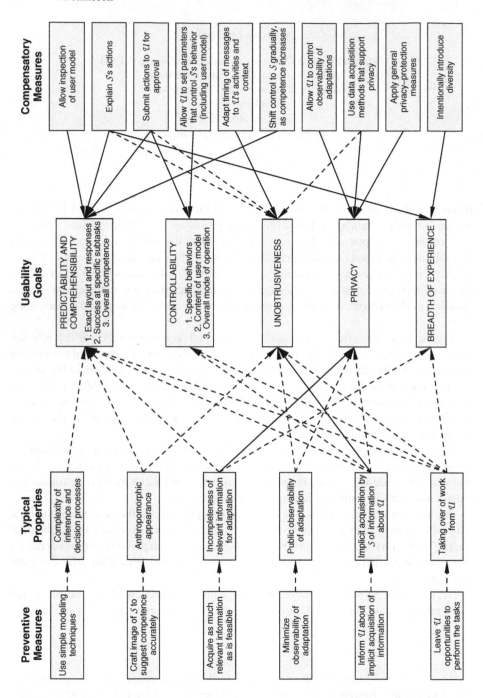

Fig. 1. Usability challenges for user-adaptive systems and ways of dealing with them. (Solid and dashed arrows denote positive and negative causal influences, respectively. $\mathcal{U}$ = "user"; $\mathcal{S}$ = "system")

References

1. Jameson, A.: Adaptive interfaces and agents. In Jacko, J.A., Sears, A., eds.: Human-Computer Interaction Handbook. Erlbaum, Mahwah, NJ (2003) 305–330
2. Bohnenberger, T., Jacobs, O., Jameson, A., Aslan, I.: Decision-theoretic planning meets user requirements: Enhancements and studies of an intelligent shopping guide. In: Proceedings of Pervasive 2005, Munich (2005)

Hey, That's Personal!

Lorrie Faith Cranor

Carnegie Mellon University, Pittsburgh, PA, USA
lorrie@cmu.edu
http://lorrie.cranor.org/

Personalized online commerce systems, context-aware pervasive computing applications, and other personalized computing systems often sacrifice privacy for added convenience or improved service. Some systems provide users with substantial benefits from personalization; other systems profile users to the primary benefit of the service provider. In many cases users are not fully informed about how their profile information will be used and are not given adequate opportunities to control the use of their personal information. If developers of personalized systems do not consider privacy issues in the design of their systems they risk building systems that are unable to comply with legal requirements in some jurisdictions. In addition, concerns about privacy may slow adoption of some personalized systems or prevent them from ever gaining acceptance. In this talk I will discuss the privacy risks associated with personalization systems and discuss a number of approaches to reducing those risks, including approaches to minimizing the amount of profile information associated with identified individuals and approaches to better informing users and giving them meaningful opportunities to control the user of their personal information.

L. Ardissono, P. Brna, and A. Mitrovic (Eds.): UM 2005, LNAI 3538, p. 4, 2005.
© Springer-Verlag Berlin Heidelberg 2005

Inhabited Models: Supporting Coherent Behavior in Online Systems

Thomas Erickson

IBM T. J. Watson Research Center, P.O. Box 704, Yorktown Heights,
NY 10598 USA
snowfall@acm.org
http://www.visi.com/~snowfall/

Abstract. A principal focus of user modeling has been on modeling individuals, the aim being to support the design of interactive systems that can fluidly adapt to their users' needs. In this talk I shift the focus from interactions between a human and a computer, to interactions amongst people that are mediated by a digital system. My interest has to do with how to design online systems that can support the blend of flexibility and coherence that characterizes face to face interaction. I describe my approach, which involves creating shared visualizations of people and their activities in online situations such as chats, presentations, and auctions. This kind of visualization – which serves as a sort of inhabited model of an activity – plays a number of roles in supporting group interaction that is both flexible and coherent.

1 Coherent Behavior

Think about the last time you attended the theatre. When the play is ready to begin, the doors are closed, the house lights are lowered, and the audience responds, their collective murmur subsiding into silence, punctuated by the occasional cough. When the play ends, the audience makes an effort – each individual acting on his or her own – to give signs of their enthusiasm. Typically the result is applause, in which an individual's hand claps are rapidly taken up by others, swelling into a uniform texture of sound. This is a simple example of a pervasive phenomenon: groups of people – even when the individual members do not know one another – are remarkably good at behaving coherently as a group. Of course, this is not happening in a vacuum. Theatres are carefully designed to support performances and the events that surround them; effects like lighting are used not just to enhance the play, but to provide cues to the audience about when the performance begins and ends. To produce coherent behavior, the audience makes use of its knowledge of the situation, cues from the environment, and its members' mutual awareness of one another's action.

Our daily life is rife with examples. We queue up, in a more or less orderly manner, at the ticket window. We wait for the traffic signal to change, or, if there is a break in the traffic and enough willing 'conspirators', we may cross *en mass* against the light. Of course, behaving coherently does not necessarily mean that everyone does the same thing. Pedestrians passing through Victoria Station at rush hour do a

L. Ardissono, P. Brna, and A. Mitrovic (Eds.): UM 2005, LNAI 3538, pp. 5 – 8, 2005.

remarkable job of avoiding one another: a glance, a slight alteration in direction or gait, and collision is averted, time after time after time. In more ordered circumstances such as meetings, groups orchestrate their behavior: someone waits for a turn to talk, judges how his or her words are being received, and shifts course depending on the audience's reaction. And in most cases we do all of this with the greatest of ease. None of this is a surprise: these skills are basic aspect of being social creatures, and examples pervade the work of sociologists (e.g. [3]), anthropologists (e.g. [5]), and other scholars (e.g. [4]).

2   Coherent Behavior in Online Systems

However, when our interactions are mediated by digital systems, things that were easy in face to face situations become more difficult. When we use instant messaging, email or even telephony, many of the cues that we effortlessly use to coordinate our face to face behavior are absent. Conversational practices that are simple in face to face situations – such as taking turns when talking, or 'going around the room' with one person speaking after another – become awkward and cumbersome in a conference call. Other practices, such as an audience's spontaneous applause at the end of an excellent performance, become difficult or impossible.

The problem is not only that digital mediation makes it difficult for us to coordinate behavior as we wish; there is a subtler problem. To see this, let's return to our example of an audience applauding. We are back in theater: the house lights have come up, the cast has come out on the stage to take their bows, and the audience is applauding with vigor. As the applause continues, one or two people stand up, and they are rapidly joined by more and more, giving rise to a standing ovation. Now let us suppose that there is a member of the audience who is less enthusiastic about the performance and doesn't believe it should receive a standing ovation. Nevertheless, in spite of this reluctance, he or she may well be even more reluctant to be seen to be the only one *not* standing. In fact, there is an almost palpable pressure to join with rest of the audience in giving a standing ovation. What this example demonstrates is that the cues and mutual visibility that structure our face to face behavior do not just make it easier to do what we want to do, but also encourage us to do that which we may not be inclined to do: wait in the queue, wait for the traffic signal, or stand, applauding politely if not enthusiastically. This pressure to conform, to join with others in producing a coherent collective outcome, is absent or greatly weakened in digitally mediated situations.

In summary, in online environments where collective behavior is mediated by digital systems, group interaction loses much of the grace and unity that characterizes its face to face counterpart. As an interaction designer, I am interested in remedying this situation.

3   Social Proxies as Inhabited Models

My approach to this problem is to design visualizations of the activities of participants in an online system. These visualizations, which I call "social proxies," function by

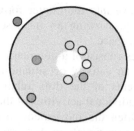

Fig. 1. A social proxy for Babble: the circle depicts a chat room, and dots depict the users

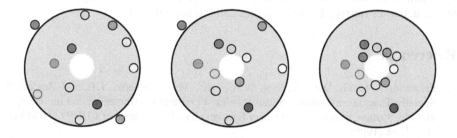

Fig. 2. Three states of the Babble proxy with increasingly focused degrees of activity

depicting the fine structure of individuals' activities relative to an implicit model of the activity the system is intended to support. Social proxies typically contain representations of the participants in the activity, and thus are, in a sense, inhabited. Because the proxies are made visible to all users of the system, they can be used as a shared resource, and serve as a common ground from which individuals can draw inferences about various aspects of the system's state.

Fig. 1 shows a simple example, implemented in a multi-user, persistent chat system called "Babble" [1]. The Babble social proxy depicts the current chat room as a large circle, and participants as small colored dots; dots shown inside the circle are in the chat room being viewed. Thus, the social proxy in Fig. 1 depicts eight people logged into Babble, seven of whom are in the same room. Dots move to the circle's inner core when their users type or are otherwise active, and slowly drift to the periphery of the circle over the course of about 20 minutes of idleness. Thus, of the seven participants in the chat room, five have been active very recently, one has been idle for about 10 minutes, and the last has been idle for 20 minutes.

Although this social proxy is very simple, it allows users of the system to get a sense of how many people are in the same room, and how many of those are active in the chat. Typically, a cluster of dots at the center of the circle indicates that 'something is going on.' The experience, to a Babble user, is somewhat similar to walking down a street and noticing a crowd: it provokes curiosity and (often) a desire to see what's going on. Because the Babble system can be minimized so that only the proxy is visible (while Babble users are involved in other computer-based activities), a cluster of dots in the proxy often can pull other people back into Babble, causing their idle, side-lined dots to move into the center forming a 'crowd.' Fig. 2 shows three states of the Babble proxy, showing an increase in focus as more and more people become active in the chat space.

More generally, social proxies consist of a geometric background figure that serves as a sort of model of a particular activity or situation, and small colored dots that represent participants. Movements of the dots relative to the background figure provide information about the individual activities of the participants, and express the overall state of the system. Often the movements and groupings of the dots are analogous to the ways in which participants in the corresponding face to face activity would move and position their bodies, in the same way in which the clustering of the dots in the Babble proxy represent a crowd gathering. Although minimal, this approach turns out to be remarkably powerful, and provides ways of supporting online activities ranging from conference calls to auctions [2].

References

1. Erickson, T. Smith, D.N., Kellogg, W.A., Laff, M.R., Richards, J.T., and Bradner, E.: Socially Translucent Systems: Social Proxies, Persistent Conversation, and the Design of 'Babble.' Human Factors in Computing Systems: The Proceedings of CHI '99. ACM Press, New York (1999)
2. Erickson, T. and Kellogg, W.A.: Social Translucence: Using Minimalist Visualizations of Social Activity to Support Collective Interaction. In: Höök, K., Benyon, D. and Munro, A. (eds.): Designing Information Spaces: The Social Navigation Approach. Springer, London (2003) 17-42
3. Goffman, E.: Behavior in Public Places: Notes on the Social Organization of Gatherings. Macmillan Publishing Co., New York (1963)
4. Jacobs, J.: The Death and Life of Great American Cities. Random House, New York (1961)
5. Whyte, W. H.: City: Return to the Center. Anchor Books, New York (1988)

Integrating Open User Modeling and Learning Content Management for the Semantic Web

Ronald Denaux[1], Vania Dimitrova[2], and Lora Aroyo[1]

[1] Computer Science Department, Eindhoven Univ. of Technology,
The Netherlands
[2] School of Computing, University of Leeds, UK
r.o.denaux@student.tue.nl
l.m.aroyo@tue.nl, vania@comp.leeds.ac.uk

Abstract. The paper describes an ontology-based approach for integrating interactive user modeling and learning content management to deal with typical adaptation problems, such as cold start and dynamics of the user's knowledge, in the context of the Semantic Web. An integrated OntoAIMS system is presented and its viability discussed based on user studies. The work demonstrates some novel aspects, such as (a) ontological approach for integration of methods for eliciting and utilizing of user models; (b) improved adaptation functionality resulted from that integration, validated with real users; (c) support of interoperability and reusability of adaptive components.

1 Introduction

A key factor for the successful implementation of the Semantic Web vision [2] is the ability to deal with the *diversity of users* (who differ in their capabilities, expectations, goals, requirements, and preferences) and to provide *personalized access* and *user-adapted services*. Recently, the Semantic Web community is acknowledging the need to consider the user's perspective to provide personalization functionality [8]. Personalization has been a prime concern of the user-modeling community which has developed methods for building user models (UMs) and using these models to tailor the system's behavior to the needs of individuals. However, for UM methods to be deployed on the Semantic Web, they should deal with semantics defined with *ontologies* [3], and should enable *interoperability* of algorithms that elicit and utilize UMs[8] based on common ontology specification languages, for example OWL [10].

We present here how interactive user modeling (UM elicitation) and adaptive content management (UM utilization) on the Semantic Web can be integrated in a *learning domain* to deal with typical adaptation problems, such as cold start, inaccuracy of assumptions about a user's cognitive state drawn only on the basis of interaction tracking data, and dynamics of the student's knowledge. The paper demonstrates the following novel aspects: (a) ontological approach for integration of methods for eliciting and utilizing user models; (b) improved

L. Ardissono, P. Brna, and A. Mitrovic (Eds.): UM 2005, LNAI 3538, pp. 9–18, 2005.
© Springer-Verlag Berlin Heidelberg 2005

adaptation functionality resulted from that integration, validated in studies with real users; (c) support of interoperability and reusability on the educational Semantic Web. We illustrate these in an adaptive system called OntoAIMS.

Our work on providing users with a structured way to search, browse and access large repositories of learning resources on the Semantic Web relates to research on adaptive *Learning Content Management Systems* (LCMS). Similarly to existing LCMS, e.g. [4, 12], OntoAIMS employs student models to allocate tasks and resources for individual students. Distinctively, we use OWL ontologies to represent the domain and the UM. The latter extends the notion of a domain overlay by including students' beliefs that are not necessarily in the system's domain knowledge. In contrast with more general UMs for the Web, e.g. Hera [11], which consider merely user attributes, OntoAIMS uses an enhanced, interoperable, ontology-based user model built via a dialog with the user.

The interactive user modeling component in OntoAIMS, called OWL-OLM, elicits an *OWL-based open learner model* built with the active user's participation. This extends an interactive open learner modeling framework [7] to deal with dynamic, ontology-based, advanced learner models [6]. Similarly to [9, 13], the open user modeling approach in OWL-OLM deals with a user's conceptual state. Distinctively, we exploit OWL-reasoning to maintain diagnostic interactions and to extract an enhanced user model represented in OWL. This shows a novel open user modeling approach that deals with important issues of modeling users to enable personalization and adaptation for the Semantic Web.

The focus of this paper is the *integration* and the *benefits* of both *interactive user modeling* and *adaptive task recommendation*. We first introduce the integrated architecture of OntoAIMS (Sect. 2) and then briefly describe its main components: ontology-based user modeling (Sect. 3) and task recommendation and resource browsing (Sect. 4). Section 5 discusses how users accept the integrated environment. Finally, we conclude and sketch out future work.

2   Integrated OntoAIMS Architecture

OntoAIMS[1] is an <u>Onto</u>logy-based version of the AIMS <u>A</u>daptive <u>I</u>nformation <u>M</u>anagement <u>S</u>ystem [1] providing an information searching and browsing environment that recommends to learners the most appropriate (for their current knowledge) task to work on and aids them to explore domain concepts and read resources related to the task. Currently, OntoAIMS works in a Linux domain.

OntoAIMS uses ontologies (see Fig. 1) to represent the aspects of the application semantics, to allow a strict separation of domain-dependent data, application-related data and resources, and to further enable reusability and sharing of data on the Semantic Web. The learning material is specified in terms of a *Resource Model* that describes the documents in the resource repository and is linked to the *Domain Ontology* which represents the domain concepts and their re-

---

[1] The system is available with username *visitor* and password *visitor* at `http://swale.comp.leeds.ac.uk:8080/staims/viewer.html`

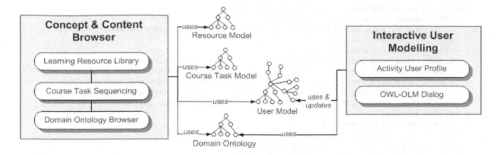

Fig. 1. OntoAIMS Integrated Architecture

lationships. The course structure is represented as a hierarchy of tasks in a *Course Task Model*. To enable adaptivity, OntoAIMS utilizes a *User Model* that covers learner preferences, personal characteristics, goals and domain understanding.

The success of adaptation in OntoAIMS depends on the accuracy and completeness of the user model. Unobtrusive ways to collect user data have been considered. The user's interaction with the system (e.g. tasks/resources chosen and searches performed) is gathered in the *Activity User Profile*, which provides information about user preferences and personal characteristics. However, this data is insufficient for modeling a user's domain understanding (called here *conceptual state*, see Sec. 3.1), moreover, such data is unavailable when the user logs for a first time. Hence, to build a model of the user's conceptual state, OntoAIMS employs an interactive UM component that maintains a dialog to elicit a user's conceptual model, see Sect. 3.2. Both the User Model and the Course Task Model are used for recommending the learner a task to study, so that he can navigate efficiently through the course structure, while the Resource Model is used to allocate resources and rank them according to the appropriateness to the learning task, see Sect. 4.

3   Ontology-Based User Modeling in OntoAIMS

Throughout the user interaction, information about concepts visited, searches performed, task status (current, started, finished, not started yet), resources opened, and bookmarks saved is stored in the Activity User Profile. It is useful for deducing user preferences and characteristics, and to make initial assumptions about the user's domain understanding. To have an *in-depth* representation of aspects of the user's domain understanding, OntoAIMS uses a User's Conceptual State. This section will outline how it is represented and maintained.

3.1   User's Conceptual State

The main reason for maintaining a conceptual state is to have an intermediate model that *links* a user's conceptualization to an existing domain ontology. The conceptual state is a model of the user's conceptualization inferred during in-

```
<rdf:Description rdf:about="blo:Filesystem_node">
  <rdfs:comment rdf:datatype="xmls:string">
      Any set of data that has a pathname on the filesystem.</rdfs:comment>
  <rdfs:label>file</rdfs:label>
  <rdf:type rdf:resource="owl:Class"/>
  <aimsUM:times_used rdf:datatype="xmls:long">12</aimsUM:times_used>
  <aimsUM:times_used_correctly rdf:datatype="xmls:long">10</aimsUM:times_used_correctly>
  <aimsUM:times_used_wrongly rdf:datatype="xmls:long">2</aimsUM:times_used_wronlgy>
  <aimsUM:times_affirmed rdf:datatype="xmls:long">3</aimsUM:times_affirmed>
  <aimsUM:times_denied rdf:datatype="xmls:long">1</aimsUM:times_denied>
</rdf:Description>
<rdf:Description rdf:nodeID="A273">
  <rdf:type rdf:resource="rdf:Statement"/>
  <rdf:subject rdf:resource="blo:Move_file_operation"/>
  <rdf:predicate rdf:resource="rdfs:subClassOf"/>
  <rdf:object rdf:resource="blo:Command"/>
  <aimsUM:times_used rdf:datatype="xmls:long">1</aimsUM:times_used>
  <aimsUM:times_used_wrongly rdf:datatype="xmls:long">1</aimsUM:times_used_wrongly>
</rdf:Description>
```

Fig. 2. An extract from a student's Conceptual Model based on a dialog episode from the second study described in Sect 5

teractions with the user. To distinguish between a temporary, short-term state that gives a snapshot of a user's knowledge extracted during an interaction session and a long-term state that is built as a result of many interactions with the system, we consider *short term conceptual states* (STCS) and a *long term conceptual state* (LTCS), respectively. The former is a *partial* representation of some aspects of a user's conceptualization and is used as the basis for extracting the latter that forms the User Model in OntoAIMS.

STCS is defined as a triple of URIs pointing to a *Conceptual model*, a set of *Domain ontologies* and a *LTCS*. The *Conceptual model* is specified in OWL, which is well-suited for defining conceptualization and for reasoning upon it. The Conceptual Model resembles an ontology specification, i.e. it defines classes, individuals, and properties, and uses OWL properties to define relationships. By using OWL, concepts in the conceptual state are mapped to the domain ontology.

Fig. 2 shows an extract from a conceptual model. The user has used the concept Filesystem_node[2] 12 times[3] - 10 of these cases are supported by the domain ontology and 2 are not. He has also stated 3 times that he knows the concept Filesystem_node and once that he does not know it. Fig. 2 also shows that conceptual models keep track of specific relationships between concepts like Move_file_operation being a subclass of the concept Command. Note that the last relationship has been marked as *used wrongly*, which means that it is not supported by the domain ontology and a *mismatch* between the user's conceptualization and the domain ontology is indicated. Note also that a mismatch only indicates that there is a discrepancy between the conceptual state and the domain ontology, it does not indicate that the relationship is not true.

---

[2] This concept is defined in the domain ontology, which can be found at http://wwwis.win.tue.nl/~swale/blo

[3] The RDF specification of the properties used to annotate conceptual states can be found at http://wwwis.win.tue.nl/~swale/aimsUM

STCS is used to update LTCS which associates a *belief value* for each domain concept. The belief value is calculated based on the conceptual model. The first time the concept is used its belief value is assigned to 50 (out of 100). From then on, $Belief\_value(c) = x + (100 - x)/2$, if there is evidence for knowing c and $Belief\_value(c) = x/2$, if there is evidence for not knowing c, where x is the current belief value of c and evidence is calculated depending on the situation, e.g. `times_used_correctly/times_used`.

3.2   Dialog for Extracting a User's Conceptual Model

OntoAIMS uses OWL-OLM – an <u>OWL</u>-based framework for <u>O</u>pen <u>L</u>earner <u>M</u>odeling to (a) validate the analysis of the user data, (b) elicit a learner's conceptual model, and (c) build and maintain a dynamic UM. OWL-OLM follows the STyLE-OLM framework for interactive open learner modeling [7] but amends it to work with a domain ontology and user model built in OWL. OWL-OLM builds a conceptual model of a user by interacting with him in a graphical manner (see Fig. 3). During these interactions, both OWL-OLM and the user can ask domain-related questions and give their opinions about domain-related sentences. To maintain the dialog, OWL-OLM uses a discourse model and infers knowledge from the domain ontology and from the current conceptual model. Because OWL is used as the representation language, OWL-OLM can deploy existing OWL reasoners for the Semantic Web, currently, it uses Jena [4].

The OWL-OLM screenshot in Fig. 3 shows the dialog history in the upper-left corner and the last utterance in the graphical area. The user composes utterances by constructing diagrams using basic graphical operations – 'create', 'delete' or 'edit' a concept or a relation between concepts – and selecting a sentence opener to define his intention, e.g. to 'answer', 'question', 'agree', 'disagree', 'suggest topic'. For a detailed description of OWL-OLM see [6, 5].

OWL-OLM analyzes each user utterance to determine how to update the user's conceptual model based on the domain concepts and relations used in the utterance. It determines whether the user's statement

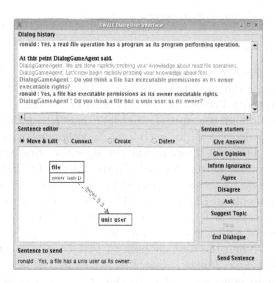

Fig. 3. Graphical User Interface of OWL-OLM

---

[4] `http://jena.sourceforge.net/`

is supported by the domain ontology, and, if this is not the case, marks a mismatch. Reasoning over the domain ontology and the conceptual model is also used to determine how OWL-OLM continues the dialog, e.g. asking the user a question, initiating a clarification dialog to discuss a mismatch, or answering a user's question.

Currently, OntoAIMS calls OWL-OLM to probe about a user's domain understanding, and, based on the task model, specifies what domain aspects have to be discussed. The dialog can be terminated either by the user whenever he wishes or by OWL-OLM when the required aspects of the user's conceptualization have been covered. OWL-OLM then uses the extracted STCS to update the belief values in the LTCS that is used by the task recommendation in OntoAIMS.

4   Task Recommendation and Resource Browsing

The OntoAIMS Course Task Model consists of a hierarchy of tasks. An example extract from a simplified representation of the Course Task Model used in the current instantiation of OntoAIMS is given below.

```
Course: Introduction to Linux
T1. Introduction
 T1.1 Operating Systems
  T1.1.1 Definition and Description; concepts={operating system, kernel, system program,...}
    ...
 T1.2 Files and Filesystems
  T1.2.1 Files and operations on files; concepts={file, filename, copy files, view files,...}
    ...
T4. The Gnome environment
```

Each course task T is represented as $(T_{ID}, T_{in}, T_{out}, T_{concepts}, T_{pre})$, where T_{in} is the input from the user's Activity Profile, T_{out} is the output for the user's Activity Profile and for STCS based on the user's work in T, $T_{concepts}$ is a set of domain concepts studied in T, and T_{pre} indicates the prerequisites for T (e.g. knowledge level for each $T_{concept}$, other tasks and resources required).

The task recommendation algorithm first selects a set of potential tasks to recommend from all tasks in the Course Task Model, by checking whether their T_{in} and T_{pre} are supported by the Activity Profile and the *belief_values* for the concepts in LTCS. OntoAIMS checks the concept knowledge threshold for the concepts in $T_{concepts}$ and recommends either to follow the task if the knowledge is not sufficient or to skip the task otherwise.

When the user chooses to perform the recommended task, the *OntoAIMS Resource Browser* (see Fig. 4) helps the user to learn more about the domain concepts related to that task. He can search for and read learning resources, browse domain concepts and study their definitions in the context of this task. For each resource in the search result list OntoAIMS provides two types of ranking - relevancy to the current task, and relevancy to the current user query. In this way, OntoAIMS can recommend resources for those concepts the user does not know or which contain mismatches with the domain ontology. The user's activities for a task and T_{out} are used to update the user

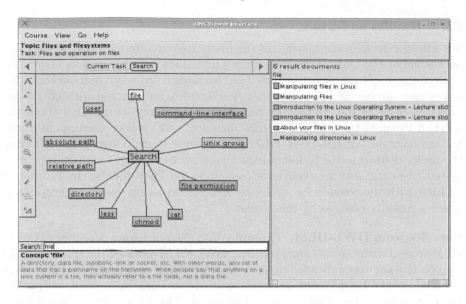

Fig. 4. OntoAIMS resource browser

model once the task is completed. It is possible to employ OWL-OLM to validate the updates to the Conceptual State in T_{out}, although this is not currently implemented.

5   Initial Evaluation of OntoAIMS with Users

We have conducted user studies with OntoAIMS to: (a) verify the functionality of its components (user modeling, task recommendation, and resource browser); (b) examine how users accept the integrated environment and its adaptive behavior; (c) identify how the system can be improved with additional adaptive features.

5.1   Observational Studies

Two user studies were conducted with the current instantiation of OntoAIMS in a domain of Linux. Initially, *six users*, postgraduate students and staff from the universities of Leeds and Eindhoven, took part. An improved version of the system was used in a second study with *ten first year Computing undergraduates* at Leeds. It followed a two-week introductory course on Linux. In both studies, the users attended individual sessions, which lasted about an hour and were video recorded and monitored by an observer. OntoAIMS did not have data about the users prior to their logon to ensure realistic *cold start* conditions. The users were asked to study resources on Linux, which would be recommended by the system. At times, the observer interrupted the users to clarify their behavior with the system. At the end, the users were given a questionnaire related to their satisfaction and suggestions for system improvements.

5.2   Results and Discussion

We will discuss here the benefits of the integrated architecture, see [5] for more details about the OntoAIMS evaluation. OntoAIMS was regarded as helpful for both tuning one's knowledge in Linux and learning more about domain concepts. Every user appreciated the *integrated functionality* and worked with *all components*. Because at the start the system did not have any information about the users, it directed them to OWL-OLM (see Sect. 3.2), where users spent about half an hour on average. OWL-OLM probed their domain knowledge following the topics defined in the task ontology. Based on the dialog, the users were suggested tasks suitable for their level (see Sect. 4). They then spent about half an hour with the resource browser (see Sect. 4) exploring domain concepts and reading resources offered by the system.

Benefits from OWL-OLM. The evaluation showed strong potential of OWL-OLM to deal with the *cold start problem*. OWL-OLM assessed the students' level of expertise and recommended them appropriate tasks to study. The expert users followed the OWL-OLM dialog answering most questions, and occasionally asked the system to confirm their domain statements. These users were pleased to be able to show their familiarity and to engage in discussions on more advanced domain topics. Less knowledgeable users struggled to answer the system's questions and often sought the answer from OWL-OLM. These users explored a variety of dialog moves, e.g. they disagreed with system's statements, composed new concepts and links, and asked several types of questions. There were occasions when discrepancies with the domain ontology were shown, which triggered corresponding clarification dialog games.

OWL-OLM was regarded by all users as a component that helped them learn. The students used the dialog to study about the domain and commented that the OWL-OLM dialog made them think about their knowledge, so they became aware of which concepts they were familiar with or struggling with. Indeed, as reported in [7], interactive open user modeling provides the means for reflection.

Benefits from Task Recommendation. The user models generated with OWL-OLM were used to inform the task proposal. Some users were offered to skip tasks, as OWL-OLM found that they already knew quite a bit about that topic, while less knowledgeable users were directed to introductory topics. Most users agreed that the task recommended by the system was appropriate for their level, two students disagreed with this as they found the resources insufficient for the recommended topics. All users were pleased that the system could recommend them a task, they followed the recommended tasks, and regarded them as compliant with their learning goals. All users but one, said that they were aware why the task recommendation was made, which was due to the preceding OWL-OLM interactions. This gives a strong argument for the benefits of integartion.

Benefits from Resource Browsing. The resource browser was regarded as *"a flexible way of looking at resources"*. The users found it intuitive and easy to

Table 1. Additional adaptive features in OntoAIMS as pointed out by the ten users in the second study (the numbers show how many students support the feature)

Feature	No
I want the resources ranked according to my preferences and knowledge	10
I want the resources ordered according to my preferences and knowledge	8
I want the resources filtered according to my preferences and knowledge	4
I would like to be able to choose when the system should be adaptive	10
I would like to know what the system's thinks about my knowledge	10
I would like to know how my interaction with the system is used to form the system's opinion about my knowledge	8
I would like to know how the system's behavior is affected by its opinion about me	9
I would like to be able to inspect and change what the system thinks of me	10

use. All users agreed that the graphical representation gave them an overview of the conceptual space: *"it allows to map your path through sequences of topics"*, *"demonstrated exactly where I was in relation to the suggested topic"*. The users were offered a set of resources ranked according to their appropriateness to the task. Depending on the goal (e.g. learning more about a concept, checking the syntax of a command, or tuning the student's domain knowledge), the resources the students were looking for differed in size, structure, and depth of domain knowledge. All users were pleased to see document ranking, but, again all of them, wanted this to be done not according to the the task but the user's preferences, knowledge, and current goal. This points at the need for further improvement of the integration, as discussed below.

Improving the Integration and Adaptation. The evaluation pointed at improvements needed with regard to the integration between OWL-OLM and the resource browser. All students wanted to use a *flexible switch* between both modes. They stressed that this should be the user's choice, not something imposed by the system, and pointed at ways to implement it, e.g. offering the users a choice to go to the resource browser when they ask a question in OWL-OLM or enabling them go to a dialog to check their domain understanding after reading resources in the browser. The users in the second study were asked about *additional adaptive features*. The study pointed at future extensions of OntoAIMS to further integrate OWL-OLM and resource recommendation, see Table 1.

6   Conclusions and Future Work

The paper proposed an ontology-based approach for integrating interactive user modeling and learning content management to deal with typical adaptation problems on the Semantic Web, such as cold start, unreliability of user interaction for building conceptual UMs, and dynamics of a user's knowledge. We exemplified the approach in the integrated learning environment OntoAIMS for adaptive task recommendations and resource browsing on the Semantic Web. Initial results from two user studies were discussed. OntoAIMS shows a promising approach for dealing with adaptation on the Educational Semantic Web and contributes to this newly emerging strand.

Our immediate plans relate to improving OntoAIMS by adding additional integration and adaptation features, as suggested by the user studies. In the long run, we consider studies to (a) produce a good classification of users' mismatches and patterns for clarification dialog (b) design effective knowledge elicitation tools suited not for ontology engineers, but for users with a wide range of experiences, and (c) use Semantic Web services for the dynamic allocation of learning resources which are then flexibly integrated in OntoAIMS.

Acknowledgments. The research was supported by the UK-NL Partnership in Science and the EU NoE PROLEARN. The authors thank Michael Pye for implementing the OWL-OLM GUI and the participants in the evaluative study.

References

1. Aroyo, L., Dicheva, D.: Aims: Learning and teaching support for www-based education. Int. Journal for Continuing Engineering Education and Life-long Learning (IJCEELL) **11** (2001) 152–164
2. Berners-Lee, T., Hendler, J., Lassila, O.: The semantic web. Scientific American (2001) 35–43
3. Bra, P.D., Aroyo, L., Chepegin, V.: The next big thing: Adaptive web-based systems. Journal of Digital Information, 5(1) (2004)
4. Brusilovsky, P., Eklund, J.: A study of user model based link annotation in educational hypermedia. Journal of Universal Computer Science, 4(4) (1998) 429–448
5. Denaux, R.: Ontology-based interactive user modeling for adaptive information systems. Master's thesis, Technische Universiteit Eindhoven (2005)
6. Denaux, R., Aroyo, L., Dimitrova, V.: An approach for ontology-based elicitation of user models to enable personalization on the semantic web. In: Proc. of WWW05. (to appear)
7. Dimitrova, V.: Style-olm: Interactive open learner modelling. Int. Journal of Artificial Intelligence in Education **13** (2003) 35–78
8. Henze, N.: Personalization functionality for the semantic web: Identification and description of techniques. Technical report, REWERSE project: Reasoning on the Web with Rules and Semantics (2004)
9. Kay, J.: The um toolkit for cooperative user modeling. User Modeling and User-Adapted Interaction **4** (1995) 149–196
10. McGuinness, D.L., van Harmelen, F.: Owl web ontology language overview. Technical report, W3C Recommendation (2004)
11. Vdovjak, R., Frasincar, F., Houben, G., Barna, P.: Engineering semantic web information systems in hera. Journal of Web Engineering, 2(1&2) (2003) 3–26
12. Weber, G., Kuhl, H., Weibelzahl, S.: Developing adaptive internet-based courses with the authoring system netcoach. In: Int. Workshop on Adaptive Hypermedia. (2001) 41–54
13. Zapata-Rivera, D., Greer, J.: Student model accuracy using inspectable bayesian student models. In: Proc. of AIED03. (2003) 65–72

Modeling Suppositions in Users' Arguments*

Sarah George, Ingrid Zukerman, and Michael Niemann

School of Computer Science and Software Engineering,
Monash University, Clayton,
VICTORIA 3800, Australia
{sarahg, ingrid, niemann}@csse.monash.edu.au

Abstract. During conversation, people often make assumptions or suppositions that are not explicitly stated. Failure to identify these suppositions may lead to mis-communication. In this paper, we describe a procedure that postulates such suppositions in the context of the discourse interpretation mechanism of BIAS – a *Bayesian Interactive Argumentation System*. When a belief mentioned in a user's discourse differs from that obtained in BIAS' user model, our procedure searches for suppositions that explain this belief, preferring suppositions that depart minimally from the beliefs in the user model. Once a set of suppositions has been selected, it can be presented to the user for validation. Our procedure was evaluated by means of a web-based trial. Our results show that the assumptions posited by BIAS are considered sensible by our trial subjects.

1 Introduction

During conversation, people often make assumptions or suppositions that are not explicitly stated. The identification of these suppositions is important in order to understand the intentions or reasoning of one's conversational partner, and to provide cooperative responses. For instance, if someone says "Jack is tall, so Jill must be tall", s/he is probably assuming that Jack and Jill are related. This assumption must be taken into account in order to respond cooperatively. In this example, rather than responding "I disagree, Jill may or may not be tall", it would be more helpful to say "Actually, Jack and Jill are not related, so we can't infer that Jill is tall".

In this paper, we describe a procedure that postulates such suppositions in the context of the discourse interpretation mechanism of BIAS – a *Bayesian Interactive Argumentation System* [8, 7]. This mechanism receives as input arguments for a goal proposition, and generates *interpretations*.

An interpretation is a representation of what an interlocutor said in terms of the mental model maintained by the addressee. When the addressee is a computer, this representation is constrained by the knowledge representation and reasoning formalism employed by the system, and by the purpose for which the system is used. The interpretations generated by the version of BIAS described in [8, 7] consist of propositions asso-

---

* This research was supported in part by the ARC Centre for Perceptive and Intelligent Machines in Complex Environments. The authors thank David Albrecht and Yuval Marom for their help with the analysis of the evaluation results.

L. Ardissono, P. Brna, and A. Mitrovic (Eds.): UM 2005, LNAI 3538, pp. 19–29, 2005.

ciated with degrees of belief, and relations between propositions. For example, if a user said "If I walk to the main road, then I'll probably be in Sydney tomorrow", one possible interpretation would be "*WalkMainRoad* → *TakeBus* → *ArriveSydney* [Likely]", and another would be "*WalkMainRoad* → *HitchRide* → *ArriveSydney* [Likely]".

The procedure described in this paper incorporates suppositions into such interpretations in order to account for the beliefs stated by a user. For example, if the user had been previously discussing the perils of hitchhiking, and then said "If I walk to the main road, I'll have to hitch a ride to Sydney", the system could posit that the user is supposing that no buses are available. If such a supposition departs significantly from the beliefs recorded in the user model, it is presented to the user for confirmation, whereupon it is incorporated into the user model.

In the next section, we discuss related research. Section 3 outlines our interpretation-generation process, and Section 4 describes our mechanism for positing suppositions. We then present a user-based evaluation of this mechanism, and concluding remarks.

2   Related Research

An important aspect of discourse understanding involves filling in information that is omitted by the interlocutor. In our previous work, we have considered *inferential leaps*, where BIAS filled in intermediate reasoning steps left out by a user [8, 7], and *unstated premises*, where BIAS postulated which premises from the user model were considered by the user, but omitted from his/her argument [9]. In this paper, we consider *suppositions*, which according to the Webster dictionary "consider as true or existing what is not proved". Suppositions are beliefs that *differ* from those in the user model, but are posited by the system to account for the beliefs expressed in the user's argument.

Several researchers have considered *presuppositions*, a type of suppositions implied by the wording of a statement or query [3, 5, 4, 2]. For instance, "How many people passed CS101?" presupposes that CS101 was offered and that students were enrolled in it [3]. Mercer [4] used default logic together with lexical information to identify a speaker's presuppositions. Gurney *et al.* [2] used active logic plus syntactic and lexical information to update the discourse context presupposed by an utterance. Kaplan [3] considered the information in a database and applied language-driven inferences to identify *presumptions* in database queries, and generate indirect cooperative responses, e.g., "CS101 was not offered" rather than "nobody passed CS101". Motro [5] extended this work using information about the database, such as integrity constraints, in addition to the information in the database.

The presuppositions considered by these researchers are typically few and can be unequivocally inferred from the wording of a single statement. In contrast, the suppositions considered in this paper are postulated to justify the relations between statements made by a user, and differ from what our system thinks that the user believes. Furthermore, there may be several alternative suppositions that explain a user's statements, and their probability depends on the other beliefs held by a user.

3   Outline of BIAS

BIAS uses Bayesian networks (BNs) [6] as its knowledge representation and reasoning formalism.[1] Our domain of implementation is a murder mystery, which is represented by a 32-node binary BN. That is, each node in the BN may be set to either True or False. In addition, an unobserved node may remain unset (with a probability between 0 and 1 inferred by means of Bayesian propagation).

In the context of a BN, an interpretation consists of the tuple $\{SC, IG\}$, where SC is a *supposition configuration*, and IG is an *interpretation graph*.

- A **Supposition Configuration** is a set of suppositions made by BIAS to account for the beliefs in a user's argument.
- An **Interpretation Graph** is a subnet of the domain BN which links the nodes that correspond to the antecedents in an argument to the nodes that correspond to the consequents. Each node is associated with a degree of belief.

Figure 1 shows a sample argument (left-hand side) and interpretation (the Bayesian subnet on the right-hand-side). The argument is composed of propositions (obtained from a menu in an argument-construction interface [7]) linked by argumentation connectives. The italicized nodes in the Bayesian subnet are those mentioned in the argument, and the boxed node is a supposition (posited by the system) that accounts for the beliefs in the argument. If the time of death is unknown according to the user model, then GreenInGardenAt11 does not necessarily imply that Mr Green was in the garden at the time of death, yielding a belief of LessThanEvenChance in GreenMurderedBody. In order to account for the user's belief of BetterThanEvenChance for this consequent, BIAS posits that the user supposes TimeOfDeath11=True.

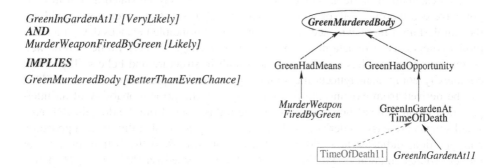

GreenInGardenAt11 [VeryLikely]
AND
MurderWeaponFiredByGreen [Likely]

IMPLIES

GreenMurderedBody [BetterThanEvenChance]

Fig. 1. Sample argument and interpretation

The problem of finding the best interpretation $\{SC, IG\}$ is exponential. Hence, we use the anytime algorithm in Figure 2 for this task [1]. This algorithm activates the following three modules until it runs out of time (after 20 seconds), retaining the top N

---

[1] However, BNs are not essential. Our mechanism requires a set of propositions that represent the system's domain knowledge, and a representation of relations between propositions.

(=4) interpretations at any point in time: one module for proposing a supposition configuration, one for proposing an interpretation graph, and one for evaluating the resultant interpretation.[2] This algorithm typically generates a few supposition configurations (Section 4), and several interpretation graphs for each supposition configuration.

Algorithm *GenerateInterpretations(UserArg)*
while {there is time}
{

1. Propose a supposition configuration SC that accounts for the beliefs stated in the argument.
2. Propose an interpretation graph IG that connects the nodes in *UserArg* under supposition configuration SC.
3. Evaluate interpretation $\{SC, IG\}$.
4. Retain top N (=4) interpretations.

}

Fig. 2. Anytime algorithm for generating interpretations

An interpretation is evaluated by calculating its posterior probability, where the best interpretation is that with the highest posterior probability.

$$SysIntBest = \text{argmax}_{i=1,...,n} \Pr(SC_i, IG_i | UserArg)$$

where n is the number of interpretations.

After applying Bayes rule and making independence assumptions, we obtain

$$SysIntBest = \text{argmax}_{i=1,...,n} \{ \Pr(UserArg | SC_i, IG_i) \times \Pr(IG_i) \times \Pr(SC_i) \} \quad (1)$$

This calculation implements Occam's Razor, which may be stated as follows: "If you have two theories both of which explain the observed facts, then you should use the simplest until more evidence comes along". This principle balances data fit against model complexity. The data fit component ($\Pr(UserArg | SC_i, IG_i)$) reflects how well an interpretation matches a user's argument both in structure and beliefs. The model complexity component reflects the simplicity of the interpretation, or how easily it can be derived from existing information. $\Pr(IG_i)$, the prior probability of an interpretation graph, reflects how easy it is to obtain this graph from the domain BN (e.g., small graphs are easy to derive); and $\Pr(SC_i)$, the prior probability of a supposition configuration, indicates how close are these suppositions to the beliefs in the user model. The calculation of $\Pr(UserArg | SC_i, IG_i)$ is based on $\Pr(UserArg | IG_i)$ (the calculation of $\Pr(UserArg | IG_i)$ and $\Pr(IG_i)$ is described in [7], where we considered only interpretation graphs, not suppositions). In this paper, we describe the calculation of $\Pr(SC_i)$ and the influence of suppositions on the probability of an interpretation (Section 4).

---

[2] We have also implemented a module that matches Natural Language (NL) sentences in an argument with nodes in the domain BN, This module, which should be called before the other modules, is not part of the version of BIAS described here, where the propositions in an argument are copied from a menu.

4   Positing Suppositions

As stated in Section 3, the nodes in our BNs are binary. Hence, the possible supposition states are: SET TRUE – suppose that a node is True; SET FALSE – suppose that a node is False; and UNSET – suppose that a node has not been observed (i.e., ignore any evidence supplied by this node). Making a supposition may strengthen the influence of a node on its consequents, as shown in the example in Figure 1, or weaken it.

A supposition configuration describes the state of every node in the BN, hence there are 3^N such configurations (where N is the number of nodes in the BN). Since the number of nodes in the BNs implemented in BIAS ranges between 32 and 85, we cannot consider all possible supposition configurations, and we certainly cannot combine them with large numbers of interpretation graphs in the next step of algorithm *GenerateInterpretations*. We therefore find promising supposition configurations by generating only a limited number (=200) of supposition configurations that are close to the beliefs in the user model, and selecting from these the best three configurations as the basis for the generation of interpretation graphs. This is done by applying algorithm *GetSuppositionConfig* (Figure 3).

Algorithm *GetSuppositionConfig*, which is called in Step 1 of algorithm *GenerateInterpretations*, receives as input an argument *UserArg* and returns a supposition configuration randomly selected from a short-list of k (=3) configurations. This short-list, which is denoted *SuppositionConfigList*, is generated by calling *MakeNewConfig(Supposition)* K (=200) times, and selecting the best three configurations.

Algorithm *MakeNewConfig*, which is called in Step 1(a) of *GetSuppositionConfig*, maintains a priority queue of configurations and their probabilities. Each time it is called, it removes the configuration at the top of the queue (which has the highest probability), generates its "child configurations" (derived from the removed one), inserts them in the queue according to their probability, and returns the removed configuration.[3] The bold-italicized segments of the algorithm are explained later in this section.

We have adopted this process for the generation of supposition configurations, because observations of our system's behaviour indicate that there are only a few promising supposition configurations among the many possible options, but these configurations generally do not follow a monotonic pattern. Hence, a procedure that just descends a priority queue will not yield good results reliably. Further, trials performed during system development show that the top 200 supposition configurations (obtained by repeatedly accessing a priority queue) provide a suitable basis for selecting three promising configurations.

The generation of supposition configurations and their children employs a structure called *Supposition Score Table*, which maps nodes to suppositions (Table 1). Each column in the Supposition Score Table corresponds to a node in the BN. Each node is associated with a list of <supposition: probability> pairs – one pair for each supposition – sorted in descending order of probability. Each pair represents the probability of

---

[3] This algorithm is also used to generate interpretation graphs and node configurations that match NL sentences, but here we focus on its use for generating supposition configurations.

Algorithm *GetSuppositionConfig(UserArg)*

1. If *SuppositionConfigList* is empty
   (a) Call *MakeNewConfig(Supposition)* K (=200) times, where each time *MakeNewConfig* returns the best supposition configuration.
   (b) Assign the top k (=3) supposition configurations to *SuppositionConfigList*.
2. Select an element from *SuppositionConfigList* at random.
3. Return the chosen configuration.

Algorithm *MakeNewConfig(ConfigType)*

1. If the priority queue is empty, **propose an initial configuration, calculate its probability**, and add the configuration and its probability to the priority queue.
2. Remove the first configuration from the queue.
3. **Generate the children of this configuration, calculate their probability**, and insert them in the queue so that the queue remains sorted in descending order of the probability obtained for a configuration.
4. Return the chosen (removed) configuration.

Fig. 3. Algorithm for generating suppositions

Table 1. Sample Supposition Score Table

$node_1$		$node_2$		...	$node_{32}$	
UNSET:	0.7	SET TRUE:	0.8	...	UNSET:	0.7
SET TRUE:	0.21	UNSET:	0.15	...	SET TRUE:	0.15
SET FALSE:	0.09	SET FALSE:	0.05	...	SET FALSE:	0.15

making this supposition about the node in question, which is obtained by applying the following heuristics:

- *No change is best:* There is a strong bias towards not making suppositions.
- *Users are unlikely to change their mind about observed evidence:* If a user has observed a node (e.g., its value is True or False), s/he is unlikely to change his/her belief in this node.
- *Small changes in belief are better than large changes:* If a node that is left unset has a propagated value of 0.9, then it is more likely that the user is assuming it True than if the propagated value was 0.6.

These heuristics are implemented by means of the probabilities in Table 2. The left side of Table 2 specifies the probabilities of making suppositions about nodes that have been observed by the user. For example, if the user knows that GreenInGarde-nAt11=True, then the probability of setting this node to True (leaving it unchanged) is 0.8, the probability of unsetting this node is 0.15, and the probability of setting it to False is 0.05. The right side of Table 2 specifies the probabilities of making suppositions about nodes which have not been observed by a user (i.e., nodes that are unset). As per the above heuristics, the bulk of the probability mass is allocated to leaving a node unset. The remainder of the probability mass is allocated in proportion to the propagated probability of the node ($\mathrm{Pr}_{floating} = 0.2$ is used to normalize this component). However, we include a fixed component of $\mathrm{Pr}_{fixed} = 0.05$ to ensure that some probability mass is

Table 2. Probability of making suppositions

	Node has been observed by the user		Node has not been observed by the user
Probability	**Node = FALSE**	**Node = TRUE**	
Pr(UNSET)	0.15	0.15	Pr_{unset} (=0.7)
Pr(SET FALSE)	0.8	0.05	$Pr(\text{FALSE}) \times Pr_{floating} + Pr_{fixed}$
Pr(SET TRUE)	0.05	0.8	$Pr(\text{TRUE}) \times Pr_{floating} + Pr_{fixed}$

allocated to every value (i.e., the probability of setting a node to True or False can not go below 0.05). For instance, if the propagated belief of unobserved node GreenHad-Means is Pr(GreenHadMeans) $= 0.8$, then the probability of leaving it unset is 0.7, the probability of setting it to True is $0.8 \times 0.2 + 0.05 = 0.21$ and the probability of setting it to False is $0.2 \times 0.2 + 0.05 = 0.09$.

The Supposition Score Table is used by elements of algorithm *MakeNewConfig* (Figure 3) to generate supposition configurations as follows.

Propose an initial configuration (Step 1 of MakeNewConfig). Select the first row from the Supposition Score Table. This yields supposition configuration $\{node_1:$ UNSET, $node_2:$ SET TRUE, $\ldots, node_{32}:$ UNSET$\}$ for the Supposition Score Table in Table 1.

Generate the children of a configuration (Step 3). The ith child is generated by moving down one place in column i in the Supposition Score Table, while staying in the same place in the other columns. For the Supposition Score Table in Table 1, this yields $\{\underline{node_1:}$ SET TRUE, $node_2:$ SET TRUE, $\ldots, node_{32}:$ UNSET$\}$, $\{node_1:$ UNSET, $\underline{node_2:}$ UNSET, $\ldots,$ $node_{32}:$ UNSET$\}, \ldots,$ where the underlined node-supposition pair is the element being replaced in the parent supposition configuration.

Calculate the probability obtained for a configuration (Steps 1 and 3). According to Equation 1 (Section 3), the probability of an interpretation is given by

$$Pr(UserArg|SC_i, IG_i) \times Pr(IG_i) \times Pr(SC_i)$$

The probability of a supposition configuration, $Pr(SC_i)$, is the product of the probabilities of the entries in the Supposition Score Table for the configuration in question. For instance, the initial configuration selected above has probability $0.7 \times 0.8 \times \ldots \times 0.7$, and configuration $\{\underline{node_1:}$ SET TRUE, $node_2:$ SET TRUE, $\ldots, node_{32}:$ UNSET$\}$ has probability $\underline{0.21} \times 0.8 \times \ldots \times 0.7$. Thus, the more SC_i departs from the beliefs in the user model, the lower is $Pr(SC_i)$, thereby reducing the overall probability of the interpretation.

However, recall that $Pr(UserArg|SC_i, IG_i)$ depends both on the structural match between IG_i and *UserArg* and the match between the beliefs in IG_i (influenced by the suppositions in SC_i) and those in *UserArg*. Thus, if SC_i yields a better match between the beliefs in the interpretation and those in the user's argument, then the probability of Pr(beliefs in $UserArg|SC_i, IG_i$) increases. As a result, the "cost" incurred by the suppositions in SC_i may be overcome by the "reward" resulting from the better match between the beliefs. This cost-reward balance is represented by the product Pr(beliefs in $UserArg|SC_i, IG_i$) $\times Pr(SC_i)$, which determines the position of configuration SC_i in the priority queue maintained by algorithm *MakeNewConfig* (this product is also used to calculate Equation 1). Thus, the configurations that yield the best cost-reward balance *among those inspected until now* are at the top of the queue (children that are more promising may be discovered next time *MakeNewConfig* is called).

Our process for generating supposition configurations proposes promising configurations in terms of improvements in the belief match between an argument and an interpretation. However, it does not take into account other types of interactions which may cause locally optimal supposition configurations and interpretation graphs to combine into interpretations that are sub-optimal as a whole or even invalid. For example, if a user says $A \rightarrow C$ and the most direct path between A and C in the BN is $A \rightarrow B \rightarrow C$, then if B has been set to True in the user model, this path is *blocked* [6], as B prevents A from influencing C (which does not reflect the reasoning employed in the user's argument). Thus, the shortest interpretation graph together with the best supposition configuration (which retains the beliefs in the user model) yield an invalid interpretation. In this case, unsetting the value of B (supposing that it was not observed) makes the above interpretation valid. However, this may still not be the best interpretation, as there may be a longer interpretation, e.g., $A \rightarrow D \rightarrow E \rightarrow C$, which is not blocked and requires no suppositions. Such global effects are considered during the evaluation of an interpretation as a whole (Step 3 of algorithm *GenerateInterpretations*).

5   User Evaluation

Our evaluation of the module for postulating suppositions was conducted as follows. Using a Web interface, we presented four scenarios: Crimson and Lemon (Figure 4), Sienna and Mauve. These scenarios test various supposition alternatives as follows. The Crimson and Sienna scenarios required supposing that a node is True in order to strengthen the belief in the goal proposition of an argument; the Lemon scenario required a True supposition in order to unblock a path; and the Mauve scenario required unsetting or "forgetting" the value a node to weaken the belief in the goal proposition of an argument. Each scenario contained background evidence (not shown in Figure 4) and two versions of a short argument for a goal proposition in our BN. One version (denoted "We think that") stated the belief obtained for the goal proposition by performing Bayesian propagation from the evidence, and the other version (denoted "If someone says") gave a different belief for this proposition. The trial subjects were then asked to determine what this "someone" may be assuming in order to account for his/her belief in the goal proposition.

We have used this "indirect" evaluation method (instead of having subjects interact freely with the system), because we wanted to remove extraneous factors (such as interface usability) from the evaluation, and we wanted to focus on a particular behaviour of the system (the postulation of suppositions) that does not occur for every argument.

Since the purpose of our evaluation is to determine whether BIAS generates sensible suppositions in the context of its domain knowledge, we needed to limit the suppositions available to our trial subjects to the propositions known to BIAS. However, at the same time, we did not wish to burden our subjects with the need to look through BIAS' knowledge base to find out what BIAS knows. Additionally, we wanted to allow respondents some freedom to state their views, if they disagreed with BIAS' supposi-

CRIMSON SCENARIO	LEMON SCENARIO
We think that *If forensics matched the bullets in Mr Body's body with the found gun, then the suspect Mr Green **possibly** had the means to murder Mr Body.*	**We think that** *If broken glass was found, then Mr Body's window **probably wasn't** broken from outside.*
If someone says *Forensics matching the bullets with the found gun means Mr Green **very probably** had the means to murder Mr Body.*	**If someone says** *Broken glass being found means Mr Body's window **probably was** broken from outside.*
Then it would be reasonable to think that they are assuming	
S1) Mr Green fired the gun found in the garden.	S1) Broken glass was found inside the window.
S2) The gun found in the garden is the murder weapon.	S2) The suspect Mr Green argued with Mr Body last night.
S3) Mr Green fired the murder weapon.	S3) Mr Body was killed from outside the window.
S4) Mr Green murdered Mr Body.	S4) Mr Green was in the garden at the time of death.
S5) None of the above are suitable as assumptions. A more likely assumption (in light of what our system understands) is .... [LINK TO LIST OF PROPOSITIONS]	
S6) It is not appropriate to think they are assuming anything.	

Fig. 4. Crimson and Lemon scenarios for user trials

tions. These requirements were addressed by presenting our subjects with the following options (Figure 4): (S1-S4) a list of four candidate suppositions (one was the top supposition recommended by BIAS, and most of the others were considered by BIAS to be reasonable options); (S5) an option to include an alternative supposition (the subjects were provided a link to a list containing the propositions in the BN, but could also write a supposition of their own); and (S6) an option to state that they didn't believe that any suppositions were required.

The order of presentation of the suppositions was randomized across the scenarios. However, for the discussion in this paper, BIAS' preferred supposition is always S1. The trial subjects had to award a rank of 1 to one option and could optionally rank additional alternatives (with inferior ranks). This allowed respondents to ignore suppositions that didn't make sense to them, while enabling them to include more than one option that seemed reasonable. At the same time, the results obtained by this method enable us to determine whether BIAS' suppositions are considered sensible, even if they are not our subjects' top-ranked preferences.

Our four scenarios were considered by 34 participants. Many of the respondents had not been exposed to BIAS previously and were from outside the industry. The responses for the Lemon and Mauve scenarios were clear cut, while the responses for the Crimson and Sienna scenarios were more ambiguous, but still positive. The results for these scenarios are shown in Table 3. The top rows for each scenario contain the suppositions that were preferred by the trial subjects, and the bottom row lists the total responses for each scenario and for the different ranks (recall that the only rank that had to be given was 1). The columns contain the total number of respondents that ranked a supposition (Total), and the number of respondents that ranked it first (R1), second (R2) or gave it a lower rank (Other). Our results are summarized below.

Table 3. Ranking of candidate suppositions for the four scenarios

LEMON SCENARIO	Total	R1	R2	Other	MAUVE SCENARIO	Total	R1	R2	Other
Supposition S1	30	30	0	0	Supposition S1	25	19	4	2
Supposition S3	11	0	11	0	Supposition S5	14	8	5	1
Total responses	51	34	12	5	Total responses	62	34	16	12
CRIMSON SCENARIO	Total	R1	R2	Other	SIENNA SCENARIO	Total	R1	R2	Other
Supposition S1	20	10	8	2	Supposition S1 + S3	30	20	6	4
Supposition S2	18	11	3	4	Supposition S4	16	7	6	3
Total responses	75	34	21	20	Total responses	69	34	19	16

- Supposition S1 was clearly the most favoured choice for the **Lemon** scenario, with 30 of the 34 respondents ranking it first. Supposition S3 was clearly the next best choice, with 11 trial subjects giving it a rank of 2.
- Supposition S1 was the preferred choice for the **Mauve** scenario, with 19 of the 34 respondents giving it a rank of 1. The next best choice was the Alternate Supposition, with only 8 subjects ranking it first. There were no clear preferences for rank 2, with all options receiving this rank at least once, but never more than five times.
- Suppositions S1 and S2 for the **Crimson** scenario were similarly ranked (each ranked first by about 1/3 of the subjects), with Supposition S1 being favoured slightly over S2, but not significantly so. The other options were ranked first only by a few trial subjects.
- The responses for the **Sienna** scenario presented us with a special case. The results of the first 22 responses and the comments provided by our trial subjects indicated that there was some confusion due to the wording of the instructions and the fact that, unlike the other scenarios, the Sienna scenario included a True and False version of the same node (Supposition S1 was "The time of death was 11 pm last night" and S3 was the negation of S1). Further, Supposition S3 supports the "We think that" version, while S1 supports the "If someone says" version. As a result, most of the respondents were divided between giving a rank of 1 to Supposition S1 or Supposition S3. Nonetheless, the main outcome from this scenario is that regardless of how the respondents read it, they clearly felt that a supposition had to be made about the "time of death" node, which was ranked first by 20 of the 34 respondents.
- Overall, very few trial subjects felt that no suppositions were warranted (9 for all the scenarios combined). Further, BIAS' preferred supposition was consistently ranked first or second, with its average rank being the lowest (best) among all the options.

These results justify the importance of making suppositions, and indicate that the suppositions made by BIAS not only are considered reasonable by people, but also have significant support.

6   Conclusion

We have offered a mechanism that postulates suppositions made by users in their arguments, and have shown how this mechanism is incorporated into our argument interpretation process. Our mechanism includes a procedure for generating suppositions, a method for calculating the probability of a set of suppositions, and a formalism for incorporating this probability into the probability of an interpretation.

An important feature of our system is its stability, in the sense that it does not match spurious beliefs (that don't follow a "sensible" line of reasoning). That is, the system will posit a supposition for a node only if it yields a payoff, i.e., a substantially better match between the beliefs in an interpretation and those in a user's argument. This behaviour is a result of BIAS' inherent reluctance to posit suppositions, combined with its reliance on a rigorous reasoning formalism, such as BNs, which requires the beliefs in the system to be consistent.

Finally, the results of our evaluation show that our trial subjects found BIAS' suppositions to be both necessary and reasonable, with its preferred suppositions being top-ranked or top-2 ranked by most subjects.

References

1. Sarah George and Ingrid Zukerman. An anytime algorithm for interpreting arguments. In *PRICAI2004 – Proceedings of the Eighth Pacific Rim International Conference on Artificial Intelligence*, 311–321, Auckland, New Zealand, 2004.
2. John Gurney, Don Perlis, and Khemdut Purang. Interpreting presuppositions using active logic: From contexts to utterances. *Computational Intelligence*, 13(3):391–413, 1997.
3. S. J. Kaplan. Cooperative responses from a portable natural language query system. *Artificial Intelligence*, 19:165–187, 1982.
4. Robert E. Mercer. Presuppositions and default reasoning: A study in lexical pragmatics. In J. Pustejovski and S. Bergler, editors, *ACL SIG Workshop on Lexical Semantics and Knowledge Representation (SIGLEX)*, 321–339. 1991.
5. Amihai Motro. SEAVE: a mechanism for verifying user presuppositions in query systems. *ACM Transactions on Information Systems (TOIS)*, 4(4):312–330, 1986.
6. Judea Pearl. *Probabilistic Reasoning in Intelligent Systems*. Morgan Kaufmann Publishers, San Mateo, California, 1988.
7. Ingrid Zukerman and Sarah George. A probabilistic approach for argument interpretation. *User Modeling and User-Adapted Interaction, Special Issue on Language-Based Interaction*, 2005.
8. Ingrid Zukerman, Sarah George, and Mark George. Incorporating a user model into an information theoretic framework for argument interpretation. In *UM03 – Proceedings of the Ninth International Conference on User Modeling*, 106–116, Johnstown, Pennsylvania, 2003.
9. Ingrid Zukerman, Michael Niemann, and Sarah George. Improving the presentation of argument interpretations based on user trials. In *AI'04 – Proceedings of the 17th Australian Joint Conference on Artificial Intelligence*, 587–598, Cairns, Australia, 2004.

Generative Programming Driven by User Models

Mauro Marinilli and Alessandro Micarelli

Dipartimento di Informatica e Automazione,
Laboratorio di Intelligenza Artificiale,
Università "Roma Tre", via della Vasca Navale 79, 00184 Rome, Italy
{marinil, micarel}@dia.uniroma3.it

Abstract. This paper discusses the automatic generation of programs by adapting the construction process to the user currently interacting with the program. A class of such systems is investigated where such generation process is continuously repeated making the program design and implementation evolve according to user behaviour. By leveraging on existing technologies (software generation facilities, modelling languages, specific and general standard metamodels) an experimental proof of concept system that is able to generate itself while interacting with the user is introduced and tested. The findings are discussed and a general organization for this class of adaptive systems is briefly proposed and compared with existing literature.

1 Introduction

Generative Programming (GP) is a set of techniques that enables programs to be automatically constructed from smaller domain-specific artifacts [5]. We focus here on *model* artifacts only, and on Model Based Generative Programming. With the term model we mean representations of generic discrete information (including application domains, algorithms, user models etc.) expressed as UML 2.0 [4] diagrams. By using this representation formalism we can take advantage of the large diffusion of this language and the wide array of supporting technologies and existing domain-specific standard models available. UML 2.0 is a powerful language that allows expressing sophisticated representations and some fine-grained behavior thanks to the Object Constraint Language[1] (OCL). Model Based Generative Programming with UML is commonplace in some GP technologies that transform business domain models into software executables for a given technology scenario such as the Model Driven Architecture (MDA) approach [8], that unfortunately lack user-adapted features. This paper is structured following a general-to-particular organization. The following section 2 discusses some general introductory concepts. Section 3 briefly introduces a proposed class of user-adapted systems of interest and section 4 shows a concrete prototype application of such systems. The paper concludes with a comparison with existing literature and a summary.

---

[1] An introduction of the OCL language can be found at http://www.klasse.nl/ocl/ocl-definition.pdf. In the following for brevity we will report only structural class diagrams while avoiding other details such as other diagram types or OCL code.

L. Ardissono, P. Brna, and A. Mitrovic (Eds.): UM 2005, LNAI 3538, pp. 30–39, 2005.
© Springer-Verlag Berlin Heidelberg 2005

2 Modeling Abstraction Layers

Following [1, 4] our generic models are organized in abstraction layers. This approach to knowledge organization involves descriptions of abstraction levels placed on top of other abstraction levels. Each level (except the lowest one) can be thought of a model and the "level below" as an instance of that model. Figure 1 shows such organization[1] (focusing only on UML models for simplicity). The abstraction levels in Figure 1 are discussed in the following.

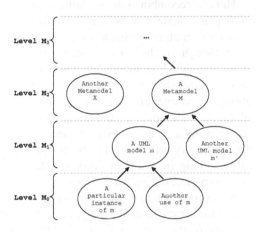

- Level 0 represents the instance level, i.e. the execution of a give program in a given time in a given context (user, underlying hardware and OS, etc.). For uniformity we call (inexactly) models also the items in level 0, which are not models but rather real world "runs" of a given program.

- Level 1 represents the abstraction model common to most programming languages. We will make the assumption that Object-Oriented (OO) code and UML diagrams are equivalent and rep-

Fig. 1. Layers of abstraction for models

resented at this level of abstraction. A source code (or an equivalent level 1 model M_1) can be thought of as an abstraction over a set of executions (i.e. M_0 instances).

- Level 2 represents a model for expressing level 1 models, i.e. a *metamodel*. The UML modeling language can be thought of as a general metamodel representing a vast set of models (OO models). More specific metamodels can be defined for specific domains. For example, the JCP26 specification could be seen as a partial metamodel that describes the technical details of Enterprise Java Beans (EJB) technology architecture[2]. EML and its successor IMS Learning Design are metamodels that describe the design of units of learning from a pedagogical perspective [11, 12].

- Level 3 is yet another level of abstraction upon level 2 and it is a model representing metamodels (or, alternatively, a meta-metamodel). An example is the Meta Object Facility (MOF) for Model Driven Architectures (MDA)[8].

- Theoretically, more abstraction layers can be thought on top of M_3 [14]. For simplicity we will deal in this paper only at most with level 2 models.

In order to generate a model from level M_{i+1} to M_i specific model transformations are applied. Usual compilation techniques (including linking and all other processes that transform source code and other artifacts in an executable for a given execution platform) can be thought of as the standard transformation for mapping M_1 to M_0 models.

---

[2] The JCP26 specification is available at http://www.jcp.org/en/jsr/detail?id=26.

3   A Class of Generative Systems

As a particular class of Generative Systems we define Recombining Systems (RS) as a class of interactive Generative Systems that are able to modify themselves at runtime by means of a set of explicit models while interacting with the user and or other external sources. The typical runtime cycle of a RS is shown in Figure 2.

Hence, recombination is defined as particular model transformation that preserves runtime session consistency even though it alters (recombines) the system from M_i down to M_0. Runtime session consistency is defined as the ability of maintaining a substantial part of the runtime application's state. Intuitively, using a term from Self-Organizing System theory [10], RS could be thought of remaining in a sort of (very simple) stationary state during their evolution[1].

Fig. 2. The basic cycle of RS

Software that is generated only once at deployment time (a common application of GP) is not considered a RS because does not satisfy the cycle in Figure 2. Differently from non-RS software systems, RS evolve their (user-perceived) runtime state through explicit models at various levels of abstraction. The *level of a RS* is defined as the highest abstraction layer that is affected (i.e. modified) during the recombination phase. A level 2 RS is a system that is able to modify at runtime its own generating metamodels (M_2) and possibly also its models (M_1)[3]. For brevity we don't discuss here RS. In this paper we will focus on a particular class of RS that use an explicit model of the user for driving the recombination process. We will call these systems User-Adapted Recombining Systems (UARS).

3.1   User-Adapted Recombining Systems

UARS are systems that are defined in terms of models at various abstraction layers and that modify some of these models in order to evolve following user's needs. UARS can be thought of user-centered RS. UARS recombine themselves basing upon particular representations of the user called Recombining User Models (RUM). These models drive the transformations from higher level models down to executable code.

Ideally, RUM could be thought of models of the user *as a software designer*. When manufacturing traditional software, designers and developers go through cycles of application tuning and testing before releasing the product to end users. By distilling this knowledge in very specialized models (both for technology and domain logic) it

---

[3] Usual interactive adaptive systems can be thought of as level 0 RS in that the adaptive model is defined once for all at level 1 (i.e. in the system source code or some equivalent models) and it is actuated at level 0 (i.e. in the various execution instances).

is possible to automate part of this process for some limited domains and technologies. Through recombination cycles UARS evolve accordingly to user needs. UARS (and RS as well) can be seen as systems where the design and execution phase (habitually two distinct phases in traditional software manufacturing) collapse into a unique augmented runtime phase, where the System converges on (model-represented) user's needs through recombination cycles. Of course, in order to enable this architecture a number of complex models and model transformations need to be built up front. We now introduce some definitions that will be used in the following (the subscript i to indicate a generic abstraction level): *Recombining User Model* (RUM$_i$) is the model that drives the user-adapted generation of the system. *System User Model* (SUM$_i$) is the representation of user as of the adaptation performed outside the Recombining phase. Classic user adaptation falls into this category of models. *System Model* (SM$_i$) is the model that describes the system functional domain.

Recapping, UARS embody a generic[4], radical form of user-driven adaptation that hides both underlying technology and other non-meaningful details providing a very high level of representation (the models could even be shown to those end users familiar with UML). If well designed, models and ontologies can be reused in other contexts as well. In the following we introduce a simple prototype UARS Computer-based training system (CBT) modeled for training students in basic OO design.

4   A Case Study on a CBT System for OO Design

As a proof of concept of the UARS approach to adaptive systems, to test its practical feasibility and effectiveness we developed a number of prototypes refining a number of techniques that were used to design and implement a simple UARS prototype that will be presented in the following. We simplified in a number of ways the power of the system: the recombining level has been kept to a minimum and preexisting standards have employed as much as possible in the design of the metamodels.

4.1   Domain Choice

In order to stress the UARS approach in a challenging application domain we developed a simple user-adapted computer-based learning system training students on basic OO class diagrams (OOCD) design focused on OO design patterns (OODP)[5]. A number of reasons influenced our decision: (i) computer-based learning and the related fields are domains with an already relatively large number of standard metamodel initiatives and specifications that speeded up the design of the metamodel for our test system; (ii) knowledge of the domain helped the design and development; (iii) user adaptation has been studied and applied extensively in this and related fields providing an important research background for our work.

---

[4]   The proposed approach is both technology and application agnostic; for example Adaptive Hypermedia systems can be developed as UARS, as well as Web-based adaptive applications, wireless applets, etc.

[5]   A list can be found at: http://home.earthlink.net/~huston2/dp/patterns.html.

Learners use a well-known software development platform, Eclipse[6] for designing their class diagrams; in case of need they can ask advice to our prototype for designs having a similar use. The System suggests learners with the class diagrams which most closely match the current learner's software design style retrieved from a predefined library of recurring designs drawn from standard OODP. A screenshot of the prototype System is provided in Figure 3.

Our objective was to use UARS to represents explicitly the learner's design style and experience. In order to do so we employed the concept of learner's *perceived affordance* for a given design. In general this term refers to the actionable properties of some objects as perceived from an actor [9] and successively was adapted to the design of interactive artifacts [13]. Our hypothesis is that designers maintain an (often implicit) conceptual representation of the possible *use* of a given design while crafting or employing it. These representations are subjective. Design in general (and OO software design in particular) is a rather subjective process and there may not exist the right design for a given situation but rather a set of valid alternatives. We assumed that learners develop their own subjective design style by evolving an implicit set of affordances for designs. We explicitly represented these styles in our system by means of user-perceived relevance functions (RF) between different designs, that we will call m_u.[7]

Our prototype's user model contained a set of software implementations of RF $\{M_u^i\}$ evolved by means of user feedback f_u. These $\{M_u^i\}$ are algorithms (represented as executable Java classes) generated through the UARS cycle exposed before, returning a value $\in [0,1]$ and a confidence measure $c_u^i \in [0,1]$. We assumed that during their learning process learners continuously refine m_u adapting it to new scenarios and solutions. The final value M_u (our prototype's representation of m_u) is obtained as: $M_u | \max(c_u^i) \ \forall M_u \in \{M_u\}$. If no RF has a confidence value higher than a minimum (that we set empirically to 0.35) then a new recombination phase is launched, as discussed later, and the result value obtained from the new RF is provided to the learner. Recombination comes into play in those situations where no $\{M_u^i\}$ returns a confidence value higher than a minimum.

In these cases our prototype resorts to obtain a new M_u^j that is inserted in $\{M_u\}$ as follows. Randomly[8], 10 new RF are generated from the SUM_2 metamodel in Figure 4,

---

[6]   Eclipse was employed both as the application domain technology –our prototype was packaged as an Eclipse plug-in- and as the technology for implementing code generation (thanks to technologies like EMF and JET). The Eclipse project can be accessed at: http://www.eclipse.org.

[7]   The function $m_u(d_1, d_2) \rightarrow [0,1]$ represents the distance between two OOCD designs d_1, d_2 as perceived by the user. Two designs that afford similar uses have a small distance m_u. As regards the suggestion phase, given the user design d_u the System provides another design $d_R | m_u(d_u, d_R) \leq m_u(d_u, d_X) \ \forall \ d_X \in$ Library.

[8]   The SUM_2 transformations used in our prototype are capable of providing 6×6×8×8 combinations, thus generating 2304 different RF (i.e. SUM_1 instances) drawn from standard Machine Learning algorithms taken from the WEKA library (http://www.cs. waikato.ac.nz/ml/weka/) and from a family of ad-hoc, keyword based algorithms.

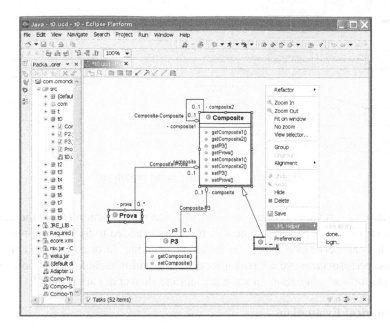

Fig. 3. A prototype screenshot

each represented as a Java class (equivalent to a SUM_1 model) that are used to train all M_u^j, but only one is kept (the others are discarded) by choosing the one that better resembles the last (chronologically) feedback f_u (used as the *fitness parameter* [8]). This is the recombination algorithm, driven by RUM_0 (note that f_u are also used for classic SUM_0 user adaptation). A "renting" parameter is used to delete those RF that don't provide anymore values close enough to user's feedbacks. The user provides a feedback f_u by indicating the closest design available in the Library together with a distance value.

To recap, an instance of SUM_0 in our prototype contains a set of RF $\{M_u^i\}$ tracking the evolution of user's m_u. An instance of RUM_0 instead contains past learner's feedbacks $\{f_u\}$. Figure 4 shows the structure of both the RUM_1 and the SUM_2 designed for the prototype.

The following transformations occur at every recombination cycle (see Figure 2) after a cold-start preliminary phase (where 10 feedbacks were preliminary provided in order to tune a default startup RF): (1) User provides feedback to the System.

The feedback is added to the runtime instance RUM_0 and to the SUM_0[9]. (2) RUM_0 is used for seeding the adaptation of the level 1 model generation (see discussion above). (3) After the level 1 models have been generated, they are assembled together to provide executable code. In our prototype we generate only a new class representing a new M_u^i. (4) The newly generated executable code is deployed and dynamically

---

[9] The same user feedback thus performs a twofold purpose: as a part of SUM_0 is provided to past generated metrics for fine parameters tuning, while as part of RUM_0 is used to drive the recombination process and create new metrics.

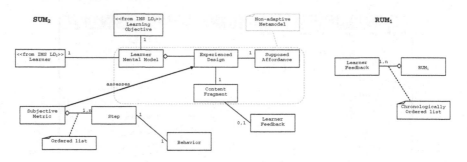

Fig. 4. Some models used in the prototype[10]

loaded into the previous running session, in a seamless fashion (from the end user point of view). In our prototype a new metric class is added to SUM_0. The recombination cycle is all performed locally on the client machine. In order to curb complexity and boost performances we adopted a focused generation technique that concentrates recombination and adaptation on some model (and then code) areas only[11].

4.2 Empirical Evaluation

For evaluating our prototype, following carefully the advice provided by [3], we prepared a special version of the system that was used to support 16 users in solving 4 design problems in diverse application domains that could be solved using a single OODP. Users did not know that there was an adaptive system behind the graphic UML editor. The first and the second problem could be solved using the same OODP; so did the third and fourth problem. Between a problem and the next users were asked to pay attention to 5 suggested tentative solutions provided by the system. Some of these suggestions were provided by the prototype (using the user design), others were provided non-adaptively[12]. Users were asked to assess if, in their opinion, those suggested designs could solve the given problem. Users' designs were judged blindly by an expert and a score was obtained for each design. Differences between scores of paired designs were calculated separating those pairs where suggestion was provided adaptively from those where suggestions were not adapted.

---

[10] The SUM_2 metamodel presented in Fig. 4 was designed as a test bed of complex modeling situations for testing the UARS approach rather than a reusable asset. The UML stereotype `<<from IMS LD2>>` represents the IMS Learning Design metamodel. In order to promote metamodel reuse a number of decompositions have been performed on the metamodels that are not reported here for brevity.

[11] Runtime deployment of the newly generated code is performed using custom Java class loaders. Runtime context (i.e. level 0 data) is passed from one generation to the next through object serialization.

[12] Non-adaptive suggestions were provided by randomly picking 4 designs and adding the correct answer among them, in the form of the abstract template of the OODP solving that problem.

Table 1. Empirical Evaluation Results

(i)	-.2	.4	-.2	.4	.2	.5	.2	.4	.5	.4	.3	.4	.5	.5	.4	.5	0	0
(ii)	-.3	-.3	.1	-.2	.1	.3	.1	-.3	.1	.1	.2	.1	.1	.1	0	.1	0	0

The results from Table 1 (first row are the scores obtained with the adaptive tool, in the second row there are the scores obtained without adaptive support) clearly show the benefit of the adaptive tool. Furthermore, we used the Wilcoxon Signed-Rank Test for paired data [6] to detect whether the two samples (from two continuous, assumed independent and non-normal distributions) were statistically unrelated or not. The Null hypothesis in our experiment was "The statistical populations are the same, i.e. there is no difference in performance between the adaptive and the non-adaptive metric". Given the test results found[13] we can conclude that the Null hypothesis can be rejected and the alternative hypothesis ("The differences observed between the two distributions are not due to chance but are due to the difference between the populations they belong to") can be accepted proving the usefulness of the UARS approach in our prototype.

4.3 Lessons Learned

We found that UARS have a number of advantages over more traditional adaptive systems, even if they are much more labor-intensive to set up (at least with current technology): (i) they represent adaptive and system functional models at a high level of abstraction, isolated from implementation and other non meaningful details. Clear and more maintainable representations are thus encouraged; (ii) they may take advantage of existing standard metamodels, ontologies and other modeling facility (which are growing in many application domains) thus reusing knowledge representations; (iii) by taking advantage of generative technologies they provide a very powerful and general adaptation mechanism that includes as a particular case classic adaptation techniques; (iv) such systems are particularly useful for generating user-tailored software for devices where computing resources don't allow for sophisticated client-side user adaptation.

5 Related Work

User-adapted generative technologies are increasingly being studied in user-tailored ubiquitous software [2, 15] for computing devices with limited resources where user-adapted code generation can be performed on remote servers at deployment time. Despite some research in the convergence area of GP and user modeling ([2] introduces an architecture for personalizing applications based on a model-driven, user

---

[13] We obtained a pValue= 8.4104E-4, less than the Significance Level set at the beginning of the experiment ($\alpha=0.01$). We used an open source implementation of the test available at: http://rana.lbl.gov/~nix/.

centered approach), the adoption of GP techniques together with "strong" user adaptation for general systems is still missing.

Some work focused on investigating the adoption of Software Engineering techniques and approaches to Adaptive Hypermedia (AH) systems. The Munich Reference Model [16], aimed at providing a formal reference model for AH systems, using UML (with OCL) and providing a user and adaptation metamodels together with a comprehensive design method and development process for AH applications. These initiatives focused on engineering AH applications development by adapting state-of-the-art techniques and methodologies, providing a comprehensive framework that anyway lacks enough flexibility and expressive power to handle powerful adaptation models and non-standard situations (quite the norm in intelligent adaptive applications). The use of the UML language for generating navigation sequences for Web-based systems was investigated [7].

Our proposed approach is different in several ways from the previous contributions in that it embodies a somehow visionary yet general programming approach (see section 3) that still needs to be fully explored. Far from being limited to technological aspects only (model-based knowledge representation and GP techniques) our proposed approach allows the definition of technology-independent, powerful user models at several abstraction layers. Moreover, the introduction in the field of user adaptation of rich metamodels suitable for code generation can foster standardization and reuse both in vertical domains (as it is happening on the software technology front) and as a general modeling foundation for an infrastructure for a rich set of user modeling services. As an example of the proposed approach we crafted a simple yet powerful and innovative UARS capable of modeling explicitly and at a high level user's subjective OO software design styles.

6 Summary and Conclusions

We introduced an original application of GP and user modeling technologies and approaches for designing and building highly adaptive interactive systems. One prototype that adopts this approach has been developed and preliminarily tested showing the effectiveness of the proposed concepts. Such a prototype system is able to track and represent user-perceived relevance metric by means of models that drive the generation of its own code. The preliminary prototype tests revealed an added value compared to non-adaptive representations, even if more accurate testing are needed.

Concluding, the UARS approach seems extremely promising given its ability to express complex systems by means of high-level abstraction models that can be used to drive code generation, shielding both end-users and knowledge engineers from technology details. The simultaneous emergence of standard modeling specifications expressed in UML for specific domains and the development of GP technologies supporting UML will simplify the adoption of user model-driven GP. In the future we expect certain application fields (like the user models-based generation of ubiquitous computing software or user interfaces) to benefit from the technologies and approaches discussed here.

References

1. Bézivin J.: From Object Composition to Model Transformation with the MDA. In Proceedings of TOOLS USA, Vol. IEEE TOOLS-39. pages 195-200.Santa Barbara. USA (2001)
2. Bonnet S.: Model Driven Software Personalization. In: Proceedings of Smart Objects Conference. Grenoble (2003) available at: http://www.grenoble-soc.com/proceedings03/Pdf/50-Bonnet.pdf
3. Chin, D.: Empirical Evaluation of User Models and User-Adapted Systems. Journal of User Modeling and User-Adapted Interaction vol.11 pages 181-194. (2001)
4. Cranefield, S. and Purvis M.: UML as an Ontology Modelling Language In: Proceedings of the Workshop on Intelligent Information Integration, 16th International Joint Conference on Artificial Intelligence. IJCAI 99 (1999) available at: http://nzdis.otago.ac.nz/download/papers/Dis-arch-6-99.pdf
5. Czarnecki K., Eisenecker U. Generative Programming: Methods, Tools, and Applications. Addison-Wesley (2000)
6. Devore, J.L. Probability and Statistics for Engineering and the Sciences. Brooks/Cole Publishing Company, Monterrey, California, fourth edition (1995).
7. Dolog, P. and Nejdl W.: Using UML and XMI for Generating Adaptive Navigation Sequences in Web-Based Systems. In: "UML" 2003 - The Unified Modeling Language: Modeling Languages and Applications. Lecture Notes in Computer Science. Vol.2863 Springer-Verlag Heidelberg (2003)available at: http://www.l3s.de/~dolog/pub/uml 003.pdf
8. Frankel, D.: Model Driven Architecture: Applying MDA to Enterprise Computing. J. Wiley & Sons. (2003)
9. Gibson, J. J.: The theory of affordances. In R. E. Shaw & J. Bransford (Eds.), Perceiving, Acting, and Knowing. Hillsdale, NJ: Lawrence Erlbaum Associates (1977)
10. Heylighen F., The Science Of Self Organization And Adaptivity. (2001) Available at: http://pespmc1.vub.ac.be/papers/EOLSS-Self-Organiz.pdf
11. IMS Learning Design Best Practice and Implementation Guide. IMS Global Learning Consortium (2003) available at http://www.imsglobal.org/profiles/lipbest01.html.
12. Koper R.: Modeling Units of Study from a Pedagogical Perspective – The Pedagogical Meta-Model Behind EML. Open University of the Netherlands (2001)
13. Norman, D. A.: The psychology of everyday things. New York: Basic Books. (1988)
14. Nytun, J. P. and Prinz A.: Metalevel Representation and Philosophical Ontology. In: ECOOP 2004 workshop: Philosophy, Ontology, and Information Systems. Oslo. Norway (2004) available at: http://ikt.hia.no/janpn/papers/Art_philosophy_Ontology.pdf
15. Pazzani, M.: Adaptive Interfaces for Ubiquitous Web Access In: Proceedings of the 9th International Conference on User Modeling UM 03 page 1. Springer-Verlag (2003)
16. Parcus de Koch, N.: Software Engineering for Adaptive Hypermedia Systems – Reference Model, Modeling Techniques and Development Process. PhD Dissertation University of Munich (2001)

Data-Driven Refinement of a Probabilistic Model of User Affect

Cristina Conati and Heather Maclaren

Dept. of Computer Science, University of British Columbia,
2366 Main Mall, Vancouver, BC,
V6T 1Z4, Canada
{conati, maclaren}@cs.ubc.ca

Abstract. We present further developments in our work on using data from real users to build a probabilistic model of user affect based on Dynamic Bayesian Networks (DBNs) and designed to detect multiple emotions. We present analysis and solutions for inaccuracies identified by a previous evaluation; refining the model's appraisals of events to reflect more closely those of real users. Our findings lead us to challenge previously made assumptions and produce insights into directions for further improvement.

1 Introduction

The assessment of users' affect is increasingly recognized as an informative task when attempting to improve the effectiveness of interactive systems. Information on the user's affective state is particularly important when the user is focused on a highly engaging task where inappropriate system interventions may be especially disruptive, such as learning in simulated environments and educational games.

Educational games attempt to stimulate student learning by embedding pedagogical activities within a highly engaging, game like environment. We are working to improve the pedagogical effectiveness of these games by producing intelligent agents that monitor the student's learning progress and generate tailored interactions to improve learning during game playing. To avoid interfering with the student's level of engagement, these agents should take into account the student's affective state (in addition to her cognitive state) when determining when and how to intervene.

Assessment of emotions, particularly the multiple specific emotions that educational games can generate, is very difficult because the mapping between emotions, their causes, and their effects is highly ambiguous [10]. However, we believe that information on specific emotions may enable more precise and effective agent's interventions than a simpler assessment of arousal or valence (e.g.[1]), or stress [7]. To handle the high level of uncertainty in this modeling task, we have devised a framework for affective modeling that integrates in a Dynamic Bayesian Network (DBN) information on both the *causes* of a user's emotions and their *effects* on the user's behavior. Model construction is done as much as possible from data, integrated with relevant psychological theories of emotion and personality. The inherent difficulties

L. Ardissono, P. Brna, and A. Mitrovic (Eds.): UM 2005, LNAI 3538, pp. 40–49, 2005.

of this task include: the novel nature of the phenomena that we are trying to model, the limited existing knowledge of users' emotional reactions during system interaction, especially within the context of educational games, and the difficulty of observing variables that are key to the assessment of affect.

We have been using data collected in a series of studies (e.g. [3,11]) to construct a probabilistic model of the user's affective state that is based on the OCC model of emotions [9]. The data from our most recent study [4] was used to evaluate the model we have built so far. Although there have been evaluations using aggregated data [6] and evaluations of sources of affective data (e.g.[2]), to the best of our knowledge this is currently the only evaluation of an affective user model embedded in a real system and tested with individual users. Our results showed that if the user's goals could be correctly assessed then the model could produce reasonably accurate predictions of user affect, but also revealed some sources of inaccuracy that needed to be addressed. We recognize that the assessment of the user's goals must be improved before the model can be used autonomously within a real system. However, solutions for the other sources of inaccuracy within the model's emotional assessment will help clarify the full requirements of the goal assessment task.

In this paper we address previously identified inaccuracies within the model's mechanism of emotional appraisal. We then rc-evaluate the refined model, producing insights into additional refinements that would produce further improvement.

2 The Affective User Model

Fig. 1 shows a high level representation of two time slices of our affective model. The part of the network above the nodes *Emotional States* represents the relations between possible causes and emotional states, as they are described in the OCC theory of emotions [9]. In this theory, emotions arise as a result of one's *appraisal* of the current situation in relation to one's goals. Thus, our DBN includes variables for *Goals* that a user may have during the interaction with an education game and its embedded pedagogical agent (for details on goal assessment see [11]). Situations consist of the outcome of any event caused by either a user's or an agent's action (nodes *User*

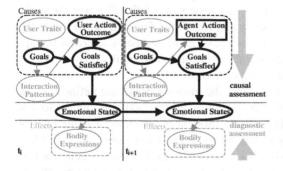

Fig. 1. Two slices of our general affective model

Fig. 2. Prime Climb interface

Action Outcome and *Agent Action Outcome*). An event's desirability in relation to the user's goals is represented by *Goals Satisfied,* which in turn influences the user's *Emotional States.* The part of the network below the nodes *Emotional States* provides diagnostic assessment from bodily reactions known to correlate with emotions.

We have instantiated and evaluated the causal part of the model to assess players' emotions during the interaction with the Prime Climb educational game. In the rest of the paper we will focus on the refinement and evaluation of the appraisal part of this causal model (the bold nodes and links in Figure 1).

2.1 Causal Affective Assessment for Prime Climb

Figure 2 shows a screenshot of PrimeClimb, a game designed to teach number factorization to 6th and 7th grade students. In the game, two players must cooperate to climb a series of mountains that are divided in numbered sectors. Each player should move to a number that does not share any factors with her partner's, otherwise she falls. Prime Climb provides two tools to help students: a *magnifying glass* to see a number's factorization, and a *help box* to communicate with the pedagogical agent we are building for the game. In addition to providing help when a student is playing with a partner, the pedagogical agent engages its player in a "Practice Climb" during which it climbs with the student as a climbing instructor.

The affective model described here assesses the student's emotions during these practice climbs. Figure 3 shows the appraisal part of this model created after the student makes a move. As the bottom part of the figure shows, we currently represent in our DBN 6 of the 22 emotions defined in the OCC model. They are *Joy/Distress* for the current state of the game, *Pride/Shame* of the student toward herself, and *Admiration/Reproach* toward the agent, modeled by three two-valued nodes: *emotion for game, emotion for self* and *emotion for agent*.

Let's now consider the workings of the part of the model that assesses the student's situation appraisal in Prime Climb. In this part of the model the links and Conditional Probability Tables (CPTs) between *Goal* nodes, the outcome of the student's or agent's action, and *Goal Satisfied* nodes were based on subjective judgment because our previous studies focused on collecting data to refine the model's assessment of student goals. For some links, the connections were quite obvious. For instance, if the student has the goal *Avoid Falling,* a move that results in a fall will lower the probability that the goal is achieved. For other goals, like *Have Fun* and *Learn Math,* the connections were not obvious and we did not have good heuristics to create the appraisal links. Thus we postponed including them in the model until we could collect data from which to determine an appropriate structure.

The links between *Goal Satisfied* nodes and the emotion nodes are defined as follows. We assume that the outcome of every agent or student action is subject to student appraisal. Thus, each *Goal Satisfied* node influences *emotion-for-game* (*Joy* or *Distress*) in every slice. If a slice is generated by a student action then each *Goal Satisfied* node influences *emotion-for-self* (slice t_i in Fig. 3). If a slice is generated by an agent's intervention, then *emotion-for-agent* is influenced instead (slice not shown

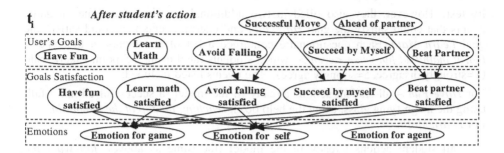

Fig. 3. Sample sub network for appraisal after student action

due to lack of space). We also assume that a student either has a goal or does not (i.e. we do not model goal priority) and that the student has the same goals throughout the game session. The CPTs for emotion nodes were defined so that the probability of the positive emotion is proportional to the number of true *Goal Satisfied* nodes.

When we evaluated the affective model that included this version of the appraisal component [4], we discovered two main sources of inaccuracy:

Source 1: *Joy* and *Distress* due to student actions. The absence of links (as shown in Fig. 3) between the outcome of a student's move and the satisfaction of goals *Have Fun* and *Learn Math* made the model underestimate the positive emotions towards the game for students that only had these goals. This reduced the model's accuracy for *Joy* from 74% to 50% and highlighted the need to collect data to create the missing links. The model also underestimated the negative emotions felt by some students when falling repeatedly and thus had low accuracy for *Distress* of 57%.

Source 2: *Admiration* and *Reproach* towards the agent. The subjective links between agent actions and goal satisfaction had caused the model to underestimate the students' positive feelings towards the agent. This produced an accuracy of 20.5% for *Admiration* and 75% for *Reproach*, further highlighting the need to collect data to refine the connections in the appraisal part of the model.

3 User Study

The general structure of this new study was similar to the previous one. Sixty-six 6th and 7th grade students from 3 local schools interacted with Prime Climb, and, during the interaction, were asked to report their feelings towards the game and towards the agent using simple dialogue boxes. However, while in the previous study the agent was directed in a Wizard of Oz fashion, in this study the agent was autonomous and based its interventions on a model of student learning [5]. While the model of student affect was dynamically updated during interaction, the pedagogical agent did not use it to direct its interventions. However, the assessments of the affective model were included in the log files, for comparison with the student's reported emotions.

As in the previous study, students completed a pre-test on number factorization, a post-questionnaire to indicate the goals they had during game playing, and a personality test. However, they also filled in two additional questionnaires, one on game events that could satisfy the goal *Have Fun* and one on events that could satisfy the goal *Learn Math*. Each questionnaire contained a list of statements of the type '*I learnt math/had fun when <event>*' which students rated using a 5-point Likert scale (1=strongly disagree, 5=strongly agree). The events listed included:

For *Have Fun* – all student actions already in the model (a successful climb, a fall, using the magnifying glass, using the help box), *reaching the top of the mountain*.
For *Learn Math*

- all student actions already in the model (the same as above), *following the agent's advice,* and *encountering big numbers.*
- agent interventions already in the model that were intended to help the student learn math (reflect on reasons for success, reflect on reasons for failure), *think about common factors,* and *use the magnifying glass.*

The italicized items at the end of each list above had not been explicitly included in the model before, but were added based on anecdotal evidence suggesting that they may help to satisfy these goals. We did not ask students about agent actions that satisfied the goal *Have Fun* or other events that already satisfied other goals within the model due to limitations on time and to avoid students becoming fatigued.

4   Refinement of the Model's Causal Affective Assessment

Before discussing how we refined the model using data from the new study we describe how well the existing model performed on the new data set.

We measured the model's accuracy as the percentage of assessments that agreed with the students' reports for each emotion pair (e.g. *Joy/Distress*). If the model's corresponding assessment was above a simple threshold then it was predicting a positive emotion, if not then it was predicting a negative emotion. The threshold was determined using the data from our previous study [4].

Table 1 shows the accuracy obtained using three-fold cross-validation when the goals students declared in the questionnaire are used as evidence in the model; each iteration used one-third of the data as a test set. The results show that the inaccuracies discussed earlier still affect the model's performance on the new data set. The high variance for *Joy* is due to one test set containing some students who only had the goals *Have Fun* or *Learn Math*, thus the model underestimated their positive re-

Table 1. Emotional belief accuracy of the initial model for the new data set

Emotion	Accuracy (%)		
	Mean	Std. Dev.	Total data points
Joy	66.54	17.38	170
Distress	64.68	29.14	14
Combined J/D	65.61		
Admiration	43.22	12.53	127
Reproach	80.79	6.05	28
Combined A/R	62.00		

sponses. The high variance of *Distress* is due in part to the small number of data points, but it is also due to the model underestimating the negative feelings of some students who fell repeatedly. The low accuracy for *Admiration* and high accuracy for *Reproach* agree with the results of our previous study.

4.1 Assessment of Joy Due to Student Actions

The students' answers to the questionnaires indicated that all of the events related to student actions were relevant to some degree. We therefore scored all possible network structures using their log marginal likelihood [8], as we did for [11], in order to determine which events made a difference to the model's assessments. We found that (i) the outcome of the student's move influenced the satisfaction of the goal *Have Fun* and (ii) whether the student encountered a big number influenced the satisfaction of the goal *Learn Math*.

We included these findings in the model as follows. First, we added a node for the new event, *Big number*, and corresponding links to goal satisfaction nodes. We based our definition of a big number on the large numbers frequently incorrectly factorized in the students' pre-tests. Second, we used the study data to set the CPTs for the goal satisfaction nodes for *Have Fun* and *Learn Math*. Fig. 4 shows the revised time slice. Each new node and link is drawn using heavier lines.

4.2 Appraisal of Agent Actions

As mentioned earlier, the model's initial accuracy of assessing emotions towards the agent showed that we needed to revise and refine the existing links modeling how appraisal of the agent's actions affects players' emotions. Data analysis targeting this goal consisted of two stages.

Stage 1. First, we analyzed students' questionnaire items related to the influence of agent's actions on the goal *Learn Math*. We scored all possible network structures using their log marginal likelihood and found that our current structure received the highest score. Therefore our only refinement to the model based on these findings was to use the study data to refine the CPTs linking agent actions to the satisfaction of the goal *Learn Math*. However, a preliminary evaluation of these changes showed that the model was still underestimating students' admiration toward the agent. Thus, we moved to a second stage of data analysis.

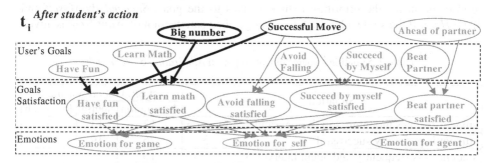

Fig. 4. Revised sub-network for appraisal after student action

Stage 2. We analyzed the log files of each student's session to identify situations in which students gave positive or negative reports towards the agent. The results are shown in Table 2. Congratulation by the agent (first row in Table 2) was already included in the original model as satisfying the goal *Have Fun*. Our data confirms that this action generates students' admiration, although it cannot tell whether this happens through the satisfaction of the goal *Have Fun*.

The second situation in Table 2 shows that students who are generally successful are usually either happy or neutral towards the agent, regardless of their goals. This suggests that the students' positive feelings toward the game will positively influence their attitude towards the agent. We translated this finding into the model by adding a link from the student's emotion towards the game in the previous time slice to the student's emotion towards the agent. This new link, and all the additions described below, can be seen in Figure 5.

The final two situations in Table 2 show reported feelings towards the agent when the student was falling and either received help or did not. Analysis of these situations revealed that approximately half of the students who reported reproach and half of the students who reported admiration when the agent intervened had declared the goal *Succeed By Myself*. This seems to indicate that, although some of the students may have wanted to succeed by themselves most of the time, when they began to fall they reduced the priority of this goal in favor of wanting help. This invalidates two of the choices previously made in the model implementation: (i) to ignore goal priority; (ii) to assume that goals are static during the interaction. Because we currently don't have enough data to model goal evolution in a principled way, we only addressed the implementation of multiple priority levels to model the relation between *Succeed By Myself* and wanting help. The model was changed as follows.

First, we added an additional goal, *Want Help*. The satisfaction of *Want Help* is dependent on two factors: the outcome of the student's move (i.e. a successful climb or a fall) and the agent's action. When the student falls, *Want Help* can only be satisfied if the agent provides help. If the agent congratulates the student, or does not perform any action, then this goal is not satisfied. If the student does not fall then satisfaction is neutral.

Second, we tried to determine which students' traits influenced their attitude towards receiving help during repeated falls. From our data, the only factor that seems to play a role is students' math knowledge. A Fisher test on the students' pre-test scores and whether they demonstrated that they wanted help showed a significant relationship (Fisher score = 0.029). Thus, a new node, representing prior math knowledge, was used to influence the priorities a student gives to the goals *Succeed By Myself* and *Want Help*. If the student has high knowledge, then satisfaction of *Want Help* is given

Table 2. Situations where students reported *Admiration* or *Reproach*

Situation	# Students reporting		
	Admiration	Neutral	Reproach
Student reaches mountain top, is congratulated by agent	12	13	2
Student is generally successful	26	19	4
Student falls frequently and agent intervenes	10	6	7
Student falls frequently and agent doesn't intervene	6	8	7

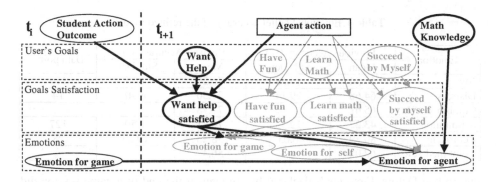

Fig. 5. Revised sub-network for appraisal after agent action

higher weight in the CPT defining the influence of goals satisfaction on emotion to-wards the agent. If the student has low knowledge, satisfaction of *Succeed By Myself* is given higher weight instead.

Third, the node representing the available agent's actions was refined to include the agent choosing not to intervene. All *Goal Satisfied* nodes other than *Succeed By My-self* and *Want Help* were given a neutral satisfaction for this new action. *Want Help* was discussed earlier, *Succeed By Myself* was given a small probability of satisfaction to reflect possible mild positive feelings towards the agent for not interrupting in general rather than at specific events.

4.3 Evaluation of the New Model

To evaluate the model changes discussed above, we replayed the event logs recorded during the study using a simulator that used the refined model. We added an addi-tional 'no action' event after each student action that was not followed by an agent intervention. We performed cross-validation using the data from our current study; each iteration used two-thirds of the data to train the refined CPTs and one-third as a test set. Table 3 shows the results of the re-evaluation, when students' goals from the post-questionnaires are used as evidence in the model. To get evidence on the newly added goal *Want Help*, we relied on student answers to the questionnaire item '*I wanted help when I became stuck*', originally used together with another item to as-sess the goal *Succeed By Myself*.

We start by discussing the accuracy results for *Admiration/Reproach*, because that will facilitate the discussion of *Joy/Distress*.

Accuracy of *Admiration/Reproach*. Table 3 shows that, although accuracy for *Admi-ration* improved considerably, accuracy for *Reproach* dropped off a comparable amount, bringing the combined accuracy to be slightly lower than the accuracy of the previous model. However, the high accuracy for *Reproach* in the previous model was a fortunate side effect of underestimating *Admiration*. Instead, an analysis of the model's assessment in relation to the interactions simulated from the log files shows that high accuracy for *Admiration* in the new model is mostly due to the addedchanges. The same analysis revealed that low accuracy for *Reproach* is mainly

Table 3. Emotional belief accuracy of the refined model

Emotion	Previous Accuracy (%)		Revised Accuracy (%)		Data points
	Mean	Std. Dev.	Mean	Std. Dev.	
Joy	66.54	17.38	76.26	1.75	170
Distress	64.68	29.14	71.30	40.48	14
Combined J/D	65.61		73.78		
Admiration	43.22	12.53	74.71	1.50	127
Reproach	80.79	6.05	38.23	19.23	28
Combined A/R	62.00		56.47		

due to two factors. First, goals declared by students at the end of a game session did not seem to match their goals throughout the game. Some students did not declare the goal *Want Help*, but their reports showed that they wanted help when they began to fall. Other students declared the goal but then did not want help. This is additional evidence that goal's priority can change during the interaction, and shows that the model is sensitive to these changes, confirming that in order to improve the model's accuracy we will have to lift the current model's assumption of static goals. Second, using only previous math knowledge to help assess each student's attitude toward wanting help incorrectly modeled some of the students. There appear to be other factors that should be taken into account, such as personality traits. We collected personality data during the study but encountered difficulties due to the general integrity of the students when describing their personality. We are investigating other methods for obtaining more reliable personality measurement.

Accuracy of *Joy/Distress*. As we can see from Table 3, the accuracy for *Joy* and *Distress* increased to about 76% and 71% respectively in the new model. The increase in *Joy* accuracy is mostly due to the changes discussed in Section 4. However, we should note that the impact of these changes is partially reduced by the goal fluctuation issues discussed above. Recall that the model's appraisal of agent actions also affects the assessment of *Joy* and *Distress* toward the game (Figure 5). From log file analysis, we saw that fluctuations of the goal *Want Help* made the model overestimate the negative impact of episodes of not receiving help for another group of 8 students who reported this goal, did not receive help when they were falling, but still reported joy toward the game and neutral or positive feelings toward the agent. It appears that, while we are correctly modeling the priority that these students give to the *satisfaction* of receiving help (thus the improved accuracy for admiration), we are overestimating the importance that they give to this goal *not being satisfied*. Thus, as it was the case for *Admiration/Reproach*, there appear to be other student traits that, if modeled, could further improve model accuracy.

The refinements made to assess *Admiration/Reproach* are the main reason for the improvement in *Distress*, because they correctly classified the *Distress* reports given by a student who was falling repeatedly, had the goal *Want Help* and did not receive help. These few correctly classified reports have high impact because of the limited number of *Distress* reports in the dataset (as the high variation for *Distress* shows). Note that this same student did not report *Reproach* during the same falling episodes, so he does not improve the model's *Reproach* accuracy.

5 Summary and Future Work

Building a user model of affect from real data is very difficult; the novel nature of the phenomena that we are trying to model, the limited existing knowledge of emotional reactions during system interaction, especially within the context of educational games, and the difficulty of observing key variables all contribute to the inherent complexity of the task.

In this paper, we have addressed sources of inaccuracy found within our model of user affect during a previous evaluation by refining the model's appraisal of both student and agent actions. We used data collected from real users to revise the relationship between game events and the satisfaction of two goals, *Have Fun* and *Learn Math*. We also used the data to analyze students' attitudes towards the agent and determined the common situations in which they changed. This analysis led to the introduction of a new goal, *Want Help*, the appraisal of the agent not giving help, and the first steps towards accommodating students giving different priorities to goals.

Our analysis has challenged two assumptions that were made during model construction; firstly that the set of goals the user is trying to achieve remains the same throughout the game session, secondly that we can make assessments using these goals without modeling goal priority. As part of our future work on revision of the model's goal assessment we intend to construct a clearer picture of how user's goals fluctuate during game sessions. We can then use this information to further improve the model's emotional assessment.

References

1. Ball, G. and Breese, J.: Modeling the Emotional State of Computer Users. Workshop on 'Attitude, Personality and Emotions in User-Adapted Interaction', UM'99, Canada (1999)
2. Bosma, W. and André, E.: Recognizing Emotions to Disambiguate Dialogue Acts. International Conference on Intelligent User Interfaces (IUI 2004). Madeira, Portugal (2004)
3. Conati, C.: Probabilistic Assessment of User's Emotions in Educational Games. Journal of Applied Artificial Intelligence 16(7-8), special issue: "Merging Cognition and Affect in HCI", (2002) 555-575
4. Conati, C. and Maclaren, H.: Evaluating A Probabilistic Model of Student Affect. Proceedings of the 7th Int. Conference on Intelligent Tutoring Systems, Maceio, Brazil (2004)
5. Conati, C. and Zhao, X.: Building and Evaluating an Intelligent Pedagogical Agent to Improve the Effectiveness of an Educational Game. IUI 2004. Madeira, Portugal (2004)
6. Gratch, J. and Marsella, S.: Evaluating the Modeling and Use of Emotion in Virtual Humans, 3rd Int. Jnt. Cnf. on Autonomous Agents and Multiagent Systems, New York (2004)
7. Healy, J. and Picard, R.: SmartCar: Detecting Driver Stress. 15th Int. Conf. on Pattern Recognition. Barcelona, Spain (2000)
8. Heckerman, D.: A Tutorial on Learning with Bayesian Networks, in Jordan, M. (ed.): Learning in Graphical Models (1998)
9. Ortony, A., Clore, G.L., and Collins, A.: The Cognitive Structure of Emotions. Cambridge University Press (1988)
10. Picard, R.: Affective Computing. Cambridge: MIT Press (1995)
11. Zhou, X. and Conati, C.: Inferring User Goals from Personality and Behavior in a Causal Model of User Affect. Int. Conference on Intelligent User Interfaces. Miami, FL (2003)

Recognizing Emotion from Postures: Cross-Cultural Differences in User Modeling

Andrea Kleinsmith, P. Ravindra De Silva, and Nadia Bianchi-Berthouze

Database Systems Laboratory, University of Aizu,
Aizu Wakamatsu 965-8580, Japan
andi@andisplanet.com
{d8052201, nadia}@u-aizu.ac.jp

Abstract. The conveyance and recognition of human emotion and affective expression is influenced by many factors, including culture. Within the area of user modeling, it has become increasingly necessary to understand the role affect can play in personalizing interactive interfaces using embodied animated agents. Currently, little research focuses on the importance of emotion expression through body posture. Furthermore, little research aims at understanding cultural differences within this vein. Therefore, our goal is to evaluate whether or not differences exist in the way various cultures perceive emotion from body posture. We used images of 3D affectively expressive avatars to conduct recognition experiments with subjects from 3 cultures. The subjects' judgments were analyzed using multivariate analysis. We grounded the identified differences into a set of low-level posture features. Our results could prove useful for constructing affective posture recognition systems in cross-cultural environments.

Keywords: Affective communication, affective body postures, embodied animated agents, intercultural differences, user modeling.

1 Introduction

As Picard [20] points out, the manner in which humans convey emotion or affective messages in general is affected by many factors, such as age, gender, posture, physical body characteristics, culture, context, and so on. Each individual has his/her own way to express affective states. Understanding these factors has become increasingly important in the area of user modeling. More than ever, it is necessary to personalize interactive interfaces to be capable of communicating with the user through an affective channel. While we acknowledge the importance of other modalities, such as face and voice, whole body postures are also shown to be quite important for conveying emotion, and remains a novel area of research. Indeed, while there are formal models for classifying affective facial expressions [6], there are no equivalent models for affective posture. These models are necessary to develop embodied animated agents capable of affective communication.

L. Ardissono, P. Brna, and A. Mitrovic (Eds.): UM 2005, LNAI 3538, pp. 50–59, 2005.
© Springer-Verlag Berlin Heidelberg 2005

Although it has previously been argued that the importance of body postures and gestures is not the primary channel for conveying emotion [3], more recent findings indicate that the body is used for emotional display more than formerly thought [1] [24] [2]. In fact, the role of posture in affect recognition, and the importance of emotion in the development and support of intelligent and social behavior has been accepted and researched within several fields including psychology, neurology, and biology. According to several researchers, central nervous system structures are responsible for the perception of emotion, and furthermore, its placement in these structures may be specific to both emotion and modality [14] [22]. Ekman [5] posits that body postures are used to express general emotions. Furthermore, according to Mehrabian and Friar [17], changes in a person's emotional state are reflected by changes in posture.

There is evidence to support that the way in which emotions are expressed and controlled [17], as well as the interpretation of emotion [14] is clearly shaped by culture. Many researchers have used cross-cultural emotion recognition studies to validate evidence in favor of emotion universality [8]. For some emotions, there is cross-cultural support for the universality of many modes of nonverbal behavior, including face, voice, and body expressions, as well as changes in a person's physiology [18]. However, the majority of the research on emotion universality concentrates on the recognition of facial expressions using still photographs [4] [21]. Currently, few researchers are examining the cross-cultural differences of emotion recognition in whole body posture [15]. Much research has been conducted comparing emotion differences between Japan and the United States. In a study by Friesen [10], cross-cultural differences were compared in the facial expressions of Japanese and American subjects while viewing both neutral films, and films intended to cause stress. As a support to the universality of facial expressions, it was shown that both groups expressed almost exactly the same facial expressions when watching the films alone. In a study by Scherer et al. [23], it was reported that the Japanese use fewer hand, arm, and whole body gestures than Americans when in emotional situations.

The goal of this paper is to evaluate the possible cultural differences between Japan, Sri Lanka, and the US in the perception of emotion through whole body postures. If, in fact, differences do exist, our aim is twofold. One, we will attempt to qualify these differences through an examination of how the cultures vary in recognizing emotion and its intensity. Two, we will ground these differences into a set of low-level posture features by identifying which features are used by all 3 cultures, and which features play a different role in each of the 3 models. In our studies, we use images of a 3D avatar created from original motion capture data in an attempt to eliminate bias due to culture and/or gender. Each avatar always has the same body. Furthermore, by using the avatar, the subjects are not affected by facial expressions. We chose to study two Asian cultures (Japanese and Sri Lankan), as the way each of these cultures interacts socially, on a nonverbal level, is quite different. Sri Lankans are considered to have a more Latin way of interacting [16].

While the above research examines the ways in which emotions are conveyed, our study aims to understand cross-cultural differences in the ways in which emotions are recognized. The remainder of this paper is organized as follows. Section 2 gives a description of the posture data collection method and our tri-cultural (Japanese, Sri Lankan, and American) posture recognition experiment. In Sect. 3 we examine the cultural differences, and how the different cultures rated emotion and intensity. Section 4 describes how we grounded these differences into a set of low-level postural features. We conclude in Sect. 5.

2   Method

2.1   Posture Data Collection

As a first step, we used a motion capture system to collect 3D affective postures of 13 human subjects (called actors hereafter) of different age, gender, and race. In this context we define a posture as any *stance involving the hands and/or body that can convey emotions or feelings.*

Each actor, dressed in the same suit with 32 markers attached to various joints and body segments, was asked to perform an in-place posture expressing *anger, fear, happiness* and *sadness.* As a starting point, these emotions were chosen on the basis that they are included in the set of universal emotions defined by Ekman and Friesen [7]. The actors were allowed to perform the emotion postures in her/his own way, as no constraints were placed on them. Moreover, the actors were not allowed to observe each other during the capturing sessions in an effort to avoid influencing the individual performances. Each affective posture was captured by 8 cameras and represented by contiguous frames describing the position of the 32 markers in the 3D space. In total, we captured 108 affective postures. We then used the original motion capture data to build affectively

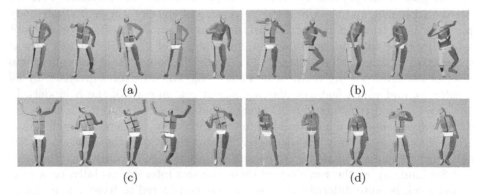

(a)   (b)

(c)   (d)

Fig. 1. Examples of the 3D affectively expressive avatars for each emotion category. (a) Angry (b) Fear (c) Happy (d) Sad

expressive avatars, shown in Fig. 1, by selecting the frame (i.e., a static posture) that the actor evaluated as being the most expressive instant of the posture.

2.2 Posture Evaluation Experiment

We used an 8 word forced-choice experimental design to evaluate potential cultural differences in emotion perception through whole body posture. This method was purposely chosen as it has been widely used in studies aimed at assessing cross-cultural agreements in the expression of emotion [13]. 25 Japanese, 25 Sri Lankan, and 20 Caucasian American subjects (called observers hereafter) participated in the experiment. We used 108 affective posture images as the data set (refer to Fig. 1 for examples).

The experiment was conducted online as a series of webpages. The postures were presented in a randomized order, differing for each participant. For each page (one posture per page), subjects were asked to (1) rate the intensity of the emotion, defined by a value between 1 and 5 to indicate how emotional is the posture, and (2) choose an emotion label to represent the posture displayed based on an 8-word list comprised of pairs of labels indicating two intensities of the same emotion: anger (*angry, upset*), fear (*fearful, surprised*), happiness (*happy, joyful*), and sadness (*sad, depressed*).

2.3 Concordance Between Actors and Observers Across 3 Cultures

The results for each of the 3 cultures are represented in Table 1. The rows indicate the frequency of use by the subject of a culture for each emotion label to classify the set of postures corresponding to the emotion intended by the actors. Overall, a high correlation is observed between the observer-selected pairs of labels (i.e., *happy/joyful*) and the actors' intended emotions, with the

Table 1. The observers' ratings from the 3 cultures for each of the 8 emotions. This table depicts the frequency of use (percentage) of the 8 emotions (combined as pairs of labels indicating 2 intensities of the same emotion). (sur. = surprised and dep. = depressed)

Actors	Japanese Observers				Sri Lankan Observers				American Observers			
Emotion Labels	Angry (angry upset)	Fear (fear sur.)	Happy (happy joyful)	Sad (dep. sad)	Angry (angry upset)	Fear (fear sur.)	Happy (happy joyful)	Sad (dep. sad)	Angry (angry upset)	Fear (fear sur.)	Happy (happy joyful)	Sad (dep. sad)
Angry	**41.7**	4.4	10.4	7.3	**22.9**	5.5	10.8	8.5	**22.2**	4.9	19.2	3.9
	14.4	9.2	7.9	4.4	**25**	10.7	7.7	7.1	**22.3**	9.2	8.4	4.3
Fear	15.5	**26.1**	9.4	2.3	18.7	**30.4**	8.8	4.5	17.3	**23.2**	10.7	1
	4.4	**28.7**	10.9	2.6	10	**13.4**	9	3.3	1.2	**26.3**	5.5	1.8
Happy	13.6	1.4	**22**	1	8.2	4.5	**29.3**	4.4	11.6	1.8	**29**	1.5
	5.7	20.7	**32.4**	3.2	7.9	11.9	**30.2**	2.3	10.2	15.3	**26.2**	1.7
Sad	5.4	2.8	2.2	**34.6**	5.4	1.8	1	**29.5**	6.6	2.2	2.6	**35.8**
	23.9	3.7	1.4	**25.6**	22.6	1.5	1	**35.4**	14.1	4.3	1.8	**29.2**

sad/depressed categories showing the overall highest agreement for all 3 cultures with an average of 63.4%. The emotion category with the lowest agreement was different for each culture. We hypothesize that this may be due to each culture placing greater importance on different features for distinguishing between postures within those emotion categories. To evaluate the agreement between the 3 cultures, each posture was associated with the most frequent emotion category for each culture. The most frequent label was the same across the 3 cultures for 71 of the 108 postures (i.e., 66% agreement).

3   Intensity Ratings and Cultural Differences

3.1   Method

The second aim was to assess the cultural differences in the evaluation of emotional intensity on the 71 common postures. Toward this goal, we analyzed the data using two approaches. First, we aimed to assess the intensity according to the intensity value (i.e., a number from 1 to 5) associated by the observers of the 3 cultures to each posture during the posture evaluation experiment presented in Sect. 2. Second, we attempted to assess how each culture used the pair of labels within each emotion category. For both of these examinations we used the repeated measurement method [9] and either a mulivariate test or a univariate test[1] to identify the existence of statistically significant differences between the cultures. This method was applied to each emotion case separately. There are 21 postures for *angry*, 19 for *fear*, 15 for *happy*, and 16 for *sad*. Subsequently, to better qualify which differences occurred between which cultures, for each of the emotion categories, we used a post hoc test with the Bonferroni correction.

3.2   Discussion

Table 2 shows the results of the analysis of the intensity rating. Overall, we can see that only in the case of the fear category is there no significant difference between the intensity ratings of the observers belonging to the 3 different cultures. In fact, its p-value is well above a significance level of 0.05. This could confirm brain studies in which the fear emotion seems to be triggered more at the sensorial level than at the cognitive one [11]. Table 3 shows the results of the analysis in the use of label as an index of intensity. The overall results point out that in the case of angry and fear postures, there is no significant difference in the use of the pair of labels between the 3 cultures.

---

[1] We used Mauchly's test for checking the assumption of sphericity. The *sphericity* assumption is an assumption about the structure of the covariance matrix in a repeated measures design. Following [9] (pp. 337-338), we used a univariate test (Greenhouse-Geisser) to treat cases in which the sphericity was statistically satisfied, while we used a multivariate test (Wilks' Lambda) in the cases of significant violation of the sphericity assumption.

Table 2. Testing the differences in intensity ratings. JA=Japanese, SL=Sri Lankans, US=Americans

Emotion	Multivariate test	Post hoc p-value	Cultural diffs
Angry	Significant differences p-value=0.032	JA-SL=0.896 JA-US=0.756 **SL-US=0.032**	US > SL p-value=0.043
Fear	No significant diff. p-value=0.176	No significant diff.	No significant diff.
Happy	Significant diff. differences p-value=0.021	**JA-SL=0.021** JA-US=0.089 SL-US=0.742	JA > SL p-value=0.034
Sad	Significant diff. differences p-value=0.041	**JA-SL=0.022** JA-US=0.976 SL-US=0.0876	JA > SL p-value=0.012

Table 3. Testing the differences in the use of the 8 emotion labels

Emotion	Univariate test	Post hoc p-value	Cultural diffs
Angry	No significant p-value=0.432	No significant differences	No significant differences
Fear	No Significant p-value=0.078	No significant diff. differences	No significant differences
Happy	Significant diff. p-value=0.022	**JA-SL=0.032** JA-US=0.073 SL-US=0.987	JA used the **joyful** label more than SL
Sad	Significant diff. p-value=0.033	**JA-SL=0.001** JA-US=0.323 SL-US=0.625	JA used the **depressed** label more than SL

For both analyses, when significant differences were detected by the multivariate test (p-value below 0.05), a post hoc test was conducted to better qualify these differences. The results of this test are represented in the third column of each table. This column indicates in which pairs of cultures a significant difference exists (p-value below 0.05). For these pairs, we applied a paired t-test to assess if one culture used a higher intensity rating than the other. The results, shown in the last column of Table 2, points out that the Japanese are more likely than the Sri Lankans to associate a higher intensity to both happy and sad postures. In the case of angry, it is the Americans who are more likely than the Sri Lankans to assign a higher intensity to these postures. We compared these culture pairs in their use of the emotion labels. The results, shown in the last column of Table 3, suggest that the Japanese again tended to use stronger labels, i.e., *joyful* and *depressed*, than did the Sri Lankans. We can summarize the results shown in these tables by saying that intensity plays an important role in the way the 3 cultures will differently perceive the same affective avatar.

4   Grounding Cultural Differences in Posture Features

The final goal of the study was to ground the perceptual differences between the 3 cultures into a set of features describing the affective postures. Toward this objective, we used the set of 24 low-level postural features (Table 4) proposed in [24] to create a numerical description of our 108 postures. Hence we applied the non-linear Mixture Discriminant Analysis (MDA) [12] modeling technique to create a model for discriminating between affective postures on the basis of this set of features. Using the MDA dimensions, it is possible to map the postures onto a multidimensional discriminant space defined by the axes that maximize the separation between groups and minimize the variance within groups.

For each culture, an MDA model was created using the 108 postures. Specifically, for each posture we used the vectors describing its postural features (computed on the original motion capture data) and the most frequent emotion category (4 categories) that was assigned by the observer of that culture to the avatar associated with that posture. For each of the 3 models, the classification performances are very high. The Japanese model correctly classifies (with respect to the Japanese observers) 90% of the postures. The Sri Lankan model correctly classifies (according to the Sri Lankan observers) 88% of the postures and the American model correctly classifies (according to the American observers) 78% of the postures.

Table 4. The table lists the set of posture features used. The "Code" column indicates the feature codes used in the paper. The following short-cuts are used: L: Left, R: Right, B: Back, F: Front

Code	posture features	Code	posture features
V4	$Orientation_{XY}$: B.Head - F.Head axis	V5	$Orientation_{YZ}$: B.Head - F.Head axis
V6	$Distance_z$: R.Hand - R.Shoulder	V7	$Distance_z$: L.Hand - L.Shoulder
V8	$Distance_y$: R.Hand - R.Shoulder	V9	$Distance_y$:L.Hand - L.Shoulder
V10	$Distance_x$:R.Hand - L.Shoulder	V11	$Distance_x$:L.Hand - R.Shoulder
V12	$Distance_x$:R.Hand - R.Elbow	V13	$Distance_x$:L.Hand - L.Elbow
V14	$Distance_x$: R.Elbow - L.Shoulder	V15	$Distance_x$: L.Elbow - R.Shoulder
V16	$Distance_z$: R.Hand - R.Elbow	V17	$Distance_z$:L.Hand - L.Elbow
V18	$Distance_y$: R.Hand - R.Elbow	V19	$Distance_y$:L.Hand - L.Elbow
V20	$Distance_y$: R.Elbow - R.Shoulder	V21	$Distance_y$:L.Elbow - L.Shoulder
V22	$Distance_z$: R.Elbow - R.Shoulder	V23	$Distance_z$:L.Elbow - L.Shoulder
V24	$Orientation_{XY}$: Shoulders axis	V25	$Orientation_{XZ}$: Shoulders axis
V26	$Orientation_{XY}$: Heels axis	V27	$3D - Distance$: R.Heel - L.Heel

Table 5. The table shows the features selected by the 3 MDA models. The first and the third columns indicate the set of features, the second and the fourth columns the culture-models using them (Cults = cultures)

Selected features	Cults.	Selected features	Cults.
V5-$Orientation_{YZ}$: B.Head - F.Head	JA,SL,US	V6-$Distance_z$: R.Hand - R.Shoulder	JA
V11-$Distance_x$:L.Hand - R.Shoulder	JA,SL,US	V8-$Distance_y$: R.Hand - R.Shoulder	JA
V15-$Distance_x$: L.Elbow - R.Shoulde	JA,SL,US	V9-$Distance_y$:L.Hand - L.Shoulder	JA
V13-$Distance_x$:L.Hand - L.Elbow	JA,SL	V17-$Distance_z$:L.Hand - L.Elbow	JA
V16 -$Distance_z$: R.Hand - R.Elbow	JA,SL	V22-$Distance_z$: R.Elbow - R.Shoulder	SL
V7-$Distance_z$: L.Hand - L.Shoulder	SL,US	V4-$Orientation_{XY}$: B.Head - F.Head	US
V18-$Distance_y$: R.Hand - R.Elbow	SL,US	V20-$Distance_y$: R.Elbow - R.Shoulder	US
V25-$Orientation_{XZ}$: Shoulders axis	SL,US	V26-$Orientation_{XY}$: Heels axis	US

As the models perform quite well, we can use them to ground the differences between cultures on the features. Hence, we analyzed the equations of the discriminant functions within each of the 3 MDA models, and extracted the set of features that were identified by MDA as most relevant for the discrimination process. We observed that the 3 models share only 3 features, while the overall set of important features is different for each model. Table 5 shows the feature sets for each culture. From this we can see that the Sri Lankans only have one feature unique to their culture while the Japanese and Americans have several. This discovery may indicate that the Sri Lankans are in the middle of the other 2 cultures in their way to perceive emotion from posture.

In evaluating the feature sets for each culture, one interesting finding was that the arm stretched along the body ($v6$) and the head bent ($v5$) are necessary features for the Japanese in recognizing sadness in the avatar. Indeed, $v6$ is considered to be important only to the Japanese, and seems to reflect a typical posture they frequently use to express saddness or remorse. Refer to postures 1 and 3 (from left to right) in Fig. 1(d) to see examples. However, while the other 2 cultures generally associated this type of posture to sadness, many avatars with the face up and the hands close to the chest (a combination of $v18$ and $v22$) were also considered as sad (Fig. 1(d) posture 4). We can see that this feature is shared between the Sri Lankans and the Americans, while it is not considered important by the Japanese. Another relevant finding is that the Japanese seem to attribute happy to postures in which the arms remain close to the body's side (again $v6$), and both fear and happy when the arms are raised to mid-level, whereas the Sri Lankans more often appear to consider these postures as angry. In general, fear and angry for all 3 cultures consist of a wide variety of postures (as referenced by Fig. 1(a)(b)), differing from a study by Paiva et al. [19] in which angry is represented by a dynamic motion in which the avatar/doll is moved rapidly forward and backward, and fear is associated with the hands placed directly over the eyes. Specifically, in the case of fear for the Sri Lankans, the elbow is always below the shoulder, and very low in the case of sad. This feature, $v22$, is the single unique feature for the Sri Lankans. Furthermore, we notice that when the Japanese associated a posture with fear, the Sri Lankans did not agree. In fact, we see that angry was typically selected as the most frequent label by the Sri Lankans for these postures. This result seems to correlate to the distance between the heels (refer to Fig. 1(b)) ($v27$), which is a feature shared by the Japanese and the Sri Lankans, however, it appears to be used differently within those cultures. We can see this difference in the Sri Lankan selected angry postures, which have a wider stance and a tilted or turned head.

5   Conclusions

In this paper we have statistically evaluated the cultural differences between Japanese, Sri Lankan, and American subjects in perceiving the emotional state of an avatar's body posture. When considering the frequency of label use for each posture according to actor-intended emotion label, a fairly high agreement was obtained between the 3 cultures, with the sad/depressed categories showing the highest agreement. This may indicate the existence of a cross-cultural stereotype for the sad emotion. In further analysis, significant cultural differences were observed when considering intensity ratings, specifically, that the Japanese easily assigned a stronger intensity to the animated body postures than did the other cultures, which may support Scherer's [23] findings discussed in the Introduction. These results were grounded into a set of low-level posture features from which a separate model was created for each culture. We found that classification rates were quite significant when testing these models on our set of affective avatars, and moreover, that each culture considers different features important for recognizing affective postures. To further evaluate our findings, the next goal is to examine the interaction between posture features and to collect a larger set of postures for each nuance (8 labels) of the emotions to also ground the differences in emotional intensity onto postural features.

Acknowledgment

This study was supported by a Grants-in-Aid for Scientific Research from the Japanese Society for the Promotion of Science.

References

1. Argyle M., Bodily Communication – 2nd Edition, Methuen & Co. Ltd., (1988)
2. Coulson M., Attributing emotion to static body postures: recognition accuracy, confusions, and viewpoint dependence, Journal of Nonverbal Behavior, **28**, (2004), 117-139
3. Ekman P., Emotion in the Human Face, Cambridge University Press, (1982)
4. Ekman, P., Strong evidence for universals in facial expressions: A reply to Russell's mistaken critique, Psychological Bulletin, **115**, (1994), 268–287
5. Ekman, P. and Friesen, W., Head and Body Cues in the Judgment of Emotion: A Reformulation, Perceptual and Motor Skills, **24**, (1967), 711–724
6. Ekman P. and Friesen W., Manual for the Facial Action Coding System, Palo Alto, California: Consulting Psychology Press, (1978)

7. Ekman P. and Friesen W., Unmasking the Face: A Guide to Recognizing Emotions from Facial Expressions, Prentice Hall, (1975)

8. Elfenbein, H. A. and Mandal, M. K. and Ambady, N. and Harizuka, S. and Kumar, S., Cross-Cultural Patterns in Emotion Recognition: Highlighting Design and Analytical Techniques, Emotion, **2:1**, (2002), 75–84

9. Field, A., Discovering statistics: Using SPSS for WIndows, London: Sage, (2000)

10. Friesen, W., Cultural Differences in Facial Expressions in a Social Situation: An Experimental Test of the Concept of Display Rules, Doctoral dissertation, University of California, San Francisco, (1972)

11. de Gelder, B. and Snyder, J. and Greve, D. and Gerard, G. and Hadjikhani, N., Fear fosters flight: A mechanism for fear contagion when perceiving emotion expressed by a whole body, Proc. of the National Academy of Science, **101**, (2003), 16701–16706

12. Hastie, T. and Tibshirabi, R., Discriminant analysis by Gaussian mixture, Journal of the Royal Statistical Society, **B:58**, (1996), 155–176

13. Keltner, D. and Ekman, P., Expression of Emotion, Handbook of Affective Sciences, Eds. R. Davidson and K. Scherer and H. Goldsmith, Oxford University Press, New York, (2003)

14. Keltner, D. and Ekman, P. and Gonzaga, G. C. and Beer, J., Facial Expression of Emotion, Handbook of Affective Sciences, Eds. R. Davidson and K. Scherer and H. Goldsmith, Oxford University Press, New York, (2003)

15. Kudoh, T. and Matsumoto, D., Cross-Cultural Examination of the Semantic Dimensions of Body Postures, Journ. of Personality and Social Psychology, **48:6**, (1985), 1440–1446

16. Lewis, R. D., When cultures collide: Managing successfully across cultures, Nicholas Brealey, London, (1999)

17. Mehrabian, A. and Friar, J., Encoding of Attitude by a Seated Communicator via Posture and Position Cues, Journal of Consulting and Clinical Psychology, **33**, (1969), 330–336

18. Mesquita, B., Emotions as Dynamic Cultural Phenomena, Handbook of Affective Sciences, Eds. R. Davidson and K. Scherer and H. Goldsmith, Oxford University Press, New York, (2003)

19. Paiva, A. and Prada, R. and Chaves, R. and Vala, M. and Bullock, A. and Andersson, G. and Hook, K., Towards tangibility in gameplay: Building a tangible affective interface for a computer game, Proc. of the International Conference on Multimodal Interfaces, ACM, (2003), 60–67

20. Picard R., Toward Agents that Recognize Emotion, Actes Proc. IMAGINA, 153-165, Monaco, March, (1998)

21. Russell, J. A., Is there universal recognition of emotion from facial expressions? A review of the cross-cultural studies, Psychological Bulletin, **115**, (1994), 102–141

22. Scherer, K. R. and Johnstone, T. and Klasmeyer, G., Vocal Expression of Emotion, Handbook of Affective Sciences, Eds. R. Davidson and K. Scherer and H. Goldsmith, Oxford University Press, New York, (2003)

23. Scherer, K. R. and Wallbott, H. G. and Matsumoto, D. and Kudoh, T., Emotional Experience in Cultural Context: A Comparison Between Europe, Japan, and the United States, Faces of Emotions, Ed. K. R. Scherer, Erlbaum, Hillsdale, New Jersey, (1988)

24. de Silva, R. and Bianchi-Berthouze, N., Modeling human affective postures: An information theoretic characterization of posture features, Journal of Computer Animation and Virtual Worlds, **15**, (2004), 269—276

Recognizing, Modeling, and Responding to Users' Affective States

Helmut Prendinger[1], Junichiro Mori[2], and Mitsuru Ishizuka[2]

[1] National Institute of Informatics, 2-1-2 Hitotsubashi,
Chiyoda-ku, Tokyo 101-8430, Japan
helmut@nii.ac.jp
[2] Dept. of Information and Communication Engineering,
University of Tokyo, 7-3-1 Hongo, Bunkyo-ku,
Tokyo 113-8656, Japan
{jmori, ishizuka}@miv.t.u-tokyo.ac.jp

Abstract. We describe a system that recognizes physiological data of users in real-time, interprets this information as affective states, and responds to affect by employing an animated agent. The agent assumes the role of an Empathic Companion in a virtual job interview scenario where it accompanies a human interviewee. While previously obtained results with the companion with were not significant, the analysis reported here demonstrates that empathic feedback of an agent may reduce user arousal while hearing interviewer questions. This outcome may prove useful for educational systems or applications that induce user stress.

1 Introduction

Computers sensing users' physiological activity are becoming increasingly popular in the human–computer interface and user modeling communities, partly because of the availability of affordable high-specification sensing technologies, and also due to the recent progress in interpreting physiological states as affective states or emotions [10]. The general vision is that if a user's emotion could be recognized by the computer, human–computer interaction would become more natural, enjoyable, and productive. The computer could offer help and assistance to a confused user or try to cheer up a frustrated user, and hence react in ways that are more appropriate than simply ignoring the user's affective state as is the case with most current interfaces.

Our particular interest concerns interfaces that employ animated or embodied agents as interaction partners of the user. By emulating multi-modal human–human communication and displaying social cues including (synthetic) speech, communicative gestures, and the expression of emotion, those agents may trigger social reactions in users, and thus implement the "computers as social actors" metaphor [14]. This type of social and affect-aware interface has been demonstrated to enrich human–computer interaction in a wide variety of applications, including interactive presentations, training, and sales [2, 12].

L. Ardissono, P. Brna, and A. Mitrovic (Eds.): UM 2005, LNAI 3538, pp. 60–69, 2005.

In this paper, we propose an interface that obtains information about a user's physiological activity in real-time and provides affective feedback by means of an embodied agent. The interface is intended to respond to the user's emotion by showing concern about user affect, sometimes called *empathic* (or *sympathetic*) behavior. Empathic interfaces may leave users less frustrated in the case of a stressful event related to the interaction [5]. Potential application fields include software (assuming unavoidable software-related failures), computer-based customer support, and educational systems. The web-based (virtual) job interview scenario described here serves as a simple demonstrator application that allows us to discuss the technical issues involved in real-time emotion recognition as well as the implementation of an empathic agent. In this paper, we will extend and complement our previous investigations on empathic agents.

- *Virtual Quizmaster.* An agent providing empathic feedback to a deliberately frustrated user can significantly reduce user arousal or stress when compared to an agent that ignores the user's frustration [13].
- *Empathic Companion.* An empathic agent has no overall positive effect on the user's interaction experience in terms of lower levels of arousal [11].

The rest of this paper is organized as follows. In Sect. 2, we describe related work. Section 3 is dedicated to introducing the Empathic Companion. There, we first describe our system for real-time emotion recognition, and then explain how physiological signals are mapped to named emotions. The final part of Sect. 3 discusses the decision-theoretic agent that is responsible for selecting the Empathic Companion's actions. In Sect. 4, we illustrate the structure an interaction with the Empathic Companion in the setting of a virtual job interview, and provide new results of an experiment that recorded users' physiological activity during the interaction. Section 5 concludes the paper.

2   Related Work

There are various research strands that share the methodology and motivation of our approach to affective and empathic interfaces. The tutoring system developed by Conati [3] demonstrates that the user's physiological state can play a key role in selecting strategies to adapt an educational interface. When the user's frustration is detected, an interface agent can try to undo the user's negative feeling. Bickmore [1] investigates empathic agents in the role of health behavior chance assistants that are designed to develop and maintain long-term, social-emotional relationships with users, so-called 'relational agents'.

The investigation of Klein et al. [5] is most closely related to our work on empathic interfaces. They describe the design and evaluation of an interface implementing strategies aimed at reducing negative affect, such as active listening, empathy, sympathy, and venting. The resulting affect–support agent used in a simulated network game scenario could be shown to undo some of the users' negative feelings after they have been deliberately frustrated by simulated network delays inserted into the course of the game. The Emphatic Companion interface differs from the one used in [5] in two aspects. First, the user in our system is given feedback in a more timely fashion, i.e. shortly after the emotion actually occurs, and not after the interaction session, in response to the subject's questionnaire entries. While providing immediate response to user affect is certainly preferable in terms of natural interaction, it assumes that affect is processed in real-time. Hence, in order to assess a user's emotional state online, we implemented a system that takes physiological signals of the user during the interaction with the computer.

Second, affective feedback to the user is communicated by means of an embodied agent, rather than a text message. Although the study of Klein and coworkers [5] supports the argument that embodiment is not necessary to achieve social response, it has been shown that embodied characters may boost the tendency of people to interact with computers in a social way [12].

3   The Empathic Companion

The Empathic Companion is an embodied agent that was developed in the context of a web-based job interview scenario (Fig. 1), where it addresses the user's emotion resulting from an interview situation (see also the 'affective mirror' in [10, p. 86]). Being interviewed is likely to elicit emotions in the user, especially when the interviewer (Fig. 1, left) asks potentially unpleasant or probing questions, such as "What was your final grade at university?" or "Are you willing to work unpaid overtime?", and comments pejoratively upon the interviewee's (i.e. the user's) unsatisfactory answer. In order to emphasize the training aspect of the interview situation, the user is led by a companion agent (Fig. 1, right) that addresses the user's (negative) emotions by giving empathic feedback, e.g.

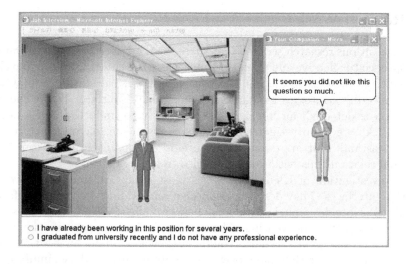

Fig. 1. Job Interview Scenario

"It seems you did not like this question so much" or "Maybe you felt a bit bad to be asked this kind of question". The user is told that the companion is invisible to the interviewer and present for his or her comfort only. Although a web-based (virtual) interview cannot induce the stress level of a face-to-face or phone interview, it provides a convenient training platform for job seekers.

3.1   System Architecture

Since the Empathic Companion application assumes real-time emotion recognition, the system architecture depicted in Fig. 2 has been implemented on the Windows XP platform.

Data Capturing and Processing. The user is attached to sensors of the Pro-Comp+ unit [15]. The ProComp+ encoder allows to use input from up to eight sensors simultaneously. Currently, we only use galvanic skin response (GSR) and electromyography (EMG) sensors. Data capturing is achieved by a module written in Visual C++ that employs the ProComp+ data capture library.

When prompted by the application (i.e. interface events), the Data Processing component retrieves new data every 50 milliseconds, stores and evaluates them. Given the baseline information for skin conductance (GSR signal) and muscle activity (EMG signal), changes in physiological activity are computed by comparing the current mean signal values to the baseline value. The baseline is obtained during a relaxation period preceding the interaction. The current mean value is derived from a segment of five seconds, the average duration of an emotion [7]. If skin conductance is 15–30% above the baseline, is assumed as "high", for more than 30% as "very high". If muscle activity is more than three times higher than the baseline average, it is assumed as "high", else "normal". Emotions are hypothesized from signals using a Bayesian network, as part of the decision network discussed below.

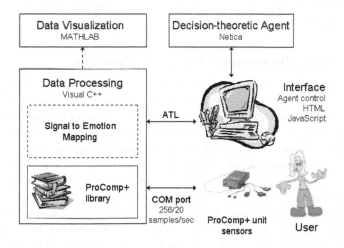

Fig. 2. System architecture

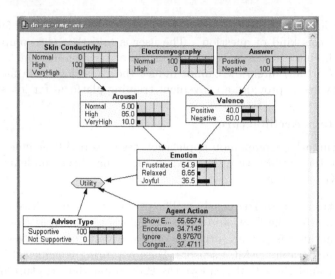

Fig. 3. Simple decision network

User Interface. The User Interface component contains the job interview scenario and runs under Internet Explorer 5.5 (or higher). It is written in HTML and JavaScript and utilizes the Microsoft Agent package [8] to control the verbal and non-verbal behavior (such as gestures or facial displays) of characters. This package includes an animation engine to trigger about 50 pre-defined 2D animation sequences and a text-to-speech engine.

Decision-theoretic Agent. A decision network is used to combine bio-signals and other facts about the interaction, and relate them to emotions as well as agent decisions (see Fig. 3). The decision-theoretic agent will be discussed in Sect. 3.3. Before that, we will explain the modeling and interpretation of the user's physiological activity as emotions.

3.2   Relating Physiological Signals to Emotions

Lang [6] claims that all emotions can be characterized in terms of judged valence (pleasant or unpleasant) and arousal (calm or aroused), and therefore named emotions can be identified as coordinates in the arousal–valence space. For instance, the "Angry" emotion is located in the 'arousal=high'&'valence=negative' segment. The relation between physiological signals and arousal/valence is established in psychophysiology that argues that the activation of the autonomic nervous system changes while emotions are elicited [7]. The following two signals have been chosen for their high reliability (other signals are discussed, e.g. in [10]). Galvanic skin response (GSR) is an indicator of skin conductance (SC), and increases linearly with a person's level of overall arousal. Electromyography (EMG) measures muscle activity and has been shown to correlate with negatively valenced emotions [6].

3.3   Decision-Theoretic Agent

The decision-theoretic agent is responsible for deriving the user's emotion given physiological data and the valence of the user's answer (to the question of the interviewer), and to suggest an appropriate action. The agent is implemented with Netica [9], a software package that allows solving decision problems and provides convenient tools, including an API in Java.

The decision network depicted in Fig. 3 represents a simple decision problem. A decision-theoretic agent selects actions that maximize the outcome in terms of some utility function [4]. The subnet consisting only of chance nodes is the Bayesian network used to derive the user's emotional state. It relates physiological signals (GSR, EMG) and the user's answer to arousal and valence which are employed to infer the user's emotional state by applying the model of Lang [6]. The probabilities have been set in accord with the literature (whereby the concrete numbers are made up). "Relaxed (happiness)" is defined by the absence of autonomic signals, i.e. no arousal (relative to the baseline), and positive valence. "Joyful" is defined by increased arousal and positive valence, whereas "Frustrated" is defined by increased arousal and negative valence. The node "Answer" in the network represents situations where the user gives a 'positive answer' (that satisfies the interviewer's question) or a 'negative answer' (that does not satisfy the interviewer's question). This ('non-physiological') node was included to the network in order to more easily hypothesize the user's positive or negative appraisal of the question, as the user's EMG value changes (in this application) are often too small to evaluate valence.

Besides nodes representing probabilistic events in the world (chance nodes), decision networks contain nodes representing agent choices (decision nodes), and the agent's utility function (utility or value node). The utility function is set to the effect that negatively aroused users receive empathic feedback, by assum-

Table 1. Example responses of the Empathic Companion

Actions	Example Response
Show Empathy	The agent displays concern for a user who is aroused and has a negatively valenced emotion, e.g. by saying "I am sorry that you seem to feel a bit bad about that question".
Encourage	If the user is not aroused, the agent gives some friendly comment, e.g. by saying "You appear calm and don't have to worry. Keep going!".
Ignore	The agent does not address the user's emotion, and simply refers to the interview progress, by saying, e.g. "Let us go on to the next question".
Congratulate	If the agent detects that the user is aroused in a positive way, it applauds the user ("Well done!", "Good job! You said the right thing", etc.).

ing that negative states are a hindrance to performing successfully in stressful situations (including interviews).

Table 1 lists some responses of the Empathic Companion associated to the action types (see also Fig. 3). The actual implementation of the job interview scenario provides linguistic variations for each response category. If the advisor type is supportive, the utility function is set to respond to the user's affective state. "Advisor Type" is a deterministic (rather than chance) node that allows us to characterize the agent as supportive or non-supportive. If set to "Not Supportive", the "Ignore" action is selected for all inputs. This node is needed to compare empathic vs. non-empathic versions of the companion.

4   Interacting with the Empathic Companion

In an interaction session with the Empathic Companion, the user is seated in front of a computer running the job interview, with the GSR sensors attached to two fingers of the non-dominant hand, and the EMG sensors attached to the forearm of the same body side. The baseline for subsequent bio-signal changes is obtained during an initial relaxation period of one minute, where the user listens to music from Caf del Mar (Vol. 9), as the mean of GSR and EMG values.

4.1   The Structure of the Interview

An interview session is composed of (interview) episodes, whereby each episode consists of four segments (see below). The entire interview session contains ten episodes, and concludes with the interviewer agent's acceptance or rejection of the user as a new employee of the company, depending on how many 'credits' the user could collect.

- *Segment 1*: The interviewer agent asks a question, e.g. "Tell me about your previous work experience".
- *Segment 2*: The user chooses an answer from the set of given options (see Fig. 1, lower part), by clicking on the button next to the selected answer, e.g. the user admits the lack of experience by clicking the lower button.
- *Segment 3*: The interviewer responds to the user's answer, e.g. "Then you are not the kind of person we are looking for" or "I am happy to hear that you have extensive experience in the field".
- *Segment 4*: The companion agent responds to the emotion derived from the data gathered during the third segment and the user's answer given in the second segment.

4.2   Exploratory Study

While a questionnaire method is certainly possible to evaluate the impact of the Empathic Companion agent, we are using physiological data to assess the user's perception of the interface. A signal processor has been developed in-house that reads users' skin conductance (SC) and heart rate (HR). Like EMG, HR also correlates with negative emotions and Lang's [6] model can be applied.

Observe that unlike the experiment reported in [13], tight experimental controls are not practicable in the job interview application as the interaction is not designed to invoke specific emotions at specific moments. In particular, depending on their answers to the interviewer's questions, users may receive positive or negative feedback. Facing a comparable situation – users' physiological responses to different web page designs – Ward and Marsden [16] thus propose to compare signal values for whole interaction periods rather than for specific interface events.

Following this paradigm, we *initially* hypothesized that, averaged over the entire interview period (see Fig. 4), the presence of a (supportive) Empathic Companion will have users with lower levels of arousal and less negatively valenced affective states. As the control condition, the "Not Supportive" advisor type was used, where the "Ignore" action is always selected. However, no significant results could be obtained.

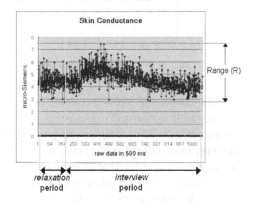

Fig. 4. SC data of one subject

The main reason might be that the user interacts with the interviewer rather than the empathic agent most of the time. Other possible reasons include: (i) The responses intended to have a calming effect on the user might actually not do so; (ii) heart rate might not be a reliable indicator of negative valence for all users; (iii) a measurement spanning the whole interaction period is too coarse.

Extending the analysis of [11], a more fine-grained data analysis has been carried out, based on an affective concept that we call "anticipatory emotion". This type of emotional response occurs when a person expects a certain event to happen that will likely elicit a particular emotion. In the interview scenario a user might be assumed to experience stress when being asked a question for which he or she will not be able to give a satisfying answer. In order to investigate the effect of the Empathic Companion on subjects' anticipatory emotion, we compared the normalized SC and HR data from the period when the interviewer asks the question (Segment 1) for the "Supportive" and "Not Supportive" versions of the Empathic Companion application, abbreviated as Em and NEm, respectively.

In the study subjects are connected both to the GSR sensors of the Pro-Comp+ unit with the first two fingers of their non-dominant hand,[1] and to our in-house encoder that provides a wristband for SC and an ear-clip to measure HR. Participants were 10 staff and students from the University of Tokyo, aged 23–40, who were randomly assigned to the two versions (5 subjects in each).

---

[1] For simplicity, the EMG sensors have not been used.

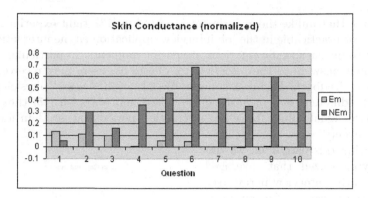

Fig. 5. Normalized SC data for anticipatory emotion

The result for SC is depicted in Fig. 5. Here the t-test (two-tailed, assuming unequal variances) demonstrates a significant effect of the companion in the "Supportive" (Em) version ($t(8) = -5.49$; $p = 0.0002$). The companion displaying empathy effects a decrease in the subject's arousal level for the period of being questioned by the interviewer, which eventually stabilizes at the baseline level. On the other hand, when the companion ignores the subject's emotion, the arousal level increases over the interview session. In the case of HR, the average (normalized) value is even higher in the Em version than in the NEm version (contrary to our expectation). Hence the core finding of the experiment can be stated as: *Users (as interviewees) receiving empathic feedback are significantly less aroused when hearing the interviewer's questions, independently of whether they are able to give a satisfying answer or not.*

In summary, the results of the experiment indicate that while an overall positive effect of the Empathic Companion cannot be shown, the presence of an agent that 'cares' can have a positive effect on the way users perceive questions in terms of lower levels of arousal (or stress).

5   Conclusions

This paper describes the Empathic Companion, an animated agent based interface that takes physiological signals of the user in real-time, models and interprets them as affective states, and addresses user emotions derived from those signals. A virtual job interview serves as an exploratory application that can be seen as an instance of stress-inducing interaction scenarios such as educational or training interfaces.

While results of statistical relevance of the Empathic Companion could not be obtained for the whole interview period [11], interestingly, empathic feedback is shown to have a significant impact on users' arousal level while being queried. This result relates to the importance of the timing of data assessment in emotion recognition [7] – when an emotion occurs. The Empathic Companion only responds to a user's emotional reaction that happens when the interviewer responds to the user's answer to the interviewer question. A more advanced system, however, must allow to react user emotion in a more flexible manner.

The study described in this paper was not designed to test a model of emotion recognition but employed a widely used two-dimensional emotion theory [6]. Future work will be directed toward a richer emotion model that takes into account situational and task-specific parameters of emotion elicitation during human–computer interaction.

Acknowledgments. This research is partly supported by the JSPS Research Grant (1999-2003) for the Future Program and a Memorandum of Understanding between the National Institute of Informatics and the Univ. of Augsburg.

References

1. Bickmore, T.: Relational Agents: Effecting Change through Human-Computer Relationships. PhD thesis, Massachusetts Institute of Technology (2003)
2. Cassell, J., Sullivan, J., Prevost, S., Churchill, E. (eds.): Embodied Conversational Agents. The MIT Press, Cambridge, MA (2000)
3. Conati, C.: Probabilistic assessment of user's emotions in educational games. Applied Artificial Intelligence 16 (2002) 555–575
4. Jensen, F.: Bayesian Networks and Decision Graphs. Springer, Berlin New York (2001)
5. Klein, J., Moon, Y., Picard, R.: This computer responds to user frustration: Theory, design, and results. Interacting with Computers 14 (2002) 119–140
6. Lang, P.J.: The emotion probe: Studies of motivation and attention. American Psychologist 50 (1995) 372–385
7. Levenson, R.W.: Autonomic specifity and emotion. In: Davidson, R.J., Scherer, K.R., Goldsmith, H.H. (eds.): Handbook of Affective Sciences, Oxford University Press, Oxford (2003) 212–224
8. Microsoft: Developing for Microsoft Agent. Microsoft Press, Redmond, WA (1998)
9. Norsys Software Corp. Netica: URL: http://www.norsys.com (2003)
10. Picard, R.W.: Affective Computing. The MIT Press, Cambridge, MA (1997)
11. Prendinger, H., Dohi, H., Wang, H., Mayer, S., Ishizuka, M.: Empathic embodied interfaces: Addressing users' affective state. In: Tutorial and Research Workshop on Affective Dialogue Systems, Springer Verlag, LNAI 3068, Berlin Heidelberg (2004) 53–64
12. Prendinger, H., Ishizuka, M. (eds.): Life-Like Characters. Tools, Affective Functions, and Applications. Cognitive Technologies. Springer Verlag, Berlin Heidelberg (2004)
13. Prendinger, H., Mori, J., Ishizuka, M.: Using human physiology to evaluate subtle expressivity of a virtual quizmaster in a mathematical game. International Journal of Human-Computer Studies 62 (2005) 231–245
14. Reeves, B., Nass, C.: The Media Equation. How People Treat Computers, Television and New Media Like Real People and Places. CSLI Publications, Center for the Study of Language and Information. Cambridge University Press (1998)
15. Thought Technology Ltd.: URL: http://www.thoughttechnology.com (2002)
16. Ward, R., Marsden, P.: Physiological responses to different WEB page designs. International Journal of Human-Computer Studies 59 (2003) 199–212

Using Learner Focus of Attention
to Detect Learner Motivation Factors

Lei Qu, Ning Wang, and W. Lewis Johnson

Center for Advanced Research in Technology for Education (CARTE), USC / ISI
4676 Admiralty Way, Suite 1001, Marina del Rey, CA, 90292
{leiqu, ning, johnson}@isi.edu

Abstract. This paper presents a model for pedagogical agents to use the learner's attention to detect motivation factors of the learner in interactive learning environments. This model is based on observations from human tutors coaching students in on-line learning tasks. It takes into account the learner's focus of attention, current task, and expected time required to perform the task. A Bayesian model is used to combine evidence from the learner's eye gaze and interface actions to infer the learner's focus of attention. Then the focus of attention is combined with information about the learner's activities, inferred by a plan recognizer, to detect the learner's degree of confidence, confusion and effort. Finally, we discuss the results of an empirical study that we performed to evaluate our model.

1 Introduction

Animated pedagogical agent technology seeks to improve the effectiveness of intelligent tutoring systems, by enabling them to provide various interactive actions in more natural and engaging ways. However, work to date has focused mainly on improving the output side of the interface, through the inclusion of expressive, lifelike behaviors [2]. The focus of the work described in this paper is on the input side, to enable the agent to track the learner's activities and focus of attention, so that it can detect the learner's motivational factors such as confidence and confusion.

Our approach involves monitoring of the learner's activities - both interface actions and focus of eye gaze. It infers the learner's focus of attention using a Bayesian model [5], which allows reasoning under uncertainty with various sources of information. And it combines the method for tracking learner focus of attention with a plan recognition capability for interpreting the learner's actions and forming expectations of future actions. Our particular motivation for conducting this work is to create pedagogical agents that are able to interact with learners in more socially appropriate ways, sensitive to rules of politeness and etiquette and able to influence the learner motivational as well as cognitive state [3, 4].

L. Ardissono, P. Brna, and A. Mitrovic (Eds.): UM 2005, LNAI 3538, pp. 70 – 73, 2005.
© Springer-Verlag Berlin Heidelberg 2005

2 Background Tutoring Studies

In an earlier study, we investigated how human tutors coach learners while interacting with Virtual Factory Teaching Systems (VFTS) [1, 4], an on-line factory system for teaching industrial engineering concepts and skills. We found that tutors used the following types of information, observed and inferred the learner motivation:

- The task that the learner was expected to perform next.
- The learner's focus of attention.
- The learner's self-confidence, inferred from the questions the learner asked.
- The learner's effort expended, as evidenced by the amount of time that the learner spent reading the tutorial and carrying out the tasks described there.

We therefore designed the user interface of our new system to enable an agent to have access to sufficient information about the learner, her/his activities, cognitive and motivational state. The new interface includes three major components:

- The VFTS interface, which reports each keyboard entry and mouse click that the learner performs on it.
- WebTutor, which is an on-line tutorial used to teach learner instruction and concepts of industrial engineering.
- Agent window, in which the left part of this window is a text window used to communicate with the agent (or a human tutor in Wizard-of-Oz mode) and the right part is an animated character that is able to generate speech and gestures.

The input devices consist of keyboard, mouse, and a small camera focused on the learner's face. This interface thus provides information that is similar to the information that human tutors use in tracking learner activities.

3 Description of Our Model

Our model includes four components for pedagogical agent to access the learner's focus of attention and track the learner's activities to detect the learner's motivation.

- WebTutor provides information about what task the learner is working on, as well the actions the learners perform as they read through the tutorial.
- The plan recognizer in VFTS monitors the learner's actions and tracks learner progress through the task.
- The focus of attention model takes input from the WebTutor interface, the VFTS interface and Agent interface as well as eye gaze information, in order to infer learner focus of attention.
- The detection model calculates the learner motivational factors based on outputs from focus of attention model and plan recognizer.

These four components can provide agents with capabilities to gather information about the learners' states and their expected tasks. Therefore agents are able to track learner attention and detect the learners' motivation.

3.1 Tracking Learner Focus of Attention Under Uncertainty

Information about eye gaze is extremely useful for detecting user focus of attention. In our system we want an eye tracking approach that is unobtrusive, that requires no special hardware and no calibration. We use a program developed by Larry Kite in the Laboratory for Computational and Biological Vision at USC to track eye gaze. It estimates the coordinates on a video display that correspond to the focus of gaze. The agent uses two types of information to infer the learner's focus: (1) information with certainty, i.e., mouse click, type and scroll window events in VFTS, WebTutor and Agent Window, and (2) information with uncertainty, namely data from eye track program and inferences about current state based upon past events. Then agents use Dynamic Bayesian Networks (DBNs) to infer the learner's focus of attention based on various sources of information.

3.2 Plan Recognition System

To help pedagogical agents track learner activities, we need to be able to track the learner's actions as well as track the learner's focus. We developed a plan recognition system to track learner actions and progress. The plan recognition system has four main components: .NET server, Student Interaction Database (SID), Plan Library and Action Pattern file in VFTS. The .NET server has two services: data service and agent service. All student interaction data in VFTS are captured and encoded into SOAP messages, sent to the data service and then saves it to SID. Interaction data represent learner action on the current object in the VFTS. An object in VFTS could be a textfield, a tab panel or a combobox. Interaction data include mouse clicks, mouse movements and keyboard input. A plan in the plan library consists of a list of tasks the user needs to achieve given a tutorial or problem. The VFTS action pattern XML file defines the actions a user could perform in VFTS.

3.3 Utilizing Focus of Attention

The above analyses make it possible for the agent to track learner's attention and actions. There are many factors that influence learner's motivation. We focus here on the learner's confidence, confusion and effort, factors that were shown to be important in the background tutor studies.

- Confidence represents the confidence of learners in solving problems in the learning environment. The learner's confidence is modeled as one of three levels: High, Normal and Low.
- Confusion reflects the learner's failing to understand the tutorial or deicide how to proceed in the VFTS. A learner with high confusion is most likely to be stuck or frustrated.
- Effort is the duration of time that the learner spends on performing tasks. It is an important indicator of intrinsic motivation in learners, and expert human tutors often praise learners for expending effort even when they are not successful.

4 Evaluation and Conclusion

To evaluate our method, we designed and conducted an experimental study. With new interfaces and models, we ran 24 subjects at the University of California at Santa Barbara. The 24 participants were all undergraduate students. Most of them had computer skills but little or no knowledge of industrial engineering. With the human tutor's observation as the baseline, the recognition accuracies of our model are 82% for confidence, 76.8% for confusion, and 76.3% for effort. With the learner's self-reports as the baseline, the recognition accuracies dropped to 70.7%, 75.6% and 73.2% for the learner's motivation. In conclusion, we can say that the results of our evaluation suggest that such model can provide agents accurate information about learner's motivation. It is possible for pedagogical agents to detect learner's motivation with confidence and provide learner with proactive help in order to motivate the learner's learning.

Furthermore we wish to extend the user monitoring capability to handle a wider range of ambiguous contexts. Based upon these results, pedagogical agent can then interact with learners through a conversational system in more socially appropriate ways.

Acknowledgements

This work was supported in part by the National Science Foundation under Grant No. 0121330, and in part by a grant from Microsoft Research. Any opinions, findings, and conclusions or recommendations expressed in this material are those of the author and do not necessarily reflect the views of the National Science Foundation.

References

1. Dessouky, M.M., Verma, S., Bailey, D., Richel, J.: A methodology for developing a Web-based factory simulator for manufacturing education. IEEE Transactions, 33 (2001) 167-180
2. Johnson, W.L., Rickel, J.W., Lester, J.C.: Animated pedagogical agents: Face-to-face inter-action in interactive learning environments. International Journal of Artificial Intelligence in Education, 11 (2000) 47-78
3. Johnson, W.L.: Using Agent Technology to Improve the Quality of Web-Based Education. In N. Zhong and J. Liu (Eds.), Web Intelligence, Springer-Verlag, Berlin Heidelberg New York (2002)
4. Johnson, W.L.: Interaction Tactics for Socially Intelligent Pedagogical Agents. In Proceedings of the Intelligent User Interfaces (2003) 251-253
5. Pearl, J.: Probabilistic Reasoning in Intelligent Systems: Networks of Plausible Inference. Morgan-Kaufmann, San Mateo, CA (1988)

Player Modeling Impact on Player's Entertainment in Computer Games

Georgios N. Yannakakis[1] and Manolis Maragoudakis[2]

[1] Centre for Intelligent Systems and their Applications,
The University of Edinburgh, AT, Crichton Street, EH8 9LE, UK
g.yannakakis@sms.ed.ac.uk
[2] Wire Communication Lab, Electrical and Computer Engineering Department,
University of Patras, 26 500 Rio, Greece
mmarag@wcl.ee.upatras.gr

Abstract. In this paper we introduce an effective mechanism for obtaining computer games of high interest (i.e. satisfaction for the player). The proposed approach is based on the interaction of a player modeling tool and a successful on-line learning mechanism from the authors' previous work on prey/predator computer games. The methodology demonstrates high adaptability into dynamical playing strategies as well as reliability and justifiability to the game user.

1 Introduction

In [6], we introduced an efficient generic measure of interest of predator/prey computer games. We also presented a robust on-line (i.e. while the game is played) neuro-evolution learning mechanism capable of increasing the game's interest at high levels while the game is being played. The test-bed used for these experiments was the well-known Pac-Man computer game.

In the work presented here, we attempt to study the player's contribution to the emergence of interest of the aforementioned computer game. We do that by investigating a Player Modeling (PM) mechanism's impact on the game's interest when it is combined with the aforementioned on-line learning procedure. More specifically, we use Bayesian Networks (BN), trained on computer-guided player data, as a tool for inferring appropriate parameter values for the chosen on-line learning (OLL) mechanism. Results obtained show that PM positively affects the OLL mechanism to generate games of higher interest for the player. In addition, this PM-OLL combination, in comparison to OLL alone, demonstrates faster adaptation to challenging scenarios of frequent changing playing strategies.

2 Player Modeling in Computer Games

Player modeling in computer games and its beneficial outcomes have recently attracted the interest of a small but growing community of researchers and game developers. Houlette's [4] and Charles' and Black's [1] work on dynamic player

L. Ardissono, P. Brna, and A. Mitrovic (Eds.): UM 2005, LNAI 3538, pp. 74–78, 2005.

modeling and its adaptive abilities in video games constitute representative examples in the field.

Bayesian networks [5] provide a comprehensive means for effective representation of independent assumptions and a mechanism for effective inference under conditions of uncertainty. In the field of PM, BN can cope with uncertainty on the model of the player, allowing for inference on the class variable given a subset of the input features, rather than a complete representation of them.

3   The Pac-Man Game

The test-bed studied is a modified version of the original Pac-Man computer game released by Namco. The player's (*PacMan's*) goal is to eat all the pellets appearing in a maze-shaped stage while avoiding being killed by the four *Ghosts*. For the experiments presented here, the game field (i.e. stage) is a 19×29 grid maze where corridors are 1 grid-cell wide.

Three fixed *Ghost*-avoidance and pellet-eating strategies for the *PacMan* player, differing in complexity and effectiveness are used (see [6]). Each strategy is based on decision making applying a cost or probability approximation to the player's four neighbor cells (i.e. up, down, left and right). On the other hand, a multi-layered fully connected feedforward neural controller is employed to manage the *Ghosts'* motion.

4   Interest Metric

In order to find an objective estimate of interest in the Pac-Man computer game we first need to define the criteria that make a game interesting. Then, second, we need to quantify and combine all these criteria in a mathematical formula. The three criteria, presented in [6], which collectively define interest for the Pac-Man game, are briefly as follows.

1. When the game is neither too hard nor too easy.
2. When there is diversity in *Ghosts'* behavior over the games.
3. When *Ghosts'* behavior is aggressive rather than static.

The metrics (as presented in [6]) for the three criteria are given by T (challenge metric; based on the difference between maximum and average player's lifetime over N games — N is 50 in this paper), S (diversity metric; based on standard deviation of player's lifetime over N games) and $E\{H_n\}$ (aggressiveness metric; based on stage grid-cell visit average entropy of the *Ghosts* over N games) respectively. All three metrics are combined linearly (1)

$$I = \frac{\gamma T + \delta S + \epsilon E\{H_n\}}{\gamma + \delta + \epsilon} \tag{1}$$

where I is the interest value; γ, δ and ϵ are criterion weight parameters ($\gamma = 1, \delta = 2, \epsilon = 3$ in this paper). The metric given by (1), can be effectively applied to any predator/prey computer game (e.g. see [7]) because it is based on generic quantitative features of this genre of games.

5   On-line Learning

On-line learning (see [6] for more details) is a genetic search mechanism based on the idea of *Ghosts* that are reactive to any player's behavior and learn from its strategy instead of being the predictable and, therefore, uninteresting characters that exist in all versions of this game today. The OLL parameters e_v (simulation time for the evaluation of each group of *Ghosts*) and p_m (probability of mutation) strongly influence the performance of the mechanism. Naive selection of these values may result in disruptive phenomena on the *Ghosts'* behavior through the mutation operator. Sect. 6 presents a BN-based mechanism designed to lead to more careful OLL parameter value selection and furthermore to an increasingly interesting game.

6   PM-OLL Mechanism

This work's target is to investigate whether player modeling can contribute to the satisfaction of the player. Towards this aim we combine PM, by the use of BN, with the OLL algorithm to form the PM-OLL mechanism presented here. The two mechanisms' interaction flows through the OLL parameters which are set by inferences from the PM mechanism.

In order to construct a model of the player we have considered the following features obtained from a play of 10 games: 1) Score; 2) time played; 3) grid-cell visits entropy of the player — this metric corresponds to the player's aggressiveness; 4) initial interest of the game; 5) relative interest difference after 10 games; 6) e_p; and 7) p_m.

Our objective, given that we desire maximum interest change in the game, is to find the optimal values for the features p_m and e_p that correspond to the player input variables. The BN which embodies the PM mechanism, is trained off-line on feature instances obtained by multiple simulation runs within a fixed set of empirically selected and representative e_v and p_m values.

7   Results and Analysis

For PM in our test-bed we used the Bayesian Network Augmented Naïve Bayes (BAN), by Cheng et al. [2]. For the BN training we have utilized the *Bayesian scoring function* [3] which provides a metric of relation among two candidate networks. Upon completion of the BN structure learning mechanism, the Expectation Maximization (EM) algorithm is used in order to estimate the parameters of the conditional probability table.

7.1   Adaptability Test

In order to test a learning mechanism's ability to adapt to a changing environment, the following experiment is proposed. Beginning from five significantly different (by means of interest) initial behaviors we apply the examined mechanism against a specific *PacMan* type. During the on-line process we keep changing the *PacMan* type every 20 games played. The process stops after 60 games when all three types of player have played the game. These thirty (6 different player type sequences times 5 different initial behaviors) experiments (scenarios) illustrate the overall picture of the mechanism's behavior against any sequence of the fixed strategy *PacMan* types.

7.2   Comparative Study

In [6], we empirically chose the OLL parameters to be $p_m = 0.02$ and $e_p = 50$. Our empirical hypothesis is well supported by a sensitivity analysis based on experiments with all combinations of pairs of (p_m, e_p) fixed set parameters values. Results obtained — which are not presented analytically due to space considerations — show that the $(0.02, 50)$ values constitute the most appropriate pair of fixed OLL parameters and, therefore, are selected for all experiments in this paper.

To test the PM impact on the OLL mechanism's ability to generate games of high interest we apply the adaptability test for the OLL alone (fixed parameter values — $p_m = 0.02, e_p = 50$) and for the PM-OLL approach. For the latter, player modeling occurs every 10 games inferring values for p_m and e_p. Fig. 1 shows that the PM-OLL mechanism is able to generate more interesting games than the OLL mechanism in 23 out of 30 playing scenarios examined; in 12 of these cases the difference is statistically significant.

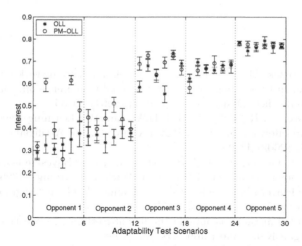

Fig. 1. Adaptability test: average interest values and interest intervals

7.3   Randomness Testing

In order to assess the truth of the hypothesis that random selection of the set of p_m and e_p values, instead of BN produced values, has a better impact on the generated interest value, we apply the adaptability test for PM-OLL where p_m and e_p values are picked randomly. The test is conducted for all thirty scenarios. In 27 out of 30 cases examined, the random fashion of selecting values for p_m and e_p generates lower average interest value than the interest value generated by PM-OLL (in 16 cases the difference is statistically significant). These results imply that appropriate selection of OLL parameter values correlates to the improvement of the player's satisfaction.

8   Conclusions

Successful applications of the on-line learning approach [6, 7] have already shown the mechanisms' robustness in generating computer games of higher interest and fast adaptability to changing playing strategy situations. In this paper we demonstrated a PM mechanism's positive impact on the generation of more interesting games. Moreover, the proposed PM-OLL mechanism shows game reliability since it demonstrates adaptive behaviors in the scale of decades of games played and it is computationally inexpensive (1-3 seconds of CPU time for the BN to infer OLL parameter values; few milliseconds for the OLL to evaluate the *Ghost* population on-line). The subsequent step of this work is to discover whether the interest value computed by (1) for a game correlates with human judgement of interest. Preliminary results on a survey with a statistically significant sample of human subjects show that human players' notions of interest of the Pac-Man game are highly correlated with the proposed measure of interest.

References

1. Charles, D., Black, M.: Dynamic player modelling: A framework for player-centric digital games. In Proceedings of the International Conference on Computer Games: Artificial Intelligence, Design and Education (2004) 29–35
2. Cheng, J., Greiner, R., Kelly, J., Bell, D.A., Liu, W.: Learning Bayesian Networks from Data: an Information-Theory Based Approach. The Artificial Intelligence Journal, Vol. 137. (2002) 43–90
3. Heckerman, D., Geiger, D., Chickering, D.M.: Learning Bayesian networks: the combination of knowledge and statistical data. Machine Learning, (1995) 20:197–243
4. Houlette, R.: Player Modeling for Adaptive Games. AI Game Programming Wisdom II, Charles River Media, Inc (2004) 557–566
5. Pearl, J.: Probabilistic Reasoning in Intelligent Systems, Networks of Plausible Inference. Morgan Kaufmann Publishers, Inc (1988)
6. Yannakakis, G.N., Hallam, J.: Evolving Opponents for Interesting Interactive Computer Games. In Proceedings of the 8th International Conference on Simulation of Adaptive Behavior, The MIT Press (2004) 499–508
7. Yannakakis, G.N., Hallam, J.: Interactive Opponents Generate Interesting Games. In Proceedings of the International Conference on Computer Games: Artificial Intelligence, Design and Education (2004) 240–247

Using Learning Curves to Mine Student Models

Brent Martin and Antonija Mitrovic

Intelligent Computer Tutoring Group,
Department of Computer Science and Software Engineering,
University of Canterbury,
Private Bag 4800, Christchurch, New Zealand
{brent, tanja}@cosc.canterbury.ac.nz

Abstract. This paper presents an evaluation study that measures the effect of modifying feedback generality in an Intelligent Tutoring System (ITS) based on Student Models. A taxonomy of the tutor domain was used to group existing knowledge elements into plausible, more general, concepts. Existing student models were then used to measure the validity of these new concepts, demonstrating that at least some of these concepts appear to be more effective at capturing what the students learned than the original knowledge elements. We then trialled an experimental ITS that gave feedback at a higher level. The results suggest that it is feasible to use this approach to determine how feedback might be fine-tuned to better suit student learning, and hence that learning curves are a useful tool for mining student models.

1 Introduction

Analysing adaptive educational systems such as Intelligent Tutoring Systems (ITS) is hard because the students' interaction with the system is but one small facet of their education experience. Pre- and post-test comparisons provide a rigorous means of comparing two systems, but they require large numbers of students and a sufficiently long learning period. The latter confounds the results unless it can be guaranteed that the students do not undertake any relevant learning outside the system being measured. Further, such experiments can only make comparisons at a high level: when fine-tuning parts of an educational system (such as the domain model), a large number of studies may need to be performed. In this research we explored using a more objective measure of domain model performance, namely learning curves, to see if we could predict what changes could be made at the level of individual knowledge elements (concepts), or sets of concepts, to improve student performance.

A key to good performance in an ITS is its ability to provide the most effective feedback possible. Feedback in ITS' is usually very specific. However, in some domains there may be low-level generalisations that can be made where the generalised concept is more likely what the student is learning. For example, Koedinger and Mathan [2] suggest that for their Excel Tutor, one of the cognitive tutors [1], the concept of relative versus fixed indexing is independent of the direction the information is copied; this is a generalisation of two concepts, namely horizontal

L. Ardissono, P. Brna, and A. Mitrovic (Eds.): UM 2005, LNAI 3538, pp. 79–88, 2005.
© Springer-Verlag Berlin Heidelberg 2005

versus vertical indexing. We hypothesised that this might be the case for our tutor (SQL-Tutor), which contains of a set of rules (constraints) that represent the concepts of the model. For example, an analysis of the feedback messages found that often they are nearly the same for some groups of rules. Other rules may differ only by the clause of the SQL query in which they occur (for example, the WHERE and HAVING clauses of an SQL query have substantially similar rule sets).

Some systems use Bayesian student models to represent students' knowledge at various levels (e.g. [10]) and so theoretically they can dynamically determine the best level to provide feedback, but this is difficult and potentially error-prone: building Bayesian belief networks requires the large task of specifying the prior and conditional probabilities. We are interested in whether it is possible to infer a set of high-level rules that generally represent concepts being learned while avoiding the difficulty of building a belief network, by analysing past student model data to determine significant subgroups of rules that represent such concepts.

One method of analysing rules is to plot learning curves: if the objects being measured relate to the actual concepts being learned, we expect to see a "power law" between the number of times the object is relevant and the proportion of times it is used incorrectly [8]. Learning curves can be plotted for all rules of a system to measure its overall performance. In [2] Koedinger and Mathan used learning curves to argue that differences in learning existed between a specific "six-rule" and a more general "four-rule" model of the Excel domain. Learning curves can also be used to analyse groups of objects within a system, or to "mine" the student models for further information. We used this latter approach to try to determine which groups of domain rules appear to perform well when treated as a single rule. To decide which rules to group, we used a (man-made) taxonomy of the learning domain [3], and grouped rules according to each node of the taxonomy. This enabled us to measure how well the rules, when combined into more general rules of increasing generality, still exhibited power laws, and hence represented a concept that the students were learning. We then used this information as the basis for building a new version of the domain model where feedback was now given when students violated one of a set of rules that describes the new concept, rather than giving feedback specific to each individual rule. We then compared the performance of this system with that of the original SQL-Tutor.

In the next section we describe the system we used in the study, and the two different versions of it that utilise the two feedback strategies. In Section 3 we present our hypotheses and discuss how we used the student models to predict the performance of groups of rules. Section 4 presents the results, while the conclusions are given in Section 5.

2   SQL-Tutor

The goal of this project is to investigate whether we can predict the effectiveness of different levels of feedback by observing how well the underlying group of rules appears to measure a single concept being learned. We performed an experiment in the context of SQL-Tutor, an intelligent tutoring system that teaches the SQL database language to university-level students. For a detailed discussion of the system, see [4, 5]; here we present only some of its features. SQL-Tutor consists of an interface, a pedagogical module—which determines the timing and content of pedagogical actions—and a student modeller, which analyses student answers. The system contains definitions of several databases and a set of problems and their ideal solutions. To check the correctness of the student's solution, SQL-Tutor compares it to an example of a correct solution using domain knowledge represented in the form of more than 650 constraints. It uses Constraint-Based Modeling (CBM) [9] for both domain and student models. Fig. 1 shows a screen shot of SQL-Tutor. Like all constraint-based ITS, feedback is attached directly to the rules, or "constraints", which make up the domain model. An example of a constraint is:

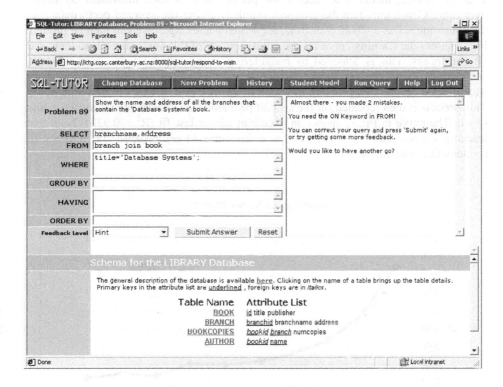

Fig. 1. A screen shot of SQL-Tutor

```
(147
"You have used some names in the WHERE clause that are not from
this database."

; relevance condition
  (match SS WHERE (?* (^name ?n) ?*))
; satisfaction condition
  (or  (test SS (^valid-table (?n ?t))
       (test SS (^attribute-p (?n ?a ?t)))))
; Relevant clause
"WHERE")
```

Constraints are used to critique the students' solutions by checking that the concept they represent is being correctly applied. The relevance condition first tests whether or not this concept is relevant to the problem and current solution attempt. If so, the satisfaction condition is checked to ascertain whether or not the student has applied this concept correctly. If the satisfaction condition is met, no action is taken; if it fails, the feedback message is presented to the student. In this case the relevance condition checks whether the student has used one or more names in the WHERE clause; if so, the satisfaction condition tests that each name found is a valid table or attribute name. The student model consists of the set of constraints, along with information about whether or not it has been successfully applied, for each attempt where it is relevant. Thus the student model is a trace of the performance of each individual constraint over time. Constraints may be grouped together, giving the average performance of the constraint set as a whole over time, for which a learning curve can then be plotted. Fig. 2 shows the learning curve for the control group of this study, for all students and all constraints. This is achieved by considering every constraint, for every student, and calculating the proportion of constraint/student instances for which the constraint was violated for the first problem in which it was relevant, giving the first data point. This process is then repeated for the second problem each constraint was used for, and so on. The curve in Fig. 2 shows an excellent power law fit ($R^2 = 0.978$). Note that learning curves tend to deteriorate as n becomes large, because the number of participating constraints reduces.

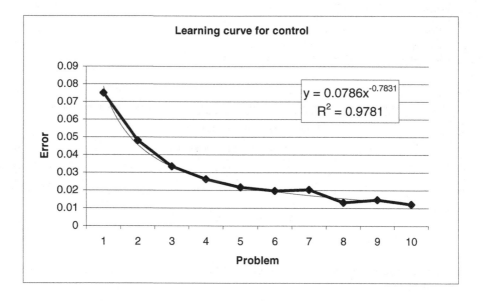

Fig. 2. Example learning curve for the control group

The experimental version of SQL-Tutor was identical to the control, except feedback was no longer directly supplied by the constraints. Instead, a lookup table was provided that contained definitions of 63 high-level constraints being tested, where each was a tuple of the form (new constraint num, <constraints>, feedback), where <constraints> is a list of the constraints this new generalised constraint represents. The generalised constraint set is described in the next section.

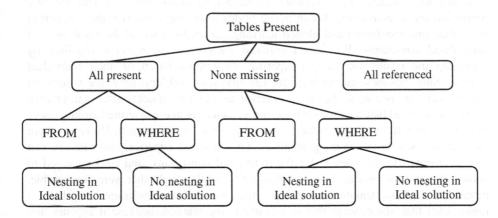

Fig. 3. Example subtree from the SQL –Tutor domain taxonomy

3 Experiment Design

We hypothesized that some groupings of constraints would represent the concepts the student was learning better than the (highly specialised) constraints themselves. We then further hypothesised that for such a grouping, learning might be more effective if students were given feedback about the general concept, rather than more specialised feedback about the specific context in which the concept appeared (represented by the original constraint). To evaluate the first hypothesis, we analysed data from a previous study of SQL-Tutor on a similar population, namely second year students from a database course at the University of Canterbury, New Zealand. To decide which constraints to group together, we used a taxonomy of the SQL-Tutor domain model that we had previously defined [3]. This taxonomy is very fine-grained, consisting of 530 nodes to cover the 650 constraints, although many nodes only cover a single constraint. The deepest path in the tree is eight nodes, with most paths being five or six nodes deep. Fig. 3 shows the subtree for the concept "Correct tables present". Whilst developing such a hierarchy is a non-trivial task, in practice this can actually aid construction of the domain model [6, 7].

We grouped constraints according to each node in the taxonomy, and rebuilt the student models as though these were real constraints that the system had been tracking. For example, if a node N1 in the taxonomy covers constraints 1 and 2, and the student has applied constraint 1 incorrectly, then 2 incorrectly, then 1 incorrectly again, then 2 correctly, the original model would be:

(1 FAIL FAIL)
(2 FAIL SUCCEED)

while the entry for the new constraint is:

(N1 FAIL FAIL FAIL SUCCEED)

Note that several constraints from N1 might be applied for the same problem. In this case we calculated the proportion of such constraints that were violated. We performed this operation for all non-trivial nodes in the hierarchy (i.e. those covering more than one constraint) and plotted learning curves for *each* of the resulting 304 generalised constraints. We then compared each curve to a curve obtained by averaging the results for the participating constraints, based on their individual models. Note that these curves were for the first four problems only: the volume of data in each case is low, so the curves deteriorate relatively quickly after that. Overall the results showed that the more general the grouping is, the worse the learning curve (either a poorer fit or a lower slope), which is what we might expect. However, there were eight cases for which the generalised constraint had superior power law fit and slope compared to the average for the individual constraints, and thus appeared to better represent the concept being learned, and a further eight that were comparable. From this result we tentatively concluded that some of our constraints may be at a lower level than the concept that is actually being learned, because it appears that there is "crossover" between constraints in a group. In the example above, this means that exposure to constraint 1 appears to lead to some learning of constraint 2, and vice versa. This supports our first hypothesis.

We then tested our second hypothesis: that providing feedback at the more general level would improve learning for those high-level constraints that exhibited superior learning curves. Based on the original analysis we produced a set of 63 new constraints that were one or two levels up the taxonomy from the individual constraints. This new constraint set covered 468 of the original 650 constraints, with membership of each generalised constraint varying between 2 and 32, and an average of 7 members (SD=6). For each new constraint, we produced a tuple that described its membership, and included the feedback message that would be substituted in the experimental system for that of the original constraint. An example of such an entry is:

```
(N5 "Check that you are using the right operators in
numeric comparisons." (462 463 426 46 461 427 444 517
445 518 446 519 447 520 404 521 405 522))
```

This generalised constraint covers all individual constraints that perform some kind of check for the presence of a particular numeric operator. Students for the experimental group thus received this feedback, while the control group were presented with the more specific feedback from each original constraint concerning the particular operator.

To evaluate this second hypothesis we performed an experiment with the students enrolled in an introductory database course at the University of Canterbury. Participation in the experiment was voluntary. Prior to the study, students attended six lectures on SQL and had two laboratories on the Oracle RDBMS. SQL-Tutor was demonstrated to students in a lecture on September 20, 2004. The experiment was performed in scheduled laboratories during the same week. The experiment required the students to sit a pre-test, which was administered online the first time students accessed SQL-Tutor. The pre-test consisted of four multi-choice questions, which required the student to identify correct definitions of concepts in the domain, or to specify whether a given SQL statement is appropriate for the given context.

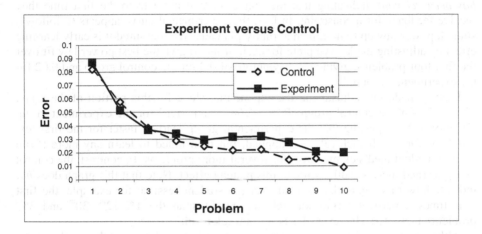

Fig. 4. Learning curves for the two groups

The students were randomly allocated to one of the two versions of the system. The course involved a test on SQL on October 14, 2004, which provided additional motivation for students to practise with SQL-Tutor. A post-test was administered at the conclusion of a two-hour session with the tutor, and consisted of four questions of similar nature and complexity as the questions in the pre-test. The maximum mark for the pre/post tests was 4.

4 Results

Of the 124 students enrolled in the course, 100 students logged on to SQL-Tutor at least once. However, some students looked at the system only briefly. We therefore excluded the logs of students who did not attempt any problems. The logs of the remaining 78 students (41 in the control, and 37 in the experimental group) were then analysed. The mean score for the pre-test for all students was 2.17 out of 4 (sd=1.01). The students were randomly allocated to one of the two versions of the system. A t-test showed no significant differences between the pre-test scores for the two groups (mean=2.10 and 2.24 for the control and experimental groups respectively, standard deviation for both=1.01, p=0.53).

Fig. 4 plots the learning curves for the control and experimental groups. Note that the unit measured for both groups is the *original* constraints, because this ensures there are no differences in the unit being measured, which might alter the curves and prevent their being directly compared. Only those constraints that belong to one or more generalised constraints were included.

The curves in Fig. 4 are comparable over the range of ten problems, and give similar power curves, with the experimental group being slightly worse (control slope = -0.86, R^2 = .94; experiment slope = -0.57, R^2 = 0.93). However, the experimental group appears to fare better between the first and second problem *for which each rule has been relevant*, indicating that they have learned more from the first time they receive feedback for a constraint. In fact, the experimental curve appears to follow a smooth power law up to n=4, then abruptly plateaus. We measured this early learning effect by adjusting the Y asymptote for each group to give the best power law fit over the first four problems, giving a Y asymptote of 0.0 for the control group and 0.02 for the experimental group.

Having made this adjustment, the exponential slope for this portion of the graph was –0.75 for the control group (R^2 = 0.9686) and –1.17 for the experiment group (R2=0.9915), suggesting that the experimental group learned faster for the first few problems for which each rule was applied, but then failed to learn any more (from each individual feedback message) for several more problems. In contrast, the control group learned more steadily, without this plateau effect. Note that this graph does *not* indicate how this feedback is spread over the student session: for example, the first four times a particular rule was relevant might span the 1st, 12th, 30th and 35th problems attempted. However, this is still a weak result.

Although the generalised constraints used were loosely based on the results of the initial analysis, they also contained generalisations that appeared feasible, but for which we had no evidence that they would necessarily be superior to their individual counterparts. The experimental system might therefore contain a mixture of good and bad generalisations. We measured this by plotting, for the control group, individual learning curves for the generalised constraints and comparing them to the average performance of the member constraints, the same as was performed for the *a priori* analysis. The cut-off point for these graphs was at n=4, because the volume of data is low and so the curves rapidly degenerate, and because the analysis already performed suggested that differences were only likely to appear early in the constraint histories. Of the 63 generalised constraints, six appeared to clearly be superior to the individual constraints, a further three appeared to be equivalent, and eight appeared to be significantly worse. There was insufficient data about the remaining 46 to draw conclusions. We then plotted curves for two subsets of the constraints: those that were members of the generalised constraints classified as better, same or 'no data' (labelled "acceptable"), and those classed as worse or 'no data' (labelled "poor"). Fig. 5 shows the curves for these two groups.

For the "acceptable" generalised constraints, the experimental group appears to perform considerably better for the first three problems, but then plateaus; for the "poor" generalised constraints the experimental group performs better for the first two problems only. In other words, for the "acceptable" generalisations the feedback is more helpful than the standard feedback during the solving of the first two problems in which it is encountered (and so students do better on the second and third one) but is less helpful after that; for the "poor" group this is true for the first problem only. We tested the significance of this result by computing the error reduction between n=1 and n=3 for each student and comparing the means.

The experimental group had a mean error reduction of 0.058 (SD=0.027), compared to 0.035 (SD=0.030) for the control group. The difference was significant at p=0.01. In contrast, there was no significant difference in the means of error reduction for the "poor" group (experimental mean=0.050 (SD=0.035), control mean=0.041 (SD=0.028), p>0.3). This result again suggests that the individual learning curves do indeed predict to some extent whether generalised feedback at this level will be effective.

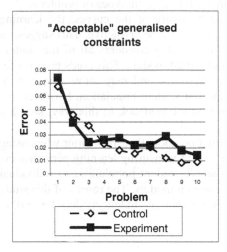 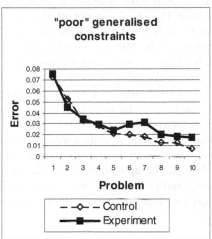

Fig. 5. Power curves based on predictions of goodness

5 Conclusions

In this experiment we explored whether learning curves could be used to analyse past student model data for predicting the behaviour of feedback that is based on generalised domain concepts. We analysed an existing set of student models by plotting learning curves for various groups of constraints (based on a taxonomy of the domain) and showed that some of these groupings appeared to perform better as a generalised concept than the underlying constraints. Such generalisations tended to be moderate, with very general concepts exhibiting poor performance. We then hypothesised that feedback applied at the level of these general concepts would be more effective than more specific feedback from the highly specific constraints currently in the domain model. We developed a feedback set that mapped to a set of moderately general concepts, and found that for some of these learning performance did appear to improve, although only for the first two or three problems, after which learning performance deteriorated. For other generalisations, performance was better only for the very first problem, and worse afterwards. We also showed that we could predict to some extent which generalised constraints would produce better performance by analysing their apparent performance in the control group.

There are several tentative conclusions we can infer from these results. First, generalised feedback (when the generalisation is valid) appears to be more effective in the early stages of learning a new concept, but then becomes worse. This suggests a dynamic approach may work best. A conservative approach might be to use generalised feedback only for the first problem (for a given concept), and then revert to more specialised feedback. Alternatively, we might measure the performance of each generalisation: when it appears to be losing its effectiveness, the system could switch to specific feedback. However, the small amount of data available makes this a difficult task. More general feedback may also increase the generality of what is learned, thus leading to better knowledge transfer for different types of problems.

Despite the small amount of data and poor quality of the curves, the learning curves for individual generalised concepts did appear to be predictive. This suggests a system might be able to tailor feedback on-the-fly if it considers all of the student models when making decisions, rather than individual models. This holds promise for increased adaptability in Intelligent Tutoring Systems, and may allow a system to quickly tailor its feedback responses to the current student population. However, the data volume may be too small to individually tailor feedback in this way, so other measures may need to be employed.

Students' models contain a wealth of information about their behaviour when using an adaptive system. Learning curves are one way of measuring learning performance, and they can be applied at various levels to whole student populations or individual students, and to groups of rules versus entire domain models. The results of this study suggest that learning curves are a useful tool for mining student models for further insight.

References

1. Anderson, J.R., Corbett, A.T., Koedinger, K.R., Pelletier, R.: Cognitive Tutors: Lessons Learned. Journal of the Learning Sciences 4(2) (1995) 167-207
2. Koedinger, K.R., Mathan, S.: Distinguishing qualitatively different kinds of learning using log files and learning curves. ITS 2004 Log Analysis Workshop Maceio, Brazil (2004) 39-46
3. Martin, B.: Constraint-Based Modelling: Representing Student Knowledge. New Zealand Journal of Computing 7(2) (1999) 30-38
4. Mitrovic, A.: An Intelligent SQL Tutor on the Web. Artificial Intelligence in Education 13(2-4) (2003) 173-197
5. Mitrovic, A., Martin, B., Mayo, M.: Using evaluation to shape ITS design: Results and experiences with SQL-Tutor. User Modelling and User Adapted Interaction 12(2-3) (2002) 243-279
6. Mitrovic, A., Suraweera, P., Martin, B.: The role of domain ontology in knowledge acquisition for ITS. Seventh international conference on Intelligent Tutoring Systems, Maceio, Brazil (2004) 207-216
7. Mizoguchi, R., Bourdeau, J.: Using Ontological Engineering to Overcome Common AI-ED Problems. International Journal of Artificial Intelligence in Education 11 (2000) 107-121
8. Newell, A., Rosenbloom, P.S.: Mechanisms of skill acquisition and the law of practice. Cognitive skills and their acquisition, J.R. Anderson, Editor. Lawrence Erlbaum Associates, Hillsdale, NJ (1981) 1-56
9. Ohlsson, S.: Constraint-Based Student Modeling. Student Modeling: The Key to Individualized Knowledge-Based Instruction, J. Greer and G. McCalla, Editors, Springer-Verlag, New York (1994) 167-189
10. Zapata-Rivera, J.D., Greer, J.E.: Interacting with Inspectable Bayesian Student Models. Artificial Intelligence in Education 14(2) (2004) 127-163

Exploiting Probabilistic Latent Information for the Construction of Community Web Directories

Dimitrios Pierrakos[1,2] and Georgios Paliouras[1]

[1] Institute of Informatics and Telecommunications, NCSR "Demokritos",
15310 Ag. Paraskevi, Greece
{dpie, paliourg}@iit.demokritos.gr
[2] Department of Informatics and Telecommunications, University of Athens,
Panepistimiopolis, Ilissia Athens 15784, Greece

Abstract. This paper improves a recently-presented approach to Web Personalization, named Community Web Directories, which applies personalization techniques to Web Directories. The Web directory is viewed as a concept hierarchy and personalization is realized by constructing user community models on the basis of usage data collected by the proxy servers of an Internet Service Provider. The user communities are modeled using Probabilistic Latent Semantic Analysis (PLSA), which provides a number of advantages such as overlapping communities, as well as a good rationale for the associations that exist in the data. The data that are analyzed present challenging peculiarities such as their large volume and semantic diversity. Initial results presented in this paper illustrate the effectiveness of the new method.

1 Introduction

The hypergraphical architecture of the Web has been used to support claims that the Web will make Internet-based services really user-friendly. However, due to its almost unstructured and heterogeneous environment, as well as its galloping growth, the Web has not realized the goal of providing easy access to online information. Information overload is one of the Web's major shortcomings that place obstacles in the way users access the required information.

An approach towards the alleviation of this problem is the organization of Web content into thematic hierarchies, also known as Web directories, such as Yahoo! [14] or the Open Directory Project (ODP) [9], that allow users to locate required information. However their size and complexity are canceling out any gains that were expected with respect to the information overload problem, i.e., it is often difficult to navigate to the information of interest to a particular user. A different approach is Web personalization [8], which focuses on the adaptability of Web-based information systems to the needs and interests of individual users, or groups of users. A major obstacle though towards realizing this solution is the acquisition of accurate and operational models for the users. Reliance to manual

L. Ardissono, P. Brna, and A. Mitrovic (Eds.): UM 2005, LNAI 3538, pp. 89–98, 2005.
© Springer-Verlag Berlin Heidelberg 2005

creation of these models, either by the users or by domain experts, is inadequate for various reasons, among which the annoyance of the users and the difficulty of verifying and maintaining the resulting models. An alternative approach is that of Web Usage Mining [13], which provides a methodology for the collection and preprocessing of usage data, and the construction of models representing the behavior and the interests of users [10].

In recent work [11], we proposed, the concept of *Community Web Directories*, which combines the strengths of Web Directories and Web Personalization, in order to address some of the above-mentioned issues. Community Web Directories are usable Web directories that correspond to the interests of groups of users, known as user communities. The members of a community can use the community directory as a starting point for navigating the Web, based on the topics that they are interested in, without the requirement of accessing vast Web directories. For the construction of Community Web directories, we have presented the *Community Directory Miner, (CDM)* algorithm, which was able to produce a suitable level of semantic characterization of the interests of a particular user community. This approach, similar to other clustering approaches, is based on relations between the users, that correspond to observable patterns in the usage data. However, there also exists a number of latent factors that are responsible for the observable associations. These latent factors can be thought of as the motivation of a particular user accessing a certain page, and therefore groups of users, can be constructed sharing common latent motives. In the case of Web directories this method could provide a more thorough insight of the patterns that exist in the usage data. A common method for discovering latent factors in data is Probabilistic Latent Semantic Analysis (PLSA), a technique that has been used extensively in Information Retrieval and Indexing [5]. In this work we employ this method in order to identify user communities.

The rest of this paper is organized as follows: Section 2 presents existing approaches to Web personalization with usage mining methods, as well as approaches to the construction of personalized Web directories. Section 3 presents our methodology for the construction of Community Web directories. Section 4 provides results of the application of the methodology to the usage data of an Internet Service Provider (ISP). Finally section 5 summarizes interesting conclusions of this work and presents promising paths for future research.

2   Related Work

In recent years, Web personalization has attracted considerable attention. To realize this task, a number of applications employ machine learning methods and in particular clustering techniques, that analyze Web usage data and exploit the extracted knowledge for the recommendation of links to follow within a site, or for the customization of Web sites to the preferences of the users. In [10] a thorough analysis of the above methods is presented, together with their pros and cons in the context of Web Personalization. Personalized Web directories, on the other hand, are mainly associated with services such as Yahoo! [14] and

Excite [4], which support the manual personalization of their directories by the user. An initial approach to automate this process, is the Montage system [1], which is used to create personalized portals, consisting primarily of links to the Web pages that a particular user has visited, while also organizing the links into thematic categories according to the ODP directory. A technique for WAP portal personalization is presented in [12], where the portal structure is adapted to the preferences of individual users. A related approach is presented in [3], where a Web directory, is used as a "reference" ontology and the web pages navigated by a user are mapped onto this ontology using document classification techniques, resulting in a personalized ontology. The scalability of the content-based classification methods and their questionable extensibility to aggregate user models such as user communities, raise important issues for the above methods.

Probabilistic Latent Semantic Analysis has already been used for Web Personalization, in the context of Collaborative Filtering [6], and Web Usage Mining [7]. In the first case, PLSA was used to construct a model-based framework that describes user ratings. Latent factors were employed to model unobservable motives, which were then used to identify similar users and items, in order to predict subsequent user ratings. In [7], PLSA was used to identify and characterize user interests inside certain Web sites. The latent factors derived by the modeling process were employed to segment user sessions and personalization services took the form of a recommendation process.

In this paper we extend the methodology of our previous work for building Web directories according to the preferences of user communities which are now modeled with the use of PLSA. The methodology presented in this paper proposes a new way of exploiting the knowledge that is extracted by the analysis of usage data. Instead of link recommendation or site customization, it focuses on the construction of Community Web directories, as a new way of personalizing the Web. The construction of the communities is based on usage data collected by the proxy servers of an Internet Service Provider (ISP). This type of data, in contrast to the work mentioned above, has a number of peculiarities, such as its large volume and its semantic diversity, as it records the navigational behavior of the user throughout the Web, rather than within a particular Web site. The methodology presented in this paper handles these problems, focusing on the new personalization modality of Community Web directories.

3   Constructing Community Web Directories

The construction of Community Web directories is seen here as the end result of an analysis of Web usage data collected at the proxy servers of a central service on the Web. The details of the process are described in our previous work [11]. In brief, this process involves the thematic categorization of Web pages, thus reducing the dimensionality and semantic diversity of the data. A hierarchical agglomerative clustering approach [15], is used to build a taxonomy from Web pages included in the log files, based on terms that are frequently encountered in the Web pages. The resulting taxonomy of thematic categories forms the base

Web directory. Furthermore usage data are transformed into access sessions, where each access session is a sequence of accesses to Web pages by the same IP address, when the time interval between two subsequent entries does not exceed a certain time interval. Pages are mapped onto thematic categories that correspond to the leaves of the hierarchy and therefore an access session is translated into a sequence of categories from the Web directory.

3.1   Building the Probabilistic Model

Most of the work on Web usage mining uses clustering methods or association rule mining, in order to identify navigation patterns based solely on the "observable" behavior of the users, as this is recorded in the usage data. For instance, pages accessed by users are a typical observable piece of navigational behavior. However, it is rather simplifying to assume that relations between users are based only on observable characteristics of their behavior. We are relaxing this assumption and consider a number of latent factors, that control the user behavior and are responsible for the existence of associations between users. These latent factors can be exploited to construct clusters of users which share common motivation. The existence of latent factors that rule user behavior provides a more generic approach for the identification of patterns in usage data and thus provides better insight into the users' behavior.

As an example, assume that user u navigates through Web pages that belong in the *category*="computer companies" because of the existence of a latent cause-factor z. This cause might be the user's interest in finding information for business-to-business commerce. However, another user u' might arrive at the same category because she is interested in job offers. Hence, the interest of the second user corresponds to the existence of a different latent factor z'. Despite the simplicity of this example, we can see how different motives may result in similar observable behavior in the context of a Web directory.

A commonly used technique for the identification of latent factors in data is the PLSA method [5], which is supported by a strong statistical model. Applying PLSA to our scenario of Web directories we consider that there exists a set of user sessions $U=\{u_1, u_2, \ldots, u_i\}$, a set of Web directory categories $C=\{c_1, c_2, \ldots, c_j\}$, as well as their binary associations (u_i, c_j) which correspond to the access of a certain category c_j during the session u_i. The PLSA model is based on the assumption that each instance, i.e. each observation of a certain category inside a user session, is related to the existence of a latent factor, z_k that belongs to the set $Z=\{z_1, z_2, \ldots, z_k\}$. We define the probabilities $P(u_i)$: the a priori probability of a user session u_i, $P(z_k|u_i)$: the conditional probability of the latent factor z_k being associated with the user session u_i and $P(c_j|z_k)$: the conditional probability of accessing category c_j, given the latent factor z_k. Using these definitions, we can describe a probabilistic model for generating session-category pairs by selecting a user session with probability $P(u_i)$, selecting a latent factor z_k with probability $P(z_k|u_i)$ and selecting a category c_j with probability $P(c_j|z_k)$, given the factor z_k. This process allows us to estimate the probability of observing a particular session-category pair (u_i, c_j), using joint probabilities as follows:

$$P(u_i, c_j) = P(u_i)P(c_j|u_i) = P(u_i) \sum_k P(c_j|z_k)P(z_k|u_i). \tag{1}$$

Using Bayes's theorem we obtain the equivalent equation:

$$P(u_i, c_j) = \sum_k P(z_k)P(u_i|z_k)P(c_j|z_k). \tag{2}$$

Equation 2 leads us to an intuitive conclusion about the probabilistic model that we exploit: each session-category pair is observed due to a latent generative factor that corresponds to the variable z_k and hence it provides a more generic association between the elements of the pairs. However, the theoretic description of the model does not make it directly useful, since all the probabilities that we introduced are not available a priori. These probabilities are the unknown parameters of the model, and they can be estimated using the *Expectation-Maximization* (EM) algorithm, as described in [5].

3.2   Extraction of User Communities

Using the above probabilities we can assign categories to clusters based on the k factors z_k that are considered responsible for the associations between the data. This is realized by introducing a threshold value, named *Latent Factor Assignment Probability, (LFAP)* for the probabilities $P(c_j|z_k)$ and selecting those categories that are above this threshold. More formally, with each of the latent factors z_k we associate the categories that satisfy:

$$P(c_j|z_k) \geq LFAP. \tag{3}$$

In this manner and for each latent factor, the selected categories are used to construct a new Web directory. This corresponds to a topic tree, representing the community model, i.e., usage patterns that occur due to the latent factors in the data. A number of categories from the initial Web directory have been pruned, resulting in a reduced directory, named community Web directory. This approach has a number of advantages. First is the obvious shrinkage of the initial Web directory, which is directly related with the interests of the user community, ignoring all other categories that are irrelevant. Second, the selected approach allows us to construct overlapping patterns, i.e. a category might belong to more than one community directories, i.e. affected by more than one latent factor. A pictorial view of a "snapshot" of such a directory is shown in Figure 1, where the community directory is "superimposed" onto the original Web directory. For the sake of brevity we choose to label each category using a numeric coding scheme, representing the path from the root to the category node, e.g. "1.4.8.19" where "1" corresponds to the root of the tree. Each category is also labelled by the most frequent terms of the Web pages that belong in it. Grey boxes represent the categories that belong in a particular community directory, while big white boxes represent the rest of the categories in the Web directory, which are not included in the model. The categories "12.2" and "18.79" (the smaller white boxes) have been pruned, since they do not have more than one child in the community directory and are thus redundant.

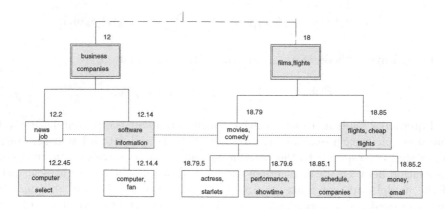

Fig. 1. An example of a Community Web Directory

4   Experimental Results

The methodology introduced in this paper for the construction of community Web directories has been tested in the context of a research project, which focuses on the analysis of usage data from the proxy server logs of an Internet Service Provider. We analyzed log files consisting of 781,069 records and using hierarchical agglomerative clustering [15] we obtained 998 distinct categories. We also constructed 2,253 user sessions, using a time-interval of 60 minutes as a threshold on the "silence" period between two consecutive requests from the same IP. At the next step we built the PLSA models, varying the number of the latent factors. We used 10-fold cross validation, in order to obtain an unbiased estimate of the performance of the method. We train the model 10 times, each time leaving out one of the subsets from training, and employ the omitted subset to evaluate the model. Therefore, the results that we present are always the average of 10 runs for each experiment.

As an initial measure of performance, we measured the shrinkage of the original Web directory, compared to the community directories derived by the PLSA model. This was measured via the average path length of the original directory and the community directories. These values were computed by calculating the number of nodes from the root to each leaf of a directory. The results are depicted in Figure 2, taken for various values of the LFAP threshold discussed in Section 3.2. From these results we can derive that the length of the paths is dramatically reduced, up to 50%, as the threshold increases. This means that the users have to follow much shorter paths to arrive at their interests. Furthermore, the method seems to be robust to the choice of the number of factors.

The community directories are further processed for the evaluation tasks as follows: a user session is assigned to a community directory based on its conditional probability against the latent factor, $P(u_i|z_k)$, that defines the community directory. However, the PLSA model, allows user sessions to belong to more than one community directory, and hence we identified the most prevalent community

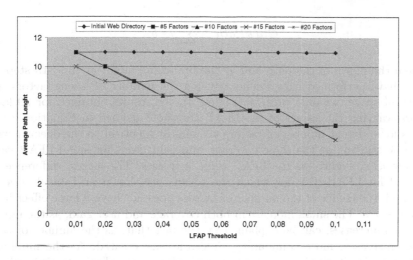

Fig. 2. Average Path Length

directories, i.e. the community directories where user sessions have the highest conditional probabilities for the respective factors. For our scenario we select the three most prevalent directories. From these prevalent community directories a new and larger directory is constructed by joining the respective hierarchies, resulting in a session-specific community directory. The resulting, session-specific directories are used in further evaluation.

The next stage of the evaluation process consisted of analyzing the usability of our models, i.e. the way that users benefit from the community Directories. We have focused on: (a) how well our model can predict what the user is looking for, and (b) what the user gains by using a community directory against using the original directory. In order to define suitable metrics, we followed a common approach used for recommendation systems [2], i.e., we have hidden each hit, i.e. category, of each user session, and tested to see whether and how the user can get to it, using the community directory to which the particular user session is assigned. The hidden category is called the "target" category here. The first metric that we used measured the coverage of our model, which corresponds to its predictiveness, i.e. the number of target categories that are covered by the corresponding community directories. This is achieved by counting the number of user sessions, for which the community directory, as explained before, covers the target category. The second metric that we used was an estimate of the actual gain that a user would have by following the community directory structure, instead of the complete directory. In order to realize this, we followed a simple approach that is based on the calculation of the effort that a user is required to exert in order to arrive at the target category. We estimated this effort based on the user's navigation path inside a directory, towards the target category. This is estimated by a metric, introduced in [11], named *ClickPath*, which takes into account the depth of the navigation path as well as the branching factor at each step. More formally:

$$ClickPath = \sum_{j=1}^{d} j * b_j, \tag{4}$$

where d the depth of the path and b_j the branching factor at the j-th step.

We have performed experiments varying the number of latent factors. Due to lack of space, we only present (Figure 3), the results obtained for 20 latent factors, varying the values of the LFAP threshold defined in Equation 3. The results for different number of factors are almost identical to the ones shown in Figure 3, starting at the same coverage and gain levels for small LFAP values and deviating slightly as the LFAP value increases. The largest difference was obtained for LFAP=0.1, for which the results are shown in Table 1. Even at that level, the choice of the number of factors does not have a large effect in the two measures. The small increase in both coverage and user gain, as the number of factors increases, can be explained by the fact that, as the number of latent factors increases, more community directories are created. As the number of community directories increases, more categories get the chance to appear in one of the directories, thus increasing coverage. At the same time, smaller community directories are constructed, resulting in higher user gain. However, even this small effect disappears as the number of community directories increases above 15. We also provide the results of applying the CDM algorithm to the same dataset (Figure 4).

From the above figures we conclude that at least 70% of the target categories are included in the community directories. At the same time the user gain reaches values higher than 50%, as more categories are pruned from the original Web directory. Practically this means that the user requires half of the effort to arrive at the required information. The results also follow a rather deterministic behaviour, i.e. large values of coverage are related with small values of user gain, as compared with the results of the CDM algorithm. These figures provide an indication of the behavior and the effectiveness of the application of PLSA

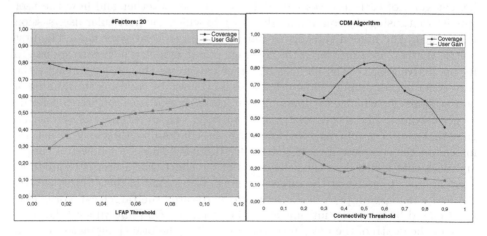

Fig. 3. PLSA Results   **Fig. 4.** CDM Results

Table 1. Coverage and User Gain for LFAP 0.1

	#5 Factors	#10 Factors	#15 Factors	#20 Factors
Coverage	0.63	0.67	0.71	0.70
User Gain	0.47	0.50	0.55	0.57

to community modeling. Furthermore, they give us an initial measure of the
benefits that we can obtain by personalizing Web directories to the needs and
interests of user communities. However, we have only estimated the gain of the
end user and we have not weighted up any "losses" that could be encountered
in the case that the users would not find the interesting category that they are
looking for in the personalized directory. This issue will be examined in future
work.

5   Conclusions and Future Work

This paper has presented work on the concept of the Community Web Directory, introduced in our recent work, as a Web Directory that specializes to the
needs and interests of particular user communities. In this case, user community
models take the form of thematic hierarchies and are constructed by employing
Probabilistic Latent Semantic Analysis. The initial directory is generated by a
document clustering algorithm, based on the content of the pages appearing in
an access log. We have tested this methodology by applying it on access logs
collected at the proxy servers of an ISP and have provided initial results, indicative of the behavior of the mining algorithm and the usability of the resulting
Community Web Directories. The results lead us to the conclusion that the application of PLSA to the analysis of user behavior in Web directories appears to
be a very promising method. It has allowed us to identify latent information in
the users' behavior and derive high-quality community directories that provide
significant gain to their users.

In general, the combination of two different approaches to the problem of
information overload on the Web, i.e. thematic hierarchies and personalization,
as proposed in this paper, together with the exploitation of PLSA for the construction of community models, introduces a promising research direction, where
many new issues arise. Further analysis of the PLSA method could be performed
and compared with other machine learning methods, in the task of discovering
community directories. Another important issue that will be examined in further work is the scalability of our approach, to larger datasets, i.e. for larger
log files that would result in a larger number of sessions. However, the performance of the whole process, together with the PLSA modeling, gave us promising indications for the methods's scalability. Finally, more sophisticated metrics
could also be employed for examining the usability of the resulting community
directories.

References

1. Anderson, C. R. and Horvitz, E.: Web Montage: A Dynamic Personalized Start Page. In: 11th International World Wide Web Conference. Honolulu, Hawaii, (2002)
2. Breese, J. S., Heckerman, D. and Kadie, C.M.: Empirical Analysis of Predictive Algorithms for Collaborative Filtering. In: 14th Conference on Uncertainty in Artificial Intelligence. Madison, WI, USA. (1998), 43–52
3. Chaffee, J. and Gauch, S.: Personal ontologies for web navigation. In: 9th Conference on Information and Knowledge Management, McLean, Virginia, USA, (2000), 227–234
4. Excite: http://www.excite.com
5. Hofmann, T.: Probabilistic Latent Semantic Analysis. In: 15th Conference on Uncertainty in Artificial Intelligence San Francisco, CA, (1999), 289–296
6. Hofmann, T.: Learning What People (Don't) Want. In: 12th European Conference in Machine Learning, Springer-Verlag, (2001), 214–225
7. Jin, X., Zhou, Y and Mobasher, B.: Web usage mining based on probabilistic latent semantic analysis. In: SIGKDD international conference on Knowledge discovery and data mining, (KDD 2004) Seattle, WA, USA (2004), 197–205
8. Mobasher, B., Cooley, R. and Srivastava, J.: Automatic personalization based on Web usage mining. Communications of the ACM, **43**, (8), (2000), 142–151
9. Open Directory Project: http://dmoz.org
10. Pierrakos, D., Paliouras, G., Papatheodorou, C. and Spyropoulos, C. D.: Web Usage Mining as a Tool for Personalization: a survey. User Modeling and User-Adapted Interaction, **13**, (4), (2003), 311–372
11. Pierrakos, D., Paliouras, G., Papatheodorou, C., Karkaletsis, V. and Dikaiakos, M.: Web Community Directories: A New Approach to Web Personalization. In: Berendt B. et al. (eds.): Web Mining: From Web to Semantic Web, EMWF 2003, Lecture Notes in Computer Science, Vol. 3209. Springer-Verlag, (2004) 113–129
12. Smyth, B. and Cotter, C.: Personalized Adaptive Navigation for Mobile Portals. In: 15th European Conference on Artificial Intelligence, IOS Press, (2002)
13. Srivastava, J., Cooley, R., Deshpande, M. and Tan, P. T.: Web Usage Mining: Discovery and Applications of Usage Patterns from Web Data. SIGKDD Explorations, **1**, (2) (2000), 12–23
14. Yahoo: http://www.yahoo.com
15. Zhao, Y. and Karypis, G.: Evaluation of hierarchical clustering algorithms for document datasets. In: 11th Conference on Information and Knowledge Management, McLean, Virginia, USA, (2002), 515–524

ExpertiseNet: Relational and Evolutionary Expert Modeling

Xiaodan Song[1], Belle L. Tseng[2], Ching-Yung Lin[1], and Ming-Ting Sun[1]

[1] Department of Electrical Engineering,
University of Washington, Box 352500, Seattle, WA 98195, USA
{song, cylin, sun}@ee.washington.edu
[2] NEC Labs America, 10080 N. Wolfe Road, SW3-350, Cupertino, CA 95014, USA
belle@sv.nec-labs.com

Abstract. We develop a novel user-centric modeling technology, which can dynamically describe and update a person's expertise profile. In an enterprise environment, the technology can enhance employees' collaboration and productivity by assisting in finding experts, training employees, etc. Instead of using the traditional search methods, such as the keyword match, we propose to use relational and evolutionary graph models, which we call ExpertiseNet, to describe and find experts. These ExpertiseNets are used for mining, retrieval, and visualization. We conduct experiments by building ExpertiseNets for researchers from a research paper collection. The experiments demonstrate that expertise mining and matching are more efficiently achieved based on the proposed relational and evolutionary graph models.

1 Introduction

Finding experts in an enterprise is a challenging problem. It is important for enterprises to understand and leverage their most valuable assets – employees' minds and knowledge bases. For instance, when a service-personnel faces problems at a customer's site, it would be desirable to have some technology to help identify the best experts for solving the problem within the company, and thus the solution may only be a phone call away. In another scenario, if employees' skills can be explicitly described, a manager can easily assemble a team for a new project, or an HR person can suggest what kind of skills an employee should learn.

Currently in an enterprise, the expertise information of employees is usually established by manual updates. However, this results in serious drawbacks. For instance, employees may not invest the necessary efforts in creating rich profiles, or they may not keep the information up-to-date as their interests, responsibilities, and expertise change. Many employees just provide a few keywords, without any timing information and the relationships between different expertises. Also, it is often difficult to differentiate who are the more suitable experts from people with similar expertise skills.

A number of automatic expert finding prototypes have been reported in literature. Liu *et al.* [6] and Mockus *et al.* [9] proposed to solve the expert-mining problem by using traditional information retrieval techniques. In their approaches, a person's expertises are described in terms of a vector without relational or timing information.

L. Ardissono, P. Brna, and A. Mitrovic (Eds.): UM 2005, LNAI 3538, pp. 99–108, 2005.
© Springer-Verlag Berlin Heidelberg 2005

HelpNet uses the user-filled information to provide the expertise profile [7]. *Expert-Locator* uses a representative collection of users' technical documents to build expertise indices [17]. Recently, NASA's *Expert Finder* [1][16] uses the name-entity extraction to process employees' published resumes and documents as well as corporate newsletters. It identifies keywords to create expertise profiles. *Expert Finder* presents a ranked list of employees that best matches the query. *I-Help* [2], an agent-based system, models a user's characteristics so that it can assist him/her in identifying a peer who can help. To select the most appropriate peer for a particular request, it uses a matchmaking agent that communicates with the personal agents of other users, by accessing various kinds of vector-based user information.

To capture the relationships between entities, link analysis has been studied for some time [18]. For instance, the Google search engine [10] and Kleinberg's HITS algorithm [5] both use link analysis on the web to find "hubs" and "authorities". The success of these approaches, and the discovery of widespread network topologies with nontrivial pro- perties, had led to a flurry of research on introducing link analysis into the traditional infor mation retrieval area [4]. In the user modeling area, a related technology – collabo- rative filtering – is used to help people make choices based on other people's opinions [11].

The goal of our paper is to develop a user-centric modeling technology, which can dynamically describe and update a person's expertise profile. The most important feature of our approach is to use expertise graphs for user modeling. A graph model is built to describe the relationship as well as the temporal evolution of the person's expertises. We refer to this expertise profile represented as graphs as an ExpertiseNet. Figure 1 shows an illustration of the proposed scheme. Both text content and citation linkages of papers are analyzed to extract the relation and the evolution information of the person's expertises. Exponential random graph models (ERGM) [15] and stochas- tic actor-oriented models [14], which deal with the relations between the entire network and individual entities, are incorporated to describe the structural properties and dyna- mics. Also, in this paper, we propose to add the citation linkages to boost the expertise classification accuracy. After we get the ExpertiseNets, expert mining and matching can be performed accurately and easily. To the best of our knowledge, our work is the first to explicitly use relational and evolutionary graph models for user profiling.

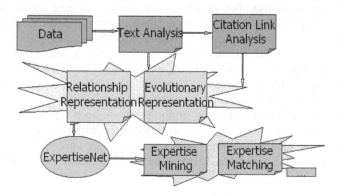

Fig. 1. Illustration of the ExpertiseNet building and expertise mining process

The main contributions of this paper are summarized as follows:

◇ We propose a scheme to represent user profiles by graphs.
◇ We propose an ExpertiseNet that provides relational and evolutional information for user modeling.
◇ We incorporate the exponential random graph models and evolutionary social network models into the user model analysis.
◇ We propose to boost the text classification accuracy by including the citation linkages in the classification algorithm.

The rest of the paper is organized as follows. In Section 2, we present the processes to build relational and evolutionary ExpertiseNets. We discuss the expertise mining and matching in Section 3. In Section 4, we show the experimental results of mining and matching. Finally, conclusions and future work are addressed in Section 5.

2   ExpertiseNet

In this paper, we use a dataset, Cora Research Publication Corpus [8], to simulate the information we may get in real applications. This set includes 24,778 authors with more than 50,000 research papers and about 715,000 citation links. The dataset also provides bibliographic information for each paper, which includes the authors' names, affiliations, email addresses, paper title, abstract, and references. These papers were pre-classified into a hierarchical ontology consisting of 69 expertise categories [8].

2.1   Classifying a Person's Expertises

We use a text classification algorithm to detect and extract expertise information of each person. Among the state-of-the-art classification algorithms, we choose the boosting algorithm [13], which is evaluated as one of the most accurate text classification algorithms [12]. This algorithm finds a "strong hypothesis" by combining many "weak" hypotheses for fusing features in different forms.

Previous techniques extract expertise using the words from the title and the abstract of one's publications. After a pre-processing stage which excludes "stop words" (common words that do not really provide any meaning to the document, such as "the", "it", "or"), and conducts "stemming" which collapses multiple forms of a term into the same term, we can get the terms as the features. In our work, the citation linkages are also used to form a feature vector (citation ratio) for classification as defined below.

$$P(X = x) = c_x / R \tag{1}$$

where X is a variable which indicates the citation information for each publication, x represents one of the 69 categories, c_x is the number of the citations belonging to category x, and R is the number of the references in the publication. The intuition of incorporating this feature is that the paper from one category tends to cite the papers in the same category. This relational structure is useful to describe the strength of a person's expertise on specific categories by his/her publications. In Section 4, we show that this feature can significantly increase the classification accuracy of a person's expertise. After document classification, we have the information about the number of published papers in each category for one person, which represents the expertise skills of the person, and is used for building ExpertiseNet for that person.

2.2 Relational ExpertiseNet

The relational ExpertiseNet of a specific person is formulated as a directional graph $G(V,E)$, where V represents the node set, and E represents the edge set. Two nodes v_i and v_j are adjacent, if edge $e_{ij} = (v_i, v_j)$ or $e_{ji} = (v_j, v_i)$ is in the set of edges E. In the relational ExpertiseNet, each node represents an expertise. The strength of each expertise is defined as:

$$s_i = p_i \tag{2}$$

where s_i represents the strength of the expertise i for the person, and p_i is the number of publications in category i. Edges represent the relationship between expertise nodes.

The correlations of a person's published papers and all papers in the research society decide the weights of the edges in the graph model. Citation linkages provide solid evidence of correlations among different expertise. When the citation linkages are not available, the correlation can be explored by the text similarity analysis. The process is illustrated in Figure 2, and explained as follows.

For each paper, the dataset contains citation linkages that include both the information of how this paper cites other papers (out-direction), and how other papers cite this paper (in-direction). From the publications of a person P, it is reasonable to infer that his/her expertise X is influenced by Y if papers in category X cite papers in category Y. For example, in Figure 2, paper #1 is one of the papers in Natural Langrage Processing (NLP). It cites paper #5, #6, #7 (out-direction citation linkages) in NLP, Machine Learning (ML), and Information Retrieval (IR) respectively. Papers #2, #3, #4 in NLP, NLP, and IR, cite paper #1 (in-direction citation linkages). We can infer that for this person, his/her NLP expertise is influenced by NLP, ML, and IR, and at the same time, affects IR. With this consideration, the strengths of the edges of the relational ExpertiseNet are determined by:

$$e_{A->B} = \left. \left(\sum_{i=1}^{K} n_{iAB} \middle/ N_i \right) \middle/ K \right. \tag{3}$$

where $e_{A->B}$ represents the strength of the edge from expertise A to expertise B, K is the total number of the publications for the person, n_{iAB} represents, the number of papers in category A cited by the papers in category B, and N_i represents the number of citations in paper i.

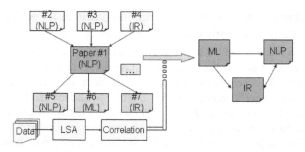

Fig. 2. Building the relational ExpertiseNet from text and citation linkages

For those people without papers, ExpertiseNet will be built upon the documents they generated. Latent Semantic Analysis (LSA) [3] is applied on the occurrence matrix which includes the frequency of occurrence of the words in the document. LSA is a method for extracting and representing the contextual meaning of words. It has been used as a technique to measure the coherence of texts. By comparing the vectors formed by the keywords of two documents in a high-dimensional semantic space, this method provides a characterization of the degree of semantic relatedness between documents. LSA starts with a sparse matrix in which the rows represent the documents and the columns represent the keywords. The values in the matrix are proportional to the number of times the keywords appear in the document, where rare terms are upweighted to reflect their relative importance. The correlation matrix is calculated to determine the edges of the relational ExpertiseNet.

An observation of the ExpertiseNet profile is obtained from the above analysis. Then, the exponential random graph model (or p* model) [15] is used to estimate an underlying distribution to describe the relational ExpertiseNet. The strong point of this statistical model is that they can represent structural tendencies (such as transitivity which represents the number of transitive patterns) that define complicated dependence patterns not easily modeled by deterministic models. Given a set of n nodes, let Y denote a random graph on those nodes, and y denotes a particular graph on those nodes. Then

$$P_\theta(Y = y) = \frac{\exp(\theta^T s(y))}{c(\theta)} \tag{4}$$

where θ is an unknown vector of parameters, $s(y)$ is a known vector of graph statistics on y(Density(defined by the out-degrees), reciprocity (defined by the number of recipro-cated relations), transitive triads (defined by the number of a set of edges {$(i$->$j)$, $(j$->$k)$, $(i$->$k)$}), and the strengths of the nodes as well as the edges as considered in this paper), $c(\theta)$ is a normalization term. This probabilistic expression has advantages on descrybing the insights of the network, thus can help to describe the evolution of Expertise Nets.

2.3 Evolutionary ExpertiseNet

In the evolutionary ExpertiseNet, the dynamics and the evolution of expertises are explored. Two tasks are performed: evolution segmentation (detect changes between expertise cohesive sections) and expertise tracking (keep track of the expertise similar to a set of previous expertises). The strength of the nodes as well as the structure of the network is considered in the evolution segmentation. Temporal sliding windows are applied. An exponential random graph model is estimated from the data in each window, i.e., time period. We can obtain a series of parameters which indicate the network configurations. Then the change points of an evolutional ExpertiseNet are deter mined by:

$$\sum_{k=1}^{M}\left|\theta_{t,k} - \theta_{t-1,k}\right| > th \tag{5}$$

where $\theta_{t,k}$ indicates the parameters of the exponential random graph model at time t, M represents the number of parameters, th is a threshold. The goal is to find all t satisfy (5).

The evolution segments are obtained from these change points. Based on the correlation between the citations and the development of related research areas, the tracking edges are determined by

For those people without papers, ExpertiseNet will be built upon the documents they generated. Latent Semantic Analysis (LSA) [3] is applied on the occurrence matrix which includes the frequency of occurrence of the words in the document. LSA is a method for extracting and representing the contextual meaning of words. It has been used as a technique to measure the coherence of texts. By comparing the vectors formed by the keywords of two documents in a high-dimensional semantic space, this method provides a characterization of the degree of semantic relatedness between documents. LSA starts with a sparse matrix in which the rows represent the documents and the columns represent the keywords. The values in the matrix are proportional to the number of times the keywords appear in the document, where rare terms are upweighted to reflect their relative importance. The correlation matrix is calculated to determine the edges of the relational ExpertiseNet.

An observation of the ExpertiseNet profile is obtained from the above analysis. Then, the exponential random graph model (or p* model) [15] is used to estimate an underlying distribution to describe the relational ExpertiseNet. The strong point of this statistical model is that they can represent structural tendencies (such as transitivity which represents the number of transitive patterns) that define complicated dependence patterns not easily modeled by deterministic models. Given a set of n nodes, let Y denote a random graph on those nodes, and y denotes a particular graph on those nodes. Then

$$P_\theta(Y = y) = \frac{\exp(\theta^T s(y))}{c(\theta)} \qquad (4)$$

where θ is an unknown vector of parameters, $s(y)$ is a known vector of graph statistics on y(Density(defined by the out-degrees), reciprocity (defined by the number of recipro-cated relations), transitive triads (defined by the number of a set of edges $\{(i\text{->}j), (j\text{->}k), (i\text{->}k)\}$), and the strengths of the nodes as well as the edges as considered in this paper), $c(\theta)$ is a normalization term. This probabilistic expression has advantages on descrybing the insights of the network, thus can help to describe the evolution of Expertise Nets.

2.3 Evolutionary ExpertiseNet

In the evolutionary ExpertiseNet, the dynamics and the evolution of expertises are explored. Two tasks are performed: evolution segmentation (detect changes between expertise cohesive sections) and expertise tracking (keep track of the expertise similar to a set of previous expertises). The strength of the nodes as well as the structure of the network is considered in the evolution segmentation. Temporal sliding windows are applied. An exponential random graph model is estimated from the data in each window, i.e., time period. We can obtain a series of parameters which indicate the network configurations. Then the change points of an evolutional ExpertiseNet are deter mined by:

$$\sum_{k=1}^{M} |\theta_{t,k} - \theta_{t-1,k}| > th \qquad (5)$$

where $\theta_{t,k}$ indicates the parameters of the exponential random graph model at time t, M represents the number of parameters, th is a threshold. The goal is to find all t satisfy (5).

The evolution segments are obtained from these change points. Based on the correlation between the citations and the development of related research areas, the tracking edges are determined by

4.1 Classification Results

We use text classification to automatically extract the strength of each person's expertise in different topic categories. Figure 3 shows the classification accuracy vs. the use of other labeled data over the whole dataset. The highest curve illustrates the performance of our method. We can achieve about 5% improvement, which is considered significant in the text classification area.

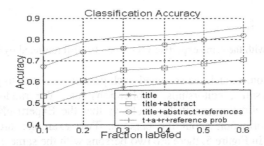

Fig. 3. Incorporation of citation ratio as a feature boosts classification accuracy

4.2 ExpertiseNet Profiles and Expert Searching

ExpertiseNet provides a dynamic model of semantics evolution in which expertise as well as inter-expertise relationships exhibit. In this experiment, we show two mining processes which are based on the relational and evolutionary ExpertiseNets. In the first experiment, by placing a query term "machine leaning – planning", we get a list of persons with expertise of Machine Leaning and Planning (Figure 4 (a)). Figure 4(b) shows another example, where "machine leaning → planning" is set as the input. A list of people with machine learning expertise in an earlier stage and planning in a later stage shows up.

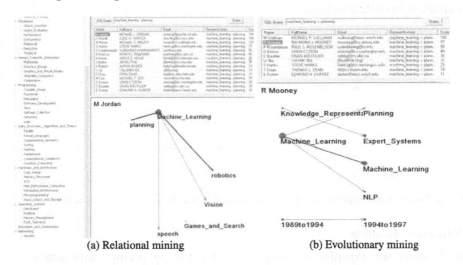

(a) Relational mining   (b) Evolutionary mining

Fig. 4. Our expertise mining system allows relational and evolutionary mining that results in a ranked people list, along with visualizations of ExpertiseNets and the 69 categories from Cora

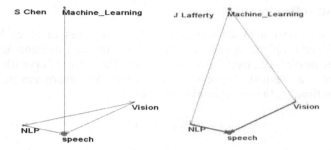

Fig. 5. Two persons with the same expertise vector can be differentiated by ExpertiseNet

In order to validate our model, we searched each person's website to get more information from one's resume, editorships, publications, etc. We randomly chose 50 persons and did this validation manually. It shows that the ExpertiseNet models can represent accurate information about the persons. Two examples are illustrated in Figure 5 and Figure 6. In Figure 5, there are two persons with the same expertise, "Prof. Chen"(http://www.cise.ufl.edu/~suchen/DrChen.htm) and "Prof. Lafferty" (http://www-2.cs.cmu.edu/~lafferty). By vector-based representation, it is difficult to differentiate them. However, it is easy to illustrate the differences by relational ExpertiseNets. From their websites, we know that Prof. Chen has background in speech/signal processing, while Prof. Lafferty is mainly interested in machine learning and statistical methods. This information validates our models: Speech contributes more to other expertises for Prof. Chen, and machine learning contributed more to other expertises for Prof. Lafferty.

Figure 6 illustrates the necessity of using evolutionary ExpertiseNets. In this example, we try to distinguish two professors. We can see that Prof. Langley mainly contributed in machine learning, and later, he applied this expertise to other areas, while Prof. Durfee's expertise on planning, agents, robotics seems to be developed at the same time, and interacts to each other a lot. This conclusion is also validated by the information from their websites.

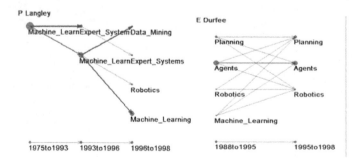

Fig. 6. Two persons' expertise evolutions are accurately captured by the ExpertiseNets

4.3 Expertise Matching

Figure 7 shows the expertise matching result for finding persons with similar expertise and relationship among expertise. Here we use Professor "Michael Jordan"

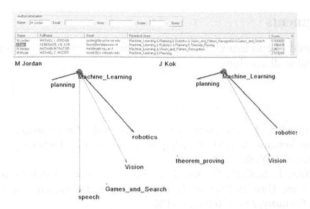

Fig. 7. A system for searching similar persons based on the ExpertiseNets

as the query input (http://www.cs.berkeley.edu/~jordan/). We can get a list of ranked experts according to the similarity to "Michael Jordan" in terms of ExpertiseNet.

To complement quantitative evaluation, we have set up an online evaluation system as well as a demo system which allow interactive exploration of expert searching and matching (http://students.washington.edu/~xdsong/index_files/Demos/ expertisenet.htm). In the online evaluation system, experts in the database are allowed to evaluate their own ExpertiseNet as well as the expert searching and matching results.

5 Conclusions and Future Work

In this paper, we propose a relational and evolutionary graph model called ExpertiseNet for expert modeling, which discovers both the relational and evolutionary information. Citation linkages and textual data are used to build the ExpertiseNets. The temporal evolution and relational information of expertises are explicitly described in the ExpertiseNet graph profiles that are used for mining, retrieval, and visualization. The parameters from ERGM and dynamic actor-oriented graph models are used to describe the structural properties and dynamics of the ExpertiseNet. We also introduce a new feature that boosts the expertise text classification accuracy by approximately 5%. Manual validations demonstrate the effectiveness of the proposed relational and evolutionary ExpertiseNets on applications of expert mining and matching. So far, the studies are complemented by qualitative evaluation. We have set up an online evaluation system for further quantitative evaluation.

Both the relational and the evolutionary ExpertiseNets are scalable since when new data arrive, only parts of the models need to be updated with the new info. For relational ExpertiseNet, only the related nodes and edges need to be updated without changing of other nodes and edges in the graph. For evolutionary ExpertiseNet, new information from the recent time period only affects the last level, or generates another level in the graph.

To the best of our knowledge, we are the first to explicitly use relational and evolutionary graph models for user profiling. Our ongoing work includes extending this graph-based user modeling frame work for user behavior modeling, and finding and predicting people's information dissemination behaviors and roles in various events.

Acknowledgments

The authors would like to thank: NEC Laboratories America for their support and Yi Wu for her valuable discussions.

References

1. Becerra-Fernandez, I.. Searching for Experts with Expertise-Locator Knowledge Management Systems. ACL 01 Workshop Human Language Technology and Knowledge Management: New York, (2001), 9-16
2. Bull, S., Greer, J., McCalla, G., Kettel, L., Bowes, J.. User Modelling in I-Help: What, Why, When and How. In Proc. of the 8th International Conference on User Modeling, Sonthofen, Germany, July, (2001), 117-126
3. Deerwester, S., Dumais, S. T., Furna, G. W., Landauer, T. K., Harshman, R.. Indexing by Latent Semantic Analysis. Journal of the American Society for Information Science, 41(6), (1990), 391-407
4. Henzinger, M.. Hyperlink Analysis on the Web. IEEE Internet Computing, 5(1): (2001), 45-50
5. Kleinberg, J.. Authoritative sources in a hyperlinked environment, In Proc. 9th ACM-SIAM Symposium on Discrete Algorithms, (1998), 604-632
6. Liu, P., Curson, J., Dew, P. M.. Exploring RDF for Expertise Matching within an Organizational Memory. In Proc. of the 14th International Conference on Advanced Information Systems Engineering: (2002), 100–116
7. Maron, M. E., Curry, S., Thompson, P.. An Inductive Search System: Theory, Design and Implementation. IEEE Transaction on Systems, Man and Cybernetics, 16(1) (1986), 21–28
8. McCallum, A. K., Nigam, K., Rennie, J., Seymore, K.. Automating the construction of internet portals with machine learning. Information Retrieval, 3(2): (2000), 127-163
9. Mockus, A., Herbsleb, J. D.. Expertise Browser: a quantitative approach to identifying expertise," In Proc. of the 24th International Conference on Software Engineering: (2002), 503–512
10. Page, L., Brin, S., Motwani, R., Winograd, T.. The PageRank Citation Ranking: Bringing Order to the Web. Stanford Digital Libraries Working Paper, (1998)
11. Resnick, P., Iacovou, N., Suchak, M., Bergstrom, P., Riedl, J.. Grouplens: An open architecture for collaborative filtering of netnews. In Proc. of the ACM Conference on Computer Supported Cooperative Work: (1994), 175-186
12. Sebastiani, F.. Machine learning in automated text categorization. ACM Computing Surveys, 34(1), (2002), 1-47
13. Schapire, R. E., Singer, Y.. BoosTexter: A boosting-based system for text categorization, *Machine Learning*, 39(2/3): (2000), 135-168
14. Snijders, T. A. B.. Models for Longitudinal Network Data. To appear as Chapter 11 in P. Carrington, J. Scott, & S. Wasserman (Eds.), Models and methods in social network analysis. New York: Cambridge University Press (in press), (2004)
15. Snijders, T. A. B.. Markov Chain Monte Carlo Estimation of Exponential Random Graph Models. Journal of Social Structure, 3(2), (2002)
16. Staab, S.. Human language technologies for knowledge management. Intelligent Systems, 16(6): (2001), 84–94
17. Steeter, L. A., Lochbaum, K. E.. An Expert/Expert Locating System based on Automatic Representation of Semantic Structure. In Proc. of the Fourth IEEE Conference on Artificial Intelligence Applications: San Diego, CA, (1988), 345–349
18. Wasserman, S., Faust, K., Iacobucci, D.. Social Network Analysis: Theory and Methods. Cambridge University Press: Cambridge, (1995)

Task-Oriented Web User Modeling
for Recommendation

Xin Jin, Yanzan Zhou, and Bamshad Mobasher

Center for Web Intelligence, School of Computer Science,
Telecommunication and Information Systems,
DePaul University, Chicago, Illinois, USA
{xjin, yzhou, mobasher}@cs.depaul.edu

Abstract. We propose an approach for modeling the navigational behavior of Web users based on task-level patterns. The discovered "tasks"
are characterized probabilistically as latent variables, and represent the
underlying interests or intended navigational goal of users. The ability to
measure the probabilities by which pages in user sessions are associated
with various tasks, allow us to track task transitions and modality shifts
within (or across) user sessions, and to generate task-level navigational
patterns. We also propose a maximum entropy recommendation system
which combines the page-level statistics about users' navigational activities together with our task-level usage patterns. Our experiments show
that the task-level patterns provide better interpretability of Web users'
navigation, and improve the accuracy of recommendations.

1 Introduction

Web users exhibit different types of behavior according to their interests and
intended tasks. These interests and tasks are captured implicitly by a collection
of actions taken by users during their visits to a site. For example, in a dynamic
application-based e-commerce Web site, they may be reflected by sequences of
interactions with Web applications to search a catalog, to make a purchase, or to
complete an online application. On the other hand, in an information intensive
site, such as a portal or an online news site, they may be reflected in a series of
user clicks on a collection of Web pages with related content.

Web usage mining is a collection of techniques for modeling Web users' navigational behavior. Beginning from Web server log data, Web usage mining involves the application of data mining and machine learning techniques, such as
association rule mining, clustering, or sequential pattern analysis to identify usage patterns. Web usage mining has achieved great success in various application
areas such as Web personalization [13, 14], link prediction and analysis [11, 20],
Web site evaluation or reorganization [21, 22], Web analytics and e-commerce
data analysis [10], Adaptive Web sites [17, 12].

Since users' activities are recorded in terms of visited pages at the session
level, after the data mining process, the discovered *page-level patterns* only provide limited interpretability in terms of the underlying users interests and the

L. Ardissono, P. Brna, and A. Mitrovic (Eds.): UM 2005, LNAI 3538, pp. 109–118, 2005.

intended tasks. For example, we may find an association rule $A \rightarrow B$ involving pages A and B. This page-level pattern, by itself, provides no clue as to nature of association between A and B or the reasons why they are commonly visited together. However, if we are able to view user interactions at a "higher" level of abstraction, we may be able to explain the association in terms of a common task or content category involving these pages. The ability to better explain or interpret the patterns at the higher abstraction level, in turn, can lead to more accurate predictive models such as those used in personalization and recommender systems.

Some recent work has focused on methods to model users' behavior at "higher" abstraction levels. In [16], Web items (documents) are first clustered based on users' navigational data, and then user behavior models are built at this item-cluster level. In [4], an aggregated representation is created as a set of pseudo objects which characterize groups of similar users at the object attribute level. While these approaches have proved useful in some applications, they generally rely on manually pre-defined semantic features or ad hoc clustering methods which limit their flexibility.

In this paper, we propose a new Web user modeling approach called *task-oriented user modeling*. The basic assumption we make is that, in a Web site there exists a relatively small set of common navigational "tasks" which can explain the behavior of numerous individual Web users at different points in their interactions with the site. We use the Probabilistic Latent Semantic Analysis (PLSA) model [6] to probabilistically characterize these tasks, as well as the relationships between the tasks and Web pages or users. We then propose an algorithm based on Bayesian updating to discover individual user's underlying tasks, as well as the temporal changes in these tasks, thus generating *task-level usage patterns*. These task-level patterns enable us to better understand users' underlying navigational goals or interests. We also propose a Web recommendation system based on a maximum entropy model [18, 1], which can flexibly combine knowledge about Web users' navigational behavior by integrating the standard page-level and our proposed task-oriented models.

This paper is organized as follows. We present our task-oriented user model in Section 2. In Section 3, we introduce our recommendation system which takes into account both the page-level and task-level usage patterns. We evaluate this recommendation system and report our experimental results on two real data sets in Section 4. Finally, in Section 5, we identify avenues for future work and conclude this paper.

2   Task-Oriented User Modeling with PLSA

In [9], we introduced a general and flexible approach for Web usage mining based on Probabilistic Latent Semantic Analysis (PLSA). Here we employ the PLSA framework to quantitatively characterize users' navigational tasks, as well as the relationships between these tasks and Web pages or users.

The first step in Web usage analysis is the data preparation process. Raw Web log data is cleaned and sessionized to generate user sessions. Each user session is a logical representation of a user's single visit to the Web site (usually within certain time interval). After data preparation (see [3] for details), we have a set of user sessions $U = \{u_1, u_2, \cdots, u_m\}$, a set of pages $P = \{p_1, p_2, \cdots, p_n\}$. The Web session data can be conceptually viewed as a $m \times n$ session-page matrix $UP = [w(u_i, p_j)]_{m \times n}$, where $w(u_i, p_j)$ represents the weight of page p_j in user session u_i. The weights can be binary, indicating the existence or non-existence of the page in the session, or they may be a function of the occurrence or duration of the page in that session. We use a set of hidden (unobserved) variables $Z = \{z_1, z_2, ..., z_l\}$, which in our framework, correspond to users' common tasks. Our goal is to automatically discover and characterize these tasks, and then obtain a view of the users' behavior in the site by associating their actions with the discovered tasks.

Each usage observation, which corresponds to an access by a user to a Web resource in a particular session which is represented as an entry of the $m \times n$ co-occurrence matrix UP, can be modeled as

$$Pr(u_i, p_j) = \sum_{k=1}^{l} Pr(z_k) \bullet Pr(u_i|z_k) \bullet Pr(p_j|z_k), \qquad (1)$$

summing over all possible choices of z_k from which the observation could have been generated.

Now, in order to explain a set of usage observations (U, P), we need to estimate the parameters $Pr(z_k)$, $Pr(u_i|z_k)$, $Pr(p_j|z_k)$, while maximizing the log-likelihood of the observations.

$$L(U, P) = \sum_{i=1}^{m} \sum_{j=1}^{n} w(u_i, p_j) \log Pr(u_i, p_j). \qquad (2)$$

We use the Expectation-Maximization (EM) algorithm to perform maximum likelihood parameter estimation of $Pr(z_k)$, $Pr(u_i|z_k)$, $Pr(p_j|z_k)$. These probabilities quantitatively measure the relationships among users, Web pages, and common interests (tasks). For example, $Pr(p_j|z_k)$ represents the probability of page p_j being visited given a certain task z_k is pursued. While $Pr(u_i|z_k)$ measures the probabilities of a user engaging in a certain task.

Given the estimated probabilities from the PLSA model, our next goal is to identify user's tasks from individual user sessions. Taking into account the order of pages being visited in user sessions, each user session can also be represented as a sequence of pages, as $u_i = \langle p_i^1, p_i^2, \cdots, p_i^t \rangle$, where $p_i^j \in P$. Here we use a Bayesian updating method, to compute the posterior probability of each task within each individual user session, given the assumption that pages are independent given a task. These probabilities measure the relative importance of each task within the session. Also, we use a sliding window over the user's click-stream history reflecting our assumption that the most recently visited pages are better predictors of user's current interests. The algorithm is as follow.

Input: a user session u_i, $Pr(p_j|z_k)$. Each user session is represented as a page sequence, $u_i = \langle p_i^1, p_i^2, \cdots, p_i^t \rangle$, $p_i^j \in P$.

Output: a user session represented as a task sequence.

1. Get the first L pages from u_i and put them into a sliding window W.
2. Using Bayesian updating [19], we compute the probability of each task given all the pages in W:

$$Pr(z|W) = \frac{Pr(W|z)Pr(z)}{Pr(W)} \propto Pr(z) \prod_{p \in W} Pr(p|z) \qquad (3)$$

3. Pick those tasks with probability exceeding a pre-defined threshold as the current tasks and output them.
4. Move the sliding window to the right (remove the first page from the window, and add the next page in u_i into the window), recompute the probability of each task given the current sliding window, and pick the dominant tasks.
5. Repeat this process until the sliding window reaches the end of this session.

After running this algorithm, each user session can be represented as a sequence of tasks, $u_i = \langle z_x', \cdots, z_y' \rangle$, where z' is either a single task or a small set of dominant tasks. This representation gives us a direct understanding of users' interests and the temporal changes in these interests.

Given these task sequences, we can discover task-level patterns from these task sequences. For example, we can identify the most popular task(s) and the least popular task(s), or we can run simple first-order Markov model to compute probabilities of task transitions, $Pr(z_b|z_a)$, etc. These task-level patterns demonstrate the Web site's functionalities from the users' point of view, and may help the site designer to evaluate and reorganize the site. Another direct application is to generate recommendations based on users' tasks and task transitions. In the next section, we will present a flexible and accurate recommendation system which combines both the page-level and task-level patterns.

3   Recommendations Based on Maximum Entropy

In this section, we present our maximum entropy based recommendation system. The system consists of two components. The offline component accepts constraints from the training data and estimates the model parameters. The online part reads an active user session and runs the recommendation algorithm to generate recommendations (a set of pages) for the user.

To make predictions or generate recommendations for active users, we aim to compute the conditional probability $Pr(p_d|H(u_i))$ of a page p_d being visited next given a user's recent navigational history $H(u_i)$, here $p_d \in P$, and $H(u_i)$ represents a set of recently visited pages by u_i. Since the most recent activities have greater influence on reflecting a user's present interests, we only use the last several pages to represent a user's history.

3.1   The Maximum Entropy Model

To discover $Pr(p_d|H(u_i))$, we adopt a maximum entropy model, a powerful statistical model, which has been widely applied in many fields, including statistical language learning [18], information retrieval [8] and text mining [15]. The goal of a maximum entropy model is to find a probability distribution which satisfies all the constraints in the observed data while maintaining maximum entropy. One main advantage of using maximum entropy model is that one or more knowledge sources can be integrated at different levels of abstraction in a natural way. Here we extract two levels of statistics about Web users' navigational behavior, and use them as features and constraints to fit our model.

In our model, we use page-level and task-level usage patterns extracted from Web users' navigation data. For each type of patterns, we define features that capture certain statistics of users' navigational behavior.

1. Features Based on Page-level Usage Patterns
   For simplicity, here we adopt the first-order Markov model to generate page transitions. For each page transition $p_a \to p_b$ where $Pr(p_b|p_a) \neq 0$, we define a feature function as:

$$f_{p_a,p_b}(H(u_i),p_d) = \begin{cases} 1 \text{ if page } p_a \text{ is the last page in } H(u_i), \text{ and } p_b = p_d, \\ 0 \text{ otherwise} \end{cases}$$

2. Features Based on Task-Level Usage Patterns
   Similarly, given a task transition $z_a \to z_b$, we define a feature as $f_{z_a,z_b}(H(u_i),p_d)$:

$$f_{z_a,z_b}(H(u_i),p_d) = \begin{cases} 1 \text{ if the dominant task of } H(u_i) \text{ is } z_a, \text{ and after moving} \\ \quad \text{sliding window right to include } p_d, z_b \text{ will be the} \\ \quad \text{dominant task,} \\ 0 \text{ otherwise} \end{cases}$$

Based on each feature f_s, we represent a constraint as:

$$\sum_{u_i} \sum_{p_d \in P} Pr(p_d|H(u_i)) \bullet f_s(H(u_i),p_d) = \sum_{u_i} f_s(H(u_i),D(H(u_i))) \quad (4)$$

where $D(H(u_i))$ denotes the page following u_i's history in the training data. Every constraint restricts that the expected value of each feature w.r.t. the model distribution should always equal its observation value in the training data. After we have defined a set of features, $F = \{f_1, f_2, \cdots, f_t\}$, and accordingly, generated constraints for each feature, it's guaranteed that, under all the constraints, a unique distribution exists with maximum entropy [7]. This distribution has the form:

$$Pr(p_d|H(u_i)) = \frac{exp(\sum_s \lambda_s f_s(H(u_i),p_d))}{Z(H(u_i))} \quad (5)$$

where $Z(H(u_i)) = \sum_{p_d \in P} Pr(p_d|H(u_i))$ is the normalization constant ensuring that the distribution sums to 1, and λs are the parameters needed to be estimated. Thus, each source of knowledge can be represented as constraints (captured by the corresponding features) with associated weights. By using Equation 5, all such constraints are taken into account to make predictions about users' next action given their past navigational activity.

There have been several algorithms which can be applied to estimate the λs. Here we use the Sequential Conditional Generalized Iterative Scaling (SCGIS) [5], which seems to be more efficient especially when the number of outcomes is not very large (in our case, the number of pages in a site). We also apply the smoothing technique suggested by Chan and Rosenfeld [2], which has shown to be able to improve the model by using some prior estimates for model parameters.

3.2   Generating Recommendations

After we have estimated the parameters associated with each feature, we can use Equation 5 to compute the probability of any unvisited page p_i being visited next given certain user's history, and then pick the pages with highest probabilities as recommendations. Given an active user u_a, we compute the conditional probability $Pr(p_i|u_a)$. Then we sort all pages based on the probabilities and pick the top N pages to get a recommendation set. The algorithm is as follows:

Input: active user session u_a, parameters λs estimated from training data.
Output: Top N pages sorted by probability of being visited next given u_a.

1. Consider the last L pages of the active user session as a sliding window (these pages are considered as this user's history), and identify all the task(s) with probability exceeding a pre-defined threshold using Equation 3 in Section 2. (L is the size of the sliding window, also the length of the user history.)
2. For each page p_i that does not appear in the active session, assume it is the next page to be visited, and evaluate all the features based on their definitions (above).
3. Using Equation 5 to compute $Pr(p_i|u_a)$.
4. Sort all the pages in descending order of $Pr(p_i|u_a)$ and pick the top N pages to get a recommendation set.

4   Experimental Evaluation

We used two real Web site data sets to empirically measure the accuracy of our recommendation system. Our accuracy metric is called *Hit Ratio* and is used in the context of top-N recommendation framework: for each user session in the test set, we take the first K pages as a representation of an active session to generate a top-N recommendations. We then compare the recommendations with page $K + 1$ in the test session, with a match being considered a *hit*. We define the Hit Ratio as the total number of hits divided by the total number of user sessions in the test set. Note that the Hit Ratio increases as the value of

N (number of recommendations) increases. Thus, in our experiments, we pay special attention to smaller number recommendations (between 1 and 10) that result in good hit ratios.

The first data set is based on the server log data from the host Computer Science department. The site is highly dynamic, involving numerous online applications, including admissions application, online advising, online registration, and faculty-specific Intranet applications. After data preprocessing, we identify 21,299 user sessions (U) and 692 pageviews (P), with each user session consisting of at least 6 pageviews. The number of tasks is set to 30, and the length of user history is set to 4. This data set is referred to as the "CTI data". Our second data set is based on *Network Chicago* Web servers representing the Chicago Public Television and Radio. A total of 4,987 user sessions and 295 Web pageviews were selected for analysis. Each user session consists of at least 6 pageviews. In contrast to the CTI data, this site is comprised primarily of static pages grouped together based on their associations with specific content areas. In this case, we expect users' navigational behavior reflect their interests in one or more programs represented by the content areas. In the experiment, task number is set to 15 and the length of user history is set to 4. We refer to this data set as the "NC data".

We tried different number of tasks and picked the one achieving the maximum likelihood of the training data. User history length was determined based on the average session length in the training data. Each data set was randomly divided into multiple training and test sets to use with 10-fold validation.

4.1 Examples of Task and Task-Level Usage Patterns

We applied the PLSA model to each of the training data sets, and then ran the task-level pattern discovery algorithm to generate task-level usage patterns. An example of a task-level usage pattern from the CTI data, and the associated task transition tracking within a selected user session, is depicted in Figure 1.

The user visited 12 pages in the selected session (the upper table in Figure 1). After we ran the algorithm in Section 2 for this session, we generated a task sequence depicted in the lower table. The sliding window moves from the beginning of the session to the end. At each position, we show the top two tasks with corresponding probabilities (in each row). We can see that the user was mainly performing two tasks in this session: Task 10 and Task 21. The figure also shows the top pages associated with Task 10 and Task 21. Task 10 clearly represents prospective international students looking for admission information, while Task 21 represents the activity of prospective students who are actually engaged in the process of submitting an application. As evident from the task transition model, this user gradually finished Task 10 and moved to Task 21. The changes of the probabilities associated with these tasks clearly reflect the change of the user's interests.

After identifying the tasks and their temporal changes in each user session, we are able to generate recommendations not only based on the page transitions, but also based on users' current task and next possible task.

A real user session (page listed in the order of being visited)	Task 10 (in descending order of Pr(page|task))	Task 21 (in descending order of Pr(page|task))
1. Admission main page	Department main page	Online application – start
2. Welcome information – Chinese version	Admission requirements	Online application – step1
3. Admission info for international students	Admission main page	Online application – step2
4. Admission - requirements	Admission costs	Online application - finish
5. Admission – mail request	Programs	Online application - submit
6. Admission – orientation info	Online application – step 1	Online application - newstart
7. Admission – F1 visa and I20 info	Admission – Visa & I-20 information	Department main page
8. Online application - start	Admission – international students	Admission requirements
9. Online application – step 1		
10. Online application – step 2		
11. Online application - finish		
12. Department main page		

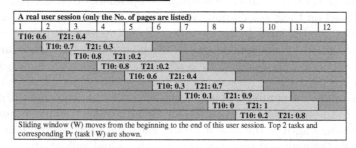

A real user session (only the No. of pages are listed)											
1	2	3	4	5	6	7	8	9	10	11	12
T10: 0.6 T21: 0.4											
	T10: 0.7 T21: 0.3										
		T10: 0.8 T21 :0.2									
			T10: 0.8 T21 :0.2								
				T10: 0.6 T21: 0.4							
					T10: 0.3 T21: 0.7						
						T10: 0.1 T21: 0.9					
							T10: 0 T21: 1				
								T10: 0.2 T21: 0.8			

Sliding window (W) moves from the beginning to the end of this user session. Top 2 tasks and corresponding Pr (task | W) are shown.

Fig. 1. Task Transition Example from CTI Data

4.2   Experimental Results

We identified page-level and task-level features as discussed in Section 3 and built our recommendation system according to the algorithm of Section 3. For comparison, we built another recommendation system based on the standard first-order Markov model to predict and recommend which page to visit next. The Markov-based system models each page as a state in a state diagram with each state transition labeled by the conditional probabilities estimated from the actual navigational data from the server log data. It generates recommendations based on the state transition probability of the last page in the active user session.

Figure 2 depicts the comparison of the *Hit Ratio* measures for the two recommender systems in each of the two data sets. The experiments show that the maximum entropy recommendation system has a clear overall advantage in terms of accuracy over the first-order Markov recommendation system on the CTI data, which demonstrates that the incorporation of task-level usage patterns actually help achieve better recommendation accuracy. As for the NC data, our model also performs better in general, but the overall advantage is not as apparent as that in the CTI data. One explanation of the difference in the results is that the CTI Web site provides many distinct functionalities for users. Student users can collect admission information, submit online applications, and

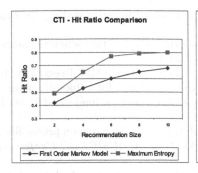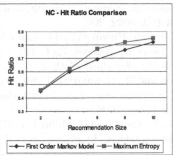

Fig. 2. Recommendation accuracy: maximum entropy model vs. Markov model

perform degree audits, while faculty members can do online advising, etc. While the content-based functionalities from NC site are not so distinct as those of CTI site. Therefore, the benefit of using tasks there is not so impressing.

5   Conclusions and Future Work

In this paper, we have presented a framework for modeling Web users' navigational behavior based on the automatically discovered task-level patterns. We have employed a probabilistic approach which can characterize the user tasks as a set of latent variables. We also demonstrated that the task-level patterns can be seamlessly integrated with the standard page-level patterns in Web usage mining to provide the basis for a more flexible and accurate Web recommender system. To achieve this integration, we employed a maximum entropy model which can be used to effectively combine knowledge from multiple sources described as various constraints imposed on the data.

In the future, we plan to conduct work in several directions. We intend to further explore the work on modeling Web users' navigational behavior at the task-level, such as modeling the hierarchical structure of users' interest and tasks. We also intend to incorporate other source of knowledge, such as from the Web site content and linkage into the user modeling process.

References

1. A. Berger, S. Della Pietra, and V. Della Pietra. A maximum entropy approach to natural language processing. *Computational Linguistics*, 22(1), 1996.
2. S. Chen and R. Rosenfeld. A guassian prior for smoothing maximum entropy models. Technical report, CMU, 1999.
3. R. Cooley, B. Mobasher, and J. Srivastava. Data preparation for mining world wide web browsing patterns. *Journal of Knowledge and Information Systems*, 1(1), 1999.
4. H. Dai and B. Mobasher. Using ontologies to discover domain-level web usage profiles. In *Proceedings of the 2nd Semantic Web Mining Workshop at ECML/PKDD 2002*, Helsinki, Finland, August 2002.

5. J. Goodman. Sequential conditional generalized iterative scaling. In *Proceedings of NAACL-2002*, 2002.
6. T. Hofmann. Unsupervised learning by probabilistic latent semantic analysis. *Machine Learning Journal*, 42(1):177–196, 2001.
7. F. Jelinek. *Statistical Methods for Speech Recognition*. MIT Press, MA, 1998.
8. J. Jeon and R. Manmatha. Using maximum entropy for automatic image annotation. In *Proceedings of the International Conference on Image and Video Retrieval (CIVR-2004)*, 2004.
9. X. Jin, Y. Zhou, and B. Mobasher. Web usage mining based on probabilistic latent semantic analysis. In *Proceedings of the Tenth ACM SIGKDD Conference(2004)*, 2004.
10. R. Kohavi, L. Mason, R. Parekh, and Z. Zheng. Lessons and challenges from mining retail e-commerce data. *To appear in Machine Learning*, 2004.
11. N. Kushmerick, J. McKee, and F. Toolan. Towards zero-input personalization: Referrer-based page prediction. In P. Brusilovsky, O. Stock, and C. Strapparava, editors, *Proceedings of the Adaptive Hypermedia and Adaptive Web-Based Systems International Conference (AH 2000)*, LNCS 1892, pages 133–143. Springer, 2000.
12. B. Mobasher, R. Cooley, and J. Srivastava. Creating adaptive web sites through usage-based clustering of urls. In *Proceedings of the 1999 IEEE Knowledge and Data Engineering Exchange Workshop (KDEX'99)*, Chicago, Illinois, November 1999.
13. B. Mobasher, R. Cooley, and J. Srivastava. Automatic personalization based on web usage mining. *Communications of the ACM*, 43(8):142–151, 2000.
14. B. Mobasher, H. Dai, and M. Nakagawa T. Luo. Discovery and evaluation of aggregate usage profiles for web personalization. *Data Mining and Knowledge Discovery*, 6:61–82, 2002.
15. K. Nigram, J. Lafferty, and A. McCallum. Using maximum entropy for text classification. In *Proceedings of IJCAI-1999*, 1999.
16. D. Pavlov and D. Pennock. A maximum entropy approach to collaborative filtering in dynamic, sparse, high-dimensional domains. In *Proceedings of Neural Information Processing Systems(2002)*, 2002.
17. M. Perkowitz and O. Etzioni. Adaptive web sites: Automatically synthesizing web pages. In *Proceedings of the 15th National Conference on Artificial Intelligence*, Madison, WI, July 1998.
18. R. Rosenfeld. Adaptive statistical language modeling: A maximum entropy approach. Phd dissertation, CMU, 1994.
19. S. Russell and P. Norvig. *Artificial Intelligence: A Modern Approach (2nd Edition)*. Prentice Hall, 2002.
20. R.R. Sarukkai. Link prediction and path analysis using markov chains. In *Proceedings of the 9th International World Wide Web Conference*, Amsterdam, May 2000.
21. M. Spiliopoulou. Web usage mining for web site evaluation. *Communications of the ACM*, 43(8):127–134, 2000.
22. R. Srikant and Y. Yang. Mining web logs to improve website organization. In *Proceedings of the 10th International World Wide Web Conference*, Hong Kong, May 2001.

Ontologically-Enriched Unified User Modeling for Cross-System Personalization

Bhaskar Mehta[1], Claudia Niederee[1], Avare Stewart[1],
Marco Degemmis[2], Pasquale Lops[2], and Giovanni Semeraro[2]

[1] Fraunhofer IPSI, Darmstadt 64293, Germany
[2] Dipartimento di Informatica, Università di Bari, Bari 70126, Italy
{mehta, stewart, niederee}@ipsi.fraunhofer.de
{degemmis, lops, semeraro}@di.uniba.it

Abstract. Personalization today has wide spread use on many Web sites. Systems and applications store preferences and information about users in order to provide personalized access. However, these systems store user profiles in proprietary formats. Although some of these systems store similar information about the user, exchange or reuse of information is not possible and information is duplicated. Additionally, since user profiles tend to be deeply buried inside such systems, users have little control over them. This paper proposes the use of a common ontology-based user context model as a basis for the exchange of user profiles between multiple systems and, thus, as a foundation for cross-system personalization.[1]

1 Introduction

Typically, personalization occurs separately within each system that one interacts with. Each system independently builds up user profiles, i.e. information about a user's likes/dislikes, and uses this information to personalize the system's content and service offer. Most of the personalization techniques [4] rely on either the implicit collection of information about users by tracking and analyzing their system usage behavior or the users explicitly providing information about themselves or giving feedback to the system. Such approaches have two major drawbacks: 1) investments of users in personalizing a system are not transferable to other systems; 2) users have little or no control over the information that defines their *profile*. *Cross system personalization*, i.e. personalization that shares information across different systems in a user-centric way, can overcome the aforementioned problems. Information about users, which is originally scattered across multiple systems, is combined to obtain maximum leverage. In this paper we present the Unified User Context Model(UUCM), an extensible, ontology based user context model, that is the foundation of the approach to cross-system personalization as an application of unified user models. The user becomes a hub and a switch, moving, controlling and synchronizing user profile data as part of a so-called *Context Passport* [3].

---

[1] This research was partially funded under the IST-2003-507173 Project VIKEF.

L. Ardissono, P. Brna, and A. Mitrovic (Eds.): UM 2005, LNAI 3538, pp. 119–123, 2005.

2   Related Work

User models have been used in recommender systems for content processing and information filtering. Recommender systems, by observing preferences through interactions with users, keep summaries of their preferences in a user model, and utilize this model to adapt themselves to generate customized information or behavior. Systems incorporating models of users interest [2] and other cognitive patterns have been widely used to selectively filter information on behalf of users. Task models of user are considered important [1] based on the assumption that the goals of users influence their information needs. Along with the aforementioned modeling dimensions, environmental aspects are considered a key issue when modeling the user for improving the interaction between human and computer.

Besides these more generic aspects of user modeling, there are also some efforts in standardizing user model related aspects, mostly in application-specific areas. The vCard specification and X.500, known as LDAP, are related standards. The *IMS Learner Information Package (LIP)* specification offers a data model that describes characteristics of a user needed for the general purpose of recording and managing learning related history, goals and accomplishments. In addition, the *IEEE Public And Private Information (PAPI)* specification was created to represent student records.

The above standards are well known, but suffer from some drawbacks. vCard is suited for light weight user profiles like contact information or directories. While LDAP allows storing user information as entries made up of attributes, the directory schemas place restrictions on the attribute types that must be, or are allowed to be, contained in an entry. IMS and PAPI are more generic and based on standards like XML. However, they are not conceptually extensible. A unified user profiling format needs to take into account the domain knowledge that might be required for various applications. In order to support personalization across multiple systems, a broader understanding of the user is required as is also discussed in [2, 3].

3   The Unified User Context Model

The UUCM is a user context model that is structured along different dimensions and captures the fact that the user interacts with systems in different working contexts by structuring the model accordingly. In order to support cross-system personalization, the model has to be flexible and extensible enough to deal with the variations in personalization approaches and to incorporate the various aspects relevant for capturing the users' characteristics and his current situation. The main building blocks for the UUCM is an extensible set of facets representing the characteristics of the user and his current context. We use the term *facets* instead of *properties*, because we do not only capture attribute value pairs, but also probabilities and qualifiers for facet values, thus giving a richer description as it is typical for frame-based languages. An extensible set of UUCM dimensions enables the structuring of the facets into groups of user characteristics (e.g. facets related to cognitive pattern). In the context of UUCM, qualification of names as well as values of the facets is a crucial aspect. Both names and values may refer to vocabularies or ontologies, giving the possibility to connect to shared vocabularies, thus simplifying interpretation in a global (cross-system) context. Each UUCM facet is described by the following properties, part of which are optional:

- *Facet name* - name of the UUCM facet to be described;
- *Facet qualifier* - used to bind the facet to a defining vocabulary or ontology;
- *Facet value* - value of the facet, which can be a simple literal as well a reference to a structured resource depending on the domain;
- *Value qualifier* - a qualifier for the value(s) of the facet, i.e. it points to the vocabulary or ontology the value is taken from;
- *Value probability* - a weight reflecting the probability of the facet value;
- *Facet dimension* - each facet is assigned to one of the UUCM dimensions.

The UUCM defines a meta-model for the concrete dimensions and facets used in the description of a user context model. For the cross-system personalization approach, that we are aiming for, it is assumed that this *user context meta-model* is published as a shared ontology and all participating systems rely on this model. In support of the UUCM, other ontologies are required: a *facet ontology* that defines the different facets, a *dimension ontology* that defines facet dimensions and, optionally, also ontologies for the facet values. More details are available in [3]. Information for filling profiles based on UUCM context models are gathered by observing the user interactions, such as items bought, rating provided by users on items, keywords searched, etc. An alternative form to collect values for the facets is to ask the user to fill in an initial form, where the user can enter information about his/her characteristics. The main problem of this process is that its validity depends on whether the users are willing to update the information regularly. A possible solution is to integrate/update the explicits interests given by the user with the automatic generation of profiles exploiting supervised learning techniques [5]. An example of collecting information for the Relationship Dimension can be found in [6].

4   UUCM in a Real World Cross System Scenario

There are three objectives which cross-system personalization needs to address:
1) broader user models that can cope with the variety in user modeling,
2) handling heterogeneous personalization systems and approaches, and
3) giving more control to the user. In line with these objectives, we claim that user profiles should be stored closer to the user. However, maintaining user profiles on the user's side presents some challenges. Interacting with multiple information systems may lead to a large amount of interaction data. Since the individual system best understands the local interactions this should be done within the individual personalization engine and only higher level descriptions

of users should be exchanged between the information system and the unified user profile, which we call the *Context Passport*. The exchange of such information requires a negotiation between activities that an information system can perform and those activities that the user context outlines. The *Cross System Communication Protocol* (CSCP) provides a platform for such negotiations.

4.1   Example Scenario for Unified Profiling in Instant Messaging

In an examle scenario, two Instant Messaging (IM) applications: the MSN and Yahoo Messenger are considered. Essentially the user profiles of these IM networks are lists of contacts that a person is explicitly connected with. While the profiles of these applications focus on modeling relationship aspects, the profiles have a different structure to model this user information. MSN Messenger allows user to have custom names, but has predefined categories for classifying contacts (Friends, Family, etc). Yahoo Messenger does not allow custom names, but allows creation of new categories. Furthermore, with MSN Messenger, it is possible to have a person on your list, yet to block them from contacting you. Yahoo has different structure, and to block or ignore a contact, this person has to be deleted from the list and then added to a separate ignore list. Most user profile formats like PAPI and IMS will fail to store a unified profile completely.

As an concrete example, we take up a simple user profile for a fictitious user John's MSN and Yahoo (Figure 2) profiles. Both these models use common concepts, which can be represented by a common vocabulary consisting of concepts *im:Contact, im:Contact-List, im:Group* related by relationships dis-

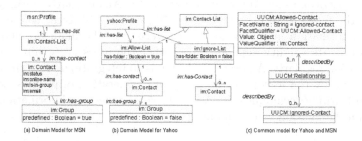

Fig. 1. User Profile Ontology for MSN and Yahoo Messenger

UUCM: Relationship		
	Facet-Name: allowed-Contact **facet qualifier** : im:Allowed-contact **Value:** {(im:status,0),(im:online-name,A), (im:is-in-group, general),(im:email, A)} **Value Qualifier:** im:Contact	**Facet-Name:** allowed-Contact **facet qualifier** : im:Allowed-contact **Value:** {(im:status,0),(im:online-name,D), (im:is-in-group, Family),(im:email, D)} **Value Qualifier:** im:Contact
	Facet-Name: allowed-Contact **facet qualifier** : im:Allowed-contact **Value:** {(im:status,0),(im:online-name,C), (im:is-in-group, Colleagues),(im:email, C)} **Value Qualifier:** im:Contact	**Facet-Name:** blocked-Contact **facet qualifier** : im:blocked-Contact **Value:** {(im:status,0),(im:online-name,B), (im:is-in-group, O),(im:email, B)} **Value Qualifier:** im:Contact

John / Friends: - A, - B (Blocked), Co-Workers, - C, Family, - D

John / Allow: General, - A, Colleagues, - C, My Family, - D   Ignore: - B

Fig. 2. (a)John's Profile for MSN and Yahoo(b)John's Yahoo Profile in UUCM

cussed in Section 3, as shown in Figure 1(a),(b). Analyzing the domain for
IM user profiles, we reach a common model shown in Figure 1(c), composed
of only two facets. The same common model can be used for AOL, ICQ and
other IM applications with minor modifications to the common vocabulary.
Thus this model represents the domain model for the IM domain. Further additions to the model are possible, but for this example, we assume the profile to be composed of only a categorized list of contacts. Using this understanding, we can represent both the profiles in the UUCM format. Figure 2(b)
shows how the Yahoo profile can be represented. The MSN profile can be similarly represented. We note that the profiles for these applications lie completely
in the Relationship dimension. By using a common format for representing
users, these two applications can more easily interoperate, and one application can connect to both networks while maintaining a common profile. Similar
models can be constructed for eCommerce websites and personalized content
providers.

5 Conclusions

This paper proposes the use of a unified user profile format, which can be extended for use with multiple applications, and potentially be used to exchange
common information between multiple systems. The UUCM provides a basis
for the realization of cross-system personalization approaches that enable the
exchange and reuse of user profiles across different systems. UUCM components
refer to common vocabularies or ontologies in order to give the possibility to
interpret the user models in the different contexts.

References

1. Kaplan, C., Fenwick, J., Chen, J.: Adaptive hypertext navigation based on user
   goals and context. User Modeling and User-Adapted Interaction Journal (1993)
   193–220
2. Kobsa, A.: Generic user modeling systems. User Modeling and User-Adapted Interaction Journal 11 (2001) 49–63
3. Niederée, C., Stewart, A., Mehta, B., Hemmje, M.: A multi-dimensional, unified
   user model for cross-system personalization. In Ardissono, L., Semeraro, G., eds.:
   Proceedings of the AVI Workshop on Environments for Personalized Information
   Access, Italy. (2004) 34–54
4. Pretschner, A., Gauch, S.: Personalization on the web. Technical Report
   ITTC-FY2000-TR-13591-01, Information and Telecommunication Technology Center (ITTC), The University of Kansas, Lawrence, KS (1999)
5. Semeraro, G., Degemmis, M., Lops, P.: User profiling to support internet customers:
   What do you want to buy today? Informatica 26 (2002) 407–418
6. Stewart, A., Niederée, C., Mehta, B., Hemmje, M., Neuhold, E.: Extending your
   neighborhood-relationship-based recommendations for your personal web context.
   In Chen, Z., Chen, H., Miao, Q., Fu, Y., Fox, E., Lim, E., eds.: Proceedings of
   the 7th International Conference on Asian Digital Libraries. Volume 3334 of LNCS.
   (2004) 523–532

Using Student and Group Models to Support Teachers in Web-Based Distance Education

Essam Kosba, Vania Dimitrova, and Roger Boyle

School of Computing, University of Leeds, UK
{essamk, roger, vania}@comp.leeds.ac.uk

Abstract. The paper illustrates how student modeling and advice generation methods can be used to address problems experienced in Web-based distance education courses. We have developed the TADV (Teacher ADVisor) framework which builds student models based on the tracking data collected by a course management system and uses these models to generate advice to the course instructors, so that they can improve their feedback and guidance to distance students. The paper introduces TADV, describes how student, group, and class models are used for generating advice to the teachers, and discusses the viability of this approach based on an evaluative study with users.

1 Introduction

Although Web-Based Distance Education (WBDE) is very popular nowadays, some problems are reported, such as the students' feeling of isolation and the instructors' communication overhead and difficulty to address the needs of individuals and groups ([5], [10]). To overcome these problems, the software used in WBDE may play the role of an *advisor* and provide *both* students and teachers with an appropriate help. While many systems include tools to provide adaptive help to students (e.g. [2], [4], [9], [12]), there is insufficient support for teachers in WBDE. Our research focuses on assisting teachers in WBDE by delivering appropriate computer-based advice to help them manage their distance courses effectively. We consider distance courses built with Web Course Management Systems (WCMS) - a platform commonly adopted in many educational organizations for learning and teaching on the Web (e.g. WebCT, Blackboard, Centra Knowledge Center, Moodle, etc.).

To effectively play their new role of facilitators who support the students' in their learning, the teachers in WBDE need to have good understanding of what is happening in distance classes. WCMS collect rich tracking data about the students' activities, but this data is rarely used by teachers due to its complexity and poor structure. We have developed a Teacher ADVisor (TADV) framework [6] which uses WCMS tracking data to build fuzzy student, group and class models, based on which appropriate advice is generated to facilitators. The TADV mechanism for fuzzy student modeling is presented elsewhere, see [7]. This paper focuses on the use of student, group, and class models to generate appropriate advice to teachers.

This paper will briefly introduce TADV (Section 2). We will then outline, in Section 3, the structure of the student, group, and class models, and will describe, in Section 4, how these models are used for advice generation. Section 5 will present a

L. Ardissono, P. Brna, and A. Mitrovic (Eds.): UM 2005, LNAI 3538, pp. 124–133, 2005.

prototype of TADV that was used in an empirical evaluation with real users, results of which will be sketched out in Section 6. Finally, in the conclusions, we will point out the contribution of our work to student modeling and intelligent WCMS.

2   Brief Overview of TADV

TADV is a computer-based advice generating framework designed to deliver advice to facilitators in a WBDE environment developed in WCMS platforms.

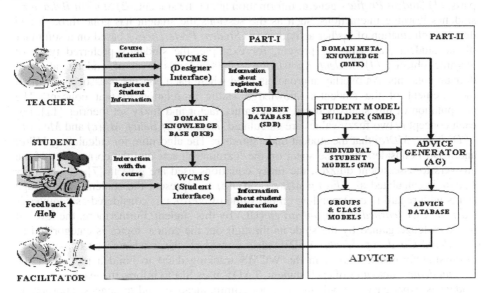

Fig. 1. The TADV Architecture

TADV consists of two parts (see Fig.1). PART-I represents the conventional structure of a course developed in WCMS. The course designers are responsible for preparing the course material incorporated in the *Domain Knowledge Base (DKB)*. TADV considers the common way a course is designed with a WCMS, i.e. a course is defined in a hierarchical way and divided into a set of *lessons*, where each lesson is decomposed into a set of *concepts* that comprise the knowledge building blocks. Each concept is illustrated by learning objects (HTML pages, presentations, etc.), assessment quizzes, and communication activities. The student tracking data that WCMS collects throughout the course is stored in a *Student Database (SDB)* - the main source for student, group and class modeling.

PART-II is an extension to WCMS to model students and generate advice. *Domain Meta-Knowledge (DMK)* is a layer upon DKB that describes the course material and how the domain concepts are related. TADV uses concept maps to represent relations between domain concepts in a hierarchical structure. *Student Models (SM)* represent the knowledge of individual students and their communication styles. *Group Models (GM) and Class Model (CM)* are derived from individual SM to represent information about specific groups of students and the whole class. *Student Model Builder (SMB)* is a module that analyzes the information supplied by the WCMS and builds SM, GM, and CM. Student modeling capabilities are briefly described in Section 3; see [6] and [7] for more details. The *Advice Generator (AG)*, which is presented in Section 4, is a module that uses the SM, GM, and CM together with relevant information in DMK to produce appropriate advice to teachers.

3   Modeling Students in TADV

Individual Student Models. The SM represents individual students and includes four parts: *(1) Student Profile* - general information about the student, *(2) Student Behavior* - student's learning interactions, such as the sessions the student has gone through and detailed information of his/her activities; *(3) Student Preferences* - based on a summary of the student's activities to present, for example, the student's preferred types of learning objects; *(4) Student Knowledge* - the student's level of understanding of domain concepts. An overlay approach is used where each concept is associated with a measurement of the student's knowledge status in relation to that concept. The computation of this status is based on certainty factor and fuzzy set theories [11]. For each concept c, two fuzzy values are calculated: *measure of Belief, MB(c)* and *Measure of Disbelief, MD(c)* that the student understands c. The algorithm for calculating $MB(c)$ and $MD(c)$ considers the time spent on the learning objects and the correctness of the answers to assessment quizzes, the fuzzy equations used are give in [7]. A *Certainty Factor* is calculated as $CF(c) = MB(c) - MD(c)$ to represent the student's knowledge status with regard to c. Depending on the value of $CF(c)$, c is considered as *completely learned* (CL), *learned* (L), or *unlearned* (UL) by this student. Furthermore, the level of the knowledge gained by the students through out the course topics is categorized as *Excellent, Good,* or *Weak.* TADV also considers the students' participation in discussion forums (as given in the WCMS tracking data) to build a picture of the *communicative activities* of each student. TADV uses SM to inform the teachers when a student is experiencing problems or is not communicative, and to suggest appropriate activities to stimulate the student. In addition, the teacher can be advised to encourage students with excellent and good knowledge to help their struggling peers.

Group and Class Models. TADV gives the teacher the choice to define groups of students to be monitored. It is, therefore, possible to model groups of students and generate advice to highlight existing group problems. The main goal of GM is to enable TADV to infer about the *common problems* that might happen to the majority of students in the group and how these problems are related to the common characteristics of the students in the group. Similarly to existing group modeling approaches (see [1]), GM is derived through the aggregation of the individual SM of the group members, i.e. it depends on the interactions made by all students in a specific group. A Group measure of belief $GMB(c)$ and measure of disbelief $GMD(c)$ in regard to a concept c are calculated using certainty factors theory using $MB(c)$ and $MD(c)$ of all group members, respectively. Then, a group Certainty Factor $GCF(c) = GMB(c) - GMD(c)$ is calculated to estimate the group understanding of c. GM also assesses the communication activities of the whole group. Similarly to GM, CM reflects the knowledge status and the communicative aspects of the whole class, considered as one big group of students. GM and CM are used, for example, to determine parts of the course that cause problems to many students, assessment quizzes that are too challenging or too easy, types of learning objects preferred by the students, communication activities commonly/rarely used, etc.

Student Model Builder. (SMB) is the module that analyses WCMS tracking data and generates SM, GM, and CM. SMB may be executed periodically (e.g. daily or weekly) or when required by the course facilitator. This depends mainly on the required interval of time between advice-generation sessions (e.g. in the study described in Section 6, SMB was executed daily). SMB contains three main modules: (a) *Interaction Interpreter* that process tracking data and stores information in the student behavior model; (b) *Individual Model Builder* that uses the student behavior model to make the necessary changes in both the student knowledge and the student preference model; and (c) *Group and Class Models Builder* that uses the individual SM to build GM and CM. The algorithms used in SMB are described in detail in [6].

4 Generating Teacher Advice in TADV

In TADV, a set of predefined conditions is used to define advising situations. For each situation, a predefined advice template(s) is described. When AG recognizes a situation (based on student SM, GM, and CM), the corresponding template is activated to generate advice to the teacher together with recommendation of what can be sent to the student. In some cases, TADV may just produce a statement that describes a situation without suggesting what the teacher should do to remedy the problem. This can happen when TADV is either unable to identify reasons for the problem or considers as appropriate to highlight the problem and let the facilitator decide what pedagogical actions are needed based on his/her subjective view.

4.1 Proposed Advice Types

TADV follows an advice taxonomy based on our analysis of problems with distance courses, as discussed in the literature and confirmed in interviews with several Web-based course teachers [6]. Three advice categories are considered:

- Advice concerning *individual student performance* (*Type-1*): includes several subtypes, such as advice related to a student's knowledge status, students who have unsatisfactory learning levels, uncommunicative students, students who have not start working or are delaying with the course, etc.
- Advice concerning *group performance* (*Type-2*): provides information about common problems that face a group of students and includes advice related to the knowledge states of groups, groups with satisfactory/unsatisfactory learning levels, uncommunicative groups, etc.
- Advice concerning *class performance* (*Type-3*): provides information about the status and behavior of the whole class and includes advice related to the class knowledge status, excellent and weak students relative to the whole class, most and least communicative students, etc.

4.2 Advice Generating Criteria

AG is based on recognizing situations when the teacher may be offered some advice. Each situation is defined by including the following:

- ***Stimulating Evidence (E):*** the situation that motivates AG to generate the advice, defined as $E(e_1, e_2, e_3)$ where e_1 is the name of the student, group, or class that cause the stimulating evidence, e_2 is the name of a domain concept, and e_3 is the status (CL, L, UL, or delayed) of the domain concept carried by e_2. For example, $E(S_1, c_b, UL)$ means that for student S_1, concept c_b is "Unlearned". If e_2 is not specified then e_3 is considered as the status of the student. For example $E(S_1, Weak)$ means that student's state of S_1 is evaluated by TADV as weak.

Table 1. Examples of defining situations for generating advice to individual students (Type-1), groups of students (Type-2) and the whole class (Type-3)

Investigated Reason (R)	Advice from TADV to facilitator (A)	Recommended advice from facilitator to the student (T)	Next AG Action
Type-1 Student advice [Stimulating Evidence is $E(S, c_b, UL)$]			
$(c_b,$ learning objects and/or assessment quizzes are not activated by S)	Student S should be advised to work on the available learning objects and assessment quizzes related to c_b	In order for you to understand c_b we suggest you refer to its available learning objects and solve related assessment quizzes.	Look for new evidence
$(c_a, Strong, UL)$	Student S should be advised to study c_a	In order for you to master c_b, it is highly recommended that you study c_a first.	Look for new evidence
$(c_a, Moderate, UL)$	It may be useful to advise student S to study c_a	In order for you to master c_b, it may be useful to study c_a first.	Look for other reasons
Type-2 Group advice [Stimulating Evidence is $E(G, c_b, UL)$]			
$(c_a, Strong, L)$	G members should be advised to work more with concept c_a	c_b appears to be a common problem for students in G. It is preferred to work more on c_a.	Look for other reasons
$(c_a, Weak, UL)$	It might be useful to advise G members to study c_a	c_b appears to be a common problem for students in G. It might be useful to study c_a	Look for other reasons
Type-3 Class advice [Stimulating Evidence is $E(C, c_b, UL)$]			
$(c_a, Strong, L)$	c_b appears to be a common problem for students in C. The prerequisite c_a is not completely mastered by the class members. It might be useful to advise class members to study c_a	Facilitator should take the necessary actions.	Look for other reasons
$(c_b,$ Uncommunicative)	c_b appears to be a common problem for students in C. TADV notes that class members are not participated in the c_b discussion forum. C members should be encouraged to participate in communication activities related to c_b.	Facilitator should take the necessary actions.	Look for new stimulating evidence

- **Investigated Reason (R):** according to the discovered E, the AG will look for reasons that cause this evidence, by using the SM, GM, and CM. The investigated reason is generally formalized as $R(r_1, r_2, r_3)$ where r_1 is the name of the domain concept related to e_2 with r_2 concept type of relation (Strong/Moderate/Weak) and r_3 is the status of r_1. For example, if $R(c_a, Strong, UL)$ is the investigated reason of $E(S_1, c_b, UL)$ then AG can reason that the unlearned status of c_a that is strongly related to c_b is the reason for this E. More examples are given in Table 1.

- **Advice from TADV to facilitator (A):** depending on the investigated reason, the AG will deliver the appropriate advice to the facilitator. A is defined as $A(P_1,..., P_n)$

where $P_1,...,$ P_n are the parameters carried with the template. There are four basic parameter types used in advice templates: concept name, student name, group name, and class name. See example templates in Table 1.

- ***Recommended advice from facilitator to student/group/class (T):*** If possible, depending on *R*, the AG will produce a predefined advice template that recommends advice that the facilitator may send to a student, a group, or the whole class. This item does not exist when the AG is unable to find reasons that might have led to the current stimulating evidence or when the advice is concerned merely with highlighting important information to the facilitator. The recommendation is generally formalized as $T(P_1,....,$ $P_n)$ where $P_1,....,$ P_n are parameters carried with the template. Table 1 shows some templates with recommendations.

- ***Next AG Action:*** For some stimulating evidence there is a possibility of having many reasons. When a reason is investigated, AG will proceed with the reason and generate the appropriate advice. At this point, depending on the investigated reason, AG will either end the processing of the current evidence or keep searching for other reasons. When a reason is considered to be sufficient then its "Next AG action" is specified as *"Look for new stimulating evidence"* to notify AG to *end* processing of the current evidence. When a reason is considered to be insufficient, its "Next AG action" is specified as *"Look for other reasons"*, i.e. AG has to continue processing of *E* by searching for other candidate reasons *R*.

Fig. 2 shows the main processes performed during generation, which include:

Process 1: Look for stimulating evidence: uses inputs mainly from SM, GM, or CM to locate the concepts with problematic learning status (i.e. unlearned and learned concepts). It also uses the course calendar to find weather the student is delayed. The major output of this process is a stimulating evidence (*E*).

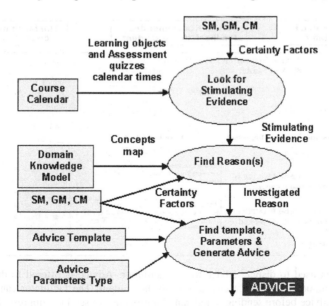

Fig. 2. Processes performed during advice generation in TADV

- **Process 2: Find possible reason:** uses E (from the last process), domain knowledge model (concept maps) and SM, GM, or CM to investigate the reason behind the given E. The major output of this process is the investigated reason R.
- **Process 3: Find template, assign parameters, and generate advice:** According to the reason R from the previous process, this process locates the appropriate advice templates and their parameter value.

5 The TADV Prototype

The TADV design is based on an extensive study of information provided by WCMS, including practical experience with several platforms [6]. One of them, the Centra Knowledge Server, has been employed to demonstrate TADV in a Discrete Mathematics distance learning course at the Arab Academy for Science and Technology (AAST), Alexandria, Egypt. In this prototype, the teacher provided the course material and the required metadata, interface for this was built. The TADV prototype is implemented on Microsoft SQL Server 2000 and Active Server Pages (ASP) technology with ODBC (Open Data Base Connectivity) drivers. The Web server is Microsoft Internet Information Server (MS-IIS) under Microsoft Windows 2000 server. Java and Visual Basic and scripts are used as development languages.

The Centra Knowledge Center has been extended, following the architecture in Fig.1. SMB was built to extract student models from student tracking data, as outlined in Section 3; and AG was implemented to highlight problems of individuals, groups, and the whole class, as described in Section 4. Fig. 3 shows part of the facilitator's interface, and Fig. 4 shows a screen used to display advice and feedback to a student. The screen shots are taken from interactions with the TADV prototype during an evaluative study with real users, which is described in the next section.

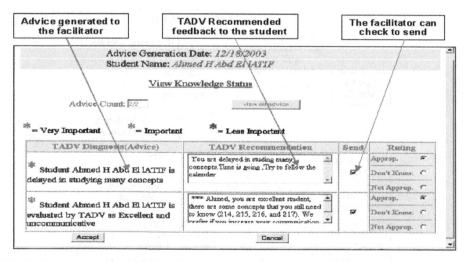

Fig. 3. A screen used to display advice to the facilitator. Advice is offered to the facilitator along with recommended text that can be sent to the student. The facilitator can modify the recommended advice before sending it and can choose either to send or suppress it. The rating section is for evaluation purposes, as described in Section 6

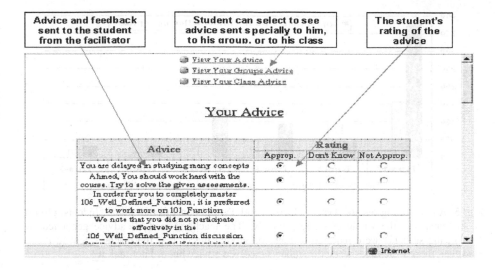

Fig. 4. A screen to display advice to a student, i.e. what the teacher has sent to this student (see Fig. 3). The rating section is for evaluation purposes, see Section 6

6   The TADV Evaluation

An empirical evaluation of the TADV prototype was conducted to verify the usability and functionality of the system's components, and to examine the benefits of the approach for facilitators and students. TADV was integrated within a distance learning environment and used by three facilitators and forty students studying a Discrete Mathematics course at AAST during December 2003-January 2004. The students were divided into two groups: *Experimental group* – using WCMS and TADV which generated advice to facilitators who then sent messages to students, and *Control group* – using just WCMS. The facilitators were observed during the study. At the end, they were interviewed, while the students were given a questionnaire. Due to space limitation, we will outline here only results that refer to suitability of the generated advice, for a full description of the study and its results see [6].

The study showed that TADV provided *practical* and *effective* advice. TADV made it easy for the facilitators to send immediate help and feedback to distance students. The facilitators felt that they *gained considerable knowledge* about the students' behavior and the problems they faced during the study of the course; and stressed the necessity of such advice to be able to manage distance classes.

The facilitators were satisfied with the advice generated regarding advice types, content, and the situations addressed. They found the generated advice *important*, *useful*, and *appropriate* for managing distance classes. They highly appreciated the advice generated regarding groups and classes, as one of them commented:

"Overall evaluation of the advising feature is good. I really appreciate the advice generated for groups and class. For me, advice that provided information like who are the most excellent or weak students, communicative or uncommunicative students, etc. is really very useful."

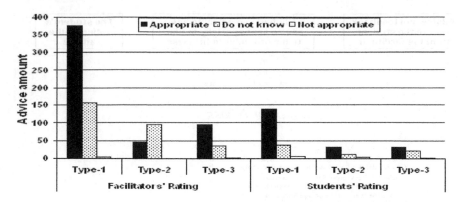

Fig. 5. Advice rating results. Type-1, Type-2, and Type-3 concern individual students, groups of students, and the whole class, respectively. The teachers rated all advice generated by TADV, the students were required to rank the advice pieces that the teachers sent to them. However, there were times when the students received advice but did not rank it

The participating students also appreciated the idea of receiving feedback from the facilitators. They found the advice sent to them helpful, especially when they were delayed with the course. Fig. 5 shows the advice rating results.

In contrast, the facilitators knew very little about the students in the control group. The students in that group received much less feedback on their progress and little guidance from the facilitators. The analysis of the students' questionnaire has showed that the student working with TADV were satisfied with the system. Moreover, comparison of pre/post-tests scores showed that the learning gains of the experimental group are slightly higher than those of the control group.

The study pointed at the need for TADV improvements. For instance, there was repetition and redundancy in Type-2, i.e. group-related, advice that was generated for each individual student in the group (see the Type-2 ranking in Fig.5). Based on this, the TADV framework was tuned to include advice filtration and aggregation features.

7 Conclusions

The work presented in this paper is a step toward increasing the effectiveness of distance education with WCMS platforms through the use of student modeling and advice generation techniques. Our research contributes to a recently emerging trend for incorporating intelligent techniques in WCMS [3]. While [8] apply visualization techniques to present student tracking data using graphical manner (which sometimes may add more cognitive loads to teachers in order to understand various graphical representations), we have demonstrated an approach of using this data to implement intelligent features that extend the functionality of conventional WCMS to support teachers managing their courses. The core of our approach is the elicitation of student, group, and class models and using these models to help teachers gain better understanding of their distance students.

The paper introduced a teacher advisor framework - TADV – aimed at helping instructors to keep close to and guide effectively their distant students. We have described the TADV advice generation mechanism and have shown that student models are crucial for providing teachers with helpful advice tailored to the specific conditions of the courses they run. The advice types and advice generation criteria proposed in this work are quite general and are not dependent on a specific domain or WCMS used. An empirical study with a TADV instantiation in a Discrete Mathematics course has shown that the teachers have gained a better understanding of the needs and problems of their students, which may result in a more effective instruction and may lessen the students' feeling of isolation. The study also showed that the students appreciated the teacher's feedback, which was based on TADV recommendations. Currently, TADV is being instantiated within another WCMS that is being developed within AAST, and will be used by a large number of students and teachers. This will enable us to conduct studies involving a large number of users in a long period of time and to further examine the impact of TADV.

Acknowledgements. This is a part of the first author's PhD studies supported by the AAST. Professor John Self's supervision at an earlier stage of this work is greatly acknowledged.

References

1. Boticario, J., Gaudioso, E., Bauer, M., Kaminka, G.: Proceeding of Workshop on User and Group Models for Web-Based Adaptive Collaborative Environments, held in conjunction with the 9th Int. Conference on User Modeling (2003)
2. Brusilovsky, P.: Adaptive and Intelligent Technologies for Web-Based Education. In: Rollinger, C., Peylo, C. (eds.): Künstliche Intelligenz, Special Issue on Intelligent Systems and Teleteaching, 4, (1999) 19-25
3. Calvo, R., Grandbastien, M. (eds.): Intelligent Management Systems Workshop, Supplementary Proceedings of AIED Conference, Sydney, Australia (2003)
4. Capuano, N., Marsella, M., Salerno, S.: ABITS: An Agent Based Intelligent Tutoring System for Distance Learning. Proceedings of ITS Conference, Montreal (2000)
5. Galusha, J.: Barriers to Learning in Distance Education. Interpersonal Computing and Technology: An electronic journal for the 21st century [online], 5(3/4) (1997) 6-14
6. Kosba, A.: Generating Computer-Based Advice in Web-Based Distance Education Environments. PhD thesis, University of Leeds (2004)
7. Kosba, E., Dimitrova, V., Boyle, R.: Using Fuzzy Techniques to Model Students in Web-Based Learning Environments. IJAIT, Special Issue on AI Techniques in Web-Based Educational Systems, World Scientific Net, 13(2) (2004) 279-297
8. Mazza, R., Dimitrova, V.: Visualizing Student Tracking Data to Support Instructors in Web-Based Distance Education. Proceedings of 13th International Conference on World Wide Web (2004) 154-161
9. Mitrovic, A., Hausler, K.: Porting SQL-Tutor to the Web. International Workshop on Adaptive and Intelligent Web-based Educational Systems, Montreal (2000) 37-44
10. Rivera, J., Rice, M.: A Comparison of Student Outcomes and Satisfaction Between Traditional and Web-based Course Offerings. Online Journal of Distance Learning Administration, 5(3) (2002)
11. Turban, E., Aronson, J.: Decision Support Systems and Intelligent Systems. Prentice Hall International, Inc. (2001)
12. Weber, G., Kuhl, H., Weibelzahl, S.: Developing Adaptive Internet Based Courses with the Authoring System NetCoach. In: Reich, S., Tzagarakis, M., de Bra, P., (eds.): Hypermedia: Openness, Structural Awareness, and Adaptivity, Springer, (2001) 226-238

Using Similarity to Infer Meta-cognitive Behaviors During Analogical Problem Solving

Kasia Muldner and Cristina Conati

Department of Computer Science, University of British Columbia,
2366 Main Mall, Vancouver, BC, V6T1Z4, Canada
{muldner, conati}@cs.ubc.ca

Abstract. We present a computational framework designed to provide adaptive support aimed at triggering learning from problem-solving activities in the presence of worked-out examples. The key to the framework's ability to provide this support is a user model that exploits a novel classification of similarity to infer the impact of a particular example on a given student's meta-cognitive behaviors and subsequent learning.

1 Introduction

Research demonstrates that students rely heavily on examples, especially in the early phases of learning (e.g., [3, 4, 14, 15]). Therefore, there is a substantial amount of work in the cognitive science and Intelligent Tutoring Systems (ITS) communities exploring how examples impact learning, and how computer-based adaptive support can be provided so that examples are used effectively (e.g., [1, 8, 18]). This support typically takes one of two forms. One form involves selecting examples for students during problem-solving activities (e.g. [1, 18]). A second form involves providing guidance on skills needed to learn from examples effectively, based on evidence that different learners have various degrees of proficiency for using examples (e.g., [4]). For instance, the SE-Coach provides support for the meta-cognitive skill of *self-explanation* (the process of explaining instructional material to one self) during example studying, *before* students start solving problems [8]. Here, we describe the E-A (Example-Analogy) Coach, a computational framework designed to provide adaptive support for meta-cognitive skills required for effective *analogical problem solving* (APS), i.e., using examples *during* problem-solving activities.

A key factor that must be taken into account when providing support for APS is the similarity between the problem and example, since there is evidence that this similarity impacts the problem-solving process. For instance, students have difficulty using examples that are not similar enough to the target problem (e.g., [10, 12]). Thus, systems that select examples for students typically aim to minimize the differences between a problem and the chosen example [18]. Although this approach has been shown to be effective, we believe that student characteristics should also play a role in a system's analysis of the example's impact on APS. For instance, problem / example

L. Ardissono, P. Brna, and A. Mitrovic (Eds.): UM 2005, LNAI 3538, pp. 134–143, 2005.

differences which the student has the knowledge to reconcile do not have the same impact on learning as differences which correspond to a student's knowledge gaps. In addition, there is evidence that even given very similar examples, students do not necessarily learn well, possibly because they engage in excessive copying that interferes with learning [15, 17]. Although it is clear that problem / example similarity affects APS, there is not much understanding on *how* this happens for different types of learners (personal communication, M. T. Chi). Here, we propose that certain kinds of similarity can have a positive impact on students who lack meta-cognitive skills needed for effective APS. We incorporate this assumption into the E-A framework, and thus extend existing work on supporting APS by: 1) proposing a novel classification of similarity, and 2) devising a user model that relies on this classification, as well as student knowledge and meta-cognitive skills, to assess the impact of various examples on APS. This assessment is used by the framework to provide tailored interventions (including example selection) to improve this process.

In the rest of the paper, we first discuss the skills needed for APS. We then describe the overall E-A framework. Finally, we present the E-A user model, and discuss how it can be used to generate adaptive support for effective APS.

2 Skills Needed for Analogical Problem Solving

Analogical problem solving consists of the example *retrieval* and *transfer* phases. The *retrieval* phase involves the selection of an example to help solve the target problem. This phase is governed by expertise, in that novice students tend to experience difficulties finding examples that both facilitate problem solving and support learning (e.g., [10]). The *transfer* phase involves incorporating information from an example into a problem's solution [2, 15, 16]. The learning outcomes from this phase are influenced by meta-cognitive skills which can be categorized along two dimensions: *analogy-type* and *reasoning*.

The *analogy-type* dimension characterizes a student's preferred style of problem solving when examples are available (e.g., [15, 17]). Min-analogy identifies students who try to solve a problem on their own, and refer to an example only when they reach an impasse. Max-analogy identifies students who copy as much as possible, regardless of whether they have the knowledge to solve the problem on their own. Students who prefer min-analogy tend to learn more, because they have opportunities to 1) strengthen their knowledge through practice, and 2) uncover knowledge gaps.

The *reasoning* dimension is characterized by how a student tries to understand the example solution prior to using it to solve the problem. A behavior that is believed to result in good learning is *explanation based learning of correctness* (EBLC), a form of self-explanation used to overcome impasses when existing domain knowledge is insufficient to understand the example solution [6, 16]. This process involves using common-sense knowledge (instead of domain knowledge), in conjunction with general rules, to derive new rules that can justify an unclear step in the example. For instance, Fig. 1 shows a problem and example in the domain of Newtonian physics, while Fig. 2 (top) shows how EBLC can be used to explain the existence of the normal force mentioned in line 3 of the example in Fig. 1 [16]. This reasoning can be compressed into a rule (Fig. 2, bottom) that the student can then use to solve the

| Problem: A 5kg block is being pushed up a ramp inclined 40 degrees, with an acceleration of 3m/s². The force is applied to the block at 15 degrees to the horizontal, with a magnitude of 100N. Find the normal force on the block. | Since the crate is in contact with the floor, it follows (from a commonsense rule) that the crate pushes down on the floor. Therefore (by a general rule), the push is an official physics force that acts on the |

Example: A workman pulls a 50 kg crate along the floor. He pulls it hard, with a magnitude of 120 N, applied at an angle of 25 degrees. The crate is accelerating at 6 m/s². What is the normal force on the crate?
  [1] To solve this problem, we apply Newton's Second Law.
  [2] We choose the crate as the body.
  [3] One of the forces acting on the crate is the normal force
  [4] It is directed straight-up

floor and is due to the crate. Therefore (by Newton's third law), there is a reaction force to it that acts on the crate and is due to the floor.

Rule: *If* an object *O1* is in surface contact with object *O2 then*
   there is a normal force on object *O1*

Fig. 1. Sample Problem & Example   **Fig. 2.** Reasoning via EBLC

problem in Fig. 1, top. There some indication that certain students have an inherent tendency for this type of reasoning [6]. Unfortunately, many students employ more shallow processes when using examples during APS, which either do not result in learning, or result in shallow forms of knowledge (e.g., [13, 15, 16]). For instance, rather than reasoning via EBLC, students could focus on adapting example line 3 (Fig. 1) to copy it over to the problem. This can be done by substituting example constants by problem ones (i.e. *crate* by *block*) to generate the correct answer in the problem (this process is known as *transformational analogy* or *mapping-application* [2, 15]). Although this reasoning does accomplish the adaptation needed for correct transfer, it doesn't lead to learning the appropriate rule. Given that learners have various degrees of proficiency for using examples (e.g., [4, 6, 15]), the overall goal of our work is to provide a framework that encourages min-analogy and EBLC and discourages its ineffective counterparts. We begin by describing the E-A architecture.

3   The E-A Architecture

The overall architecture of the E-A Coach is shown in Fig. 3. The system contains two data bases of problems: worked-out examples and problems for students to solve. The solutions to these are automatically generated by the problem *solver*, using the *problem specification* and the rules found in the *knowledge base* component. The E-A *interface* allows students to interactively solve problems from the *problem pool* and to refer to worked-out examples in the *example pool*. The E-A *coach* relies on the *user model's* assessment of a given student's knowledge and APS behaviors to provide adaptive support for APS. This support includes suggesting appropriate examples and generating hints to encourage EBLC and min-analogy when needed.

Our approach for providing tailored support for APS is domain independent and applies to any problem-solving domain for which a rule-based representation is applicable. However, the current instantiation of the E-A framework is embedded in Andes, a tutoring system for Newtonian Physics [7]. Andes provides support for problem solving and example studying in isolation. The E-A Coach is designed to provide a bridge between these two modes, allowing for a smooth transition from pure example studying to independent problem solving. We now describe the E-A user model.

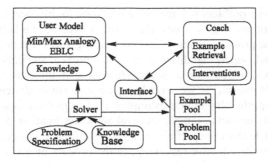

Fig. 3. The E-A Architecture

4 The E-A User Model

The E-A user model allows the framework's coach to provide individualized support to students during APS, by operating in two modes: *assessment* and *simulation*. In *assessment* mode, the model generates an appraisal of how well a student is using an example to solve a given problem, based on that student's interface actions. This allows the E-A coach to generate interventions encouraging EBLC and min-analogy only when it becomes apparent that the student is not learning effectively. In *simulation* mode, the model generates a prediction of student behavior and consequent learning for a particular problem / example pair. This allows the framework to find an example in its example pool that maximizes learning for a particular student. To perform both assessment and simulation, the model reasons about the student's cognitive skills (knowledge) and meta-cognitive traits (analogy and EBLC tendencies). To do so accurately, it takes into account the impact of problem / example similarity on these student characteristics, as we discuss below.

4.1 Impact of Similarity on the E-A User Model's Assessment

To show how the E-A user model incorporates similarity into its assessment, we need to first describe how similarity impacts APS. The similarity between a problem and example is typically classified as either *superficial* or *structural* (e.g., [5, 10]). *Superficial* similarity is assessed using features not part of the underlying domain knowledge, such as the objects in the problem specification and/or its solution (e.g., *block* and *crate* in the problem and example in Fig. 1). *Structural* similarity is assessed using the domain principles (rules) needed to generate the solution (e.g., the rule derived via EBLC, Fig. 2).

Let's now look at how these two kinds of similarity impact problem solving, and in particular, how they can be used to encourage effective APS. One of the downfalls of using examples is that some students copy from them without trying to learn the principles that generated the example solution. This could be prevented by introducing structural differences into the example. However, the benefit of doing so strongly depends on whether the student knows the rules involved in these differences. If the student knows the rules, the lack of similarity with the example forces her to do pure problem solving, which can be highly beneficial. If, however, the student does not know these rules, the example will not be helpful for acquiring them to generate the problem solution, and no learning gains will occur.

On the other hand, superficial differences do not prevent students from learning the underlying concepts, which increases the chances that they can carry on in their problem-solving. However, as we already discussed, some students do not reason effectively from superficially-similar examples. Although there is some evidence that superficial similarity impacts example retrieval and classification [5, 11], it is still not clear how different levels of superficial similarity influence students' meta-cognitive behaviors necessary for effective reasoning. In the process of investigating this issue, we realized that we needed a finer-grained classification of superficial similarity than one currently available in the literature. Thus, we developed one, based on further categorizing superficial differences as:

- *trivial*: differences between problem / example solution elements which correspond to constants that appear in *both* the example specification and its solution, and have a corresponding constant in the problem specification. In addition, in order for a difference to be classified as trivial, simple substitution of the example constant by the corresponding problem constant is sufficient (i.e. requires no further inference) to generate a correct solution step in the problem. For instance, a *trivial* difference between the problem and example in Fig. 1 corresponds to the objects chosen to be the body in their solutions: *crate* (line 2, example solution) and *block* (problem solution, not shown);
- *non-trivial*: differences between problem / example solution elements corresponding to constants that do not appear in both problem / example specifications, or that require additional inference to generate a correct problem solution. One such *non-trivial* difference in Fig. 1 relates to the problem solution step requiring that a normal force be drawn perpendicular to the ramp, as opposed to straight up for the example (line 4, example). This difference depends on a constant defining the incline of the surfaces on which the block and crate rest, which only appears in the problem specification, but which also requires additional inference in order to be reconciled (i.e. that the force is directed 90 degrees away from the surface's incline).

Note that the classification is based on comparing solutions, which the E-A Coach has access to (students only have access to the example solution). Given this classification, we have two hypotheses regarding the impact of superficial similarity on APS behaviors, which are based on cognitive theories of learning from examples [2, 15, 16]. First, trivial differences do not stimulate EBLC and min-analogy for students who do not spontaneously engage in these processes and have poor knowledge. There is some evidence backing up this assumption: students do not have difficulty reconciling trivial differences during APS to generate the problem solution, but do not always learn from doing so [13, 15]. Second, non-trivial differences can have a positive impact on learning for students with poor APS skills. This assumption is based on our observation that only the 'good' APS processes (i.e. EBLC and min-analogy) make it possible to resolve the non-trivial difference and generate a correct problem solution. For instance, students can not apply transformational analogy to

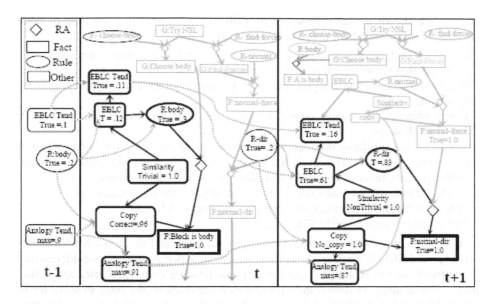

Fig. 4. Fragment of the E-A User Model (not all probabilitites/links between slices are shown)

transfer example solution line 4 in Fig. 1, and still obtain the correct solution. To correctly continue problem solving, they need to generate the rule via EBLC.

Our proposed classification allows the E-A user model to reason about the impact of superficial similarity on students' APS behaviors. This extends existing approaches to providing such support, since these do not make an explicit distinction about different *kinds* of superficial similarity, or their impact on students' meta-cognitive behaviors [1, 18]. We will now discuss in more detail how the classification and related hypotheses are incorporated into the E-A user model.

4.2   Assessment Mode

We first describe how the E-A user model operates in assessment mode to evaluate a student's APS behavior. The model relies on the Andes approach, which involves: 1) automatically generating a solution graph consisting of all the steps and corresponding knowledge needed to solve the problem, as well as paths between these steps, and 2) automatically converting this solution graph into a Bayesian network, used in real-time to perform assessment [7]. The Andes model, however, does not account for the presence of examples during problem-solving activities. Thus, we have extended this model, as is described below.

The Andes model assesses student knowledge based on problem-solving actions, but does not assess how knowledge can *evolve* through these actions. Since the E-A model does need to assess learning resulting from EBLC reasoning, we have switched to using a fully dynamic Bayesian network. In this network, each problem-solving action results in the addition of a new slice. Fig. 4 shows a small portion of this network, assuming that a student 1) is solving the problem and has access to the example in Fig. 1, and 2) has generated two problem-solving actions (key nodes of interest are shown in bold). First, we describe the semantics of each type of node (unless otherwise stated, all nodes have *True/False* values):

- *Fact*: facts and goals (F & G prefixes in Fig. 4) corresponding to solution steps
- *Rule*: whether the student knows the corresponding rule
- *RA*: whether the student can generate the corresponding fact, either by copying or by reasoning
- *Copy*: whether the student copied a step. This node has three values: *Correct, Incorrect, NoCopy*
- *Similarity*: the similarity between a problem fact node and the corresponding fact in the example solution. This node has three values: *Trivial* (no difference or trivial superficial difference), *NonTrivial* and *None* (i.e. structural difference)
- *Analogy Tend*: whether the student has a tendency for *min* or *max* analogy
- *Eblc*: whether the student has explained the step through EBLC
- *EBLC Tend:* a student's EBLC tendency.

Each slice in the network contains the solution graph and the two tendency nodes (analogy and EBLC). Each student problem-solving action is entered as evidence into the network, and results in the addition of corresponding copy, similarity and EBLC nodes. For instance, in slice t, the student chose the block as the body to solve for in the problem in Fig. 1 ('*F:Block is body*' node). In slice $t+1$, the student drew a normal force ('*F:normal dir*', '*F:normal-force*' nodes). We now describe how the model performs its various types of assessment during APS.

Assessment of Copy Episodes. The model tries to assess whether a student copied a step to evaluate: 1) the evolution of student knowledge, since self-generated entries provide a stronger indication of knowledge than copied ones, 2) student analogy tendency. If direct evidence of copying is available, the model uses it to observe the copy node to the appropriate value. In the absence of direct evidence of copying, the model uses information about student knowledge, and analogy tendency from the previous time slice, as well as problem / example similarity, to assess the probability that a copy took place in the current slice. Fig. 4 demonstrates this process. In slice t, where the student produced an entry corresponding to the '*F:Block is body*' node, the model's belief that this step was copied is high ('*Copy*', *Correct* =.96), due to the similarity with the corresponding example step ('*Similarity*', *Trivial*=1.0), this student's tendency for max-analogy (slice $t-1$, '*Analogy*', *max*=.9) and low knowledge of the rule necessary to generate the copied step (slice $t-1$, '*R:body*', *True*=.2). In slice $t+1$, the student produced a correct entry specifying the normal force, including its direction ('*F:normal-dir*' node). The corresponding copy node is observed to *NoCopy*. This happens because the superficial similarity ('*Similarity*', *NonTrivial* = 1.0) makes it impossible to copy and still generate a correct solution entry.

Assessment of EBLC Episodes. These episodes are used to assess the evolution of student knowledge. Currently, the model does not have direct evidence of positive instances of EBLC, and so aims to assess it by taking into account the following factors: 1) similarity, encoding our assumption that non-trivial superficial differences have a higher potential to stimulate EBLC than trivial ones, 2) student tendency for EBLC, and 3) knowledge, in that students who already know a rule do not need to generate it via EBLC. The impact of these factors is demonstrated by the differences in the model's assessment of EBLC in slices t and $t+1$ in Fig. 4. In slice t, the probability of EBLC is low (*'EBLC', True*=.12), because although the student has low prior knowledge of the rule (*'R:body', True*=.2, slice *t-1*), she has a poor tendency for EBLC (*'EBLC Tend', True*=.1, slice *t-1*) and the similarity type is trivial, allowing for the correct generation of the solution step even in the absence of the appropriate rule. In slice *t+1*, the probability of EBLC has increased (*'EBLC', True* =.61), because this is the only process that would allow the student to overcome the non-trivial difference between the problem and example to generate the solution step correctly.

Analogy and EBLC Tendency Assessment. An assessment of these two meta-cognitive tendencies allows the E-A Coach to generate tailored interventions when needed. To assess analogy tendency, the model uses its appraisal of students' copying behaviors. For instance, lack of copying (slice *t+1*) decreases the model's belief in the student's tendency for max analogy (*'Analogy', max*= .91 in slice *t* decreases to *max* =.87 in slice *t+1*). To assess EBLC tendency, the model uses its appraisal of EBLC episodes. For instance, given belief in occurrence of EBLC, belief in EBLC tendency increases (*'EBLC Tend', True*=.11 in slice *t* increases to *True* =.16 in slice *t+1*).

Knowledge Assessment. The model assesses knowledge both diagnostically and causally. Knowledge is assessed diagnostically from students' problem-solving actions. Specifically, the corresponding fact nodes are observed, resulting in belief propagation to either the parent rule node or the copy node. If there is a high probability of copying, the copy node explains away much of the evidence coming from student input. For instance, in slice *t* in Fig. 4, the high probability of a correct copy (*'Copy', Correct*=.96) associated with the fact node *'F: Block is body'* explains most of the evidence away from the corresponding rule node. In slice *t+1*, the copy node is observed to *NoCopy*, so the evidence does propagate up from the fact node to the rule (*'R:dir'*) and prerequisite nodes. The model also aims to assess student learning from EBLC in a causal fashion through the link between EBLC and rule node. For example, in Fig. 4, belief in EBLC in slice *t+1* increases the probability that the *'R:dir'* rule has been generated by the student.

4.3 Simulation Mode

One of the ways in which the E-A Coach supports effective APS is through example selection for students, the goal being to choose an example that maximizes learning while helping the student achieve problem-solving success. To meet this goal, the framework relies on its user model. Specifically, the network described in Section 4.2 is used to predict the impact of each example found in the E-A example pool on the student's problem-solving (PS) success and subsequent learning during APS.

To generate this prediction, the model simulates the student's reasoning and actions, as if the student was solving the target problem and had access to the candidate example. This means that for each problem-solving step required for the target problem's solution, appropriate nodes are added to the network to assess copy and EBLC behaviors, as in assessment mode. Unlike in assessment mode, however, the only evidence available in simulation mode corresponds to the similarity between the current problem and candidate example. This evidence is combined with the model's belief in the student's knowledge and tendency for analogy and EBLC to generate a prediction of that student's problem-solving success (the probabilities for the fact nodes, i.e., problem-solving steps) and consequent learning (the value of the rule nodes). Note that problem-solving success is achieved either if the student has the knowledge to generate the problem solution, or if the example helps her do so (through the absence of structural differences). Both predictions (problem-solving success, learning) are a factor of student characteristics (knowledge, EBLC and analogy tendencies), as well as the similarity between the problem and example.

Given the model's predictions of learning and problem-solving success, to choose an example in a principled manner, the framework relies on a decision theoretic approach. Specifically, to calculate the utility of a candidate example, utility nodes are added and linked to the network's rule and fact nodes (fragment shown in Fig. 5). The *'Learning'* utility node reflects the objective to maximize learning, and is calculated using individual utility nodes for each rule in the network. The *'PS Success'* utility node reflects the objective to ensure problem-solving success, and is calculated using individual utility nodes for each fact in the network. Finally, the overall utility is calculated by combing values of the individual utility nodes using a linearly-additive multi-attribute utility (MAU) node (*'Overall'* utility node, Fig. 5). This process is repeated for each example in the framework's example pool to find the one with maximum utility. A similar approach has been proposed to select tutorial actions [9]; here, we extend it to the example selection task.

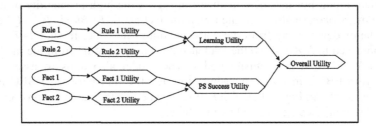

Fig. 5. E-A Utility Model

5 Summary and Future Work

We have presented a framework aimed at providing support for meta-cognitive skills needed for effective analogical problem solving. To realize this support, the framework relies on its user model, which exploits a novel classification of similarity to infer the impact of an example on a student's relevant meta-cognitive skills. This assessment allows the framework to generate tailored interventions, including hints and example retrievals for students.

The next step in our research will be to evaluate the effectiveness of the proposed model with human participants. We plan to use the outcomes of these evaluations to refine the E-A user model, as well as to determine if additional factors should be incorporated into its assessment. We also intend to use these evaluations to assess the suitability of the proposed classification of similarity.

References

1. Aleven, V. and K.D. Ashley. *Teaching case-based argumentation through a model and examples: Empirical evaluation of an intelligent learning environment.* in *Artificial Intelligence in Education.* 1997. Kobe, Japan.
2. Anderson, J.R., *Rules of the Mind.* 1993, Hillsdale, NJ: Lawrence Erlbaum Associates.
3. Atkinson, R., S. Derry, A. Renkl, and D. Wortham, *Learning from Examples: Instructional Principles from the Worked Examples Research.* Review of Educational Research, 2002. **70**(2): 181-214.
4. Chi, M.T.H., M. Bassok, M.W. Lewis, P. Reimann, and R. Glaser, *Self-explanations: How students study and use examples in learning to solve problems.* Cognitive Science, 1989. **13**: 145-182.
5. Chi, M.T.H., P. Feltovich, and R. Glaser, *Categorization and representation of physics problems by experts and novices.* Cognitive Science, 1981. **5**: 121-152.
6. Chi, M.T.H. and K. VanLehn, *The content of physics self-explanations.* The Journal of the Learning Sciences, 1991. **1**: 69-105.
7. Conati, C., A. Gertner, and K. VanLchn, *Using Bayesian Networks to Manage Uncertainty in Student Modeling .* Journal of User Modeling and User-Adapted Interaction, 2002. **12**(4): 371-417.
8. Conati, C. and K. VanLehn, *Toward Computer-based Support of Meta-cognitive Skills: A Computational Framework to Coach Self-Explanation.* International Journal of Artificial Intelligence in Education, 2000. **11**: 389-415.
9. Murray, C. and K. VanLehn. *DT Tutor: A decision-theoretic dynamic approach for optimal selection of tutorial actions.* in *5'th Int. Conf. on ITS.* 2000. Montreal, Canada.
10. Novick, L.R., *Analogical transfer, problem similarity and expertise.* Journal of Experimental Psychology: Learning, Memory and Cognition, 1988. **14**: 510-520.
11. Quilici, J. and R. Mayer, *Role of Examples in How students Learn to Categorize Statistics Word Problems.* Journal of Educational Psychology, 1996. **88**(1): 144-161.
12. Reed, S.K., *A structure-mapping model for word problems.* Journal of Experimental Psychology: Learning, Memory and Cognition, 1987. **13**: 124-139.
13. Reed, S.K., A. Dempster, and M. Ettinger, *Usefulness of analogous solutions for solving algebra word problems.* Journal of Experimental Psychology: Learning, Memory and Cognition, 1985. **11**: 106-125.
14. Sweller, J. and G.A. Cooper, *The use of worked examples as a substitute for problem solving in learning algebra.* Cognition and Instruction, 1985. **2**(1): 59-89.
15. VanLehn, K., *Analogy Events: How Examples are Used During Problem Solving.* Cognitive Science, 1998. **22**(3): 347-388.
16. VanLehn, K., *Rule-Learning Events in the Acquisition of a Complex Skill: An Evaluation of Cascade.* The Journal of the Learning Sciences, 1999. **8**(1): 71-125.
17. VanLehn, K. and R.M. Jones, *Better learners use analogical problem solving sparingly,* in *Machine Learning: Proceedings of the Tenth Annual Conference,* P.E. Utgoff, Editor. 1993, Morgan Kaufmann: San Mateo, CA. 338-345.
18. Weber, G., *Individual Selection of Examples in an Intelligent Learning Environment.* Journal of Artificial Intelligence in Education, 1996. **7**(1): 3-33.

COPPER: Modeling User Linguistic Production Competence in an Adaptive Collaborative Environment

Timothy Read[1], Elena Bárcena[2], Beatriz Barros[1],
Raquel Varela[2], and Jesús Pancorbo[3]

[1] Dpto. Lenguajes y Sistemas Informáticos, UNED
{tread, bbarros}@lsi.uned.es
[2] Dpto. Filologías Extranjeras y sus Lingüísticas, UNED
{mbarcena, rvarela}@flog.uned.es
[3] Dpto. Ingeniería Informática, Universidad Antonio Nebrija
jpancorb@nebrija.es

Abstract. This article starts from the standard conceptualization of linguistic competence as being composed of four related memories of comparable relevance: reading, listening, writing and speaking. It is argued that there is a considerable imbalance between the application of technology to the former two and the others. A system called COPPER[1] is presented, which addresses this problem by helping students to improve their linguistic production combining individual and collaborative activities in a constructivist methodology with a way to overcome technological language analysis difficulties. The knowledge models used in COPPER have been developed from the authors' previous work, undertaken to solve some of the problems of linguistic models of student competence. Methodologically, the system 'empowers' students in that it leads to shared understanding, which reinforces learning. The system is adaptive in the sense that group formation is dynamic and based upon the nature of the tasks to be performed and the features of the student model.

1 Introduction

When we speak of 'linguistic competence' we are really talking about different types of competence. As a student progresses in his/her studies of a given language, it should be expected that advancement is uniform in each of the competences. For students who have always studied in face-to-face classroom environments where a teacher has a reduced number of students to work with, progress will probably be similar. However, for the vast majority of students, who have spent some time in taught language classes but have also learnt on their own using books or computer-based language learning software or materials, the progress will almost certainly not be uniform. In this work, linguistic competence is conceptualized (from didactic and psycholinguistic perspectives) in terms of four types of memory, as illustrated in

---

[1] The work presented in this paper has been funded by the projects I-Peter (from the Vicerrectorado de Investigación of the UNED) and I-Peter II (from the Spanish Ministry of Education).

L. Ardissono, P. Brna, and A. Mitrovic (Eds.): UM 2005, LNAI 3538, pp. 144–153, 2005.

figure 1. Typically, learner comprehension will be more consolidated than production, and within it, reading (**C1**) will be more advanced than listening (**C2**). Apart from the higher cognitive demands of production competence for the average learner, it is a lot easier for a student to acquire materials that can be used to improve written comprehension (books, magazines, Web pages, etc.), and subsequently, oral comprehension (radio, television, online recordings, etc.).

	Comprehension	Production
Written	**C1** (Reading)	**C3** (Writing)
Oral	**C2** (Listening)	**C4** (Speaking)

Fig. 1. The standard four types of linguistic competence as considered in this research

Comprehension can be treated as a solitary activity whereas production requires someone (or some learning technology) that can correct what the student has produced, or at least interact meaningfully with him, something not always available. Hence, language learning typically focuses on written comprehension that is both practiced and evaluated by using simple 'gap filling' or multiple choice tests. In this article a new system, COPPER (Collaborative Oral and written language adaPtive Production EnviRonment), is proposed as a way to improve the way in which language production can be learnt. In the next section, a brief overview of the application of learning technology for linguistic production is undertaken. Subsequently, the pedagogic framework and knowledge models used in COPPER are presented. Finally, an example of the system functionality is provided and conclusions are drawn for future work.

2 Learning Technology and Linguistic Production

Considerable effort has been made over the years to apply learning technologies to support students in the development of the different linguistic competences illustrated in figure 1. As mentioned above, most progress has been made for **C1** (see [7] for a complete review). Essentially, a student's degree of understanding of a given text can be easily evaluated via simple closed tests that are easy to implement in computer systems (e.g., [3]). Recent advances in network bandwidth and digital audio, video formats and also text-to-speech systems have also enabled progress to be made for **C2**. However, progress for **C3** and **C4** has been limited due to the difficulties of using natural language processing (henceforth, NLP) techniques to analyze natural language, detect all (and only) errors produced by the student, and intervene accordingly, due to the flexibility and intricacy of language and the importance of extensive contextual and world knowledge for disambiguation. This problem is limited to some extent for the written modality by forcing a student to produce very short, controlled texts about restricted subjects, thereby simplifying analysis, or by providing a student with tagged fragments that can be combined together to form analyzable sentences.

The automatic assessment of a student's oral production entails the same NLP problems as that of written language, combined with the added difficulties of converting speech to text. Progress has been made by using automatic speech recognition (e.g., systems like FLUENCY; [4]). However, this approach is somewhat limited and problematic so, while appearing promising for the future, it is not very practical ([8], [9]). Furthermore, the majority of tools, systems and interactive materials that have been developed can be criticized due to their ad hoc nature (lacking a theoretical pedagogic framework) and or the lack of any student modeling and adaptability due to student preferences and performance.

3   The Pedagogic Framework and Knowledge Models in COPPER

COPPER is intended to address the problems presented in the previous section and other acknowledged ones (e.g., the pacification of the role of the student in the learning process and the lack of a general pedagogic framework or student models, the learning process and the educational contents). The pedagogic framework adopted for this work is that of collaborative constructivism ([6], [1]), combining elements of individual learning. Such a framework is crucial for this problem domain since, as can be seen in figure 2, for collaboration to take place, both individual learning and mutual understanding are necessary, the latter requires communication between the participants. In order to achieve such communication, participants require a certain degree of linguistic competence, which in turn, permits collaboration to take place.

Furthermore, this framework appears to be particularly suitable for this system for five additional reasons: firstly, by establishing the conditions for shared understanding, students are empowered to assume ownership of their knowledge, where the contextualised nature of the tasks enable collaboration to take place ([10], [13]). Secondly, the type of collaborative constructivism presented here, that of 'learning by doing or practicing' collectively, appears to be particularly effective for second language learning ([2]). Thirdly, the task-based learning used here has been argued to be a way to aid interaction and hence, facilitate learning in a constructivist sense ([5]). Fourthly, the collaboration between students in a group (as peers), and also as individual students with other groups of lower linguistic competence (as a monitor or tutor figure), facilitates the contextualised communicative nature of language production, and is also key to the overall technological functioning of COPPER (which is needed to sidestep the NLP difficulties presented earlier), enabling constructivist objectives to be achieved ([15]). Fifthly and finally, online linguistic production is becoming a part of our professional lives and, as such, it should become a familiar task context for students which helps motivate them ([14]).

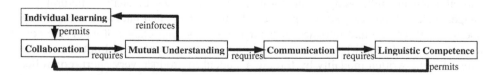

Fig. 2. Relations of dependence in the learning domain

The student model used in this system (which can be seen in figure 3) has not been designed from scratch, but is based upon the three dimensional model of student linguistic competence developed for a previous system, I-Peter ([12]). The student model used in I-Peter was developed to overcome the limitations of standard models of student linguistic knowledge. In COPPER the model of three linguistic levels previously distinguished (lexicon, grammar and discourse) has been extended, and now covers the four linguistic competences **C1, C2, C3, C4**, as presented in figure 3, each of which contains the three levels mentioned here. The two other dimensions, that of knowledge stages (the general classification of a student's linguistic knowledge) and learning phases (the extent to which knowledge has been internalized by a student) have not changed.

COPPER is composed of six knowledge models whose relation can be seen in figure 4 and are subsequently detailed.

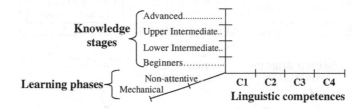

Fig. 3. The student linguistic competence model used in COPPER

KM1 - The **student model** includes the linguistic competence as defined above, together with the individual progress, learning preferences, identified problems and mistakes that a student has, etc. This model is further detailed in [12] and has been extended since then to include data related to the four linguistic competences, group participation and the results of monitoring activities. When students initially start using COPPER they have to have their linguistic competences evaluated for two reasons: firstly, so that the system is able to place them in groups and assign them tasks that are appropriate. Secondly, so that the range of tasks which they can monitor can also be identified (obviously, students that start off with low level linguistic competences are unable to monitor other students). This initial evaluation is achieved by using a battery of online multiple choice and closed production tests. The results of which are inevitably approximate and limited, due to the NLP problems presented in the previous section. Hence, newly classified students are tagged as being "newbies" and are especially monitored by other established students when undertaking tasks (or even monitoring other students) to refine the initial evaluation data.

KM2 - The **group model** represents details of the particular set of students to work together on a particular problem, detailing interactions, mistakes, logging progress towards the goal, etc. It is this model that encapsulates the adaptive part of the system since the group generation and task assignment by COPPER is dynamic. It works as a three-phase process:

1. The student models of all students currently not working on a task are analysed in terms of their current stage of linguistic learning in order to produce a list of

all the low level linguistic units that either need to be learned (basic mechanical learning) or reinforced and tested (non-attentive learning).

2. The students are initially sorted into groups by heuristically matching the unlearned / un-reinforced linguistic units in the list to the available tasks. General system wide criteria are also used for this process (established previously by a teacher). An example would be the formation of groups where not all the members have the same level of knowledge (in order to reinforce learning for certain weak students).

3. These proposed groups are subsequently refined by taking into account individual progress made in the system up to now, previous tasks undertaken (and the results), individual preferences about the type of English a student wishes to study, past experiences of collaboration with the members of the group, etc.

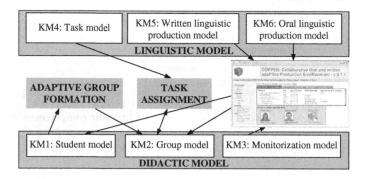

Fig. 4. Relation between the knowledge models in COPPER

KM3 - The **monitorization model** represents the relation between higher and lower level students in the tutoring function and the assessments made about the work produced, together with its later validation from other higher-level students or based upon rules and knowledge in the linguistic production models. An example of the types of monitorization possible can be seen in figure 5. A fundamental principle behind COPPER is that a student has two roles, firstly as a member of a group working collaboratively on oral and written production, and secondly, as a monitor of the production of groups in lower levels (and evaluations made by students at lower linguistic competence levels).

As such, in the context of this system, a student is not just encouraged to participate as a monitor, but is obliged to do so as part of the course, to reinforce learning. Once the dynamic group generation and task assignment process (previously summarised) has been used to form a group, a( ) monitor(s) is(are) also assigned from the student pool, depending on such factors as "previously demonstrated linguistic competence", familiarity with the given task (and underlying linguistic knowledge), past history of having monitored the members of the group, etc. Furthermore, another student with both a higher knowledge stage for the given linguistic unit and experience of monitoring this level of tasks, is also assigned as a monitor of the monitor(s); the task monitors also need to be evaluated.

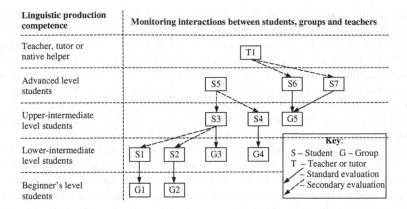

Fig. 5. Monitorization relations within COPPER

Monitors evaluate students progress with a given task not only in terms of the quality of their productions but also in terms of the effectiveness of their corrections of the productions of groups lower down in the hierarchy. When a group produces a result, it is evaluated by the monitor(s) assigned to the group, and feedback is given to the group members. A task is defined to be finished only when the monitor(s) classify it as such. Once a task is completed, the group is dissolved, the individual student models are updated, and the students return to the student pool for assignment to new tasks. Examples of such moderation can be seen in figure 5; firstly, there is a standard evaluation of the work of G1 (group number 1) by S1 (student number 1). Secondly, an example of a secondary evaluation can be seen between S3 and S1 and S2. Here, the monitoring of the latter two students is being evaluated. Finally, only teachers, tutors or native helpers can evaluate tasks undertaken at an advanced level.

The effectiveness of this methodology is founded on three pillars: firstly, the classification of student linguistic production competence; secondly, the nature of the production tasks that the groups have to undertake; and thirdly and finally, a rigorous control of group production and subsequent student evaluation to prevent errors going undetected in both group production and student evaluation.

KM4 - The **task model** contains the practical learning tasks that the groups of students must undertake. They are structured to reflect a student's knowledge stage, particular preferences and language variants.

KM5 - The **written linguistic production model** structures the linguistic knowledge that the students are supposed to use, in a bottom-up fashion, into four different levels: lexical, phrasal, sentential and supra-sentential level. A very early and somewhat simplified version of this model was developed by the authors for inclusion in a prototype of an authoring tool (VAT – Virtual Authoring Tool[2], [11]) for English as a second language. The difficulties of analyzing natural language in order to detect composition errors have been mentioned in the previous section. For this reason, current word processors offer little more help to users than basic orthographic detec-

---

[2] Partially developed with a grant from the Vicerrectorado de Investigación of the UNED.

tion and simple grammatical analysis (the results of which are presented to users as suggestions for things that may or may not be wrong!). In the literature, it is generally accepted that such tools should be considered as helpful to lazy native speakers or very advanced students, who know the rules underlying the correct way to write, but may have temporarily forgotten a particular one for one of many different reasons; e.g., they are writing quickly, concentrating on the ideas they wish to communicate, etc. However, they are generally regarded as dangerous for language learners because they will not have the necessary rules to decide if a suggestion is correct and applicable, and can even incorrectly learn certain rules if they are repeated frequently.

Hence, the objective behind the development of KM5 (and the earlier VAT) was the explicit structuring of the vast mass of linguistic knowledge and rules that a student needs to know in order to be able to write correctly, in such a way as to facilitate the steps a student needs to go through when writing, to check that what is being produced is error-free. Initially, these steps will be artificial and somewhat slow, but as the student learns and internalizes the rules, the procedure will become more normal and automatic. It should be noted that such a knowledge model does not solve the NLP problems related to text analysis. However, the pedagogic advantage that a tool based upon it offers over standard word processors is that, rather than presenting a word or text fragment as being potentially incorrect, it forces the student to go through a rigorous methodical self-diagnosis process which empowers him to detect errors in the same way that a native writer would, albeit somewhat slower.

Since oral production follows planning and written production, this model is also an important part of the oral generation process. The linguistic knowledge contained in this model can be separated into different levels: the word level (nouns, adjectives, verbs, determinatives [articles, possessives, demonstratives, indefinites, relatives, interrogatives, exclamatives], pronouns, adverbs, prepositions), the sentential level (simple, coordinative, relative, nominal, adverbial, condition, comparison, punctuation, constituent order, constituent presence), and the supra-sentential level (introduction and background, arguments and counterarguments, examples, conclusion, narration, description, dialogue, reporting).

KM6 - The **oral linguistic production model**: This model details the specific aspects of oral linguistic production that a student needs to dominate, using a template based upon the following dimensions: prosody (pronunciation, stress, intonation patterns, fluency), spoken vocabulary, idiomatic expressions, formal/informal register, slang, figures of speech, repetitions and false starts, oral syntax, mother tongue effects, regional dialect, cultural references, etc. The dimensions identified here are common to the learning of any second language; however, the exact nature of each will depend upon the language in question. Furthermore, mother tongue effects obviously depend largely on the student's first language; for native Spanish speakers learning English, typical problems include the distinction between short and long vowels and the consonant sounds not present in their language.

4   COPPER'S Environment and Functionality

Although the structure of the activities that the students at different levels undertake are different, they all contain the same basic steps: initial deliberation, planning and division of the task, formulation of a textual description / transcription of the proposed oral dialogue, initial practice of the oral production of individual words and problematic sounds (using listen / repeat and read aloud approaches), oral production of dialogue fragments, and final oral dialogue production, reflection and revision of the produced dialogue. An example of the functionality of the system can be seen in figure 6, which also presents the basic COPPER interface. Here, the system dynamically generates a group of three people (① in figure 6; each person is assigned a different colour which is used by the system to tag all input from that person) as detailed in section 3, based upon, amongst other things, a common interest in working on the sublanguage of English for Tourism, and a given knowledge stage of lower intermediate level (using task models KM1 and KM2). Once the group is formed, the task model KM4 is used to select a relevant task, in this example, that of the purchase of air tickets in a travel agency for a return trip from Madrid to London. In this example, the students are assigned the following roles: a travel agent and two tourists.

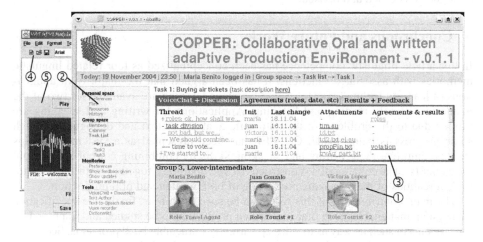

Fig. 6. Example of COPPER's interface and related tools

COPPER's interface has a generic menu on the left hand side of the screen (② in figure 6), where a student can access personal information, files and resources; use shared group resources and undertake the active tasks; monitor the work of lower level students; and finally, use the available tools (which currently include a voice recorder/player, the VAT text editor, a text-to-speech reader and a set of dictionaries). These tools are defined as services within the system so that different tools can be incorporated into the system in the future (and associated with learning tasks), without having to change the overall architecture. As can be seen (③ in figure 6), once the students start a particular task they can use the VoiceChat + Discussion tool to communicate and share ideas. It combines synchronous chat with asynchronous messaging, either via voice or text[3]. The interchanges between the students are logged by the system as in any threaded news system. As can also be seen (③ in figure 6), the discussion space has two associated tabs, one for agreements (roles assigned, dates, etc.),

---

[3] Currently, the voice input is not automatically translated into text, although in future versions of the system this option will be explored.

and another for results and the feedback of the monitors. On the right hand side of the discussion space, links to data in the other tabs are included to facilitate their access by the students without having to continually change between tabs.

Once the roles and task breakdown has been negotiated, the students can use the available tools, such as COPPER's text authoring tool and voice recorder (④ and ⑤ in figure 6, using knowledge models KM5 and KM6) to start to work on a textual description of the dialogue, and subsequently, practice the individual oral production of problematic words and sounds (identified as such by the individual student models). As the group generates results, they become available for higher-level students, working as monitors (using knowledge model KM3), to comment on them, enabling the lower level group to refine what has been produced. Once there is agreement on the form of the final dialogue, and the feedback of the monitors has been incorporated, the oral production of dialogue fragments can be undertaken, and the final oral dialogue is recorded and revised.

5   Conclusions and Future Work

In this article linguistic competence has been conceptualized as four related linguistic memories with associated functions. It has been argued that the majority of applications of learning technologies to second language learning are available for two of the memories, namely reading and listening. Applications for writing and speaking are limited due to the problems of the automatic analysis of text and dialogue, although some progress is being made. COPPER has been presented as a system that helps students improve their writing and speaking skills by combining current ideas about the benefits of a collaborative constructivist methodology together with the technological realities of the automatic processing of both written and oral production.

The main contributions of this work can be seen to be four: firstly, the specification of a system that enables both oral and written production to be studied and improved by DE students in such as way as to sidestep currently intractable NLP problems. Secondly, the knowledge models used here are based upon work that is being used in a previous system, I-Peter, which appears to solve some of the modeling difficulties with the standard conceptualization of student linguistic competence. Thirdly, the proposal is methodologically innovative for five reasons presented here: the framework empowers students and leads to shared understanding, combining individual and collaborative activities thereby reinforcing learning; learning by doing is practical for second language learning; task-based learning enhances such a practical approach and is essential for the functionality of our system; collaboration is facilitated here, something which is important for the intrinsically communicative nature of language production; online written and oral production in English is becoming a standard part of our professional lives, and hence the use of such a system as COPPER is very motivating for the students. Fourthly, this system is adaptive in the sense that group formation is dynamic and based upon the nature of the tasks to be performed and the details of the student model.

The next stage in the work presented here is to evaluate the system (something already done with the predecessor system I-Peter) with a large group of users. This is not only necessary to test the knowledge models, but also to see what practical problems arise with the group and monitoring interactions. It should be noted that the system is not devoid of problems: a reasonably large number of students is required, distributed at the different linguistic production competence levels, to enable the 'monitoring' function to be undertaken. Furthermore, the actual location of the students at each linguistic competence level needs to be very precise, which requires accurate pre-testing to be undertaken. Finally, rigorous control of moderation is required to prevent significant erroneous feedback from occurring. Such problems represent the state of the question, and as such, will be the subject of future work.

References

1. Bonk, C. & Cunningham, D. Searching for learner-centered, constructivist, and sociocultural components of collaborative educational learning tools. In C. Bonk & K. King (eds.) *Electronic collaborators*, 25-50. Mahwah, NJ: Lawrence Erlbaum. 1998.
2. Doughty, C.J. & Long, M.H. Optimal psycholinguistic environments for distance foreign language learning. *Language Learning & Technology*. Vol. 7, No. 3, 50-80. 2003.
3. Dunkel, P. (ed.). *Computer-assisted language learning and testing: Research issues and practice*. New York, NY: Newbury House. 1991.
4. Eskenazi, M. Detection of foreign speakers, pronunciation errors for second language training: Preliminary results. In *Proceedings of the International Conference on Spoken Language Processing*, 100-110. Philadelphia, PA. 1996.
5. González-Lloret, M. Designing task-based CALL to promote interaction: En busca de esmeraldas. *Language Learning & Technology*. Vol. 7, No. 3, 86-104. 2003.
6. Jonassen, D.H. Technology as cognitive tools: Learners as designers. *IT Forum*. Paper #1. http://it.coe.uga.edu/itforum/paper1/paper1.html. 1994.
7. Levy, M. *Computer-Assisted Language Learning: Context and Conceptualiztion*. Oxford: Oxford University Press. 1997.
8. Mostow, S., Roth, A., Hauptmann, G. & Kane, M. A Prototype Reading Coach that Listens. In *Proceedings of the Twelfth National Conference on Artificial Intelligence (AAAI-94), American Association for Artificial Intelligence*, 785-792. 1994.
9. Norris, J.M. Concerns with computerized adaptive oral proficiency assessment. *Language Learning & Technology*. Vol. 5, No. 2, 99-105. 2001.
10. O'Malley, C. Designing computer support for collaborative learning. In C. O'Malley (ed.) *Computer supported collaborative learning*, 283-297. New York: Springer-Verlag. 1995.
11. Read, T. & Bárcena, E. The UNED Profesor Virtual for English distance learning / practising on the Web. In *La Lingüística Aplicada a finales del siglo XX: ensayos y propuestas*. Vol. 1, 50-58. Madrid: Universidad de Alcalá de Henares. 2001.
12. Read, T., Bárcena, E., Barros, B. & Verdejo, F. Adaptive modelling of student diagnosis and material selection for on-line language learning. *Journal of Intelligent and Fuzzy Systems* Vol. 12, No. 3-4. 2002.
13. Tella, S. & Mononen-Aaltonen, M. Developing dialogic communication culture in media education: Integrating dialogism and technology. Helsinki: *Media Education Publications* 7. http://www.helsinki.fi/~tella/mep7.html. 1998.
14. Warschauer, M. & Healey, D. Computers and language learning: An overview. *Language Teaching*. No. 31, 57-71. 1998.
15. Weasenforth, D. Realizing constructivist objectives through collaborative technologies: threaded discussions. *Language Learning & Technology*. Vol. 6, No. 3, 58-86. 2002.

User Cognitive Style and Interface Design for Personal, Adaptive Learning. What to Model?

Elizabeth Uruchrutu, Lachlan MacKinnon, and Roger Rist

School of Mathematical and Computer Sciences, Heriot-Watt University,
Riccarton, Edinburgh EH14 4AS, Scotland
{ceeeu, lachlan, rjr}@macs.hw.ac.uk

Abstract. The concept of personal learning environments has become a significant research topic over the past few years. Building such personal, adaptive environments requires the convergence of several modeling dimensions and an interaction strategy based on a user model that incorporates key cognitive characteristics of the learners. This paper reports on an initial study carried out to evaluate the extent to which matching the interface design to the learner cognitive style facilitates learning performance. Results show that individual differences influence the way learners react to and perform under different interface conditions, however no simple effects were observed that confirm a relationship between cognitive style and interface affect.

1 Introduction

The implementation of web-based learning over the past few years has increasingly moved towards an individual, technology-based, learning centered model, which suggests that realizing the promise of improved learning efficiency depends on the ability of that learning technology to tailor instruction to the needs of individuals.

Accordingly, there has been considerable research on the development of learning technologies to adapt the learning experience to the individual. Two levels of adaptation are generally agreed: adaptability and adaptivity. Adaptable systems have built in flexibility allowing the user to alter its aspect or functionality. Adaptivity refers to the actual capability of a system to automatically adapt various visible aspects to new conditions, usually defined from a given model [4]. Examples of this category are the several adaptive hypermedia applications that have been introduced over the past years – in his latest review Brusilovsky [5] examined more than twenty of them.

In these adaptive systems, adaptation is mainly driven by the characteristics of their users represented in the user model, yet some applications also take into account usage data and/or environmental data. However, few attempts have been done to model cognitive attributes of the user such as their cognitive style; and while researchers agree on the importance of taking these into account, there is still "little agreement on which features can and should be used or how to use them." [5]

In determining the value of developing personal, adaptive web-based learning environments a useful starting point seems to be the analysis of individual differences, and particularly of the cognitive skills that would impact the modeling dimensions underpinning such learning systems. That is the purpose of this study.

L. Ardissono, P. Brna, and A. Mitrovic (Eds.): UM 2005, LNAI 3538, pp. 154–163, 2005.
© Springer-Verlag Berlin Heidelberg 2005

2   Learning Styles and Cognitive Styles

The term *style* has been used in the field of individual differences to describe a set of qualities, activities and behaviors that every person exhibits in a persistent way. In education, the concepts of learning style and cognitive style have been explored extensively [2, 3, 6, 19, 22], and although these have been used interchangeably, cognitive style is the "individual's preferred and habitual approach to organizing and representing information" [19]. If cognitive styles are individual and non-changing, they could provide significant basis for modeling our users towards personalization.

Relevant research on cognitive styles has however produced a myriad of models and classifications. Most of them tend to consider the position of the individual on a continuum between two extreme characteristics such as left-right cerebral hemisphere dominance, linear-holistic processing, sequential-random approach, symbolic-concrete preferences, logical-intuitive decision making, or verbal-imager tendencies.

For the purposes of our research, several of these constructs have been taken into account; as have been many of the studies carried out in the past examining the relationship between particular attributes of cognitive styles and learning variables, such as preference for computer-based learning materials [9, 10, 16, 18], learning outcomes and media types [17, 23], or the effect of different information structures [7, 8, 17, 20,]. Results have been ambiguous and while some studies find a consistent relationship between style and learning, others find no effect.

Additionally, the multiplicity of models and classifications related to cognitive styles has led to a certain extent of confusion. In an attempt to integrate much of the earlier work in the field, Riding and Cheema [16] concluded that many of the terms used could be grouped into a number of learning strategies and two principal cognitive styles: Wholist-Analytic (WA) – the tendency of individuals to *organize* information in parts or as a whole; and Verbaliser-Imager style (VI) – the tendency of individuals to represent information verbally or in mental pictures when thinking.

To measure the position of the individual in the two dimensions established, Riding also designed a computerized assessment: the Cognitive Styles Analysis (CSA) test [14], which has been used in a number of studies, all of them contributing to the validity of the construct [15, 19]. However, Peterson [13] and her colleagues found that the test had poor test re-test reliability. They designed an extended version of the WA dimension and a new test of the VI style with acceptable consistency and reliability (VICS & Extended CSA-WA test).

3   Implications for Web-Based Learning and Interface Design

While adaptive systems, and particularly adaptive hypermedia provide several techniques to afford adaptive presentation and navigation, our approach seeks to build on these to allow the convergence of several modeling dimensions, namely a model of the domain (ontology mapping, content, context, structure, composition), a learning model (derived from the rules and heuristics governing the presentation of learning materials to support a particular learning scenario), and a user model (cognitive and personal data profile). The strategy of interaction is seen as a product of the combination of these factors, but driven mainly from the personal requirements of the user, and particularly of their cognitive style.

In this conceptual structure the interaction model is regarded as an active dialogue between the system and its users, one that is capable of inferring and evaluating the user's intentions and actions in order to exhibit a more cooperative behavior. Since the dialogue between the user and the system is mediated by the interface, two issues become central: the construction and use of an explicit model of the user's key cognitive characteristics; and an interface design capable of demonstrating the adaptive behavior that is expected from the system.

To address the first point, we identified some key defining attributes and organized them under the Riding and Cheema's dimensions of analysis: *Analytics* process information from parts to the whole; they are organized, able to establish meaningful structures, sequential, conceptually oriented, and prefer individualized learning. *Wholists* process information from the whole to parts, they are factually oriented and affective, not highly organised and less likely to impose a meaningful organisation when there is no structure; they approach learning tasks randomly, and prefer collaborative work. *Verbalisers* tend to use verbal representations to depict information when thinking, and prefer words rather than images. *Imagers* tend to use images to depict information when thinking, they understand visuals.

To address the second point – the design of an adaptive interface – we proceeded to identify some instructional conditions that capitalize on the characteristics formerly acknowledged (Table 1).

Table 1. Instructional Conditions that Capitalize on Different Cognitive Styles

Analytic	Wholist
– Discovery instructional methods	– Procedural instruction sequence
– Analytical approach	– Global approach to present information
– Provide an independent learning environment	– Benefit from well-organized, well-structured material
– Offer content outlines and post organizers	– Offer structural support with salient cues, such as advance organizers
– Provide minimal guidance and direction	– Provide clear, explicit directions and the maximum amount of guidance
– Provide content resources and reference material	– Provide extensive feedback
– Instructional techniques	– Affective techniques

Verbaliser	Imager
– Learn best when information presented in verbal form	– Learn best from images, diagrams or pictures
– No trouble processing symbols	– Underlining, visual cueing in text
– -words, mathematical notations	– Presenting special text in windows or boxes

As a result, it is suggested that a learning system should exhibit an adaptive behavior based on, at least, the following variables:

Sequence of Instruction. Analytics tend to approach the learning content in a deductive manner, whereas wholists would approach the learning task following a concrete to abstract sequence. Adaptive presentation techniques can be implemented to provide the content sequence that best fits the learners.

Content Representation. Verbalisers seem to learn best when information is presented in verbal form, and imagers when diagrams and/or pictures are used. Adaptive techniques would be implemented to provide, whenever possible, the same content in either mode of presentation.

Content Structuring. Analytics would prefer an independent learning environment, and to impose their own structure on the material provided. Content outlines would be helpful, as well as post-organizers. Structured lessons would help wholists better since they seem to prefer material that is organized for them.

Control Strategy. Analytics would prefer to have control over the sequence of the learning materials, whereas wholists could be guided by the system. For that purpose, adaptive navigation techniques could be implemented.

Feedback/Advice. Wholists would perform better when explicit directions, extensive feedback and maximum guidance are provided throughout the system. On the contrary, analytics would perform better when instructions are kept to the minimum.

Interaction Techniques. Analytics are more likely to prefer a *serious* learning environment, as opposed to a playful environment, which would suit to the wholists better. The whole design of the learning system should take this issue into account.

4 The Initial Design of LEARNINT

As part of the development of an adaptive system based on the framework described previously, the approach was first tried out through a case study. A learning application was developed to assess some of the critical variables of the students' cognitive style and their impact on learning performance. LEARNINT (the Learning Interface) was developed using learning material from the "Computer Hardware" online learning module, available to students of the MSc degree in IT, at Heriot-Watt University in Edinburgh, Scotland. It comprises two extremely different interfaces. The first design is highly imager and wholist (W/I), covering concepts about "Combinational Circuit Design" (Fig. 1). The second interface (A/V) is highly verbal and analytic, covering concepts about "Relational Circuit Design" (Fig. 2).

The salient feature in the design is undoubtedly the content's mode of presentation: one interface presents information verbally, and the other in terms of images and diagrams, including elements on the screen such as buttons and navigational aids. The sequence established in the original design of the learning material was observed; however, advance organizers were included for the wholists.

In terms of the size of the information step, each page of the hypertext structure contains a complete unit of information (topic/ section/ concept), once more following the original structure used by the author. Yet an outline was placed for analytics so they are able to follow the sequence they consider best, hence increasing their sense of control. Conversely, for the W/I interface the sequence of the material is defined by the system in a linear approach. The hypertext structure is also different: the W/I interface is linear, users can proceed just to the previous or the next topic, with no additional links or deeper levels of content, but with frame arrangements allowing for the information required to be presented all at once. In contrast, the A/V interface allows the students to proceed to any page, and further levels are used such as additional pages presenting graphical content. Titles and headers are prominent in both designs since these help student understanding and give organization to the material. Other graphical components between the two interfaces: a larger, brighter combination of colors for the imager design, graphical/textual buttons on each screen, and a different layout in each case. A zigzag arrangement of information was chosen to provide a more affective/playful environment for wholists.

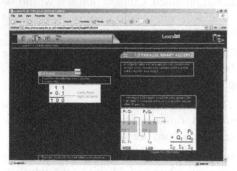   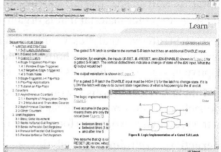

Fig. 1. Wholist/Imager Interface Design   **Fig. 2.** Analytic/Verbal Interface Design

5   The Study

In order to enquire whether matching the interface design to the cognitive style of the user can facilitate learning performance, an experiment was conducted. A within experimental design was used where all participants experienced both interfaces. Task 1 was defined as using the W/I interface to study "Combinational Circuit Design", and Task 2 as using the A/V interface to study "Relational Circuit Design".

Measures were set as performance on each topic, user satisfaction and perceived usability on each interface, and individual cognitive style. User satisfaction was measured by the users' responses to a modified-Schneidermann questionnaire. For measuring usability, the System Usability Scale (SUS) develop by John Brooke was used. Learning performance was registered in terms of information recall as measured by a test for each topic comprising 6 multiple-choice questions with degrees of confidence based on the MICE system [1]. The participants' cognitive style was assessed using the VICS and E-CSA-WA test.

Participants attended a total of three sessions, one week apart from each other. In the first session they carried out the task 1 and answered its evaluation questionnaire. The second session started with the assessment test for the content studied in task 1, followed by completion of task 2, to end by answering the corresponding evaluation questionnaire. In the last session participants answered the assessment test corresponding to task 2, and carried out the VICS and E-CSA-WA test.

5.1   The (Preliminary) Results

The actual sample consisted of 25 volunteers: 9 women and 16 men, the age average was 30.4 years (*Max= 42 years, Min= 21 years*). With just one exception, all participants were postgraduate students, 14 in computer science or IT.

The results obtained from the VICS&E-CSA-WA test showed that the participants in this study had a Verbal-Imager ratio between 0.826 and 1.819, suggesting an imager style preference *(N= 25, M=1.109, SD=.279)*. Their Wholist-Analytic ratio was between 0.973 and 1.790, showing an analytic preference *(N= 25, M=1.348, SD=.249)*. The distribution of the participants' cognitive style is shown in Fig. 3.

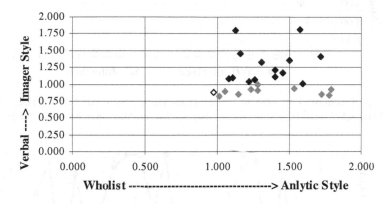

Fig. 3. Distribution of Participant's Cognitive Style: 1 individual of Wholist-verbaliser style, 10 resulted Analytic-verbalisers, and 14 Analytic-imagers

The evaluation questionnaire comprised 6 sections: Content, Navigation, Data types, Layout, User Reactions, and Usability. Considering the Likert scale used, where 9 was the most positive agreement in terms of user satisfaction, the evaluation was mainly positive towards both interfaces and, in particular, for the W/I interface. Perceived usability was also higher for the W/I interface (Table 2).

In terms of individual results, most of the participants had a preferred interface (Fig. 4). This is a key result from this study, since it demonstrates both a difference in user reaction to the interfaces (interface affect) and differences in performance are then also observed (Fig. 5). 21 participants performed differently between the two interfaces, and of these 15 (71%) demonstrated an improved performance in their preferred interface; their mean scores on each interface are compared in Fig. 6.

Table 2. Evaluation of the Interfaces, N=25

		Content	Navigation	Data Types	Layout	User Reactions	Usability
W/I Interface	M	6.5	7.1	7.2	7.1	6.8	78.8%
	SD	1.8	1.9	1.7	1.9	1.4	12.6%
A/V Interface	M	6.5	8.3	7.2	7.1	6.5	76.2%
	SD	2.0	1.1	2.0	2.1	1.9	17.1%

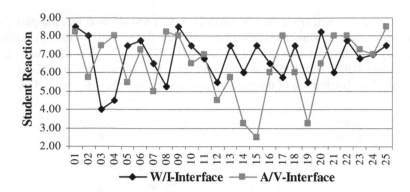

Fig. 4. User Reactions. Presented in order of the Participant's ID. W/I interface: M=6.8, SD=1.4, Max=8.5, Min=4.0. A/V interface: M=6.5, SD=1.9, Max= 8.5, Min=2.5. N=25

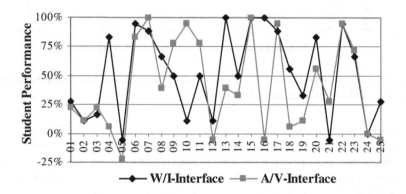

Fig. 5. Individual Performance. W/I interface: M=52%, SD=.369, Max=100%, Min=-5.56%. A/V interface: M=41.11%, SD=.401, Max= 100%, Min= -22.22%. N=25

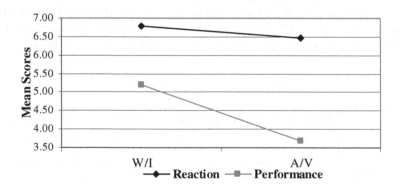

Fig. 6. User reactions and performances compared between the two Interfaces

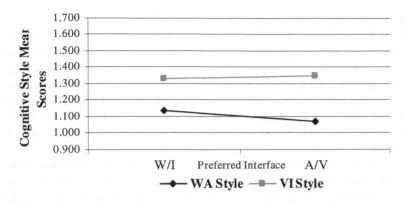

Fig. 7. User cognitive styles compared to their preferred interface condition. NP=No preference

However, as we can see from Fig. 7, no simple relationship between the individuals' cognitive style and their reaction was observed, nor was there a direct relation regarding the individuals' cognitive style and their performance.

5.2 Discussion

We recognize that this is a preliminary study with a relatively small sample and as such, the results cannot be deemed to be statistically significant. However, the results from the present study are quite conclusive as to whether matching the interface design to the learner cognitive style improves learning efficiency

It was speculated that the limited effects observed in earlier studies were due to the fact that single experimental conditions had been used [21], as has been the case for research evaluating the effects of command/menu driven interfaces [3], mode of presentation [23], medium of delivery [11], or Hypertext structure [8]. Conversely, the design of LEARNINT took into account several key characteristics derived from extensive previous research in the field of Cognitive Styles. Nonetheless, once again no simple relationship was observed between cognitive style and interface design preference, or to learning performance.

As was expected, learners responded differently to each experimental condition, reflecting their expressed preferences towards the interfaces used: 24 out of 25 participants expressed a preference for either the W/I interface or the A/V one. Differences were also observed in the learning performance of the participants, 21 performing differently between the two interfaces, 15 (71%) of these performed better in their preferred interface. This implies that students perform better in the interface they react most positively to.

The implications of the findings from this study suggest that performance of individuals is superior in certain interface conditions. The question remains then as to why Cognitive Style does not relate to the user reactions and/or to their performance given different interface designs?

Although several other factors need to be considered in future research, it is possible that the learning strategies developed by each student prevail over their cognitive style. While cognitive style is considered a fixed core characteristic of an individual, researchers also recognize that strategies are developed to deal with learning material which is not initially compatible with their cognitive style. Individual learning strategies are understood as "learning skills, strategies and study orientation displayed by the individual learner" [19]. These vary depending on the nature of the task, and are mainly driven by the experience of the user in terms of familiarity and previous success in such a learning context.

Furthermore, the sample in this study was limited in the distribution of individual cognitive styles. As shown before, 24 participants were of analytic style, and from these 14 of imager style, which might not be truly representative of the student population. Peterson [12] observed in her research a VI style ratio between .8 and 1.0 and a WA ratio between .97 and 1.25 from samples of university students.

Taking these factors into account there is clearly a need to conduct this experiment with a larger sample to verify these results. However, since our results mirror those achieved by previous studies on the relationship of cognitive style to learning performance, there is also a clear need to formally identify those parameters which influence Interface affect and determine their relationship to learning performance.

6 Conclusions

This paper describes an initial study carried out to evaluate the impact of key characteristics of individuals' cognitive style on their learning performance under different interface conditions. Its results contribute to the knowledge base on Cognitive Styles, with emphasis on how individual differences should be considered to construct user models to provide personal, adaptive learning environments.

A small sample of university students participated in the experiment, using the LEARNINT system as test vehicle. The analysis of the data suggests that interface style does have an impact on learners' preferences, which in turn have an impact on their learning performance.

The evidence of this study, supported by previous research projects, suggests little or no impact of cognitive style in learning performance. Conversely, the results indicate that certain features of the interface design and ultimately the adaptive behavior of a learning system can be matched to the user's individual differences in order to facilitate more effective learning. Further work is however required to investigate different and deeper levels of learning in this context, certainly with a greater number of participants and to investigate the contention that individual learning strategies overcome individual cognitive styles while learning.

The current findings clearly have important implications for the design of web-based learning systems as individuals would seem to benefit from using personal, adaptive learning environments designed to match their individual differences, but the mechanism for predictively matching those differences to automated adaptive design are, as yet, unclear.

References

1. Adeboye, K. and Culwin, F: Validation of the Effectiveness of a Confidence Based Multiple Choice Examination System. LTSN Conference. Galway, Ireland (2003) 44-48
2. Atkinson, S.: Cognitive Styles and Computer Aided Learning (CAL): Exploring Designer and User Perspectives. PATT-11 Conference. Haarlem, the Netherlands (2001) 2-14
3. Benyon, D.: Accommodating Individual Differences through an Adaptive User Interface (1993) http://www.dcs.napier.ac.uk/~dbenyon/publ.html
4. Benyon, D.: Employing Intelligence at the Interface (1996, unpublished). http://www.dcs.napier.ac.uk/~dbenyon/publ.html
5. Brusilovsky, P.: Adaptive Hypermedia. User Modeling and User-Adapted Interaction. 11. Kluwer Academic Publishers, Netherlands (2001) 87-110
6. Cristea, A. and De Bra, P.: ODL Education Environments based on Adaptivity and Adaptability. Proceedings of the AACE E-learn 2002 Conference (2002) 232-239
7. Graff, M.: Cognitive Style and Hypertext Structures. In: Hill, J. et al. (eds.): ELSIN 4th Annual Conference. University of Central Lancashire, Preston (1999) 233-242
8. Graff, M.: Assessing Learning from Hypertext: An Individual Differences Perspective. Journal of Interactive Learning Research Vol. 14, Issue 4 (2003) 425-438
9. Lord, D.: ICT supported Multimedia Learning Materials: Catering for Individual Learner Differences. Annual Conference of the British Educational Research Association (1998)
10. Mckenzie, J., Rose, S. and Head, C.: A study of the Relationship between Learning Styles Profiles and Performance on an Online Team-based Collaborative Learning Project. ELSIN 4th Annual Conference. University of Central Lancashire, Preston (1999) 313-332
11. Parkinson, A and Redmond, J.: Do Cognitive Styles Affect Learning Performance in Different Computer Media?. ITiCSE Conference of the ACM. Denmark (2002) 24-26
12. Peterson E. R.: Administration Guide for the Verbal Imagery Cognitive Styles Test and the Extended Cognitive Style Analysis-Wholistic Analytic Test. University of Edinburgh (2003)
13. Peterson E. R., Deary I. J., Austin E. J.: The Reliability of Riding's Cognitive Style Analysis Test. Personality and Individual Differences, 34. Elsevier Science (2003) 881-891
14. Riding, R.J.: Cognitive Styles Analysis. Learning and Training Technology, Birmingham (1991)
15. Riding, R. J.: On the Nature of Cognitive Style. Educational Psychology, 17 (1997) 29-50
16. Riding, R.J. and Cheema, I.: Cognitive Styles: an Overview and Integration. Educational Psychology 11 (1991) 193-215
17. Riding, R.J., and Douglas, G.: The Effect of Cognitive Style and Mode of Presentation on Learning Performance. British Journal of Educational Psychology 63 (1993) 297-307
18. Riding, R.J. and Grimley, M.: Cognitive Style and Learning from Multimedia CD-ROMs in 11-year-old Children. British journal of Educational Technology 30 (1999) 43-56
19. Riding, R.J. and Rayner, G.: Cognitive Styles and Learning Strategies. London: David Fulton Publishers (1998)
20. Triantafillou, E. Pomportsis, A. and Demetriadis, S.: The Design and Formative Evaluation of an Adaptive Educational System Based on Cognitive Styles. Computers and Education, 41. Elsevier Science Publishers, Holland (2003) 87-103.
21. Uruchurtu, E., MacKinnon, L. and Rist, R.J.: Interface Design for Adaptive, Personal Learning Systems. Proceedings of the 18th British HCI Conference. Leeds (2004) 239-240
22. Webster, R.: Interfaces for e-learning: Cognitive Styles and Software Agents for Web-based Learning Support. ASCILITE Annual Conference Proceedings (2001) 559-566
23. Wei, Y.: Verbaliser-Visualiser Learning on a Statistics Training Program. ACM Conference on Human Factors in Computer Systems, CHI 2001. Seattle, Washington (2001) 477-478

Tailored Responses for Decision Support

Terrence Harvey, Sandra Carberry, and Keith Decker

University of Delaware, Newark DE 19716, USA
{harvey, carberry, decker}@cis.udel.edu

Abstract. Individuals differ in the resources that they are willing to ex-
pend on information gathering and on the importance of different kinds
of information. We have developed MADSUM, a system that takes into
account user constraints on resources, the significance of propositions
that might be included in a response, and the user's priorities with respect to resource and content attributes; MADSUM produces a response
tailored to individual users in a decision support setting.

1 Introduction

We have been investigating the design of a decision support system that can
adapt to a user's resource constraints, resource priorities, and content priorities in
a dynamic environment. Our approach employs a multi-attribute utility function
as part of a user model. The utility function weighs the benefit of different
decisions about resource usage and information selection. Our approach provides
a structure in which the priorities of the user can be explicitly represented and
considered in light of the environment (information currently available, the cost
of getting the information, etc.) Furthermore, an agent architecture allows the
system to dynamically respond to changes in the environment or user priorities.

We have applied the MADSUM architecture to decision-support in a financial investment domain, where the system must support a user in making a
buy/don't-buy decision on a single investment. The MADSUM decision making algorithms and the agent hierarchy, communications, and interaction are
domain-independent. Furthermore, MADSUM is easily extendible to new domains with different attributes in its utility function. However, implementation
in a particular domain requires a set of domain-dependent information agents.
For example, tailored decision-support in an investment domain requires domain-
dependent agents that can estimate how significant a particular piece of information will be to the current user, given her current personal and financial status.

2 The User Model

The MADSUM user model has three components: User Attributes, Constraints,
and Utility Function. The User Attributes component of the user model captures
characteristics of the user, including appropriate domain-specific information.
For the financial investment domain, this component of the user model includes
the user's age, salary, expected number of years to retirement, approximate annual expenditures, current investment portfolio, and portfolio allocation goals.
The User Attributes affect the significance of certain pieces of information.

L. Ardissono, P. Brna, and A. Mitrovic (Eds.): UM 2005, LNAI 3538, pp. 164–168, 2005.

The Constraints component of the user model offers the user the option of setting both soft and hard constraints for a given attribute. Soft constraints are attribute values that the user would prefer not be exceeded in constructing a response. These soft constraints affect the utility function, as described below. Hard constraints are values that an attribute *must not* exceed in a response, and are used to pare the search space before utility is calculated.

MADSUM's utility function contains n attribute terms, each consisting of a weight w_i giving the importance of that attribute to the user, a parameter a_{value_i} that is related to the value of the attribute, and a function f_i.

$$Utility = \sum_{i=1}^{n} w_i f_i(a_{value_i})$$

The weights w_i, giving the importance of each attribute to the user, are extracted from the positions of sliders that are manipulated by the user in a graphical user interface. For resource attributes such as length of response or processing time, a_{value_i} is the actual value of the attribute, such as 75 words. On the other hand, information attributes capture propositions that might be presented to the user, and thus for information attributes, a_{value_i} captures the significance of a set of propositions in the environment of the user's personal characteristics and the application domain. We call this approximation *Decision Specificity* or *DS*. Determining DS is a domain-specific task, and thus in the MADSUM architecture, the functions that compute DS are provided by the application designer as part of the domain-specific information agents that propose propositions for inclusion in the response to the user.

In the financial investment domain, we have implemented domain-specific information agents for three categories of information: Risk (the riskiness of an investment), Value (the prospects for the investment gaining in value), and Portfolio (how the investment relates to the individual's portfolio allocation goals). For example, the significance of a proposition from the Portfolio Agent that addresses the relationship of a proposed investment to the user's portfolio allocation goals depends on the extent that the investment would cause the user's portfolio allocation to deviate from his goals, while a proposition that addresses the appropriateness of the investment from an age perspective may depend on how close the user is to retirement.

Each of the functions f_i that appear in the utility function map their parameter a_{value_i} into a utility value between 0 and 1. The particular function f_i that is used determines whether an increasing parameter value increases or decreases utility (and at what rate). For example, $f_{StartPlateauNorm}$ captures instances in which utility remains high over a plateau and then decreases for increasing values of its parameter, and $f_{LinearPlateauEnd}$ captures instances in which utility increases linearly for increasing values of its parameter until a plateau is reached. Our financial investment domain by default uses $f_{StartPlateauNorm}$ for resource attributes and $f_{LinearPlateauEnd}$ for information attributes, but advanced users can select from among MADSUM's full set of predefined utility functions.

The soft constraints entered by the user adapt the utility function f_i by determining its shape. For example, the function $f_{StartPlateauNorm}$ is used by default for the resource attribute of processing time; the soft limit determines where the plateau ends and also the rate of fall in utility after the plateau (the falling portion resembles a normal distribution whose spread is 1/2 the soft limit). This captures the notions that 1) the soft limit on processing time set by the user is the point at which the utility of the response will begin to decrease and 2) the larger the soft limit on processing time, the less severe will be the loss of utility for each second of increased processing time.

3 Agent Architecture

To address the issues of collecting and integrating information from distributed sources into a single text plan, MADSUM is implemented as a hierarchical network of independent agents. The agents bid to provide information for the response; once a highest utility set of bids is selected, the lowest level information agents pass raw information to their parent middle agents, who use the information to generate small text plan trees. As the trees are propagated further up the agent hierarchy, the middle agents assemble them using coherence rules; in doing so, the middle agents first order the text plan trees according to the utility of their highest utility proposition, and the rules for combining trees attempt to assemble larger trees with the higher ranked constituents on the left, so that the higher ranked constituents will appear earlier in the response (subject to coherence constraints). Once an assembled tree is returned to the top-level Presentation agent, it is resolved to text via templates, and the text is presented to the user. A full description of the agent architecture can be found in [2].

4 Adaptive Responses, Implementation, and Evaluation

The MADSUM architecture for adaptive response generation has been implemented and tested in a financial investment domain. The GUI interface of sliders for setting priorities is not yet part of the implemented system, so priority settings are currently entered as numbers. Formal evaluation experiments have validated MADSUM's design, such as MADSUM's strategy of balancing significance and priority in content selection and MADSUM's decisions about order of presentation of propositions.

As examples of responses produced by our system, consider a user who proposes the purchase of 100 shares of stock in IBM. The user model contains personal characteristics of the user, including her current investment portfolio and her portfolio allocation goals. Before proposing the stock purchase, the user has set soft constraints on the length of the response, the cost in dollars of any purchased information, and processing time. She has also indicated the importance she assigns to usage of different resources (length of response, cost, and processing time) and her interest in information that addresses each of the different content categories (investment risk, value, and impact on portfolio allocation).

Figure 1 displays our implemented system's response under different soft constraint and priority settings. In Figure 1a, the soft constraint on length was 75 words and the user placed a higher priority on risk information than on value

1a: Risk metrics indicate IBM has a low debt-equity ratio, suggesting the ability to weather an economic downturn; further, the company has a strong current ratio, indicating good short-term liquidity. In addition, IBM has historically maintained a moderate debt policy, and the stock has maintained a moderate risk profile. On the other hand, from a portfolio perspective you have already exceeded your allocation goal for equities. Value metrics indicate IBM has a price earnings ratio similar to the tech industry average.

1b: Risk metrics indicate IBM has a low debt-equity ratio, suggesting the ability to weather an economic downturn; further, the company has a strong current ratio, indicating good short-term liquidity. On the other hand, from a portfolio perspective you have already exceeded your allocation goal for equities.

1c: Value metrics indicate the stock has a price earnings ratio similar to the tech industry average; on the other hand, from a portfolio perspective you have already exceeded your allocation goal for equities.

Fig. 1. Three responses, derived from different soft constraints and priority settings

and portfolio information. For the responses in Figure 1b and Figure 1c, the soft constraint on length was lowered to 35 words, resulting in the exclusion of some available propositions; the relative priorities on risk, value, and portfolio information were kept the same in Figures 1a and 1b, but were altered in Figure 1c to place a much higher priority on value information than on risk or portfolio information. Due to the 35 word soft constraint on length that was set for the response in Figure 1b, propositions had to be excluded. Since risk was given highest priority, much (but not all) of the risk information was included. However, the high significance of the proposition about the proposed investment's impact on the user's portfolio allocation goals (she had already exceeded her goals for equities such as IBM) caused that proposition to increase the estimated overall utility of a response containing this proposition, and thus it was included despite the length of the resulting response slightly exceeding the soft constraint on length. In Figure 1c, the user's much higher priority for value information resulted in selection of the value proposition, even though it was of lesser significance than other available propositions. In addition, the highly significant proposition about portfolio allocation goals was included in the response. These examples illustrate the system's ability to vary its responses depending on the user's resource constraints, the significance of information, and the priority that the user assigns to different resources and kinds of information content.

5   Related Work

Adaptive systems have been using concepts of utility theory, either informally or formally, to tailor responses so that they take into account the user's preferences. In previous work[1], we used a weighted additive function to reason on a model of user preferences to detect suboptimal solutions and suggest better alternatives during a collaborative dialogue. [3] uses a similar model in ranking candidate flights in a travel domain. The MAUT Machine[5] uses a formal utility function to evaluate products in an electronic catalogue. Moore[4] and Walker[6] use a formal utility function to rank travel and restaurant options respectively, but then other mechanisms are used to identify the actual propositions that are included in the natural language response. While other systems measure the utilities of possible domain outcomes (e.g. the utilities of one purchased item vs. another) and then tailor a message accordingly, MADSUM is the first system to use a formal utility function to evaluate the utility of the message itself. This message utility includes not only a component related to the noteworthiness of a domain outcome, but also message-specific components such as length and time.

6   Conclusion

MADSUM was designed to exploit a user model in the generation of responses that are tailored to the individual user of a decision support system. MADSUM takes into account user constraints on resources, the significance of propositions that might be included in the response, and the user's priorities with respect to resource and content attributes. The output of MADSUM is a tailored response that has the highest estimated utility for the particular user. The MADSUM architecture has been implemented and tested in a financial investment domain, and the system's balancing of significance and priority in content selection and presentation order has been validated at a statistically significant level.

References

1. Elzer, S., Chu-Carroll, J., Carberry, S.: Recognizing and utilizing user preferences in collaborative consultation dialogues. In: Proc. of the Fourth International Conference on User Modeling. (1994) 19–24
2. Harvey, T., Decker, K., Carberry, S.: Multiagent decision support via user modeling. In: Proceedings of the Fourth International Joint Conference on Autonomous Agents and Multi Agent Systems. (2005) To appear.
3. Linden, G., Hanks, S., Lesh, N.: Interactive assessment of user preference models: The automated travel assistant. In: Proc. of the Sixth International Conference on User Modeling. (1997) 67–78
4. Moore, J., Foster, M.E., Lemon, O., White, M.: Generating tailored, comparative descriptions in spoken dialogue. In: Proc. of the International Florida Artificial Intelligence Research Society. (2004)
5. Schmitt, C., Dengler, D., Bauer, M.: Multivariate preference models and decision making with the maut machine. In: Proc. of the Ninth International Conference on User Modeling. (2003) 297–302
6. Walker, M., Whittaker, S., Stent, A., Maloor, P., Moore, J., Johnston, M., Vasireddy, G.: User tailored generation in the match multimodal dialogue system. Cognitive Science **28** (2004) 811–840

Decision Theoretic Dialogue Planning for Initiative Problems

Bryan McEleney and Gregory O'Hare

Department of Computer Science, University College Dublin,
Dublin 4, Ireland
{bryan.mceleney, gregory.o'hare}@ucd.ie

Abstract. The taking of initiative has significance in spoken language dialogue systems and in human-computer interaction. A system that takes no initiative may fail to seize opportunities that are important, but a system that always takes the initiative may not allow the user to take the actions he favours. We have implemented a mixed-initiative planning system that adapts its strategy to a nested belief model. In simulation, the planner's performance was compared to two fixed strategies of always taking the initiative and always declining it, and it performed significantly better than both.

1 Introduction

In cooperative dialogue one agent will consider a goal that cannot be satisfied through his own action. He may choose to act towards it and in doing so both commits to it and reveals his intention to a second agent. Then on the second agent's turn, a cooperative response is considered to satisfy the intention. Symmetrically, the second agent can act towards an intention, again obtaining recognition of his choice and his commitment. Often, the plan is so structured that there is only one option for a cooperative response, but there are also many times when the agent has two or more options. Among these, there are different levels of initiative - the agent might do nothing, he might add the next child act to the focussed goal, he might choose between different children to add, he might move the focus point, or he might introduce a new goal. An agent acting alone may have several options to choose amongst and chooses the one of maximum expected utility. Where there are two agents and a single goal, he must decide whether to act now, or wait for the other agent to decide whether the goal is important enough. Where there are two agents each with different goals, each agent must consider the coordination of their initiative with the other agent's goal. For these decisions, the agent must use a nested belief model to determine how the second agent is expected to respond to his initiative, what initiative will be taken on the third turn as a result of that, and so on. Typically, the agents will have different beliefs, so one agent may believe he should take the initiative while the other may believe he should not, or neither agent will take the initiative even though a goal was worth pursuing. With belief revision at each turn,

L. Ardissono, P. Brna, and A. Mitrovic (Eds.): UM 2005, LNAI 3538, pp. 169–173, 2005.

initiative may surface at different times, even for the same goal. For example, one agent might state that it is opportune to fix the car, which would promote the other agent's latent initiative to go to the shops and buy some tools. As an example of deeply nested initiative, the agent with the idea to fix the car might foresee the second agent's initiative to buy some milk while he is at the shops, so that as the last act in the plan, that they would have a cup of tea. For these problems, we will describe a general purpose dialogue planner that uses deeply nested, probabilistic belief models.

2   Example Problem

The planner has been tested with several initiative problems, where one agent decides upon his own goals, where two agents compete for the same goal, and where two agents decide on a sequence of different goals. Here we present an instance of the second type, a flight booking problem. The system decides whether to offer a passenger a window seat, but is wary that the passenger may not intend to have one, and would be inconvenienced by the conversation. The system's other option is to not offer the seat, and wait for the passenger to take the initiative. The passenger is also unsure whether to take the initiative since his effort will have been wasted if window seats are not available. The plan for this subdialogue is three steps deep, with two sources of variation - the travel agent's belief about the passenger's intention to have a seat, and the travel agent's belief about the passenger's belief about the travel agent having available seats. The performance of the system can be described as a function of these two variables.

A plan library was constructed for use with the planner, from which each belief set in a nested model was populated. A reward of 100 is obtained by a happy passenger, and 65 by passengers who wanted a window seat but ended up without one. A cost of 5 was uniformly assigned to each dialogue act, except for a special act chat, of cost -1, which allows the agents to decline the initiative by chatting about the weather. Lacking empirical data in the domain, these are estimated costs.

3   The Dialogue Planner

The nested belief model of the agent is a quantitative form of the BDI (belief-desire-intention) model [6]. Nested beliefs are probabilistic. At each turn, the belief revision module revises the belief model based on the preconditions and effects of the dialogue act of the last turn. On the agent's turn, the planner decides a dialogue act, using a decision tree. In the tree, there are chance nodes that represent uncertainty about the mental state of the next actor, and choice nodes that represent his options. Figure 1 illustrates the decision tree for our example problem.

Each node of the tree is grown by the plan recogniser. Plan recognition is done recursively, by recognising the tail of the history list, performing a planning step

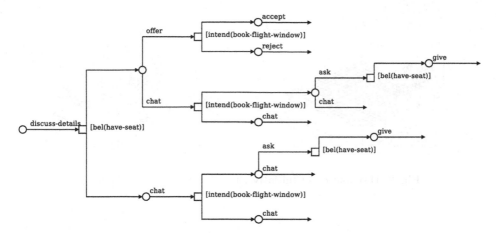

Fig. 1. Decision Tree

at the next level of nesting (in agreement with Pollack [4]), and then filtering the hypotheses that are consistent with the current history item. For example to continue an "ask" act performed at level 3, the planner at level 4 would call the recogniser at level 5 which produces a hypothesis for the first agent's intention. Then, to continue the plan, a forward planning step at level 4 adds a child node to the hypothesis. Planning can be done by both decomposition chaining and goal-effect chaining.

The decision tree is evaluated using an expected utility calculation at each chance node. At choice nodes, each agent chooses the maximum expected utility branch. Both of these calculations are done in the context of the belief model of the choosing agent. For example, the passenger may have one value for a subtree because he believes a seat is available, but the travel agent, believing none is available, has a different value for the same subtree. The planner can calculate utility in both cooperative and self-interested fashions.

4   Results

The system was evaluated by simulation rather than with a human counterpart, since evaluation over a range of belief model states is time-consuming. A similar approach to evaluating initiative strategies is advocated in [2] and [3]. The configuration of the belief model was varied for the evaluation. The first result is the distribution of initiative, shown in figure 2. The initiative rate is high when either the passenger is expected to intend a window seat, or when the passenger believes that a window seat is available. The left-hand plot represents the initiative distribution of the travel agent, whereas the right hand plot represents that of the passenger. Notice how the travel agent backs off when he believes that the passenger will pick up the initiative in the next turn, and that nobody takes the initiative when both variables have low values.

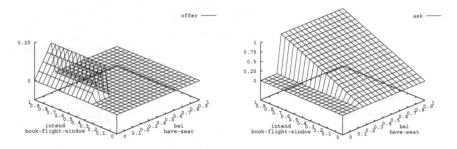

Fig. 2. Distribution of Initiative: (a) Travel Agent (b) Passenger

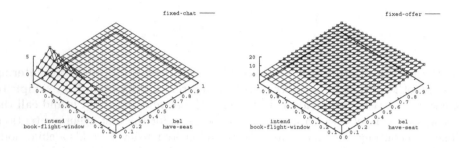

Fig. 3. Utility Gain over Fixed Strategies (a) Always Decline (b) Always Take

The second result for the system is its performance. We plotted the difference between the utility of the system and the two fixed initiative strategies of always declining the initiative (fixed-chat) and always taking it (fixed-offer). To do this, we modified the planner to prune all but the desired strategy from the relevant choice node. Figure 3 shows the results. On the left, the planner always beats the fixed-chat strategy, and by as much as 4.60 units at [1,0.2]. This is a good fraction of the length of the longest dialogue in the decision tree, which is [chat,ask,give], of length 15 units. The gain is similar for the fixed-offer strategy with a margin of as much as 12.0 units at [0,1]. Similar margins have been found across our battery of sample problems.

5   Discussion

An early approach to initiative planning was that of Smith and Hipp [5], in which a theorem prover constructs plans, employing a user model to plan subdialogues for obstacle subgoals. The planner could select between initiative modes, but it was not quantitative, and did not use a nested model. Recently, Fleming and Cohen [1] discussed a decision-theoretic approach to initiative that is similar to our own, but do not provide an implemented general purpose planner, nor do they use a nested model. There have also been two notable computer simulation studies in dialogue initiative. Guinn [2] used a quantitative negotiation system with a user model to decide between continuations to a plan, but did not use this approach to plan beyond the current move. Ishizaki et al [3] examined a map-following task and found that mixed initiative dialogue can reduce utility. However their system used an initiative policy rather than adapting to the plan and user at hand.

The results for our system are encouraging but presuppose a wide variation of belief model configurations in the dialogue system's lifetime. Otherwise, a fixed strategy is just as good. The system must have a dynamic model of the user available. This could be provided, or, using the belief revision module, the system could automatically update stereotypes as dialogue evidence accumulates. The computational demands of the system are light, with just a handful of simple calculations and comparisons performed in evaluating the decision tree. It is easy to compile the tree evaluation function to a procedural programming language. It takes little time to configure a plan library for use with a new problem. We are extending our battery of problems to widen the scope of our results.

6 Conclusion

We have evaluated a dialogue planner that decides initiative by adapting to a probabilistic nested belief model. In simulation, the planner performed better than otherwise equivalent fixed initiative planners.

References

1. Fleming, M., Cohen, R.: A User Modeling Approach to Determining System Initiative in Mixed-Initiative AI Systems. Proceedings of the Eighth International Conference of User Modelling (2001) 54–63
2. Guinn, C.: An Analysis of Initiative Selection in Collaborative Task-Oriented Dialogue. User Modelling and User Adapted Interaction 8(3-4) (1998) 255–314
3. Ishizaki, M., Crocker, M., Mellish, C.: Exploring Mixed-Initiative Dialogue Using Computer Dialogue Simulation. User Modelling and User Adapted Interaction 9 (1999) 79–91
4. Pollack, M.: A Model of Plan Inference that Distinguishes between the Belief of Actors and Observers. Proceedings of the 24th Conference of the Association of Computational Linguistics (1986) 207–214
5. Smith, R., Hipp, R., Biermann A.: A Dialogue Control Algorithm and its Performance. Proceedings of the Third Conference on Applied Natural Language Processing (1992) 9–16
6. Rao, A., Georgeff, M.: Modelling Rational Agents within a BDI architecture. Proceedings of the Second Conference on Knowledge Representation and Reasoning (1991) 473–484

A Semi-automated Wizard of Oz Interface for Modeling Tutorial Strategies

Paola Rizzo[1], Hyokyeong Lee[2], Erin Shaw[2], W. Lewis Johnson[2],
Ning Wang[2], and Richard E. Mayer[3]

[1] Dept. of Computer Science, University of Rome "La Sapienza"
Via Salaria 113, 00198 Rome, Italy
paola.rizzo@uniroma1.it
[2] Information Sciences Institute, University of Southern California
4676 Admiralty Way, Marina del Rey, CA 90292 USA
{hlee, shaw, johnson, ning}@isi.edu
[3] Dept. of Psychology, University of California,
Santa Barbara, CA, 93106-9660 USA
mayer@psych.ucsb.edu

Abstract. Human teaching strategies are usually inferred from transcripts of face-to-face conversations or computer-mediated dialogs between learner and tutor. However, during natural interactions there are no constraints on the human tutor's behavior and thus tutorial strategies are difficult to analyze and reproduce in a computational model. To overcome this problem, we have realized a Wizard of Oz interface, which by constraining the tutor's interaction makes explicit his decisions about why, how, and when to assist the student in a computer-based learning environment. These decisions automatically generate natural language utterances of different types according to two "politeness" strategies. We have successfully used the interface to model tutorial strategies.

1 Introduction

The typical approach to modeling human teaching strategies for realizing Intelligent Tutoring Systems (ITSs) and Interactive Learning Environments (ILEs) is twofold. First, one records the interactions taking place between the tutor and student in a natural setting or computer-mediated interface; then, the transcripts are analyzed to find effective teaching patterns, which are reproduced in a computational model that constitutes the basis of an artificial tutor. This approach has some shortcomings: analyzing videotaped interactions is difficult and time consuming, and the results depend on the reliability of the raters. Furthermore, the only perceivable outputs from the tutors are their utterances and non-verbal behaviors: one cannot access their teaching strategies other than by interviewing, a method that shares the typical shortcomings of indirect analyses of cognitive processes. This makes it hard to reproduce tutoring strategies within a computational model.

In order to efficiently model human tutoring strategies, we propose that the tutors use a semi-automated Wizard of Oz interface which forces them to take explicit and

L. Ardissono, P. Brna, and A. Mitrovic (Eds.): UM 2005, LNAI 3538, pp. 174–178, 2005.
© Springer-Verlag Berlin Heidelberg 2005

visible pedagogical decisions, and that automatically outputs those decisions as natural language utterances. This approach has three advantages: (a) the tutor's behavior can be analyzed much faster than transcripts and videotapes; (b) the pedagogical decisions can be easily correlated with student performance; and (c) the natural language generator can be tested for coverage and robustness.

We have realized a Wizard of Oz interface (WozUI, Fig. 1) that enables a human tutor to communicate with a student by selecting a pedagogical goal, choosing an object of discourse, and applying a communicative act to it. As a learning environment we use the Virtual Factory Teaching System (VFTS) [5], a web-based factory modeling and simulation system. The tutor can view the learner's screen activities in the VFTS, using MS NetMeeting, and exchange messages with the learner. An animated puppet speaks the comments sent by the experimenter, using text-to-speech software.

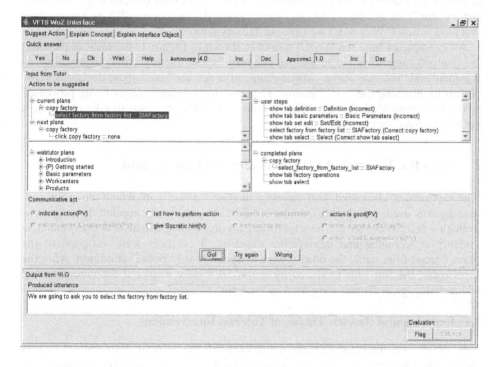

Fig. 1. Wizard of Oz interface

In order to track tutor decisions about why, what, and when to communicate with the student in the VFTS, the WozUI: (a) models the student, thanks to a plan recognizer that tracks the student's actions, and a "Web tutor" that traces the tutorial paragraphs visible to the student at any time [12], as shown in the four upper windows; and (b) embodies a model of the strategies that the tutor performs. In fact, the lower part of the WozUI enables the tutor to select a communicative act categorized according to one of the following pedagogical goals, taken from the taxonomy of pedagogical objectives proposed by Bloom and coworkers [3, 1]. *Application*: indicate an action to perform, indicate an action to perform and explain its reason, tell how to perform an action, give a Socratic hint (i.e. a cue about an action to perform). *Knowledge*: suggest to re-read a passage of the tutorial, explain a paragraph of the tutorial, provide an example for a paragraph of the tutorial. *Motivation*: tell the student that the action he has performed is good, tell the student that the action he has performed is good and describe its effect.

Together with other authors [2, 10], we are particularly interested in modeling human tutors' ability to take not only cognitive, but also affective student goals into account, according to the Politeness Theory proposed by Brown & Levinson [4]. Therefore we have realized a natural language generator (NLG), coupled with a Politeness Module, that transforms tutor communicative acts into utterances with several levels of politeness [8]. For example, a suggestion to perform an action, such as saving the current factory description, can be stated either directly (e.g., "Save the factory now"), or as a hint, ("Do you want to save the factory now?"), as a suggestion of a joint action ("Why don't we save our factory now?"), etc.

An example of how the WozUI works is shown in Figure 1: the tutor is pursuing the goal of suggesting an action; he chooses "select factory from factory list" as argument and "indicate action" as communicative act, and sends these decisions to the system by pressing the "Go!" button. The resulting utterance (after being processed by the Politeness Module), shown at the bottom, is: "We are going to ask you to select the factory from factory list".

2   Using the Wizard of Oz Interface: An Experiment

The experiment compared two tutoring modes: "direct", in which no politeness strategy was used; and "polite", where the NLG automatically applied the politeness strategies described above. The experiment involved 10 graduate and undergraduate students in technical and engineering domains: 5 of them were assigned to the "direct" condition, while the other 5 were assigned to the "polite" condition. After the experiment, the log files produced by the WozUI were analyzed for understanding which pedagogical criteria were used by the tutor.

2.1   Experimental Results: Timing of Tutorial Interventions

First of all, we analyzed the average timing of the tutorial interventions across subjects, by observing whether they were more proactive (spontaneous) or reactive (in response to student questions), both in the direct vs polite conditions and in general ("Direct + Polite"). There were slightly more proactive than reactive interventions, but the difference is not statistically significant ($t(8) = 0.58$, $p = 0.57$).

2.2   Experimental Results: Types of Tutorial Interventions

Secondly, we analyzed the average number of tutor interventions across subjects, according to the pedagogical strategies described above. The results showed that the tutor using the WozUI was pursuing the same pedagogical goals pursued by the other human tutor in a natural setting as described in [7]: in fact, the Wizard tutor provided suggestions for actions more often than providing positive feedback, and more often than explaining concepts. The difference between the number of "Application" interventions and the number of "Knowledge" interventions is statistically significant ($t(8) = 3.59$, $p = 0.007$).

2.3 Experimental Results: Types of Communicative Acts

We also analyzed the communicative acts selected within the most frequently chosen pedagogical goal (Application), in both the polite and direct mode. The two most used communicative acts were "Indicate action" and "Tell how to perform action", which are more short and explicit in telling the student what to do with respect to the "Socratic hint" and the "Indicate action & explain reason" acts. The difference between interventions of type "Indicate action" and "Tell how to perform action" is statistically significant ($t(8) = 5.33$, $p = 0.0007$). A possible reason for the larger use of concise communicative acts might be that the learning task is not very difficult, and therefore the student just needs some simple help when he seems unsure about how to operate the VFTS interface. However, another hypothesis might explain this result simply as a preference of the tutor towards given types of communicative act.

3 Related Work

While most WozUIs require the Wizard to type free text in computer-based dialogs with learners, a few examples exist where the experimenter has to produce utterances by using a limited set of options that produce canned text [6, 9]. However, a number of differences between their and our approach can be found: (a) in the other cases a domain-dependent script predefines the possible interactions with the student, while in our case the interactions between tutor and student are much less constrained; (b) the goals of the interactions, when modeled, are usually domain dependent, rather than related to a more general pedagogical taxonomy like Bloom's one; and (c) the other WozUIs do not allow to parameterize the tutor's utterances according to features like politeness.

Regarding affect, motivation and politeness in learning environments and in human-computer interaction, a number of other works have been referenced and compared with our approach in [8, 12].

4 Conclusion and Future Work

The semi-automated Wizard of Oz technique made it possible to analyze the experimental results very rapidly and systematically. If we had not employed this approach, it would have been necessary to annotate the dialogs manually. In comparison, we have found in the past that post-hoc dialog markup is time consuming, and raises the possibility of inter-rater reliability problems. We are currently analyzing the data coming from another experiment with more subjects, so as to see observe the robustness and generalizability of our current findings.

Regarding the usability of the WozUI, apparently the tutor did not find the interface difficult to use, nor overly constraining: before running the experiment, a pilot study showed that the human tutor was able to monitor the student's activities and quickly react to them. The experiment results also seem to show that working through the interface did not bias the tutor's behavior: in fact the frequencies of tutor interventions were analogous to those observed in the natural setting. Anyway, we also plan to carry out a more formal usability analysis of the WozUI.

References

1. Anderson, L. W., Krathwohl, D. R., Airasian, P. W., Cruikshank, K. A., Mayer, R. E., Pintrich, P. R., Raths, J., & Wittrock, M. C.: A taxonomy of learning, teaching, and assessing: A revision of Bloom's taxonomy of educational objectives. Longman, New York (2001)
2. André, E. Rehm, M., Minker, W. & Bühner, D.: Endowing spoken language dialogue systems with emotional intelligence. In E André et al. (Eds.): Affective Dialogue Systems: Tutorial and Research Workshop, ADS 2004. Springer, Berlin (2004) 178-187
3. Bloom, B.S. (ed.): Taxonomy of educational objectives: The classification of educational goals. Handbook I: cognitive domain. Longman, London (1956)
4. Brown, P. & Levinson, S.C.: Politeness: Some universals in language use. Cambridge University Press, New York (1987)
5. Dessouky, M.M., Verma, S., Bailey, D., & Rickel, J.: A methodology for developing a Web-based factory simulator for manufacturing education. IEE Trans. 33 (2001) 167-180
6. Fiedler A.., Gabsdil M., Horacek H.: A tool for supporting progressive refinement of Wizard of Oz experiments in natural language. In: Lester, J.C., Vicari, R. M., Paraguacu, F. (eds.): Intelligent Tutoring Systems: 7th International Conference, ITS 2004. Springer, Berlin (2004) 325-335
7. Johnson, W.L., Rizzo, P.: Politeness in tutoring dialogs: 'Run the factory, that's what I'd do'. In: Lester, J.C., Vicari, R. M., Paraguacu, F. (eds.): Intelligent Tutoring Systems: 7th International Conference, ITS2004. Springer (Lecture Notes in Computer Science, Vol. 3220), Berlin (2004) 67-76
8. Johnson, W.L., Rizzo, P., Bosma W., Kole S., Ghijsen M., Welbergen H.: Generating Socially Appropriate Tutorial Dialog. In In E André et al. (Eds.): Affective Dialogue Systems: Tutorial and Research Workshop, ADS 2004. Springer, Berlin (2004) 254-264
9. Kim J. K. & Glass M.: Evaluating dialogue schemata with the Wizard of Oz computer-assisted algebra tutor. In: Lester, J.C., Vicari, R. M., Paraguacu, F. (eds.): Intelligent Tutoring Systems: 7th International Conference, ITS2004. Springer (Lecture Notes in Computer Science, Vol. 3220), Berlin (2004) 358-367
10. Porayska-Pomsta, K.: Influence of Situational Context on Language Production. Ph.D. thesis, University of Edinburgh (2004)
11. Qu, L., Wang, N., & Johnson, W.L.: Pedagogical Agents that Interact with Learners. In: Proceedings of the Workshop on Embodied Conversational Agents: Balanced Perception and Action, Third International Conference on Autonomous Agents and Multi-Agent Systems (AAMAS 2004). New York (2004) 42-50
12. Wang N., Johnson L.W., Rizzo P., Shaw E., Mayer R.E.: Experimental Evaluation of Polite Interaction Tactics for Pedagogical Agents. In: International Conference on Intelligent User Interfaces. ACM Press, New York (2005) 12-19

Generating Artificial Corpora for Plan Recognition

Nate Blaylock[1] and James Allen[2]

[1] Saarland University, Saarbrücken, Germany
blaylock@coli.uni-sb.de
[2] University of Rochester, Rochester, New York, USA
james@cs.rochester.edu

Abstract. Corpora for training plan recognizers are scarce and difficult to gather from humans. However, corpora could be a boon to plan recognition research, providing a platform to train and test individual recognizers, as well as allow different recognizers to be compared. We present a novel method for generating artificial corpora for plan recognition. The method uses a modified AI planner and Monte-Carlo sampling to generate action sequences labeled with their goal and plan. This general method can be ported to allow the automatic generation of corpora for different domains.

1 Introduction

Over the past 10+ years, many fields in AI have started to employ corpus-based machine learning techniques. Plan recognition, however, seems to have lagged behind. For example, we are only aware of a few plan recognizers [2, 5, 8, 9] (the last two are our own) that are trained on corpora. We believe a major reason for this is the lack of appropriate corpora for plan recognition (which we will term *plan corpora*).

It is not that the field could not make use of plan corpora. Besides the machine-learning based systems mentioned above, many plan recognizers ([7, 10, 12, 17], inter alia) make use of probabilities, but only briefly mention (if at all) how such probabilities could be discovered.[1] Additionally, corpora could be used to evaluate the performance of a plan recognizer, or even compare performance across recognizers (something which, as far as we are aware, has never been done).

In this paper we present a general method for automatically generating labeled plan corpora. In Section 2, we present possible ways of getting plan corpora from human sources and discuss their disadvantages. Then in Section 3 we introduce our method for artificially generating corpora and show an example in Section 4. We then discuss some general issues in Section 5. Finally, in Section 6, we discuss related work and in Section 7, we conclude and mention future work.

---

[1] A notable exception is [4].

L. Ardissono, P. Brna, and A. Mitrovic (Eds.): UM 2005, LNAI 3538, pp. 179–188, 2005.

2   Human Sources of Plan Corpora

In this section, we mention several plausible ways of gathering plan corpora by observing humans. These can be divided into the kind of data that they make available: unlabeled, goal labeled, and plan labeled data. We discuss each in turn and then discuss the general difficulties of gathering human data.

2.1   Unlabeled Data

There are several techniques used in related fields for gathering unlabeled data, which could be useful for plan recognition.

Several projects in ubiquitous computing [3, 16] have gathered raw data of a user's state over time (location and speed from GPS data) which they use to predict user activity. Plan recognizers, however, typically take action streams as input.

Davison and Hirsh [11] collected a corpus of over 168,000 Unix commands by observing 77 users over a period of 2-6 months. The corpus consists of timestamped sequences of commands (stripped of arguments) as automatically recorded by the history mechanism of tcsh. It is unclear how useful such unlabeled data would be by itself for plan recognition (although Bauer [6] has done work on using such data to automatically construct recipe libraries).

2.2   Goal-Labeled Data

Much more useful to plan recognition are goal-labeled plan corpora, although such corpora are even harder to come by.

Albrecht et al. [2] extract a plan corpus from the logs of a Multi-User Dungeon (MUD) game. A log includes a sequence of both player location (within the game) as well as each command executed. In addition, the MUD records each successful quest completion, which can be used to automatically tag plan sessions with a top-level goal (as well as partial state with the user's location). Albrecht et al. report that the corpus data is quite noisy: first because of player errors and typos, and also because players in MUDs often interleave social interaction and other activities. We should also note that the goals in the corpus are atomic, as opposed to being parameterized goal schemas.

More tightly-controlled goal-labeled corpora have been gathered through data collection efforts in the Unix [14] and Linux [9] domains. In these experiments, test subjects are given a specific goal, such as "find a file that ends in .tex", and their shell commands are recorded as they try to accomplish the goal. The subjects then report when they have successfully accomplished the goal (as there is no way to easily compute this automatically).

In these controlled experiments, goal labeling is much more reliable because it is assigned a priori. Of course, this work can still be noisy, as when the subject misunderstands the goal, or incorrectly believes he has accomplished it. Also, this kind of data collection is expensive as compared to those mentioned above. The above-mentioned data collections monitor the normal activity of subjects, whereas these types of collections require subjects to work on tasks specifically for the collection.

2.3   Plan-Labeled Data

Of course, the most useful type of plan corpus would include not only the top-level goal, but also the plan and situation.

Bauer [5] records user action sequences (and corresponding system state) in an email program and uses a plan recognizer post hoc to label them with the appropriate goal and plan. This post hoc recognition can potentially be much more accurate than online prediction, because it is able to look at the whole execution sequence. A potential problem we see with this approach is that if the original plan recognizer consistently makes mistakes in predicting plans, these mistakes will be propagated in the corpus. This includes cases where the plan library does not cover extra or erroneous user actions.

2.4   General Challenges for Human Plan Corpora

In addition to the individual disadvantages mentioned above, we see several shortcomings to this kind of human data collection for plan recognition.

First, this kind of data collection is most feasible in domains (like operating systems) where user actions can be directly observed and automatically recorded. This, unfortunately, excludes most non-software interaction domains. In fact, the only way we can envision to gather data for other domains would be to have it annotated by hand, which could be expensive and time-consuming (not to mention error-prone).

Finally, a major shortcoming of the above work is that it is at most labeled with a top-level goal.[2] In most domains where plan recognition is used (e.g., natural language understanding), the system can benefit not only from the prediction of a top-level goal, but also partial results where a subgoal is predicted. This is especially true of domains with plans composed of large action sequences, where the top-level goal may not become apparent until very far into the plan's execution. We imagine that manual annotation of plan labeling would be quite tedious and error prone.

3   Artificial Corpus Generation

In contrast to human data collection, we propose the use of an AI planner and Monte-Carlo simulation to stochastically generate *artificial* plan corpora. This method can be used for any domain and provides a corpus accurately labeled with goal and hierarchical plan structure. It also provides a cheap way to produce the kind of large corpora needed for machine learning. The method is as follows:

1. We modify an AI planner to search for valid plans non-deterministically.
2. We model the desired domain for the planner.
3. The algorithm does the following to generate each item in the corpus:

---

[2] Except for [5], although, as we mention above, the corpus can be skewed by the original recognizer's mistakes.

(a) Stochastically generates a goal
(b) Stochastically generates a start state
(c) Uses the planner to find a valid plan for generated goal and start state

We first describe our modifications to an AI planner. Then we discuss issues of domain modeling. We then discuss stochastic generation of the goal and then of the start state. Finally, we discuss the characteristics of corpora generated by this process.

3.1   Planner Modification

For plan recognition, we want to create corpora which allow for all possible plans in the domain. Typical AI planners do not support this, as they usually deterministically return the same plan for a given goal and start state. Many planners also try to optimize some plan property (like length or cost) and therefore would never output longer, less optimal plans. We want to include all possible plans in our corpus to give us broad coverage.

We, therefore, modified the SHOP2 planner [15] to randomly generate one of the set of all possible plans for a given goal and start state.[3] We did this by identifying key decisions points in the planner and randomizing the order that they were searched.

SHOP2 [15] is a sound and complete hierarchical transition network (HTN) planner. SHOP2 is novel in that it generates plan steps in the order they will be executed, which allows it to handle complex reasoning capabilities like axiomatic inference and calls to external programs. It also allows partially ordered subtasks. The planning model in SHOP2 consists of *methods* (decomposable goals), *operators* (atomic actions), and *axioms* (facts about the state).

In searching the state space, there are three types of applicable decisions points, which represent branches in the search space:[4]

– Which (sub)goal to work on next
– Which method to use for a goal
– Which value to bind to a parameter

In order to provide for completeness, SHOP2 keeps lists of all possibilities for a decision point so that it may backtrack if necessary. We modified the planner so that these lists are randomized after they are populated but before they are used. This one-time randomization guarantees that we search in a random order but also allows us to preserve the soundness and completeness of the algorithm. We believe the randomized version is equivalent to computing all valid plans and randomly choosing one.

---

[3] In principle, the corpus generation technique described here is possible using any planner. The only caveat is that the planner must be randomized, which may or may not be a straightforward thing to do. One of the reasons we chose SHOP2 was its small code base and a modular design that was amenable to randomization.

[4] There is also a fourth which deals with :immediate tasks, but that is beyond the scope of this paper.

3.2   Domain Modeling

Each new domain must be modeled for the planner, just as it would if the intent were to use the planner for its usual purpose. As opposed to modeling for plan generation, however, care should be taken to model the domain such that it can encompass all anticipated user plans.

Usually the planning model must be written by hand, although work has been done on (semi-)automating the process (e.g., [6]). Note that, in addition to the model of the plan library, which is also used in many plan recognizers, it is also necessary to model state information for the planner.

3.3   Goal Generation

We separate goal generation into two steps: generating the goal schema and generating parameter values for the schema.

Goal Schema Generation. In addition to the domain model for the planner, the domain modeler needs to provide a list of possible top-level goals in the domain, together with their a priori probability. A priori probabilities of goals are usually not known, but they could be estimated by the domain modeler's intuitions (or perhaps by a small human corpus). The algorithm uses this list to stochastically picks one of the goal schemas.

Goal Parameter Value Generation. In domains where goals are modeled with parameters, the values of the parameters must also be generated.

Goal parameter values can be generated by using one of two techniques. For goal schemas where the parameter values are more or less independent, the domain modeler can give a list of possible parameter values for each slot, along with their a priori probabilities. For schemas where parameter values are not independent, each possible set of parameter is given, along with their probabilities.

Once the goal schema has been chosen, the algorithm uses this lists to stochastically generate values for each parameter in the schema. At this point, a fully-instantiated goal has been generated.

3.4   Start State Generation

In addition to a top-level goal, planners also need to know the state of the world — the start state. In order to model agent behavior correctly, we need to stochastically generate start states, as this can have a big effect on the plan an agent chooses.

Generating the start state is not as straightforward as goal generation for several reasons. First, in all but the simplest domains, it will not be feasible to enumerate all possible start states (let alone to assign them a priori probabilities). Second, in order to make the planning fast, we need to generate a start state from which the generated goal is achievable. Practically, most planners (including SHOP2) are **very slow** when given an impossible goal, as they must search through all of the search space before they notice that the goal is impossible.

For these reasons, only a start state which makes the generated goal achievable should be generated. Unfortunately, we know of no general way of doing this.[5] We do believe, however, that some general techniques can be used for start state generation. We discuss these here. The approach we have chosen is to separate the state model into two parts: fixed and variable. In the *fixed* part, we represent all facts about the state that should be constant across sessions. This includes such things as fixed properties of objects and fixed facts about the state (for example, the existence of certain objects, the location of cities, and so on).

The *variable* part of the state contains those facts which should be stochastically generated. Even with the fixed/variable separation, this part will probably not be a set of independent stochastically generated facts. Instead, the domain modeler must come up with code to do this, taking into account, among other things, domain objects, their attributes, and other states of the world. It is likely that values of sets of facts will need to be decided simultaneously, especially in cases where they are mutually exclusive, or one implies another, etc. This will also likely need to be closely linked to the actual goal which has been generated to ensure achievability.

3.5   The Resulting Corpus

A corpus generated by the process described above will contain a complex distribution of plan sessions. This distribution results from the interaction between (a) the a priori probabilities of top-level goals, (b) the probabilities of top-level goal parameter values, (c) the algorithm for generating start states, and (d) information encoded in the plan library itself. Thus, although it cannot be used to compute the a priori probabilities of top-level goals and parameter values (which are given as input to the generator), it can be used to e.g., model the probabilities of subgoals and atomic actions in the domain. This is information which cannot be learned directly from the plan library, since the recipes and variable fillers used are also dependent on e.g., the start state.

4   An Example: The Emergency Response Domain

We have created a domain model in an emergency response domain and used it to generate an artificial corpus. The domain includes such goals as setting up a temporary shelter and providing medical attention to victims. The coded domain consists of 10 top-level goal schemas, 46 methods and 30 operators. The plan library coded in a fairly common way and does not merit any further discussion here. For the rest of this section we discuss the generation of goals and start states in order to illustrate what may be needed in moving to a new domain (in addition to the creation of a plan library).

---

[5] One possibility might be backchaining from the goal state, although we have not explored this.

4.1   Goal and Start State Generation

As mentioned above, the domain includes 10 goal schemas which are specially marked as top-level goals (the difference is not specified in SHOP2 itself). In addition, we added a priori probabilities to each of the goal schemas.

The goal schema was chosen based on those probabilities as discussed above. The schema is then passed to a function which generates the parameter values and the start state simultaneously. In particular, we start with the fixed start state, then stochastically generate locations for movable objects, and then generate other domain facts based on goal schema specific code. We mention these in order here.

Fixed State. The fixed state consists mostly of fixed locations (such as towns and hospitals), objects and their properties. It also includes inference rules supported in SHOP2 which represent things like object types and properties (e.g., adult(x) $\Rightarrow$ can-drive(x)).

Object Locations. As part of the variable state, we define a set of *movable* objects. They are movable in the sense that we wanted to randomly choose where they were located (such as ambulances and workers). We define a list of *sets* of objects, for which it is not important *where* they are located, but only that all objects in the set are in the same location (such as a vehicle and its driver). We also define a list of possible locations, which is used to generate a random location for each object set. (Note, we ensure in the fixed state that locations are fully connected so we don't have to worry about goal impossibility at this step.)

Goal Schema Specific. The rest of the state is created, together with parameter values, in goal schema specific functions. In the emergency domain these were typically very simple, usually just determining which object to use for parameter values.

An example of a more complicated example is that of the goal schema of clearing a road wreck, which takes a wrecked car as a parameter. As we do not model the set of all possible cars in the world, we automatically generate a unique car object as well as its necessary properties (e.g., that it's wrecked, its location, etc.) Note that in cases where extra properties are generated, these are also stochastically generated from a priori probabilities (e.g., whether or not the roads are snowy).

5   Discussion

In this section, we raise several issues about the utility of artificial generation of plan corpora versus the collection of human plan corpora. As we have just begun to generate and use such corpora, we do not believe we are in a position to definitively answer these. Rather, we raise the questions and give some initial thoughts, which we hope can lead to a discussion in the plan recognition community. The questions treat three general areas: the effort needed to generate artificial corpora; the accuracy of such corpora; and the general power of the technique.

Effort. Obviously, the technique we describe above requires a certain amount of work. Minimally, one needs to create a plan library as well as an algorithm for generating start states. Plan library creation is known to be difficult and is a problem for the planning community in general (cf. [6]). This may not be a unique problem to artificial corpora, however, as a plan library would likely be necessary anyway in hand-labeling human corpora. Start state generation is also not trivial, although in our experience, it was much less work than the building the plan library.

The main question which needs to be answered here is how the effort to create the machinery for generating an artificial plan corpus compares to the effort needed to gather and annotate a human corpus. Before we can answer this, we not only need more experience in generating artificial corpora, but also experience in producing human corpora - especially plan-labeled corpora.

Accuracy. Another point is how accurately an artificial corpus can model human behavior. Ideally, to test this, one would want to gather a human corpus and independently generate an artificial corpus in the same domain and then make some sort of comparison. Of course, care must be taken here, as we suspect that the accuracy of an artificial corpus will be highly-dependent on the plan library as well as the algorithm for generating start states. Another, more practical, evaluation would be the comparison of the performance of a plan recognizer on human data when it has been trained on artificial data versus human data.

Power. Another question is in which situations an artificial corpus could be successfully used to approximate human behavior. The technique presented here makes the simplifying assumption (which is also present in most plan recognizers) that the agent first creates an entire plan and then executes it, and that each action is successfully executed. This obviously will not work well in domains where this is not the case. In future work, we would like to adapt this technique to use an artificial agent instead of a planner, to plan and simulate execution of the plan in creating a corpus. This would allow us to simulate such phenomena as action failure, replanning, and so forth. In general, we believe that the techniques reported here can build on existing work in agents in modeling human behavior and can be useful in most domains of interest in plan recognition.

6   Related Work

Conceptually, our work is based on work in NLP which uses grammars to stochastically generate artificial corpora for training language models for speech recognition [13]. Of course, there are many differences in methodology. Surface string generation from a stochastic grammar typically assumes no context (state), whereas state is very important in plan recognition. Also, in surface string generation, there is no "goal" which restricts acceptable output.

Probably the closest work to our own in the plan recognition field was done by Lesh [14], who uses the Toast reactive planer [1] to generate action sequences given a goal. However, none of the generation process was stochastic. It appears that goals were hand-generated, the state was constant, and the planner was not modified to make decisions non-deterministically, meaning that it would always produce the same action sequence given the same set of goals.

7   Conclusions and Future Work

We have presented a novel technique for generating corpora for plan recognizers. We combine the rich representation of an AI planner with Monte-Carlo sampling to generate corpora of action sequences tagged with goal and plan. Also, as it is artificially generated, it is easy to produce a very large corpus.

In future work, we want to move beyond just plans, and model an actual agent. We believe this would allow us to more closely model agents that we would want to perform plan recognition on, and would include phenomena such as plan failure and replanning. This corpus generation method would allow us to have access to this additional information (when an action failed, when replanning occurs, etc.), which would not be readily available from hand-annotated human data.

Acknowledgments

We would like to thank the anonymous reviewers for their comments and especially bringing up some of the issues discussed in Section 5.

This material is based upon work supported by a grant from DARPA under grant number F30602-98-2-0133; two grants from the National Science Foundation under grant number IIS-0328811 and grant number E1A-0080124; and the TALK project. Any opinions, findings, and conclusions or recommendations expressed in this material are those of the authors and do not necessarily reflect the views of the above-mentioned organizations.

References

1. Agre, P., Horswill, I.: Cultural support for improvisation. In: Proceedings of the Tenth National Conference on Artificial Intelligence (AAAI). (1992)
2. Albrecht, D.W., Zukerman, I., Nicholson, A.E.: Bayesian models for keyhole plan recognition in an adventure game. User Modeling and User-Adapted Interaction 8 (1998) 5–47
3. Ashbrook, D., Starner, T.: Using GPS to learn significant locations and predict movement across multiple users. Personal and Ubiquitous Computing 7 (2003)
4. Bauer, M.: Quantitative modeling of user preferences for plan recognition. In: UM, Hyannis, Massachusetts (1994)
5. Bauer, M.: Acquisition of user preferences for plan recognition. In: Proceedings of the Fifth International Conference on User Modeling, Kailua-Kona, Hawaii (1996)
6. Bauer, M.: Acquisition of abstract plan descriptions for plan recognition. In: Proceedings of the Fifteenth National Conference on Artificial Intelligence (AAAI-98), Madison, WI (1998) 936–941

7. Bui, H.H., Venkatesh, S., West, G.: Policy recognition in the Abstract Hidden Markov Model. Journal of Artificial Intelligence Research **17** (2002) 451–499

8. Blaylock, N., Allen, J.: Corpus-based, statistical goal recognition. In: IJCAI, Acapulco, Mexico (2003)

9. Blaylock, N., Allen, J.: Statistical goal parameter recognition. In: ICAPS, Whistler, British Columbia (2004)

10. Charniak, E., Goldman, R.P.: A Bayesian model of plan recognition. Artificial Intelligence **64** (1993) 53–79

11. Davison, B.D., Hirsh, H.: Predicting sequences of user actions. In: Notes of the AAAI/ICML 1998 Workshop on Predicting the Future: AI Approaches to Time-Series Analysis, Madison, Wisconsin (1998)

12. Huber, M.J., Durfee, E.H., Wellman, M.P.: The automated mapping of plans for plan recognition. In de Mantaras, R.L., Poole, D., eds.: UAI94 - Proceedings of the Tenth Conference on Uncertainty in Artificial Intelligence, Seattle, Washington, Morgan Kaufmann (1994) 344–351

13. Kellner, A.: Initial language models for spoken dialogue systems. In: Proceedings of ICASSP'98, Seattle, Washington (1998)

14. Lesh, N.: Scalable and Adaptive Goal Recognition. PhD thesis, University of Washington (1998)

15. Nau, D., Au, T.C., Ilghami, O., Kuter, U., Murdock, J.W., Wu, D., Yaman, F.: SHOP2: An HTN planning system. Journal of Artificial Intelligence Research **20** (2003) 379–404

16. Patterson, D.J., Liao, L., Fox, D., Kautz, H.: Inferring high-level behavior from low-level sensors. In: UBICOMP. (2003)

17. Pynadath, D.V., Wellman, M.P.: Accounting for context in plan recognition, with application to traffic monitoring. In: Proceedings of the Eleventh Conference on Uncertainty in Artificial Intelligence, Montreal, Canada, Morgan Kaufmann (1995)

Reasoning About Interaction
in a Multi-user System

Michael Y.K. Cheng and Robin Cohen

School of Computer Science, University of Waterloo
{mycheng, rcohen}@uwaterloo.ca

Abstract. This paper presents a model for an agent to reason about interaction with multiple users in a collaborative environment. Central to this model is the concept of an interaction strategy, determining both who to ask and what to ask, towards maximizing overall expected utility. We allow for the case of a user not responding at all, after a period of waiting, and a user responding "I don't know". Our model determines how long to wait for a response, and provides for follow up questions to users. All of this is done in a user modeling approach, with decisions based on specific factors being modeled for each user. We present the model in detail, using examples to illustrate its effectiveness and contrasting with related work.

1   Introduction

This paper introduces a model for reasoning about when and how an agent should initiate interaction with a user in a multi-user setting. The research is motivated by decision-theoretic reasoning about interaction with users in multi-agent settings, such as the meeting scheduling environment of the Electric Elves project[1]. In our framework, we allow for users who either do not respond or who respond that they do not know, when asked for information by an agent. As such, we reason not only about different possible conversational partners but also about how long to wait for a response and when to initiate a follow up question, before deciding on a course of action. Our model is intended to be used in a setting where agents can collaborate with users to determine the best actions to take. We discuss how this research relates to other efforts in clarification dialogue and mixed-initiative design.

2   Background

One starting point for our research is the work of Fleming[2][1] who developed a domain-independent decision-theoretic model for an agent to reason about whether or not it should initiate an information gathering dialogue with a human user. Fleming's algorithm consists of first determining the expected *benefit* of

---

[1] An earlier version of this model appeared in *Proc. of User Modeling 2001*.

L. Ardissono, P. Brna, and A. Mitrovic (Eds.): UM 2005, LNAI 3538, pp. 189–198, 2005.

interaction (i.e., by how much the agent's performance is expected to improve after asking the user a question), and then determining the *costs* of interaction (e.g., bother to the user, and time required for interaction). Then, the agent would proceed with the interaction only if the benefit exceeds the costs. One issue with this approach is that once the agent takes initiative and queries the user, it will wait indefinitely for a response. While acceptable in some domains, there are, however, domains (e.g., real-time systems with hard deadlines) for which the agent cannot wait forever, and so there is merit for the agent to stop waiting, and to take another action. In this case, we want to allow the agent the option of interacting with other users. Another beneficial extension to the model is for it to account for the possibility of follow-up questions.

The second starting point for our research is the prominent adjustable autonomy project of Electric Elves (E-Elves)[1], aimed at creating personal assistant agents that can help with the day-to-day activities of a human organization. One of the main issues that the E-Elves[1] work addresses is the problem that once an agent transfers decision making control to the user, the user might not respond in a timely fashion, hence incurring very high waiting costs. So, a key component to this model is the notion of a *transfer-of-control* strategy, which specifies what transfers will occur at what times. Essentially, the agent will plan ahead and determine how long it should wait for the user to respond, before transferring control away to another user, or perhaps back to itself. For example, the strategy $User_1(5)User_2(11)Agent$ is one where the agent will first transfer control to $User_1$, and if $User_1$ hasn't responded with a decision by the five minute mark, then control gets transferred away to $User_2$, and finally if $User_2$ hasn't responded by the eleven minute mark, then the agent gives up and decides autonomously. The E-Elves[1] model has only two extreme levels of agent autonomy. Either the agent can decide to operate autonomously, or it can give up control completely to a user[2]. We are proposing a middle ground, where the agent can interact with the user for information, but still retain decision making control. This is especially important in domains where the user is not equipped to make a decision, yet the agent lacks sufficient information to make a good decision.

3   Model for Reasoning About Interaction

Our primary research goal is to develop a model that an agent can use to reason about the trade-offs between interacting with one or more users over a series of questions, against the costs of such an interaction.

The output of our model will be an *interaction strategy* (adapted from E-Elves[1]) that the agent should follow to maximize overall expected utility. An interaction strategy tells the agent what query to ask who for how long, and depending on the response, what to do next (e.g., ask another query, or make

---

[2] E-Elves[1] also considers transfers to other agents. In this paper, we focus on users.

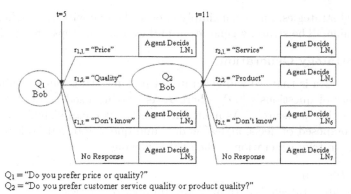

Q_1 = "Do you prefer price or quality?"
Q_2 = "Do you prefer customer service quality or product quality?"

Fig. 1. Example interaction strategy - Preference elicitation for product purchase

a decision)[3]. Visually, one can imagine a strategy as a tree, with two types of nodes, *query/internal nodes*, and *decision/leaf nodes*. A decision node represents the agent taking action and making a decision based on the information obtained from previous queries. A query node represents the agent asking a user a query at time t_{i-1} and waiting until time t_i for a response. Each possible response to a query will be represented as a branch from the query node to a strategy subtree representing what the agent should do when it gets that response. Figure 1 illustrates an example interaction strategy for an agent to use to acquire user preferences in order to make an 'informed' product purchase decision. Note that Q_j denotes a particular question, and $r_{j,1}$, $r_{j,2}$, $r_{j,n}$ denote its possible answer responses. We also include "I don't know" as a valid response, denoted as $r_{j,?}$, and allow for the no response case, $r_{j,\neg resp}$, which occurs when the user does not respond in time.

So, an interaction strategy is similar in spirit to the transfer-of-control strategy in E-Elves[1], except that the agent queries users, instead of transferring control. It should be noted that a transfer-of-control strategy is linear, in the sense that at any time point t_x, the agent knows in advance exactly who should have control. A major distinction then is that unlike a transfer-of-control strategy, an interaction strategy has branches, like a tree, and so the agent does not know exactly what it will do at a future time point t_x, since that depends on the responses it gets from the queries. For brevity's sake, we will now denote interaction strategy as simply strategy. Note that it is important that the agent has a strategy, and reasons about future actions, since the best action to do at the moment often depends on what can be done afterwards. For instance, the usefulness of a user query depends on what the agent can do with the response.

The procedure for the agent to find the optimal strategy is to generate all possible strategies, containing up to a fixed number of queries K, evaluate the

---

[3] An interaction strategy can also contain no queries, signifying the case where the agent should decide immediately without first querying users.

generated strategies, and then simply choose the one with the highest expected utility value. The strategy generation and evaluation steps are outlined below.

3.1   Strategy Generation

The basic idea is that we will generate all possible strategies containing zero to K number of questions ($\#Q$), where K is roughly used to limit the depth of strategies that we search. As mentioned earlier, you can visualize a strategy as a tree, composed of decision/leaf nodes, and query/internal nodes. Using this analogy, strategy generation is then the following:

1. Set $\#Q := 0$
2. Generate strategies containing $\#Q$ number of queries:
   - Base Case ($\#Q = 0$): Generate a strategy s that is just a single leaf node, to represent the case where the agent decides without querying.
   - General Case ($\#Q = i$): For each strategy s_{i-1} generated in the previous iteration of step#2, do the following: (*)Generate a new strategy s_i by replacing a leaf node with a query node consisting of the pairing of a question $Q_j \in Q$ and user $U_k \in U$, where Q is the set of all relevant questions, and U is the set all of users in the system. Note that the newly attached query node has a branch and a leaf node for each possible response to Q_j. Do (*) for all the leaf nodes in s_{i-1} and Q_j, U_k pairs. Discard any duplicate s_i strategies generated.
3. Set $\#Q := \#Q + 1$
4. If $\#Q \leq K$, goto step#2, else stop.

3.2   Strategy Evaluation

The optimal strategy s^* is simply the generated strategy that is evaluated to have the highest expected utility (EU). The first step is to instantiate the timings of the queries in the strategy. For example, for a simple strategy consisting of one query, we need to determine the optimal time point T that the agent should stop waiting for a response, and just make a decision.[4]

The expected utility of a strategy s is calculated as follows:

$$EU(s) = \sum_{LN}[P(LN) \times (EQ(LN) - W(T_{LN}) - BC_{LN})]$$

Considering Figure 1, each possible strategy includes many possible paths of execution, each of which ends in a step of *Agent Decide*, represented by a leaf node LN.[5] $EQ(LN)$ and $W(T_{LN})$ are adapted from E-Elves[1] and refer to the expected quality of the agent's decision at that particular leaf node, and the costs of waiting until the time of the leaf node to finish the interaction, respectively. As such, the utility of a particular path will be determined in part according

---

[4] The optimal time T can be found in several ways. For well-behaved model parameter functions, differentiate the EU equation and solve for 0. Or, use numerical methods.
[5] Note: A leaf node can be viewed as $r_1, r_2, ..., r_n$, the sequence of responses that lead to the leaf node.

to how useful the ultimate decision will be, given the information the agent has gathered on that path, and tempered by how long it may take to reach that decision point. We then include as well the bother incurred by users who may have been asked, along the path to the leaf node, and refer to this as *Bother Cost* (BC_{LN}). Note that BC_{LN} would be computed as the cumulative bother to all the users queried along the path.

The expected utility of the overall strategy is a sum of the utility of each of the individual paths in it, factoring in the probability that the particular path will be taken. We denote this term as $P(LN)$, defined as follows: $P(LN) = \prod_{r_{j,k}} P_{Q_j}^{U_i}(resp = r_{j,k})$ where we iterate $r_{j,k}$ over all the response branches that lead to the leaf node LN, and $P_{Q_j}^{U_i}(resp = r_{j,k})$ refers to the probability of user U_i responding with $r_{j,k}$ to the question Q_j.

One of the main criteria for querying one user over another is the user's $PUK_{Q_j}^{U_i}$ value, denoting the probability that user U_i knows the answer to question Q_j (as in [2]). Another criterion is the user's $PR_{Q_j}^{U_i}(t)$ value, denoting the probability distribution over time that U_i responds to Q_j at time point t (as in [1]). These two model parameters determine how much of the response probabilities will be 'shifted' from the answer responses to the "I don't know" and 'No Response' case. The idea is that the probability of getting to an answer response is contingent on the user responding, and the user knowing the answer. The three possible cases for how to compute the value of $P_{Q_j}^{U_i}(resp = r_{j,k})$, are as follows:

[No response]: $P_{Q_j}^{U_i}(resp = r_{j,\neg resp}) = 1 - \int_{T_s}^{T_e} PR_{Q_j}^{U_i}(t)dt$

["I don't know"]: $P_{Q_j}^{U_i}(resp = r_{j,?}) = \int_{T_s}^{T_e} PR_{Q_j}^{U_i}(t)dt \times (1 - PUK_{Q_j}^{U_i})$

[Answer response]: $P_{Q_j}^{U_i}(resp = r_{j,a}) = \int_{T_s}^{T_e} PR_{Q_j}^{U_i}(t)dt \times PUK_{Q_j}^{U_i} \times PA(r_{j,a})$

where T_s is the time point at which the question was asked, and T_e is the time point that the agent will wait until for a response, and $PA(r_{j,a})$ denotes the probability that the answer to question Q_j is $r_{j,a}$. Note that $\int_{T_s}^{T_e} PR_{Q_j}^{U_i}(t)dt$ gives the probability of U_i responding to Q_j during time frame $[T_s, T_e]$.

We illustrate the above calculations with an example. Consider that on average, there is a 60% chance of the weather being sunny, and a 40% chance of it being rainy. So $PA(sunny) = 60\%$, and $PA(rainy) = 40\%$. Suppose that the agent wants to reduce its uncertainty by asking user Bob the question Q_j = "What is the weather?". Starting from the initial start time of 0, the agent gives Bob until time T to respond. Then, the probability of Bob responding is $\int_0^T PR_{Q_j}^{Bob}(t)dt$. Suppose the probability of Bob knowing the answer is $PUK_{Q_j}^{Bob} = 90\%$. So, overall, when asking Bob question Q_j, the response probabilities are $P_{Q_j}^{Bob}(resp = r_{j,sunny}) = \int_0^T PR_{Q_j}^{Bob}(t)dt \times 90\% \times 60\%$, $P_{Q_j}^{Bob}(resp = r_{j,rainy}) = \int_0^T PR_{Q_j}^{Bob}(t)dt \times 90\% \times 40\%$, $P_{Q_j}^{Bob}(resp = r_{j,?}) = \int_0^T PR_{Q_j}^{Bob}(t)dt \times (100\% - 90\%)$, and $P_{Q_j}^{Bob}(resp = r_{j,\neg resp}) = (1 - \int_0^T PR_{Q_j}^{Bob}(t)dt)$. Note that the sum of the response probabilities is 1.

4   Plan Recognition Example

Consider the following scenario where an agent faces uncertainty. Bob, an avid sports fan, tells his shopping agent "Buy me a ticket to a football movie." Unfortunately, the agent cannot ascertain Bob's true intention, due to the difference in nomenclature between the usage of the term 'football' in North America versus Europe. The European definition of 'football' (EF) is actually soccer in North America, which is quite different than North American football (NAF).

From history logs of past users, the agent predicts that the probability that Bob meant NAF is $PA(NAF) = 40\%$ and that the probability that Bob meant EF is $PA(EF) = 60\%$.

After searching its movie database, the agent finds two potential movies: $Movie1$ which is a great NAF movie but has nothing to do with EF, and $Movie2$ which is a less than stellar movie containing EF and a little bit of NAF content. In this example, the expected quality of an agent's decision (EQ) will be equated with the utility to the user for that decision. Suppose the utility values to a user are the following:

User's intention	Movie Choice	Utility
NAF	$Movie1$	100
NAF	$Movie2$	30
EF	$Movie1$	0
EF	$Movie2$	80

Without information, the expected utility of choosing $Movie1$ is $EU(Movie1)$ $= 0.4 \times 100 + 0.6 \times 0 = 40$, whereas $EU(Movie2) = 0.4 \times 30 + 0.6 \times 80 = 60$. So $EQ(\{\})$, the expected decision quality of the agent with no other information, is $\max_{M \in Movies} EU(M) = \max(40, 60) = 60$ where M is $Movie2$.

However, by obtaining user information, the agent is then able to make informed choices, i.e., it selects the best movie depending on the user's intention. So, EQ $(\{NAF\}) = 100$ (by choosing $Movie1$) and $EQ(\{EF\}) = 80$ (by choosing $Movie2$).

In this scenario, there is only one relevant query, which is $Q_j =$ "Do you mean North American Football or European Football (aka soccer)?". Since Bob knows what Bob wants, $PUK_{Q_j}^{Bob} = 100\%$. To make things more interesting, suppose there's another user in the system, Oscar, whom the agent can ask about Bob's intentions[6]. Since Oscar does not know Bob all that well, $PUK_{Q_j}^{Oscar} = 70\%$.

The model parameters used will depend on the domain. Different users will have different response behaviour and bother reaction to queries. For this sample scenario, we'll use $PR_{Q_j}^{U_i}(t) = \rho_i e^{-\rho_i t}$ to denote the probability of the user U_i responding at time point t, and ρ_i controls how quickly the user responds (the higher the ρ_i, the faster). Suppose that on average, $\rho_{Oscar} = 0.5$, while $\rho_{Bob} = 0.4$ (Bob procrastinates a little bit more).

For this example scenario, we model the waiting cost as $W(t) = t^{1.5}$. This reflects the fact that the longer the agent takes to make a decision, the less time

---

[6] For Oscar, Q_j should be phrased as "Does Bob ..." rather than "Do you ..."

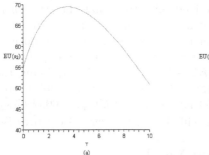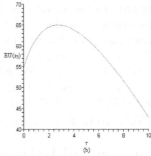

Fig. 2. Graph showing how $EU(s_2)$ and $EU(s_3)$ vary as transfer time T varies. Notice that the choice of waiting time T greatly affects the EU values

Bob has to get to the movie (and that Bob gets more and more anxious as time passes). Also, assume asking query Q_j gives a bother cost BC_j of 5, and is the same for both Bob and Oscar.

For a strategy generation bound of $K = 1$, the agent has three possible strategies, s_1 where the agent decides autonomously, s_2 where the agent asks Bob for clarification and waits until time T for a response before deciding, and s_3 which is the same as s_2 except Oscar is asked.

The expected utility formula for strategy s_1 is simply: $EU(s_1) = EQ(\{\}) - W(0)$. The expected utility formula for strategy s_2 is the following: $EU(s_2) =$
$[\int_0^T PR_{Q_j}^{Bob}(t)dt \times PUK_{Q_j}^{Bob} \times PA(NAF)] \times [EQ(\{NAF\}) - W(T) - BC_j] +$
$[\int_0^T PR_{Q_j}^{Bob}(t)dt \times PUK_{Q_j}^{Bob} \times PA(EF)] \times [EQ(\{EF\}) - W(T) - BC_j] +$
$[\int_0^T PR_{Q_j}^{Bob}(t)dt \times (1 - PUK_{Q_j}^{Bob})] \times [EQ(\{\}) - W(T) - BC_j] +$
$[(1 - \int_0^T PR_{Q_j}^{Bob}(t)dt] \times [EQ(\{\}) - W(T) - BC_j]$

The expected utility formula for strategy s_3 is just like s_2 above, except we replace Bob with Oscar. Note however, the optimal time T to stop waiting for a response will probably be different between the two strategies.

Computing the expected utility values then, $EU(s_1) = 60$, $EU(s_2) = 69.55$ at its optimal time point $T = 3.47$, and $EU(s_3) = 65.08$ at its optimal time point $T = 2.74$. As we can see, for this particular example, it is worth it for the agent to query a user, and more specifically, to query Bob. Figure 2 shows how $EU(s_2)$ and $EU(s_3)$ vary depending on the transfer time T. Notice that we initially gain EU by giving more time for the user to respond, but that after some optimal time point, the waiting cost accumulation overwhelms any extra benefit from waiting for the user's response. Note that the optimal time point for s_3 is sooner than for s_2. This is primarily because Oscar is expected to respond sooner (so there is less need to give him more time), and also because he is likely to say "I don't know", which does not benefit the agent, and so it is less worthwhile to give him more time, since waiting costs are accumulating. It is interesting to note that our model is able to select the best user to query, even though this is not immediately clear (given that Bob has a higher probability of knowing the answer, but Oscar has a higher response probability).

Keeping true to the spirit of mixed-initiative, that the style of interaction between the system and the user is not fixed in advance, our model will select different strategies[7] in different situations. For instance, if the bother cost were raised to 20 (i.e., the users really don't like to be bothered), then we'll have $EU(s_1) = 60$, $EU(s_2) = 54.55$, $EU(s_3) = 50.08$, with s_1 being the winning strategy (i.e., don't query the users). Also, if Oscar knows Bob better, then we might have $PUK_{Q_j}^{Oscar} = 0.95$, and this results in $EU(s_1) = 60$, $EU(s_2) = 69.55$, $EU(s_3) = 70.51$, so then the agent will choose to query Oscar over Bob.

5   Discussion and Related Work

Our work builds upon that by Fleming[2] and the E-Elves project[1] to create a domain-independent decision-theoretic model that can reason about the trade-offs between interacting with one or more users over a series of questions, against the costs of such an interaction.

We extended Fleming's[2] model in several ways. First, we address the issue of how to plan for follow-up questions. We also allow the agent to stop waiting and move on to another action if the queried user does not respond in time. A consequence of this approach is that we have a new category of 'response' that Fleming does not, namely 'no response'. In general, Fleming's model reasons about whether to interact with a user, while ours reasons about whether to interact, with any one of a number of users, which question to ask, when to stop waiting for a response, and whether to generate a follow-up question, depending on the response, towards an overall strategy that maximizes expected utility. Overall, we show that the concept of a *strategy*, that worked so well in the E-Elves project[1] for adjustable autonomy, is also applicable to domains where agents need to reason about information seeking dialogue with users.

We make a contribution to the E-Elves[1] work by proposing a new type of agent action that allows the agent to gather information from the user, while still retaining the decision making authority. This causes strategies in our model to be more like a tree, rather than the straight linear path of an E-Elves strategy, since now an agent will be flexible enough to do different actions depending on the user responses. A result of this is that while the E-Elves model requires that the model parameters remain static, our model allows for a dynamically changing world. For instance, our model can handle cases where the agent's decision making ability improves, as the interaction proceeds. We also incorporate relevant user modeling factors, such as bother cost.

Our work also contributes to the literature on clarification dialogues. In Chin & Porage's[3] work on IONA, they select the query that reduces the most uncertainty. As pointed out in [3] however, a major drawback to this approach is that sometimes reducing uncertainty is not important if the final outcomes remain unchanged. This is similar to the work by van Beek & Cohen[4], where they forgo clarification if the ambiguity does not matter. In our model, the

---

[7] Note that in more elaborate examples, there may be both multiple possible queries and multiple possible users to ask in a strategy.

query that gets selected is the one that results in the highest expected quality of decision (relative to the costs of interaction), and this is influenced by both uncertainty and what the agent can do with the extra information. While [3] discusses how planning ahead may be computationally expensive, we keep our computation tractable by limiting the generation of possible strategies to those containing K or fewer queries. We feel that for most domains, the waiting and bother cost will eventually overwhelm the benefit of repeatedly asking questions, and so the value of K can be kept fairly small. Our use of expected utility to drive the possible generation of clarifying questions is also similar in spirit to the work of Wu[5], that uses active acquisition goals, arising from reasoning failure, to drive the generation of queries, as long as the expected utility of doing so is higher than some current plan.

Raskutti and Zukerman's RADAR system[6] includes another proposal to generate disambiguating queries, which is issued when the user's plan is uncertain, or if there are multiple ways to meet the user's goal. Two factors used to determine which query to issue are the *nuisance factor*, aimed at avoiding irrelevant queries, and the *estimated queries factor*, to reduce the number of queries overall. This is similar to our model, where our bother cost term can incorporate the question irrelevance criterion, and the waiting cost helps temper the number of queries generated, though we will still generate more queries if the benefits exceed the costs.

A key aspect our overall model is that the choice of interaction is user dependent, and hence requires good user modeling. For instance, $PR^{U_i}_{Q_j}(t)$ can vary wildly between different situations. As reported in [7], a user in her office communicating with the agent will respond on average in five minutes, while a user outside the office and communicating with the agent via Palm pilot will require an hour to respond. Therefore, how we model the user will determine which interaction strategies are used by our agent.

6   Future Work

One direction for future research that is particularly relevant to user modeling is to further investigate the bother cost factor, including: how to model bother to the user when an agent stops waiting for a response, how to properly account for collective bother cost, and in case of multiagent systems, how to coordinate the possible interactions to a single user from multiple agents, so as to minimize excessive bother. To develop accurate models of the bother incurred by a user, it would be useful to draw from more detailed studies such as that of Horvitz[8] that learns about the user over time. A related issue is how bother affects a user's probability of response. Another factor that can be explored is the possibility of incorrect responses by the user (currently subsumed in the user response of "I don't know"). As for reasoning about generating a question for a user, it is also useful to explore options of providing more detailed responses that help to prevent further follow up, as discussed in the work of Ardissono[9]. And for best representing the probability of an answer during preference elicitation, user preference modeling such as that by Carberry[10] may be useful.

At the moment, our model computes a conservative estimate of the expected utility of a strategy, since a user can respond earlier than the time the agent allotted for the interaction. In a sense, we are giving the lower bound of a strategy's real expected utility. Therefore, a future work would be to derive a more precise calculation of a strategy's expected utility. Nonetheless, it should be noted that the model still achieves its purpose of reasoning about which strategies are good to employ.

We are also working on heuristics to reduce the number of strategies generated and searched. For instance, if one user clearly dominates other users in the relevant user dimensions, then we just need to go with that user. Likewise, by reducing the number of queries considered, we can decrease the number of strategies that we need to evaluate. Simulations could be used to demonstrate the value of the heuristics used and having real users evaluate the resulting model would be useful.

Acknowledgements

We thank NSERC for the support and Michael Fleming for his feedback.

References

1. Scerri, P., Pynadath, D.V., Tambe, M.: Why the elf acted autonomously: Towards a theory of adjustable autonomy. In *Proc. of AAMAS'02* (2002)
2. Fleming, M., Cohen, R.: A decision procedure for autonomous agents to reason about interaction with humans. In *Proc. of the AAAI 2004 Spring Symposium on Interaction between Humans and Autonomous Systems over Extended Operation* (2004) 81-86
3. Chin, D.N., Porage, A.: Acquiring User Preferences for Product Customization. In *Proc. of User Modeling 2001*, Vol. 2109 (2001)
4. van Beek, P., Cohen, R.: Resolving plan ambiguity for cooperative response generation. In *Proc. of the 12th International Joint Conference on Artificial Intelligence* (1991) 938-944
5. Wu, D.: Active acquisition of user models: Implications for decision-theoretic dialog planning and plan recognition. *User Modeling and User-Adapted Interaction*, Vol. 1, Issue 2 (1991) 149-172
6. Raskutti, B., Zukerman, I.: Generating Queries and Replies during Information-seeking Interactions. *International Journal of Human Computer Studies*, Vol. 47, Issue 6 (1997) 689-734
7. Scerri, P., Pynadath, D.V., Tambe, M.: Towards adjustable autonomy for the real world. *Journal of AI Research*, Vol. 17 (2002) 171-228
8. Horvitz, E., Apacible, J.: Learning and Reasoning about Interruption. In *Proc. of ICMI 2003, ACM International Conference on Multimodal Interfaces* (2003)
9. Ardissono, L., Lombardo, A., Sestero, D.: A flexible approach to cooperative response generation in information-seeking dialogues. In *Proc. of the 31st Annual Meeting of the Association of Computational Linguistics* (1993) 274-276
10. Carberry, S., Chu-Carroll, J., Elzer, S.: Constructing and utilizing a model of user preferences in collaborative consultation dialogues. *Computational Intelligence*, Vol. 5, Issue 3, (1999) 185-217

A Comparison of HMMs and Dynamic Bayesian Networks for Recognizing Office Activities

Nuria Oliver and Eric Horvitz

Adaptive Systems & Interaction, Microsoft Research, Redmond, WA USA
{nuria, horvitz}@microsoft.com

Abstract. We present a comparative analysis of a layered architecture of Hidden Markov Models (HMMs) and dynamic Bayesian networks (DBNs) for identifying human activites from multimodal sensor information. We use the two representations to diagnose users' activities in S-SEER, a multimodal system for recognizing office activity from real-time streams of evidence from video, audio and computer (keyboard and mouse) interactions. As the computation required for sensing and processing perceptual information can impose significant burdens on personal computers, the system is designed to perform selective perception using expected-value-of-information (EVI) to limit sensing and analysis. We discuss the relative performance of HMMs and DBNs in the context of diagnosis and EVI computation.

1 Introduction

We explore in this paper a better understanding of the relative performance of Hidden Markov Models (HMMs) and dynamic Bayesian networks (DBNs) for recognizing office activities within a component of a multilevel signal processing and inference architecture, named S-SEER. S-SEER is a multimodal probabilistic reasoning system that provides real-time interpretations of human activity in and around an office [15, 13]. Our research to date on the system has addressed two main challenges. On one front, we have explored the use of a hierarchical reasoning architecture for processing low-level signals into higher-level interpretations. We have demonstrated several valuable properties of the multilevel architecture, including its value in significantly shrinking the dimensionality of the parameter space, thus reducing the training requirements of the system [15]. On another front, we have investigated the use of value of information to limit computation by selecting in a dynamic manner specific subsets of sensors to use. We have shown how the selective use of sensors and associated computation reduces the overall computational burden in return for small degradations in the accuracy of the system [13].

To date, we have employed HMMs at all levels of S-SEER. In this paper we extend S-SEER with a comparative analyis of HMMs and DBNs at the highest level of reasoning. The research was motivated by the challenge of reasoning with unobserved sets of variables –a situation underscored by our work with selective perception.

L. Ardissono, P. Brna, and A. Mitrovic (Eds.): UM 2005, LNAI 3538, pp. 199–209, 2005.

This paper is organized as follows: We first provide background on multi-modal systems in Sect. 2. Section 3 describes our work on learning dynamic graphical models (HMMs and DBNs) to model office activities. In Sect. 4 we briefly describe the decision-theoretic selective perception strategy that we have incorporated in S-SEER. Section 5 provides background on the S-SEER system. Experimental results with the use of a layered architecture of HMMs and DBNs in S-SEER are presented in Sect. 6. We also perform a supportive study to probe the value of richer temporal relationships among states and unobserved variables with DBNs. Finally, we summarize our work in Sect. 7.

2   Prior Related Work on Human Activity Recognition

We shall review here some of the most relevant previous work on human activity recognition from perceptual data using dynamic graphical models. For a more complete overview of the prior related work, we direct the reader to [15, 13].

Most of the early work in this area centered on the identification of a specific activity in a particular scenario, and in particular, single events such as "waving the hand" or "sitting on a chair". More recently there has been increasing interest on modeling more complex patterns of behavior, and especially patterns that extend over long periods of time. Hidden Markov Models (HMMs) [16] and extensions have been one of the most popular modeling techniques. Some of the earliest work was done by Starner and Pentland in [18] where they used HMMs for recognizing hand movements in American Sign Language and by Oliver *et al* [12] to recognize facial expressions. More complex models, such as Parameterized-HMMs [19], Entropic-HMMs [1], Variable-length HMMs [7], Coupled-HMMs [2], structured HMMs [17] and context-free grammars [8] have been used to recognize more complex activities such as the interaction between two people.

Moving beyond the HMM representation and solution paradigm, researchers have investigated more general temporal dependency models, such as dynamic Bayesian networks (DBNs) (also known as dynamic graphical models). DBNs have been adopted by several researchers for the modeling and recognition of human activities [3, 5, 10].

HMMs can be viewed as a specific case of the more general dynamic graphical models, where particular dependencies are assumed. Thus, HMMs and their variants can be interpreted as examples of DBNs.

DBNs present several advantages to the problem of user modeling from multi-sensory information: they can handle incomplete data as well as uncertainty; they are trainable and provide means for avoiding overfitting; they encode causality in a natural way; algorithms exist for learning the structure of the networks and doing predictive inference; they offer a framework for combining prior knowledge and data; finally, they are modular and parallelizable. However, they pose, in the general case, difficult inference problems, especially with loopy graphs and continous data. Several efficient optimizations available for learning and solving HMMs are not available for general DBNs.

With different representations available, there is still the open question of how suitable a particular representation might be for a specific task. We explore in this paper the power and tradeoffs of HMMs versus more general DBNs when applied to the task of recognizing in real-time typical office activities from sensor data. Our main contribution is a comparison of a layered architecture of HMMs with a layered architecture of HMMs and DBNs for modeling office activities. We examine base-level inference as well as the use of value of information to select the best subset of sensors to use.

3   Layered Dynamic Graphical Models for User Modeling

We shall now review the layered dynamic graphical model approach that we have used for modeling the user's behavior in and around the office. We direct the reader to [15] for more detail on the motivation of our layered architecture and its performance compared to standard single-layer HMMs.

3.1   Layered HMMs (LHMMs)

In [15] we describe the use of a multilayer representation of HMMs, named LH-MMs, that reasons in parallel at different levels of temporal detail. Such an architecture has the ability to decompose the parameter space in a manner that reduces the training and tuning requirements. Each layer of the architecture is connected to the next layer via its inferential results. The representation segments the problem into distinct layers that operate at different temporal granularities[1] — allowing for temporal abstractions from pointwise observations at particular times into explanations over varying temporal intervals. This architecture can be characterized as a *stacked classifier*.

The layered formulation makes it feasible to decouple different levels of analysis for training and inference. As we review in [15], each level of the hierarchy is trained independently, with different feature vectors and time granularities. Thus, the lowest signal-analysis layer that is most sensitive to variations in the environment can be retrained, while leaving the higher-level layers unchanged.

3.2   Layered HMMs and DBNs

We focus here on extending the layered HMM architecture to include DBNs at the highest level,while the lower level is still based on HMMs for simplicity[2].

We learn the DBNs from observed data using structural learning [6, 11]. In particular, we have extended a Bayesian network tool named WinMine [4] developed by Microsoft Research, to consider variables at different time steps and therefore learn a DBN. WinMine uses a Bayesian score to learn the structure

---

[1] The "time granularity" in this context corresponds to the window size or vector length of the observation sequences in the HMMs.

[2] This level interfaces with the sensor data which is a continous dynamic time series.

and parameters of the model, given some basic constraints supplied *a priori*, such as prohibiting edges between nodes at time t and nodes at time $t - 1$, *i.e.* forcing the connections to be either co-temporal or go forward in time. The learned distributions are decision trees and the Bayesian score is used to choose the splits in the trees. The tree-growing algorithm for Bayesian networks is to score every possible split in every leaf of every node, and then perform the best one that does not result in a cycle in the network (a split in a tree corresponds to a parent in the DBN).

4   Decision Theoretic Selective Perception

An important challenge in multimodal real-time perceptual systems is CPU consumption. Processing video and audio sensor information to make inferences usually consumes a large portion of the available CPU time. We integrated into S-SEER several methods for selecting features dynamically [13], including an *EVI-based* method, based on calculations of the expected value of information. In the experiments described in [13] we studied the performance and overall computational cost of the system using these methods.

In this paper we focus on using an *EVI-based* method to perform real-time, one step look-ahead sensor selection both in HMMs an DBNs.

5   Implementation of S-SEER

S-SEER consists of a two-level architecture with three processing layers as illustrated in Fig. 1. For a more detailed description we direct the reader to [15, 13].

5.1   Sensors and Feature Extraction

In S-SEER we explore the challenge of fusing information from three different sensors. The raw sensor signals are preprocessed to obtain feature vectors (*i.e.* observations) for the first layer of HMMs.

(1) **Audio:** Two mini-microphones ($20 - 16000$ Hz, SNR 58 dB) capture ambient audio information. They are used for sound classification and localization. The audio signal is sampled at 44100 KHz. We compute Linear Predictive Coding coefficients [16] on the audio signal. Feature selection is applied to these coefficients via principal component analysis. We select the number of coefficients such that at least 95% of the variability in the data is kept, which is typically achieved with no more than 7 features. We also extract higher-level features from the audio signal such as its energy, the mean and variance of the fundamental frequency over a time window, and the zero crossing rate [16]. The source of the sound is localized using the Time Delay of Arrival (TDOA) method.

(2) **Video:** A standard Firewire camera, sampled at 30 f.p.s, is used to determine the number of persons present in the scene. We extract four features

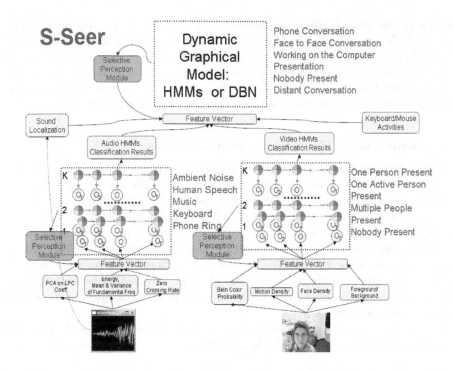

Fig. 1. Architecture of S-SEER

from the video signal: the density[3] of skin color pixels in the image (obtained by discriminating between skin and non-skin models, consisting of histograms in YUV color space), the density of motion pixels in the image (obtained by image differences), the density of foreground pixels in the image (obtained by background subtraction, using an adaptive background technique), and the density of face pixels in the image (obtained by means of a real-time face detector [9]).

(3) **Keyboard and Mouse:** A history of the last 1, 5 and 60 seconds of mouse and keyboard activities is logged.

5.2   Continuous HMMs at the First Level

The first level of HMMs includes two banks of distinct HMMs for classifying the audio and video feature vectors. The feature vectors at this level are a stream of continous floating point data. The structure for each of these HMMs is determined by means of cross-validation on a validation set of real-time data. On the audio side, we train one HMM for each of the following office sounds: *human speech, music, silence, ambient noise, phone ringing*, and the sounds of *keyboard typing*. In the architecture, all the HMMs are run in parallel. At each time slice, the model with the highest likelihood is selected and the data −*e.g.* sound in

---

[3] By "density" we mean the number of pixels that satisfy a certain property, divided by the total number of pixels.

the case of the audio HMMs– is classified correspondingly. We will refer to this kind of HMMs as *discriminative* HMMs. The video signals are classified using another bank of discriminative HMMs that implement a person detector. At this level, the system detects whether *nobody, one person (semi-static), one active person, or multiple people* are present in the office. Each bank of HMMs can use selective perception strategies [13] to determine which features to use.

5.3   Second Level Dynamic Graphical Models

The next level in the architecture processes the inferential results[4] from the previous layer (*i.e.* the outputs of the audio and video classifiers), the derivative of the sound localization component, and the history of keyboard and mouse activities. This layer handles concepts with longer temporal extent and of discrete nature. Such concepts include the user's typical activities in or near an office. In particular, the activities modeled are: (1) *Phone conversation*; (2) *Presentation*; (3) *Face-to-face conversation*; (4) *User present, engaged in some other activity;* (5) *Distant conversation* (outside the field of view); (6) *Nobody present*. Some of these activities can be used in a variety of ways in services, such as those that identify a person's availability.

This is the level of description where we have implemented and compared two different models: discrete HMMs and DBNs, both learned from data.

(1) HMMs: A bank of discriminative HMMs with selective perception policies to determine which inputs from the previous layer to use. Figure 2 (a) (left) illustrates the architecture with HMMs at the highest level.

(2) DBNs: A single DBN with selective perception and a hidden "Activity" node is learned from data. Figure 2 (a) (right) depicts the network learned and used in our experiments.

The figure shows two time slices of the DBN, corresponding to time $T0$ and time $T1$. The complete network consists of extending the DBN up to time $T9$, *i.e.* for 10 time steps. There are five different discrete variables to be modeled, all of them with a subscript corresponding to the time slice: "Activity", which is a hidden variable that contains the value of current activity that is taking place in the office, i.e. (0) *Phone conversation*; (1) *Presentation*; (2) *Face-to-face conversation*; (3) *User present, engaged in some other activity;* (4) *Distant conversation* (outside the field of view); (5) *Nobody present*; "Video", an observed variable that contains the inferential results of the bank of HMMs classifying the video signal. It has one of the following values: (0) *One person present*; (1) *Multiple people present*; (2) *One active person present*; (3) *Nobody present*; "Audio", an observed variable corresponding to the inferential results of the bank of HMMs classifying the audio signal. Its possible values are: (0) *Ambient Noise*; (1) *Speech*; (2) *Music*; (3) *Phone Ringing;* (4) *Keyboard typing*; "SL", an observed variable with the sound localization results: (0) *Left of the monitor*; (1)

---

[4] See [14] for a detailed description of how we use these inferential results.

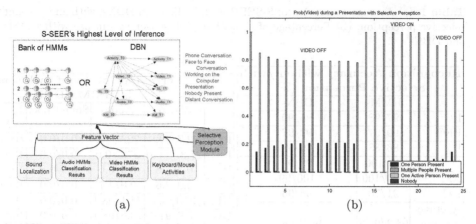

(a)   (b)

Fig. 2. (a) Highest level of S-SEER with HMMs (left) and a DBN (right); (b) Evolution over 25 consecutive time slices of the probability distribution of a "Video_T" node in the DBN with selective perception and during a *Presentation*

Center of the monitor; (2) *Right of the monitor*; "KM", an observed variable with the history of keyboard and mouse activities. Its values are: (0) *No activity*; (1) *Current Mouse Activity*; (2) *Current Keyboard Activity*; (3) *Keyboard or mouse activity in the past second.*

The learned model highlights the enhanced expressiveness of more general dynamic graphical models. Note how the learned structure of the DBN differs from that of an HMM. The DBN has new dependencies that are missing on the HMM, such as the edge between the keyboard and mouse node and the video node, the edge between the video node at time $T0$ and the sound localization node at time $T1$, and the edge between the video node at time $T0$ and the audio node at time $T1$. The DBN has discovered in the data: (1) A co-temporal dependency between the sound localization and the audio nodes, and between the keyboard and mouse, and the video nodes; (2) A causal relationship between the presence information obtained from the video sensor and the audio and sound localization nodes. These new connections make intuitive sense. For example, if the keyboard and mouse are in use at time $T0$ it is very unlikely that the video sensor would determine that there is nobody there at that same time $T0$; or if the vision sensor detects that there is one person present at time $T0$, it is quite likely that there will be some speech at time $T1$ and that the sound will come from the center of the monitor.

6   Experiments

In our experiments we were particularly interested in comparing: (1) The accuracy of HMMs versus DBNs with and without selective perception, and (2) evaluating the advantages and disadvantages of both models from a practical perspective.

Table 1. (a) Average accuracies for S-SEER with HMMs and DBNs, with and without selective perception; (b) Percentage of time that each sensor was in use with HMMs and DBNs

Recognition Accuracy without/with Selective Perception (%)		
	HMMs	DBNs
PC	97/98	95/90
FFC	99/97	97/97
P	86/88	99/99
O	93/100	99/99
NP	100/100	100/99
DC	91/70	96/96
Average Accuracy	94.3/92.2	97.7/96.7

(a)

	Percentage of use of each sensor in HMMs/DBN			
	Video	Audio	Sound Loc.	Keyboard Mouse
PC	22.7/99.8	22.7/2.3	0.0/0.0	100.0/10
FFC	27.3/100.0	27.3/0.0	0.0/0.0	100.0/10
P	0.3/5.6	0.3/0.0	0.0/0.0	100.0/10
O	0.0/2.6	0.0/4.7	0.0/0.0	100.0/10
NP	24.1/3.4	24.1/98.1	0.0/0.0	100.0/10
DC	23.6/97.4	23.6/98.1	0.0/0.0	100.0/10

(b)

We trained S-SEER both with HMMs and with the DBN at the highest processing level[5] with 1800 samples (300 samples per activity) of each of the office activities of interest, i.e., *Phone conversation; Presentation; Face-to-face conversation; User present, engaged in some other activity; Distant conversation* (outside the field of view); *Nobody present*. All the samples in the experiments below correspond to the same user. We used leave-one-out cross-validation to determine that 10 was the optimal number of time steps for the DBN.

To test the performance of both models we collected about 90 minutes of activity data (about 15 minutes per activity). We ran accuracy tests of the HMMs and the DBN with and without selective perception. The results are displayed in Table 1 (a) where we use the abbreviations: PC=Phone Conversation; FFC=Face to Face Conversation; P=Presentation; O=Other Activity; NP=Nobody Present; DC=Distant Conversation.

Observations that can be noted from our experiments are that the DBN has better recognition accuracies than HMMs for the problem we are solving, and that employing selective perception policies leads to a more significant degradation in the performance of HMMs than that of the DBN. An important factor for this difference in behavior is how unobserved variables are treated in each model. In HMMs, we marginalize over the unobserved variables whereas in DBNs we do not enter evidence in the unobserved nodes. Rather previous states and observations in the last time slice influence inference about the state of the unobserved variables. We will return to this below.

We also observed that in most of our experiments, S-SEER –both with HMMs and DBNs, never turned the *sound localization* feature on, due to its high computational cost versus the relatively low informational value this acoustical feature

---

[5] Note that the signal processing module and the first level of HMMs is identical in both cases. We are comparing HMMs with DBNs at the highest level of inference in S-SEER.

provides. On the other hand, the keyboard and mouse sensors were at use all the time. Thus, we have learned information that is valuable in learning designs for an activity sensing system in this domain.

To better understand the behavior of the EVI-based selective perception policy in HMMs and DBNs we tracked the percentage of time that each sensor was used in our experiments. Table 1 (b) reflects the results. Note how HMMs tend to use the video and audio sensors quite in synchrony, whereas the DBN exhibits are more asymmetric behavior. On top of the keyboard and mouse – that are constantly used, there are activities where the DBN heavily relies on one other sensor, such as the video sensor during a *Phone Conversation* (99.8% use) or the audio sensor when there is *Nobody Present* (98.1% use).

We note that S-SEER's high accuracy without selective perception, may indicate that the task is too easy for the model and that is the reason why the selective perception policies have reasonable accuracies as well. We emphasize that the results reflected on the table correspond to a particular test set. We are also exploring more challenging scenarios for S-SEER, both in terms of the number of activities to classify from and their complexity.

Persistence of the Observed Data

As mentioned above, we use HMMs in a discriminatory fashion, which implies learning one HMM per class, running all HMMs in parallel and choosing the HMM with the highest likelihood as the most likely model. On the other hand, we learn a single DBN that has a hidden "Activity" node that provides us with the likelihood of each office activity at each time slice[6].

We are interested in understanding the persistence versus volatility of observational states in the world. Rather than consider findings unobserved at a particular time slice if the corresponding sensory analyses have not been immediately performed, we would like to smooth out the value of the unobserved variables over time. DBNs allow for such a consideration because we have a single model for all activities, they encode a probability distribution for each variable and inference is performed with the network moving forward in time for any number of time slices with or without entering new evidence.

In a second set of experiments, we tracked the evolution of the probability distribution over all possible values of a particular node when using selective perception. Our goal was to see how the values of such variables change over time when a particular sensor is not used. Figure 2 (b) illustrates a typical behavior of S-SEER with a DBN and selective perception. The figure shows the probabilities over 25 consecutive time slices of a "Video_T" node during a *Presentation*. At time 1 the video sensor was used and therefore the probability of *One Active Person Present* was clamped to 1.0. From time slice 2 until time 14 the video sensor was not in use. The probability of *One Active Person Present* smoothly declines over time while the probability of *One Person Present* increases over

---

[6] The duration of a time slice depends on the level of inference: typical durations for the time slices at the lowest level are of 50ms, and of .5s at the highest level.

time. Then, at time 15, the system decides to use the video sensor again until time 22 when it turns off the video sensor. We believe that this probabilistic smoothing over time in the presence of missing data is a valuable property of DBNs.

7   Summary

We have explored and compared the use of HMMs and DBNs for recognizing office activities with and without selective perception. Our testbed is a multi-modal, multi-layer, real-time office activity recognition system named S-SEER.

HMMs have been used successfully in the area of human behavior modeling and this representation formed the core of the early work in S-SEER. Motivated by the case of missing observations associated with the use of a selective perception policy, we pursued a comparative analysis of the use of dynamic Bayesian network models in a component of S-SEER. In experiments, we have identified some differences and tradeoffs in the use of DBNs when compared to HMMs. We found that (1) DBNs can learn dependencies between variables that were assumed independent in HMMs; (2) DBNs provide a unified probability model as opposed to having one model per activity as in discriminative HMMs; and (3) the accuracy of inference by DBNs seems to be less sensitive than HMMs to the loss of access to sets of observations, per a specific selective perception algorithm that we have implemented. We believe that one reason for their lower degradation of the performance is the fact that unobserved variables in DBNs change smoothly over time, whereas HMMs marginalize over the unobserved variables. On the other hand, HMMs are simpler to train and to do inference with, they can handle continous data, and they impose less computational burden than arbitrary DBNs.

Thus, the best representation depends on several factors, including the resources available for training and testing, the likelihood that variables will not be observed, the nature of the data and the complexity of the domain. We advocate considering the merits of each approach in building human activity recognition systems.

References

1. M. Brand and V. Kettnaker. Discovery and segmentation of activities in video. *IEEE Transactions on Pattern Analysis and Machine Intelligence*, 22(8), 2000.
2. M. Brand, N. Oliver, and A. Pentland. Coupled hidden markov models for complex action recognition. In *Proc. of CVPR97*, 994–999, 1996.
3. Hilary Buxton and Shaogang Gong. Advanced Visual Surveillance using Bayesian Networks. In *International Conference on Computer Vision*, 111–123, Cambridge, Massachusetts, June 1995.
4. D.M. Chickering. The winmine toolkit. Technical Report MSR-TR-2002-103, Microsoft, Redmond, WA, 2002.

5. J. Forbes, T. Huang, K. Kanazawa, and S. Russell. The batmobile: Towards a bayesian automated taxi. In *Proc. Fourteenth International Joint Conference on Artificial Intelligence, IJCAI'95*, 1995.

6. N. Friedman, K. Murphy, and S. Russell. Learning the structure of dynamic probabilistic networks. In *Proceedings of the 1st Annual Conference on Uncertainty in Artificial Intelligence (UAI-98)*, 139–147, New York, NY, 1998. Elsevier Science Publishing Comapny, Inc.

7. A. Galata, N. Johnson, and D. Hogg. Learning variable length markov models of behaviour. *International Journal on Computer Vision, IJCV*, 398–413, 2001.

8. Y. Ivanov and A. Bobick. Recognition of visual activities and interactions by stochastic parsing. *IEEE Trans. on Pattern Analysis and Machine Intelligence, TPAMI*, 22(8):852–872, 2000.

9. S.Z. Li, X.L. Zou, Y.X. Hu, Z.Q. Zhang, S.C. Yan, X.H. Peng, L. Huang, and H.J. Zhang. Real-time multi-view face detection, tracking, pose estimation, alignment, and recognition, 2001.

10. L. Liao, D. Fox, and H. Kautz. Learning and inferring transportation routines. In *Proceedings of AAAI'04*, 348–353, 2004.

11. K. Murphy. *Dynamic Bayesian Networks: Representation, Inference and Learning*. PhD thesis, U.C. Berkeley, 2002.

12. N. Oliver, F. Berard, and A. Pentland. Lafter: Lips and face tracking. In *Proceed. of IEEE International Conference on Computer Vision and Pattern Recognition, CVPR'97*, S.Juan, Puerto Rico, June 1997.

13. N. Oliver and E. Horvitz. Selective perception policies for guiding sensing and computation in multimodal systems: a comparative analysis. In *Proc. of Int. Conf. on Multimodal Interfaces*, 36–43, 2003.

14. N. Oliver, E. Horvitz, and A. Garg. Layered representations for human activity recognition. In *Proc. of Int. Conf. on Multimodal Interfaces*, 3–8, 2002.

15. N. Oliver, E. Horvitz, and A. Garg. Layered representations for human activity recognition. *Computer Vision and Image Understanding Journal*, 96:2:163–180, 2004.

16. L. Rabiner and B.H. Huang. *Fundamentals of Speech Recognition*. 1993.

17. F. Bremond S. Hongeng and R. Nevatia. Representation and optimal recognition of human activities. In *Proc. of the IEEE Conference on Computer Vision and Pattern Recognition, CVPR'00*, 2000.

18. T. Starner and A. Pentland. Real-time american sign language recognition from video using hidden markov models. In *Proceed. of SCV'95*, 265–270, 1995.

19. A. Wilson and A. Bobick. Recognition and interpretation of parametric gesture. In *Proc. of International Conference on Computer Vision, ICCV'98*, 329–336, 1998.

Modeling Agents That Exhibit Variable Performance in a Collaborative Setting*

Ingrid Zukerman and Christian Guttmann

School of Computer Science and Software Engineering,
Monash University, Clayton, Victoria 3800, Australia
{ingrid, xtg}@csse.monash.edu.au

Abstract. In a collaborative environment, knowledge about collaborators' skills is an important factor when determining which team members should perform a task. However, this knowledge may be incomplete or uncertain. In this paper, we extend our *ETAPP (Environment-Task-Agents-Policy-Protocol)* collaboration framework by modeling team members that exhibit non-deterministic performance, and comparing two alternative ways of using these models to assign agents to tasks. Our simulation-based evaluation shows that performance variability has a large impact on task performance, and that task performance is improved by consulting agent models built from a small number of observations of agents' recent performance.

1 Introduction

Collaboration plays a critical role when a team is striving for goals which are difficult to achieve by an individual. When a team is trying to perform a task, knowledge about collaborators' skills is necessary in order to determine which team members should perform which portions of the task. However, this knowledge may be incomplete, e.g., when collaborators are new to a team or face a new task, or uncertain, e.g., when the performance of collaborators is variable.

Our work focuses on how teams of agents make decisions when allocating tasks to team members. Group decisions are based on the opinions of team members, which in turn are based on their models of their collaborators. In previous work, we investigated joint decision making under the *ETAPP* framework [4], which expresses the collaboration of a team of agents in terms of five operating parameters (Environment, Task, Agents, Policy and Protocol). An important result from this research is that the main factor that influences task performance is the ability of the agents in a team to learn the models of team members from observations of their performance. However, this insight was obtained under a simplistic assumption whereby agents' performance is deterministic and invariant. This assumption implies that an agent's performance is the same every time a task is performed under the same conditions. Hence, an agent's level of performance under a particular set of conditions can be determined from a single observation of its actions.

---

* This research was supported in part by Linkage Grant LP0347470 from the Australian Research Council, and by an endowment from Hewlett Packard. The authors thank Yuval Marom for his assistance with the evaluation.

L. Ardissono, P. Brna, and A. Mitrovic (Eds.): UM 2005, LNAI 3538, pp. 210–219, 2005.

In this paper, we extend the ETAPP framework to build agent models under more realistic assumptions whereby the performance of agents is non-deterministic. That is, an agent's level of performance may change every time it performs a task due to the influence of factors that are not explicit. This extension requires a probabilistic representation of an agent's *task-related capabilities*, such as mean level of performance and stability; a procedure for building agent models from a sequence of observations; and a representation of an observer's *observation capacity*, i.e., how many observations can the observer remember. To illustrate these representations, a stable, high-performing agent exhibits a consistently high level of performance, while an unstable, medium-performing agent may sometimes perform well and other times poorly. An observer with a high observation capacity (it recalls many actions performed by team members) will derive an accurate model of the task-related capabilities of both types of agents, while an observer with a low observation capacity (it can recall only the last few observations) may still derive an accurate model of the stable agent, but its model of the unstable agent may be quite skewed.

In addition to our agent-modeling extensions, in this paper we compare two policies for assigning agents to tasks based on the proposals made by the agents in a team: an "optimistic" policy, which chooses the proposed agent with the most promising performance compared to all the other proposed agents [4], and a "majority" policy, which chooses the agent preferred by most team members.

We assessed the influence of these factors on task performance by means of a simulation where we varied the level of performance and stability of agents and their observation capacity, and applied the two policies for selecting agents for tasks.

Section 2 outlines the ETAPP framework and discusses the above mentioned extensions. Our evaluation is described in Section 3. In Section 4, we consider related research, followed by our conclusions.

2   The ETAPP Framework

The *ETAPP* [4] framework is designed for a decentralized setting, where agents act autonomously based on their knowledge of their team members. Our framework provides an explicit representation of five operating parameters of a collaboration: *Environment, Task, Agents, Policy* and *Protocol*. The *Task* given to the group is to be performed in the *Environment*, and the *Policy* and *Protocol* are procedures agreed upon by all the agents in the group, but performed autonomously (this is similar to abiding by certain rules in order to belong to a society). Central to the *ETAPP* framework is the idea that the real capabilities of the agents in a team are not known to the team members. Hence, individual agents employ models of collaborators' capabilities in order to estimate the contributions of team members to a task. The *Agents* component stores these models and the mechanisms to reason about them.

The elements of the ETAPP framework are outlined below (for more details see [4], but note that the *Agents* component has been substantially modified since that publication). Our extensions are described in Section 2.1.

An ***Environment*** $\mathcal{E}$ is a state space described by predicates, which represent properties of objects and relations between objects. A state in the environment describes the values of these predicates at a particular step in a collaboration.

A **Task** $\mathcal{T}$ is represented by a tuple with two elements $< EC_T, EF_T >$.

- EC_T specifies the *Evaluation Criteria* relevant to task $\mathcal{T}$, e.g., speed, quality or profit. The value for each criterion ranges between 0 and 1, where 0 corresponds to the worst possible performance and 1 corresponds to the optimal performance.
- EF_T denotes the *Evaluation Function* for the task, which specifies the weights assigned to the Evaluation Criteria (i.e., their relative importance to the task), and the way in which the values for these criteria are combined. For instance, the Evaluation Function $EF_T = \max \sum_{i=1}^{n} ec_i w_i$ specifies that the task should maximize a linear combination of n Evaluation Criteria, where w_i for $i = 1, \ldots, n$ are the weights assigned to these criteria. These weights range between 0 and 1, where 0 indicates no impact of a criterion on task performance, and 1 indicates maximum impact.

A team of **Agents** $\mathcal{A}$ comprises agents $\{A_1, \ldots, A_m\}$, where m is the number of agents in $\mathcal{A}$. Individual agents have *Internal Resources (IR)*, which represent the task-related capabilities of an agent, and *Modeling Resources (MR)*, which represent the ability of an agent to model agents and reason about them.

The *IR* of an agent represent how well it can perform an action in terms of the Evaluation Criteria of the task. The values for *IR* range between 0 and 1, with 0 indicating the worst performance and 1 the best. For instance, if the Evaluation Criteria of a task are time and quality, and one of the actions in the environment is *drive*, then $IR_{A_i}(drive)$ represent the driving performance of agent A_i in terms of time and quality, i.e., $IR_{A_i}(drive) = \{Perf_{A_i}^{time}(drive), Perf_{A_i}^{qual}(drive)\}$. These capabilities are *not* directly observable (only the resultant behaviour can be observed). Hence, they cannot be used to propose agents for tasks (but they are necessary to simulate agent performance, Section 3).

The *MR* of an agent comprise its *Models (M)* of the Internal Resources of agents, the *Resource Limits (RL)* of the agent in question, and its *Reasoning Apparatus (RA)*.

- M_{A_i} are the models maintained by agent A_i to estimate IR_{A_j} for $j = 1, \ldots, m$. A_i's estimation of the capabilities of the agents in the team (including its own capabilities) may differ from their actual performance, in particular if agent A_i has never observed the team in action. This estimation may be updated as agent A_i observes the real performance of the agents in the team.
- The *RL* of an agent pertain to the amount of memory available to store models of agents, the agent's ability to update these models and generate proposals, and its ability to send and receive proposals (an agent that has become disconnected cannot send proposals, even if it can generate them).
- The *RA* consists of the processes applied by protocol $\mathcal{P}$, which enable an agent to act in an environment and interact with collaborators. These processes are: (1) proposing agents for an action (selecting agents from a list of candidates); (2) communicating this proposal to other agents; (3) applying a policy $\mathcal{P}_A$ to select a proposal from the communicated proposals; and (4) updating *M* based on the observed performance of the selected agent(s).

A **Policy** $\mathcal{P}_A$ is a joint policy (adopted by all the agents in the team) for making decentralized group decisions about assigning agents to activities. As stated above, each agent proposes one or more agents for an action (according to its models *M* and its *RA*). Upon receiving all the proposals, each agent uses $\mathcal{P}_A$ for selecting one proposal.

In the future, we plan to compare this decentralized decision-making process with a centralized process, where a leader assesses proposals and communicates the outcome to team members. It is expected that the centralized process would require less communication and computations than our current procedure, while our procedure would be more resistant to being subverted by corrupt or incompetent leaders.

A **Protocol** $\mathcal{P}$ is a process that is followed by all the agents in the group to coordinate their interaction. According to this protocol, all agents generate a proposal and communicate it to the other agents. Next, each agent applies $\mathcal{P}_A$ to select a proposal, observes the performance of the selected agent(s), and updates its model(s) accordingly.

2.1   Extensions of ETAPP

In this paper, we extend the ETAPP framework along three agent-modeling dimensions – Internal Resources, Resource Limits and Reasoning Apparatus, and consider a new Policy for agent selection.

Internal Resources. As mentioned in Section 1, in the original framework we assumed that agents' performance is deterministic and invariant. Thus, $IR_{A_i}(action)$ comprise a set of numbers between 0 and 1. However, in realistic settings, agents exhibit variable performance (e.g., they could be having a bad day). We represent such a performance by means of a truncated normal distribution, where the mean represents the ability of an agent, and the standard deviation represents its stability (truncation is required so that we don't exceed the [0,1] thresholds). As stated above, these values are not observable, but they are the basis from which the observed performance of an agent is obtained during simulations.

Resource Limits. Originally, due to the deterministic performance of agents, a single observation of an agent's performance yielded an accurate model of its ability. However, this is clearly not the case if the performance is non-deterministic. In order to cope with this situation, we include *Observation Capacity (OC)* in our model of the Resource Limits of agents. This parameter, which is similar to attention span [8], specifies how many observations of the performance of each agent can be stored by an agent in its memory. When this limit is exceeded, the observer agent retains a window of the last K observations (forgetting the initial ones).

Reasoning Apparatus. The variable performance of agents also demands the implementation of a new model-updating procedure. As for Resource Limits, our previous single-update method is unlikely to yield accurate results. We therefore propose a simple procedure whereby an agent re-calculates the mean and standard deviation of the observed performance of an agent every time it performs an action. Notice, however, that the results obtained by this procedure are moderated by the observation capacity of the observing agent. That is, if the observing agent can remember only the last K observations of an agent's performance, then the mean and standard deviation are calculated from these observations.

Policy. In previous work, we implemented an *optimistic* policy, where the agent with the most promising performance was chosen for an action. We now consider the *majority* policy, where the agent that receives the most votes is chosen.

2.2   Example – Surf Rescue Scenario

In this section, we present an example that illustrates the ETAPP framework in the context of the Surf Rescue (SR) scenario used in our simulation-based evaluation (Section 3). In this scenario, the environment $\mathcal{E}$ consists of the *beach* and the *ocean*, and the task $\mathcal{T}$ is to rescue a distressed person (DP) in the shortest time possible. This means that the set of evaluation criteria is $EC_T = \{ec_{time}\}$, and the evaluation function is $EF_T = \max \{ec_{time}\}$ (recall that the best performance has value 1, i.e., a short time has a high score).

In this example, we have three lifesavers $\mathcal{A} = \{A_1, A_2, A_3\}$ at the beach. The task consists of performing one action – to rescue the distressed person. The values for the *IR* of A_1, A_2 and A_3 for this action are $IR_{A_1}(rescue) = 0.5$(STDV=0.4), $IR_{A_2}(rescue) = 0.8$ (STDV=0.3), and $IR_{A_3}(rescue) = 0.3$ (STDV=0.2). That is, agent A_1 has a medium performance and is unstable, agent A_2 has a high performance and is a bit more stable, and agent A_3 has a low performance and high stability.

For clarity of exposition, we assume that only agents A_1 and A_2 can select agents for a rescue. These two agents (which are both observers and lifesavers) maintain models of lifesaver agents A_1, A_2 and A_3 ($M_{A_1}(A_1)$, $M_{A_1}(A_2)$ and $M_{A_1}(A_3)$, and $M_{A_2}(A_1)$, $M_{A_2}(A_2)$ and $M_{A_2}(A_3)$), and generate proposals involving the lifesaver agents. The models are initialized randomly (i.e., each agent has an *a priori*, random opinion of the other agents). Both A_1 and A_2 store the last three observations made of the performance of the lifesavers ($OC=3$), and apply the majority policy for selecting a lifesaver for a rescue. This policy chooses the lifesaver that most agents voted for (in the event of a tie, the top agent in an ordered list of agents is selected).

Table 1 illustrates the assignment of agents to a sequence of rescues under the majority selection policy (the values obtained after each rescue are boldfaced). The first column shows the time of the rescue; the second column lists the observer agents; the third and fourth columns show the agent proposed by each observer agent and the agent selected by the majority selection policy, respectively. Columns 5-7 contain the observed performance of the lifesaver agents; and columns 8-10 contain the models resulting from these observations (we have listed only the mean of the observed performance).

The first two rows in Table 1 (for time T_0) contain the initial conditions of the collaboration. Columns 8-10 contain the initial values of the models maintained by A_1 and A_2 for the Internal Resources (rescue performance) of A_1, A_2 and A_3. These initial values, which are *not* consistent with the real performance of the agents in question, are also recorded as the first "observed" performance of A_1, A_2 and A_3. This is done to model a behaviour whereby an agent's initial "opinion" of the members of its team can be influenced, but not immediately replaced, by observations of their performance.

According to the models maintained by A_1 and A_2, A_3 has the best performance. Hence, A_3 is selected by both A_1 and A_2 when a rescue is announced at time T_1. However, as expected from the *IR* of A_3, the agent's actual performance (0.4 at time T_1, Column 7) is poorer than that anticipated by the observer agents. Both agents observe this performance, and update their models accordingly (Column 10).

Now, when a new rescue must be performed (at time T_2), agent A_1 proposes A_3, as it is still the best according to its models, but agent A_2 proposes A_1. As indicated above, according to our tie-breaking rule, the first agent in the ordered list of agents is chosen. This is A_1, as it appears in the list before A_3. However, A_1 does not perform

Table 1. Sample agent assignment to a sequence of rescues

Time	Observer agent	Proposed agent	Selected agent	Observed performance of A_1	A_2	A_3	Models $M(A_1)$	$M(A_2)$	$M(A_3)$
T_0	A_1			0.3	0.4	0.5	0.3	0.4	0.5
	A_2			0.6	0.5	0.7	0.6	0.5	0.7
T_1	A_1	A_3	A_3	0.3	0.4	0.5 **0.4**	0.3	0.4	**0.45**
	A_2	A_3		0.6	0.5	0.7 **0.4**	0.6	0.5	**0.55**
T_2	A_1	A_3	A_1	0.3 **0.3**	0.4	0.5 0.4	**0.3**	0.4	0.45
	A_2	A_1		0.6 **0.3**	0.5	0.7 0.4	**0.45**	0.5	0.55
T_3	A_1	A_3	A_3	0.3 0.3	0.4	0.5 0.4 **0.2**	0.3	0.4	**0.37**
	A_2	A_3		0.6 0.3	0.5	0.7 0.4 **0.2**	0.45	0.5	**0.43**
T_4	A_1	A_2	A_2	0.3 0.3	0.4 **0.8**	0.5 0.4 0.2	0.3	**0.6**	0.37
	A_2	A_2		0.6 0.3	0.5 **0.8**	0.7 0.4 0.2	0.45	**0.65**	0.43
T_5	A_1	A_2	A_2	0.3 0.3	0.4 0.8 **0.7**	0.5 0.4 0.2	0.3	**0.63**	0.37
	A_2	A_2		0.6 0.3	0.5 0.8 **0.7**	0.7 0.4 0.2	0.45	**0.67**	0.43

well in the rescue (0.3 at time T_2, Column 5), which significantly lowers $M_{A_2}(A_1)$ to 0.45 (Column 8). As a result, A_3 is once more the top choice of both observer agents for the next rescue (at time T_3). But A_3 performs quite badly (0.2 at time T_3, Column 7), thereby further lowering its expected performance according to the models maintained by the observers (Column 10).

At this stage, the bad performance of both A_1 and A_3 has yielded models with low mean values for these agents. Hence, for the next rescue, A_2 is chosen by both observer agents (at time T_4). This is a high-performing agent that has been under-estimated by both observers. Its good performance (0.8 at time T_4, Column 6) raises the expected value in the models maintained by both observers (Column 9). As a result, A_2, who is now clearly preferred by both observers, is chosen for the rescue at time T_5, rendering once more a good performance (0.7 at time T_5, Column 6).

At this point, the models maintained by the observer agents are closer to the IR of the lifesavers than the initial (random) models. Since both observer agents have an observation capacity of three observations, the next time a rescue is performed, the initial value will be dropped, which will further increase the accuracy of the models.

3   Simulation-Based Evaluation

We evaluated our extensions of the ETAPP framework by means of simulation experiments which assess the impact of the following parameters on task performance: (1) Internal Resources, (2) Observation Capacity, and (3) Agent-Selection Policy. The same model-updating procedure was used in all our experiments (when $OC=1$, this procedure reverts to that used in our original framework). Our simulation is based on the Surf Rescue (SR) scenario introduced in Section 2.2, where the task is to rescue a person in distress. However, in our simulation the team of lifesavers is composed of five agents.

3.1   Simulation Parameters

The parameters corresponding to our extensions were varied as follows.

- **Internal Resources** – We defined teams of agents with different degrees of stability: *Invariant, Stable, Medium, Unstable* and *Mixed*. The agents in Invariant teams exhibit the same performance in all the rescues. Agents in Stable teams exhibit low performance variability – the standard deviation of their performance distribution ranges between 0 and 0.2. The standard deviation for the performance of agents in Medium teams ranges between 0.2 and 0.8, and for agents in Unstable teams between 0.8 and 1. The Mixed team includes a mixture of stable, medium and unstable agents. The mean of the performance distribution is randomly initialized for the agents in all types of teams. In the future, we propose to conduct experiments with high-performing, medium-performing and low-performing teams.

- **Observation Capacity** – We varied the *OC* of the agents between 1 and 8. When *OC=i*, agents retain the last *i* observations made, and when *OC=1*, their observation capacity is as for the original ETAPP framework.

- **Agent Selection Policy** – We experimented with the two policies mentioned in Section 2.1: *optimistic* and *majority*.

In addition, we constructed two benchmark collaboration settings: RAND and OMNI.

- The RAND (or random) setting defines a lower bound, where a rescue is conducted by an agent that has been chosen randomly from the team. In this setting, agents do not maintain or update models of their collaborators' resources, and do not communicate proposals.

- The OMNI (or omniscient) setting defines an upper bound, where the best-performing agent in the team is always assigned to a rescue. This setting is consistent with the traditional assumption of multi-agent systems whereby agents have accurate knowledge about the performance of team members prior to the collaboration (i.e., $M_{A_i}(A_j) = IR_{A_j}$ for $i, j = 1, \ldots, m$). In this setting, all agents have the same accurate models, and hence do not update their models or communicate proposals.

3.2   Methodology

We ran one simulation for each combination of the simulation parameters ($IR \times OC \times \mathcal{P}_A = 5 \times 8 \times 2 = 80$), plus one simulation for each of the benchmark settings, RAND and OMNI. Each simulation consists of ten trials, each divided into 1000 runs (we selected this number of trials and runs because it yields stable and continuous behaviour patterns). Each run consists of a rescue task that is repeated until convergence is reached.

The *IR* and *M* for each agent are initialized at the beginning of each run. *IR* are initialized as specified by the type of the team (e.g., Stable or Unstable), and *M* are initialized with random values.[1] The *IR* of each agent remain constant throughout a run (the agent's performance is drawn from the distribution specified in the *IR*), while *M* are updated from the observations made for each rescue in the run.

The process for reaching convergence works as follows. At the beginning of a run, different lifesavers may be proposed for a rescue task due to the discrepancy between

---

[1] We also conducted experiments where all the models are initialized with a value of 0.5 (medium expected performance), and with a value of 1.0 (high expected performance). The overall results are similar to those obtained with the randomly initialized models, except for the Invariant and Stable group of agents and the 0.5 initialization, which yield a worse average performance. This is because a run terminates when the chosen agent's performance is repeatedly better than 0.5, and so other agents who may be better are not given a chance, thereby converging to a local maximum (Section 3.3).

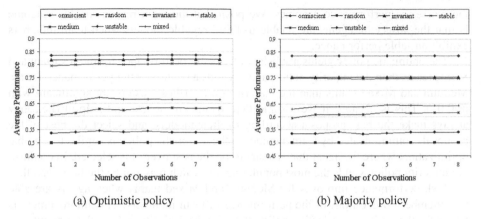

(a) Optimistic policy   (b) Majority policy

Fig. 1. Average task performance obtained with the optimistic and the majority agent-selection policy plotted against observation capacity for several types of teams

the models maintained by the different agents. After each rescue, the agents update their models based on the performance of the chosen agent. Hence, when a rescue task is announced in the next turn, more agents are likely to propose the same lifesaver (but not necessarily the lifesaver chosen for the previous task). A run is terminated when the same lifesaver is chosen in N consecutive turns (we have experimented with $N = 2$ and $N = 5$; the results presented in Section 3.3 are for $N = 5$).

3.3   Results

The results of our experiments are shown in Figure 1, which depicts the average task performance obtained with our two selection policies as a function of OC for our seven types of teams – RAND, OMNI, Invariant, Stable, Medium, Unstable and Mixed. Figure 1(a) shows the results obtained with the optimistic policy, and Figure 1(b) shows the results for the majority policy.

Our measure of task performance for a run is the mean of the IR distribution for the agent on which the observers eventually converged. For instance, in the example in Table 1, this agent is A_2, whose $IR_{A_2}(rescue)$ has mean 0.8 (STDV=0.3). This measure reflects the final outcome of the combination of the parameters of the simulation for the run in question.

As expected, the results for the RAND and OMNI settings correspond to the worst and best performance respectively, and are used as a benchmark for comparison with the other settings. The performance for the Invariant team is slightly lower than that for the OMNI setting. This is due to the fact that the Invariant team sometimes converges to a local maximum, which is reached when the agents in the team repeatedly select an agent that is not the best. This happens when the agents under-estimate the performance of the best agent to the extent that it will never be proposed by any agent in the group, and hence will never perform the task. These results are consistent with the results obtained for the RAND, OMNI and default scenarios in our previous work [4].

As seen in Figure 1, the average performance obtained for the other types of teams is generally worse than that obtained for the Invariant team. This is due to the higher variability in agent performance. In fact, the more unstable the agents in the team are, the worse the performance becomes. We posit that the main reason for this outcome is that the observing agents are unable to build reliable models when team members exhibit unstable performance.

The optimistic policy yields a substantially better performance for the Invariant and Stable teams than the majority policy, and it yields a slightly better performance for the Medium and Mixed teams than the majority policy (these results are significant with p=0.01). This is because if we assume that agents are honest and helpful (i.e., they always make the best proposal according to their models, and select the best of the proposals communicated by team members), the optimistic policy is similar to a global optimization, where the agent that appears to be the best overall is selected. In contrast, the majority policy yields the most popular agent, which may not be the best overall.

Task performance improves for Medium and Mixed teams when agents are able to remember observations of the performance of team members. This improvement is larger for the optimistic selection policy than for the majority policy (these results are significant with p=0.01). Further, this improvement is achieved with only 3 observations for the optimistic policy, and with 5 observations for the majority policy. This discrepancy may be caused by the need for additional "evidence" in order to get several agents to prefer the same agent, as required by the majority policy.

Finally, the performance of Unstable teams is not affected by the agent-selection policy or the agents' observation capacity, as the agents in these teams exhibit too much performance variation for the observer agents to reach reliable conclusions.

4   Related Research

Several research projects have demonstrated that maintaining models of features of collaborators can benefit different aspects of task performance [6, 3, 7].[2]

Suryadi and Gmytrasiewicz [6] and Gmytrasiewicz and Durfee [3] investigated agents that apply a decision-theoretic procedure to make decisions that maximize their own individual payoffs. This procedure takes into account the "payoff matrix" of collaborators, which in turn is learned from observations of their behaviour. Our system also learns the behaviour of other agents from observations (although we learn only the mean and standard deviation of their performance). However, whereas Suryadi and Gmytrasiewicz's agents make individual decisions and do not communicate with each other, our agents communicate proposals in order to make a joint decision. Vassileva et al. developed I-Help [7], which is a large scale multi-agent system that provides students with distributed help resources. Personal agents represent students' personal preferences. Matchmaker agents collect this information from personal agents, and match students that require help in a certain topic with students that are able to provide help. The incorporation of our model-update mechanism into the models maintained by the matchmaker agents would increase the accuracy of these models, and hence improve their usefulness for help-seeking students.

Our OC parameter is similar to the attentional limitations considered by Walker [8], and is related to the memory boundedness investigated by Rubinstein [5]. However,

---

[2] Garrido et al. [2] and Suryadi and Gmytrasiewicz [6] provide an overview of research on modeling other agents.

both Walker and Rubinstein also considered inferential limitations, while we consider agent-modeling limitations.

Finally, our agents' ability to build models of agents from observations resembles the work of Davison and Hirsh [1]. Their model gave greater weight to more recent events than to earlier events, while we achieve a similar behaviour through our *OC* parameter, which specifies that only the last K observations should be considered.

5   Conclusion

We have extended our ETAPP collaboration framework to model team members that exhibit variable performance. This requires a probabilistic representation of agent performance, the specification of the number of observations retained by observer agents, and a procedure for building agent models from these observations. In addition, we have offered the majority policy for assigning agents to tasks, and compared its impact on task performance with the impact of the optimistic policy.

We evaluated our extensions by means of a simulated rescue scenario, where we varied the performance stability of teams of agents, the number of observations retained by observer agents, and the policy used to allocate agents to tasks. Our results show that performance variability has a large impact on task performance, that a small number of observations of agent behaviour is sufficient to improve task performance, and that the task performance obtained by applying the optimistic selection policy is at least as good as that obtained with the majority policy.

References

1. Brian Davison and Haym Hirsh. Predicting sequences of user actions. In *Notes of the AAAI/ICML 1998 Workshop on Predicting the Future: AI Approaches to Time-Series Analysis*, Madison, Wisconsin, 1998.
2. Leonardo Garrido, Katia Sycara, and R. Brena. Quantifying the utility of building agents models: An experimental study. In *Proceedings of the Agents-00/ECML-00 Workshop on Learning Agents*, Barcelona, Spain, 2000.
3. Piotr J. Gmytrasiewicz and Edmund H. Durfee. Rational communication in multi-agent environments. *Autonomous Agents and Multi-Agent Systems*, 4(3):233–272, 2001.
4. Christian Guttmann and Ingrid Zukerman. Towards models of incomplete and uncertain knowledge of collaborators' internal resources. In Jörg Denzinger, Gabriela Lindemann, Ingo J. Timm, and Rainer Unland, editors, *Second German Conference on MultiAgent system TEchnologieS (MATES) 2004*, LNAI 3187, 58–72, Erfurt, Germany, 2004. Springer.
5. Ariel Rubinstein. *Modeling Bounded Rationality*. Zeuthen lecture book series. MIT Press, Cambridge, Massachusetts, 1998.
6. Dicky Suryadi and Piotr J. Gmytrasiewicz. Learning models of other agents using influence diagrams. In *Proceedings of the Seventh International Conference on User Modeling*, 223–232, Banff, Canada, 1999.
7. Julita Vassileva, Gordon McCalla, and Jim Greer. Multi-agent multi-user modeling in I-Help. *User Modeling and User-Adapted Interaction*, 13(1-2):179–210, 2003.
8. Marilyn A. Walker. The effect of resource limits and task complexity on collaborative planning in dialogue. *Artificial Intelligence*, 1-2(85):181–243, 1996.

Detecting When Students Game the System, Across Tutor Subjects and Classroom Cohorts

Ryan Shaun Baker, Albert T. Corbett, Kenneth R. Koedinger, and Ido Roll

Human-Computer Interaction Institute, Carnegie Mellon University,
5000 Forbes Avenue, Pittsburgh, PA, 15217, USA
{rsbaker, corbett, koedinger, idoroll}@cmu.edu

Abstract. Building a generalizable detector of student behavior within intelligent tutoring systems presents two challenges: transferring between different cohorts of students (who may develop idiosyncratic strategies of use), and transferring between different tutor lessons (which may have considerable variation in their interfaces, making cognitively equivalent behaviors appear quite different within log files). In this paper, we present a machine-learned detector which identifies students who are "gaming the system", attempting to complete problems with minimal cognitive effort, and determine that the detector transfers successfully across student cohorts but less successfully across tutor lessons.

1 Introduction and Prior Work

In the last couple of decades, there has been considerable work in creating educational systems that adapt to their users – offering help and feedback targeted to a student's specific cognitive or motivational needs. However, just as educational systems can adapt to their users, users can adapt to their educational systems, sometimes in ways that lead to poorer learning [2,5]. For instance, students who game the system, attempting to perform well in an educational task by systematically exploiting properties and regularities in the system used to complete that task, rather than by thinking about the material, learn less than other students [2]. Examples of gaming include systematic guessing, and repeatedly requesting help until the system gives the answer. It may be possible to substantially improve learning environments' educational effectiveness by adapting to how students choose to use the learning environment. In order to do this, we need to be able to detect when a student is selecting strategies that lead to poorer learning.

In [1], we presented a Latent-Response Model [4] that accurately detected if a student was gaming the system, within a specific tutor lesson, cross-validated across students in 4 classes. This model distinguished "GAMED-HURT" students who gamed the system in a fashion associated with poor learning both from students who were never observed gaming, and from "GAMED-NOT-HURT" students who gamed in a different fashion not associated with poor learning. The model did so by first predicting whether each individual student action was an instance of gaming (using tutor log files), and then aggregated these predictions to predict what proportion of time each student was gaming (comparing the predicted proportions to data from

L. Ardissono, P. Brna, and A. Mitrovic (Eds.): UM 2005, LNAI 3538, pp. 220–224, 2005.

classroom observations). The classifier's ability to distinguish gaming was assessed with A' values, which give the probability that if the model is given one gaming student and one non-gaming student, it will accurately identify which is which [3].

A model in this framework consists of features selected from linear, quadratic, and interaction effects on a set of 26 base features describing a student action (for instance, what interface widget it involved and how long it took), and its historical context (for instance, how many errors this student made on this skill in past problems). The model presented here improves on the model reported in [1] in three fashions: First, by adding two features to the set used in [1], in order to represent asymptotic skills (which students on the whole either knew before starting the tutor, or failed to learn while using the tutor). Second, by switching from using forward selection to select model features to testing a set of search paths constrained by fast correlation-based filtering [6] (in both cases, Leave One Out Cross Validation was used to prevent over-fitting). Third, by switching from treating both types of gaming as identical during training to training to detect just GAMED-HURT students, considerably improving our model's ability to distinguish between types of gaming, $\Delta Z=6.57$, $p<0.01$. After these changes, our model was significantly better than chance at distinguishing GAMED-HURT students from non-gaming students (within the original classroom cohort and lesson), A' $=0.85$, $p<0.01$, and at distinguishing GAMED-HURT students from GAMED-NOT-HURT students, A' $=0.96$, $p<0.01$.

Though this detector is effective within a single population and tutor lesson, it will be more useful if it can generalize across student populations and cognitive tutor lessons (or even across types of interactive learning environments). There appear to be multiple ways to game a given system, and we have observed students teaching each other new strategies for gaming – therefore, different cohorts of students may game differently. Similarly, different tutor lessons often have different patterns of interaction, because of differences in subject matter. In this paper, we present work towards detecting gaming in a fashion robust to differences between tutor lessons and classroom cohorts, through analyzing how well a model trained on one population or lesson transfers to other populations and lessons, and how the features that correlate to gaming differ across data sets.

2 Detecting Gaming Across Classroom Cohorts

In this section, we discuss how well our detector transfers between our original student cohort (termed the 2003 cohort) and a newly recruited cohort of students (termed the 2004 cohort). At a surface level, the two cohorts were similar: both were drawn from students in 8th and 9th grade non-gifted/non special-needs cognitive tutor classrooms in the same middle schools in the suburban Pittsburgh area. However, our observations suggested that the two cohorts behaved differently. The 2004 cohort gamed 88% more frequently than the 2003 cohort, $t(175)=2.34$, $p=0.02$, but a lower proportion of the gaming students had poor learning, $\chi^2(1, N=64)=6.01$, $p=0.01$. This data does not directly tell us whether gaming was different in kind between the two populations – however, if gaming differs substantially in kind between populations, two populations as different as these are likely to manifest such differences, and thus these populations provide us with an opportunity to test whether our gaming detector is robust to differences between distinct cohorts of students.

Table 1. Our model's ability to transfer between student cohorts. Boldface signifies both that a model is statistically significantly better within training cohort than within transfer cohort, and that the model is significantly better than the model trained on both cohorts [1]

Training Cohort	G-H vs no game, 2003 cohort	G-H vs no game, 2004 cohort	G-H vs G-N-H, 2003 cohort	G-H vs G-N-H, 2004 cohort
2003	*0.85*	*0.76*	***0.96***	0.69*
2004	*0.77*	***0.92***	*0.75*	***0.94***
Both	*0.8*	*0.86*	*0.85*	*0.85*

The most direct way to evaluate transfer across populations is to see how successfully the best-fit model for each cohort of students fits to the other cohort. As shown in Table 1, a model trained on either cohort could be transferred as-is to the other cohort, without any re-fitting, and perform significantly better than chance at detecting GAMED-HURT students (marginally significantly better at distinguishing them from GAMED-NOT-HURT students in the 2004 cohort; significantly better in all other comparisons). However, in 3 of the 4 comparisons, the models were statistically significantly better in the student population within which they were trained than when they were transferred to the other population of students.

It was also possible to train a model, using the data from both student cohorts, which achieved a good fit to both data sets, shown in Table 1. This model was significantly better than chance in all 4 comparisons conducted. However, models trained in single cohorts did better than the unified model, in 3 of the 4 comparisons.

3 Detecting Gaming Across Tutor Lessons

In this section, we discuss how well our detector transfers between two tutor lessons, within a single student population. One lesson (the "scatterplot" lesson) involved creating and interpreting scatterplots of data; the other lesson (the "geometry" lesson) involved computing the surface area of 3D solids. Both lessons were drawn from the same middle-school mathematics curriculum and were designed using the same general pedagogical principles, although the scatterplot lesson had a greater variety of widgets and a more linear solution path. Our observers did not notice substantial differences between the types of gaming they observed in these two lessons. Overall, the same students gamed between lessons – a student's frequency of gaming was also correlated across lessons, $r=0.22$, $p=0.02$.

The most direct way to evaluate transfer across lessons is to see how successfully the best-fit model for each tutor lesson fits to the other tutor lesson. As shown in Table 2, the results were poor. Though both models were significantly better than

---

[1] All numbers are A' values. Italics denote a model which is statistically significantly better than chance ($p<0.05$); asterisks (*) denote marginal significance ($p<0.10$).

Table 2. Models trained on the scatterplot lesson, the geometry lesson, and both lessons together. All models trained using only the 2004 students.[1] Boldface denotes the model(s) which are statistically significantly best in a given category

Training Lesson	G-H vs no game, SCATTERPLOT	G-H vs no game, GEOMETRY	G-H vs G-N-H, SCATTERPLOT	G-H vs G-N-H, GEOMETRY
SCATTERPLOT	*0.92*	0.55	*0.94*	0.63
GEOMETRY	0.53	*0.80*	0.41	*0.90*
BOTH	*0.82*	*0.77*	0.70*	*0.82*

chance within the training lesson, neither model was significantly better than chance when transferred to the other lesson. It was possible to train a model, using both data sets, which achieved a good fit to both data sets, as shown in Table 2. This model was significantly better than chance on 3 of 4 measures (and was marginally significant on the fourth); however, on 2 of 4 measures it was statistically significantly worse than a model trained on one lesson alone. But while this unified model performed well in the units it was trained in, it transferred very poorly to the 2003 cohort of students using the scatterplot tutor, only reaching A'=0.54,p=0.77 (G-H versus non-gaming) and A'=0.54,p=0.78 (G-H versus G-N-H). This result is surprising, considering that a model trained just on the 2004 cohort using the scatterplot tutor was quite effective at detecting gaming within the 2003 cohort (see Table 1). Hence, although we can develop a unified model at this point, our modeling approach has not yet delivered a unified model which transfers across lessons in a generalizable fashion.

But why not? The difference in gaming between these lessons is small enough that our observers did not notice a qualitative difference in gaming between them. Additionally, the top candidate features considered for each lesson (which are highly correlated to gaming but not to each other) appear conceptually similar (see Table 3). In both sets, gaming corresponds to errors and repeated quick actions. However, the top 6 features for scatterplots averaged an unimpressive correlation of 0.06 to gaming in the geometry data set, and the top 6 features for geometry averaged a correlation of 0.09 to gaming in the scatterplot data set, suggesting that the difficulty in transferring between models is not just an artifact of the specific features chosen during model selection. It is possible that the overall strategic choice underlying gaming is consistent across the two lessons, but that the interface and pedagogical differences between the two lessons may be causing our models to differ considerably at the detailed grain size our approach relies upon to make predictions.

Table 3. Top 3 non-intercorrelated GAMED-HURT features in each lesson (2004 data)

SCATTERPLOT
1) Several quick actions in a row
2) A high percentage of errors on skills that involve popup menus (ie multiple choice)
3) Quick actions on problem steps that need a numerical answer

GEOMETRY
1) Requesting help several actions in a row on skills the student has a history of getting wrong
2) Several very brief help requests in quick succession
3) Several very quick errors in succession

4 Discussion and Conclusions

In this paper, we have presented a system that detects when a student is gaming the system. This system transfers successfully across cohorts of students. However, the same detector can not, at this point, transfer without re-training to different tutor lessons. Furthermore, training data from two lessons together does not produce a model which can transfer across student cohorts. Despite this, detectors for different lessons are detecting qualitatively similar behavior. One approach would be use our knowledge of what actions are gaming in different lessons to develop a system that maps from a tutor interface to gaming actions. However, given that our approach can train successful models for fairly different tutor lessons, it may not actually be necessary to make individual models that can generalize across lessons. For example, if the detector is deployed in a year-long curriculum, it may be possible to develop interventions which guide students to stop gaming, where the effect s maintained even after the intervention is no longer present. In this event, we would only need to detect gaming in a few lessons during the course of a curriculum, and could train a detector for each of those lessons. This approach would not afford rapidly extending our detector to new curricula, but may still be quite effective in improving student learning. Regardless, a gaming detector such as ours will only be useful if combined with an intervention that persuades students to change how they use the tutor. If the tutor responds to gaming in a fashion that gives students an incentive to learn how to game the gaming detector, the gaming detector will quickly become ineffective. Systems that detect intentional mis-use must adapt in a fashion that makes it in the student's interest to use the software appropriately.

Acknowledgements. We would like to thank James Fogarty, Vincent Aleven, Angela Wagner, Tom Mitchell, Brian Junker, Amy Hurst, Cristen Torrey, and Amy Ogan for helpful suggestions and assistance. This work was funded by an NDSEG Fellowship.

References

1. Baker, R.S., Corbett, A.T., Koedinger, K.R. Detecting Student Misuse of Intelligent Tutoring Systems. Proceedings of the 7th International Conference on Intelligent Tutoring Systems (2004), 531-540.
2. Baker, R.S., Corbett, A.T., Koedinger, K.R., Wagner, A.Z. Off-Task Behavior in the Cognitive Tutor Classroom: When Students "Game the System". Proceedings of ACM CHI 2004: Computer-Human Interaction (2004) 383-390
3. Donaldson, W. Accuracy of d' and A' as Estimates of Sensitivity. Bulletin of the Psychonomic Society Vol. 31(4) (1993) 271-274.
4. Maris, E. Psychometric Latent Response Models. Psychometrika vol.60(4) (1995) 523-547.
5. Stevens, R., Soller, A., Cooper, M, Sprang, M. Modeling the Development of Problem-Solving Skills in Chemistry with a Web-Based Tutor. Proceedings of the 7th International Conference on Intelligent Tutoring Systems (ITS 2004), 580-591.
6. Yu, L., Liu, H. Feature Selection for High-Dimensional Data: A Fast Correlation-Based Filter Solution. Proc. of the Intl. Conference on Machine Learning (ICML-03), 856-863.

A Bayesian Approach to Modelling Users' Information Display Preferences

Beate Grawemeyer and Richard Cox

Representation & Cognition Group, Department of Informatics,
University of Sussex, Falmer, Brighton BN1 9QH, UK
{beateg, richc}@sussex.ac.uk

Abstract. This paper describes the process by which we constructed a user model for ERST - an External Representation Selection Tutor - which recommends external representations (ERs) for particular database query task types based upon individual preferences, in order to enhance ER reasoning performance. The user model is based on experimental studies which examined the effect of background knowledge of ERs upon performance and preferences over different types of tasks.

1 Introduction

Successful use of external representations (ERs) depends upon skillful matching of a particular representation with the demands of the task. [2] and [4] provide numerous examples of how a good fit between a task's demands and particular representations can facilitate search and read-off of information. [5] provides a review of studies that show that tasks involving perceiving relationships in data or making associations are best supported by graphs, whereas 'point value' read-off is better facilitated by tabular representations. But people differ in their representational expertise and in their individual ER preferences for particular task types.

We describe the development of a user model for ERST - an External Representation Selection Tutor. This has been constructed on the basis of empirical data gathered from two psychological experiments. The study reported earlier in [3] investigated the representation selection and reasoning behaviour of participants who were offered a choice of information-equivalent data representations (e.g. tables, bar charts, etc.) upon various types of database query tasks. Following that earlier study, the aim of the experiment reported here was to investigate the degree to which task types are more representation-specific[1] than others, with respect to reasoning performance and response latency. For both experiments, a prototype automatic information visualization engine (AIVE) was used to present a series of questions about the information in a database. The results of the experiments indicated that ERST needs to take into account

---

[1] These are tasks for which only a few, specialised, representational forms are useful.

L. Ardissono, P. Brna, and A. Mitrovic (Eds.): UM 2005, LNAI 3538, pp. 225–230, 2005.

a) individual differences (like user's ER preferences), b) their level of experience and c) the domain task characteristics, in order to provide effective ERs that reflect individual needs and therefore enhance ER reasoning performance. A Bayesian network for ERST has been constructed based on the experimental results.

2   Experiment

The aim of the study reported here was to investigate the degree to which some task types are more representation-specific than others in terms of reasoning performance and response latency. We were interested to discover what task types can be answered successfully with a variety of different representations and which tasks were more constrained in terms of useful representations. We define representation-specificity as follows: For highly representation-specific tasks only a few, specialised, representational forms are useful. Whereas for low representation-specific tasks a range of different types of representations can be used successfully to solve the problem.

This study builds on previous work [3] in the following ways: The AIVE system has been changed from a Java Applet to a stand alone Java Application in order to produce more accurate timing data[2]. The system has been extended with a new set of more representation-specific critical task types. We also employ a new approach to the assessment of subjects 'graphical literacy' [1].

Our hypotheses were, that different degrees of representation-specific tasks types influence participants' performance on a) their ER selection *skill*; b) time to answer the database query (latency); and c) the correctness of their response on the database query task.

Procedure
Twenty participants were recruited (5 software engineers, 1 graphic designer, 1 html programmer, 2 IT business managers, 7 postgraduate students, and 4 research officers/fellows). Each participant completed 4 pre-experimental ER tasks followed by the AIVE database query problem solving session.

The ER pre-tasks [1] assessed the visual recognition of particular ERs requiring real/fake decisions, ER categorisation, functional knowledge of ERs, and specific naming. This represents an information processing approach to the assessment of 'graphical literacy' [1] and these ER tasks were employed as pre-tests of ER knowledge. Participants then performed the AIVE database query tasks using the same procedure as that used in [3]. Participants were asked to make judgments and comparisons between cars and car features based on database information. The database contained information about 10 cars: manufacturer, model, CO^2 emission, engine size, *etc.* Each subject responded to 30 database questions, of which there were 6 types: identify; correlate ; quantifier-set; locate;

---

[2] The timing data in the previous experiment lacked precision because of time delays caused by the internet connection.

cluster; compare negative. Participants were informed that to help them answer the questions, the system (AIVE) would supply the appropriate data from the database. AIVE also offered participants a choice of representations of the data. They could choose between various types of ERs, *eg.* set diagram, scatter plot, bar chart, sector graph, pie chart and table (the full range of representations were offered by the system on all queries). The options were presented in the form of an array of buttons each with an icon depicting - in stylised form - an ER type (table, scatterplot *etc*). Participants were told that they were free to choose any ER, but that they should select a form of display they thought was most likely to be helpful for answering the question. Participants then proceeded to the first question, read it and selected a representation. The spatial layout of the representation selection buttons was randomized across the 30 query tasks in order to prevent participants from developing a set pattern of selection. Based on the literature (eg.[2]) a single 'optimal' ER for each task was identified[3]. After the participant made his/her representation choice, AIVE generated and displayed the representation instantiated with the data required for answering the question. Participants then answered the question using the chosen display. Participants were not permitted to select a different representation following their initial selection. This constraint was imposed in order to encourage participants to carefully consider which representation was best matched to the task. Following a completed response, participants were presented with the next task and the sequence was repeated. The following data were recorded: (1) the randomized position of each representation icon from trial to trial; (2) the user's representation choices; (3) time to read question and select representation; (4) time to answer the question using chosen ER; and (5) participants' responses to questions.

Results and Discussion

To recapitulate, each of 20 subjects performed 30 AIVE tasks (600 data points in total). The simple bivariate correlations across all AIVE tasks for display selection accuracy (DSA), database query answering accuracy (DBQA), display selection latency (DSL) and database query answering latency (DBQL) were: DSA correlated significantly and positively with DBQA ($r=.30$, $p<.01$); DSA is significantly negatively correlated with DSL ($r=.-17$, $p<.01$); DSA and DBQL are significantly negatively correlated ($r=-.32$, $p<.01$); There is a significant negative correlation between DBQA and DBQL ($r=-.28$, $p<.01$); DSL and DBQL are significantly positively correlated ($r=.30$, $p<.01$). The results across all AIVE task types show that good display-type selection will lead to better query answering performance. The selection latency results show that a speedy selection of a display type in AIVE is associated with a good display-type choice. Less time spent responding to the database query question is associated with a good

---

[3] However, each AIVE query type could *potentially* be answered with any of the representations offered by the system with the exception of quantifier-set tasks for which the only real effective representation was a set diagram.

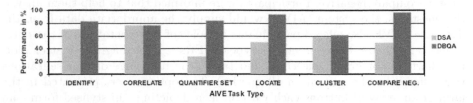

Fig. 1. AIVE task type performance

display-type choice and correct query response. This suggests that the selection and database query latencies may be used in ERST as predictors of users' DSA and DBQA performance. Looking at the different task types, these results differ extensively in terms of representational specificity. As shown in figure 1, 77% of AIVE *correlate* type queries were answered correctly by participants. Moreover, in 77% of the cases they chose the most appropriate ER display (scatter plot) from the array of display types offered by AIVE. The correlation coefficients for AIVEs' *correlate* tasks were: DSA and DBQA are significantly positively correlated (r=.67 , p<.01); DSL and DBQL are significantly positively correlated (r=.56, p<.01). The results suggest that good display-type selection is associated with accurate query answering performance. Longer display selection latency is associated with longer time spent responding to the database query question. Hence there does not seem to a be a speed/accuracy trade-off in display selection - participants either know which ER to choose and get on with the task, or they don't. In contrast, the locate task could be answered effective with different kinds of data displays. Overall, subjects locate task queries were answered with a high degree of accuracy (94%). However, in only in 51% cases did participants choose the 'right' representation (table or matrix ER). A range of other AIVE display forms were also effective (bar and pie charts, scatterplots). No significant correlations between AIVEs variables were detected. The results show that the correlate task is more representation-specific than the locate task. Therefore in order to predict DSA and DBQA performance ERST needs to include a variety of tasks that differ in terms of their representational specificity.

3   ERST's Bayesian Network

ERST's user model needs to track selection accuracy and database query answering performance for various display and response accuracy relationships within and across the various database query task types. ERST will need to be more stringent in its interventions on highly representationally-specific task types such as correlate tasks but will be able to be more lenient on more display-heterogeneous tasks. Various machine learning techniques differ in the advantages and disadvantages they have for particular applications. They also differ in terms of the user data need for the adaptation process. According to our experimental findings, the most appropriate implementation for ERST's user model is a Bayesian network. The network is being constructed and 'seeded' with the

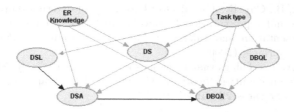

Fig. 2. ERSTs' Bayesian network

empirical data so that it can monitor and predict users' ER selection preference patterns within and across query types, relate query response accuracy and latencies to particular display selections (DS) and contrive query/display option combinations to probe an individual user's degree of graphical literacy. The structure of the Bayesian network based on the experimental data can be seen in Figure 2. For example the arc between DSA and DBQL represents the association that good display selection results in better query performance and the link between DSL and DSA represents the finding that a speedy selection of a display type in AIVE is associated with a good display-type choice.

The empirical data is used to instantiate values in the relevant conditional probability tables (CPTs) at each node of the model.

4   Conclusion and Future Work

In this paper we described our process of constructing a Bayesian network for modelling user's ER preferences, based on experimental data. The aim of this model is to provide effective ERs that reflect individual needs and therefore enhance ER reasoning performance. The resulting Bayesian network structure is based on empirical findings and the gathered data is reflected in the CPTs. The next step in our research will focus on ERST's adaptation decisions. For example, when and how to recommend ERs and the manner in which ERST utilises data from new users. The user model will need to be evaluated through user studies and will be iteratively refined. We also plan to investigate how well ERST is able to accommodate individual differences in ER selection preference.

References

1. Cox, R., Romero, P., du Boulay, B., Lutz R.: A Cognitive Processing Perspective on Student Programmers' 'Graphicacy'. In Diagrammatic Representation and Inference: Third International Conference, Diagrams 2004, Berlin, Springer (2004)
2. Day, R.: Alternative representations. In Bower, G., ed.: The Psychology of Learning and Motivation **22**, New York, Academic Press (1988) 261–305

3. Grawemeyer, B., Cox, R.: The effect of knowledge-of-external-representations upon performance and representational choice in a database query task. In Diagrammatic Representation and Inference: Third International Conference, Diagrams 2004, Berlin, Springer (2004)
4. Norman, D.A., ed: Things that make us smart. Addison-Wesley, MA (1993)
5. Vessey, I.: Cognitive fit: A theory-based analysis of the graphs versus tables literature. Decision Sciences **22**, (1991) 219–241

Modeling of the Residual Capability for People with Severe Motor Disabilities: Analysis of Hand Posture

Rachid Kadouche[1], Mounir Mokhtari[1], and Marc Maier[2]

[1] Institut National des Télécomunications-GET, Handicom Lab. Evry, France
[2] INSERM-U742 Université Pierre & Marie Curie, Paris, France
Rachid.kadouche@int-evry.fr

Abstract. People with severe motor disabilities use mainly their residual motor capability for the use of technical aids, and for the control of input devices to technical aids. This paper describes our work on characterizing the motor capability of the upper arm for patients with severe motor disabilities. This work is a continuation of a project aimed at modeling the arm posture of quadriplegic patients using STS (Spatial Tracking System) and at analyzing the compensatory strategies developed by hemiplegic patients while accessing physical interfaces for technical aids [5]. Here we report work undertaken for analyzing the posture of the hand: we have developed two calibration methods for the Cyberglove and compare their utility and ergonomics in applications on patients with motor disabilities. The first type of calibration proceeds sequentially and takes into account one joint after the other (of the hand and each digit), whereas the second procedure is based on a few key postures calibrating several joints at once. To compare the precision of both methods, four healthy subjects participated in experiments using the Cyberglove. We show that the first type of calibration is more accurate but takes longer, whereas the second is less accurate but shorter. This trade-off might be acceptable for assessing the manual workspace in patients with motor disabilities. In particular, excessive muscular fatigue and limited dexterity are decisive factors for choosing the calibration by key postures in patients. We applied the calibration by key postures to three myopathic patients and individually quantified their restricted manual working space.

1 Introduction

In order to evaluate the behavioral characteristics of users while they access different input devices, we have designed a quantitative methodology based on a newly developed software. We evaluate the use of different computer interfaces such as a mouse, a trackball, a joystick, etc, in order to determine the most suitable input device for each user. [1]. However to measure the motor capabilities when acting on different human-machine interfaces and to characterize the work-space, a 3D representation of the upper limb is necessary. We modeled the shoulder, arm and wrist with the use of the STS Spatial Tracking System, [5],[6]. However, because the hand was not represented in our model, the 3D representation of the upper limb remained incomplete and therefore, we

L. Ardissono, P. Brna, and A. Mitrovic (Eds.): UM 2005, LNAI 3538, pp. 231–235, 2005.

were not able to quantify the dexterity of the hand. Subsequently, we wanted to develop a complementary measurement system to study the manual dexterity, grip formation and digit movements, which would enable us to quantitatively model manual gestures used during human-machine interaction. In order to analyze and model hand postures and grip configurations, we opted for the use of the CyberGlove.

2   Calibration Method

The CyberGlove (Virtual Technologies, Palo Alto, CA) is a numerical single-sized glove which allows the measurement of up to 22 joint angles of the hand including the wrist. The torsion of the piezo-electric sensor generates an associated electrical signal, that is called RawValue after digital acquisition. To obtain the relationship between the raw sensor data and the actual joint angle (in degrees), a conversion factor gain and a constant term offset need to be determined for each sensor. Once both variables of calibration (gain and offset) are determined, the joint angle is calculated by equation (1). This procedure is called **calibration** of the CyberGlove [4].

$$Angle = gain \times (RawValue - offset) \tag{1}$$

To calculate gain and offset in equation (1), we need two different angles, angle1 and angle2. The relevant formulea are:

$$gain = (angle1 - angle2)/(RawValue1 - RawValue2) \tag{2}$$

$$offset = RawValue1 - (angle1/gain) \tag{3}$$

For our purposes, we assumed that wrist-related sensors (Palm Arch and Wrist Flexion sensor) would not provide significant information and would not be needed, since similar, redundant information is provided by the STS sensors. Usually, the calibration is performed by using key postures [3],[2], however, this depends on the purpose of the CyberGlove measurements. For our work, we have developed two calibration strategies: first a method based on single joint measurements ('detailed' calibration) and second a method based on predefined postures.

2.1   Calibration by Single-Joint Measurements

This method consists in calibrating each sensor on its own. For that the subject must hold two different and predefined angles for each articulation, which allows us to calculate the corresponding *gain* and *offset*. This procedure is sequentially applied for each of the 20 sensors.

2.2   Calibration by Key Postures

The use of 6 different key postures allows us to determine two different angles for all glove sensors (to resolve the equation (2) and (3)). We propose the following 6 postures (figure1):
Posture 1 corresponds to an angle of 0 for all glove sensors.
Posture 2 defines the angles for the thumb sensors: thumb roll sensor (90), metacarpal (45) and proximal (90) sensor.

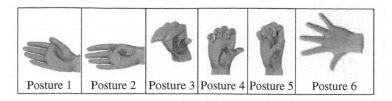

Fig. 1. The 6 proposed key postures

Posture 3 defines an angle of 90 for all metacarpal sensors except for the thumb.
Posture 4 defines an angle of 90 for all proximal sensors except for the thumb.
Posture 5 defines an angle of 90 for all distal sensors except for the thumb.
For posture 6, the hand is placed on a pre-drawn diagram that indicates the abduction angles of 10 between the little and ring finger, between the ring and middle finger, between the middle and index finger, and an angle of 45 for the Thumb-Index abduction, as well as 150 for the Wrist abduction.

3   Experimentation and Results

The goal was to assess the accuracy of two different calibration procedures and to quantify the work-space of the hand for patients with spinal cord injury or with muscular dystrophy by using the CyberGlove system.

3.1   Calibration in Health Subjects

First, we compared the accuracy of the calibration methods in 4 healthy subjects. For each subject, we calibrated the glove with both methods. The average time for the calibration by single-joint measurements was 10 minutes and demanded over 40 different postures. Calibration by the 6 key postures demanded less than 5 min. Then a particular posture with a predefined angular configuration of the hand was recorded. The results indicated that the joint-by-joint calibration is more accurate with deviations of about 5 or less degrees, whereas the calibration by key postures often shows errors larger than 5 degrees. However, the calibration by key postures may still be of sufficient accuracy for applications in the field of rehabilitation and ergonomics.

3.2   Application in Subjects with Motor Disabilities

We applied the CyberGlove system to 3 adult patients with severe motor disabilities. Two patients suffer from muscular dystrophy, the first (U1), male, 28 years of age, shows very little voluntary digit movements, except for small movements of the thumb and of the index. For obtaining the calibrations, U1 was actively assisted by the experimenter, who moved and held the joints passively. The second patient (U2), male, 25 years of age, suffers from Duchenne muscular dystrophy where the digits are only partially affected. Another patient (U3), male, 45 years of age, is affected by a degenerative neuromuscular disease provoking spasticity and tremor. In all three patients we used the calibration by key postures, which took about 5 min. The joint-by-joint calibration was impractical or simply impossible due to fatigue, limited dexterity, spasticity

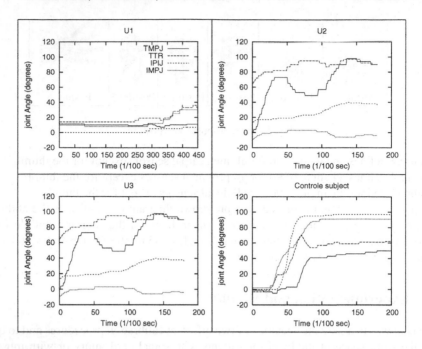

Fig. 2. Thumb and index finger joint rotations (in deg.) for movement 2 (flexion) in three patients and a control subject

or insufficient muscular forces. We asked the patients to perform two hand movements: i) Movement 1: starting from a relaxed initial position the subjects were asked to fully extend all fingers. ii) Movement 2: starting from a relaxed initial position the subjects were asked to fully flex digits II-V at the distal, proximal and metacarpal joints. For the thumb, the final posture corresponded to about a joint angle of 90 for Thumb roll and the proximal thumb joint, and about 45 for the thumb metacarpal joint. We compared the observed movements of the patients to those of a healthy control subject. The time-varying joint angles of movement 2 (flexion) for the three patients and the control subject are depicted in (figure 2) TMPJ (Thumb metacarpal joint), TTR (Thumb carpometacarpal rotation), IPIJ (Index proximal interphalangeal joint) and IMPJ (Index metacarpal joint) angular values are represented.

The movement time of the control subject was about 0.5 s and three of the four measured joint angles flexed simultaneously. Movement amplitude, depending on the joint, varied between 40 and 100. In contrast, the movement time and amplitude in patients varied to a large degree: Patient U1, due to weak muscular strength, showed low-amplitude movements, i.e. smaller than 35 for the proximal thumb metacarpal (TMPJ) and index metacarpal (IMPJ) joints and even smaller for the thumb carpometacarpal joint (TTR) and the index proximal interphalangeal joint (IPIJ). Movement time was prolonged (up to 4 s). Patient U2 showed almost normal movement amplitudes in index metacarpal joint (IMPJ), but much more smaller amplitudes in the other three joints (TMPJ, TTR and IMPJ). Movement time was about 1.5 s. Patient U3, showed close to normal amplitudes, however, the timing among the different joints was very disparate and he was incapable of holding the final posture: this was due to his spasticity. In summary, these results provide a quantitative kinematic description of the reduced working space in three patients.

4   Conclusion

This work attempts to study the grip formation and grip postures of people having severe motor disabilities. We have used the CyberGlove system to do so. The adopted calibration method and the obtained results suggest that the CyberGlove provides sufficient kinematic parameters and sufficient accuracy to characterize the residual motor capacity of patients with upper limb disabilities.

We first compared and validated our calibration method for the CyberGlove system based on 6 key postures. These postures are simple and take a few minutes to perform, however the accuracy is less than can be obtained with the more sophisticated joint-by-joint calibration. We then applied the CyberGlove to three patients affected by muscular dystrophy or neuro-muscular degenerative disease in order to calculated their residual work-space (dexterity). Based on the time-varying rotations of the thumb and index finger joints the work-space of the patients was characterized in terms of movement kinematics. Compared to healthy control subjects, the residual work-space was very limited and movement time was increased. However, in ergonomic terms, the routine use of the CyberGlove in patients with severe motor disabilities seems limited. We will explore other measurement systems such us Optotrak that employ active marker technology to precisely measure rapid, complex motions in three-dimensional space[7].

References

1. Kadouche, R., Abdulrazak, B., Mokhtari, M.: Toward an evaluation methodology for computer accessibility. IOS. Press, ICOST. Singapore (2004) 49–56
2. Kessler, G.D., Hodges, L.F., Walker, N.: Evaluation of the CyberGlove as a whole-hand input device. Vol 2. Issue 4. ACM (TOCHI). New York. (1995) 263–283
3. Maciel, A., Sarni, S., Buchwalder, O., Boulic, R., Thalmann, D.: Multi-Finger Haptic Rendering of Deformable Objects. EGVE (2004)
4. Rabinowitz, P.:4. Griffin, W.B., Findley, R.P., Turner, M.L., Cutkosky, M.R.: Calibration and Mapping of a Human Hand for Dexterous Telemanipulation. ASME IMECE (2000)
5. Roby-Brami, A., Bennis, N., Mokhtari, M., Baraduc, P.: Hand orientation for grasping depends on the direction of the reaching movement. Brain. Res. **869** (2000)121–9
6. Roby-Brami, A., Laffont, I., Mokhtari, M., Heidmann, J.: Compensation des incapacités du membre supérieur du sujet tétraplégique. Entretiens de l'Institut Garches. Paris. (2001)
7. http://www.ndigital.com/

Non-intrusive User Modeling for a Multimedia Museum Visitors Guide System

Tsvi Kuflik[1], Charles Callaway[2], Dina Goren-Bar[2], Cesare Rocchi[2],
Oliviero Stock[2], and Massimo Zancanaro[2]

[1] MIS Department, University
[2] ITC-irst, via Sommarive 18, 38050 Povo, Italy
{kuflik, callaway, gorenbar, rocchi, stock, zancana}@itc.it

Abstract. A personalized multimedia museum visitor's guide system may be a valuable tool for improving user satisfaction in a museum visit. Personalization poses challenges to user modeling in the museum environment, especially when several different applications are supported by the same user model, where it is required to operate in a non-intrusive manner. This work presents the PEACH experience of non-intrusive user modeling supporting online dynamic multimedia presentation production and additional applications such as visit summary report generation.

1 Introduction

A museum visit is a personal experience encompassing both cognitive aspects (such as the elaboration of background and new knowledge) and emotional aspects, which may include the satisfaction of interests or the fascination with the exhibit itself. Despite the inherently stimulating environment they create, cultural heritage institutions often fall short of successfully supporting conceptual learning, inquiry-skill-building, analytic experiences or follow-up activities at home or at school [7]. The value of multimedia for a museum mobile guide is discussed in [4] with an extended user study conducted at Modern Tate in 2002. Yet the optimal multimedia tourist guide should support strong personalization of all the information provided in a museum, in an effort to ensure that each visitor can accommodate and interpret the visit according to his or her own pace and interests. Simultaneously, a museum guide should also provide the appropriate drive to foster learning and self-development so as to create a richer and more meaningful experience.

In the context of the PEACH[1] project, we are building and evaluating a number of prototypes aimed at providing the visitor with a personalized experience. Common to all these prototypes is a user model that gathers information about the visitor and guides the adaptation of information presented to the user.

The PEACH museum visitors' guide consists of a *Dynamic Presentation Composer* that generates personalized presentations seen by the user, detailed in [6] and currently a

---

[1] http://peach.itc.it. The PEACH project is funded by the Autonomous Province of Trento.

L. Ardissono, P. Brna, and A. Mitrovic (Eds.): UM 2005, LNAI 3538, pp. 236–240, 2005.

Report Generator that generates a personalized visit summary for the visitor, as detailed in [1]. Both components employ a common *Domain Knowledge Base* (KB) and are supported by a *Dynamic User Modeler* (UM) for generating personal presentations for the visitor.

There are two unique challenging aspects for personalization in the context of the PEACH project. The first challenge is that user modeling is required to be "non-intrusive"; hence visitors are not required to provide any personal information and user modeling is based solely on users' behavior. The second challenge is that user modeling component needs to support different applications, with different requirements: the main one is online production of personalized presentations delivered to the visitor during the visit; another is supporting a personalized visit summary report.

2 User Modeling Challenges in the PEACH Scenario

Non-Intrusive User Modeling means that the model is built solely by observing the visitor's behavior. The information that is available for modeling includes the sequence of visitor's positions (exhibits) and time spent at each position, presentations presented to the user, and an enjoyment feedback from the user (the user is able to respond to and rate the presentations delivered). This information then drives the inference mechanism for assessing user interests.

Dynamic Presentation Generation requires a lot of personal and contextual information: for example, spatial information (current user position and whether the user has already been here, is in front of an artwork, or just near it), visitor interests with respect to the current exhibits, discourse history (what particular presentations were delivered to the visitor).

These attributes can be used in set of rules guiding the dynamic generation of personalized presentation for the user during her visits, as presented in [6]. In addition to specific details regarding the current visit, which consist of the visitor's path through the museum, presentations delivered and visitor's feedback, there is a need for a more abstract representation of user interests to guide future generations of presentations. Several works have dealt with adaptable guides. For instance in HIPS [4] work on adaptation has included the classification of users' patterns of movements in the course of the visit. Here the situation is different: our UM must support dynamic multimedia, including video generation, seamless presentations on mobile and stationary devices [5] and additional applications as discussed below.

Visit Summary Report Generation requires the consideration of various different aspects; factual aspects of the visit (such as exhibits visited, the visit sequence, the time spent at different locations, the presentations delivered to the visitor, and visitor's actions), cognitive aspects related to the exhibitions (such as interest for themes, pleasure, boredom etc), extra subject-centered aspects[2] (such as persons met, discussions held and additional events that occurred), attention-grabbing elements and hints for subsequent reading and visiting and the appearance of the report (combining text, images and possibly additional forms of media, in a personalized manner either on paper or in an electronic form).

---

[2] At least in principle, not implemented so far.

The quality of the report is crucial: it should be a memory aid for later consultation, something one can share with others, and an entry point for getting deeper into a subject. It should be short but readable and concrete. Detailed descriptions are important, but only when relevant to the specific visitor [1]. As such the user model that supports report generation should provide detailed descriptions of information presented to the user that seemed specifically interested in it.

3 User Modeling in PEACH

The PEACH *Dynamic User Modeler* (UM) works in a "non-intrusive" manner. Currently there is no initial information about the visitor when starting each visit, and as a result, the model is built solely by observing the visitor's behavior. We are studying ways of importing and adapting pre-existing models of the specific visitor obtained from other applications.

The user is tracked during the visit by recording the visitor's positions (in terms of the visited exhibits) and the time spent at each position are recorded by the UM, as well as the presentation delivered. User interests are defined in terms of domain concepts, which are associated with individual presentations. These concepts provide a description of the content of the presentation, thus representing its theme. The concepts are drawn from a domain knowledge-base that is primarily designed for natural language generation for visit summary reports. Since there is no prior knowledge about the user, the knowledge base and the concepts associated with the individual presentation are the only source of information for user preferences with respect to the exhibits visited and presentations delivered in the current museum visit.

In addition to the various events recorded, the UM also contains inferred information about the level of interest the visitor has in the concepts associated with the presentations delivered to her. In addition to the specific concepts associated with the presentation, an inference mechanism that follows ontological links in the KB, from the specific concepts associated with the presentations to related concepts augments the user model with additional, more abstract concepts extending the UM to categories of concepts beyond those that were associated with the presentation seen by the visitor. For example, if a presentation that seems to be of interest to the visitor is represented by the concept "knight", this concept is added to the UM, with an initial value, the interest in "knight" is now propagated to the more abstract concept "aristocracy", which is added to the UM.

The visitor's interests in the various concepts are defined in a 5-level scale. Explicit and implicit visitor's feedbacks are used to infer user interest in the various concepts associated with the presentations delivered to the visitor. Explicit user feedback is in the form of pressing a "More" button (for positive reaction) or an "Enough" button (for negative reaction). Implicit positive feedback is the completion of a presentation delivery to the user, without objection (e.g. no "Enough" button pressed or position changed). Explicit feedback has a higher priority than implicit feedback in the sense that explicit feedback is more reliable so it drives an immediate change in level of interest in the concepts associated with the delivered presentation, while implicit feedback requires accumulation of evidence for every concept (several implicit responses) before changing a visitor's interest level in that given concept. Several implicit responses are required for updating a level of interest. Whenever a new concept is added to the list of interests, it gets a neutral value – "interested a little". As mentioned above, the interest level is propagated to a more abstract concept related to them, following ontological links among the concepts as represented in the system KB. The level of interest associated with the concepts that are related to the original concepts decays as a function of the distance from the initial concept.

The information stored in the UM includes both recorded information of all events that happened during the visit and inferred information regarding level of interest is dynamically updated and used during the visit to help prepare the presentation for the visitor. This is done by tailoring the presentations to the current visit context – what the user has already seen, visitor's current location and specific interests. Finally, the UM drives generation of a visit summary report. This report includes details about the visit, and suggestions for future activities for future visits to this and other museums

4 Planned Evaluations

We are performing several user studies aimed at evaluating the PEACH guide user interface and the adaptive report. We will address in short to both of them.

1. User studies on PEACH guide user interface. In order to assess if the user perceive the adaptive dimensions depicted in the guide we conducted a simulation study assessing four dimensions of adaptivity: location awareness, follow-ups, content adaptation with respect to user interests, and content adaptation with respect to history of interaction. The results of this study are reported in [2]. Currently we are assessing real visitors in the museum using the implemented visitor guide. At the end of the visit users are interviewed about the same four adaptivity dimensions. We resort to an action-protocol and retrospective-interview qualitative study; in particular, we target the expression of the affect and the delegation of control paradigm implemented that are the main events that affect the UM component. The results of this iterative evaluation cycle will lead to the final design of the PEACH guide interface. We expect that users will be able to properly carry out the task with a reasonable understanding the conceptual model of the system. Furthermore, we expect that the interface is easy to use and that their expectations about the interest model will be fulfilled.

2. User studies on PEACH adaptive report. In order to assess if the user perceive the adaptive dimensions depicted in the summary reports we are currently conducting a simulation study. We compare three types of summary visits: Adaptive Sequential Report, Adaptive Thematic Report and a Non Adaptive Generic Report that differ on the following adaptivity dimensions: (1) Sequential vs. thematic (2) Personalized vs. generic (3) Reference to related topics in unseen frescos (4) Reference to related topics in other museums and sites (5) Reference to the most interesting scene (6) Comparison between topics within and between frescos. At the end of the visit using the PEACH multimedia guide the experimenter give the three simulated summary visit reports in different order and let the users read them all. Then the visitors are interviewed in order to assess all six dimensions. The preliminary results indicate that visitors perceive the differences between the sequential and the thematic reports; they like more the personalized over the non personalized reports, rather because of the personal reference present in the adaptive versions than for the adaptive contents of them. The full results of the current user study will be reported in the future.

5   Conclusions and Future Work

This paper presented user modeling challenges in the PEACH scenario, where "nonintrusive" user modeling is required to support personalization of dynamic presentation generation and other applications, including summary visit reports for museum visitors. Concepts drawn from a domain KB, used primarily for natural language generation are associated with presentations delivered to the visitor and used to represent visitor's interests. User behavior is used to determine the level of interest the visitor has in the various concepts. In the next phase we are going to apply different user modeling techniques working in parallel (as competing user modeling agents). We are also studying ways of importing and adapting pre-existing models of the specific visitor obtained from other applications. Finally, research will focus on evaluation of the user modeling activities as part of the whole system evaluation.

References

1. Callaway C., Kuflik T., Not E., Novello A., Stock O. and Zancanaro M. Personal Reporting of a Museum Visit as an Entrypoint to Future Cultural Experience. In *Proceedings of Intelligent User Interfaces IUI'05*,San Diego,275-277, January 2005
2. Goren-Bar D., Graziola I., Pianesi F. and Zancanaro M. Dimensions of Adaptivity in Mobile Systems: Personality and People's Attitudes. In *Proceedings of Intelligent User Interfaces IUI'05*. San Diego,223-230, January 2005
3. Marti P., Rizzo A., Petroni L., Tozzi G., and Diligenti M. Adapting the Museum: a Nonintrusive User Modeling Approach. *Proceedings of the Seventh International Conference on User Modeling (UM99)*, 311-313, Banff, 1999
4. Proctor N. and Tellis C. The State of the Art in Museum Handhelds in *Proceedings of Museums and the Web Conference*, 227-237, 2003
5. Rocchi C., Stock O., Zancanaro M., Kruppa M. and Krueger A. 'The Museum Visit: Generating Seamless Personalized Presentations on Multiple Devices' *Proceedings of Intelligent User Interfaces IUI'04*, 316-318, Madeira, 2004.
6. Rocchi C. and Zancanaro M. Rhetorical Patterns for Adaptive Video Documentaries. In *Proceedings of Adaptive Hypermedia and Adaptive Web-Based Systems AH-2004*, Eindhoven, 324-327, 2004.
7. Semper R. and Spasojevic M. The Electronic Guidebook: Using Portable Devices and a Wireless Web-Based Network to Extend the Museum Experience. In *Proceedings of Museums and the Web Conference*, 18-20, Boston, 2002

Modelling the Behaviour of Elderly People as a Means of Monitoring Well Being

Nick Hine[1], Andrew Judson[1], Saqib Ashraf[1], John Arnott[1],
Andrew Sixsmith[2], Steve Brown[3], and Paul Garner[3]

[1] Applied Computing, University of Dundee, Dundee DD1 4HN,
United Kingdom
{nhine, ajudson, sashraf, jarnott}@computing.dundee.ac.uk
[2] University of Liverpool, United Kingdom
sixsmith@liverpool.ac.uk
[3] BT Research, United Kingdom
{paul.2.garner, steve.j.brown}@BT.com

Abstract. The care of elderly people in their own homes is being promoted throughout the world. The proportion of older people within western societies is rising, and it is anticipated that the already stretched resources of both the informal and formal care sectors will be unable to meet demand for home based care in the near future. This paper reports on work being undertaken within the BT Care in the Community project to model the lives of older people in order to understand, anticipate and respond to their home based care needs.

1 Introduction

The UK population is ageing. At the time of the 2001 census there were 8.1 million people aged over 65 living in the UK, 3.1 million of them living alone. By 2011 the number of over 65s is projected to reach just under 12 million, and by 2026 over 13 million [23]. The extra workload this will place on health and care services will be compounded by political ambitions aimed at meeting the challenges of rising patient expectations [16]. In addition to this, the Department of Health aims to promote the independence of older people by providing enhanced services from the National Health Service (NHS) and councils to prevent unnecessary hospital admission [7]. As a result we can expect to see a continuing rise in the number of elderly people living at home and requiring good quality health and social care services.

The Department of Health in the UK, in common with health care providers worldwide, hopes for a substantial increase in the uptake of telecare and other electronic assistive technologies to increase independence for older people [12]. Telecare can be defined as the application of electronic information and communication technologies to support elderly people who live alone. Existing telecare solutions currently provide elderly and vulnerable individuals (clients) with the means of raising an alert should assistance be required. This type of Telecare solutions can characterised as either first or second generation systems. First generation systems are simple

L. Ardissono, P. Brna, and A. Mitrovic (Eds.): UM 2005, LNAI 3538, pp. 241–250, 2005.

means by which a client can call for help when they find themselves in difficulties. Second generation systems incorporate a degree of intelligence that enables the system to alert the carer without client intervention if the client is incapacitated. Future telecare is intended to include the ability to predict the onset of an acute situation by monitoring long-term changes in activity trends to assess the well-being of the client. The goal of those deploying such so called third generation systems is to inform a dialogue between those responsible for care, and the client in order to promote a change in lifestyle that will not only prevent acute conditions from arising, but will contribute positively to the general well-being and quality of life of the client.

To this end, the Care in the Community Centre [5] is researching the possibility of developing and deploying third generation telecare systems capable of monitoring long-term activity trends which may indicate a general decline in the 'well-being' of the client. BT Research is leading the DTI funded Care in the Community Centre in collaboration with several UK universities. This centre consists of four projects. The foundation is being laid by the Domain Specific Modelling project (DSM), which is utilising the domestic environment sensor development work of the Sensornet project, and feeding concepts, models and test data to the Intelligent Data Analysis (IDA) for to guide and inform the data analysis and interpretation process. The work is coming together in a Demonstrator project where systems will be deployed in the homes of elderly people and the data generated analysed.

Pioneering work in this field was undertaken by BT in the mid 1990's in a project together with the Anchor Trust [18]. This project demonstrated that it was possible to gather data about activity in domestic environments by placing sensors within those environments. The trials in that project did not employ enough sensors however, to reliably define and measure specific activities within the home, nor was the technology available sufficiently reliable to ensure that a complete record of activity was gathered. In recent years a number of studies have begun to explore the technical possibilities of monitoring the lifestyle of older people or people with disabilities [1, 2, 21, 17, 20]. The general goal of these studies has been to build a model of the lifestyle of these people, in order to detect changes that indicate an alarm condition. These studies have resulted in new alarm products [15, 22] and deployed services [3]. Current research has begun to consider the possibilities for more sophisticated analysis of the lifestyle data that can detect more subtle changes of lifestyle leading to changes in health and well-being. [6, 11, 19, 10], and ensure that the technology deployed in the homes of older people is suitable for use by them [4, 8, 9].

A key element in the success of well-being monitoring systems depends on an understanding of the expected or normal lifestyle and the degree to which the behaviour of the older person has deviated from that norm. The first task, therefore, of the work within the DSM project was to outline a conceptual model that would serve as a "roadmap" of the territory of well-being amongst older people. The starting point for this is a well-established literature base that includes both the subjective (e.g psychological well-being, life satisfaction) and objective (e.g. life circumstances and personal capacities) aspects of quality of life [14, 13] While this provided a useful perspective, it became very clear, in the context of the present work on activity monitoring, that a key theoretical weakness is the lack of attention to how well-being is grounded within the everyday activities. Fig 1. presents the conceptual framework used within the DSM project, comprising person and context as " background" factors that determine well-being "outcomes".

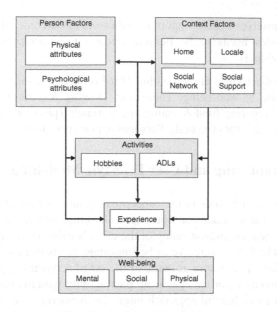

Fig. 1. Conceptual Framework of factors affecting well-being

The person factors include physical attributes, such as physical and mental abilities, while psychological attributes include needs, preferences, motivation, goals, etc. Key context factors include the home environment, the local neighbourhood, care provision and social network. Well-being outcomes include social participation, psychological well-being and physical health. Our model, however emphasises the role of everyday activities, such as activities of daily living (ADLs) including bathing, hygiene, looking after the home etc. and hobbies and leisure that are important for well-being. Social interaction is also an important component of well-being.

These different activities are important from a well-being monitoring perspective because:

- A person's activities are indicative of the precursors of well-being. A person's general lifestyle and their everyday activities are seen as a function of their goals and abilities within a particular context. For example, changes in patterns of activities could indicate changes in the motivation or physical competencies of the individual. They could also indicate changes in contextual factors, such as the loss of informal support from a carer.
- Activities are also predictive of well-being outcomes. For example, people who are able to maintain valued activities and hobbies into old age may experience higher levels of life satisfaction. Our sense of well-being is affected by our own subjective interpretation of everyday life, so that one person's experience of a particular incident or activity may be very different from another's. For example, social isolation and lack of contact with others is predictive of well-being, but this largely depends on whether the person "feels" lonely or not. While this experiential domain is obviously outside the domain of monitoring and sensing, the

activities themselves remain important indicators of outcome. However, monitoring of activities needs to be flexible enough to encompass key differences between individuals.

The initial set of activities chosen within DSM reflects the wide range of activities that may contribute to well-being. These are: Leaving & returning home (social), Visitors (social), Preparing food & eating appropriately (physical), Sleeping patterns (physical), Leisure activities (mental), Personal appearance (mental).

2   Activity Monitoring and User Lifestyle Modelling

The set of six general activities in the conceptual framework cover a wide variety of detailed activities that together contribute to well-being. Before such abstract activities can be interpreted, an understanding of the client's existing lifestyle and factors of their well-being which they perceive to be important needs to be collated. There is a temptation, therefore, to measure as many of the set of activities as possible, and then to integrate the deviations or changes from past activity patterns into a general well-being measure. A more helpful approach might be, however, to consider these high-level activities as primary activities that can be broken down into progressively more detailed classes of activities. This maps onto the type of questions that carers would ask as they consider each person in their case-load. Initial questions would be at the level of "tell me how the client is sleeping" or "tell me how the client is eating". More detailed questions such as "is the client eating fresh fruit?" would follow. At the most detailed level, a client with known specific risks would be monitored at the level of individual activities such as the way they cook a specific meal. This would result in activity interpretation model that is a hierarchical question tree, with abstract questions at the top drilling into more specific questions.

An overview of the top level of the tree is shown in fig. 2 below.

If then, for example, the client feels that on a bad day they just cannot be bothered to make a proper meal, and this happens increasingly frequently, this could be an indicator of a reduction in well-being and subsequently a reduction in health. A sensor network would be designed and installed into the client's home to observe the activity of preparing fresh meals versus ready-made processed foods.

Whilst the monitoring of detailed activities will require the comprehensive deployment of activity specific sensors, a comprehesive highlevel insight of activities, or lack of them, can be gained from a small set of well-placed sensors. In the tree in fig. 3 below, 3 durations of activity, A, B, and C, are outlined. Duration A is the period during which the client is definitely not doing the activity of interest. Duration B is the time they might be doing the activity or it is probable that a proportion of the time is being spent doing the activity. The duration C is the time where it is highly probable or certain that they are doing the activity. With this approach, if the client is not spending the amount of time involved in an activity as would be expected, further more detailed questions can be explored with a more targeted deployment of additional sensors.

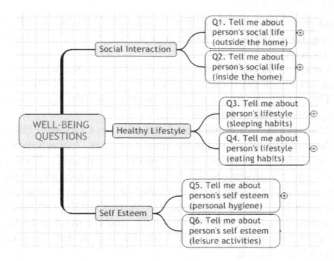

Fig. 2. Top level well-being questions

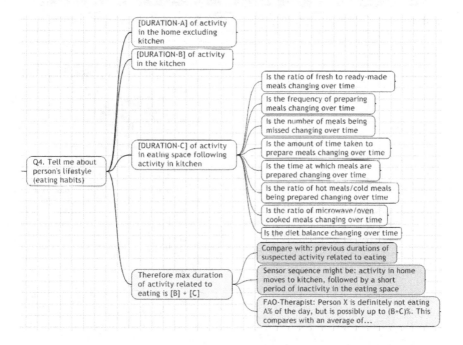

Fig. 3. Second level well-being questions related to eating habits

In order to validate this approach, a home is being instrumented with a network of sensors. This sensor network consists of a portfolio of low-powered, unobtrusive sensors such as PIRs, door/cupboard switches, beam breakers and pressure mats networked to a National Instruments fieldpoint terminal. When each sensor is fired, the timestamp and state change is read by a application (developed in National Instruments LabView IDE) and stored within a SQL Server database. This data is then available for analysis.

In order to assist in the verification of the data prior to analysis, a set of visualisation interfaces have been developed. The screenshot in fig 4 below shows this system in use. This system is provided as the interface for the technical support team developing and running the installation.

On the left, we can see a floorplan of the test house. Coloured circles indicate the locations of the installed sensor within the sensor network. As each sensor is fired, the colour of these circles will change to indicate the current state. This representation shown has two clusters of sensors installed, at the front door and at the entrance to one of the bedrooms. These sensors have enabled the research team to put in place the chain of equipment between the house and the University lab, with data being logged locally on a computer acting as the data gateway, and the main archiving server. Using this architecture the issues associated with the local or remote storage and processing of data can be explored.

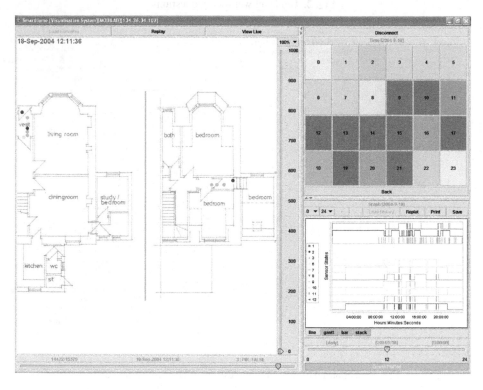

Fig. 4. Raw data visualisation interface

In the top right, we have a calendar view. The calendar view allows an overview of the volume of data generated over a whole year, a month or a day to be viewed. The view currently showing is the 24 hours of the day. Each hour is shaded based on how much activity has occurred in that hour. The redder the colour, the more activity oc-curred within the hour.

In the bottom right, there is the graph view. There are four different types of graphs available, each showing the data in a different visual representation. The graph visible is the line graph with individual plots for each of the sensors. This gives an indication of sensor activity to monitor the data collection technology, but it is recognised that this is not the most helpful representation for understanding user activities, as activities that span hours will not be readily visible. In order to understand the user, activities should be grouped according to activity zone times such as "breakfast time" or "lunchtime", or "evening time". The setting of these zones is an iterative process that will need to be tuned to the specific user based on their activity patterns. This will be done in the subsequent data analysis.

A simplified visualisation (figure 6) is being prepared that will present the status of the user relative to the initial six well-being parameters, and the subsequent hierarchi-cal set of activities associated with these high level parameters. This visualisation will allow the carers and the clients to have an overview of the client's well-being over time.

The design of this simplified interface reflects detailed discussions with care service personal both in Dundee, Scotland and in Liverpool, England, and enables an overview of both the status and the trends in the well-being of the older person to be seen.

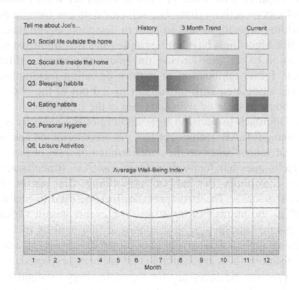

Fig. 5. High level questions and well-being level view

In the upper section of the screen, there are the six well-being questions that the carers are interested in. Beside each question, there are coloured blocks showing three states, with the following colour coding: Red = Bad, Yellow = OK, Green = Good.

The three states are: History state showing the known or observed normal state for the person; 3 Month Trend state showing a colour gradient indicating the trend of the state over the past 3 months; Current state showing the perceived state of the person at this moment in time.

Finally, along the bottom section of the screen, there is a graph showing the trend of the well-being index over the last 12 months. The well-being index is an integrated values of the various well-being factors, weighted according to the aspirations of the user.

When the carer selects a question from the overall summary screen.

This interface is currently being discussed with the carers that contributed to the original design. Initial impressions suggest that as the carers drill down into the details of the issue affecting well being, a more detailed presentation of the state of the individual sensors might be useful.

The additional analysis that will subsequently be applied to this data gathered from the client's home utilises data mining techniques. A significant task within the sequence of data mining operations to be performed in this analysis deals with the selection of relevant data from within the total available data set. This is a particularly important phase in the analysis of the home data as it is clear from the initial installation and data gathering work that sensors detect many activities that are not associated with the activities of interest. A promising technique for selecting the required data from within the pool of sensor firings is detection of temporal sequence patterns. Initial results of the application of such a technique to this data has shown that it can indeed select the required data when presented a data set within which human users have identified blocks of activity data. The selected data can then be presented to rule decision tree building algorithms and to pattern detection algorithms. Initial application of decision tree algorithms have built simple rules that highlight regular activities such as the detection of the user leaving the house at particular times on particular days of the week. Initial application of pattern detection techniques have detected clusters of patterns associated with movement in and out of the house, and of movements within the house associated with activities at the front door.

An alternative approach to decision trees and clustering analysis is to use On-Line Analytical Processing (OLAP) techniques to form predetermined answers to questions that have numerical values based on the consideration of a set of factors. Initial application of these techniques has focused on factors such as time, location, direction of movement. The algorithms depend on structuring the sensor data as multi-dimensional data structures. The structures can then be used to precalculate answers to questions such as the number of house leaving events within various time periods ranging from gross periods such as years down to fine periods such as hours. These techniques are being applied extensively in commerce decision situations, so a variety of intuitive visualisations tools are available and are being explored.

Whilst it may prove to be necessary for the technology to identify the specific activities being performed in the homes, the research approach is initially more concerned with the identification of change in the activity levels of people within the context of home space most likely to be associated with the well-being activities identified. As the need of carers and older people to identify specific activities becomes clear in order to correlate the changes of activities to changes in well-being, additional sensors and more targeted analysis algorithms will be deployed. In these cases, it will be necessary to validate the insights being gained through the sensors and algorithms in order to confirm that the activity being assumed to be apparent in the data is in fact the one taking place. An early example of this approach being piloted in the facility is that all occupants swipe a personal RFID card against a reader as they enter the dwelling so that the researchers can validate the entry and leaving patterns against the person. Such interventions would be in place as a temporary measure until the system had been trained.

Having verified the validity of the user activity modelling and exploration approach, and the utility of the data coming from the clients' homes with these techniques, the experiences and models are fed into the Intelligent Data Analysis (IDA) team within the Care in the Community Centre who are producing fuzzy set rules of normal activity patterns to apply to the raw sensor data recorded from the client's home. The fuzzy rules can then be used to test the data for variations over time from the normal trend of an activity. More powerful data mining techniques are being investigated as a means of discovering a user's pattern of activity from the raw data to refine or even generate rules for the IDA fuzzy rule set.

3 Conclusion

In this paper we have presented the user modelling working taking place in the DSM project of the BT Care in the Community Centre. This modelling is intended to guide the analysis of sensor data being gathered from the homes of older people in order to identify changes in activities that might be an indication of decline in well being and quality of life. This work is continuing to evolve to inform the dialogue between clients and their carers, and will be extended to consider an increasing spectrum of domestic activities within the core framework presented here.

References

1. Abowd, G.D. et al: Living laboratories: the future computing environments group at the Georgia Institute of Technology. Proceedings of CHI '00: Conference on Human Factors and Computing Systems, The Hague, The Netherlands (2000) 215-216.
2. Barnes, N.M., Edwards, N.H., Rose D.A.D., Garner P.: Lifestyle monitoring – technology for supported independence. IEE Computing and Control Engineering Journal, volume 9, number 4 (1998)
3. Bowes, A., McColgan, G.: Pilot evaluation of 'Open Doors for Older People' in 'wired' West Lothian – Report to West Lothian Council. West Lothian Council and the University of Stirling, Stirling, Scotland, UK (2002)
4. Brownsell S.J., Bradley D.A. Bragg R., Catlin P., Carlier J.,: Do community alarm users want Telecare? Journal of Telemedicine and Telecare, 6, (2000) 199-204
5. Care in the Community Centre — http://www.nextwave.org.uk/centres/care.htm
6. Das, S.K. et al: The role of prediction algorithms in the MavHome smart home architecture, IEEE Journal of Wireless Communications, Vol. 9, No. 6, (2002) 77-84
7. The Department of Health: National Service Framework for Older People, Standard three — Intermediate care. 47 (March 2001) At: http://www.dh.gov.uk/assetRoot/04/07/12/83/04071283.pdf

8. Fellbaum, K., Hampicke, M.: Integration of smart home components into existing residences. In: C. Bühler and H. Knops (eds.) Assistive Technology on the Threshold of the New Millennium. Amsterdam, The Netherlands: IOS Press. (1999) 497-501

9. Hirsch, T. et al: The ELDer Project: Social, Emotional, and environmental Factors in the Design of Eldercare technologies. In: Proceedings of CUU '00: ACM Conference on Universal Usability, Arlignton, Virginia, USA. (2000) 72-79

10. Intel: Digital Home Technologies for Aging in Place (2004) At: http://www.intel.com/research/exploratory/digital_home.htm

11. Jahnke, J.H., D'Entremont, M., Stier, J.: Facilitating the programming of the smart home. IEEE Journal of Wireless Communications, Vol. 9, No. 6, (2002) 70-76

12. Ladyman, S: Integration of community equipment service (ICES) conference. Homing in 1 (March 2004) At: http://www.dh.gov.uk/NewsHome/Speeches/SpeechesList/SpeechesArticle/fs/en?CONTENT_ID=4075877&chk=k9YRoU

13. Lawton, M.P.: Environment and other determinants of well-being in older people. The Gerontologist, 4, (1983) 349-357

14. Lawton, M.P.: A multidimensional view of quality of life in frail elders. In Birren, J., Lubben, J,. Rowe, J., Deutchman, D. (eds) The Concept of Measurement of Quality of Life in Frail Elders. Sandiego: Academic Press. (1991) 3-27

15. Living Independently (2003) At: http://www.livingindependently.com/

16. Milburn, A: The NHS plan' — introduction by the secretary of state. (July 2000) — http://www.nhs.uk/nationalplan/intro.htm

17. Mynatt, E.D., Rowan, J., Craighill S., Jacobs A.: Digital family portraits: Providing peace of mind for extended family members. In Proceedings of the ACM Conference on Human Factors in Computing Systems (2001)

18. Porteus, J. and Brownsell, S.: Using Telecare: Exploring Technologies for Independent Living for Older People. Anchor Trust, Oxfordshire, England, UK: Pavilion Publishing (Brighton) Ltd (2000)

19. Rialle, V., Noury, N., Hervé, T.: An experimental health smart home and its distributed internet-based information and communication system: First steps of a research project, Proceedings of MEDINFO 2001, London, England, UK. (2001) 1479-1483

20. Siio, I., Rowan, J., Mynatt E.D.: Peek-a-drawer: Communication by furniture. In Extended Abstracts of the ACM Conference on Human Factors in Computing Systems (2002)

21. Tang, P., Venables, T.: 'Smart' homes and telecare for independent living. Journal of Telemedicine and Telecare, 6. (2000) 8-14

22. Tunstall Ltd (2003) At: http://www.tunstall.co.uk/4_1_2_1telecare.htm

23. UK Population Projections by Age Group, Population Trends 32 — Spring. National Statistics. Georgia Institute of Technology (2003)

Bayesphone: Precomputation of Context-Sensitive Policies for Inquiry and Action in Mobile Devices

Eric Horvitz, Paul Koch, Raman Sarin, Johnson Apacible,
and Muru Subramani

Microsoft Research, One Microsoft Way Redmond,
Washington 98052 USA
{Horvitz, Paulkoch, Ramans, Johnsona, Murus}@microsoft.com

Abstract. Inference and decision making with probabilistic user models may be infeasible on portable devices such as cell phones. We highlight the opportunity for storing and using precomputed inferences about ideal actions for future situations, based on offline learning and reasoning with the user models. As a motivating example, we focus on the use precomputation of call-handling policies for cell phones. The methods hinge on the learning of Bayesian user models for predicting whether users will attend meetings on their calendar and the cost of being interrupted by incoming calls should a meeting be attended.

1 Introduction

Over the last decade, there has been increasing research on the use of probabilistic user modeling for inferring user goals and states of the world [6,7] under uncertainty. The user models have been applied typically in desktop settings, where designers can assume that a personal computer is available for performing inferences. We focus in this paper on the precomputation of ideal decision-theoretic policies from probabilistic user models and the caching of the policies on a cell phone for decision making in a mobile setting. We believe that such precomputation and caching of policies will enable probabilistic learning and reasoning to be applied to the large and growing number of devices and appliances in the world with limited computational abilities.

We focus on the example of using probabilistic models to guide the handling of telephone calls, so as to deliberate about the cost of interruption versus the cost of deferral of an incoming call. Such decisions can be made locally at cell phones, based on a consideration of context and multiple properties of meetings. We analyze the case of local decision making based on sensed properties of meetings on a user's calendar and on properties of callers based on caller identification, as well on real-time sensing of motion and ongoing conversation.

We first discuss the learning of predictive models of attendance and of interruptability. We present the computation of the expected cost of interruption from the output of these models. Then we discuss the computation of value of information to reason about the value of acquiring additional information from users in real time. We review how we can precompute and cache policies on cell phones that consider whether calls should interrupt users. We discuss how the methods have been used to field a prototype call handling system that we call Bayesphone.

L. Ardissono, P. Brna, and A. Mitrovic (Eds.): UM 2005, LNAI 3538, pp. 251–260, 2005.
© Springer-Verlag Berlin Heidelberg 2005

2 Learning Models of Interruptability and Attendance

Efforts over the last several years have demonstrated that relatively accurate models can be constructed for predicting the interruptability of users from such contextually relevant observations as sensed activity and calendar properties [2,3,4,5,8]. We shall focus first on the construction of two Bayesian network models via supervised machine learning. One model predicts the interruptability of a user. More specifically, we build a model that is used to infer a probability distribution over the cost of interruption of users. The second model outputs the probability that users will attend meetings that appear on their electronic calendar. Inferences from both models are used to predict the expected cost of interruption at different times for a user. Additionally, we show how we compute from the output of the models, the value of information associated with asking users in real time about their situation. Such an analysis considers the inferences from the models as well as the frequency and types of calls coming in over time.

2.1 Models of a User's Interruptability

We have been investigating predictive models of the cost of interruption from evidence associated with a user's context, including a stream of sensed data generated by a user's interaction with a desktop computer and properties of items on a user's electronic calendar [4,5]. Online calendars are central for coordinating meetings in many enterprises. For example, the Outlook calendaring subsystem is used universally at our organization for extending invitations to meetings, monitoring responses about planned attendance, and scheduling and tracking daily agendas. As part of the Coordinate project, we constructed an appointment crawler and assessment tool that searches through users' online calendars, as represented in the Microsoft Outlook messaging and calendaring application [3]. The appointment crawler sifts through online appointments and records sets of properties associated with each appointment. The appointment crawler notes, for each appointment, a set of properties drawn from the Outlook application, including the time of day and day of week of the meeting, meeting duration, subject, location, organizer, the response status of the user (responded yes, responded as tentative, did not respond, or no response request was made), whether the meeting is recurrent or not, whether the time is marked as busy or free on the user's calendar, whether the user was required or optional, the number of invitees, the organizational relationships of the invitees to the user, and the role of the user (user was the organizer versus a required or optional invitee). The system accesses the Microsoft Active Directory service to identify the organizer of the meeting and invitees and notes whether the organizer and attendees are organizational peers, direct reports, managers, or managers of the user's manager.

The crawled data is used to build an assessment view that displays a form to users. The form consists of a list of titles of meetings and provides fields for indicating the state of interruptability of users. Fig. 1 shows the assessment palette for assigning a cost of interruption to each crawled calendar item and a form used to define the meaning of high, medium, and low cost of interruption states. Users use this form to assign scalar values to each state of interruptability. For this assessment, we ask users to estimate the cost associated with a ringing phone during states of high, medium, and low cost of interruption. To ground the semantics of cost throughout the system, we consider the decision-analytic notion of *willingness to pay*; and assess dollar values that users would be willing to pay to avoid a call in each setting.

Given the interruptability tags and appointment properties, we build a library of cases, and then employ a Bayesian structure search procedure, based on methods developed by Chickering, et al. [1], to build a Bayesian network. The methods employ a greedy search across different structures to identify the probabilistic dependency structure that best explains the data, based on a score known as the Bayesian Information Criterion. The resulting Bayesian network can be used later to infer probability distributions over the states of interruptability for previously unseen meetings, based upon a consideration of a set of observations consisting of the properties of meetings.

Date	Subject	Cost	
Oct 8, 2004	10/8/2004 Computational History In Ac	☐ High ☑ Medium ☐ Low	
Oct 8, 2004	10/8/2004 Structural Comparison of Ex	☐ High ☑ Medium ☐ Low	
Oct 7, 2004	Attila's going away party, B30 cafeteria	☐ High ☑ Medium ☐ Low	
Oct 7, 2004	UW CSE Colloquium - 10/7/04 - "The	☐ High ☑ Medium ☐ Low	
Oct 7, 2004	10/7/2004 The totally nonnegative part	☐ High ☑ Medium ☐ Low	
Oct 7, 2004	10/7/2004 ME++; Bill Mitchell - MIT	☐ High ☑ Medium ☐ Low	
Oct 7, 2004	Updated: Adaptive Systems & Interact	☑ High ☐ Medium ☐ Low	
Oct 7, 2004	10/7/2004 Data Mining & Machine Lea	☐ High ☑ Medium ☐ Low	
Oct 6, 2004	UW CSE Televised Talks for October 2	☐ High ☑ Medium ☐ Low	
Oct 6, 2004	10/6/2004 Toolkit for Construction and	☐ High ☑ Medium ☐ Low	
Oct 6, 2004	10/6/2004 Some uses of orthogonal po	☐ High ☑ Medium ☐ Low	
Oct 6, 2004	10/6/2004 Command Post of the Futur	☑ High ☐ Medium ☐ Low	
Oct 6, 2004	ASI dev group mid-week meeting	☑ High ☐ Medium ☐ Low	
Oct 6, 2004	10/6/2004 SHARK - A Pen Gesture Si	☐ High ☑ Medium ☐ Low	
Oct 6, 2004	10/6/2004 1 Vision: Extraordinary Com	☐ High ☑ Medium ☐ Low	
Oct 6, 2004	ASI dev group mid-week meeting	☑ High ☐ Medium ☐ Low	
Oct 5, 2004	UW CSE Colloquium - 10/5/04 - "Rese	☐ High ☑ Medium ☐ Low	

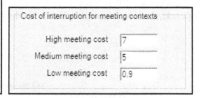

Cost of interruption for meeting contexts

High meeting cost   7

Medium meeting cost   5

Low meeting cost   0.9

Fig. 1. Cost of interruption assessment palette that enables users to view a list of prior appointments and to assess the cost of a phone call during each meeting (left). Overall dollar-valued costs are assigned to each state (right)

Fig. 2 displays a Bayesian network model learned from a set of cases tagged by cost of interruption. The model can be used to infer a probability distribution over states of interruptability, outputting for each previously unforeseen appointment the likelihood that the meeting has a high, medium, or low cost of interruption. A study of a model constructed from the same 559 appointments and tested on 100 hold out cases showed a classification accuracy of 0.81 for assigning interruptability.

2.2 Models of Meeting Attendance

Beyond models of the cost of interruption associated with a context associated with the attendance of a meeting, we also assess and learn in an analogous manner Bayesian network models that predict the likelihood that the meetings will be attended, based on meeting properties. Fig. 3 shows a sample Bayesian network learned from training data for inferring the likelihood that a user would attend meetings, based on meeting properties. The model was trained with the same appointments as were used to train the model for the cost of interruption. In use, the personalized attendance model generates, for previously untagged meetings, the likelihood that users will attend the meetings. For this model, a study of the accuracy on 100 cases held out for testing found that attendance was classified at an accuracy of 0.92.

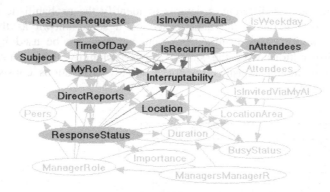

Fig. 2. Bayesian network learned from case library that can be used to infer the probability distribution over states of a variable representing the interruptability of a user, given attendance of a meeting with particular properties. The most influencing variables and their probabilistic dependencies are highlighted with shading

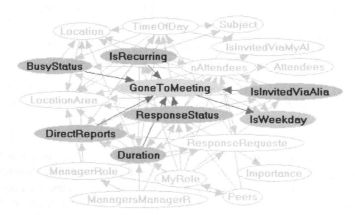

Fig. 3. Bayesian network learned from case library that can be used to infer whether a user will attend a meeting or not, based on meeting properties. The most influencing variables and their probabilistic dependencies are highlighted with shading

3 Computing Expected Cost of Interruption

We can employ the Bayesian networks for predicting attendance and the cost of interruption to compute the *expected cost of interruption* (ECI) associated with calls that ring through to users who are attending different kinds of meetings. To perform the computation of expected cost of interruption, we consider the probability distribution over the cost associated with the meeting at hand, as provided by the interruptability model, and the likelihood that a user will attend the meeting indicated on the user's calendar, as provided by the attendance model. To compute the ECI of interrupting a user when a meeting on a user's calendar is recognized as being in progress, we need one additional piece of information—the *default cost* associated with receiving a phone call when a user does not attend a meeting indicated on a user's calendar. Such a default cost is typically a function of the time of day, as receiving a call during the early hours of the morning or very late at night is likely to be different than receiving a call during business hours, and the cost of interruption may also be dependent on the day of week. To assess default costs of interruption, we allow users to sweep over default high, medium, and low cost regions within a seven day by twenty-four hour time palette, and to define default costs of interruption to each value. Fig. 4 displays the palette for assessing the default of interruption by time.

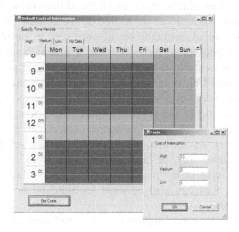

Fig. 4. Time palette for assessing costs of interruption by time via a sweeping out of regions of time, and assessing default costs for non-meeting times assigned high, medium, and low costs

Given (1) an inferred probability distribution over the interruptability of a meeting, (2) the likelihood that a user will attend a meeting on their calendar, and (3) the default cost associated with the no-meeting situation, the ECI at any moment is computed by weighting the cost of interruption for the no-attendance and attendance situations in accordance with the likelihoods of these states. Taking the expectation, the ECI is,

$$ECI = p(A \mid E)\sum_i p(c_i \mid E)c_i + (1 - p(A \mid E))c^b(S) \qquad (1)$$

where $p(A|E)$ is the likelihood that users will attend a meeting, given evidential properties E associated with the meeting, obtained via Outlook appointment properties, $p(c_i|E)$ is the probability that users will assign a cost c_i to the meeting, where i indexes the meeting as being either in low, medium, or high cost, and $c^b(S)$ is the background cost of being interrupted in the default situation S, representing the case where a user does not attend a meeting, as captured by the time of day and day of week. The default cost can be extended to be dependent on multiple aspects of a user's overall context S. Also, special mutually-exclusive contexts can be considered as active in a priority-order relationship. In the current Bayesphone prototype, the special contexts of *user driving* (*stop-and-go* versus *smooth highway* driving) and *local conversation in progress* are sensed from a Bluetooth-based GPS system and headset, respectively. If neither of these situations is sensed, the meeting and default day and time context is considered as active. Otherwise the costs of interruption assessed for the special contexts are assumed.

4   Performing Cost-Benefit Analysis in Real Time

We can balance a computed cost of interruption with the cost of deferring a conversation until later. A key piece of the decision is the cost of deferring calls from different callers. We thus obtain from users the dollar-value cost associated with delayed communication when a call is routed to voicemail rather than a real-time conversation. For such an assessment, we allow users to define groups of callers, based on properties of people, so as to provide a manageable set of classes. The deferral-cost assessment tool allows users to create groups of people based on sets of properties of people including organizational relationships and activities. The tool allows users to create such organization-related groups as peers, direct reports, manager, position higher-up in the organizational chart, person within organization, and people identified in a user's list of contacts. Users can also pick activity-based groups, so as to have their device recognize people who are scheduled in meetings in the next hour, on the same day, or later in the same week. Another activity-based group provided by the system is "people I have called today" and "people I have called this week." The tool can also be used to build ad hoc groups like "critical associates," and "close friends."

We employ Equation 1 to precompute the expected cost of interruption based on meeting properties for any time during the day. We shall return to the desktop and mobile device application in Section 5. First, we review the precomputation of value of information for making decisions about when to acquire additional information from users.

5   Precomputing Ideal Interactions with Users

Beyond storing policies for making the best decision based on information that is *currently available* to a system, we have extended the basic cost-benefit analysis with precomputation about whether it is worthwhile for the phone to ask users at run time to assist with resolving key uncertainties about the user's situation. More specifically, we precompute the *value of asking users* for information about whether they are attending a meeting that appears on their calendars. Answers to such queries can resolve key uncertainties used in the ECI computation, potentially increasing the value of the call-handling policies.

To identify ideal queries, we compute the expected value of information (EVI) of asking users a question. EVI is a decision-theoretic measure of the value of gathering additional information that considers the current uncertainties, the likelihood of different answers to a query for more information, and the ultimate influence of the different answers on ideal policies. For the case of Bayesphone, we precompute the value of asking a user if they intend to attend a meeting before a meeting is scheduled to begin. The question itself incurs a cost of interruption that must be balanced with the gains in value based in the new information.

To compute the value of asking the user about attendance, we must consider the ECI before and after asking, and cost of querying the user. Given an answer, the ECI will be either be the expected cost associated with the meeting (the first term in Equation 1), or the background cost of the time of day (the second term Equation 1). To compute the value of information, we introduce the concept of the overall communication cost over a period of time. The *expected communication cost* (ECC) for a period of time is the cost of deferral and cost of interruption for all incoming calls during the period. We wish to interact with a user only if the reduction in ECC is greater than the cost of asking. Bayesphone precomputes the value of information for all meetings and uses this information to drive selective question asking.

The ECC is computed by maintaining a log of incoming calls. Bayesphone records a log of incoming calls by group. This log is segmented into calls that arrive at different time periods. For the current prototype, we consider eight periods: *mornings, afternoons, evenings*, and *late night* for weekdays and weekends. For each period, we compute the rates at which calls associated with different caller groups arrive each hour. Given this information, we can compute the ECC for any value of the cost of interruption. We simply note the expected number of calls that will be deferred and the calls that will ring through to a user given the computed ECI. The expected numbers of each class of calls are computed as a product of the stored rates for each caller group and the duration of the period. The ECC for a meeting of duration t based on a consideration of current evidence E only about properties of the upcoming meeting is,

$$ECC(E,t) = (\sum_i f_i c_i^{defer} + \sum_j f_j c_j^{ring})t \qquad (2)$$

where f_i is frequency of calls in each caller group i that has a cost of deferral lower than the cost of interruption, f_j is the frequency of calls in each caller group j that has a cost of deferral higher than the cost of interruption, and c^{defer} and c^{ring} are the costs of deferral and cost of interruption of each of these caller classes, respectively. We note that c^{ring} is just the current expected cost of interruption, ECI, as computed with Equation 1, so we can rewrite Equation 2 as,

$$ECC(E,t) = (\sum_i f_i c_i^{defer} + \sum_j f_j ECI(E))t \qquad (3)$$

To compute the EVI of asking the user a question, we recompute ECI and ECC separately for the answers of "attending" and "not attending," identifying the changes in the numbers of calls in the deferral and the ring-through classes for the updated values of ECI, and finally combine these two ECC values together, weighted by the probability of hearing each answer. The communication cost for the answer, "attending meeting" considers the expected cost associated with being at the meeting,

$$ECC(E,a,t) = (\sum_i f_i^{'} c_i^{defer} + \sum_j f_j^{'} \sum_k p(c_k \mid E)c_k)t \qquad (4)$$

The communication cost for the answer, "not attending" takes as the cost of interruption, the background cost associated with the time of day,

$$ECC(E,\bar{a},t) = (\sum_i f_i^{''} c_i^{defer} + \sum_j f_j^{''} c^b)t \qquad (5)$$

Putting these terms together, we can compute the expected value of asking the user as,

$$EVI(E,t) = ECC(E,t)$$
$$-[p(A \mid E)ECC(E,a,t) + (1 - p(A \mid E))ECC(E,\bar{a},t)] \qquad (6)$$
$$-C^a$$

where C^a is the cost of asking the user before the meeting, just the ECI before the meeting begins. The system also considers the added value of directly asking a user about the interruptability of a meeting, given that the user has answered that the meeting will be attended, using an analogous value of information computation. Users are asked to optionally answer a second question about the cost of interruption, if acquiring that information is worth the incremental cost of asking the second question.

6 Bayesphone Desktop and Mobile Applications

Bayesphone consists of two applications: (1) a desktop application, running on WindowsXP, that performs inference, cost-benefit analyses, and value of information precomputation of ideal real-time actions and inquiries, and (2) an application running on Smartphones that downloads the precomputed policy file from the desktop via a device synchronization program. The Bayesphone desktop application analyzes each forthcoming meeting, making inferences with the Bayesian network models for both attendance and interruptability. The client application considers these inferences along with the costs of deferral of calls from callers in different groups, the expected cost of interruption with taking calls for each meeting, and the history of incoming calls in the user's call log, and precomputes the ideal call-handling actions and interactions for each meeting. The desktop system creates an XML-encoded file, which includes for each meeting, the meeting title, date, and time, whether the user should be asked with an alert about meeting attendance before the meeting, and the list of caller groups who are allowed to breakthrough to the user during the meeting for the no-interaction or no-answer case, and for each answer.

In use, a user may be asked before a meeting occurs about whether they plan to attend the forthcoming meeting. A special alert tone is used to inform the user about the question, and a screen appears that allows the user to specify whether they will attend the meeting. The maximum likelihood answer is displayed on the device, allowing the user to either confirm or to change the guess. If no answer is available with three minutes, the question times out and the title of the meeting appears on the screen, along with the groups who can breakthrough. Users can directly change their attendance status or the cost of interruption directly at any time via a menu, and the ideal precomputed policy for the state will be accessed and displayed. Figure 6 displays two screens of the Bayesphone application executing the call-handling policies of one of the authors. In this case, the system has alerted the user to the value of answering a question about attendance before a meeting. The system has guessed that the user will not attend the meeting, and the user confirms this guess. After the interaction, the system shows the users the caller groups that will be allowed to breakthrough. At run time, Bayesphone intercepts incoming calls and takes control of the ringing of the phone. The application checks caller ID, examines the list of callers allowed via the precomputed cost-benefit analysis, and decides whether to ring the phone versus transfer the call to voicemail.

Although the primary intent of this paper is to share with the User Modeling community methods for precomputing user models for fielding ideal policies on mobile devices that do not have the computational power of desktop machines, we are interested also in the value of these methods for the call-handling domain. The initial Bayesphone prototype has been used by two people on our team for four months. We have not yet performed a formal validation of satisfaction with call handling, but the system has been reported by both users to perform well overall in a qualitative survey. Both users provided us with feedback on the effort with setting up the system. The users found that the assessments of caller groups, costs of deferral, and costs of interruption were straightforward, taking under 15 minutes to complete. However, they found the assessment of the Bayesian models to be more burdensome, taking about two hours of time to assess crawled events from their online calendars. We are working on means for easing this burden via experience sampling along the lines of [5], and on the use of lighter-weight, but less precise models. Such an approach includes the reliance on the direct assessments of probability distributions for attendance and interruptability for classes of appointments.

7 Summary

We have described a project highlighting the opportunity for precomputing inferences from Bayesian networks and coupling these inferences with cost-benefit policies for fielding policies for action and dialog with users on simple end-point devices like cell phones. We reviewed the construction of probabilistic models that can infer the expected cost of interruption and the likelihood that users will attend meetings on their calendar. We showed how these models can drive a cost-benefit analysis of call-handling policies and reviewed a prototype application. We are now studying the difficulties that users may have in building probabilistic models for the prototype, and the overall experience with using the system. We are also working to extend the evidential considerations beyond meeting properties and time, to include such observations as local sensing of location, motion, and ambient acoustical signals, such as those representing a nearby conversation in progress.

Fig. 5. Bayesphone application, showing the case where it is best to ask the user about attendance of a forthcoming meeting. When the meeting starts, the application displays the title of the meeting in progress, the input from the user, and the callers who can break through

Moving beyond the motivating example we selected to explore the precomputation of personalized policies, we are excited about the prospects for precomputing user models for fielding adaptive behavior that can be executed on a variety of small devices—especially on mobile devices that may have minimal computational power.

References

1. Chickering, D.M., Heckerman, D. and Meek, C. (1997). A Bayesian approach to learning Bayesian networks with local structure. In *Proc. of UAI 1997*, pp. 80-89.
2. Fogarty, J., Hudson, S.E., and Lai, J. (2004). Examining the Robustness of Sensor-Based Statistical Models of Human Interruptability, *Proc. of CHI 2004*.
3. Horvitz, E. Koch, P., Kadie, C.M. Jacobs, A. (2002). Coordinate: Probabilistic Forecasting of Presence and Availability. *Proc. of UAI 2002*, pp. 224-233.
4. Horvitz, E. and Apacible, J. (2003) Learning and Reasoning about Interruption, *Proc. of ICMI 2003*, pp. 20-27.
5. Horvitz, E. Apacible, J. and Koch, P. (2004) BusyBody: Creating and Fielding Personalized Models of the Cost of Interruption, *Proc. of CSCW 2004*.
6. Jameson, A. (1996) *User Modeling and User-Adapted Interaction, Volume 5,* pp. 193-251.
7. Jameson, A. (2003). Adaptive Interfaces and Agents In J. Jacko and A. Sears (Eds.), *Human-computer interaction handbook* (pp. 305-330). Erlbaum Publishers.
8. Mynatt, B. and Tullio, J. (2001). Inferring Calendar Event Attendance, *Proc. of Intelligent User Interfaces* 2001, pp. 121-128. ACM Press.

Just Do What I Tell You: The Limited Impact of Instructions on Multimodal Integration Patterns

Sharon Oviatt, Rachel Coulston, and Rebecca Lunsford

Center for Human-Computer Communication,
Department of Computer Science & Engineering,
Oregon Health & Science University, 20000 NW Walker Road,
Beaverton, OR 97006, USA +1 503-748-1342
{oviatt, rachel, rebeccal}@cse.ogi.edu

Abstract. Large individual differences have been documented among users in their multimodal integration patterns, which suggest that new user-adaptive approaches to multimodal fusion may be opportune. Before pursuing such an approach, this study explores whether people can be successfully encouraged to switch their multimodal integration pattern to one that is easier to process through the use of explicit instructions. Longitudinal data were collected from young and elderly adults as they used speech and pen input with a simulated map system. Results revealed that only 37% of users switched their integration pattern and maintained it, whereas another 19% never switched their natural pattern and 31% switched but then reverted during a follow-up session. In addition, significant destabilization of elderly users' integration pattern was one "cost" of attempting to instruct a change in pattern. This research underscores the need for user-centered design in future multimodal system development, especially for vulnerable users such as the elderly.

1 Introduction

Research has documented large individual differences among users in multimodal integration patterns, with greater variability among the elderly than younger adults [6,9]. However, state-of-the-art multimodal systems still are based on *fixed temporal thresholds* to determine when modality fusion is "legal" [1]. These temporal thresholds are used to resolve when a person's input is unimodal versus multimodal, and also when sequential signals separated by a lag should be fused into one multimodal interpretation. Since multimodal systems based on fixed temporal thresholds are inaccurate for many users and do not permit tailoring to handle departures from modal patterns, one key direction for future multimodal interfaces is the development of a new class of *adaptive temporal thresholds* that can *detect and adapt to a user's dominant multimodal integration pattern*. Adaptive thresholds are expected to reduce system response delays to approximately 44% of what they currently are for fixed thresholds, and also to significantly improve the synchrony of user-system interaction and overall system reliability.

As a new class of adaptive multimodal interfaces begins to be prototyped, engineers might reasonably ask whether users can't just be trained to deliver their multi-

L. Ardissono, P. Brna, and A. Mitrovic (Eds.): UM 2005, LNAI 3538, pp. 261–270, 2005.
© Springer-Verlag Berlin Heidelberg 2005

modal commands in a simultaneously integrated manner. This could greatly simplify the development of temporal constraints that are needed to build new time-sensitive multimodal architectures. The present research explores this theme of the potential malleability of users' multimodal integration patterns, as well as examining possible differences between younger adults and the elderly.

1.1 Related Research on Multimodal Integration Patterns

Recent research has revealed an unusual bimodal distribution of multimodal integration patterns when users interact with computers. As illustrated in table 1, studies conducted with users across the lifespan have indicated that individual child, adult, and elderly users all adopt either a predominantly *simultaneous* or *sequential* integration pattern during production of speech and pen multimodal constructions [6,8,9]. During a simultaneous integration, speech and pen input is at least partly overlapped in time, whereas during a sequential construction one input mode begins and ends before the second starts. A user's dominant integration pattern can be identified almost immediately, typically on the very first multimodal command, and it remains highly consistent (88-97%) throughout an interactive computer session [6,8,9]. Interestingly, large individual differences and within-subject stability likewise have been documented in the perception of multisensory synchrony [4,7].

Table 1. Percentage of simultaneously-integrated multimodal constructions (SIM) versus sequentially-integrated constructions (SEQ) for children, adults, and seniors

Children			Adults			Seniors		
U	SIM	SEQ	User	SIM	SEQ	User	SIM	SEQ
SIM integrators:			SIM integrators:			SIM integrators:		
1	100	0	1	100	0	1	100	0
2	100	0	2	94	6	2	100	0
3	100	0	3	92	8	3	100	0
4	100	0	4	86	14	4	97	3
5	100	0	SEQ integrators:			5	96	4
6	100	0	5	31	69	6	95	5
7	98	2	6	25	75	7	95	5
8	96	4	7	17	83	8	92	8
9	82	18	8	11	89	9	91	9
10	65	35	9	0	100	10	90	10
SEQ integrators:			10	0	100	11	89	11
11	15	85	11	0	100	12	73	27
12	9	91				SEQ integrators:		
13	2	98				13	1	99
						Non-dominant integrators:		
						14	59	41
						15	48	52
Average Consistency 93.5%			Average Consistency 90%			Average Consistency 88.5%		

In many respects, these data on individual differences in multimodal integration patterns present an ideal opportunity for adaptive processing, since users are divided into two basic types, with early predictability and high consistency in their integration pattern. Furthermore, recent work has indicated that users' natural dominant integration pattern, whether simultaneous or sequential, spontaneously remains stable over extended time periods [5]. In addition, their dominant integration pattern is resistant to change even when a strong training contingency is delivered [6].

1.2 Goals of This Study

The present research assesses whether an individual's natural dominant multimodal integration pattern, either simultaneous or sequential, can be changed via explicit instructions. It also examines whether this changed pattern then remains stable during a longitudinal follow-up one month later. It was predicted that: (1) most users would switch their integration pattern if explicitly instructed to do so (from simultaneous to sequential, or vice versa), with younger adults more likely than elderly ones to change. One related goal was: (2) to investigate how gradual or abrupt this change in patterns would be as people consolidated their new integration pattern. During the longitudinal follow-up, it was hypothesized that: (3) some users would revert to their natural integration pattern, with elderly users more likely to do so than younger ones due to memory limitations and greater individual differences [2,3]. It also was expected that: (4) elderly users would be more likely to report having forgotten the original instruction than younger ones. Finally, it was hypothesized that: (5) one byproduct or "cost" of attempting to change people's natural integration pattern, whether this attempt was successful or not, would be to destabilize or reduce the overall consistency of their pattern.

The long term goal of this research is the development of empirically-based models on users' multimodal integration patterns, which will be needed for deriving optimal temporal thresholds for signal fusion in a new generation of time-sensitive multimodal architectures. One expected outcome of such work is the design of high-performance multimodal systems that are capable of adapting to a full spectrum of diverse users, thereby supporting more tailored and robust multimodal systems.

2 Methods

2.1 Participants, Task and Procedure

There were 16 participants, 6 elderly adults 66-89 years of age, and 10 younger adults 18-61 years of age. Among the elderly 4 were female and 2 male, whereas the young adults included 6 females and 4 males. All participants were native English speakers and paid volunteers and represented varied professional backgrounds. They were healthy and physically active, had no major physical limitations or cognitive impairments, and were not on medications known to influence speech or motor performance.

Participants were instructed to act as volunteers assisting during a flood management exercise. They used a simulated multimodal map system. Instructions from headquarters were displayed as text near the bottom of their screen. The experimenter gave them instructions and practice until they were ready to work. Participants were told that they could use speech and pen input in any way they wished, as long as they used both modalities for each task. The experimenter's instructions initially were unbiased with respect to how users could integrate modalities. Then the experimenter left the room, and the participant completed the first 10 tasks, which constituted an identification band to determine their natural dominant multimodal integration pattern.

Instructional manipulation – After determination of the user's integration pattern, the experimenter then reentered the room to check on the user, and explained that she had forgotten to mention that the system would work best if speech and pen input were integrated together/separately (i.e., whichever was not their natural dominant pattern). This was done without making reference to the user's pattern. If the volunteer had just been identified as a sequential integrator, then he was instructed to provide speech and pen *together, or in an overlapped way*. However, if he was identified as simultaneous, he was instructed to complete one input mode before starting the second so they *would not be presented at the same time*. If the volunteer asked, he was told that it did not matter which mode was used first. To one subject, for example, whose dominant integration pattern was simultaneous, the experimenter said "I forgot to tell you something. I was talking to the programmer, and the system actually works best if you give your spoken and pen input not overlapping; so do one, then do the other. It doesn't matter which one you do first." Following this instructional intervention, the experimenter watched while the participant completed one task correctly as instructed. Then she left the room and the participant completed another 82 tasks while working alone for about one hour.

Longitudinal follow-up – One month after their initial session, each participant returned for a second one. After a brief reorientation and practice using the same system, they completed 83 tasks while working alone for about one hour. On this visit, no instructions were given on how to integrate speech and pen, and no mention was made of the previous instructions they received during their earlier session.

Post-experimental Interview – An oral interview was conducted by the experimenter at the end of the second longitudinal session to determine whether participants were aware of their own integration pattern, and whether they recalled the experimenter's instructions. Participants also were debriefed on the purpose of the study, and it was confirmed that everyone believed they were interacting with a fully functional system.

Simulation Technique – Data collection was accomplished using a dual-wizard high-fidelity semiautomatic simulation technique, as described in previous work [6], with a simulated recognition error rate of 20% throughout each session.

2.2   Research Design, Data Capture and Coding

The research design involved an initial identification band phase, during which a user's dominant multimodal integration pattern was classified based on the first 10 tasks. After this, the user received the main instructional manipulation, which entailed giving different instructions depending on what the user's dominant pattern was, as described above. The main data collection phase followed, with a second longitudinal session following one month later. The experimental design involved two within-subject factors: (1) Longitudinal session (first, second) and (2) Age group (younger, elder). Both sessions and the interviews were videotaped, and multimodal integration patterns, consistency levels, and self-report data then were analyzed as such:

Integration Pattern Classification– All multimodal constructions were classified as either simultaneous or sequential in their temporal integration pattern. A multimodal construction was *simultaneous* if the gesture and speech components were executed with any portion temporally overlapping. A multimodal construction was considered *sequential* if the gesture and speech contained no overlap, and instead a temporal lag was present between the modes. Based on a subject's percentage of simultaneous versus sequential integration patterns for a given session, that person's session also was classified as either a simultaneous (M) or sequential (Q) dominant integration pattern if 60% or more of the constructions for that session represented that pattern, and as non-dominant (ND) if the 60% criterion was not reached for either pattern (i.e., falling between 40-60% consistency range). The dominant pattern identified during a person's baseline identification band (i.e., before instructions) was termed their *natural integration pattern*. If a person responded to instructions by reversing their integration pattern, this was termed the *instructed integration pattern*.

Integration Pattern Change Score– For a given participant, change scores were calculated between the subject's percentage of constructions delivered in their natural integration pattern as defined during the identification band, and the percentage of constructions delivered in that same pattern on a later session following instructions (i.e., either session 1 or 2). This change score was computed by subtracting the percentage on the later session from the original baseline (e.g., %ID - %Session 1).

Integration Pattern Consistency– The percentage of a person's total constructions delivered in their dominant integration pattern was calculated for a given session.

Post-Experimental Interview – Participants' responses to interview questions were summarized as a percentage within each category.

2.3 Reliability

The dual-wizard simulation technique permitted real-time identification and logging of users' integration pattern throughout the session, and previous analyses have revealed it to be 99% accurate when compared with hand codings [9]. Participants' multimodal integration pattern during the baseline identification band was hand verified. The integration pattern for all multimodal constructions throughout the rest of the participants' sessions also was calculated by measuring the start and end of both the speech and pen signal, and programmatically identifying overlap (simultaneous) or lag (sequential) between the two signals. Measurements of start and end of the speech and pen signals were compared between coders for 6% of the data in the first session, and over 80% matched to within 0.1 second.

3 Results

Analyses were based on longitudinal data from approximately 2770 multimodal constructions, including 1740 from younger adults and 1030 from elderly adults.

3.1 Changes in Dominant Integration Pattern

Of the sixteen subjects, all displayed a clear dominant multimodal integration pattern during their identification band - their first ten constructions. Fourteen were identified as simultaneous integrators, and two as sequential. Following the explicit instructional manipulation, twelve subjects or 75% reversed their integration pattern during session 1 as expected. One dropped below the 60% threshold for dominance, but did not actually switch to the reverse pattern completely as instructed. The remaining three subjects never changed their dominant integration pattern at all. These data are summarized in table 2. Of the elder adults, four out of six (67%) switched integration patterns but two did not (33%), whereas eight out of ten younger adults switched (80%) and only two did not (20%). An analysis of the integration pattern change score between the ID band and session 1 for younger versus elder adults revealed that these two groups were not significantly different by Wilcoxon Rank Sum test, z < 1, N.S., one-tailed.

Table 2. Dominant multimodal integration pattern and percentage consistency for each elder or younger adult during their ID band, first session, and second follow-up session, with consistency levels broken down by first versus second half for the main sessions [M-Simultaneous; Q-Sequential; ND-No dominant pattern]

Subject Age	ID Band Natural Dominant Pattern	Session 1 Dominant Pattern (Overall)	1st half	2nd half	Session 2 Dominant Pattern (Overall)	1st half	2nd half
79	M (100.0%)	Q (81.7%)	82.9%	80.5%	M (80.3%)	85.7%	75.6%
71	M (88.9%)	Q (95.1%)	97.6%	92.7%	M (61.4%)	81.0%	41.5%
78	M (100.0%)	Q (66.3%)	57.1%	75.6%	M (91.6%)	85.7%	97.6%
66	M (80.0%)	Q (81.5%)	78.6%	84.6%	Q (89.2%)	83.3%	95.1%
69	M (90.0%)	M (83.8%)	81.1%	86.5%	M (96.2%)	97.4%	94.9%
89	M (100.0%)	M (67.5%)	73.8%	61.0%	M (85.2%)	85.0%	85.4%
Elder Avg	**93.2%**	**79.3%**	**78.5%**	**80.1%**	**84.0%**	**86.4%**	**81.7%**
26	M (100%)	Q (86.7%)	88.1%	85.4%	ND (56.6%)M	42.9%	70.7%
61	M (70%)	Q (79.5%)	83.3%	75.6%	M (60.0%)	42.5%	77.5%
45	M (100%)	Q (82.9%)	78.0%	87.8%	M (97.6%)	95.2%	100.0%
27	M (100%)	Q (85.0%)	80.5%	89.7%	Q (97.3%)	100.0%	95.1%
19	M (80%)	Q (98.8%)	97.6%	100.0%	Q (98.8%)	100.0%	97.6%
23	M (100%)	Q (100.0%)	100.0%	100.0%	Q (100.0%)	100.0%	100.0%
18	M (100%)	Q (94.0%)	88.1%	100.0%	Q (100.0%)	100.0%	100.0%
53	Q (70%)	M (91.6%)	85.7%	97.6%	M (91.5%)	87.8%	95.1%
33	M (100%)	M (96.4%)	97.6%	95.1%	M (98.8%)	97.6%	100.0%
19	Q (70%)	ND (51.25%)Q	55.0%	47.5%	M (100.0%)	100.0%	100.0%
Younger Avg	**89.0%**	**86.6%**	**85.4%**	**87.9%**	**90.1%**	**86.6%**	**93.6%**
Overall Avg	**90.6%**	**83.9%**	**82.8%**	**85.0%**	**87.8%**	**86.5%**	**89.1%**

By the second longitudinal session one month later, figure 1 illustrates that only six of the twelve participants who had initially switched their dominant integration pattern (i.e., 6 of original 16) continued with this instructed pattern, or just 37%. Five others reverted back to their natural integration pattern (i.e., 5 of 16), or 31%, and the remaining person reverted back partially but fell within the non-dominant zone. Of the 3 participants who had maintained their natural integration pattern during the first session (i.e., 3 of 16), all or 19% continued to maintain this pattern during the longitudinal follow-up. The last person, who had partially switched patterns during the first session but remained within the non-dominant zone, eventually did switch to the instructed pattern in a delayed manner during the second session.

With respect to differences between elder and younger adults on the longitudinal follow-up, three of the four elders, or 75% of those who had switched to the instructed pattern during the first session reverted back to their natural pattern. In contrast, only two of the eight younger adults, or 25% who had switched, reverted back. As shown in figure 2, by the second session, six out of ten younger adults were displaying the instructed integration pattern as their dominant one (60%, as compared with 80% on session 1), whereas only one of six elderly adults did so (16.5%, as compared with 67% on session 1). An analysis of the integration pattern change score between the ID band and session 2 for younger versus elder adults revealed a significant difference between the two groups by Wilcoxon Rank Sum test, $z = 1.37$, $p < 0.05$, one-tailed.

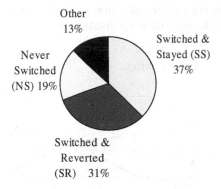

Fig. 1. Percentage of all participants who switched to the instructed integration pattern and maintained it through the longitudinal follow-up (SS), switched but reverted back to their natural integration pattern (SR), or never switched from their natural integration pattern (NS)

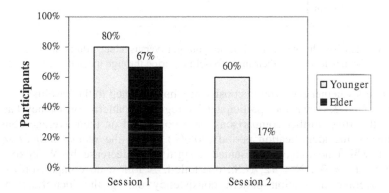

Fig. 2. Percentage of younger versus older adults who displayed instructed integration pattern on session 1 and session 2

3.2 Changes in Consistency of Integration Pattern

Table 2 (see preceding page) summarizes participants' dominant integration pattern (M, Q, ND) and also their average consistency level during the identification band, session 1, and session 2. Since one hypothesis was that the instructional intervention itself might destabilize people's integration pattern and result in reduced consistency of this pattern, this was evaluated in the results. As shown in table 2, participants' average consistency level during the identification period was 90.6%, which decreased to 82.8% *immediately following instructions* in the first half of session 1, a significant drop by Wilcoxon Signed Rank test, T+ = 90, N = 15, p < 0.05, one-tailed. A follow-up within-subject comparison by age group revealed that elderly adults' average integration pattern consistency decreased from 93.2% to 78.5% between the identification band and first half of session 1, which was a significant drop by Wilcoxon Signed Rank test, T+ = 19, N = 6, p < 0.05, one-tailed. However, younger adults' decrease in consistency from 89.0% to 85.4% for this same interval was not a statistically significant one, Wilcoxon Signed Rank test, T+ = 28, N = 9, NS, one-tailed. Figure 3 illustrates this difference between elder and younger adults in the destabilization of their integration pattern immediately following instructions.

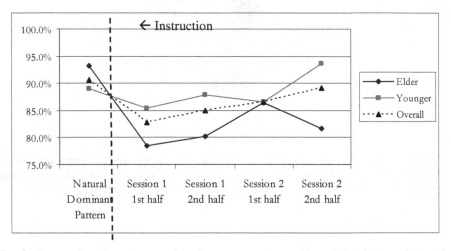

Fig. 3. Progressive changes over time in younger versus elder adults' average integration pattern consistency level from their initial baseline period through the end of session 2

To assess whether this drop in consistency had returned to the baseline level by the end of session 2, or whether participants' integration pattern consistency had recovered by this time, further comparisons were conducted on their average consistency level during the identification period (90.6%) versus the *second half of session 2* (89.1%), which no longer represented a significant decrease by Wilcoxon Signed Rank test, T+ = 39, N = 12, N.S., one-tailed. A follow-up comparison of elderly adults' average integration pattern consistency during the identification period (93.2%) versus the *second half of session 2* (81.7%), revealed that the gap they originally displayed did not continue to reflect a significant decrease one month later, Wilcoxon Signed Rank test, T+ = 15, N = 6, N.S., one-tailed. A similar comparison on younger adults for this same time interval revealed that their average consistency had returned from 89.0% back up to 93.6%, which actually exceeded their original level. Figure 3 also illustrates this difference between elder and younger adults in the return of stability in their integration pattern by the end of session 2.

3.3 Self-report on Integration Patterns

All subjects reported being aware of their integration pattern, although only 12 of the 16 (75%) were correct in reporting whether it was mainly simultaneous or sequential.

The other four (25%) self-reported the wrong integration pattern. When asked whether their integration pattern had changed between the first and second sessions, six people (38%) reported correctly but another nine (56%) were wrong about whether their integration pattern changed and one (6%) did not remember.

When asked whether they remembered the instruction in session 1 about how to integrate the two input modes, 9 of 16 subjects (56%) correctly recalled that the experimenter had asked them to change their integration pattern and what the instruction had been. The other 7 (44%) either did not remember receiving an instruction at all or failed to remember what it was. In addition, for 63% of participants the ability to recall instructions correctly corresponded with having switched and/or maintained their integration pattern accordingly by session 2. Among younger adults, 50% correctly recalled the original instruction, although 67% of the elderly actually remembered it, which clearly did not support the interpretation of greater selective forgetting among the elderly group.

4 Discussion

This research underscores that future multimodal systems need to accurately model users' existing natural integration patterns, rather than naively assuming that instructions can prompt users to adopt a particular style that may be easier for the system to process. Only 37% of users in this study switched their natural integration pattern to the instructed one and maintained it one month later, whereas 19% never switched their natural pattern at all, and another 31% switched but then reverted back to their natural pattern during the follow-up session. That is, permanent switching was uncommon in spite of the fact that all users had demonstrated their understanding of the experimenter's original instruction by composing an appropriately integrated construction. However, the self-report data indicated that 25% of users were not aware of what the temporal organization of their multimodal communication had been over the last hour, and 62% of users either failed to recall or incorrectly remembered whether their integration pattern had changed from session 1 to 2. These data on users' limited awareness of their multimodal integration patterns at least partially explain why explicit instructions were so ineffective in prompting the desired change.

As illustrated in figure 2 and confirmed by the analysis of younger and elderly adults' change scores between their baseline and session 2, elderly users also were significantly less likely than younger ones to switch and maintain the instructed integration pattern. By the longitudinal follow-up, only 16.5% of the elderly still maintained the instructed pattern, whereas 60% of younger adults did so. Perhaps surprisingly, self-report data did not support the interpretation that the elderly forgot the instructions more frequently than younger adults. They simply were more likely to either persist or to revert back to their natural dominant pattern. In addition, a significant temporary destabilization of participants' integration pattern was a *cost* of attempting to instruct them to change their natural pattern, as shown in figure 3. There was a significant drop in elderly adults' average consistency level from 93.2% during their baseline period to 78.5% immediately following instructions on the first half of session 1. By the second half of the longitudinal follow-up, their consistency level had climbed back up to 81.7%, which no longer represented a significant departure from baseline. Although younger adults were not completely immune from the destabilizing impact of instructions, they nonetheless were not significantly disrupted by them to the same extent as the elderly.

Taken together, these results underscore that a user-centered design perspective is needed to guide successful multimodal system development, since (1) the majority of users cannot be expected to change their natural multimodal integration pattern to suit system processing capabilities, and (2) attempts to change their pattern incurs a cost by destabilizing user-system interaction. The present data also clarify that user-centered design is more critical for elderly users, since they are less likely to adapt to the system, and also are more adversely affected by attempts to instigate change in their interaction patterns. These results have implications for the effective design of "aging-in-place" and other emerging elder interfaces.

The long-term goal of this research is the development of empirically-based models on users' multimodal integration patterns. Such models will be needed for deriving optimal temporal thresholds for signal fusion for a new generation of time-sensitive multimodal architectures. One outcome of such work will be the design of high-performance multimodal systems that are capable of adapting to a full spectrum of diverse users, thereby supporting more tailored and robust multimodal systems.

Acknowledgements

Thanks to B. Xiao and K. Hollingshead for data collection, scoring and programming, to M. Wesson for acting as wizard, and to members of CHCC for insightful discussions. This research was supported by DARPA Contract No. NBCHD030010 and NSF Grant No. IIS-0117868.

References

1. Cohen, P.R., Johnston, M., McGee, D.R., Oviatt, S., Pittman, J., Smith, I., Chen, L., Clow, J.: QuickSet: Multimodal interaction for distributed applications. Proc. Multimedia'97 (1997) 31-40
2. Craik, F.I.M., Salthouse, T.A., (eds.): Handbook of Aging and Cognition. 2 ed. LEA, Mahwah, NJ (2000)
3. Czaja, S.J., Lee., C.C.: Designing computer systems for older adults. In: J. Jacko, A. Sears, (eds.): Handbook of Human-Computer Interaction. LEA, New York (2003) 413-427
4. Mollon, J.D., Perkins, A.J.: Errors of judgement at Greenwich in 1796. Nature, Vol. 380. (1996) 101-102
5. Oviatt, S., Lunsford, R., Coulston, R.: Individual differences in multimodal integration patterns: What are they and why do they exist? Proc. Human-Factors in Computing Systems (CHI) (2005) in press
6. Oviatt, S.L., Coulston, R., Tomko, S., Xiao, B., Lunsford, R., Wesson, M., Carmichael, L.: Toward a theory of organized multimodal integration patterns during human-computer interaction. Proc. ICMI (2003) 44-51
7. Stone, J.V., Hunkin, N.M., Porrill, J., Wood, R., Keeler, V., Beanland, M., Port, M., Porter, N.R.: When is now? Perception of simultaneity. Proc. Royal Society: Biological Sciences, Vol. 268. (2001) 31-38
8. Xiao, B., Girand, C., Oviatt, S.L.: Multimodal integration patterns in children. Proc. ICSLP (2002) 629-632
9. Xiao, B., Lunsford, R., Coulston, R., Wesson, M., Oviatt, S.L.: Modeling multimodal integration patterns and performance in seniors: Toward adaptive processing of individual differences. Proc. ICMI (2003) 265-272

Motion-Based Adaptation of Information Services for Mobile Users

Mathias Bauer[1] and Matthieu Deru[2]

[1] DFKI, Stuhlsatzenhausweg 3, 66123 Saarbrücken, Germany
bauer@dfki.de
[2] mineway GmbH, Im Stadtwald, Geb. 34, 66123 Saarbrücken, Germany
mderu@mineway.de

Abstract. Adaptive information systems typically exploit knowledge about the user's interests, preferences, goals etc. to determine what should be presented to the user and how this presentation should take place. When dealing with *mobile* users, however, information about their motions—the places visited, the duration of stays, average velocity etc.—can be additionally exploited to enrich the user model and better adapt the system behavior to the user's needs. This paper discusses the use of positioning data and background knowledge to achieve such a motion-based adaptation of information provision.

1 Introduction

"Conventional" adaptive systems tend to characterize their users in terms of their preferences, interests, goals, etc. Location-aware systems additionally use the user's position to provide information or support that is somehow associated with a geographical point. When dealing with *mobile* persons, an additional, rich source of information about the user becomes available (at least in principle): the user's motion itself that lead her to her current position.[1]

A *motion profile* derived from observations about the user moving in the physical space can reflect both the sequence of places visited by the user before reaching the current position—at various levels of abstraction—and additional features of the movement itself. The latter can be used to infer user characteristics such as her degree of commitment to a certain goal, her cognitive load and so forth. Combining both aspects of the motion profile, a mobile application can determine both what information (or service) is most appropriate to the user in the given situation and how it can (or should) be presented to her. This paper presents a machine-learning approach to the computation of a two-part motion profile from low-level position data as provided e.g. by GPS receivers.

2 Related Work

Hidden Markov Models (HMMs) are a standard technique to the characterization and description of users' typical motions. While the straightforward application of HMMs

---

[1] Throughout this paper, users will be referred to in the female form.

L. Ardissono, P. Brna, and A. Mitrovic (Eds.): UM 2005, LNAI 3538, pp. 271–276, 2005.

as in [1] leads to problems when trying to relate the observations to higher-level goals, *hierarchical* HMMs as used in [4] overcome this limitation using a hierarchy of abstract goals associated with places and trip segments.

In the HIPS system [3] information about the user's movements in physical space is exploited to adapt the presentation of pieces of art to the user's preferences. Similar to our approach described below, two aspects of the user's motions are taken into account: the set of artworks visited before and the user's *visitor style*—one of a collection of four patterns characterizing the typical behavior of most museum visitors in general, but neglecting the concrete location.

One of the purposes of characterizing the user's motion is to determine her current attentiveness. Other approaches rely on data derived e.g. from her speech input (such as articulation rate, disfluencies etc.) [5]. While this provides additional relevant information about the user, we will concentrate on location- and motion-related aspects here.

3   Computing a Motion Profile

Let $S = \langle p_1, ..., p_n \rangle$ be the sequence of positions passed by the user where $p_i = \langle x_i, y_i, z_i, t_i \rangle$. In the case of GPS data, x_i and y_i correspond to latitude and longitude values, respectively, z_i measures the current elevation, t_i is a time stamp.[2]

A *motion profile* $MP_S = \langle mod_p(S), mod_m(S) \rangle$ based on S consists of two components. $mod_p(S)$ encodes properties of the various positions contained in S. $mod_m(S)$, on the other hand, characterizes the motion itself—without referring to the positions actually visited—in terms of abstract features and mainly serves the purpose to form the basis for adapting the information presentation.

The ultimate objective of modeling the user's motion is to derive recommendations of what information might become relevant to her in the foreseeable future. In the context of location-based information systems, the relevance of some piece of information is connected to the places a user is likely to visit. In order to arrive at a reliable estimation of this relevance, there basically exist two different approaches. We can either compare the user's behavior to that of other users, thus deriving a kind of collaborative recommendation or produce a prediction model based on structural properties of the user's motion itself.

Collaborative Recommendation Rules. Assume we are given some background knowledge in the form of annotations to the locations a user has visited. This knowledge comes in the form of unique identifiers for the various GPS coordinates (e.g. "Kultur-cafe") or additionally contains classification information about the type of this place (e.g. restaurant, department store).

In either case, the user's motion history S can be reduced to the set of (named) locations or location types visited. Collecting such information across all users allows the derivation of association rules using standard techniques known from market bas-

---

[2] Due to lack of space, preprocessing steps required to cope with imprecise or incorrect measurements will not be discussed here.

ket analysis (e.g. the well-known *a-priori* algorithm or the *CAPRI* algorithm in case the temporal order of visits is additionally taken into account). Depending on the background knowledge available, these rules then have the form

- "If the user has visited 'Kulturcafe' and (then) 'Sport Scheck', then she will also visit 'H&M'. " (*confidence* = 40%, *support* = 85)   or
- "If the user has visited a shoe shop and a department store, then she will also visit a restaurant." (*confidence* = 27%, *support* = 145).

Confidence and *support* are measures for the quality of such rules that represent their accuracy and the number of occurrences in the past, respectively.

Given these rules, information items connected to the places or types of places occurring in the conclusions can be considered relevant, the reliability of these estimations being determined by the rule quality measures. $mod_p(S)$ in this case corresponds to the set of rules applicable.

Abstraction of the Position History. Another way of predicting the relevance of some piece of information is trying to extrapolate the user's route observed so far and select the information associated with the locations to be possibly visited in the near future. In Section 2 we already discussed HMM-based approaches for predicting a user's presence at a particular place. Here we sketch a simple algorithm for quickly assigning an observed motion sequence to one of a number of prototypical patterns which forms the basis for relevance assessment of information.

The basic idea is to collect a number of motion sequences in a certain area and then determine clusters of similar motions. Each cluster then represents a particular type of navigation behavior that differs significantly from the others. To this end, we need a distance measure between motion sequences.

Let $S_1 = \langle p_1^{(1)}, ..., p_n^{(1)} \rangle$ and $S_2 = \langle p_1^{(2)}, ..., p_m^{(2)} \rangle$ be motion sequences. Then the distance between S_1 and S_2 can be defined as

$$dist_s(S_1, S_2) = w_e \cdot min(dist_e(S_1, S_2), dist_e(S_2, S_1)) + w_o \cdot disorder(S_1, S_2).$$

Here $dist_e(S_1, S_2)$ corresponds to the *edit distance* between both sequences.[3] The *disorder* measure adds a penalty for each pair of positions $p_i^{(1)}$ and $p_{i+1}^{(1)}$ that are mapped onto positions $p_k^{(2)}$ and $p_l^{(2)}$, resp., where $t_l^{(2)} < t_k^{(2)}$, i.e. where the temporal order in S_2 differs from that in S_1. w_e and w_o are weights controlling the influence of both factors on the overall distance measure. In particular, w_o can be set to 0 if the directions of motion sequences can be ignored, i.e. whenever it is irrelevant whether the user is moving from A to B or in the opposite direction.

With a distance measure defined this way, it is possible to determine clusters of similar motion sequences using an algorithm such as k-means. Each cluster can be compactly represented by its *medoid*, the element with the smallest average distance to

---

[3] The edit distance $dist_e(S_1, S_2)$ is a concept known e.g. from string comparisons. It measures the minimum number of operations required to transform S_1 into S_2 where each such operation contributes a certain "penalty" to the overall distance measure. See e.g. www.csse.monash.edu.au/~lloyd/tildeAlgDS/Dynamic/Edit.

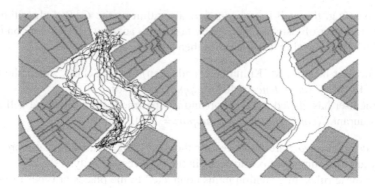

Fig. 1. Typical motion patterns in a city (left) and the medoids of three clusters (right)

all cluster members. Figure 1 depicts a set of motion sequences observed (left) and 3 cluster medoids found in these data (right).

Given this compact representation of all the training sequences, a newly observed sequence S_0 can be efficiently classified by computing its distance to all medoids available and associating it with the nearest one. Note that the cluster membership of S_0 can change over time and thus has to be re-confirmed regularly.

This classification—including the set of visited places predicted—then constitutes $m_p(S)$, the location-dependent part of the motion profile. Preselection of relevant information can either take place by searching for information associated with the locations predicted by the cluster membership or by combining this prediction with the recommendation rules as discussed above, thus applying an additional filter to the candidate information items.

Abstract Motion Features. As mentioned above, the HIPS project [3] distinguished between only 4 prototypical motion patterns specific to museums. In order to be able to appropriately address a wide spectrum ranging from people strolling leisurely through a pedestrian zone to people searching for a certain place under great time pressure, it is necessary for the system to reliably identify these different types of behavior.

The criteria for this distinction can be directly derived from a motion sequence S. They characterize motion sequences in terms of *loops* (including average duration and velocity, frequency per km etc.), *stays* at certain positions (average duration, prevalent type of places visited etc.), and *deviations* from the previous direction, measured at various time scales. Additional information such as the local weather can help to correctly interpret the values so determined. Rainfall tends to speed up even the most relaxed ambler.

Once a sufficient number of such feature vectors resulting from observed motion sequences is available, standard machine-learning algorithms can be applied to identify classes of mobile users that can then be used to classify the user currently being observed.

Knowledge about the user's class membership can be used to adapt the presentation of the information determined on the basis of $mod_p(S)$ to her estimated cognitive load, attentiveness, estimated time pressure etc. (see also [5]). Information that appears inappropriate in the current situation can be filtered out. For example, even the most relevant product offer is little helpful when the user is obviously speeding up to try and catch her bus.

An Application Scenario. The techniques introduced above are currently being investigated in the context of a project dealing with the installation of numerous WLAN hotspots throughout the city center of Saarbrücken. The basic idea is to provide the mobile user with up-to-date information about the closer neighborhood of her current position. As these hotspots do not cover the entire city, there are regions in which the user is disconnected and no high-level information about her interests can be gathered (while at the hotspot, her browsing behavior is a rich source of information). While walking in those parts not covered with WLAN, it is still possible to collect information about the user. These profiles are then used to provide a personalized collection of information items such as news regarding the user's current environment, navigation aids, or marketing messages from stores in the neighborhood.

4   Conclusions and Future Work

We presented an approach to the personalization of location-based information services for mobile users based on the observation and classification of their motions in space. The motion profiles determined using a variety of machine-learning techniques serve the purpose to both identify *what* information might be relevant to the user in the current situation and find out *how* this information can be best presented to her.

While the WLAN-based information service mentioned above is an obvious candidate for the application of such techniques, the overall goal is the integration of the motion-profile approach into SPECTER [2], a context- and affect-aware mobile personal assistant in particular for instrumented environments. It aims at observing and recording as much as possible about its user—including actions, emotions, and movements—in order to create a kind of episodic memory called *personal journal*. The latter serves the purpose to support the user in information access and decision making. The experience from the WLAN project will help limit the number of features that have to be recorded in order to arrive at a reliable classification.

Acknowledgments. This research was supported by the German Ministry of Education and Research (BMB+F) under grant 524-40001-01 IW C03 (project SPECTER).

References

1. Ashbrook, D. and Starner, T. Using GPS to learn significant locations and predict movement across multiple users. *Personal & Ubiquitous Comp.*, 7(5):275–286, 2003.
2. Bauer, M. Transparent User Modeling in SPECTER . In *Proc. of the 7th International Conference on Work with Computing Systems (WWCS 2004)*, 2004.
3. Benelli, G.,Bianchi, A., Marti, P.,Not, E., and Sennati, D. HIPS: Hyper-Interaction within Physical Space. In *Proceedings of IEEE Multimedia Systems '99, International Conference on Multimedia Computing and Systems*, 1999.

4. Liao, L., Fox, D., and Kautz, H. Learning and Inferring Transportation Routines. In *Proceedings of AAAI-04*, 348–353, 2004.
5. Müller, C., Grossmann-Hutter, B., Jameson, A., Rummer, R., and Wittig, F. Recognizing time pressure and cognitive load on the basis of speech: An experimental study. In *Proc. of the 8th International Conference on User Modeling (UM2001)*, 24–33, 2001.

Interaction-Based Adaptation
for Small Screen Devices*

Enrico Bertini[1], Andrea Calì[1,2], Tiziana Catarci[1], Silvia Gabrielli[1],
and Stephen Kimani[1]

[1] Università di Roma "La Sapienza", Dipartimento di Informatica e Sistemistica,
via Salaria 113, I-00198 Roma, Italy
[2] Free University of Bozen/Bolzano, Faculty of Computer Science,
piazza Domenicani 3, I-39100 Bolzano, Italy

Abstract. This paper explores an original approach to overcome current issues in the use of mobile devices, such as limited screen space
and interaction modalities, based on exploiting interface adaptation and
adaptive techniques. Specifically, the paper describes the application of
this approach to a web searching prototype, which collects usage data to
model interaction and provide a personalized version of the web facility
visited by the user.

1 Introduction

Mobile devices can provide many potential benefits, such as: ubiquity, portability,
context exploitation, and democratization of information systems. However, they
have also proved to bring costs and design challenges, mostly related to some of
their inherent limitations like small output space, constrained input modalities,
memory, network, disk space, energy-supply limitations. Recent studies have
tried to tackle the issues of device input-output limitations by exploring the
application of adaptive techniques to the context of mobile devices [5]. Most of
the solutions proposed suggest the construction of complex representations to
describe users interests on a certain topic (e.g., books, hotels, electronics), to
predict their goals, as well as to modelling their knowledge through machine
learning and pattern matching algorithms. By contrast, the approach proposed
here suggests to base personalization on usage data that, similarly to the work
presented in [4], are derived from the analysis of how interface elements are
used during interaction. The idea behind this is to enable both users and system
to gradually adapt the web facility visited, in order to maximize their rate of
gaining valuable information, when accessing it through a mobile device [9]. More
precisely, the aim is to arrive at presenting the user with a minimal subset of
the available information that is the most relevant for the task at hand (thus

* Work supported by the DELOS Network of Excellence on Digital Libraries (http://www.delos.info) and the MIUR-FIRB "MAIS" (http://www.mais-
project.it).

L. Ardissono, P. Brna, and A. Mitrovic (Eds.): UM 2005, LNAI 3538, pp. 277–281, 2005.
© Springer-Verlag Berlin Heidelberg 2005

optimizing display resources) as well as to reduce the amount of typing and clicking required to carry out the tasks (thus saving input effort). The rest of the paper is organized as follows: Section 2 introduces some related studies on interface adaptation for small screen devices. Section 3 sketches our adaptation approach that has been partially implemented into the prototype described in Section 4. Section 5 provides conclusions and future directions.

2   Related Work

Interesting contributions, relevant to our work, have recently been provided from different research areas. Among studies in the field of screen real estate, Brewster [1] has investigated the idea of enhancing interaction with non-speech sound, that has consisted on attempts to reduce the size of screen objects and replace the lack of visual feedback with audio feedback. In [3], Power Browser exploits the idea of page summarization, since the content of a standard web page is provided together with a hierarchical list of links extracted from current and subsequent pages. From the area of usability studies on small screen devices a comparative study on PC, PDA, and cell phone devices [8] has shown that the way small screens affect performance, strongly depends on the success of the adopted strategy: when users find the right information they do it in comparable time, when they fail they fail badly. Further contributions from adaptive hypermedia research have demonstrated that adaptivity can offer great potential to overcome the limits of mobile devices, by offloading to the system some of the burden related to search and browsing. Adaptive stretch text is addressed to saving screen space [2]. Some page fragments can be collapsed or expanded according to a user model, so that only interesting information are fully displayed, while the rest is maintained in a compact format, although it remains still accessible if required [6]). Finally, in [10] an adaptive web portal is proposed which monitors the users selection of menu items of a WAP service to promote frequently used menu items to become more easily accessible.

3   The Overall Adaptation Strategy

In this section we focus our attention to a common usage pattern: searching information within a web site, and take this as reference to point to sources of user input user interface adaptations.

Sources of User Input. We consider four types of user input: *Requests for sorting*: the user sorts the result according to some criteria (e.g., order books by price); *Form input*: the user inputs parameters in the form to guide the search; *Further actions*: the user is on the details page and selects further actions to request services (e.g., reserve the hotel), ask for related objects, activate procedures; *Explicit requests for adaptation*: the user selects some parameters to adapt the user interface explicitly. For instance, she/he requests the system to display results without including images.

Adaptations. On the basis of this user input, we envision the following potential adaptations: *Push-forward/pull-back*: User interface objects can be moved up or down in the navigation hierarchy according to usage frequencies. Those that are rarely used can be *pushed forward* to a page one step away, so that screen space can be saved, while those frequently used can be *pulled back* to permit early access; *Defaulting*: In the input page the system can provide defaults for frequently used form elements, automatically selecting parameters and filling text fields; *Filtering*: Information considered not relevant for the specific user or for the current task can be filtered out; *Sorting*: In the result list the results can be ordered according to some criteria; *Level of detail*: Objects can be represented at different levels of detail (e.g., different resolution/size)

All the adaptations have the potential to enhance the interaction either by saving screen space or limiting requests for user input. In order to detect effective combinations, it is necessary to find adaptations that prove useful and do not affect usability, and find the right combination of user input and adaptations. In the reminder of the paper we focus our attention on the combination of *explicit requests for adaptation* and *filtering*.

4   Filtering Out Information with Interaction-Based Adaptation

We developed a system that accepts explicit input for adaptation when searching, and accordingly adapts the format of the result list filtering out unwanted item attributes. The prototype is a web based mobile access to the Amazon.com book search facility [1], and it is organized around the pattern described above. As shown in Figure (1), when the user accesses the web site, she/he is presented with an input form to search books by keyword and an option to ask for an adapted result list. If the adapted result option is selected, the system chooses a set of item attributes to display and uses it to display the result. Then, the user can either move on a detail page, request a new search, or refine the current one and, in the latter case, she/he can ask a different set of features to display.

The user interface has been designed by taking into account the usability principles for adaptive user interfaces suggested by Höök in [7]: *controllability, predictability, transparency*. In accordance with these principles we have designed our system with the following design criteria: (i) *The user can always use a completely non-adaptive search* as a way to support controllability; (ii) *The adaptation can be previewed* as a way to alleviate low predictability problems; *The user can access a history of past selections and see their ranking* as a way to support transparency.

The user model relies on the frequency of selected combinations: every time an adaptation preference is issued, the system stores it, recording how many times and when the user has issued it. Our model resembles the one proposed

---

[1] The prototype is publicly accessible at the following address: http//www.dis. uniroma1.it/∼madui/. It has been tested with Nokia phones and HP PDAs.

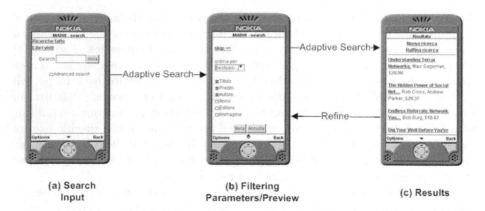

(a) Search
Input

(b) Filtering
Parameters/Preview

(c) Results

Fig. 1. The results adaptation pattern: (a) keyword search and option for requesting an adaptive result; (b) the user can preview the adaptation parameters selected by the system and eventually change them; (c) the adapted result lists displays the items with the selected features

by Debevc et al. in [4], where the frequency of selections of URLs is recorded to present an adaptive list of visited web sites.

For each attribute we draw the following measures: *Total Frequency (TF)*: the total frequency of a selection from the first time the system has been used; *Recent Frequency (RF)*: the frequency of selections made in the lapse of time going from the last time the service has been used back to the last K sessions; *Session Frequency (SF)*: the frequency of selections made in the current session. The adaptations come in two fashions: within sessions and between sessions. When a new session starts, the system proposes adaptations based on the whole history of user's interaction. While in the current session, it proposes adaptations that give more relevance to the choices made within it. In order to achieve the proposed behavior, we need two values, as shown in the following; we start by the *Between Sessions* value: $BS = \beta TF + \gamma RF$ where $0 \le \beta \le 1$, $0 \le \gamma \le 1$, and $\beta + \gamma = 1$. The value BF is obtained by summing the value of the total frequency (TF) and the recent frequency (RF), properly weighted with the values β and γ, set by the system administrator. The rationale behind this is that TF takes into account the whole history of the system and gives relevance to combinations that are often repeated in the long term. In other words, it privileges patterns that steadily recur during time. Recent Frequency on the other hand carries weight in the case the user begins to adopt a new strategy that will be maintained for the future. If we have not this parameter, these changes may take too long to show up. Of course, a higher value of γ makes the value TF more sensitive to the recent user's behavior.

When the user is in the middle of a running session the following values is used: $WS = \alpha SF + \beta TF + \gamma RF$ where $0 \le \beta \le 1$, $0 \le \gamma \le 1$, and $\alpha + \beta + \gamma = 1$. It is the weighted sum of session frequency (SF) total frequency and recent frequency. The rationale here is that we want to give relevance to departing behaviors within a single session. The session frequency counts for a fraction α to consider this aspect. Obviously, a higher value of α makes the value WS more sensitive to the user's behavior in the current session.

5   Conclusion and Future Work

This paper has proposed and described an approach that exploits interaction and usage data (e.g., how the user uses interface elements, selects parameters, inputs data, and navigates among pages) in order to optimize small screen usage and how the user interacts with a mobile device. Plans are underway for evaluation studies corresponding to the forthcoming new level of system development to provide some quantitative evaluation results and to run user studies based on long term usage adaptations. Finally, we are also planning to extend the current prototype with some of the adaptation techniques described in Section 3 that are not part of the system yet.

References

1. Stephen Brewster. Overcoming the lack of screen space on mobile computers. *Personal Ubiquitous Comput.*, 6(3):188–205, 2002.
2. Peter Brusilovsky. Adaptive hypermedia. *User Modeling and User-Adapted Interaction*, 11(1-2):87–110, 2001.
3. Orkut Buyukkokten, Hector Garcia-Molina, Andreas Paepcke, and Terry Winograd. Power browser: efficient web browsing for pdas. In *Proc. SIGCHI Conference*, pages 430–437. ACM Press, 2000.
4. Matjaz Debevc, Beth Meyer, and Rajko Svecko. An adaptive short list for documents on the world wide web. In *Proc. Conference on Intelligent User Interfaces*, pages 209–211. ACM Press, 1997.
5. Josef Fink and Alfred Kobsa. User modeling for personalized city tours. *Artif. Intell. Rev.*, 18(1):33–74, 2002.
6. Kristina Höök. Evaluating the utility and usability of an adaptive hypermedia system. In *Proc. Conference on Intelligent User Interfaces*, pages 179–186. ACM Press, 1997.
7. Kristina Höök. Steps to take before iuis become real. *Journal of Interacting with Computers*, 12:409–426, 2000.
8. Matt Jones, George Buchanan, and Harold W. Thimbleby. Sorting out searching on small screen devices. In *Proceedings of the 4th International Symposium on Mobile Human-Computer Interaction*, pages 81–94. Springer-Verlag, 2002.
9. Peter Pirolli and Stuart Card. Information foraging in information access environments. In *Proc. SIGCHI Conference*, pages 51–58. ACM Press/Addison-Wesley Publishing Co., 1995.
10. Barry Smyth and Paul Cotter. The plight of the navigator: Solving the navigation problem for wireless portals. In *Proc. Conference on Adaptive Hypermedia and Adaptive Web-Based Systems*, pages 328–337. Springer-Verlag, 2002.

Adapting Home Behavior to Its Inhabitants

Berardina De Carolis

Dipartimento di Informatica -Università di Bari
http://www.di.uniba.it/~nadja

Abstract. In this paper, we propose a multiagent system for simulating the control of an intelligent home able to adapt its behavior to the user situation. Central to the adaptation process is the concept of *influence sphere* that is defined in function of the type of service it provides to house inhabitants (i.e. comfort, security, entertainment, etc.). Each influence sphere is controlled by a Supervisor Agent (SA) that is responsible for taking decisions relative to that scope. Decisions about actions involve device behaviors that, in our system, are controlled by Operator Agents (OAs). Each OA is responsible for deciding the utility of an action in the current user context. Then, according to this organization, the adaptation process is performed at two levels: globally for the relevant influence sphere and locally at the device level.

1 Introduction

An intelligent home aims at handling the house control and management from several points of view (security, communications, comfort, power saving, ...) with the main objective of making inhabitants life easier. However, most of the time, solutions to this problem result in using new complex remote controls or a new computer-based interfaces and this does not always produce an improvement of the quality of interaction. Changing this trend and making home automation systems more accepted and spread through different user categories and type of services, in our opinion, requires creating environments in which technology interacts with the user in a transparent and unobtrusive way. This goes in the direction of Weiser's vision, in which the technology is going to be "invisible, everywhere that does not live on a personal device of any sort, but is in the woodwork everywhere" [8].

AMbient Intelligence (AMI) solutions may help in making the house services fruition easy, natural and adapted to the user needs [5]. In the AMI information technology paradigm, people will be surrounded by intelligent and intuitive interfaces embedded into objects of daily use that will be able to recognize them and answer to their presence in a transparent way. Then, an AMI environment is composed of independent and distributed devices (artifacts) interacting to support user-centered goals and tasks. The key characteristics of these artifacts are autonomy, distribution, adaptation, proactiveness, etc: therefore, in a way, they share the characteristics of agents [1]. According to this view, we propose a MultiAgent System (MAS) called C@sa[1]

---

[1] The word "casa" in Italian means "home".

L. Ardissono, P. Brna, and A. Mitrovic (Eds.): UM 2005, LNAI 3538, pp. 282–286, 2005.

which is aimed, on one side, at simulating the control of an intelligent home from the functional point of view and, on the other side, at providing an interface layer for interacting with the house. As we will see in the rest of the paper, the system adapts the house behavior to inhabitant's needs, adjusting the control of devices according to the considered "Influence Sphere" (IS). An IS is defined in function of the type of service(comfort, wellness, power saving, etc.) it provides to the house inhabitants.

The paper is structured as follows: the next section shows an overview of the architecture of our system. Section 3 illustrates how the 3DUI is used for simulating the house behaviour and how it will be used for evaluation purposes. Conclusions and future work directions are illustrated in the last Section.

2 Overview of C@sa Architecture

There are several projects concerning the realization of a Smart Home. For instance, in the MavHome project [4], the house is seen as an intelligent agent that perceives the environment and acts upon it through the use of actuators. Another example of intelligent home that uses agent technology is the UMASS simulated IHome environment that is controlled by intelligent agents that are associated with particular appliances (i.e. WaterHeater, CoffeeMaker, Heater, A/C, etc.) [3].

In developing our system, we were concerned about control, simulation and interaction with the home environment not only at a low abstraction level (single appliances behavior) but also at a higher one, closer to the user needs and goals. If every appliance is controlled by an agent, achieving this aim requires the establishment of a form of organization in which agents come together to form coherent groups able to achieve some higher level goals matching user needs and desires. To this aim, central to the system organization and coordination model is the concept of "Influence Sphere" (IS). In this phase of the project, we focus the modeling and development of the system on the Comfort IS since, this type of service, seems appropriate for testing our approach: achieving comfort involves several devices and, according to several definition, its perception is highly individual and involves different human senses (temperature, light, intimacy, sounds, level of noise, etc.) [6]. Then, we will use examples in this context for explaining how the system works.

In C@sa, each IS is controlled by a **Supervisor Agent** (**SA**) that is responsible for taking decisions for fulfilling user needs related to that scope. Its decisional behavior is modeled as a Bayesian Network (BN) that, according to the user situation, will be used to infer which are the possible user goals related to that influence sphere (Figure 1). Decisions about actions have an impact on device behaviors; to this aim each device is controlled by an **Operator Agent** (**OA**). Then, the global adaptation process is achieved through the coordination between single OAs and a Supervisor. OAs are responsible for deciding locally the utility of that action, using an influence diagram as a decision model (Figure 2), while the SA is responsible for considering which are the best actions to do in that context according to the answers of OAs and taking into account user preferences. To this aim, C@sa includes an agent dedicated to the management of user profiles: the **Butler Interactor Agent** (**BIA**). It has been designed as a kind of user assistant and provides an interface between the house and its inhabitants; in particular, it knows users' habits and preferences.

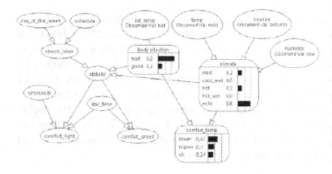

Fig. 1. BN modelling the Comfort SA

The general coordination protocol between a Supervisor Agent and the other agents is represented in Figure 3. Cyclically or, as an answer to actions of the user, the SA, according to the context and user situation, infers which are the possible user goals related to that influence sphere. In the example shown in Figure 1, the SA will infer that, since "the internal situation is *hot*, and therefore the user is very probably in a not comfortable situation" then the user would like to have *a lower internal temperature*. Then, for each triggered goal, the SA will ask to the **HouseKeeper** (*HK*) who is able to fulfil that goal. The HK, that acts as a facilitator, will return the list of active OAs able to achieve the goal. The SA will request, then, to each of them, the utility of their action that is calculated locally at the operator level. In case there are action decisions that have the same effect in terms of utility, these are weighted according to the user habits and preferences profile that is handled by the BIA. Then, the SA will ask for the execution of the "best" one.

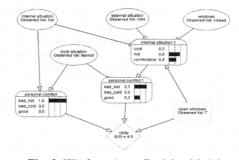

Fig. 2. *Windows Agent* Decision Model

However, in order to design guidelines for including intelligence into daily living, it is important to test the effectiveness of the system and, in particular, of its decisional behaviour. Evaluating prototypes of this type is difficult and expensive since it would require installation in a considerable number of real houses. For this reason, we decided to simulate the system behaviour before testing it in a "real" environments with a 3D "Environment Simulation & Control" Interface (3DUI). In order to control the interaction between this interface and the other agents, we developed the *Simulation Interface Agent*

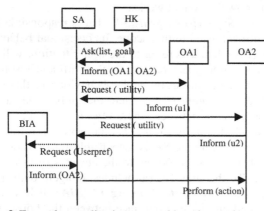

Fig. 3. Example coordination protocol based on action utility

(*IntA*) that communicates to the system, on one side, actions that are performed in the simulated world and, on the other side, the rendering, at the interface level, of changes decided by Supervisor Agents.

The system has been developed using the JADE [2] framework.

3 Simulating the Interaction

The 3DUI has been created using 3D Studio Max and then exported and transformed into VRML [7].

Figure 4 shows a portion of the 3DUI where active entities, controlled by operator agents, are the *internal temperature* sensor, the *air-conditioner,* the *windows,* the *light* and the *hi-fi.*

In order to use the 3DUI for simulation and control purposes, it has been necessary to establish a connection with C@sa. This relation works in two directions: i) when a SA

Fig. 4. 3DUI showing the air-conditioner cooling the room

ask to an OA to execute an action (i.e. to turn on the air-conditioning or to open the window) it sends a message to the *IntA* controlling the 3D World in order to show this change in the interface. This message will be received by a Java class able to parse it and to render, at the interface level, what is specified in the message. This protocol is used also to simulate the house behavior on a set of sensor data representing the evolution of the context for a time period (a day, one week, etc.). This is important to test the stability of the decisional model. On the other side, the user that is simulating or controlling the interaction with the house may want to: i) set some simulation conditions; ii) check the state of a particular device (exact parameters like the *temp* of the internal temperature sensor, etc.); iii) change the state of a particular device in order to simulate what changes as a consequence of a user action. In this case, the 3DUI interface agent sends an ACL message specifying a state change or the need to read some state attributes to the OA responsible for that device.

A change has an impact on the decisional behavior of the supervisor agent and operators involved in the control of a certain influence sphere. Actions performed in the virtual world are collected by the usage model that according to the type of action will be used to update decision model. In order to understand how these actions impact on the high level Supervisor decision and/or on the local decision of an Operator agent, we are running an experiment in order to add a learning capability to our agents. In particular, we collected a diary of 300 people concerning comfort habits. This data corpus will be annotated and used as a training set for a learning tool that will be used for understanding which are the relevant relation, for most of people, between comfort appliances behaviour and contextual parameters.

4   Conclusions and Future Work Directions

The idea of an house equipped with technical and life-enhancing devices is already old. What is new in this area is the added value of the transparency and interactivity of ambient intelligence where, following Weiser's vision, the technological devices fade into the background and be embedded into daily objects. In this optics, we have designed and developed a MAS called C@sa aiming at modeling and simulating the behaviour of an intelligent home. In particular, we proposed a distributed approach that tries to satisfy users' needs and preferences concerning particular service classes. In this phase of the project we are testing and evaluating the system behaviour using a simulation 3D interface. The collected data will be used not only for system evaluation by architects involved in the system but also as a set of examples to add a learning capability to the system, that will be able to refine its decision behaviour on the basis of the users' reactions. Furthermore, we started to investigate how to model the house behaviour in presence of more than one member of the family.

Acknowledgements

I wish to thank those Giovanni Cozzolongo, Grazia Ricco, Vito Campanella, Anna Rowe and Vincenzo Silvestri for their contribution in implementing the system. Fiorella de Rosis and Sebastiano Pizzutilo for their useful comments on the MAS organization.

References

1. Grill, T. Ibrahim I.K., Kotsis G. Agents for Ambient Intelligence - Support or Nuisance.ÖGAI Journal 23/1.http://www.tk.uni-linz.ac.at/download/oegai_article_final.pdf
2. JADE: http://jade.tilab.com/
3. Lesser, V., Atighetchi, M., Benyo, B. et al.. *The UMASS intelligent home project*. In Proceedings of the Third Annual Conference on Autonomous Agents, pages 291--298, Seattle, USA, 1999.
4. Rao S. and D. J. Cook, Predicting Inhabitant Actions Using Action and Task Models with Application to Smart Homes, *International Journal of Artificial Intelligence Tools*, 13(1), pages 81-100, 2004.
5. Shadbolt N.Ambient Intelligence. IEEE Intelligent Systems.July/August(Vol.18, No.4).
6. Spronk, B. A House is not a Home: Witold Rybczynski Explores the History of Domestic Comfort. Aurora Online, 2001.
7. VRML: http://www.vrmlsite.com/
8. Weiser M. The Computer for the 21st Century. Scientific American, september 1991.

Design and Evaluation of a Music Retrieval Scheme That Adapts to the User's Impressions

Tadahiko Kumamoto

Keihanna Human Info-Communication Research Center,
National Institute of Information and Communications Technology,
Kansai Science City, Kyoto 619-0289, Japan
kuma@nict.go.jp
http://www2.nict.go.jp/jt/a133/kuma/

Abstract. We have developed a scheme for music retrieval that adapts to the user's impressions of the musical pieces. First, we conducted impression-estimation experiments in which 100 subjects gave their impression of 80 musical pieces, and then, using a clustering method, we classified the 100 subjects into 20 groups based on the results. Next, we created a user model for each group consisting of formulas for numerically expressing the impressions and a set of vectors calculated using the formulas. We then developed a procedure for identifying the most suitable model for an unidentified user. Testing of the models and procedure in an existing impression-based music-retrieval system demonstrated the effectiveness of the proposed scheme.

1   Introduction

With the rapid development of information and communications technology, a huge, ever-increasing volume of multimedia data is being provided everyday on the Internet. A large portion of this data is music-related and image-related data-bibliographical information, such as the names of pieces, producers, and artists, and content information, such as songs, melodies, and sketches. Searching for specific items from the enormous volume of multimedia data is relatively easy as long as the user can identify the item specifically [1, 2, 7, 11, 14, 16]. However, users cannot always specifically identify the item they want. Instead, they simply want an item that matches their preferences, feelings, or mental state, so they are unable to input retrieval keys that match specific items. Several impression-based retrieval systems have thus been developed for locating multimedia data such as musical pieces and images [3, 4, 5, 6, 8, 9, 10, 12, 13, 15] that provide a heuristic means of retrieval enabling the presentation of novel and unexpected items.

Impression-based systems for retrieving multimedia data must deal with two kinds of variation between individuals [6]: in the impressions of the data and in the words used to represent the impressions. Conventional studies have focused on the latter and have defined the relationships between the words and the impressions as a user model. With this approach, the model for a user is either

L. Ardissono, P. Brna, and A. Mitrovic (Eds.): UM 2005, LNAI 3538, pp. 287–296, 2005.

created through a learning process in which the user specifies the relationship between impressions of multimedia data used for training and the target impression words [10, 15], or it is created by modifying a model for an average user prepared beforehand so that the difference between the average user model and the true relationship that the user has in mind is minimized [4, 5, 6].

We focused on the variation in impressions and developed a retrieval scheme that adapts to the user's impressions. The impressions of the retrieved items are classified into various patterns, and a user model is created for each pattern. The best model for a user is then identified. We limited the target multimedia data to musical pieces.

The remainder of this paper is organized as follows. In Section 2, we describe our experiments in which 100 subjects listened to 80 musical pieces and gave their impression of each piece. We classified the 100 subjects into an adequate number of groups by applying a clustering method to the results of the experiments. That is, subjects with the same or similar impressions were placed into the same group. In Section 3, we describe how we create the user models. Each one consists of both formulas for expressing the impressions numerically and a set of vectors calculated using the formulas. A model is created for each group, and each model is created so that it can effectively be used for the subjects in the corresponding group. These models should be effective for unknown users who can be classified into one of the groups. In Section 4, we present our procedure for identifying the model best suited for a user using a relevance feedback technique. Finally, in Section 5, we describe the testing of the user models and procedure implemented in an existing impression-based music-retrieval system [8] and present the results, which demonstrate the effectiveness of our scheme.

2   Diversity and Similarity of Impressions of Music

To investigate user impressions of music pieces in terms of diversity and similarity, we conducted impression-estimation experiments.

2.1   Impression-Estimation Experiments

One hundred people comprising 61 women and 39 men participated in our experiments; two were under 20, 45 were in their twenties, 44 were in their thirties, 8 were in their forties, and 1 was over 50. Each subject listened to 80 musical pieces [1] once or twice and gave their impression of each piece using one or more of ten impression scales (listed in Table 1). A series of related words describing an impression on a seven-step scale was used as the "impression scale". For

---

[1] The pieces were shortened versions for use as background music for Web pages and software applications; the average length was about one minute. They were obtained from two Web sites: `http://nocturne.vis.ne.jp` and `http://k2works.com/nerve/`, both of which permit their use for secondary purposes and redistribution.

Table 1. Ten impression scales

No.	Polar opposite words	No.	Polar opposite words
1	Quiet — Noisy	6	Leisurely — Restricted
2	Calm — Agitated	7	Pretty — Unattractive
3	Refreshing — Depressing	8	Happy — Sad
4	Bright — Dark	9	Calm down — Arouse
5	Solemn — Flippant	10	The mind is healed — The mind is vulnerable

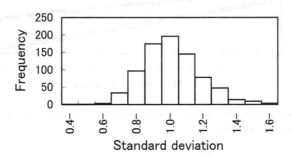

Fig. 1. Distribution of standard deviations for each musical piece and each impression scale

instance, impression scale No. 8 had the steps "very happy (7)," "happy (6)," "a little happy (5)," "medium (4)," "a little sad (3)," "sad (2)," and "very sad (1)," where the number in parentheses denotes the assigned score. We obtained 80,000 data items (80 pieces × 10 impression scales × 100 subjects). (The items corresponding to instances where the subject indicated "*don't care*" are shown as "*nil*" in the data; that is, the impression scale was not used in the estimation.)

2.2   Diversity of Impressions

To investigate the diversity in user impressions of the musical pieces, we calculated the standard deviations of the data obtained in the experiments for each piece and each impression scale. The results are shown as in Fig. 1.

The mean and median of the standard deviations were 1.06 and 1.04, respectively. This indicates that half or more of the standard deviations were larger than 1. Assuming that the data for each piece and each impression scale had a normal distribution with a mean of 4 and a standard deviation of 1, the theoretical number of subjects who gave a score between 3 and 5 is about 68, and the theoretical number of subjects who gave a score between 2 and 6 is about 95. This means that user impressions of the musical pieces differed significantly and that the number of subjects who had quite opposite impressions was not negligible.

2.3   Similarity of Impressions

While there was a rich diversity in user impressions of the musical pieces, as described above, we can reasonably assume that a number of people had the same

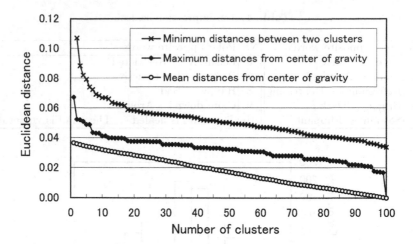

Fig. 2. Mean and maximum distances from center of gravity and minimum distances between two arbitrary clusters

or similar impressions. We therefore applied Ward's clustering method using the squared Euclidean distance [2] to the 80,000 data items and investigated the similarity of impressions. The squared Euclidean distance $D(E_A, E_B)^2$ between impression E_A of subject S_A and impression E_B of subject S_B is defined as

$$D(E_A, E_B)^2 = \sum_{m=1}^{80} \sum_{i=1}^{10} (x_{m,i}(E_A) - x_{m,i}(E_B))^2,$$

where $x_{m,i}(E_A)$ denotes the score on impression scale i given by subject S_A for musical piece m. The value of $x_{m,i}(E_A)$ is replaced with 4 when $x_{m,i}(E_A) = nil$.

To clarify the clustering process, we calculated two distances at each step of the clustering: $d(E_j, G_k)$ and $d(G_A, G_B)$. The former denotes the distance between the E_j of subject S_j forming cluster C_k and the center of gravity G_k of cluster C_k:

$$d(E_j, G_k) = \sqrt{\sum_{m=1}^{80} \sum_{i=1}^{10} (x_{m,i}(E_j) - x_{m,i}(G_k))^2 \Big/ 800},$$

where $x_{m,i}(G_k)$ denotes the value in musical piece m and impression scale i of the center of gravity G_k of cluster C_k. The $d(G_A, G_B)$ denotes the distance between the centers of gravity of two arbitrary clusters, C_A and C_B:

$$d(G_A, G_B) = \sqrt{\sum_{m=1}^{80} \sum_{i=1}^{10} (x_{m,i}(G_A) - x_{m,i}(G_B))^2 \Big/ 800}.$$

---

[2] A representative hierarchical clustering method.

Figure 2 plots the mean and maximum values of $d(E_j, G_k)$ and the minimum value of $d(G_A, G_B)$ at each step of the clustering. All the values changed rapidly when the subjects were classified into ten or less clusters, and they changed gradually when they were classified into 20 or more clusters. Apparently, the subject(s) who gave comparatively peculiar scores formed a cluster when the number of clusters was ten or less.

3   Creation of User Models

We previously proposed a method for generating a ten-dimensional impression vector representing a listener's impressions of a musical piece based on its features (height, length, and strength of a tone, and tone color) [9]. Each component of an impression vector corresponds sequentially to an impression scale and has a value, a real number, ranging from 0 to 8 that is related to the seven steps on the impression scale. We have now constructed a system for generating an impression vector from a musical piece or standard MIDI file using all the data obtained in our experiments. That is, we regarded the features extracted from each of the 80 musical pieces as explanatory variables and regarded a mean value in the corresponding experimental data as a criterion variable. We performed multiple regression analysis (forward selection) for each impression scale and obtained ten multiple regression equations for calculating the value of the corresponding impression scale. These equations are used in the system to generate an impression vector.

In our proposed scheme, each user model consists of ten multiple regression equations for generating impression vectors and a set of impression vectors generated using the equations. Creating a model suitable for a user means obtaining ten multiple regression equations for the cluster into which the user would be classified. We applied the above method not to all the data obtained in our experiments, but only to the data corresponding to each cluster. We selected 20 as the number of user models to create based on the trade-off between the results shown in Fig. 2 and the cost of the multiple regression analysis. As a result, we obtained ten multiple regression equations for each cluster. In addition, we created 10 user models to compare with the 20 user models in terms of effectiveness. That is, the 10 user models were created by classifying the 100 subjects into ten clusters, and obtaining ten multiple regression equations for each cluster. The

Table 2. Modified coefficients of determination in multiple regression analysis

Scale	Mean value	Max. value	Min. value	Scale	Mean value	Max. value	Min. value
1	0.785	0.866	0.607	6	0.764	0.847	0.649
2	0.802	0.869	0.698	7	0.665	0.742	0.541
3	0.680	0.791	0.592	8	0.675	0.794	0.608
4	0.679	0.780	0.550	9	0.748	0.851	0.569
5	0.689	0.772	0.595	10	0.699	0.846	0.580
				Total	0.719	0.869	0.541

modified coefficients of determination when the 20 user models, i.e., 200 multiple regression equations, were created were larger than 0.5, as shown in Table 2, so excellent results were obtained.

4   Identification of Best User Model

The best model for a user is identified based on the user's estimated score for the first candidate retrieval result based on the following procedure.

1) Select the first candidate, m_n, for the user's input query for each user model, M_n (where $n = 1, 2, \cdots, 20$).
2) Unless set U_{high} of the user models for which the fitness values, f_n, are *nil*, denoting no estimation or a value not smaller than threshold value H_{high}, is empty, select the m_{min} with the minimum distance. If U_{high} is empty, select m_{min} out of set U_{med} of the user models for which f_n are not smaller than threshold H_{med}. If U_{med} is also empty, select m_{min} out of all the user models.
3) Present m_{min} to the user as the first candidate retrieval result.
4) If the user estimated a fitness between impressions caused by the first candidate and impressions represented by the input query on a five-step scale, the user should enter 5 for a very good match and 1 for a poor match. Otherwise, execution ends.
5) In all the user models for which m_{min} was selected as the first candidate, update f_n and the number of estimated pieces, k_n, using the following rules. If $f_n = nil$ then $f_n = score$. Otherwise, $f_n = (f_n \times k_n + score)/(k_n + 1)$. And $k_n = k_n + 1$, where *score* is 1 when the score the user gave is 2 and -1 when it is 1, taking some penalty into consideration, although *score* is equal to simply the value when the value is larger than 2.
6) If *score* is not 5, the user can request another retrieval without modifying the query. In this re-retrieval, the user models for which m_{min} was selected as the first candidate are excluded from the retrieval objects, and step 2 is executed. If all 20 user models are excluded, the text "Retrieval failed" is presented to the user, and execution ends.

5   Performance-Evaluation

We evaluated the effectiveness of the proposed scheme using three different systems based on an existing impression-based music-retrieval system [8]. **System A** uses ten user models for adaptation, **System B** is a proposed one and uses twenty models, and **System C** uses one model. **Systems A** and **B** have a user adaptation facility; **System C** does not. Instead, it advances the Nth candidate to the $N - 1^{th}$ candidate and presents the first candidate newly obtained when the user requests another retrieval.

We added 80 musical pieces to the 80 musical pieces used in the impression-estimation experiments, creating a database of 160 musical pieces. The impression vectors in each user model were generated using the ten multiple regression

Table 3. Examples of impression vectors for model M_1

Names of musical pieces	Impression vectors
ave_maria	(1.9 3.6 4.3 5.3 4.3 5.4 4.9 7.1 4.5 5.3)
eine_kleine1_str	(2.4 1.0 6.8 5.4 5.6 5.5 6.0 6.4 0.7 5.6)
gimnopedie1_pi	(3.8 4.3 5.0 2.4 5.7 5.1 5.1 1.6 4.6 2.0)
je_te_veux_pi	(4.8 5.4 5.9 4.9 7.6 5.1 5.3 5.7 5.6 4.6)
la_primavela1_str	(3.1 4.3 6.3 6.4 2.1 5.1 6.0 4.0 3.1 5.1)

(The values were rounded to one decimal place to save space)

equations designed for that model. Examples of impression vectors for model M_1 are shown in Table 3. Note that we set $H_{high} = 4.0$ and $H_{med} = 3.0$ as threshold values.

Thirty people participated in the experiment-15 women and 15 men; three were under 20, 23 were in their twenties, two were in their thirties, and two were over 40. We randomly classified them into three groups of equal size. We assigned the three systems to the three groups one by one. For her/his assigned system, each subject inputted ten queries or sentences using a list of 164 impression words and 119 degree modifiers, which any retrieval system can understand. The process was as follows.

(1) The subject entered the Nth sentence ($N = 1, 2, \cdots, 10$).
(2) If at least one retrieval result was presented, the subject listened to the first candidate and, using a five-step scale, estimated how well it matched her/his target result: very good match (5 points), good match (4 points), fair match (3 points), questionable match (2 points), and poor match (1 point). If no retrieval results were presented, the subject returned to step (1) and entered the next sentence.
(3) If the match was very good, the subject returned to step (1), and entered the next sentence. Otherwise, the user requested another retrieval and returned to step (2). The maximum number of retrievals was set to five.

Once the subject finished this process, she/he took a break for about 30 minutes. The subject then repeated the process using the same ten sentences to investigate the effectiveness of user adaptation facilities. The results of these experiments are shown in Tables 4 and 5.

Table 4 shows the mean values and standard deviations for the first retrieval, and Table 5 shows them for the second. They do not include the results for when the system failed to generate impression vectors for some reason. When the first candidate in the second retrieval was the same as the first candidate in the first retrieval, the result for the second retrieval was replaced with that for the first.

Comparing the results of these two tables, we see that the difference in retrieval accuracy between the two retrievals for **System B** was statistically significant at the 1% level, while those for the other two systems were not statistically significant even at the 5% level. This indicates that using 20 user models is more effective than using 10 models or 1 model and that using user models created

Table 4. Results for first retrieval

System	Mean value	Standard deviation	Number of estimations
A (10 user models)	3.38	1.28	106
B (20 user models)	3.39	1.36	99
C (one user model)	3.69	1.09	97

Table 5. Results for second retrieval

System	Mean value	Standard deviation	Number of estimations
A (10 user models)	3.73	1.24	92
B (20 user models)	4.02	1.16	96
C (one user model)	3.70	1.10	97

Table 6. Change in score from first to second retrieval

Diff. in estimation	-3	-2	-1	0	1	2	3
Frequency	1	2	19	107	30	15	2
Ratio (%)	0.6	1.1	10.8	60.8	17.0	8.5	1.1

Table 7. Examples of sentences the subjects made, which were translated into English by the author

Tune with confused power / Fresh and refreshing tune / Lilting and comical tune / Super-impressing tune / Intonational and passionate tune / Profound, solemn, and dignified tune / Lyrical tune with a quiet mood / Tune of considerably settled feeling / Powerful and dynamic tune / Tune by which one hundred percent of the mind is healed / Beautiful, sad, and transparent tune

Table 8. Numbers of different impression words and degree modifiers used in sentences

System	Impression words	Degree modifiers	Examples (Ones that appeared five times or more)
A	74	30	Comical / Mind is healed / Transparent / Blight / Very
B	66	20	Vigorous / Confused power / Beautiful / Classical / Powerful / Pretty / Very
C	63	47	Bright / Lilting / Fantastic / Passionate / Calm / Powerful / So / Very / Moderately

based on the proposed scheme improves the retrieval accuracy of impression-based music-retrieval systems.

The change in the score for the same candidates from the first to the second retrieval is shown in Table 6. These results suggest that the impressions depended on the situation, for example, the retrieval context or mental state. Consequently, a person's impressions of a musical piece may differ under different conditions. This situation dependency must be taken into account to obtain a system that produces better matches.

For the reader's reference, we show some of the sentences that were entered and the numbers of different impression words and degree modifiers appearing in the sentences in Tables 7 and 8, respectively.

6   Conclusion

People listening to the same music can have different impressions of it. We have thus developed a music retrieval scheme that adapts to the user. We had 100 people give us their impressions of 80 music pieces, and, based on the results, we classified them into 20 groups. The people in each group generally had the same or similar impressions. We then created a user model suitable for each group and a procedure for identifying the model best suited for an unidentified user. Each model consisted of formulas for generating impression vectors representing the impressions of a musical piece and a set of impression vectors generated using the formulas. Testing using another 30 people showed that our scheme is effective.

We plan to tackle the problems of individual variations in the interpretation of the impression words and degree modifiers. We also plan to develop a more flexible scheme that takes into account the situational dependency of impressions.

References

1. Blackburn, S. G., DeRoure, D. C.: A Tool for Content Based Navigation of Music, Proc. 6th ACM International Multimedia Conference, Bristol, UK (1998) 361–368
2. Cascia, M. L., Sethi, S., Sclaroff, S.: Combining Textual and Visual Cues for Content-based Image Retrieval on the World Wide Web, Proc. IEEE Workshop on Content-based Access of Image and Video Libraries, Santa Barbara, USA (1998) 24–28
3. Ikezoe, T., Kajikawa, Y., Nomura, Y.: Music Database Retrieval System with Sensitivity Words Using Music Sensitivity Space, Trans. IPS of Japan, Vol. 42, No. 12 (2001) 3201–3212
4. Kawabe, K., Ezawa, Y., Hirashima, T., Toyoda, J.: A Tuning Method of User Models Reflecting Personal Sensual Disposition, Technical Report of IPS of Japan, Vol. Human Interface 45-1 (1992) 1–8
5. Kimoto, H.: An Image Retrieval System Using Impressional Words and the Evaluation of the System, Trans. IPS of Japan, Vol. 40, No. 3 (1999) 886–898
6. Kiyoki, Y., Kaneko, Y., Kitagawa, T.: A Semantic Search Method and Its Learning Mechanism for Image Databases Based on a Mathematical Model of Meaning, Trans. IEICE of Japan, Vol. J79-D-II, No. 4 (1996) 509–519
7. Kosugi, N., Nagata, H., Nakanishi, T.: Query-by-Humming on Internet, Proc. International Conference on Database and Expert Systems Applications (2003) 589–600

8. Kumamoto, T.: Design and Implementation of Natural Language Interface for Impression-based Music-retrieval Systems, Proc. 8th International Conference on Knowledge-Based Intelligent Information and Engineering Systems, KES2004, LNAI3214, Springer, Wellington, New Zealand (2004) 139–147

9. Kumamoto, T., Ohta, K.: A Query by Musical Impression System Using N-gram Based Features, Proc. IEEE Conference on Cybernetics and Intelligent Systems (2004) 992–997

10. Kurita, T., Kato, T., Fukuda, I., Sakakura, A.: Sense Retrieval on an Image Database of Full Color Paintings, Trans. IPS of Japan, Vol. 33, No. 11 (1992) 1373–1383

11. Mukunoki, M., Minoh, M., Ikeda, K.: A Retrieval Method of Outdoor Scenes Using Object Sketch and an Automatic Index Generation Method, Trans. IEICE of Japan, Vol. J79-D-II, No. 6 (1996) 1025–1033

12. Omae, H., Ishibashi, N., Kiyoki, Y., Anzai, Y.: An Automatic Metadata Creation Method for Music with Multiple Musical Instruments, Technical Report of IPS of Japan, Vol. 2001-DBS-125, No. 84 (2001) 145–152

13. Sato, A., Ogawa, J., Kitakami, H.: An Impression-based Retrieval System of Music Collection, Proc. 4th International Conference on Knowledge-Based Intelligent Engineering Systems and Allied Technologies, Brighton, UK (2000) 856–859

14. Sonoda, T., Goto, M., Muraoka, Y.: A WWW-Based Melody Retrieval System, Proc. International Computer Music Conference, Michigan, USA (1998) 349–352

15. Tsuji, Y., Hoshi, M., Ohmori, T.: Local Pattern of a Melody and Its Applications to Retrieval by Sensitivity Words, Technical Report of IEICE of Japan, Vol. SP96-124 (1997) 17–24

16. Yang, C., Music Database Retrieval Based on Spectral Similarity, Proc. International Symposium on Music Information Retrieval, Indiana, USA (2001) 349–352

The Pursuit of Satisfaction:
Affective State in Group Recommender Systems

Judith Masthoff

University of Aberdeen, Scotland, UK
jmasthoff@csd.abdn.ac.uk

Abstract. This paper describes three algorithms to model and predict the satisfaction experienced by individuals using a group recommender system which recommends sequences of items. Satisfaction is treated as an affective state. In particular, we model the wearing off of emotion over time and assimilation effects, where the affective state produced by previous items influences the impact on satisfaction of the next item. We compare the algorithms with each other, and investigate the effect of parameter values by comparing the algorithms' predictions with the results of an earlier empirical study. We show a way in which affective state can be used in recommender systems, which is useful for recommendations not only to groups but also to individuals.

1 Introduction

Inspired by Interactive TV, we are interested in recommending *sequences* of items (e.g. news stories, music clips) to *groups* of users. In [6], we have discussed various strategies to combine ratings by individuals into ratings for the group as a whole. For instance, given individual ratings as in Table 1 from 1 (really hate) to 10 (really like), we can take the average of ratings (so called Average Strategy) and recommend item sequence EFHDJA when there is time to see six items. Or, we can take the minimum of ratings (so called Least Misery) and recommend sequence FEHJDG. We have empirically evaluated which strategy performs best (the Multiplicative strategy which multiplies ratings) in the sense of keeping all individuals in the group satisfied.

Table 1. Example of individual ratings for ten items (A to J) for a group of three

	A	B	C	D	E	F	G	H	I	J
John	10	4	3	6	10	9	6	8	10	8
Adam	1	9	8	9	7	9	6	9	3	8
Mary	10	5	2	7	9	8	5	6	7	6
Average	7	6	4.3	7.3	8.7	8.7	5.7	7.7	6.7	7.3

In a recommender system that adapts to individuals, we are only interested in maximizing *individual* satisfaction, and for this it suffices to always recommend the item with the highest rating. So, there is no need to predict satisfaction accurately. However, if we are interested in keeping a *group* satisfied, then suddenly it becomes more important to accurately predict individual satisfaction. To keep the rest of the group happy, an individual might need to be confronted occasionally with items they

L. Ardissono, P. Brna, and A. Mitrovic (Eds.): UM 2005, LNAI 3538, pp. 297–306, 2005.

do not like. It is important then to know whether the items chosen do not make an individual too dissatisfied. Accurate predictions of individual satisfaction can also help to evaluate group adaptation strategies. It may even be possible to use these predictions as part of a strategy. For these reasons, we started investigating satisfaction. In [6], we have presented several functions to model individual satisfaction, and have empirically evaluated which function performs best. However, the satisfaction functions used in [6] did not really show whether and to what extent somebody would be satisfied or dissatisfied. Rather, they showed the relative satisfaction of individuals in the group: so, for instance, whether we expected John to be more satisfied than Adam, and whether Mary would be more satisfied with one sequence or another. In this paper we will attempt to model satisfaction in more detail. As part of this, we will argue that so far a vital element in the modelling of satisfaction has been overlooked, namely affective state.

2   About Individual Satisfaction

The satisfaction functions proposed in [6] were all based on a summation: the satisfaction after viewing another item was modelled as the summation of that before viewing the item, and the impact of the item itself. In the simplest satisfaction function, the impact of an item was taken to be its rating. So, the satisfaction with a sequence of items was the summation of the items' ratings. We investigated whether low ratings (noting dissatisfaction) needed to be included, or only high ratings. We investigated normalization: whether one should take the ratings of not chosen items into account when deciding the impact of an item. We investigated whether to use a linear impact of ratings or a quadratic one: the difference between a rating of 9 and a 10 might feel larger than the difference between a 5 and a 6. Including low ratings, normalization, and a quadratic impact all improved the satisfaction function [6].

One limitation of the satisfaction functions in [6] is that satisfaction increases with the length of the sequence. Another serious limitation is that the *order* of items in the sequence did not affect satisfaction. Nevertheless, several reasons were given that suggest that order may be important (some related to advertising research, others to comments of subjects in experiments like "it is better to end on a high"). In this paper, we want to refine the satisfaction function to take this into account.

It seems reasonable to regard satisfaction as an affective state or mood. Since the seventies, psychologists have researched the cognitive effects of mood: how mood influences perception, attention, memory, information processing, and judgement. Effects have been found in all of these areas [8]. More recently, several psychologists and economists have started to research Affective Forecasting: how accurately people can predict what will make them happy, by how much, and for how long. Many studies have found that people are not good at predicting happiness [10]. People tend to be good at predicting whether they will be happy or unhappy, but not by how much and for how long. Additionally, in our own field, there has been a lot of interest recently into Affective Computing (e.g. [9]). We will briefly discuss those results out of these three areas that seem most relevant to the topic of this paper.

Researchers have consistently found an impact of mood on evaluative judgement (see [8] for a review). Much research has been done in the context of persuasion theory: individuals in a happy mood were persuadable to a higher extent than individuals in a neutral or sad mood (see e.g., [4]). Mood effects are studied and used in commercial and political advertisement (e.g., [1, 3]): influencing people's mood to make them judge a subsequent ad more favourably. So, when our recommender system presents subjects with a sequence of items, viewing the first items could induce a mood, which could impact subjects' opinions on the next items.

Film clips are often used to elicit emotions in a laboratory setting, with empirical research having resulted in a set of film clips that consistently elicit a certain emotion, like happiness, fear, anger [2]. We will need to differentiate between the emotions elicited by the content of a clip, and the satisfaction with having seen it. For instance, one might be revolted by the content of a news item (e.g. on happenings in Iraq), but still be satisfied with having seen it. For our modelling, we will for now ignore the emotion elicited by the content, and concentrate on satisfaction in isolation. However, this issue will need to be addressed in future, and it will also complicate evaluation.

Kahneman and colleagues (as reported in [10]) found that the actual feelings experienced (e.g., self-reported pain during a colonoscopy) differed from those reported retrospectively. The retrospective reports were heavily influenced by the intensity of the emotional experience when it ended and the peak intensity of the experience.

People's affective forecasting can change their actual emotional experience (e.g., [12]). Several studies have shown that if you expect to like something, than you might end up liking it more than if you did not have any expectations. This is called assimilation.[1] If our recommender system has presented several items you liked, than you might expect to also like the next item, and therefore your perceived satisfaction with that item might be higher than its actual rating merits.

People's emotional reactions become less intense with time [11]. When something has made you happy, this happiness does not last, but wears off. This is explained in [10] as needed to save energy and to protect the emotions' role as a signalling device.

Picard discusses the use of emotions and moods in computer systems [9]. She describes emotions as being regulated by moods: for instance, in a good mood smaller positive events can have an emotional impact. She proposes to model mood as a weighted summation of positive events and subtraction of negative events, with recent events receiving extra weight. She argues that mood can not be of unbounded intensity, so a limit should be used (or a saturation function).

3 Satisfaction Functions Chosen

In [6], satisfaction with a (fixed-length) sequence of items was calculated as the summation of the impact of the individual items of the sequence:

Satisfaction($items+<i>$) = Satisfaction($items$) + Impact(i),
for item i and item sequence[2] $items$.
Satisfaction($<>$) = 0

---

[1] It has been suggested that the opposite can also happen [12], but there is not much evidence.
[2] Whenever we talk about an item sequence, we mean a sequence of distinct items.

Based on the literature review above, we will henceforth assume that Satisfaction will decrease in intensity over time. Also, we give more weight to recent items[3].

Variant 0. Satisfaction(items+<i>) = δ * Satisfaction(items) + Impact(i), with 0≤δ≤1

With δ=1 no decrease occurs, and with δ=0 no memory of past items would be used. The value of δ could depend on the person or the time duration of items.

To calculate the impact of an item, we perform three steps.

1. *Normalizing.* In [6], not the individual rating, but the satisfaction produced was normalized, using for item sequence *items*:

> NormSatisfaction(*items*) = Satisfaction(*items*) / PossSatisfaction(*items*)
> with PossSatisfaction(*items*) =
> > Max *s*: item sequence *s* and length(*s*)=length(*items*): Satisfaction(*s*)

Our introduction of δ into the Satisfaction function means that normalization now needs to be handled differently. We would like to apply normalization to the rating, not to the satisfaction as a whole, to make it independent of the selections so far:

> Normalized(*r*) = *r**TotalRatingsExpected / TotalRatingsPossible, for rating *r*
> with TotalRatingsExpected = Σj: item *j*: AverageRating
> TotalRatingsPossible = Σj: item *j*: Rating(*j*)

We could have taken the AverageRating to be the midpoint of the scale (5.5), but have decided instead to use the average rating over all individuals in the group over all items (6.93 in our case).

Note that our normalization results in ratings 10-10-10-10 being treated as the same as 5-5-5-5. This was also the case in the normalization in [6]. In as sense, this is also a form of assimilation.

2. *Rebalancing.* We have been using ratings from 1 to 10. As we want our satisfaction function to give an easy indication of whether somebody is satisfied or not, it would be good if negative numbers meant dissatisfaction, and positive numbers satisfaction. Therefore, we will rebalance the rating scale, by deducting its mid-point value. For our scale this value is 5.5.

> Rebalanced(*r*) = *r* – midpoint,   for rating *r*

3. *Making the impact quadratic.* We will use the following formula[4]:

> Quadratic(*r*) = r^2,   if $r \geq 0$; $-r^2$,   if $r < 0$,   for rating *r*

---

[3] This deviates from the proposal in [9] of a linear decrease in weight, and only consideration of the last four events.

[4] This deviates from [6], where no rebalancing happened and Quadratic(r) = $(r-5)^2$, if r ≥6, and $-(r-6)^2$ if r<6. This makes it easier to deal with the new normalization of ratings.

Combining these three steps, we obtain:

Impact(i) = Quadratic(Rebalanced(Normalized(Rating(i)))) , for item i

The satisfaction function discussed above sums the (weighted) satisfaction so far with the impact of the new item. This has as effect that if you see a series of items you like, your satisfaction is predicted to keep increasing. The question arises whether summation is indeed the right operation. An alternative could be to take the average. We therefore propose the following variant:

Variant 1. Satisfaction($items$+<i>)=(δ*Satisfaction($items$)+Impact(i)) / (1+δ)

We divide by 1+δ rather than 2, to get Satisfaction($items$+<i>) = Impact(i) when δ=0.

The satisfaction function discussed above takes into account that emotion wears off. However, it does not yet take into account that the mood you are in can change your judgement, and that expectation can influence emotion. Inspired by the literature discussed above, we want the impact of an item to depend upon the mood you are in, showing an assimilation effect. We therefore propose the following variant:

Variant 2. Satisfaction($items$+<i>) = δ*Satisfaction($items$) +
$$\text{Impact}(i, \delta*\text{Satisfaction}(items))$$
with   Impact(i, s) = Impact(i) + (s-Impact(i))*ε, for all s and $0 \leq \varepsilon \leq 1$

With ε=0, we have the same satisfaction function as Variant 0. With ε=1, the new item would not have any impact (so, satisfaction would always remain 0).

It is easy to come up with more variants, but we would first like to understand the effects of the satisfaction functions proposed so far.

4 Simulations

In this section, we will report on the results of simulations of the satisfaction functions. The main purpose of these simulations is to get a feeling of the difference in predictions between the satisfaction functions discussed. We will also compare the predictions with the empirical data of Experiment 2 in [6], mainly to decide what values are most appropriate for δ and ε. In that experiment, subjects were shown ratings of items for John, Adam and Mary (as in Table 1) and sequences (e.g. FEAHD) and asked to predict how satisfied John, Adam and Mary would be with those sequences.

Satisfaction Function Variant 0 has been applied to the same sequences as in Experiment 2 of [6], which are the recommended sequences by various group modelling strategies. For each sequence, the satisfaction of John, Adam and Mary has been calculated at each moment in the presentation of the sequence, for varyingvalues of δ. Table 2 shows the results. As can be expected, a lower value of δ tends to result in a lower predicted satisfaction. Comparison of the results for sequences AIEFD and AEFID shows the impact the order of a sequence can have, particularly for small δ. To judge the group modelling strategies, we will look at the curves as a whole, not just the end point. So, we judge the Borda strategy to have made Adam

Table 2. Predicted satisfaction for Variant 0 per sequence per individual, for several values of δ: ◆—0 ■—0.2 ▲ 0.4 ✕ 0.6 ✳—0.8 ●—0.9 +—1 . Y-axis shows satisfaction, X-axis time (first item shown, second shown, etc)

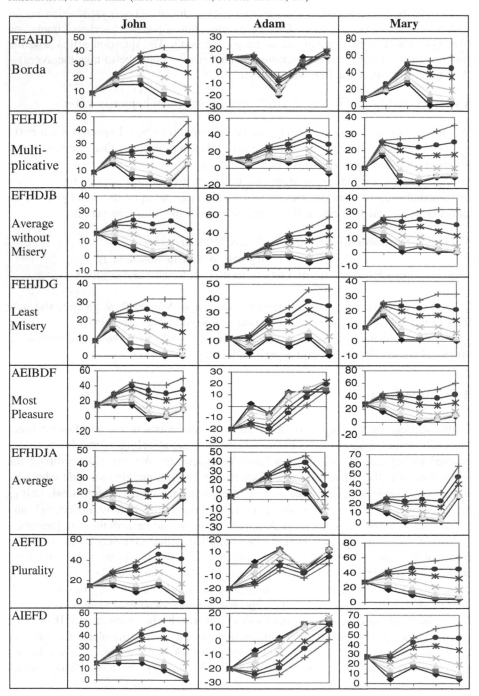

Table 3. Predicted satisfaction for Variant 1 per sequence per individual, for several values of δ: ◆ 0 ■ 0.2 0.4 ✕ 0.6 ✳ 0.8 ● 0.9 ╋ 1 . Y-axis shows satisfaction, X-axis time (first item shown, second shown, etc)

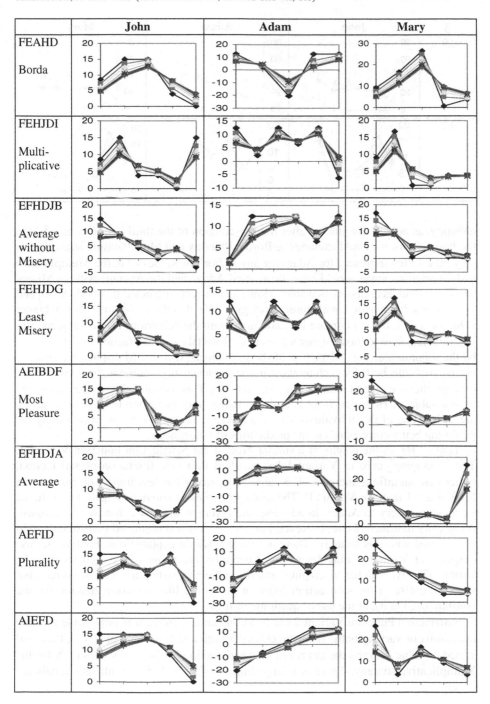

Table 4. Predicted satisfaction of Variant 2 for sequence FEHJDI chosen by the Multiplicative strategy per individual, for several values of ε: ◆—0 ■—0.2 0.5 ✕—0.8, and two values of δ. Y-axis shows satisfaction, X-axis time (first item shown, second shown, etc)

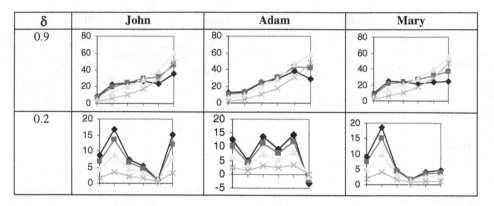

δ	John	Adam	Mary
0.9			
0.2			

unhappy, as he was dissatisfied after the presentation of the third item (for any δ). On the basis of this, we could exclude the Borda, Plurality and Most Pleasure strategies, as they all resulted in misery for Adam for any δ. For low values of δ, the Multiplicative and Average strategies would have dissatisfied Adam, and the Average without Misery strategy would have dissatisfied John. However, subjects predicted that both Adam and John would be satisfied with those strategies. We therefore conclude that a higher value of δ (0.8, 0.9, 1) is more in accordance with the behaviour of our subjects. Restricting ourselves to those higher values of δ, if we take the satisfaction of the group to be the minimum of the satisfaction of the individuals, then the Multiplicative strategy clearly performs best: for each moment in the sequence, it gives the highest satisfaction (except after the second item for δ is 0.8 and 0.9). This was also the strategy preferred by our subjects. However, if we take the satisfaction of the group to be the average of the satisfaction of the individuals, then the Average strategy performs best. Taking the minimum better corresponds to the predictions of our subjects.

Table 3 shows the results of a similar process for Satisfaction Function Variant 1. The 'averaging' used in Variant 1 has resulted in a nice limitation of satisfaction, rather than an infinite increase. The value of δ clearly has less impact on satisfaction for Variant 1 than for Variant 0. The same strategies as above can again be excluded as causing misery to Adam. In addition, the Average strategy can now be excluded. As already indicated above, however, human subjects had predicted that Adam would be satisfied with this strategy. There are three possible explanations. Firstly, the 'averaging' in Variant 1 may be wrong. Secondly, the subjects' predictions may be wrong. Thirdly, both the 'averaging' and the subjects' predictions may be correct, but something else in the satisfaction function is wrong, like the normalization (or the constant used in it), or the use of quadratic ratings.

Satisfaction Function Variant 2 has two constants: δ and ε. It is impossible to show the results of varying both. We have chosen a high and low value of δ (0.9, 0.2), and varied ε. Table 4 shows the impact of ε on satisfaction for the two values of δ, for the Multiplicative strategy. There is a large impact of δ: with δ=0.9, all individuals are about equally satisfied and the impact of ε is low. With δ=0.2, the satisfaction profiles of John, Adam and Mary are quite different, and the impact of ε is high. With δ=0.2, Adam is predicted to be dissatisfied at the end, independent of ε. As our subjects predicted Adam to be satisfied, again a higher value of δ seems better. With δ=0.9, it is hard to see which value of ε is best. Our subjects predicted Adam and Mary to be equally satisfied and John to be slightly more satisfied. When looking at the end of the sequence, a lower value of ε seems to perform slightly better. When looking at the curves as a whole (e.g., averaging satisfaction over the sequence), John would be more dissatisfied than Adam, regardless of ε.

5 Inherent Complexity of Evaluation

We have shown how we can use satisfaction functions to reason about group modelling strategies, even when these functions are not yet completely validated. For instance, we could dismiss several strategies as they were shown to perform badly independent of δ, and independent of 'averaging' being a good idea. Comparing the satisfaction functions with predictions by subjects, allowed us to conclude that δ should have a high value, and given such a high value, we could even conclude that the Multiplicative strategy performed best, in accordance with our subjects. However, there is a problem: the empirical data used comes from an indirect experiment, where subjects were not shown items, but only ratings, and had to predict satisfaction. As discussed above, the Affective Forecasting literature shows that people are very poor in predicting the intensity of emotions[5]. So, a next step should be to empirically compare the real satisfaction experienced by subjects with that predicted by the satisfaction functions. However, this seems particularly challenging[6]:

Firstly, we need accurate ratings for the individuals. We could ask subjects to rate items. But if our assumption is right, then the rating given would depend on the order in which the items are presented. This could be avoided by having large time gaps between the items, but we would need to ensure that the mood of our subjects does not vary. Attempts in [6] to construct items for which the ratings are the same for all subjects (e.g. "your favourite team has won an important game") failed miserably.

Secondly, we need items that are topically unrelated, as topical relatedness between items can influence judgement (e.g. an item about an earthquake in Bulgaria getting a higher rating after an item on their football team playing Bulgaria) [6].

Finally, we need to know how satisfied each subject is after each item has been presented. If we ask them at the end of the experiment to judge their satisfaction at the various time points, we are likely to get inaccurate data (given the difference between retrospective and experienced emotions). If we ask subjects to report their satisfaction during the experiment, it takes time and therefore influences the results (given the decrease in emotions over time). If we determine satisfaction on the basis of facial expressions and sensor data, then the emotional content of items can influence results.

---

[5] People are, however, good at predicting valence, so this does not invalidate our conclusions about δ on the basis that subjects predicted Adam to be satisfied.

[6] So challenging indeed that the evaluation of this system is the topic of an "evaluation competition" for the 2005 UM workshop on the Evaluation of Adaptive Systems.

6 Conclusions

Modelling satisfaction is important when recommending sequences of items to groups: it provides a way to evaluate group modelling strategies and it can inspire a better strategy. In this paper, we have modelled satisfaction as a mood, drawing on the mood literature for inspiration. We have discussed satisfaction functions, which incorporate assimilation and decline of emotions with time. We have shown through simulations the impact these factors can have on satisfaction, and have drawn some conclusions about group modelling strategies. We have compared the satisfaction functions with empirical data from [6], and have drawn some conclusions (e.g. about δ). We have discussed the inherent difficulties in doing empirical evaluations.

Models of individual satisfaction are not only useful when adapting to groups. As argued in [5, 7], adaptation to individuals can sometimes also benefit from group modelling strategies, for instance, when ratings on multiple criteria need to be combined, or when virtual group members are added, e.g. representing a teacher.

Accurate predictions of individual satisfaction can also be used to improve the transparency of adaptive systems: showing how satisfied others in your group are, or how satisfied criteria are, could improve the users' understanding of the working of the system and perhaps make it easier to accept items they do not like.

References

1. Aylesworth, A.B., MacKenzie, S.B. Context is key: The effect of program-induced mood on thoughts about the ad. *Journal of Advertising, 27* (1998) 17-33
2. Gross, J.J., Levenson, R.W. Emotion elicitation using films. *Cognition & Emotion, 9* (1995) 87-108
3. Isbell, L.M., Ottati, V.C., Burns, K.C. Affect and politics: Effects on judgment, processing, and information selection. As accessed on 16 October 2004. http://www.cbrss.harvard.edu/events/ppbw/papers/isbell.pdf (2003)
4. Mackie, D.M., Worth, L.T. Processing deficits and the mediation of positive affect in persuasion. *Journal of Personal and Social Psychology, 57* (1989) 1-14
5. Masthoff, J. Modeling the multiple people that are me. In P. Brusilovsky, A. Corbett, & F. de Rosis (Eds.) *Proceedings of the User Modeling Conference*, Johnstown, PA, Berlin: Springer Verlag (2003) 258-262
6. Masthoff, J. Group modeling: Selecting a sequence of television items to suit a group of viewers. *User Modeling and User Adapted Interaction, 14*, (2004) 37-85
7. Masthoff, J. Selecting news to suit a group of criteria. *Proceedings of the Personalization in Future TV workshop*, AH Conference, Eindhoven (2004) 252-263
8. Oatley, K., Jenkins, J.M. *Understanding emotions.* Malden, MA: Blackwell (1996)
9. Picard, R.W. *Affective computing.* Cambridge, MA: MIT Press (1997)
10. Wilson, T.D., Gilbert, D.T. Affective forecasting. *Advances in Experimental Social Psychology, 35* (2003) 345-411
11. Wilson, T.D., Gilbert, D.T, Centerbar, D.B. Making sense: The causes of emotional evanescence. In I. Brocas & J. Carrillo (Eds.), *The psychology of economic decisions. Vol. 1: Rationality and well being.* New York: Oxford Uni Press (2003) 209-233
12. Wilson, T.D., Klaaren, K. The role of affective expectations in affective experience. In M.S. Clark (Ed.), *Review of personality and social psychology* (Vol. 14: Emotion and social behaviour). Newbury Park, CA: Sage (1992) 1-31

An Economic Model of User Rating in an Online Recommender System

F. Maxwell Harper[1], Xin Li[2], Yan Chen[2], and Joseph A. Konstan[1]

CommunityLab*

[1] University of Minnesota, Minneapolis, MN, 55406 USA
{harper, konstan}@cs.umn.edu
[2] University of Michigan, Ann Arbor, MI, 48109 USA
{xinl, yanchen}@umich.edu

Abstract. Economic modeling provides a formal mechanism to understand user incentives and behavior in online systems. In this paper we describe the process of building a parameterized economic model of user-contributed ratings in an online movie recommender system. We constructed a theoretical model to formalize our initial understanding of the system, and collected survey and behavioral data to calibrate an empirical model. This model explains 34% of the variation in user rating behavior. We found that while economic modeling in this domain requires an initial understanding of user behavior and access to an uncommonly broad set of user survey and behavioral data, it returns significant formal understanding of the activity being modeled.

1   Introduction

Designers of online communities struggle with the challenge of eliciting participation from their members. Butler [4] found that 50% of social, hobby, and work mailing lists had no traffic over a 122 day period. Under-contribution is a problem even in communities that do survive; in a majority of active mailing lists, fewer then 50% of subscribers posted even a single message in a four month period [4].

Recommender systems built on collaborative filtering [14] are particularly vulnerable to the problem of undercontribution. If users do not contribute ratings to the community, especially for new and rarely-rated items, the system loses its ability to produce recommendations–its main purpose for existence.

We have been conducting research on how to increase the number of ratings contributed to MovieLens [8, 13], a movie recommendation web site. In this paper we report on our activity using economic modeling to build a parameterized model of the motivations underlying user rating behavior. We model factors that affect users' willingness to rate movies, such as the desire to view accurate movie recommendations and the time and effort needed to rate movies. We

---

* CommunityLab is a collaborative project of the University of Minnesota, University of Michigan, and Carnegie Mellon University. http://www.communitylab.org/

L. Ardissono, P. Brna, and A. Mitrovic (Eds.): UM 2005, LNAI 3538, pp. 307–316, 2005.

believe that economic modeling will guide future site development by providing us with insights into user motivations, predictions about user behavior, and opportunities to personalize the site to match user goals.

As far as we know, this is the first use of economic analysis to build models of user incentives and behavior in an adaptive web site. Accordingly, we discuss in detail the modeling process and the ways in which such a model can be applied. We discuss why economic modeling in this domain is difficult, and what benefits modelers can expect.

2   Related Work

Informal economic analysis has been used to inform the design and analysis of computer-supported cooperative work (CSCW) applications. Grudin, for example, assessed relative costs and benefits of using digital voice versus text in a groupware application [7]. More formal economic modeling has been applied to develop probabilistic models of human interruptibility [9].

The design of online trust and reputation management systems has been heavily influenced by economic theories. For example, Keser used experimental economics to demonstrate the effects of reputation management systems such as eBay's on marketplace success [10]. Friedman and Resnick examined the theoretical effects on trust and reputation based on enforcing costly or permanent pseudonyms in online communities [5].

More broadly, economic theories have informed research investigating the design of e-commerce and auction sites. Bakos examined the theoretical implications of the accessibility of product descriptions and pricing information in e-commerce Web sites, including cases where sellers have intentionally introduced difficulties into the search process to increase revenue [2].

To our knowledge, economic analysis has not been used to inform the design of user adaptive Web sites. Adaptive hypermedia researchers have traditionally used a variety of approaches to explicitly or implicitly gather data about users' knowledge, goals, background, or preferences [3]. This work extends these approaches by modeling incentives and behavior in the language of economics.

3   An Economic Model of MovieLens Users

The primary purpose of economic modeling is to generate insights into complex problems [15] and to make predictions about rational agents' behavior. In a canonical economic model, agents act in order to maximize their objectives, subject to constraints. To create an effective model, we make simplifying assumptions while still keeping the essential features of the real world situation.

3.1   A Theoretical Model

In a typical session in MovieLens, users spend time rating movies and viewing movie recommendations. Their activity can be modeled mathematically as follows: let x_i be the number of movies user i has rated, and $X_{-i} = \sum_{j \neq i} x_j$ be the total number of ratings from all other users in MovieLens. Based on survey data and our understanding of user behavior from interactions with users, a user's benefit from using MovieLens comes from three sources:

- Recommendation quality, $Q_i(x_i, X_{-i})$: Users enjoy viewing useful movie recommendations. Based on the characteristics of the MovieLens recommendation algorithm, we assume this function is concave in both its components. That is, it increases along with each rating count, but at a decreasing rate.
- Rating fun, $f_i(x_i)$: Users enjoy expressing opinions about movies. We assume that $f'(x_i) > 0$, and $f''(x_i) \leq 0$. Again, rating more movies brings more enjoyment, but at a decreasing rate.
- Non-rating fun, h_i: Users enjoy activities such as searching for movies and reading information about movies.

We further assume that there is cost associated with rating. The cost function of rating movies, $c_i(x_i)$, represents the amount of time that user i needs to rate x_i movies. Assume that $c_i(x_i)$ is convex, i.e., the marginal cost is positive, $c_i'(x_i) > 0$, and $c_i''(x_i) \geq 0$ for all $i \in N$. Thus, the marginal cost of rating either remains constant or increases with the number of ratings. This fits with our experience that users rate popular, easily remembered movies first.

For analytical tractability, we assume that various components of the utility function are additively separable. Let γ_i denote the marginal benefit to recommendation quality of rating one movie. We can represent user i's utility, π_i, as

$$\pi_i = \gamma_i Q_i(x_i, X_{-i}) + f_i(x_i) + h_i - c_i(x_i). \tag{1}$$

To calibrate this model with survey and behavioral data, we now parameterize various components of the utility function, and solve for the optimal number of ratings. Based on features of the recommendation algorithm, we assume that $Q_i(x_i, X_{-i}) = \min(\bar{R}, X_{-i}^{\alpha} x_i^{\beta_i})$. This is a Cobb-Douglas production function[1] with an upper bound, $\bar{R}$. The upper bound is included to represent the fact that average recommendation quality has a theoretical limit. $\alpha \in [0, 1]$ measures the impact of system-wide ratings on recommendation quality. $\beta_i \in [0, 1]$ measures user i's taste in movies. A higher β_i indicates that a user has rare taste, while a lower β_i indicates that a user has mainstream taste.

Furthermore, assume that both the rating fun function and the cost function are linear such that $f_i(x_i) = f_i x_i$ and $c_i(x_i) = c_i x_i$, respectively. While neither function is necessarily linear in general, we do not have enough data to estimate their shape.

Under these assumptions, we consider two cases. In the first case, when $\min(\bar{R}, X_{-i}^{\alpha} x_i^{\beta_i}) = \bar{R}$, a user is getting the best possible recommendation quality from MovieLens. In this case, a user will continue to rate movies as long as the marginal fun is greater than or equal to the marginal cost.

In the second case, when $\min(\bar{R}, X_{-i}^{\alpha} x_i^{\beta_i}) = X_{-i}^{\alpha} x_i^{\beta_i}$ and $\alpha \to 0$, a user's recommendation quality will improve via ratings, but will not improve due to

---

[1] The Cobb-Douglas production is one of the most commonly used production functions in economics [12].

others contributing ratings to the system - a simplifying assumption possible in MovieLens where there is a large stock of total ratings. In this case, we solve Equation (1) for the optimal number of ratings, x_i^*:

$$x_i^* = \left(\frac{\beta_i \gamma_i}{c_i - f_i}\right)^{\frac{1}{1-\beta_i}}. \tag{2}$$

Taking a log transformation of Equation (2), we get

$$\ln x_i^* = \frac{1}{1-\beta_i}[\ln \beta_i + \ln \gamma_i - \ln(c_i - f_i)]. \tag{3}$$

As a sanity check, we change various parameters and see if the optimal number of ratings is moving in the right direction. An increase in marginal cost leads to a decrease in rating quantity, while an increase in marginal fun or marginal benefit from recommendation quality leads to an increase in rating quantity. When $\frac{1-\beta_i}{\beta_i} + \ln \beta_i + \ln \gamma_i - \ln(c_i - f_i) > 0$, an increase in β_i also leads to more rating, indicating that, other things being equal, a user with rare taste will rate more movies than one with mainstream taste. These results are consistent with our intuition.

3.2   Data to Calibrate the Model

To calibrate our model, we collected both survey and behavioral data. An online survey consisting of ten multi-part questions was given to 357 users in June and July, 2004[2]. Only users who had logged in at least 3 times and who had rated at least 30 movies were presented with an invitation to participate. The survey was promoted on the MovieLens main page.

The survey focused on understanding users' motivations. Motivations are not only important for understanding user costs and benefits, but can later be used to calibrate reduced models for new users with little history data.

We found that MovieLens users do have differing motivations. 92% of users listed viewing movie recommendations as one of their top-three reasons for using the system. However, we found that people rate movies for a wider variety of reasons: to keep a personal list of movies they've seen, to influence others, and because they find rating itself to be fun. We also found that users perceive that the quality of movie recommendations provided by the system improves over time.

We also gathered historical behavioral data about the volunteers who took the survey. This data includes, for example, information about the use of MovieLens features and the quality of recommendations received. Table 1 summarizes some of the key behavioral variables we used in this study.

The users that we studied were disproportionately "power users", i.e., those users who use the system often and rate a lot of movies. They also tended to be quite happy with MovieLens, based on their survey responses. However, the

---

[2] See http://www.grouplens.org/data/mlsurvey0604.html for a list of survey questions and a summary of responses.

Table 1. Selected MovieLens Survey-Taker Behavioral Data

	Mean	Median	Min.	Max.	Std. Dev.
# Ratings, User Lifetime	693.52	556	41	3235	525.16
# Ratings, Last 3 Months	86.67	37	0	1041	150.34
Recent Error of Recommendations[a]	0.54	0.50	0.13	1.57	0.22
Unusual Taste[b]	0.65	0.64	0.32	1.24	0.14
Fraction of Ratings that are Rare Movies[c]	0.07	0.05	0	0.33	0.06
Number of Movie Suggestions Contributed	3.00	0	0	218	13.87
# Saved Movie Searches	3.68	3	0	93	5.54
# Sessions, Last 3 Months	24.61	12	1	299	35.99
Fraction of Sessions w/ Ratings, Last 3 Months	0.60	0.60	0	1	0.26
Weeks Since Registration	33.21	34	1	72	22.99

[a] Measured by the mean absolute error (MAE) of last 20 ratings.
[b] Measured by the mean distance between a user's ratings and system average ratings.
[c] We define a rare movie as one with fewer than 250 ratings from the 88,000 users in MovieLens. By comparison, the top 100 movies average about 23,500 ratings each.

users in our study did exhibit a great deal of variety in a number of areas such as movie taste, interface customization and usage, and in the average quality of movie recommendations they receive.

3.3 Calibration and Results

We now describe an empirical model that we will calibrate using survey and behavioral data. Recall that Equation (3) characterizes the optimal number of ratings for a user. Since the distribution of ratings is skewed, we use a logarithm transformation of the number of ratings as the dependent variable. The main explanatory variables include a user's marginal benefit (MB) from the quality of recommendations, γ_i, the taste parameter, β_i, the fun score, f_i, and the marginal cost (MC) of providing additional ratings, c_i. We also control for other characteristics, $\vec{Z}$, such as a user's age in MovieLens and how many times a user has used MovieLens recently. Our empirical model is defined as

$$\ln x_i = a_0 + a_1\gamma_i + a_2\beta_i + a_3f_i + a_4c_i + \vec{A}\,\vec{Z} + \varepsilon_i. \qquad (4)$$

Calibrating the marginal cost and benefit parameters proved challenging in constructing the empirical model. Our survey questions designed for calibrating these parameters were phrased in terms of money, but many survey takers resisted assigning monetary values to a free web service. As such, many respondents failed to answer these questions, and many responded with $0 values or very unlikely costs. To handle this type of truncated data, we employed a Tobit maximum likelihood approach[3] to predict marginal benefit and cost using other survey and behavioral data.

---

[3] The Tobit model is an econometric model able to handle the case where the dependent variable is zero for a nontrivial fraction of the sample.[16, 6].

Table 2. Tobit Analysis: Estimating Marginal Benefit and Marginal Cost

	(1) Reported MB	(2) Reported MC
Freq of Picking Movies to Watch	1.358 (0.515)***	
Freq of Searching for a Particular Movie	0.198 (0.431)	
Freq of Looking Only at 1st Screen of Recs	-0.786 (0.333)**	
Freq of Looking at 5+ Screens of Recs	0.420 (0.447)	
# "Hide this Movie" Ratings	0.001 (0.003)	
# Saved Searches	0.100 (0.053)*	
Reported Time Estimate to Rate 10 Movies		4.231 (1.076)***
# Ratings/Login, Last 3 Months		0.184 (1.066)
Constant	-4.246 (1.551)***	-13.391 (3.880)***
Observations	339	338
Pseudo R-squared	0.02	0.03
Corr(predicted, user reported)	0.228	0.320
p-value	0.000	0.000

Notes:
1. Standard errors in parentheses.
2. Significant at: * 10-percent level; ** 5-percent level; *** 1-percent level.

The results of the Tobit estimation are presented in Table 2. The strongest indicator of marginal benefit is the frequency of using MovieLens to pick movies to watch. This indicator, along with other data reflecting usage patterns, provide an estimated value for γ_i that correlates with the monetized survey responses at 0.228. The estimation of marginal cost is based on survey responses concerning the time required to rate movies along with behavioral data on the number of ratings provided per session. The correlation between our estimated measure of c_i and the monetized value provided in the survey is 0.320. We report later on the strength of these measures in the discussion of the final model.

The taste and fun parameters are constructed more directly. The taste parameter is constructed from how often a user rates rare movies (as defined above, in Table 1) and how different a user's ratings are from movie averages. The fun score is derived from the frequency of using MovieLens to rate just-seen movies, the number of ratings sessions per month, and several other behavioral factors reflecting enjoyment of the rating process.

Table 3 reports the results of the empirical analysis, where we explain individual users' rating behavior in terms of Equation (4). Column (1) shows the explanatory variables used in the analysis. Column (2) shows only behavioral data to demonstrate the relative power of a reduced model without survey data. We focus on column (1) when interpreting the results.

The results are consistent with the theoretical predictions. Marginal cost has the expected significant and negative correlation with the quantity of ratings. Marginal benefit from movie recommendation shows a positive but not statistically significant correlation with number of ratings.

As suggested by survey responses, many MovieLens users consider rating movies to be an entertaining activity. This is reflected by the positive coefficient

Table 3. Regression Analysis: Predicting the Quantity of User Ratings

	Dependent Variable: log(ratings)	
	(1)	(2)
	Behavioral+Survey	Behavioral only
MC of Rating 10 Movies, c_i	-0.042 (0.019)**	
MB of 10 Recommendations, γ_i	0.028 (0.053)	
Fun Score, f_i	0.353 (0.104)***	
Uncommon Taste, β_i	0.974 (0.284)***	0.922 (0.290)***
% Ratings that are Rare Movies, β_i	1.906 (0.379)***	2.137 (0.382)***
Altruism Score, $\vec{Z}$	-0.053 (0.030)*	
Weeks Since Registration, $\vec{Z}$	0.001(0.001)**	
Helpful Subject Score, $\vec{Z}$	0.171(0.050)***	0.195 (0.050)***
# Logins, Last 3 Months, $\vec{Z}$	0.004 (0.001)***	0.006 (0.001)***
% Sessions with Rating Activity, $\vec{Z}$	0.732 (0.144)***	0.872 (0.141)***
Recent Error of Recommendations, $\vec{Z}$	-0.477 (0.186)**	-0.427(0.191)**
Constant, a_0	4.351 (0.308)***	4.606 (0.210)***
Observations	356	356
Adjusted R squared	0.342	0.304
Corr(predict #ratings, actual #ratings)	0.622	0.514
p-value	0.000	0.000

Notes:
1. Standard errors in parentheses.
2. Significant at: * 10-percent level; ** 5-percent level; *** 1-percent level.

of the fun score, statistically significant at 1 percent. Both measures of taste are significant and have strong effects, which confirms the theoretical prediction that users with rare tastes tend to rate more.

Our control variables, used to account for user-specific characteristics, also improve the overall predictive power of the model. The percentage of sessions over the last three months that includes rating activity has a strong, significant effect. Recent error of recommendations, measured in terms of a user's mean absolute error (MAE) over the last 20 ratings has a significant negative effect on predicted ratings.

The regression analysis has an adjusted R-squared of 0.342 and the correlation between the predicted and actual number of ratings is 0.622 ($p < 0.001$). As is common practice in the social sciences, we report the adjusted R-squared, which imposes a penalty for adding additional but irrelevant independent variables. In terms of a cross-sectional economic study, this is a strong result.[4]

---

[4] "In the social science, low R-squared in regression equations are not uncommon, especially for cross-sectional analysis."[16] For cross-section data, such as those we have, a R-squared above 0.2 is usually considered decent. For example, Ashenfelter and Krueger report R-squared in the range of 0.2 and 0.3, with a sample size of 298 [1]. Levitt reports R-squared in the range of 0.06 and 0.37 with a sample size between 1,276 and 4,801 [11].

Table 3 also shows the results of our reduced model, which consists of only behavioral data. The adjusted R-squared is 0.304 and the correlation between the predicted number of ratings and the actual number of ratings is 0.514 ($p < 0.001$), both slightly worse than the full model. However, the advantage of the reduced model is that the necessary data are available without extensive surveying.

We have conducted ten-fold cross-validation for both the full and reduced empirical models. The results are robust and are available upon request.

4   Discussion

Achieving an R-squared value of 0.34 implies that we are able to explain a significant portion of individual rating behavior. This has two direct applications. First, we use these results to increase our understanding of user motivations and behavior. We have identified markers of behavior that guide us in further site development. To be specific, before conducting this analysis we believed that a particularly effective way of increasing ratings would be to reveal to users the extent of their effect on others. In view of the results we found, we now believe it may be more effective to focus on increasing the fun and non-prediction personal benefits of rating through better interfaces for rating and making lists, better interfaces for browsing collections of one's own ratings, and increased use of games that engage users in the system. At the same time, we originally were quite skeptical of any "pre-surveys" or other barriers to entering the system, but now see that using them may serve as an indicator of good citizenship and might well lead to increasing the percentage of new users who become high raters.

Second, we can use these results to start thinking about personalized interfaces, to go along with the already-personalized content. Now that we can efficiently fit users into this model, we can choose to emphasize different elements of the system to them. Users who most directly benefit from prediction quality can be given updated information on the quality of their recent predictions and the estimated increase in quality from the next quantum of ratings. Users who are more interested in the fun of rating itself can receive different cues and prompts.

Of course, we must include a very important caveat. We discovered quite early that the users in our sample are very much power users. Before making major site changes that would affect all users we would want to extend this analysis to include a broader range of newer and infrequent users.

Lessons Learned. The entire process of conducting this analysis was filled with lessons, many of them the direct result of a first-time collaboration between a pair of computer scientists and a pair of economists. While the process was rewarding, we should warn those attempting it the first time that there is a substantial learning curve. The computer scientists in the team not only had to re-learn the Greek alphabet, but had to learn to formalize years of intuition about user behavior in new ways. This led to challenging but rewarding attempts to operationalize the abstract parameters of the analysis through mixtures of survey and behavioral data. At the same time, the nature of working with the online MovieLens community handicapped the economists on our team. In contrast with most experimental economics work, our users steadfastly resisted attempts to monetize their experience with the system, adding substantial challenges to the task of estimating value and cost.

If we were to repeat this effort, we would likely take a more iterative approach to surveying the users. While our survey *design* was appropriate for our modeling task, the effect of user behavior on that design made the modeling much harder. With greater iteration we probably would have been better able to substitute time for money in the overall analysis of cost and value.

Finally, we must address the question of whether economic modeling is a valuable approach for studying and personalizing an interactive web site. While this answer certainly depends upon the details of the site, in general we think it is so long as a sufficient amount of data is available to support the process. Economic models have the nice property of building formality from a base of initial understanding. Unlike a neural network, they don't simply appear from data. But unlike a neural network, they return significant understanding of the population being analyzed.

Future Work. We are currently engaged in a series of experiments to learn whether certain laboratory-tested economic theories of collective action apply to the more real-world environment of online communities. Specifically, we plan a set of field studies that look at theories of reciprocity and inequality aversion to determine how user contributions to a collective good are affected by awareness of the contributions of others. Following this work, we plan to explore incentive-personalized interfaces to MovieLens–interfaces that provide the specific cues and information that motivate each particular user to contribute to the system.

5   Conclusions

Economic modeling is a formal method for combining initial understanding about a user population with data to refine that understanding. We developed an economic model of rating behavior of MovieLens users, tying that behavior to a number of factors that determine how much the user benefits from ratings– directly and indirectly–and how much effort the user requires to enter those ratings. The process gave us insight into the motivations of our user community, and resulted in a useful model able to explain a substantial percentage of user variation in rating behavior.

Acknowledgments. We would like to thank Dan Cosley and Sean McNee for their feedback on early drafts of this paper, and Robert Kraut for his ideas that helped guide our research. This work is supported by a grant from the National Science Foundation (IIS-0324851).

References

1. Ashenfelter, O., Krueger, A.B.: Estimates of the economic returns to schooling from a new sample of twins. American Economic Review **84** (1994) 1157–73
2. Bakos, J.Y.: Reducing buyer search costs: implications for electronic marketplaces. Manage. Sci. **43** (1997) 1676–1692
3. Brusilovsky, P.: Methods and techniques of adaptive hypermedia. User Modeling and User-Adapted Interaction **6** (1996) 87–129
4. Butler, B.S.: Membership size, communication activity, and sustainability: A resource-based model of online social structures. Info. Sys. Research **12** (2001) 346–362
5. Friedman, E.J., Resnick, P.: The social cost of cheap pseudonyms. Journal of Economics & Management Strategy **10** (2001) 173–199
6. Greene, W.H.: Econometric analysis. 4th edn. Prentice Hall, Upper Saddle River, NJ (2000)
7. Grudin, J.: Why CSCW applications fail: problems in the design and evaluation of organizational interfaces. In: Proceedings of CSCW '88, ACM Press (1988) 85–93
8. Herlocker, J., Konstan, J.A., Riedl, J.: An empirical analysis of design choices in neighborhood-based collaborative filtering algorithms. Inf. Retr. **5** (2002) 287–310
9. Horvitz, E., Apacible, J.: Learning and reasoning about interruption. In: Proceedings of ICMI '03, ACM Press (2003) 20–27
10. Keser, C.: Experimental games for the design of reputation management systems. IBM Systems Journal **42** (2003) 498–506
11. Levitt, S.D.: Using electoral cycles in police hiring to estimate the effect of police on crime. American Economic Review **87** (1997) 270–90
12. Mas-Colell, A., Whinston, M.D., Green, J.R.: Microeconomic Theory. Oxford University Press (1995)
13. McNee, S.M., Lam, S.K., Konstan, J.A., Riedl, J.: Interfaces for eliciting new user preferences in recommender systems. In: Proceedings of User Modeling 2003. (2003) 178–187
14. Resnick, P., Varian, H.R.: Recommender systems. Commun. ACM **40** (1997) 56–58
15. Varian, H.R.: How to build an economic model in your spare time. In Szenberg, M., ed.: Passion and Craft, How Economists Work. University of Michigan Press (1995)
16. Wooldridge, J.M.: Introductory Econometrics: A Modern Approach. 2nd edn. South-Western College (2002)

Incorporating Confidence in a Naive Bayesian Classifier

V. Pronk[1], S.V.R. Gutta[2], and W.F.J. Verhaegh[1]

[1] Philips Research Laboratories, Prof. Holstlaan 4, 5656 AA Eindhoven,
The Netherlands
{verus.pronk, wim.verhaegh}@philips.com
[2] Philips Research Bangalore, 1 Murphy Road, Ulsoor, Bangalore - 560 008,
India
srinivas.gutta@philips.com

Abstract. Naive Bayes is a relatively simple classification method to,
e.g., rate TV programs as interesting or uninteresting to a user. In
case the training set consists of instances, chosen randomly from the
instance space, the posterior probability estimates are random variables.
Their statistical properties can be used to calculate confidence intervals around them, enabling more refined classification strategies than
the usual *argmax*-operator. This may alleviate the cold-start problem
and provide additional feedback to the user.

In this paper, we give an explicit expression to estimate the variances
of the posterior probability estimates from the training data and investigate the strategy that refrains from classification in case the confidence
interval around the largest posterior probability overlaps with any of the
other intervals.

We show that the classification error rate can be significantly reduced
at the cost of a lower coverage, i.e., the fraction of classifiable instances,
in a TV-program recommender.

Keywords: machine learning, naive Bayes, recommenders, reliability,
confidence intervals.

1 Introduction

The rapid increase in video and audio content availability to the end user has
resulted in the emergence of recommender systems, which aim to filter interesting, or positive, from uninteresting, or negative, content for a particular user
or group of users. This filtering is more generally referred to as classification
and individual pieces of video or audio content are usually called instances. The
classes in this case are *positive* and *negative*.

A simple and popular way to classify instances is naive Bayesian classification (NBC) [10]. This classification method relies upon the availability of training
data, which is a collection of instances with known class. Each instance is characterized by a set of feature values. For example, a TV program may amongst
others be characterized by its title and genre, such as comedy or sports, its main

L. Ardissono, P. Brna, and A. Mitrovic (Eds.): UM 2005, LNAI 3538, pp. 317–326, 2005.

characters, such as actors or players, the day and time at which it is broadcast, a description, et cetera. The training data thus provides a relation between feature and class values, or classes for short. Using this relation and using Bayes' rule, a given instance is classified, based on its feature values. The approach is to obtain for each class an estimate of the probability that the instance belongs to this class. These probabilities are called the *posterior probabilities*. The instance is then classified as being of the class with the largest posterior probability, where ties are broken arbitrarily.

NBC owes its relative simplicity to the usually naive assumption of conditional independence. More precisely, it is assumed that for each instance, given its class, none of its feature values provides any information on the values of any of its other features. Despite the presence of conditional dependence in many practical applications, see Domingos & Pazzani [3] and Hand & Yu [6], NBC is often successfully applied and can compete with more complex methods such as decision trees and artificial neural networks [10].

The amount of training data has a direct influence on the accuracy of classification. With only little training data, it cannot be expected that a classifier performs flawlessly. Even with ample amounts of training data, a classifier usually does not operate error-free. It may therefore be useful to make the extent to which a classifier can classify an instance explicit, for instance by adding a measure of confidence to each individual instance classified or by adding an 'unable to classify' answer, which can be used whenever there is insufficient training data to classify a given instance. The latter leads to the notion of *coverage,* which is defined as the fraction of classifiable instances. The aim then is to increase the classification accuracy of the classifiable instances and to offset this against the coverage.

The approach we pursue is to estimate, for a given instance, confidence intervals around the posterior probability estimates. These intervals are used to decide whether or not to classify the instance. A confidence interval is obtained by considering the estimate of the corresponding posterior probability as the realization of a random variable.

We investigate how to obtain estimates of the confidence intervals and provide an example of their use. We show that the classification accuracy can be traded off against the coverage. It thus provides an alternative to the problem of a low overall classification accuracy by making explicit which instances are difficult and which ones are easy to classify, given the training data. In an alternative approach, not further elaborated upon in the paper, an explicit notion of confidence can be associated to the classification of each instance, thereby retaining a coverage of 1.

It stands to reason that the results are especially relevant for user-oriented applications such as a TV-program recommender: The user obtains valuable feedback concerning the confidence that the recommender has in the classification of a program. Furthermore, the well-known cold-start problem, where only a limited training set is available, can be alleviated by a more defensive classification strategy. These extensions may greatly enhance the user's appreciation of the recommender, or the application in which it is used, even though it does not operate error-free.

The remainder of the paper is organized as follows. Before we discuss related work in Section 3, we review naive Bayesian classification in Section 2. In Section 4 we investigate how to calculate confidence intervals around the posterior probability estimates and how to estimate them from the training data. In Section 5 we apply the results to the problem of recommending TV programs, using the viewing histories of ten users. We end with some concluding remarks in Section 6.

2   Naive Bayesian Classification

We next describe NBC, starting with some notation. An instance x is described by f feature values $x_i \in D_i$, for $i = 1, 2, \ldots, f$, where D_i is the domain of feature i. Its class is denoted by $c(x) \in \mathcal{C}$, where $\mathcal{C}$ is the set of classes. For simplicity, we do not consider missing feature values. The results, however, can easily be generalized to handle missing feature values.

Given is a non-empty set $\mathcal{X}$ of training instances and for each instance $x \in \mathcal{X}$ its class $c_x = c(x)$. Let y be an instance to be classified. The approach in NBC is that we express $\Pr(c(y) = j)$, for each $j \in \mathcal{C}$, in terms of the training data.

Let x be a random variable on the domain $\mathcal{U}$ of instances. Using Bayes' rule and assuming conditional independence of feature values for a given class, we can rephrase $\Pr(c(y) = j)$ as follows.

$$\Pr(c(y) = j) = \Pr(c(x) = j \mid x = y) \tag{1}$$

$$= \frac{\Pr(c(x) = j)\ \Pr(x = y \mid c(x) = j)}{\Pr(x = y)} \tag{2}$$

$$= \frac{\Pr(c(x) = j)\ \prod_{i=1}^{f} \Pr(x_i = y_i \mid c(x) = j)}{\Pr(x = y)}. \tag{3}$$

As the denominator can alternatively be written as the sum over all j of the numerator, it serves as a normalization constant. When comparing probabilities, this constant can be omitted.

The factors $\Pr(c(x) = j)$ are called *prior probabilities*, $\Pr(x_i = y_i \mid c(x) = j)$ *conditional probabilities*, and the expressions $\Pr(c(y) = j)$ are called the *posterior probabilities*.

The general approach in NBC is that the prior and conditional probabilities are estimated using the training data to obtain estimates of the posterior probabilities. We define

$$N(j) = |\{x \in \mathcal{X} \mid c_x = j\}| \quad \text{and} \tag{4}$$

$$N(i, v, j) = |\{x \in \mathcal{X} \mid x_i = v \land c_x = j\}|, \tag{5}$$

where $|S|$ denotes the cardinality of a set S. By assuming, without loss of generality, that $N(j) > 0$, we estimate the probabilities as

$$\Pr(c(\underline{x}) = j) \approx N(j)/|\mathcal{X}| \quad \text{and} \tag{6}$$

$$\Pr(x_i = y_i \mid c(\underline{x}) = j) \approx \frac{N(i, y_i, j)}{N(j)}. \tag{7}$$

By substituting these estimates into (3) we obtain an estimate of the probability that $\underline{y}$ belongs to class j in terms of the training data.

The NBC classification $C(\underline{y})$ of $\underline{y}$ is defined as the value of j that maximizes the estimate. Ties are broken arbitrarily. Formally, $C(\underline{y})$ is defined as

$$C(\underline{y}) = \operatorname*{argmax}_{j \in \mathcal{C}} \frac{N(j)}{|\mathcal{X}|} \prod_{i=1}^{f} \frac{N(i, y_i, j)}{N(j)}. \tag{8}$$

If $C(\underline{y}) \neq c(\underline{y})$, then we speak of a classification error. The classification error rate E, or error rate for short, is defined as

$$E = \Pr(C(\underline{x}) \neq c(\underline{x})), \tag{9}$$

and is a measure for the performance of the classifier. The classification accuracy is defined as $1 - E$. The definition of error rate can be refined by considering class-conditional error rates. Given a class j, we define

$$E_j = \Pr(C(\underline{x}) \neq c(\underline{x}) \mid c(\underline{x}) = j) \tag{10}$$

as the class-j error rate. The class-conditional classification accuracy is given by $1 - E_j$.

3   Related Work

The performance of a classifier is usually expressed in terms of its classification accuracy. Berikov [1] added to this its variance by considering the accuracy as a random variable. A recent trend, identified by Kononenko [8], is to consider the reliability of the classification of individual instances. In this respect, Kukar [9] and Zaffalon [12] complement our work.

Kukar [9] proposes the use of *transductive reliability estimation* to obtain a measure of the reliability of a classification. The method is applicable to any classifier that outputs a posterior probability distribution on the set of classes. The approach is to classify an instance using a set of training data and then to classify it again a number of times, equal to the number of classes, each time with the same training data, extended with the instance to be classified, assuming that it belongs to the respective class. Using an appropriate distance metric, the distances between the respective posterior probability distributions are used to calculate a measure for the classifier's instability or unreliability for this classified instance. A threshold for determining whether a classification is reliable or not is calculated, based on the training data.

Zaffalon [12] extends NBC by introducing *credal sets*, which are generalizations of probability distributions, and uses these sets to derive upper and lower bounds for the posterior probabilities. As such, this approach is comparable to ours, be it that the author is implicit on how to obtain these credal sets, as opposed to our explicit calculation of confidence intervals.

Ramoni & Sebastiani [11] consider the problem of missing data. Their approach is to compute bounds on the posterior probabilities by considering all possible completions in the training set. They propose various methods to rank the so-formed intervals and arrive at a trade-off between classification accuracy and coverage. These methods can be used to further extend our work.

Our contribution in the context of NBC is to give an explicit expression for the variance of each of the posterior probabilities for an individual instance and, based on that, to distinguish between reliable and unreliable classifications. The intuitive nature of the variance is an advantage over the more implicit methods described above. As such, it also provides an alternative to estimating the variance of a classification by repeatedly estimating the posterior probabilities.

4   Estimating the Confidence Intervals

Assuming that the instances in $\mathcal{X}$ are generated randomly on $\mathcal{U}$, $N(j)$ is binomially distributed with parameters $|\mathcal{X}|$ and $\Pr(c(\underline{x}) = j)$, and $N(i, v, j)$ is binomially distributed with parameters $N(j)$ and $\Pr(x_i = v \mid c(\underline{x}) = j)$. Although, of course, $N(i, v, j)$ is also binomially distributed with parameters $|\mathcal{X}|$ and $\Pr(x_i = v \wedge c(\underline{x}) = j)$, the former characterization makes the dependence of $N(i, v, j)$ on $N(j)$ explicit. The estimate of a conditional probability is thus the ratio of two dependent, random variables. The following theorem gives an expression for the variance of this estimate. Its proof is omitted for brevity, but will appear in a future publication.

Theorem 1. *Let X be a binomially distributed random variable with parameters (N, p) with $N \geq 1$ and $0 < p < 1$ and let, for each $n \geq 1$, Y_n be a binomially distributed random variable with parameters (n, q) with $0 \leq q \leq 1$. Let $\tilde{X}$ be the random variable, defined by*

$$\Pr(\tilde{X} = n) = \Pr(X = n \mid X \neq 0), \quad for \; n = 1, 2, \ldots, N. \tag{11}$$

Then the variance $VAR(Z)$ of the random variable Z, defined as

$$Z = \frac{Y_{\tilde{X}}}{\tilde{X}}, \tag{12}$$

is given by

$$VAR(Z) = q\,(1 - q)\,\frac{(1 - p)^N}{1 - (1 - p)^N}\,(H_N(1 - p) - H_N(1)), \tag{13}$$

with

$$H_N(\alpha) = \sum_{n=1}^{N} \frac{\alpha^{-n}}{n}. \tag{14}$$

Kononenko [7] also analyzes the conditional probabilities, but then to investigate the extent of dependency between two feature values. He uses the Chebyshev inequality to bound the deviation of an estimate from the actual value from above, using $p = 1$ and $q = 0.5$.

By setting N equal to $|\mathcal{X}|$, p to $\Pr(c(\underline{x}) = j)$, and q to $\Pr(x_i = v \mid c(\underline{x}) = j)$, Z stands for $N(i, v, j)/N(j)$. As we are estimating p and q with the training data, we can also estimate $VAR(Z)$ with this data.

Before aggregating the results obtained thus far, we note the following two issues. First, in case some $N(i, v, j) = 0$, the associated variance is 0 as well. The usual way to deal with zero counts is to apply a correction, known as the Laplace correction [2]. When an experiment with k possible outcomes is performed n times, the probability of a particular outcome, assuming that it occurs r times, is estimated as $(r + 1)/(n + k)$. This can intuitively be understood by assuming that the experiment has been carried out an additional k times, whereby each outcome has occurred exactly once. Hence, in case $N(i, v, j) = 0$, we set the estimate of the conditional probability q to $1/(N(j) + |D_i|)$. In case $|D_i|$ is large, the associated estimate of the standard deviation is relatively large with respect to q. This turns out to have a detrimental effect on the results. To alleviate this problem, we estimate the variance by the square of $1/(N(j) + |D_i|)$ in case $N(i, v, j) = 0$.

Secondly, the prior probabilities need not be estimated using the training data, i.e., with $N(j)/|\mathcal{X}|$. Instead, they can be based on other criteria [4,5]. For the moment, we assume that they are set to predefined values, denoted by p_j. This approach will be explained further in Section 5. We thus replace the definition of $C(\underline{y})$ in (8) by

$$C(\underline{y}) = \operatorname*{argmax}_{j \in \mathcal{C}} p_j \prod_{i=1}^{f} \frac{N(i, y_i, j)}{N(j)} . \tag{15}$$

If we assume independence among the f fractions in this equation, we can use the following rule to estimate the variance of the jth term. Assume that we have f independent random variables Z_i and a constant p. It holds that

$$VAR\left(p \prod_{i=1}^{f} Z_i\right) = p^2 \left(\prod_{i=1}^{f} \left(VAR(Z_i) + E(Z_i)^2\right) - \prod_{i=1}^{f} E(Z_i)^2\right). \tag{16}$$

However, the assumption of independence does not hold in our case. Each of the Z_is contain a common denominator, i.e., the $\tilde{X}$ from Theorem 1. Nevertheless, it can be shown that, if N and p are the parameters associated with $\tilde{X}$ and Np is large, then (16) holds by approximation.

By combining (16) with (13) for each Z_i, we obtain expressions for estimating the variance of the estimates of each of the posterior probabilities in terms of the training set and the parameters p_j. Denoting these variance estimates by $s^2(\underline{y}, j)$ and using $P(\underline{y}, j)$ to denote the estimates of the posterior probabilities, we define a confidence interval with parameter $\kappa \geq 0$ around $P(\underline{y}, j)$ by the bounds

$$P(\underline{y}, j) \pm \kappa\, s(\underline{y}, j) , \tag{17}$$

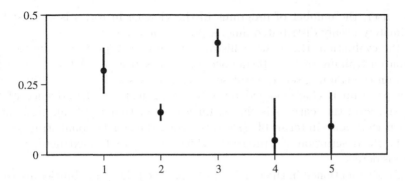

Fig. 1. An illustration of clipped confidence intervals around each of five posterior probability estimates for $\underline{y}$

Figure 1 gives an illustration of what the results for an instance $\underline{y}$ could look like for a chosen value of κ. There are five classes called 1 to 5. The dots represent the corresponding estimates for the posterior probabilities, normalized to add up to 1, whereas the associated vertical lines indicate the correspondingly scaled confidence intervals, clipped from below by 0. These confidence intervals can be used to indicate to what extent a classification can be justified.

A straightforward way to define a κ-*reliable* classification strategy using these intervals is the following. For conventional classification, we use (15) to obtain $C(\underline{y})$, but in case

$$P(\underline{y}, C(\underline{y})) - \kappa\, s(\underline{y}, C(\underline{y})) < \max_{j \neq C(\underline{y})} P(\underline{y}, j) + \kappa\, s(\underline{y}, j)\,, \tag{18}$$

the κ-reliable classification becomes 'unable to classify'. Otherwise, the κ-reliable classification equals the conventional classification. For the example in Figure 1, the κ-reliable classifier is unable to classify the instance, as the confidence interval of class 1 overlaps with that of class 3, which is the conventional classification.

The fraction of classifiable instances is called the *coverage*. This coverage should be offset against the error rate of the classifiable instances.

Instead of defining a coverage, an alternative way to use the confidence intervals is to explicitly compute a value for κ such that equality holds in (18). In this way, each instance is classified, but an additional score gives a measure for the confidence the recommender has in the classification. This approach will not be pursued here.

5   Performance Evaluation

For evaluating the performance, we use the TV-viewing histories of ten users, collected in the time frame 1999-2001. There are two classes, i.e., *positive* and *negative*. The positive programs were obtained by explicit feedback from the users, whereas the negative programs were chosen randomly. In case the negative programs by far outnumber the positive ones, then this choice is reasonable.

For each user, the number of programs in the viewing histories is at least 530, approximately evenly distributed among positive and negatives.

For the evaluation, the viewing history of a user is repeatedly divided randomly into a training set of a predefined size and a test set. After training the classifier on the training set, the test set is used to assess its performance.

Each program is characterized by a set of 22 features. In advance of the tests, a subset of the features is chosen for each user that yields approximately the best performance in terms of error rate, using the conventional strategy. For simplicity, the description of a program, which can be used to extract keywords, is not considered.

As already mentioned in the previous section, the prior probabilities are set to fixed values. Using $N(j)/|\mathcal{X}|$ as an estimate of the prior probability of class j can lead to a skewed error rate, i.e., to the situation that the positive classification error rate differs substantially from the negative classification error rate. As Gärtner, Wu & Flach [5] already suggest, by changing the prior probabilities, one can balance the positive and negative classification error rates. This approach is essentially the same as suggested by Elkan [4], who uses a cost-based approach towards classification.

For both the conventional and reliable classification strategies, we set the prior probabilities such that the positive and negative classification error rates are (approximately) the same on the training set. An advantage is that we do not have to deal with the positive and negative error rates separately, but can instead focus on the overall error rates. It should be mentioned, though, that this symmetry may not be necessary or desirable in practice. This is because there is a difference between a negative program showing up in a list of recommended programs and a positive program not showing up in this list.

For each user, we vary the value of κ from 0 to 1 in increments of 0.1. Note that a value of 0 corresponds to using the conventional classification strategy. For each setting, we consider 50 as well as 400 training instances, chosen randomly from the viewing history of the user considered. This is repeated 25 times for averaging the error rates and coverages.

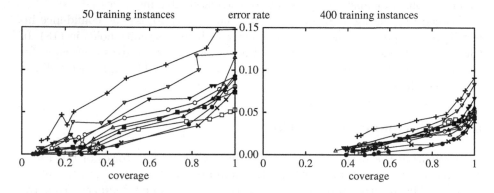

Fig. 2. The error rate versus the coverage using 50 and 400 training instances

Figure 2 illustrates the error rate versus the coverage using 50 and 400 training instances, respectively. Each line corresponds to one user and the marks correspond to the different values of κ. As the value of κ increases, both the classification error and the coverage generally decrease. The error rates shown on the right vertical axes thus correspond to the conventional classification strategy, where $\kappa = 0$.

The results clearly illustrate the trade-off between classification error and coverage. Even with few training instances, the classification error can be reduced significantly, albeit at a considerable loss of coverage. This loss diminishes as the number of training instances increases. We note that choosing an appropriate value for the coverage or the error rate is generally application as well as user dependent.

When using a small value for κ, the reduction in the error rate while still maintaining a high coverage implies that the unclassifiable instances are difficult to classify correctly. In other words, the associated reliable classification strategy can successfully separate the easy from the difficult instances and abstains from classifying the difficult ones.

6   Concluding Remarks

We have extended the naive Bayesian classifier by incorporating the notion of confidence. To each posterior probability a confidence interval is associated, based on an analysis of the training data. Using these intervals, we have defined a classification strategy that abstains from classification in case certain confidence intervals overlap.

We have shown, by a performance evaluation in the context of TV-program recommendation, that a trade-off exists between the coverage, i.e., the fraction of classifiable instances, and the error rate on the classifiable instances. The classification error can be significantly reduced at the cost of a lower coverage, effectively resulting in separating the instances that are easy to classify from those that are more difficult to classify.

Application of a confidence measure may alleviate the cold-start problem, where only a limited viewing history is available. Towards the user, an explicit indication of confidence in individual classifications may greatly enhance the user's appreciation for the recommender.

Dealing with zero counts warrants further research. The Laplace correction does not lead to satisfactory results with respect to the variance of the estimates of the conditional probabilities.

In applications where accuracy rather than coverage is of paramount importance, such as in medical diagnosis or face recognition, the technique proposed in this paper may be successfully applied. This is considered a subject for further research.

The statistical analysis of the conditional probabilities can be used in a broader sense, such as comparing profiles to investigate whether the differences are significant or not. Also this is considered a subject for further research.

Acknowledgement

Thanks are due to Dee Denteneer for our fruitful discussions on several aspects of the paper.

References

1. Berikov, V.B.: An approach to the evaluation of the performance of a discrete classifier. Pattern Recognition Letters **23:1–3** (2002) 227–233
2. Cestnik, B.: Estimating probabilities: a crucial task in machine learning. Proceedings of the European Conference on Artificial Intelligence (ECAI'90), Stockholm, Norway, August 6–10, 147–149
3. Domingos, P., Pazzani, M.: On the optimality of the simple Bayesian classifier under zero-one loss. Machine Learning **29:2–3** (1997) 103–130
4. Elkan, C.: The foundations of cost-sensitive learning. Proceedings of the 17th International Joint Conference on Artificial Intelligence (IJCAI'01), Seattle, Washington, August 4–10, 973–978
5. Gärtner, T., Wu, S., Flach, P.A.: Data mining on the Sisyphus dataset: evaluation and integration of results. Integrating Aspects of Data Mining, Decision Support and Meta-Learning, Giraud-Carrier, C., Lavrac, N., Moyle, S. (Eds.), (2001) 69–80
6. Hand, D.J., Yu, K.: Idiot's Bayes – not so stupid after all? International Statistical Review **69:3** (2001) 385–398
7. Kononenko, I.: Semi-naive Bayesian classifier. Lecture Notes in Computer Science **482**: Proceedings of the Sixth European Working Session on Learning (EWSL'91), Porto, Portugal, March 6–8, 206–219
8. Kononenko, I.: Machine learning for medical diagnosis: history, state of the art and perspective. Artificial Intelligence in Medicine **23:1** (2001) 89–109
9. Kukar, M.: Making reliable diagnoses with machine learning: a case study. Proceedings of the 8th Conference on AI in Medicine in Europe (AIME'01), Cascais, Portugal, July 1–4, 88–98
10. Mitchell, T.M.: Machine Learning. McGraw-Hill (1997)
11. Ramoni, M., Sebastiani, P.: Robust Bayes classifiers. Artificial Intelligence **125** (2001) 209–226
12. Zaffalon, M.: The naive credal classifier. Journal of Statistical Planning and Inference **105:1** (2002) 5–21

Modeling User's Opinion Relevance to Recommending Research Papers[*]

Sílvio César Cazella[1,2] and Luis Otávio Campos Alvares[2]

[1] Universidade do Vale do Rio dos Sinos, Centro de Ciências Exatas e Tecnológicas,
Av. Unisinos 950, CEP 93.022-000, São Leopoldo, RS, Brazil
cazella@exatas.unisinos.br
[2] Universidade Federal do Rio Grande do Sul , Instituto de Informática,
Av. Bento Gonçalves 9500, CEP 91.591-970, Porto Alegre, RS, Brazil
{cazella, alvares}@inf.ufrgs.br

Abstract. Finding the right material on the Web could be a worthwhile result. Users waste too much time to discover the useful information. Recommender system can provide some shortcuts to the user, but if the recommendation is based on people's opinion, one question remains — how relevant is a user's opinion? This paper presents a model to define the user's relevance opinion in a recommender system. This metric aims to help the target user to decide in what recommendation he should focus his attention. Beyond the model, we present a real experiment using an e-government database.

Keywords: User modeling, Authority, Recommender System.

1 Introduction

The Web is an excellent source of information, but it is becoming increasingly difficult to find relevant information. For this reason, considerable research has been done, which focuses on the information overload problem, and there are Internet search engines available to assist the user in his search. In order to retrieve information these systems require users to designate keywords to start a search. However, there are two main problems in this approach: the user may not know the right words to use in order to find the desired information and/or maybe the system will return a great deal of useless information [2].

Recommender systems (RS) are widely applied in e-commerce sites to assist customers in their purchasing decisions. Almost all RS do the same thing: they identify items to offer to the user based on some criteria and the user profile [5]. According to [4], items can be recommended based on the top sold items on a site, on the demographics of the consumer, and other users opinion. However, some important questions remain: How important is the opinion of this person? How much does this

---

[*] This research has been funded in part by the Brazilian agency CAPES under grant BEX1357/03-4.

L. Ardissono, P. Brna, and A. Mitrovic (Eds.): UM 2005, LNAI 3538, pp. 327–331, 2005.

person know about the product? When we relate our concerns to academic life, the relevance of a user's opinion in this specific domain has a great importance. In this work we claim that a user who has more relevance of opinion in an area of knowledge can better evaluate an item.

The main contribution of this paper is to provide a complete and generic model to define the user's relevance opinion (authority) based on attributes in a RS. The remainder of the paper is organized as follows: Section 2 presents a model to represent user's opinion relevance. Section 3 presents an extended example of a real application of the model. Finally, in Section 4, we summarize our research, and discuss some directions for future work.

2 A Model to Represent User's Opinion Relevance

To better explain our approach, we can think about people in a specific position in many different careers, for example, lawyers, musicians, professors, and so on. People in the highest position in a specific career usually have well considered opinions in the community. Another example is the research area. Consider a system can predict my interest in a paper based on other opinions, but if the others do not have so much experience or knowledge with the paper's area, maybe their opinion could not be so relevant to me, even if they rated the things like me (*like-minded*). Maybe a recommendation based on users with more relevant opinion could be more interesting. In general, if I have knowledge about the recommenders opinions relevance I can better evaluate the recommendations.

Aiming to represent the relevance of other users opinion to the target user in a RS we are proposing a model. In this model there is a metric — Recommender's Rank (RR) — it represents how much a user knows about a specific area of knowledge or item. The RR is a value in a specific predefined range of values, which can be parameterized in the model. The criteria to measure the importance of a recommender obviously are domain dependent. But we can conceive a general model based on relevant attributes, each one normalized and with a weight.

These attributes must be selected according to the specific domain to represent a user. For example, in an academic domain some attributes to calculate the RR to a user can be: academic level, number of publications in journals, number of publications in conferences and the number of supervised students. These attributes may have different scale of values, so we use Equation (1) to normalize them.

$$an = MinMax(a) = \frac{a - minA}{maxA - minA} \times (newmaxA - newminA) + newminA \qquad (1)$$

Equation (1) performs a linear transformation on the original data. Suppose that minA and maxA are the minimum and maximum values of an attribute. Min-Max normalization maps a value a of A to an in the range [newminA, newmaxA]. According to [3], this normalization is essential in order to maintain a consistency of ranges among all the attributes.

$$RR = \sum_{i=1}^{n} an_i w_i / \sum_{i=1}^{n} w_i \qquad (2)$$

Equation (2) is used to calculate the RR, and represents the weighted mean for all the selected attributes, represented by a list of attributes $(an_1, an_2, \ldots, an_n)$. This equation converts all the information into a unique quantitative value in a specific range. It represents a general user relevance of opinion.

A large domain may be subdivided in some areas of interest and the user has different knowledge and experience in each one. For instance, if we consider artificial intelligence as the general area, some specific areas of interest may be neural networks, multi-agent systems, and genetic algorithms. Then, can be important to have a RR for each specific area, which will be calculated using Equation (2), but considering for instance only publications in the specific area.

3 Extended Example

Aiming to present a real application of the model we have used it in a project named W-RECMAS (a hybrid recommender system based on multi-agent system for academic paper recommendation) [1]. This project focuses on a RS for academics and we are using an e-government database to collect the attribute values. In this database, it is possible to find information about researchers, graduate students, teachers and professors.

This database is part of the CV-Lattes system, and it was developed by CNPq (The National Council for Scientific and Technological Development), and used by the Ministry of Science and Technology (MCT) and other organizations in Brazil. The CV-Lattes database offers a number of important attributes called production metrics (quantitative data) from each researcher (e.g., number of publications in journals, number of publications in conferences) and a complete description of each publication, besides other relevant information as areas of interest, academic level, and so on.

W-RECMAS is composed by some agents, two of them present a very important role in RR calculation — Crawler Agent and Analyst Agent. In this system the user needs to enroll and give some information to enable the system to create a profile. Once the system has the user's full name, a Crawler Agent will obtain more information about this user from the Internet, accessing the database CV-Lattes. The Crawler Agent retrieves information and an Analyst Agent parses the content and then calculates the RR based on the attribute values.

The model to represent user's opinion relevance can be applied to any scale of values. In this example of the model, the range for RR was a scale from [0-10], where 0 is the lowest and 10 is the highest relevance opinion.

3.1 Domain and Attributes

The domain of our example is academics from computer science, and we do not have only one area of interest for all users, but many different areas of interest to each user. The selected attributes used to calculate the RR in order to represent the relevance of a user's opinion to others in the example are extracted from CV-Lattes, parsed and analyzed. The Analyst Agent applied a text analyze, matching the extracted Academic Level with the predefined categories. All areas of interest and publications are extracted and the publications from each area were analyzed.

Selected qualitative Researchers' attributes from CV- Lattes applied in RR calculation: Academic Level/ AL (for each value of AL there is a specific weight: Undergraduate Student (1), Graduate (2), Specialist (3), Master Student (4), Master (5), Ph.D. Student (6), Ph.D. (9) and Postdoc (10)); Areas of Interest /AI (this is a list of all areas of interest cited by the researcher in his CV-Lattes.).

All quantitative production metrics (Publications in magazines or journals/PMJ, Papers published in events / PPE, Books and chapters published / BCP, Supervised students / SS, Examining committee / EC and Students advising / SA) are measure in units and should be normalized into a specific range. Equation (1) was applied in the normalization process, and the maximum value defined to each attribute was obtained using a sample of 50 curricula of computer science researchers from the CV-Lattes database. The minimum value defined to each attribute was zero. All these attributes have a different scale of values.

When we have applied the Equation (2) to calculate the RR, the weights attributed to AL, and to each production metric were AL=2.0, PMJ=2.5, PPE=1.5, BCP=2.5, SE=1.0, EC=0.3 and SA=0.2.

We should highlight some important information here; in our example there is a distinction in importance among international and national publications. This distinction comes from a predefined list proposed by Brazil's government. It presents a categorization about importance among magazines or journals, and conferences. In consequence of this list, we are working with different weights: 1) International publications in PMJ: there are categories A, B and C for publications, with the following weights A=3.0, B=2.0, C=1.0; 2) National publications: there are categories A, B and C, with the following weights for each category: A=2.0, B=1.5 and C=1.0. The same happens in other attributes as PPE.

We have made other necessary distinction in some production metrics as supervised students (SS) and students advising (SA). In these attributes we have done a distinction between supervised undergraduate and graduate students. We defined this classification and respective weights: PhD student = 5.0, Master student = 3.0, Undergraduate student = 1.0. It is applicable to SS and SA production metrics.

3.2 Applying the Model

Table 1 shows the production metrics (attributes) and respective values extracted from the CV-Lattes of 5 researchers (users), however, the attribute values are not normalized (NN) in the first column behind each production metric. The second column behind each production metric shows the attributes normalized (N) after applying Equation (1).

Finally, we have calculated the RR_{Total}, applying Equation (2) for all selected attributes and using the respective weights. Interpreting the final values, we can observe that U3's opinion is the most relevant opinion for the recommender system. In our example, we present the calculation of RR_{Total} by user, but the same calculation can be done to each user's area of interest. More information about the model to represent user's opinion relevance can be found in [1].

Table 1. Attribute values not normalized (NN)/normalized (N)

User	AL	PMJ		PPE		BCP		SS		EC		SA		RR_{Total}
		NN	N	NN	N	NN	N	NN	N	NN	N	NN	N	
U1	9	11	3.1	11	0.6	1	0.8	19	5.3	17	8.1	3	2	5.1
U2	9	21	6	32	2.1	8	6.7	22	6.1	21	10	10	6.7	8.9
U3	9	34	9.7	65	4.6	5	4.2	36	10	19	9	8	5.3	9.2
U4	0	13	3.7	34	2.3	8	6.7	25	6.9	0	0	0	0	5.9
U5	6	24	6.9	4	0.1	0	0	16	4.4	0	0	0	0	5.2

4 Conclusions and Future Work

This paper presents a complete model to represent the user's relevance opinion to a recommender system. The main idea in this work is to create conditions for people to easily receive recommendation of relevant material, based on the relevance of opinion of users who have participated in the formulation of the recommendation.

The experimental results suggest that the model is flexible and can be easily instanced for different domains, once the attributes and their weights can be changed.

The real benefit from the model is that, it can present how relevant the recommenders opinions are, and, doing so, we believe we can provide more information to stimulate the users "consumption".

Currently, the W-RECMAS started being applied in a controlled experiment by students and professors. The aim of this experiment is evaluate the users satisfaction with the recommendations based on user's relevance opinion.

References

1. Cazella, S.C.: W-RECMAS: a hybrid recommender system based on multi-agent system to academic paper recommendation. Technical Report, PPGC-UFRGS–2003-339, Federal University of Rio Grande do Sul, Porto Alegre, Brazil (2003)
2. Flake, G.W., Laurence, S., Giles, G.L.: Efficient identification of web communities. In: Proceedings of knowledge discovery in database, Boston, MA, USA (2000) 150- 160
3. Han, J., Kamber, M.: Data mining: concepts and techniques. Morgan Kaufmann Publishers, San Francisco, CA, USA (2001)
4. Schafer, J.B. et al.: E-Commerce Recommendation Applications. Data Mining and Knowledge Discovery, Vol. 5, Issue 1-2. Kluwer Academic Publishers, Hingham, MA, USA (2001) 115–153
5. Wærn, A.: User involvement in automatic filtering: an experimental study. User Modeling and User-Adapted Interaction, Vol. 14. Kluwer Academic Publishers, Netherlands (2004) 201-237

User- and Community-Adaptive Rewards Mechanism for Sustainable Online Community

Ran Cheng and Julita Vassileva

Computer Science Department, University of Saskatchewan,
Saskatoon, SK, S7N 5A9 Canada
{rac740, jiv}@cs.usask.ca

Abstract. Abundance of user contributions does not necessarily indicate sustainability of an online community. On the contrary, excessive contributions in the systems may result in "information overload" and user withdrawal. We propose an adaptive rewards mechanism aiming to restrict the quantity of the contributions, elicit contributions with higher quality and simultaneously inhibit inferior ones. The mechanism adapts to the users preferences with respect to types of contributions and to the current needs of the community depending on the time and the number of existing contributions.

1 Introduction

The proliferation of online communities (OCs) may lead designers and researchers to the conclusion that the development of custom-made communities for particular purpose is straightforward. Unfortunately, this is not the case. Although software providing basic community infrastructure is readily available, it is not enough to ensure that the community will "take off" and become self-sustainable. A critical mass of user participation is necessary. Besides, the quality of the resources shared by users is crucial to the sustainability of the community.

Developed at the MADMUC lab at University of Saskatchewan, Comtella is a small-scale OC for sharing academic papers and class-related web-articles among students. The initial problem encountered was the scarcity of the user participation and contributions since most users tended to free-ride instead of sharing new resources. To address the problem, we introduced a set of hierarchical memberships into the system to stimulate users to contribute [2, 3]. While the strategy was effective in increasing participation in terms of *quantity* of contributions, it led to a deteriorating *quality* of contributions, catalyzed "information overload" [7] in the system, and resulted in disappointment and withdrawal of some users.

Therefore, to make OCs more self-sustaining and long-lasting, a new mechanism is needed to measure and monitor the quality of user contributions, elicit the ones of high quality and restrict the overall number of contributions.

2 Related Works

It is not easy to measure the value of contribution impartially and accurately since quality measures are usually subjective. Centralized moderation is feasible only for

L. Ardissono, P. Brna, and A. Mitrovic (Eds.): UM 2005, LNAI 3538, pp. 332–336, 2005.

small and narrowly focused communities, where members have very similar evaluation criteria. Therefore, decentralized mechanisms for quality measurement are necessary. There are two kinds of such mechanisms – implicit and explicit – depending on how evaluation is elicited from users. An example of implicit social quality evaluation mechanism is the impact factor which counts how many times a paper has been cited by other researchers. In a similar way, one can measure the quality of a posting in an OC by counting the times it was viewed (clicked). However, this method is based on the assumption that people who view a resource hold a positive attitude to its quality, which is not always the case.

Another way of evaluating the quality of resources or comments is through explicit user ratings, as in the peer-reviewing process in academia or in OCs like Slashdot. Since the final ratings of resources are computed based on ratings from many users, they are more unbiased. However, a study of the Slashdot rating mechanism showed that some deserving comments may receive insufficient attention and end up with an unfair score, especially those that were contributed late in the discussion [5]. Therefore the timeliness of making a contribution is important and a motivational mechanism should encourage early contributions. The Slashdot study showed also that comments starting their life at a low initial rating have a lower chance to be viewed and rated and are therefore more likely to end up with unfair score. In Slashdot, the initial rating depends on the "karma" of the user who made the comment. The user's "karma" is a measure of reputation computed from the quality of the user's previous contributions. In this way, good comments made by new users or the users who haven't contributed highly rated comments so far tend not to receive a deserving attention and to collect sufficient ratings to raise the "karma" level of their contributor. This causes a feedback loop resulting in the Matthew effect [6].

An important problem in systems that rely on ratings is ensuring that there are enough ratings. The evaluation of an approach to motivate users to rate movies in MovieLens through sending them email-invitations showed that users seemed to be influenced more by personalized messages emphasizing the uniqueness of their contributions and by those that state a clear goal (e.g. number of movies the user should rate) [1]. It is interesting that personalization seems important and that setting specific goals are more persuasive than general appeals. However, this approach is questionable as a long-term solution since the effect of receiving email invitations will likely wear off.

3   Rewarding Users for Rating Papers

The Comtella rating mechanism is inspired from the Slashdot moderation system. In order to have a broader source of ratings, all the users can rate others' contributions by awarding them points (either +1 or -1). However, the users with higher membership levels receive more points to give out, which means they are more influential in the community. To ensure that contributions have equal chance initially to be read and rated, the initial rating for every new contribution is zero regardless of its providers' membership level or the quality of her previous contributions. In the end, the final rating for the contribution is the sum of all the ratings it has obtained.

The summative rating for each contribution is displayed in the list of search results, which can be sorted by the user and viewed as a "top 10" list of articles for any topic.

According to the reciprocation theory from social psychology [4], it is logical to motivate users to rate papers by rewarding them for this kind of actions. As an incentive for users to rate contributions, a virtual currency is introduced, called "*c-points*". A certain number of *c-points* are awarded to a user for rating papers, depending on her reputation of giving high-quality ratings. The earned *c-points* can be used to increase the initial visibility of the users' postings in the search result list. Most users desire that their new contributions appear in salient positions, e.g. in the first place or among the top 10, because in those positions they will have a better chance to be read and rated. The Comtella search facility displays all the contributions matching a query in a sorted list according to the number of *c-point* allocated by the contributor (Fig 1). Unlike the mechanism in Slashdot, it allows the user flexibility to invest *c-point* in a particular posting. Rating papers leads to immediate reward, which we believe will be a powerful incentive for the users.

Result: **<<Previous   Next>>   Total: 8 Page(s)**

Cpoint	Paper Title	Earned Ratings	My Rating	View Times	Fake?	Fake Coun
50+	Password selection	3	▾ Rate	11	Fake	0
40+	NETSPIONAGE COSTING BILLIONS - Internet Hacking	2	▾ Rate	13	Fake	0
30+	Face-off: Hiring a hacker	2	▾ Rate	11	Fake	0
30+	Liability for computer crime in Russia	-1	▾ Rate	1	Fake	0
20+	E-Crime to Rise in 2005	2	▾ Rate	9	Fake	0
20+	When the Hacker Is on the Inside	2	▾ Rate	4	Fake	0

Fig. 1. A segment of a search result list

4   Community Model, Individual Model and Adaptive Rewards

In our previous motivation mechanism [3], the comprehensive evaluation of a user's participation was based on the times of the user engaged in cooperative activities (e.g. sharing, rating, etc.) and the weights introduced to denote the importance of each kind of the activities. The users were classified into several levels of membership depending on the evaluation of their participation. The adaptive reward mechanism is introduced as an extension of our pervious work. The basic idea is to substitute the constant weights for the cooperative activities with varying weights adaptable to the users' individual status and the current needs of the community.

Fig.2 presents an overview of the mechanism. Community model is used to describe the current phase of the whole community. It includes the expected sum of user contributions for current topic (Q_c) and the community reward factor (F_c). For each week, a new discussion topic is introduced and Q_c is set by a community administrator for the new topic depending on the feature of the topic, users' spare time and energy, etc. F_c reflects the extent to which new contributions are useful for the whole community. It has its maximum value when a new topic discussion begins and decreases gradually with the time. After the middle of the discussion period, it decreases faster (Fig.3).

Each user has an individual model that contains the average quality of his/her previous contributions and ratings (C_I and R_I) and the data describing him/her current status. The expected number of contributions of each user (Q_I) is a fraction of Q_c. The users with higher C_I will get a larger Q_I. The individual reward factor (F_I) defines the extent to which the user's contributions are being rewarded. F_I has its maximum value as long as the number of the user's contributions is less than or equal to his/her Q_I. When the number exceeds the expectation, F_I drops to its one fourth suddenly and keeps decreasing with the increment of the users' contributions (Fig.4).

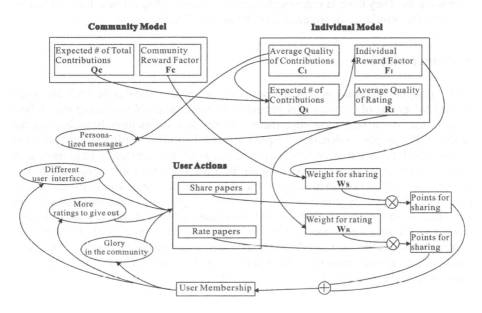

Fig. 2. An overview of adaptive motivational mechanism

Fig. 3. The change of the community reward factor (F_c)

Fig. 4. The change of the individual reward factor (F_I)

The adaptive weight for sharing resources (W_S) inherits the features of both reward factors, F_c and F_I. In this way, the user who shares many papers but does not pay enough regard to their quality gets a low C_I and a small Q_I and therefore, little reward for his/her subsequent contributions. Thus the personalized message to the user would be to contribute less in next period but improve the quality. On the other hand, if the user tends to share good resources in a small number, she obtains a high C_I and a large Q_I. Therefore, potentially she is able to earn more rewards by sharing resources. Therefore W_S is able to restrict the quantity of user contributions, inhibit low-quality ones, and stimulate users to share resources early in the discussion period, which fully exposes them to the quality control rating system.

The adaptive weight for giving ratings is proportional to the users' average quality of previous ratings (R_I). The users who have gained a good reputation in making ratings get higher weight for their subsequent ratings, which stimulates them to rate more papers. However, those with poor R_I will not get much reward for rating contributions. They have to improve the quality of their ratings to win their reputation back and this would be the suggestion of the personalized message.

5 Conclusions

While designing incentives into the software to ensure sustainable OCs has been recognized as one of the most challenging and important problems facing researchers in this area, to our best knowledge there are only few works directly addressing the problem. We propose a dynamic, adaptive mechanism for rewarding contributions in an OC which takes into account the current needs of the community (e.g. more new papers, versus more ratings, depending on the time since the topic is introduced and the current level of contributions) and the user's personal style of contributing (e.g. less but higher-quality contributions versus fewer but more mediocre ones). The hypothesis is that such a mechanism will stimulate users to contribute when and what is most useful for the community at the moment, thus achieving a level of activity that makes the community sustainable and avoids the "information overload" in OCs. Our study to test the effectiveness of the proposed mechanism is currently underway in a fourth year undergraduate class with 32 students.

References

1. Beenen, G., Ling, K., Wang, X., Chang, K., Frankowski, D., Resnick, P., Kraut, R. E.: Using Social Psychology to Motivate Contributions to Online Communities. Proceedings of CSCW, Chicago, Illinois, (2004)
2. Bretzke, H., Vassileva, J.: Motivating Cooperation in Peer to Peer Networks. User Modeling UM03, Johnstown, PA, Springer Verlag LNCS 2702, (2003) 218-227
3. Cheng, R., Vassileva, J.: User Motivation and Persuasion Strategy for P2P Communities. Proceedings HICSS'38 (Online Communities in Digital Economy), Hawaii, (2005)
4. Cialdini, R.B.: The Science of Persuasion. Scientific American, (2001) 76-81
5. Lampe, C., Resnick, P.: Slash(dot) and Burn: Distributed Moderation in a Large Online Conversation Space. Proceedings of CHI', Vienna, Austria, (2004)
6. Merton, R., Zuckerman, H. A.: The Matthew Effect in Science: the Reward and Communication Systems of Science are Considered. Science 199, 3810, (1968) 55-63
7. Shenk, D.: Data smog: Surviving the information glut. HarperCollins, New York, (1997)

Off-line Evaluation of Recommendation Functions

Tingshao Zhu[1], Russ Greiner[1], Gerald Häubl[2], Kevin Jewell[1], and Bob Price[1]

[1] Dept. of Computing Science, University of Alberta, Canada T6G 2E1
{tszhu, greiner, kjewell, price}@cs.ualberta.ca
[2] School of Business, University of Alberta, Canada T6G 2R6
Gerald.Haeubl@ualberta.ca

Abstract. This paper proposes a novel method for assessing the performance of any Web recommendation function (i.e., user model), M, used in a Web recommender sytem, based on an off-line computation using labeled session data. Each labeled session consists of a sequence of Web pages followed by a page $p^{(IC)}$ that contains information the user claims is relevant. We then apply M to produce a corresponding suggested page $p^{(S)}$. In general, we say that M is good if $p^{(S)}$ has content "similar" to the associated $p^{(IC)}$, based on the the same session. This paper defines a number of functions for estimating this $p^{(S)}$ to $p^{(IC)}$ similarity that can be used to evaluate any new models off-line, and provides empirical data to demonstrate that evaluations based on these similarity functions match our intuitions.

1 Introduction

While the World Wide Web contains a vast quantity of information, it is often time consuming and sometimes difficult for a Web user to locate the information she[1] finds relevant. This motivates the large body of research on ways to assist the user in finding relevant pages. There are, however, many Web user models that can generate recommendations, but how to evaluate their performance is a critical task. It is often costly, in terms of both time and finances, to evaluate such systems in user studies.

In this paper, we propose a novel method to evaluate the performance of these recommendation functions by an off-line computation. Our evaluation uses the data that we collected in a previous user study (Section 2). From this data, we developed several similarity functions that estimate the subject's evaluation of the suggested page. Our cross-validated empirical results verify that these similarity functions are good models of the user's judgment. Therefore, they can then be used to evaluate any new user models.

Section 1.1 discusses related work. Section 2 describes the "LILAC" user study that we conducted previously to acquire labeled session data. Section 3 outlines our ideas for how to identify these similarity functions, using this collected data.

1.1 Related Work

There is a great deal of research on generating recommendations for Web users. Some of these systems recommend pages either within a specified Web site [1], or based on

---

[1] We will use the female pronoun ("she", "her") when referring to users of either gender.

L. Ardissono, P. Brna, and A. Mitrovic (Eds.): UM 2005, LNAI 3538, pp. 337–341, 2005.

some specific hand-selected words [2]; while others seek useful pages from anywhere on the Web [9]. This paper introduces an off-line technique to evaluate such models. Below we summarize several alternative approaches, and discusses how they relate to our work.

Kobsa and Fink [3] simulate the workload to test the performance and scalability of the user model servers. In our research, we run the off-line evaluation by simulating the users' assessment, and focus on evaluating the relevance of recommended pages.

Weibelzahl and Weber [7] propose two methods to evaluate the accuracy of any predictive user model. However, their approach can only be applied to straightforward user models, which means it cannot be applied to the complex user models produced by machine learning algorithms. By contrast, our method can evaluate any user models.

Ortigosa and Carro [5, 6] describe how they infer evaluation by using some heuristics in an adaptive-course system. In our case, the evaluating functions have been verified by data from our user study, which indicate that they are consistent with the users' judgement.

2   User Study — LILAC

We developed a system, WebIC (Figure 1) that observes the user as she browses the Web, and in particular, records 35 different "browsing properties" of the words that appeared on these visited pages (e.g., for each word w, did the user tend to follow links anchored with w, or did the user "back out of" pages whose title included w, etc. [8]). WebIC then applies a trained classifer to these browsing properties, to identify which of these encountered words is "relevant" to the user's current information need; it then attempts to find pages that address these needs.

The challenge in the WebIC [8] research is finding a good classifer, for mapping the browsing properties of a word to a relevance score. To address this problem, we considered several models: the "Followed Hyperlink Word" (FHW) model as a baseline, and three "IC-models" trained from data, ICWord, ICQuery, and ICRelevant. Specifically, ICWord tries to identify the words will appear in the relevant page; ICQuery tries to identify the words that allow a search engine to locate the relevant page; and ICRelevant tries to predict the words explicitly selected by the user as being relevant.

We conducted a five-week user study, "LILAC" (Learn from the Internet: Log, Annotation, Content), both to learn the parameters for these IC-models, and also to evalu-

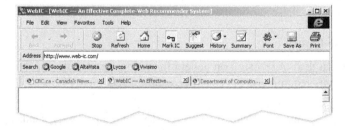

Fig. 1. WebIC — An Effective Complete-Web Recommender System

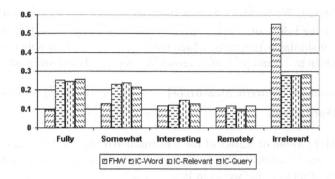

Fig. 2. Overall Results of the LILAC Study

ate their performance. During the study, each of the 100+ participants was required to install *WebIC* on their own computer and then browse their own choice of web pages.[2]

During her browsing, the user may push the "Suggest" button to ask *WebIC* to recommend a page, $p^{(S)}$. At other times, she may find a page $p^{(IC)}$ that satisfies her current information need. As part of this study, whenever she encounters such a page, she is asked to click the "MarkIC" button in the *WebIC* browser to indicate that this an "Information Content page" (i.e., "ICpage"). *WebIC* would then suggest an alternative page $p^{(S)}$ as chosen by one of the IC-models. In either case, whenever *WebIC* recommends a page, the user is then asked to characterize how well this suggested page satisfied her current information need: "*Fully* answered my question", "*Somewhat* relevant, but does not answer my question fully", "*Interesting*, but not so relevant", "*Remotely* related, but still in left field", or "*Irrelevant*, not related at all". Figure 2 shows the overall results of these evaluation responses; each bar show the relative percentage of one evaluation response for one model.

We ran the Wilcoxon test on each possible pair of models, which confirmed that each of our trained IC-models performed better than the baseline FHW model. These results confirm our basic assumption that we are able to provide useful recommendations by integrating the user's browsing behaviors into the prediction.

3   Off-line Evaluation

An effective "similarity function" $s(p_1, p_2)$, over a pair of Web pages, should return a large value iff p_1 and p_2 are similar in content. By definition the $p^{(IC)}$ found by the user satisfied her information need, as did any $p^{(S)}$ that was evaluated as "Fully". Therefore, we would expect $s(p^{(IC)}, p^{(S)})$ to return a large value iff $p^{(S)}$ was evaluated as a "Fully" page, and otherwise to return a small value.

The challenge is learning such a similarity function from the MarkIC data. Here, we only consider the two extreme kinds of suggested pages: "Fully" (S_+) and

---

[2] We requested they use only English language pages. We also provides ways to turn off the data capture part of *WebIC* when dealing with private information — e.g., email or banking.

"Irrelevant" (S_-). We basically want a function $s(\cdot, \cdot)$ that has a significant difference between the values of $s(p_i^{(IC)}, p_i^{(S_+)})$ and $s(p_i^{(IC)}, p_i^{(S_-)})$. Below we propose three different similarity functions, which use W_{IC} and W_S to denote respectively the bags of words in $p^{(IC)}$ and $p^{(S)}$, after removing stop words and stemming.

ITM: Information Theoretic Measure[4] $s_{ITM}(p^{(IC)}, p^{(S)}) = \frac{|W_{IC} \cap W_S|}{|W_{IC} \cup W_S|}$

Recall: ICWord Recall $s_{Rec}(p^{(IC)}, p^{(S)}) = \frac{|W_{IC} \cap W_S|}{|W_{IC}|}$

avRankTFIDF: Mean of Ranks of the Common Words' TFIDF (ranks all the words in an ICpage based on TFIDF weights, from the highest to the lowest, and returns the mean of ranks of the words in $W_{IC} \cap W_S$)

$$s_{Rank}(p^{(IC)}, p^{(S)}) = \frac{\sum_{w \in W_{IC} \cap W_S} \text{TFIDFRank}(w \in W_{IC})}{|W_{IC} \cap W_S|}$$

For each s we compute similarity scores using the collected sample sessions, and then perform the Mann-Whitney test to determine whether there is a significant difference between the "Fully" and "Irrelevant" cases. The results (Table 1) shows that the each of the similarity functions can detect a significant difference. For *avRankTFIDF*, the smaller the rank, the higher the similarity between pages.

Table 1. Mann-Whitney Test on Different Similarity Functions

	Hypothesis	Confidence Intervals	p
ITM	Fully>Irrelevant	>0.027	<0.0001
Recall	Fully>Irrelevant	>0.045	<0.0001
avRankTFIDF	Fully<Irrelevant	<-4.554	0.0055

3.1   Validating Similarity Functions on LILAC Data

Next, we analyzed these functions on the LILAC data without using any evaluation labels, to determine whether the results are consistent with our previous conclusions (Section 2), based on evaluation labels directly.

For around one-quarter of the MarkIC sessions, *WebIC* selected the baseline FHW model. The similarity between the user's ICpage $p^{(IC)}$ and this proposed $p^{(S_{FHW})}$ page can be computed using each of these similarity functions $s \in \{s_{ITM}, s_{Rec}, s_{Rank}\}$. We then identify three new recommended pages off-line, one using each of the IC-models (i.e., ICWord, ICRelevant, and ICQuery). We can compute the overall similarity $s(p^{(IC)}, p^{(S_\chi)})$ where $\chi \in \{ICW, ICR, ICQ\}$. Similarly, for each MarkIC session using any of the IC-models, we can also run the FHW model on the same session to produce a new recommended page $p^{(S_{FHW})}$, and then compute $s(p^{(IC)}, p^{(S_{FHW})})$.

To verify that the off-line evaluation can acheive the same conclusions as obtained previously (i.e., each IC-Model is better than FHW), we use the Wilcoxon test on the correlated samples, and view a p-value less than 0.05 as supporting each claim. Table 2 shows the p values of each hypothesis given a similarity function. This data indicates

Table 2. Wilcoxon Test on LILAC MarkIC Session Data using different similarity functions

Hypothesis →	FHW<ICWord	FHW<ICRelevant	FHW<ICQuery
ITM	<0.0001	0.0002	<0.0001
Recall	0.087	0.0213	0.003
avRankTFIDF	0.0057	<0.0001	<0.0001

that both the ITM and Rank (avRankTFIDF) functions can detect a significant difference between FHW and any of IC-Models, which is consistent with the overall results that were based on evaluations directly from LILAC.

4   Conclusion

We propose a novel method to assess the performance of Web user models off-line, which can infer the evaluation by an off-line computation. In particular, we can take advantage of the previously annotated Web logs in the LILAC study to evaluate any new user models. We have developed several similarity functions to approximate the subject's evaluation of the suggested page. By applying the similarity functions to the LILAC data, we find that the results based on these similarity functions are consistent with the evaluations made by the subjects directly in LILAC.

References

1. Agrawal, R., Srikant, R.: Fast algorithms for mining association rules. VLDB'94
2. Billsus, D., Pazzani, M.: A hybrid user model for news story classification. UM'99
3. Kobsa, A., Fink, J.: Performance evaluation of user modeling servers under real-world workload conditions. UM'03
4. Lin, D.: An information-theoretic definition of similarity. ICML'98
5. Ortigosa, A., Carro, R.: Agent-based support for continuous evaluation of e-courses. SCI 2002, Volume 2., Orlando, Florida (2002) 477–480
6. Ortigosa, A., Carro, R.: The continuous empirical evaluation approach: Evaluating adaptive web-based courses. UM'03 163–167
7. Weibelzahl, S., Weber, G.: Evaluating the inference mechanism of adaptive learning systems. UM'03
8. Zhu, T.: http://www.web-ic.com/.
9. Zhu, T., Greiner, R., Häubl, G.: An effective complete-web recommender system. WWW'03

Evaluating the Intrusion Cost of Recommending in Recommender Systems

Felix Hernandez-del-Olmo, Elena Gaudioso, and Jesus G. Boticario

Dpto. de Inteligencia Artificial, Universidad Nacional de Educacion a Distancia,
C/ Juan del Rosal 16, 28040 Madrid, Spain
{felixh, elena, jgb}@dia.uned.es

Abstract. Recommender systems suggest items, guiding the user in a personalized way in a large space of possible options. To accomplish this task, they should
try to bother users as less as possible, but each recommendation occupies expensive room in the always small user interface. Unfortunately, current evaluation
of recommender systems do not have into account this cost. This work presents
some new measures that have into account this intrusion cost while recommending. Some experiments are performed to compare our approach with traditional
ones.

1 Introduction

Adaptive recommender systems produce individualized recommendations of items [1].
In fact, the usual way to see this problem is that given a large set of items, a recommender must present a personalized *set of recommended* items to the user.

However, we could reformulate the problem as follows: given a large set of items,
a recommender must choose which of them must not be recommended. In fact, every
single recommendation presented to the user means a cost for her, because the recommendation must be read, or at least it occupies space that could be occupied by other
information, perhaps more interesting.

Unfortunately, current measures for evaluating recommenders do not have into account the intrusion cost of recommending. In this paper we show some new measures
which try to overcome this problem. Lets start recalling traditional evaluation of recommender systems.

From now on, in order to clarify the discussion which follows and without lost of
generality, we will consider alongside this paper that recommendations are composed
by a single recommended item. In that way, we will be able to focus on the intrusion
provoked by each recommendation without distracting with the (also hard) problem of
its size.

To compare the performance of recommender algorithms, usual measures have into
account the number of single recommendations that became useful or useless. Formally,
they use the so called *confusion matrix* depicted in table 1. Respectively, we define
$N = a + b + c + d$ as the total number of recommendation possibilities to be offered in
a whole session.

L. Ardissono, P. Brna, and A. Mitrovic (Eds.): UM 2005, LNAI 3538, pp. 342–346, 2005.
© Springer-Verlag Berlin Heidelberg 2005

Table 1. Confusion matrix of two classes when considering all recommended items of all recommendations. Diagonal numbers a and d count the *correct* predictions: recommend the item when it is to be followed (useful), do not recommend the item when it is to be not followed (useless). The rest of the numbers b and c count the *incorrect* predictions

	useful (u)	useless ($\neg u$)
recommend (r)	a	b
no recommend ($\neg r$)	c	d

Now, focusing on the evaluation measures, *information retrieval* is likely the parent of recommender systems field. Therefore, it is not strange evaluating recommenders by measures that come from that field. Most usual of them are:

$$Precision = \frac{a}{a+b}; \quad Recall = \frac{a}{a+c}; \quad F1 = \frac{2 \times Precision \times Recall}{Precision + Recall} \quad (1)$$

Examples of recommenders evaluated by those measures appear in [2].

Due to having more and more recommenders in which part of their user models are built by machine learning approaches, some measures from that field have appeared:

$$Accuracy = \frac{a+d}{N}; \quad MAE(Mean\ Absolute\ Error) = \frac{b+c}{N} \quad (2)$$

An example of recommenders evaluated by Accuracy is Syskill&Webert [3]. Recommenders evaluated by MAE are usually collaborative filtering approaches [4].

A big problem of the above traditional measures is that they do not account for the fact that the cost of bad recommendations (not followed) should be considered greater than not recommending at all. We will discuss it later (see section 3), now lets start introducing in the next section some new measures that consider good recommendations much better than not recommending, but also consider a bad recommendation a little worse than not recommending at all.

2   Measures to Account for Both the Efficiency and the Obtrusive Cost of Recommendations

In the last section we went over the current measures to evaluate recommenders. However, we claimed that none of those measures had into account the effort users made (intrusion) by *interacting* with a previous untrained recommender. We treat this problem throughout this section.

To this end, lets first start defining three quantities: r_+, r_-, and r_0. The first quantity (r_+) accounts for the positive fact that a previously recommended item is followed. The second quantity (r_-) accounts for the bothersome that each not followed recommended item has provoked. The third quantity (r_0) accounts for the cost of not recommending. Reader must notice that a trivial property these three quantities must pose is the next: $r_+ \geq r_0 \geq r_-$. In fact, the recommender system have to try recommending in order to get the optimum r_+. However, in the process, the recommender must notice that each bad recommendation is always a little worse (r_-) than not recommending at all (r_0).

Now, formally, we define the next measure:

Definition 1.

$$RG(Recommendation\ Gain) = r_+ \times a + r_- \times b + r_0 \times (c + d) \tag{3}$$

Unfortunately, recommendation gain or RG has the problem that only recommenders which have tried to offer the same number of recommendations (same N, see previous section) can be compared. So as to avoid the last problem, we introduce the next:

Definition 2.

$$ARG(Averaged\ RG) = \frac{r_+ \times a + r_- \times b + r_0 \times (c + d)}{N} \tag{4}$$

Now, in order to get a closer definition, we have assigned the next three values to the last three quantities: $(r_+, r_0, r_-) = (10, 0, -1)$. We have chosen those values because we believe they are near the general objectives of most recommenders. In fact, intuitively we can see that not recommending is the same as doing nothing and, because of that, it has no cost (= zero cost). However, acting has a cost: it means either a little worst than doing nothing (-1), if a bad recommendation is offered; or an order of magnitude better (10) than recommending bad, when a good recommendation is offered. Another way to see previous values is as follows: if we keep $ARG > 0$, it means we can stand a recommender that offers (on average) as much as ten bad single recommendations before offering a good single recommendation, *otherwise* $ARG \leq 0$: it would be better turn off the recommender.

Finally, if we go on considering $r_0 = 0$ as above, ARG range goes from r_- to r_+. But, we could prefer a measure whose range were mostly independent on those quantities and varied mostly from 0 to 1. Therefore, we define what follows:

Definition 3.

$$NARG(Normalized\ ARG) = \frac{r_+ \times a + r_- \times b}{N \times r_+} \tag{5}$$

Now, lets show how this measure works in a real application. The experiment will show further on that a good performance in traditional measures does not assure good performance in NARG, sometimes they even possess really conflicting properties.

Leaded by the objectives of the experiment, our recommender is only focused on recommending the best next content item to be visited in a web learning environment. There, only one item can be suggested per visited content item.

The machine learning algorithms used for testing the approach are three well known and used in the field of user modeling and machine learning: Naive Bayes, Nearest Neighbor, and C4.5. Also, we consider two extreme recommenders: "never recommend" and "always recommend". In figure 1, we show graphs which describe *Accuracy*, $F1$, and $NARG$ in every moment (visit) of the experiment. It must be noticed, on the first hand, that the most accurate recommenders are at the same time the less efficients in F1 and NARG. This fact will be discussed in the next section. On the other hand, it must be noticed the instability of F1 along the whole experiment. It can be better appreciated in the last graph where each mean derivate per measure is shown. However, the

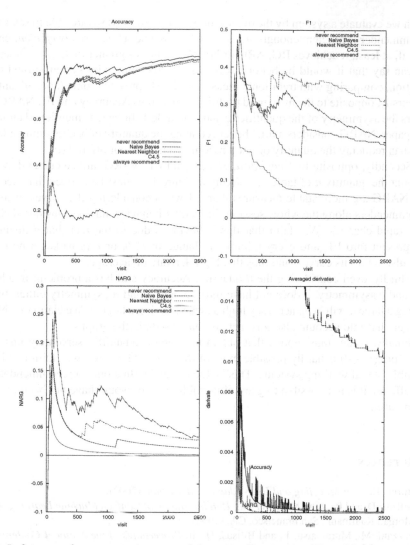

Fig. 1. Left top graph represents Accuracy, right top graph represents F1, and left bottom graph represents NARG. The last (right bottom graph) represents the average of the derivates of the last curves, a different average per measure

opposite happens in NARG or Accuracy measures, which after the visit 1000 are kept almost constant for most curves (derivate near 0). Lets conclude and discuss all these results in the next section.

3   Discussion

In this paper, we have introduced some new quantities: RG, ARG and NARG, which have into account the intrusion provoked by the recommender's interactions. Moreover, when we evaluate a system by those measures, (while $r_0 = 0$) we are able to say when a recommender is efficient enough. In fact, a recommender is *intrusively efficient* enough only if, at least, it achieves RG, ARG or NARG quantities greater than zero. Otherwise, we can say that it would be better not having the recommender system turned on. In addition, comparing with traditional measures, NARG presents some more advantages.

Firstly, opposite to the most used traditional measures Accuracy and F1, NARG considers the asymmetry of the quantities b and c of table 1. In fact, as mentioned alongside this paper, NARG considers a little better reducing the quantity of bad recommendations (b), than reducing the quantity of good recommendations not offered (c).

Secondly, opposite to *Precision*, *Recall* and F1, NARG and Accuracy have into account the quantity d of table 1. Looking at figure 1, it must be noticed that Accuracy and NARG are more stable measures than F1 when considering the curves of the five recommenders along the whole session. In fact, F1 behavior may be considered chaotic with rapid changes. We claim that this behavior is due to the fact that d quantity is not present into F1, and every minimum change in a, b, or c provokes a noticeable convulsion into its curves, and thus that high derivate on average.

Thirdly, even considering the d quantity, Accuracy still has a problem: in addition to b and c asymmetry, it does not have into account a and d asymmetry either. In fact, having a large d will keep accuracy high as when having a large a. We claim that NARG measure has into account also this fact, as can be seen in the graphs.

Finally, reader must notice that obtaining c and d quantities separately instead of their sum ($c + d$) is hardly possible most of the times. Moreover, we claim it is hardly possible in real working systems. This is due to the fact that once a recommendation is not offered, it is not possible to guess if it would have or would have not been followed by the user.

References

1. Burke, R. *User Modeling and User-Adapted Interaction* (2002).
2. Billsus, D. and Pazzani, M. J. In *Proc. 15th International Conf. on Machine Learning*, 46–54. Morgan Kaufmann, San Francisco, CA, (1998).
3. Pazzani, M., Muramatsu, J., and Billsus, D. In *Proceedings of the National Conference on Artificial Intelligence, Vol. 1*, 54–61, (1996).
4. Shardanand, U. and Maes, P. In *CHI'95: Proceedings of the Conference of Human Factors in Computing Systems*. ACM Press, (1995).

Introducing Prerequisite Relations in a Multi-layered Bayesian Student Model

C. Carmona, E. Millán, J.L. Pérez-de-la-Cruz,
M. Trella, and R. Conejo

Departamento de Lenguajes y Ciencias de la Computación, Universidad de Málaga
eva@lcc.uma.es

Abstract. In this paper we present an extension of a previously developed generic student model based on Bayesian Networks. A new layer has been added to the model to include prerequisite relationships. The need of this new layer is motivated from different points of view: in practice, this kind of relationships are very common in any educational setting, but also their use allows for improving efficiency of both adaptation mechanisms and the inference process. The new prerequisite layer has been evaluated using two different experiments: the first experiment uses a small toy example to show how the BN can emulate human reasoning in this context, while the second experiment with simulated students suggests that prerequisite relationships can improve the efficiency of the diagnosis process by allowing increased accuracy or reductions in the test length.

1 Introduction

In last years, much interest has been devoted to the development and use of user models based on Bayesian Networks (BNs). Successful examples can easily be found in research literature: in student modeling [4,7,9], for inferring user goals and needs [8], etc. All this research has shown that this probabilistic framework offers a theoretically sound methodology for accurate diagnosis in such contexts.

The main goal of our previous work on this field was the development of a generic Bayesian student knowledge model that a) could be used for any domain and b) included proposals to simplify the knowledge engineering effort required (parameters of the Bayesian network). First results in this field were described in [10]: an integrated approach for Bayesian student modeling. Later on, in this model was evaluated and proposed as the basis of computer adaptive testing based in Bayesian networks [11]. To this end, several adaptive criteria for item selection were defined and tested using simulated students. In this way, the integration of a probabilistic user model with adaptive item selection criteria was used to improve the accuracy and efficiency of the diagnosis process.

In parallel to this work, our research group was also working in the MEDEA project. MEDEA is a component-based architecture that allows the integration of different learning systems to be used intelligently for instruction. To achieve this task, MEDEA provides a built-in student model and an instructional planner. Learning components are integrated as web services following high-level pre-established protocols. Courses developed with MEDEA guide students in their learning process,

L. Ardissono, P. Brna, and A. Mitrovic (Eds.): UM 2005, LNAI 3538, pp. 347–356, 2005.

but allow them free navigation to better suit their learning needs. So it was natural to integrate our probabilistic generic student model into the MEDEA architecture.

However, there were several problems for this integration, being the most important that prerequisite relationship had been excluded from our theoretical model. In the next section, we will briefly present MEDEA's student model with special emphasis in the knowledge model. A short explanation of the reasons why this kind of relations were not considered in the first place will be provided, together with a discussion of why these relationships need to be included in the new model and how this can be achieved. The third section presents some preliminary evaluation results of the new prerequisite layer: a first qualitative experiment uses a small toy example to show how the BN prerequisite model can emulate human reasoning in this context, while a second experiment with simulated students is used to evaluate how the efficiency of the diagnosis process can be improved in accuracy and/or reductions of test lengths by using the new prerequisite layer. The paper concludes with some conclusions and future lines of research.

2   Building a Generic Student Model for MEDEA

As described in [2], MEDEA's student model is divided in two main sub-models: the *attitude model* and the *knowledge model*. The attitude model contains information such as preferred learning styles, motivation, learning goals, preferences and technical experience. This information used by the instructional planner to adjust some educational settings (for example, for students with low motivation, the way of teaching should be more interactive). But the focus of this paper is the knowledge model. As aforementioned, one of the main problems for the integration of our student model [9] into MEDEA was that it did not include prerequisite relationships. But the need for prerequisite relations was evident in the very first effort to validate the MEDEA architecture: the development of a web-based course for Logic. When the teacher on Logic built the domain model, he used *aggregation* (is_a, is_part_of) and *prerequisite* relationships, which he represented in separate graphs for better legibility. Fig 1. shows parts of such graphs:

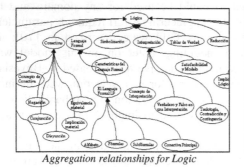
Aggregation relationships for Logic

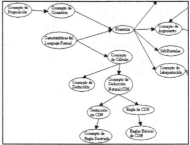
Prerequisite relationships for Logic

Fig. 1. Parts of the graphs for aggregation and prerequisite relationships for the Logic course

Aggregation and prerequisite relationships are very commonly used in educational settings (real or virtual). Fig. 2 shows an example of a domain model of a course divided in topics, subtopics and atomic concepts (modeled by a BN). Nodes in this network represent *Knowledge items* (KIs), while links are represented by light arrows for aggregation relationships, and bold arrows for prerequisite relationships.

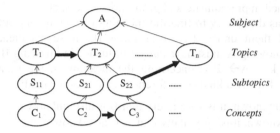

Fig. 2. Graph for relationships between the Kis

One of the main reasons for disregarding prerequisite relationships when building our integrated knowledge student model was that, if they are introduced in the model together with the aggregation relationships, the meaning of the relations between nodes becomes somehow unclear and the specification of the parameters gets more difficult. For example, in the above network, for node T_2 the parameters needed are the conditional probabilities $P(T_2/T_1,S_{21},S_{22})$. But the fact of different types of relationships are mixed in the conditioning distribution makes this probability difficult to estimate, and even in some cases it seems that the meaning of such events is unclear (for example, we would need to provide the probability of knowing a topic T_2 given that its parts S_{21} and S_{22} are *known* but its prerequisite T_1 is *unknown*).

But obviously, prerequisite relationships are useful when modelling a domain: not only they serve as guide for important instructional actions (adequate curriculum sequencing, selection of the instructional focus, generation of tailored exercises, etc.) but also they provide useful information about the student's knowledge state.

So once the need for including such relations in the model was disclosed, we had to find a way to include them in our model. Due to the problems aforementioned with combining the two kinds of relations (meaning of the causal relationships and difficulty of parameter specification), and, consistently with human way of simplifying the representation of structured knowledge by using separate graphs (as our teacher on Logic did), we decided to adopt a multi-layered approach similar to the described in other works [12]. The proposed knowledge student model for MEDEA is an overlay multi-layered model with four different layers: (a) *estimated layer*, that stores the information based on the student behavior during the instruction (pages visited, time in each page, etc.); (b) *assessed layer*, that contains the information inferred using the assessment components (e.g. SIETTE[1]); (c) *infered_by_prerequisite layer*, that is a BN that represents prerequisite relationships and (d) *inferred_ by_ granularity layer*, that is a BN that represents aggregation relationships.

---

[1] SIETTE [5] is an adaptive web-based testing tool based on IRT that can be used independently or integrated in a learning environment. By means of web services, SIETTE has been integrated in the MEDEA architecture to serve as a powerful diagnosis tool for student modeling.

In MEDEA, the instructional planner uses the information contained in such layers to take instructional decisions, so for example the planner calls to an assessment component whenever a significant difference between values stored in the estimated and assessed layers exist; or the planner selects the next concept to be taught using the information contained in prerequisite and granularity layers, etc.

Our next step was then to try to find the meaning of prerequisite relationships and the way to model them under the BN framework. It seems clear that if A is prerequisite of B, knowing A must have causal influence in knowing B, so the correct direction of the link is A$\rightarrow$ B. Concerning the meaning of the relation, if A is a prerequisite of B, at least two kinds of inferences can be performed:

- If A is unknown, it is very likely that B is also unknown.
- If B is known, it is very likely that A is also known[2].

But if A is known, we do not have any idea about the probability of B being known. Fig. 3 represents then this kind of relationship as a BN.

$$P(A) \qquad P(B/A)$$

Fig. 3. BN for a prerequisite relationship

Regarding the conditional distribution (parameters) needed, we thought that, it was sensible to assume that $P(+b/\neg a)=0+\varepsilon$ (the weaker the prerequisite relationship, the bigger the ε). For $P(+b/+a)$, we decided to use estimations based on the difficulty as supplied by the course designer: for each KI, a linguistic value (low, medium, high) is given and then internally converted into a probability d, which represents the intrinsic difficulty of the KI (given that all its prerequisites are known). This model can be easily extended for the case of a set of two or more prerequisite nodes by modifying the traditional noisy AND/OR gates (depending on whether all the prerequisites of the KI are needed or there are alternative ways of getting to know it): instead of using 1-ε we use the probability value d associated to the KI.

Let us then describe how the BNs for the aggregation and prerequisite layers have been defined: each elementary concept node C_i can take two values: *known* (represented by 1) and *not_known* (represented by 0), while for aggregated nodes (subtopics, topics, subject, etc), we use discrete random variables whose behavior will be emulated by binary nodes (*known*, *not_known*)[3]. The conditional probabilities for the aggregation and prerequisite BNs parameters are estimated in our model by pre-defined functions that use some features specified by the course designer, which namely are: *difficulty degrees* for each KI (that, as explained before, will be converted into probabilities d that represent their intrinsic difficulty, i.e, the probability of knowing the KI given that all its prerequisites are known) and *normalized weights* w_{ij} for aggregation relationships between two knowledge items K_i and K_j. From this

---

2   And this is the kind of information that would be of interest when using prerequisite relations to diagnose student's state of knowledge.

3   This emulation is possible because, as explained in [11], the probability of knowing a KI can be interpreted as the degree of knowledge reached in such KI.

information, an estimation of the parameters needed for the BNs of each layer is done as follows:

- For aggregation relationships, the following formula is used:

$$P(K_i = y/K_1 = x_1,...,K_k = x_k) = \begin{cases} 1 & \text{if } y = w_{1_i}x_1 + ... + w_{k_i}x_k \\ 0 & \text{otherwise} \end{cases}$$

- For prerequisite relationships, the following formulas are used:

$$P(K_i = 1/K_1 = x_1,...,K_k = x_k) = \begin{cases} d & \text{if } x_1 = ... = x_k = 1 \\ 0+\varepsilon & \text{otherwise} \end{cases} \quad \begin{array}{l}\text{(Modified noisy} \\ \text{AND-}gate)\end{array}$$

$$P(K_i = 1/K_1 = x_1,...,K_k = x_k) = \begin{cases} 0+\varepsilon & \text{if } x_1 = ... = x_k = 0 \\ d & \text{otherwise} \end{cases} \quad \begin{array}{l}\text{(Modified noisy} \\ \text{OR-gate)}\end{array}$$

3 Evaluation of the Prerequisite Model

When evaluating adaptive systems, it is important to separate the evaluation of the accuracy of the user model from the evaluation of the efficacy of the adaptations based on such user models [1]. In this way, possible inefficiencies are more easily isolated and identified and weakest points can be improved. This section presents a preliminary evaluation of the performance of the new prerequisite layer (the aggregation layer had previously been evaluated with satisfactory results [11]). This evaluation should be considered as an evaluation of the accuracy of the student model. To this end, two experiments have been performed: the first one is based on the use of a small toy example to study from a qualitative point of view the reasoning process in the prerequisite BN, while the second one aims to explore how the use of the prerequisite layer can improve the efficiency of the diagnosis process.

Experiment 1: A Small Toy Example
For a first informal evaluation of the performance of this approach, we used a small toy example (originally presented in [6], a previous study about prerequisite relations) about finding the Least Common Multiple (LCM). Fig. 4 shows a BN for such domain, which is an adaptation of the original undirected graph (arcs are directed).

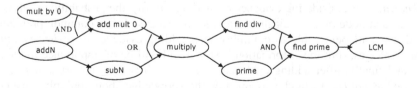

Fig. 4. BN for finding the LCM. Adapted from [6]

Each node in this network is binary and takes values *known* (1) and *not_known* (0); *addN/subN* to add/substract natural numbers, *mult*, multiply, and so on. Node *add mult 0* is an intermediate node that summarizes the abilities contained in its parent nodes. Regarding the parameters, we have used the following values:

- $P(addN = 1) = 0.8$

- $P(mult\ by\ 0 = 1) = 0.9$

- $P(add\ mult\ 0 = 1/\ addN, mult\ 0) = \begin{cases} 0.9 & \text{if } addN = mult\ 0 = 1 \\ 0 & \text{otherwise} \end{cases}$

- $P(mult = 1/\ add\ mult\ 0, subN) = \begin{cases} 0 & \text{if } add\ mult = 0 = subN = 0 \\ 0.7 & \text{otherwise} \end{cases}$

- $P(find\ prime = 1/\ find\ div, prime) = \begin{cases} 0.8 & \text{if } addN = mult\ 0 = 1 \\ 0 & \text{otherwise} \end{cases}$

- $P(prime = 1/\ multiply = 1) = 0.8$
- $P(prime = 1/\ multiply = 0) = 0$

- $P(find\ div = 1/\ multiply = 1) = 0.6$
- $P(find\ div = 1/\ multiply = 0) = 0$

- $P(LCM = 1/\ find\ prime = 1) = 0.8$
- $P(LCM = 1/\ find\ prime = 0) = 0$

- $P(sub\ N = 1/\ addN = 1) = 0.8$
- $P(subN = 1/\ addN = 0) = 0$

The set of evidences that were introduced in this network was also taken from [6] and is shown in Table 1, together with the evolution of the probabilities (of knowing the knowledge items). New evidences introduced are marked as "new ev", former evidences as "ev", arrows are used to mark if the probability has increased or decreased after considering the evidence and nodes that have already been diagnosed (one of its two values has reached probability 1) are marked as *known* or *not_ known*:

Table 1. Results of the inference as new evidence is added to the BN

	Initial state	e_1		e_2		e_3		e_4	
addN	0.8	0.704	↓	1	known	1	known	1	known
Mult by 0	0.9	0.892	↓	0.917	↑	0.917	=	0	new ev
subN	0.64	0.548	↓	0.832	↑	0.832	=	1	known
add mult 0	0.648	0.555	↓	0.842	↑	0.842	=	0	not_known
mult	0.539	0.318	↓	1	new ev	1	ev	1	ev
find div	0.667	0	new ev	0	ev	0	ev	0	ev
prime	0.431	0.255	↓	0.8	↑	1	new ev	1	ev
find prime	0.207	0	not_known	0	not_known	0	not_known	0	not_known
LCM	0.165	0	not_known	0	not_known	0	not_known	0	not_known

Results show that the use of a BNs and the modified noisy AND/OR gates allows to emulate human way of reasoning as described in [6]: after considering evidence e_1 (*find div* is *not_known*), the probability of knowing the rest of the nodes decreases and the nodes from which *find div* is a prerequisite (*find prime* and *LCM*) are diagnosed as *not_known*; after considering evidence e_2 (*mult* is *known*), the probability of all nodes increases and node *addN* is diagnosed as *known* (because it is a common prerequisite in both ways of being able to multiply); after adding evidence e_3 (*prime* is *known*) nothing changes, (but this information is stored and will be of importance in the next step), and finally, after adding evidence e_4 (*mult* by 0 is *not_known*), *add mult 0* is diagnosed as *not known* (and consequently, the knowledge about multiply must come from the other node in the modified OR-gate, so *subbN* is diagnosed as *known*).

So this small example suggests that a) prerequisite relationships can be very useful for efficiently diagnosing student's state of knowledge, because, as stated in [6], they can be used for adapting the items posed to a student so items too difficult or too easy are avoided; b) the BN framework is very suitable for emulating human's way of reasoning in such context.

Experiment 2: Using the Prerequisite Layer to Improve Diagnosis

In this section we present an empirical study with simulated students that was conducted to evaluate whether or not the use of the prerequisite layer could improve the diagnosis process. Next we present the conditions of this study together with the results obtained.

In the simulations, we used the same trial network that in our previous work [11], that consists in fourteen concepts and one hundred questions. Concepts are grouped using their intrinsic probability of being known (d) as a measure of their difficulty: C_1 to C_6 are *easy* ($d = 0.75$); C_7 to C_{10} are *medium*, ($d = 0.5$); and C_{11} to C_{14} are *difficult*, ($d = 0.25$). Each question is related with one to three concepts and each concept is related to several questions. Each question has six possible answers, and therefore a common guessing factor of 1/6. There are four different groups of twenty-five questions each, with different slips and discriminations factors (parameters that are used to determine the probability of a correct answer given the knowledge state of its related concepts, see [11] for more details).

A prerequisite relationship structure between concepts has been created for this trial network and is shown in Fig. 5. The parameters of this network are: for the nodes without parents, their prior probabilities; for the rest, the conditional probabilities required are computed using the formulas presented in section 2.

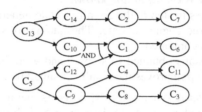

Fig. 5. Prerequisite BN defined for the trial network

Obviously, when prerequisite relationships are introduced in the model the difficulty of the KIs changes, because if for example an easy concept has several difficult concepts as prerequisites, the concept is not easy anymore. But the use of the BN allows taking this fact into account easily, because once the prerequisite BN is initialized, a prior probability r for each concept is computed. This number represents then the total difficulty of the KIs, as it is a function of its intrinsic difficulty d and the intrinsic difficulty of its prerequisite KIs. These values are then used in our approach to re-classify the concepts into categories: *easy* if $0.7 \leq r \leq 1$; *medium* if $0.3 < r \leq 0.7$; and *difficult* if $0.3 < r \leq 0$. So for example, in our experiment, after considering the prerequisite relationships, only C_5 resulted to be *easy*, C_9 and C_{12} were *medium* and the rest of the concepts *difficult*. This re-categorization of concepts has been considered also when generating the simulated students. Four categories of simulated students have been generated: *novice, intermediate, good* and *expert,* determined according to the number of concepts known and their total difficulty r.

The experiment with simulated students is described next:

1. *Random generation of simulated students* (45 of each type, making a total of 180) taking into account the total difficulty r of the concepts and consistently with prerequisite relationships.

2. *Selection of a test item to be asked.* An item is randomly[4] selected.
3. *Simulation of the student's answer.* Let Q be an item (question) node. Let $p=P(Q/Pa(Q))$. A random k number in $[0,1]$ is generated. If $k \leq p$, then the answer is correct ($Q=1$) and incorrect ($Q=0$) otherwise.
4. *Updating the probabilities.* For each C_i, $p_i=P(C_i/Q=q)$ is computed, being q the value taken by Q in the previous step (0 or 1).
5. *Stopping criterion.* As termination criterion a combination of two criteria is used: the test finishes when a previously fixed maximum number of questions is reached (in this experiment this value is 60), or when all the concepts have been evaluated. To determine whether a concept has been evaluated, a fixed threshold u is used (in this experiment, 0.2). If the probability of knowing a concept is greater than or equal to 1-u, then the concept is diagnosed as *known*, whereas if it is smaller than u, the concept is diagnosed as *not_known*. The rest are considered *not-diagnosed*.
6. *Test results.* The cognitive state generated in the previous step is compared to the true cognitive state. The number of correctly/incorrectly/not-diagnosed concepts is computed.
7. *Adding evidences.* The concepts evaluated as *known* or *not_known* in the test are introduced as evidences in the prerequisite BN. The idea is to propagate this information in the network, so we concepts that have not been diagnosed yet can be correctly classified as *known* or *not_known*.
8. *Prerequisite results.* As in step 6, the cognitive state generated in the previous step is compared to the true cognitive state. The number of correctly/incorrectly/not-diagnosed concepts is computed.
9. *Final results.* The results obtained in steps 6 and 9 are compared to see how the prerequisite relationship improves the results obtained by the test.

Steps 1 to 6 are similar to our former experiments, being the main differences: a) concepts are re-categorized according to their prior probability r of being known and b) only valid (i.e., complying with prerequisite relationships) knowledge states for simulated students are generated. Steps 7 to 9 are new and account for prerequisite relationships with the goal to improve diagnosis. The results of this new experiment are shown in

Table **2**, that presents percentages of correctly, incorrectly and not-diagnosed concepts for each of the fourteen concepts in the network (results of step 6 and 8, respectively). Overall results are also presented in the last row of the table.

The results show how the number of not-diagnosed concepts decreases, and most of them are diagnosed correctly. The best results are obtained for concepts C_{10} and C_{14}, which increase the correct percentage in 14.44 % and 20% respectively. In some cases, the number of incorrectly diagnosed concepts increases, but always in smaller proportion that the number of correct diagnosis. Overall, using prerequisites reduces the number of non-diagnosed concepts in 6.27 %, (i.e, more than two thirds of undiagnosed concepts are diagnosed) and, from them, 81.65% are correctly classified. These results supports the conclusion presented in [6]: "not considering valid prerequisites relationships does not lead to a wrong assessment of a student's knowledge state, but it renders the assessment less efficient in the sense that more answers than necessary have to be collected". Probably, the undiagnosed nodes only

---

[4] Adaptive item selection criteria could be used, but this was not the purpose of this study.

needed a few more items to be diagnosed, but, exploiting the prerequisite structure, we can further assess student's knowledge state without needing any more items.

Table 2. Correct/incorrect/not-diagnosed concepts (in %) before/after using the prerequisite BN

	BEFORE PREREQUISITES			AFTER PREREQUISITES		
	Correct	Incorrect	Not diagnosed	Correct	Incorrect	Not diagnosed
C_1	95,00	1,11	3,89	97,78	1,67	0,56
C_2	91,11	1,11	7,78	97,22	2,78	0,00
C_3	96,67	1,11	2,22	98,89	0,56	0,56
C_4	95,00	2,22	2,78	97,22	2,22	0,56
C_5	93,33	2,22	4,44	93,89	2,22	3,89
C_6	97,78	0,00	2,22	99,44	0,56	0,00
C_7	96,11	0,00	3,89	100,00	0,00	0,00
C_8	83,89	0,00	16,11	91,67	1,11	7,22
C_9	96,11	1,67	2,22	96,67	2,78	0,56
C_{10}	71,67	2,78	25,56	86,11	7,78	6,11
C_{11}	90,56	1,11	8,33	97,22	1,67	1,11
C_{12}	75,56	3,89	20,00	78,33	4,44	17,22
C_{13}	98,33	1,11	0,00	98,33	1,11	0,00
C_{14}	68,89	1,11	30,00	88,89	6,67	4,44
OVERALL	89.29	1.43	9.29	94.40	2.58	3.02

The next issue to be studied now is: how many questions are needed to reach a performance comparable to the model without prerequisites?. Table 3 shows the results of an analogous experiment in which the number of questions was reduced:

Table 3. Results with reduced test lengths

	BEFORE PREREQUISITES (60 ITEMS)	AFTER PREREQUISITES (40 ITEMS)	AFTER PREREQUISITES (50 ITEMS)
Correct	89.29	91.39	93.49
Incorrect	1.43	4.05	3.41
Not-diagnosed	9.29	3.02	3.10

We can see that using only 40 questions there are more correctly diagnosed concepts, but the number of incorrectly diagnosed concepts also increases in a very similar proportion. However, after 50 questions the percentage of correctly classified concepts increases in a bigger proportion than the incorrectly classified. So the answer in this case depends on a compromise between the reduction of the test length and the number of incorrectly diagnosed concepts that we are willing to admit, but in any case the results show that the number of questions can be reduced significantly with a similar performance of the diagnosis algorithm.

4 Conclusions and Future Work

The work presented in this paper builds upon our previous research on the field of Bayesian student modeling, in which an integrated generic student model based BNs was developed. To put this model into practice within the MEDEA architecture, we needed to find a way of adding prerequisite relationships to our model without increasing the knowledge engineering effort required. An informal first experiment was conducted to test the validity of the approach, using an existing toy example (about a prerequisite structure for finding the least common multiple) to show that the use of the defined BN allows emulating human's way of reasoning in this context. A second experiment with simulated students was then performed to see how the use of prerequisite relationships could improve the accuracy and efficiency of the diagnosis process, yielding satisfactory results.

Future lines of research include: a) improvements in the student model, like for example allowing the definition of different degrees of strength for prerequisite relationships (some ideas have already been presented in [2]), or the combination of this new model with adaptive item selection criteria and b) uses of such model, which opens up a broad research field within the MEDEA project.

References

[1] Brusilovsky, P., Karagianidis, C., Sampson, D. The benefits of layered evaluation of adaptive applications and services. Proceedings of the UM 2001 workshop on Empirical Evaluation of Adaptive Systems. Pedagogical Univ. of Freiburg (2001) 1-8

[2] Carmona, C., Conejo, R. A Learner Model in a Distributed Environment. LNCS 3137, Springer Verlag (2004) 353-359

[3] Conati C., Gertner. A., VanLehn, K. Using Bayesian Networks to Manage Uncertainty in Student Modeling. User Modeling and User-Adapted Interaction, 12(4), (2002) 371-417

[4] Conejo, R., Guzmán, E., Millán, E., Pérez, J. L., Trella, M. SIETTE: A Web-Based Tool for Adaptive Testing. International Journal of Artificial Intelligence in Education, 14(1), (2004) 29-61

[5] Dowling, C. E., Hockemeyer, C., Ludwig, A.H. Adaptive Assessment and Training Using the Neighborhood of Knowledge States. In LNCS 1086, Springer Verlag (1996) 578-585

[6] Henze, N., Nedjl, W. Student Modeling for the KBS Hyperbook System using Bayesian Networks. Technical report, University of Hannover (1998)

[7] Horvitz, E., Breese, J., Heckerman, D., Hovel, D., Rommelse, K. The Lumière Project: Bayesian User Modeling for Inferring the Goals and Needs of Software Users. Proceedings of UAI'98, Morgan Kauffman (1998) 256-265

[8] Mayo, M., Mitrovic, A. Using a Probabilistic Student Model to Control Problem Difficulty. In LNCS 1839, Springer Verlag (2000) 525-533

[9] Millán, E., Pérez-de-la-Cruz, J. L., Suárez, E. An Adaptive Bayesian Network for Multilevel Student Modeling. In LNCS 1839, Springer Verlag (2000) 534-543

[10] Millán, E., Pérez-de-la-Cruz, J. L. A Bayesian Diagnostic Algorithm for Student Modeling. User Modeling and User-Adapted Interaction, 12, (2002) 281-330

[11] Vassileva, J., McCalla, G., Greer, J. Multi-Agent Multi-User Modeling in I-Help. User Modeling and User-Adapted Interaction, 12, (2003) 179-210

Exploring Eye Tracking to Increase Bandwidth in User Modeling

Cristina Conati, Christina Merten, Kasia Muldner, and David Ternes

Department of Computer Science, University of British Columbia,
2366 Main Mall, Vancouver, BC, V6T1Z4, Canada
{conati, merten, kmuldner, ternes}@cs.ubc.ca

Abstract. The accuracy of a user model usually depends on the amount and quality of information available on the user's states of interest. An eye-tracker provides data detailing where a user is looking during interaction with the system. In this paper we present a study to explore how this information can improve the performance of a model designed to assess the user's tendency to engage in a meta-cognitive behavior known as self-explanation.

1 Introduction

One of the key dimensions that characterizes a user modeling problem is *model bandwidth* [15], i.e., the amount and quality of information available to the model to assess the user's states of interest (e.g., knowledge, goals, emotions). If a model assesses a user's task performance (or a user's *final states*, following the classification in [15]), high bandwidth is already achieved through information on task-related interface actions. However, if the model must assess the higher level *mental states* underlying a given behavior, high bandwidth requires explicit information on these states, which are seldom fully observable. In this case, bandwidth can be increased through interface mechanisms that force the user to make the states of interest explicit (e.g., by showing all the steps used to generate a problem solution). Unfortunately, this approach has the potential to be highly intrusive.

In this paper, we present research on exploring eye tracking as a means to unobtrusively raise bandwidth in user models. In particular, we discuss findings from a user study that explores the usage of users' gaze patterns to understand whether students engage in a meta-cognitive behavior known as *self-explanation* [4], during interaction with an Intelligent Learning Environment for mathematical functions.

Retrospective analysis of eye movements has been long used in Cognitive Psychology as a tool to help understand both motor and cognitive processes (e.g., [9]), as well as in HCI for off-line interface evaluation (e.g., [8]). There has also been fairly extensive research in using eye gaze as an alternative form of input to allow a user to explicitly operate an interface (e.g., [8, 11]).

There is a much smaller body of work on real-time processing of a user's gaze to interpret a user's behavior beyond interface operation to enable on-line adaptation of the interaction. Some of this work uses gaze tracking to help assess user *final states*, such as reading performance in a system for automatic reading remediation [13], or *what* task a user is performing independently from the underlying application (e.g.,

L. Ardissono, P. Brna, and A. Mitrovic (Eds.): UM 2005, LNAI 3538, pp. 357–366, 2005.

reading email vs. reading a web page) [14]. Others have explored using gaze data to assess user *mental states* such as *interest* in various elements of an interactive story [7], or *problem-solving strategies* in a tutoring system for algebra [6]).

Our work extends this body of research by exploring if and how eye tracking can help assess *mental states* related to the meta-cognitive, domain-independent skill of *self-explanation*. Self-explanation is the process of explaining to oneself a piece of instructional material, and has been shown to greatly improve learning [4]. It has also been shown that many students tend to not self-explain spontaneously. For this reason, there has been increasing interest in devising computer-based tools that can help students self-explain. The support provided by most of these tools, however, is not based on an explicit model of a student's self-explanation behavior. The Geometry Explanation Tutor prompts students to self-explain *every* problem-solving step in an Intelligent Learning Environment (ILE) for geometry [1]. Normit-SE prompts students to self-explain every *new* or *incorrect* problem-solving step in an ILE for data normalization [10]. This approach is potentially intrusive, since it may force spontaneous self-explainers to produce redundant and unnecessary self-explanations. In contrast, [5] proposes a framework that provides individualized support for self-explanation based on an explicit model of a student's self-explanation needs. The model uses information on both student knowledge and reading patterns to assess self-explanation during example studying in the domain of Newtonian physics. Reading patterns are tracked via a *poor-man-eye-tracker* interface that forces students to explicitly uncover the various parts of the studied example via mouse movements.

We have been working on a similar model of self-explanation to aid the assessment of the effectiveness of student *exploratory* behavior and consequent learning in the Adaptive Coach for Exploration (ACE) [2, 3]. ACE is an ILE designed to help students learn about mathematical functions through free exploration of interactive simulations, rather than through more traditional problem solving activities. Like [5], ACE could benefit from information on student attention patterns to more reliably assess whether a student is self-explaining the phenomena observed in the interactive simulations. However, because of the nature of the interaction, i.e. unconstrained exploration, we felt that it would be too intrusive to use a poor-man-eye-tracker mechanism to track user attention. Thus, we are exploring the usage of real-time eye-tracker data to inform our model. In the rest of the paper, we first describe ACE. We then provide a high level description of the ACE student model. Next, we illustrate a user study that we have conducted to understand what information an eye-tracker can provide about a student's self-explanation behavior. Finally, we discuss the implications of our findings.

2   The ACE Open Learning Environment

ACE is an adaptive open learning environment for the domain of mathematical functions. Open learning environments rely on the assumption that if a learner can freely explore the instructional material, she can acquire a deeper understanding of the target domain. However, various studies have shown that not all students can explore effectively on their own (e.g., [12]). Thus, ACE provides activities for students to freely explore mathematical functions, tracks their exploratory behavior and provides tailored suggestions to improve this behavior when needed.

ACE's activities are divided into units, which are collections of exercises. Figure 1 shows the main interaction window for the Plot Unit. We will focus on this unit throughout the paper because it is the most relevant to the eye tracker research presented in later sections. In the Plot Unit, a learner can explore the relationship between a function's graph and equation by moving the graph in the Cartesian plane and observing how that affects the equation (displayed below the graph area). The student can also change the equation parameters and see how these affect the graph.

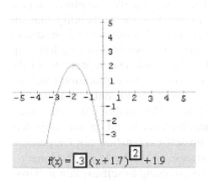

Fig. 1. The Plot Unit

All student interface actions are used to update the ACE student model, designed to assess if a student is exploring and learning effectively or if she needs help from ACE. For more detail on ACE's interface and coaching component see [2]. In the next subsection, we describe the high level structure of the ACE student model, and the components that allow the model to assess self-explanation behavior.

2.1 The ACE Student Model

ACE's student model uses a Dynamic Bayesian Network to assess the effectiveness of a student's exploratory behavior in ACE. The main source of evidence in the model comes from observing students perform *Relevant Exploration Cases* in an exercise (e.g., changing the position of a function graph in the Plot Unit, so that it has a *positive intercept* with the x-axis; changing the equation so that it has an *even exponent*). Evidence of these cases is then propagated in the model, together with the current assessment of relevant student knowledge, to assess higher level dimensions of student exploration, such as exploration of exercises and of general domain concepts (e.g., the input/output relation for different types of functions) [2].

For a student to effectively explore a case, she must both perform an action and self-explain changes that it generates in the environment [3]. Thus, the ACE student model includes self-explanation as one of the factors that influence the assessment of student exploration.

2.2 Assessing Self-explanation in the ACE Student Model

Assessing whether a student is spontaneously self-explaining is a typical user modeling problem in which it is hard to achieve high bandwidth, unless we ask students to explicitly input their self-explanation in the system. Doing so, however, can be intrusive and annoying for those students who can self-explain on their own. The alternative is to gather information from sources that may provide indirect evidence on *implicit* self-explanation, i.e. self-explanation that happens in the student's head.

Figure 2 exemplifies how we leverage these sources in the part of the ACE student model that tracks implicit self-explanation. In Figure 2, nodes e_0Case_0, e_0Case_1 and e_0Case_2, represent three relevant exploration cases of a generic exercise e_0. This model fragment corresponds to the learner having performed an action corresponding to the exploration of e_0Case_2. Nodes representing the assessment of self-explanation are shaded grey. As the figure shows, the two sources of information that the model uses to assess the occurrence of implicit self-explanation for a given exploration case are *Stimuli to SE* and *SE-related-behavior*. *Stimuli to SE* is the probability that the learner has stimuli to self-explain either from her general *SE tendency* or from one of the hints that ACE is designed to provide when a student is assessed to be a low self-explainer (node *Coach hint to SE*). The node *SE-related-behavior* represents all the available evidence that a student is actually self-explaining the exploration case just generated. The first version of this model that we proposed in [3] only included time spent on each exploration case as behavioral evidence. The conditional probabilities defining the relation between time and self-explanation were based on our subjective judgment, to represent the assumptions that (1) no self-explanation can happen if a student switches too rapidly from one exploration case to the next; (2) the longer a student dwells on a case the more likely it is that she is trying to self-explain it. Time, however, can be an ambiguous predictor. First, it is hard to define what "too rapidly" means for different students. Furthermore, a student may be completely distracted during a long interval between exploration cases.

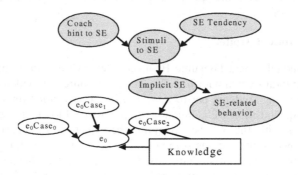

Fig. 2. The ACE student model

Thus, we chose to explore an additional source of evidence of self-explanation behavior, i.e., the student's attention patterns during the exploration of a given case. The intuition here is that self-explanation may be more likely if the student attends to the parts on the interface showing the effects of a specific exploratory action (if the student, for instance, switches attention from the graph area to the equation area after moving the graph in the Plot Unit). To unobtrusively obtain evidence on student attention patterns we used real-time processing of eye-tracking data. To collect empirical data on the mapping between actual student self-explanations, time and attention patterns, we ran a user study, described in the next section.

3   User Study

In this study, we collected data from 18 students using ACE while their gaze was tracked by an Eyelink I eye-tracker, developed by SR Research Ltd., Canada. This is a fairly intrusive head mounted eye tracker, that we used because it was available to us through the psychology department at the University of British Columbia. However, the same data could be easily obtained through a completely non-intrusive remote eye-tracker, consisting of a small camera which sits on top of the monitor or on some other flat surface (e.g. IView X Red from SensoMotoric Instruments, USA).

All the study participants were non-science university students (i.e. students that had not taken high school calculus or first-year college math). Each participant received a brief introduction to ACE and instructions to try and verbalize all his/her thought processes while using the system. The participant then went through a calibration phase with the eye tracker, and finally used the system for as much time as needed to go through all the units. This varied from 20 minutes to close to an hour. All the student exploration cases were logged (567 in total), along with raw data from the eye tracker, as well as complete video and audio data of the interaction.

3.1 Data Analysis

To understand how attention patterns and time per exploration case relate to self-explanation, we needed to obtain from the study data points on actual explicit positive and negative self-explanation episodes. (Here, "negative self-explanation" indicates situations in which students did not self-explain, not situations in which students self-explained incorrectly, consistent with the original definition of self-explanation [6].)

We had two observers analyze the recorded audio protocols in search of such episodes, and then create the link between the verbal episodes and the corresponding exploration cases in the log files. This turned out to be a much more laborious process than expected, due to two factors.

First, we quickly realized that not all verbal episodes could be unambiguously classified as positive or negative self-explanations. This is not surprising because, although there has been extensive research on what constitutes self-explanation in various problem solving domains (e.g., Newtonian physics, statistics, geometry), ours is the first attempt to understand self-explanation in an exploratory learning environment for mathematical functions. We tackled this problem by having the two observers independently label a subset of the audio data, then compare their classifications, possibly reconcile them and devise a detailed coding scheme based on this discussion. The coding scheme was then used to analyze the rest of the data, and only episodes on which the coders fully agreed were used in the rest of the analysis (the intercoder reliability was 93% in this phase). In the coding scheme, students utterances were classified as self-explanation if they expressed a conclusion about a domain-specific principle related to the exploration process (e.g., *"when I increase the coefficient here, the line gets steeper"*) regardless of correctness, or if they predicted the result of an action just before it occurred (e.g., *"putting a negative sign here will turn the curve upside-down"*). It is assumed here that if a student predicts the result of an action, she will watch to see if she is right and thus self-explain *after* the action. Simply narrating the outcome of each action once it happened (e.g., *"this number just changed to a 3"*), or isolated statements of confusion (e.g., *"I don't understand"*) were not considered self-explanation. However, tentative explanations followed by expressions of confusion were coded as self-explanation.

The second factor that increased the complexity of data analysis was difficulty in determining which action each coded utterance corresponded to. The observers at first

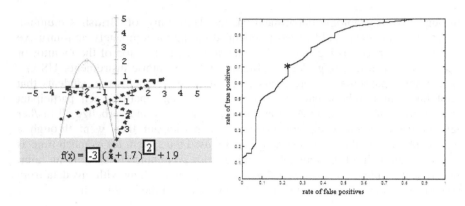

Fig. 3. Sample gaze shift

Fig. 4. ROC curve for time as a filter for self-explanation

assumed that subjects' utterances always pertained to whatever exploratory action they had just taken. However, while analyzing the video data they realized that this was not always the case, particularly for users who showed great reluctance to think aloud. These learners had to be repeatedly prompted by the observers to speak, so some of the conclusions they shared weren't reached as they spoke, but related to self explanation that occurred a few minutes earlier. The observers solved this problem by looking at every coded episode and matching it to its corresponding action. Thirteen coded episodes were discarded because the match was ambiguous.

While both parts of the above coding process resulted in the elimination of data points, the factor that had the greatest impact on the amount of data that we could get from the study was students' willingness to verbalize their thoughts. We found that a number of students were incapable or unwilling to think aloud, even if they were periodically reminded to do so. Without such verbalizations, the coders could not tell whether a student had self-explained or not. Thus, of the 567 exploration cases recorded in the log files for all students, only 149 could be classified in terms of associated self-explanation.

Once positive and negative self-explanation episodes were identified and mapped onto specific exploration cases, we proceeded to analyze the correspondence between these episodes, gaze information, and time students devoted to each case.

Raw eye tracker data was parsed by a pattern detection algorithm we developed to detect switches of attention ("gaze shifts") among the graph panel, the equation area, and any other non-conspicuous areas in the Plot Unit. As we mentioned earlier, these are the gaze patterns that we hypothesize to be associated with self-explanation in the plot unit. A sample gaze switch appears in figure 3. Here a student's eye gaze (shown as the dotted line) starts in some untracked area below the screen, moves to the equation region and then hovers around the graph region above. The data-parsing algorithm uses fixation coordinates from the eye-tracker and matches them to the appropriate ACE interface region. Next, it searches the data for the pattern of making changes in one region and then looking at the other to observe the outcome, i.e. having a gaze shift. When this pattern is found, a tag is placed in the ACE log file to synchronize the switch with the appropriate exploration case.

To analyze the relationship between time per exploration case and self-explanation, we first compared average time spent on exploration cases that were accompanied by self-explanation (24.7 seconds) and those that were not (11.6 seconds). The difference is statistically significant at the 0.05 level, suggesting that time per case is actually a fairly reliable indicator of self-explanation.

To turn time into a predictor of self-explanation, we then determined a threshold T so that an action could be classified as self-explained if the student spent more than T seconds on it. To choose the optimal threshold, we built a Receiver Operating Characteristic (ROC) curve (figure 4). The ROC curve is a standard technique used in machine learning to evaluate the extent to which an information filtering system can successfully distinguish between relevant data (episodes the filter correctly classifies as positive, or *true positives*) and noise (episodes the filter incorrectly classifies as positive, or *false positives*), given a choice of different filtering thresholds. Figure 4 shows the ROC curve we obtained for time, where each point on the curve represents a different threshold value. As it is standard practice, we chose as our final threshold the point on the curve that corresponds to a reasonable tradeoff between creating too many false positives and creating too few true positives (16 seconds, labeled by an asterisk on the curve in figure 4).

3.2 Results

Figure 5 categorizes our 149 data points into episodes with and without self-explanation (99 circles and 50 triangles, respectively). The vertical line further categorizes the points into those with and without a gaze shift (GS) between graph and equation pane in the plot unit. The horizontal line separates points with elapsed time above or below 16 seconds. The raw data is also presented in a table adjacent to the histogram. ROC curves were used to find that when time is used in combination with eye tracking data, 16 seconds continues to be the optimal threshold.

Table 1 shows different measures of self-explanation classification accuracy if we use as predictor: (i) the eye-tracker to detect gaze shift; (ii) time per self-explanation case; (iii) both predictors. Accuracy is reported in terms of true positive rate (i.e. percentage of self-explanation cases correctly classified as such, or *sensitivity* of the predictor) and true negative rate (i.e. percentage of "no self-explanation" cases correctly classified as such, or *specificity* of the predictor). We also report a combined measure, which is the average of the two accuracies. As the table shows, time alone has a higher *sensitivity* than gaze shift, i.e. the episodes involving self-explanation were more likely to take over 16 seconds than to include a gaze shift. However, the eye-tracker alone has comparably higher *specificity*, i.e. the cases without self-explanation were more likely to involve the absence of a gaze shift than shorter time per exploration case. The two predictors have comparable combined accuracy.

This may suggest that the gain of using an eye tracker is not worth the cost of adding this information to the ACE model. However, there are a few counter-arguments to this conclusion.

First, it should be noted that time accuracy here is probably artificially high. One of the drawbacks of using time as predictor of self-explanation is that the amount of time elapsed tells the model nothing about the student's behavior between actions. During

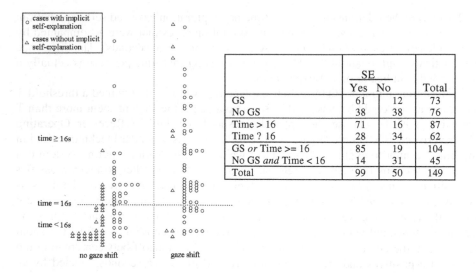

Fig. 5. Dual histogram (left) and raw time/GS data (right)

a long time spent on a given case, a student may be doing or thinking of something completely unrelated to ACE. This seldom occurs in our data, but we should bear in mind that students were in a laboratory setting with little available distractions, in the presence of an observer and wearing a rather intrusive device on their head. All these factors are likely to have made it more difficult for the students' thoughts to wander from the task at hand, resulting in time being a more reliable indicator of self-explanation than it would be in actual practice.

Table 1. Classification accuracy of different predictors

	Eye-tracker	Time	Eye-tracker + Time
True Positive Rate (*sensitivity*)	61.6%	71.7%	85.8%
True Negative Rate (*specificity*)	76.0%	68.0%	62.0%
Combined Accuracy	68.8%	69.85%	73.9%

Second, we found that the sensitivity of the eye-tracker may be higher than our data shows. The program that synchronizes gaze shifts with actions assumes that a student performs an exploratory action and then carries out a gaze shift to observe the changes it generates. Thus, each gaze shift or lack thereof is associated with the preceding action. In our logger, an action involving a change in the function equation would be captured only when a student finishes typing and presses "enter". However, it is possible that in some cases the student wanted to catch the change in the graph when it happened, and thus would look up at the graph region after typing but before pressing enter. Our logger would incorrectly record this gaze shift to be associated with the action *before* the current one. Of the 38 false negatives generated by the eye-tracker, 21 had a gaze shift associated with the preceding action in the log file, and are thus consistent with the above scenario. If we were to switch the matching of these gaze shifts with the following log file action, the sensitivity of the eye-tracker would increase to 86.8%, and that of eye tracker plus time would reach 92.5%. We plan to run more subjects with a revised logger to clarify this issue.

Third, combining gaze shift and time into one predictor substantially improves sensitivity. That is, if an action is classified as self-explained when there is *either* a gaze shift *or* more than 16 seconds elapsed time, most of the self-explanation episodes (85.8%) are correctly recognized. This increase also causes the combined accuracy to improve. However, as sensitivity increases, specificity is reduced and only 62% of the episodes that lack self-explanation are discovered by the model. This situation is shown in figure 5. With the combined model, all data points to the right of the vertical line or above the horizontal time threshold line are classified as self-explained. As a result, most of the episodes with self-explanation are found but many of those without self-explanation are incorrectly classified.

Here a tradeoff appears between sensitivity and specificity. Depending on how the system is used, it may be most important to correctly classify self-explanation when it occurs than to detect the lack thereof. This is the situation when letting natural self-explainers explore without interruption is given highest priority. Here, using the combination of eye-tracker and time data is best. Alternatively, it may be more important to make sure that the system intervenes wherever it is necessary. Then failing to identify lack of self-explanation is a bigger problem than failing to detect it when it occurs. In this case, the eye-tracker alone is a more appropriate predictor because students who need help will be more likely to get it..

3.3 Discussion and Future Work

In this paper, we have presented a study to ascertain whether using eye tracking information can increase the accuracy of a user model that needs to assess the meta-cognitive skill known as self-explanation. An alternative, easier to obtain source of evidence for this assessment is time per relevant interface action. In the study, we have collected data to compare the two sources.

Our results have shown that, in a laboratory setting, time is actually a much better predictor of self-explanation than expected. However, our data suggests that eye tracking data combined with time can increase the model bandwidth when a system that uses this model is mostly concerned with detecting the presence of self-explanation to avoid interfering with students who spontaneously self-explain. Furthermore, the eye-tracker alone may be more appropriate when the system priority is to detect when students do not self-explain. The data analysis also uncovered possible sources of inaccuracies in the data collection that may underestimate the value of eye tracker data.

Given these considerations, we plan to continue exploring the usage of eye tracker data with further experiments. One goal is to improve our data collection procedure to more reliably assess accuracy of eye-tracker data. A second goal is to collect data to test the addition to the ACE student model of nodes to represent evidence from both eye tracker and time. We plan to experiment by adding a naive Bayesian classifier structure. The advantage of this structure is that it is highly modular, allowing the eye-tracker and time data to be included or ignored as needed. In addition, the necessary conditional probabilities are readily available   from sensitivity/ specificity frequencies in our data. We are also planning to perform the analysis described in this paper for the data collected on the other ACE units during the study. This will require extending the gaze detection algorithm to attention patterns relevant for those units.

References

1. Aleven, V. and K.R. Koedinger, *An Effective Meta-Cognitive Strategy: Learning by Doing and by Explaining with a Computer-Based Cognitive Tutor.* Cognitive Science, 2002. **26**(2): 147-179.
2. Bunt, A. and C. Conati, *Probabilistic Student Modelling to Improve Exploratory Behaviour.* Journ of User Modeling and User-Adapted Interaction, 2003. **13**(3): 269-309.
3. Bunt, A., C. Conati, and K. Muldner. *Scaffolding self-explanation to improve learning in exploratory learning environments.* in *7th Int Conf on Intelligent Tutoring Systems.* 2004. Maceio, Brazil.
4. Chi, M.T.H., et al., *Self-explanations: How students study and use examples in learning to solve problems.* Cognitive Science, 1989. **15**: 145-182.
5. Conati, C. and K. VanLehn, *Toward Computer-based Support of Meta-cognitive Skills: A Computational Framework to Coach Self-Explanation.* Int Journ of Artificial Intelligence in Education, 2000. **11**.
6. Gluck, K.A. and J.R. Anderson, *What role do cognitive architectures play in intelligent tutoring systems?*, in *Cognition & Instruction: Twenty-five years of progress*, D. Klahr and S.M. Carver, Editors. 2001, Erlbaum. 227-262.
7. Iqbal, S.T. and B.P. Bailey. *Using Eye Gaze Patterns to Identify User Tasks (to appear).* in *The Grace Hopper Celebration of Women in Computing.* 2004.
8. Jakob, R., *The Use of eye movements in human computer interaction techniques: what you look at is what you get*, in *Readings in Intelligent User Interfaces*, M.T.a.W. Maybury, W., Editor. 1998, Morgan Kaufmann Press: San Francisco. 65-83.
9. Just, M. and P. Carpenter, *The Psychology of Reading and Language Comprehension*, ed. A.a. Bacon. 1986, Boston.
10. Mitrovic, T. *Supporting Self-Explanation in a Data Normalization Tutor.* in *Supplementary Proc of AIED2003.* 2003.
11. Salvucci, D. and J. Anderson. *Intelligent Gaze-Added Interfaces.* in *SIGCHI conf on Human factors in computing systems.* 2000. The Hague, The Netherlands.
12. Shute, V.J. and R. Glaser, *A large-scale evaluation of an intelligent discovery world.* Interactive Learning Environments, 1990. **1**: 51-76.
13. Sibert, J.L., M. Gokturk, and R.A. Lavine. *The reading assistant: eye gaze triggered auditory prompting for reading remediation.* in *13th annual ACM symposium on User interface software and technolog.* 2000. San Diego, California: ACM Press.
14. Starker, I. and R.A. Bolt. *A Gaze-Responsive Self- Disclosing Display.* in *CHI: Human Factors in Computing Systems.* 1990. Seattle, WA: ACM.
15. VanLehn, K., *Student modeling*, in *Foundations of Intelligent Tutoring Systems*, M. Polson and J. Richardson, Editors. 1988, Lawrence Erlbaum Associates: Hillsdale, NJ. 55-78.

Modeling Students' Metacognitive Errors in Two Intelligent Tutoring Systems

Ido Roll, Ryan S. Baker, Vincent Aleven, Bruce M. McLaren,
and Kenneth R. Koedinger

Human Compute Interaction Institute,
Carnegie Mellon University,
5000 Forbes Ave., Pittsburgh PA 15213
{idoroll, koedinger}@cmu.edu, rsbaker@andrew.cmu.edu,
{aleven, bmclaren}@cs.cmu.edu

Abstract. Intelligent tutoring systems help students acquire cognitive skills by tracing students' knowledge and providing relevant feedback. However, feedback that focuses only on the cognitive level might not be optimal - errors are often the result of inappropriate metacognitive decisions. We have developed two models which detect aspects of student faulty metacognitive behavior: A prescriptive rational model aimed at improving help-seeking behavior, and a descriptive machine-learned model aimed at eliminating attempts to "game" the tutor. In a comparison between the two models we found that while both successfully identify gaming behavior, one is better at characterizing the types of problems students game in, and the other captures a larger variety of faulty behaviors. An analysis of students' actions in two different tutors suggests that the help-seeking model is domain independent, and that students' behavior is fairly consistent across classrooms, age groups, domains, and task elements.

1 Metacognition in Intelligent Tutoring Systems

Intelligent tutoring systems offer support and guidance to learners attempting to master a cognitive skill [7,11]. When students ask for help or make a mistake in such a tutor, they receive feedback on their problem-solving actions, that is, they receive feedback at the cognitive level. However, mistakes can also be made at the higher metacognitive level, which coordinates the learning process. Such metacognitive skills include self-assessment and help-seeking strategies, among many others. When cognitive errors originate from an incorrect metacognitive decision, feedback on student metacognition would be more appropriate. A tutoring system should try to improve students' metacognitive skills, by, for example, guiding a student who avoids using help to seek help at the right moment.

Several studies have shown that students often make unproductive metacognitive decisions, which affect their learning process [9,13]. Some types of poor metacognitive decisions include avoiding or misusing help [1,16] and attempting to obtain correct answers without thinking through the material (termed "gaming the system" [4,5]). There is evidence that these types of unproductive metacognitive decisions

L. Ardissono, P. Brna, and A. Mitrovic (Eds.): UM 2005, LNAI 3538, pp. 367–376, 2005.
© Springer-Verlag Berlin Heidelberg 2005

negatively affect learning. For instance, students with a tendency to game the system on steps they find difficult (e.g., by systematic guessing) tend to learn less from their interaction with the tutor. Similarly, the ability to seek the right help at the right time is correlated with learning, whether with tutoring systems or in the classroom environment [3,16]. Nevertheless, students do not use available help resources effectively enough (for an extensive review, see [2]). For example, Aleven et al. [1] found that when asking for hints, students spent less than 1 second on 68% of the hints before reaching the most detailed hint level, which provides an answer rather than an explanation.

Fortunately, classroom studies have shown that metacognitive skills can be improved through appropriate guidance [15]. Recently, there has also been increasing interest in improving the metacognition of students using intelligent tutors [8,12,14]. While this work focused on improving students' metacognition, such interventions are likely to be more effective if the tutor can detect which students are having metacognitive difficulties, and what the nature of those difficulties is for each student. Work towards detecting such difficulties in the domain of self-explanation is done by Conati et al. [6].

In this paper we present work towards modeling students' metacognition in order to detect errors related to misuse of the system's facilities and help resources. In particular, we compare two models that attempt to capture different aspects of students' metacognition, and show how different populations of students working with different tutors behave similarly when analyzed by one of these models. We also discuss how this work will be used to help improve student metacognition.

1.1 Cognitive Tutors

We explore these issues within the context of Cognitive Tutors, a type of intelligent tutoring system, based on ACT-R theory, that are now used in approximately 5% of US high schools, as part of complete one-year curricula in various math courses. Cognitive Tutor curricula produce learning gains that are around one standard deviation higher than those produced by traditional instruction [10].

Cognitive Tutors are based on cognitive models that detail the skills to be learned and the typical errors students make. Each student's knowledge level is continuously evaluated using a Bayesian knowledge-tracing model [7], enabling the tutor to choose the most appropriate exercises for each student.

Cognitive Tutors provide on-demand help with several levels of contextualized hints. The more hints a student asks to see on a specific problem step, the more explicit the hints become, until the final "bottom out" hint typically gives the student the answer. Some Cognitive Tutors provide additional forms of information resource. For instance, the Geometry Cognitive Tutor has a decontextualized online glossary that lists and illustrates relevant problem-solving principles, theorems, and definitions.

1.2 The Help-Seeking Model

One software agent that we currently develop is the Help-Seeking Tutor. The Help-Seeking Tutor can be added to any Cognitive Tutor (with minor adaptations [1]), and is based on a prescriptive rational Help-Seeking Model. The Help-Seeking Model describes the student's ideal help-seeking behavior; it determines what type of action the student should ideally perform by taking into account the student's estimated mastery level for the skill involved in the step, the number and types of actions so far on the step, and the time the student spends answering.

According to the model (fig. 1), when a student encounters a new step, she is first expected to think about the step (1). Following that, the student judges whether the step is familiar at all (this is approximated by using the tutor's estimation of the probability the student knows the skill). If the student is not familiar with the skill, then she asks for a hint that scaffolds the solution process (2) (note, a hint is not presented automatically, to give the

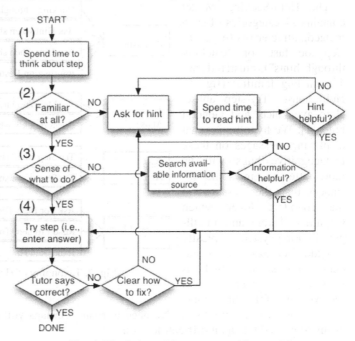

Fig. 1. The help-seeking metacognitive model

student opportunity to self-assess her lack of sufficient knowledge, and thus practice another important metacognitive skill). After spending some time reading the hint, the student evaluates the hint's helpfulness. If, in the student's own estimation, the hint provides sufficient information, she attempts to solve the step (4). Alternatively, if after reading the hint, the student still does not see how to solve the step, she asks for the next hint.

A student with a higher skill-level, who is familiar with the step (2), evaluates whether she has a sense of what to do. If the student does not know what to do, the student searches the available information resource (such as the Glossary in the Angles unit or the dictionary in foreign language tutors. Searching decontextualized information resource is an important skill that resembles searching a source such as the WWW) (3). If the information resource is not helpful, the student asks for a hint. Finally, when there is no information resource available, or when the student believes she can solve the step, she tries to solve it (4). If the answer turns out to be wrong, the student either tries to fix it (if she thinks she knows how), or asks for a hint. Upon successfully completing a step, the student proceeds to the next step and the process repeats itself.

We have implemented this model and the deviations from it as a set of 61 production rules [1]. 29 of these rules capture ideal help-seeking behavior, while the rest capture the various ways that students' help-seeking behavior diverges from the described model. These "metacognitive bug rules" enable the Help-Seeking Tutor to display a metacognitive hint, suggesting to the student what she should do in order to learn most effectively.

The Help-Seeking Model contains 11 categories of such metacognitive errors (e.g., "try step too fast" or "Clicking through hints"), clustered into 4 main bug families (fig. 2): Help abuse, Try-step abuse, Help avoidance, and General bugs [1]. We hypothesize that displaying messages on these metacognitive bugs will be more effective in some instances than the messages at the cognitive level which Cognitive Tutors and intelligent tutoring systems typically provide. For example, a student who is identified as guessing too quickly will receive the following message: "Slow down, slow down. No need to rush. Perhaps you should ask for a hint, as this step might be a bit difficult for you".

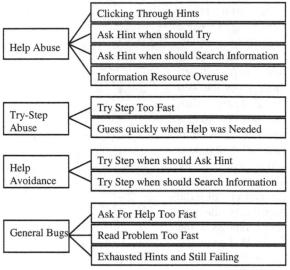

Fig. 2. Taxonomy of Help-Seeking bugs

1.3 The Gaming Detector

A second model that we have developed is the Gaming Detector. Unlike the rational Help-Seeking Model, we used machine-learning techniques to develop the Gaming Detector. Another difference form the Help-Seeking Model is that the Gaming-Detector does not attempt to model ideal behavior. Instead, it is a descriptive model, attempts to capture the behaviors characteristic of those students who use the tutor least appropriately. Specifically, this detector identifies whether a student is attempting to game the system – attempting to succeed on the assigned problems by systematically exploiting properties and regularities in the system, rather than by thinking about the material. Gaming the system has been found to have a greater negative impact on learning than several types of off task behaviors [5]. Once the system detects that a student is gaming, the system can then adapt to encourage the student to use the software more appropriately.

Through classroom observations, we determined what percentage of time each student spent attempting to game the system [5]. Two behaviors were defined to constitute gaming: systematic guessing and clicking through straight to the bottom-out hints.

The challenge that faces the Gaming Detector is to identify Gaming automatically during the interaction with the student. We used machine-learning techniques to develop a Latent Response Model that could identify gaming students by their actions, and used Leave-One-Out-Cross-Validation to be certain that the model was not over-fit to individual students through cross-validation [4]. This model first made predictions about whether each individual student action was an instance of gaming, and then aggregated these predictions to make a prediction about the frequency of time each student spent gaming. The model uses a combination of four features to predict that an action is gaming:

1. An action is more likely to be gaming if the student has already made at least one error on this problem step within this problem, and has also made a large number of errors on this problem step in previous problems.
2. Fast actions following an error are likely to be instances of gaming, unlike slow responses to an error.
3. Errors on popup menus are especially indicative of gaming.
4. Slips, where a student makes a number of errors on a well-known skill, are not counted as gaming.

Both the Help-Seeking Model and the Gaming Detector have been found to be effective at predicting how much different students learned [1,4]. In this paper, we use the two models to analyze student behavior across different units and compare the models to each other, in terms of the student behaviors they capture.

2 Comparing Students' Actions Across Tutors

Since the Help-Seeking Model captures a large variety of metacogintive errors that students make, it is of interest to compare students' metacognitive behavior across different tutor units and classrooms using this model. In addition, although the Help-Seeking model was designed to be domain-indepenedent, this premise was not validated until now.

We analyzed two datasets from different groups of students working with different tutors, and calculated the relative frequencies of each bug category in the two datasets. The first of these, collected during 1999, is of 40 students working with the Angles unit of the Geometry Cognitive Tutor for 7 hours. This data includes almost 60,000 actions. The other dataset, collected in 2003, consists of around 20,000 actions performed by 70 students over the course of an hour and a half of use of a tutor unit about Scatterplots.

There are fairly substantial differences between the units and the groups of students in these two datasets, including domain differences (one is for geometry, the other is in the domain of data analysis), age differences (one group of students was high-school age, while the other was in middle school), differences in available help resources (the Geometry Tutor had a glossary and hints, while the Scatterplot unit only had hints), and finally, differences in task elements (the Geometry Tutor had only numeric fields for the students to fill in, while the Scatterplot unit had numeric and text fields, multiple choice questions, and point plotting on a graph).

Using the help-seeking model described above, we classified each action in the datasets as either metacognitively correct or as in a bug category. Not all bugs could occur in both units. While the Angles unit has an available information resource in the form of a Glossary, the Scatterplot unit has none. In that case, the help-seeking model predicts that students that do not need hints will try to solve the step immediately. This distinction between the units creates a minor difference between the applications of the model; while a student with an intermediate skill level on a certain step is expected to consult the Glossary in the Angles unit, she is expected to try to solve the step in the Scatterplot unit.

Due to differences in the logging mechanisms, successive hint requests in the Scatterplot dataset were captured as single hint requests. In order to draw valid comparisons between the two units, we recoded successive hints in the Angles dataset as single hint requests as well, thus eliminating the "clicking through hints" category.

Results. We compare the patterns of students' metacognitive behavior by comparing the frequencies of the metacognitive bug categories (table 1). Although the domains, age groups, help opportunities and task elements were all different, the frequencies of the bug categories were remarkably similar: $r=0.89$ ($F(1,6)=18$, $p<0.01$). In other words, students tended to make similar metacognitive bugs such as overusing help across the two units.

As seen in table 1, all bug categories have similar frequencies across the units except the "Try step too fast" category. While 17% of the actions in the Angles unit are categorized as "Try step too fast", as many as 36% of the actions on the Scatterplot unit fall under the same definition. Actions categorized as "Try step too fast" are appropriate solution attempt that are done too fast (in less than 5 seconds).

The explanation for this difference possibly lies in the different interface elements between the two units. The Angles unit has only numeric fields, while The Scatterplot unit has also multiple-choice questions (implemented as radio-buttons and popup menus) that are faster to answer, thus reducing the overall duration of the action. In addition, we hypothesize that students in the Scatterplot unit reach mastery in procedural skills faster than student in the Angles unit, thus become experts more quickly, and work with the tutor more rapidly.

The Help-Seeking Model was considerably more successful in predicting learning in one data set than in the other. There was a significant correlation between students' frequencies of Metacognitively Correct Steps and their posttest scores (when controlling for pre-test) in the Angles unit, but not in the Scatterplot unit (Angles unit: partial $r=0.74$, $t(37)=4.7$, $p<0.001$; Scatterplot unit: partial $r=0.08$, $t(67)=0.7$, $p<0.5$).

A probable explanation to the lack of correlation between metacognitive bugs and leaning in the Scatterplot unit resembles the explanation for the inflation of "Try step too fast", as noted before: the Help-Seeking Model might not capture appropriately skilled students' behavior on skills they know well. Fast actions of skilled students are interpreted as being too fast, while they actually may be a result of their high knowledge level. In that case, we would expect that students who reach mastery level will perform more "Try step too fast" bugs, and indeed, there is marginally significant **positive** correlation between "Try step too fast" and posttest scores (when controlling for pretest, $r=0.2$, $t(67)=2$, $p=0.075$). Moreover, when eliminating the "Try step too fast" category, we do find a negative, marginally significant correlation between posttest scores and metacognitive bugs (when controlling for pretest, $r=-0.2$, $t(67)=-2$, $p<0.09$). In other words, besides the "Try step too fast" bug that has a positive correlation with learning, we observe a negative correlation between metacognitive bugs, as captured by the help-seeking model, and successful learning also in the Scatterplot unit.

Table 1. the properties of the databases and the frequencies of the metacognitive bugs

Unit			Angles unit		Scatterplot unit
Domain			Geometry		Data analysis
Age group			High school		Middle school
Task elements			Numeric fields		Numeric, text, plot, multiple choice
Available help resources			Hints and a glossary		Hints
Bug categories			All actions	Actions comparable to Scatterplot unit	
Help Abuse	Clicking through hints		33%	0%	Not logged
	Ask hint when should Try		1%	2%	1%
	Ask hint when should Search Information		1%	2%	N/A
	Information Resource Overuse		1%	2%	N/A
Try Step abuse	Try step too fast		11%	17%	36%
	Guess quickly when help was needed		7%	12%	11%
Help Avoidance	Try step when should Ask Hint		8%	13%	11%
	Try step when should Search Information		3%	5%	N/A
General Bugs	Ask for help too fast		3%	6%	3%
	Read problems too fast		1%	3%	1%
	Exhausted hints and still failing		1%	2%	0%
	Metacognitively Correct		28%	36%	38%

3 Comparing the Two Models of Metacognition

In addition to comparing the units, we tried to learn more about the students' meta-cognitive errors and about the way they are captured by the models, by applying both models to data from the same unit – in this case, the Scatterplot unit described above. The gaming behavior that the Gaming Detector captures consists of help abuse and systematic guessing. These behaviors are related to errors captured by the Help-Seeking Model, so a comparison between the two approaches is of interest. As mentioned before, the Help-Seeking Model is a prescriptive rational model, while the Gaming Detector is a descriptive machine-learned model. Since the two models focus on metacognition differently, there may be benefit to using them in complementary fashion.

The two models are significantly correlated; students who perform more correct metacognitive actions according to the Help-Seeking Model, engage less frequently in gaming behavior as predicted by the Gaming Detector (r= -0.42, $F(1,69)=15$, p<0.001). The correlation between the sum of the Help-Abuse and Try-step Abuse, (the two bugs in the Help Seeking Model which correspond to the observations used to train the gaming detector), and the output of the Gaming-Detector, is lower and only significant (r=0.20, $F(1,69)=3$, p<0.1).

The observed frequencies of gaming give us a standard for how successful each model detects attempts to game the system. The Gaming Detector reveals significant behavioral differences between students who game the system but still learn (these "gamed-not-hurt" students were found to game on the easiest steps) and students who game the system and fail to learn (these "gamed-hurt" students were found to game on the hardest steps [4]). To be maximally useful, a metacognitive model should accurately identify the gamed-hurt students —it is not as important to identify the gamed-not-hurt students.

As seen in Table 2, the Gaming-Detector is effective at detecting Gamed-Hurt students, while its correlation with the degree of gaming in gamed-not-hurt students is not different from random. Interestingly, the Help-Seeking Model also distinguishes between the two groups, without having been designed to. Its correlation to gamed-hurt is marginally significant, and it is not corre-

Table 2. distinguishing game-hurt from game-not-hurt students

	Gamed-Hurt	Gamed-Not-Hurt
Gaming Detector	r = 0.77 (F(1,68)=100, p<0.001)	r = 0.06 (F(1,69)=0.3, p>0.6)
Help Seeking Model	r=0.20 (F(1,68)=3, p<0.1)	r=0.03 (F(1,69)=0.1, p>0.7)
Both models in conjunction	r=0.79 (F(2,67)=54, p<0.001)	r=0.09 (F(2,67)=0.3 p>0.7)

lated to gamed-not hurt. Moreover, using the models together is more effective than either alone (t(67)=1.9, p<0.07). Though the improvement is modest, it suggests that the Help-Seeking Model captures gaming-related behavior that is not explained by the Gaming-Detector alone.

While the Help-Seeking Model identifies the Gamed-Hurt students, it does not find that they game mainly on the hardest steps (as found by the Gaming-Detector). The reason for that may be, as mentioned before, that the model might capture fast answers on mastered (and thus easy) skills as being inappropriate, and therefore has a high rate of metacognitive bugs on easy steps.

4 Discussion and Conclusions

Though tutoring systems are capable of effectively tracing students' cognition and giving relevant feedback on that level, in order to maximize learning, they should also respond to students' poor metacognitive decisions. The first step in doing so is detecting metacognitive errors. Since metacognitive behavior is not tied to a specific subject matter, improving it may improve learning across tutors and domains.

We have developed two metacognitive models: The Help-Seeking Model is a prescriptive rational model aimed at modeling appropriate help-seeking behavior and detecting ineffective help-seeking behavior. The Gaming Detector is a machine-learned model that identifies students who are trying to make progress in the curriculum by systematically exploiting the tutor's properties without thinking about the problems.

We investigated two different datasets using the Help-Seeking Model. Though the datasets differ in age group, subject matter, task elements, and help resources, we found a consistent pattern in students' metacognitive errors. This finding suggests that the help-seeking model is not tied to a specific domain, and can be generalized to tutors that include different tools. While the rates of most bug categories were remarkably similar across units, this was not the case for the "Try step too fast" category. In addition, while in the Angles unit the Help-Seeking Model was a good predictor of learning, in the Scatterplot unit we did not observe such a correlation. A probable explanation to both findings is that the Help Seeking Model falsely classifies appropriate fast actions as buggy ones, which is more relevant to the generally faster Scatterplot unit.

Beyond this, we compared the two approaches to model metacognition, within the context of one dataset. While targeted at different goals, both models successfully distinguish gaming students from other students; combining the models yields better results than either of the models can obtain alone. Though the two models are correlated, they seem to capture different properties of students' behavior. The Gaming-Detector is much more successful at identifying gaming students who do not learn, which is its main goal; the Help-Seeking Model can identify a larger span of meta-cognitively faulty behaviors. Future development of metacognitive models should combine the advantages of the different approaches.

These results show us that a tutoring system can be aware of a user's metacognition. Once refined, the models will be used to extend the Cognitive Tutors so that they provide feedback to students on their metacognitive behavior. We will examine whether students improve their metacognitive skills following targeted appropriate feedback, and ultimately whether they become better learners as a result.

Acknowledgments. We would like to thank Matthew W. Easterday and Eun-Jeong Ryu for their assistance. This research is sponsored by NSF Award IIS-0308200. The contents of the paper are solely the responsibility of the authors and do not necessarily represent the official views of the NSF.

References

1. Aleven, V., McLaren, B.M., Roll, I., Koedinger, K.R.: Toward tutoring help seeking - Applying cognitive modeling to meta-cognitive skills. In *Proceedings of the 7th International Conference on Intelligent Tutoring Systems, ITS 2004,* Springer Verlag, Berlin (2004) 227-239.
2. Aleven, V., Stahl, E., Schworm, S., Fischer, F., Wallace, R.M.: Help Seeking in Interactive Learning Environments. *Review of Educational Research,* 73(2), (2003) 277-320
3. Arbreton, A.: Student Goal Orientation and Help-Seeking Strategy Use. In S. A. Karabenick (Ed.), *Strategic help seeking. Implications for learning and teaching,* Erlbaum, Mahwah (1998) 95-116
4. Baker, R.S., Corbett, A.T., Koedinger, K.R.: Detecting Student Misuse of Intelligent Tutoring Systems. In *Proceedings of the 7th International Conference on Intelligent Tutoring Systems, ITS 2004,* Springer Verlag, Berlin (2004) 531-540

5. Baker, R.S., Corbett, A.T., Koedinger, K.R., Wagner, A.Z.: Off-Task Behavior in the Cognitive Tutor Classroom: When Students "Game the System". In *Proceedings of ACM CHI 2004: Computer-Human Interaction (2004)* 383-390

6. Bunt A., Conati C., Muldner K.: Scaffolding Self-explanation to Improve Learning in Exploratory Learning Environments. In *Proceedings of the 7th International Conference on Intelligent Tutoring Systems, ITS 2004,* Springer Verlag, Berlin (2004)

7. Corbett, A.T., Anderson, J.R.: Knowledge Tracing: Modeling the Acquisition of Procedural Knowledge. *User Modeling and User-Adapted Interaction,* 4, (1995) 253-278

8. Gama, C.: Metacognition in Interactive Learning Environments: The Reflection Assistant Model. In *Proceedings of the 7th International Conference on Intelligent Tutoring Systems, ITS 2004,* Springer Verlag, Berlin (2004) 668-677

9. Gräsel, C., Fischer, F., Mandl, H.: The Use of Additional Information in Problem-Oriented Learning Environments. *Learning Environments Research,* 3 (2001) 287-305

10. Koedinger, K.R., Anderson, J.R., Hadley, W.H., Mark, M.A.: Intelligent Tutoring Goes to School in the Big City. *International Journal of Artificial Intelligence in Education,* 8 (1997) 30–43

11. Linton, F., Bell, B., Bloom, C.: The Student Model of the LEAP Intelligent Tutoring System. In *Proceedings of the Fifth International Conference on User Modeling,* UM96 (1996) 83–90

12. Luckin, R., Hammerton, L.: Getting to Know me: Helping Learners Understand Their Own Learning Needs through Meta-cognitive Scaffolding. In *Proceedings of Sixth International Conference on Intelligent Tutoring Systems,* ITS 2002, Springer Verlag, Berlin (2002) 759-771

13. Renkl, A.: Learning from worked-out examples: Instructional explanations supplement self-explanations. *Learning & Instruction,* 12, (2002) 529-556

14. Roll, I., Aleven, V., Koedinger, K.R.: Promoting Effective Help-Seeking Behavior through Declarative Instruction. In *Proceedings of the 7th International Conference on Intelligent Tutoring Systems,* ITS 2004. Springer Verlag, Berlin (2004) 857-859

15. White, B., Frederiksen, J.: Inquiry, Modeling, and Metacognition: Making Science Accessible to all Students. *Cognition and Instruction,* 16(1) (1998) 3-117.

16. Wood, H., Wood, D.: Help Seeking, Learning and Contingent Tutoring. *Computers and Education,* 33,(1999) 153-169.

Modeling Individual and Collaborative Problem Solving in Medical Problem-Based Learning

Siriwan Suebnukarn and Peter Haddawy

Computer Science and Information Management Program,
Asian Institute of Technology, Pathumthani,
12120, Thailand
{Siriwan.Subnukarn, haddawy}@ait.ac.th

Abstract. Since problem solving in group problem-based learning is a collaborative process, modeling individuals and the group is necessary if we wish to develop an intelligent tutoring system that can do things like focus the group discussion, promote collaboration, or suggest peer helpers. We have used Bayesian networks to model individual student knowledge and activity, as well as that of the group. The validity of the approach has been tested with student models in the areas of head injury, stroke and heart attack. Receiver operating characteristic (ROC) curve analysis shows that, the models are highly accurate in predicting individual student actions. Comparison with human tutors shows that group activity determined by the model agrees with that suggested by the majority of the human tutors with a high degree of statistical agreement (McNemar test, $p = 0.774$, Kappa = 0.823).

1 Background

Over the past few decades, problem-based learning (PBL) has been introduced as an alternative to traditional didactic medical education. PBL is designed to challenge learners to build up their knowledge and develop effective clinical reasoning skills around practical patient problems. PBL instructional models vary but the general approach is student-centered, small group, collaborative problem solving activities [2]. While PBL has many strengths, effective PBL requires the tutor to provide a high degree of personal attention to the students, which is difficult in the current academic environment of increasing demands on faculty time. We are investigating the potential use of concepts from Intelligent Tutoring Systems (ITSs) and Computer-Supported Collaborative Learning (CSCL) to develop an intelligent medical training system for PBL. In this paper we focus on the student modeling aspects of the problem.

Similar to one-to-one ITSs, e.g. ANDES [4], SQL-Tutor [15], our system requires an accurate model of clinical problem solving and a model of the student's state of knowledge so that the system can guide the students effectively. But in a PBL group clinical problem solving ability can vary from student to student since students differ in their background knowledge and skill. Thus modeling individuals and the group is

L. Ardissono, P. Brna, and A. Mitrovic (Eds.): UM 2005, LNAI 3538, pp. 377–386, 2005.

necessary if we wish to develop tutoring algorithms that can do things like focus the group discussion, promote collaboration, and suggest peer helpers.

Developing successful collaborative environments that satisfy each member's needs and contribute to the effectiveness of the group as a whole is an area that researchers have recently begun to address. The Docs 'n Drugs project [13] supports intelligent tutoring for group-based medical PBL by including collaborative work and intelligent tutoring capabilities in one system. But the tutoring module in Docs 'n Drugs is still focused on guiding individual students rather than the group as a whole. Jameson et al [9] propose a generative model of individual group members, which is a computational model of relevant beliefs, preferences, motivation and other relevant properties. The work focuses on supporting asynchronous collaboration, with the models being used to predict member's responses to proposed solutions during discussion sessions when they are not present. Lock and Kudenko [12] propose a multi-component user modeling approach in which each user model contains an explicit team profile in addition to other distinct components. The models are developed in the context of personalized information briefing for military decision-making. Building upon results from Social Choice Theory, Masthoff [14] addresses the issue of combining models of individuals' preferences in order to infer group preferences in a more general framework. The work is illustrated with the problem of selecting appropriate television programming for a group. Our work departs from previous efforts to incorporate user modeling into computer supported collaborative learning environments by focusing on modeling individual *and* group problem solving behavior. The modeling technique that we present in this paper has been implemented in COMET, a collaborative intelligent tutoring system for medical PBL [17]. Medical PBL is challenging due to the complexity of the knowledge involved, and the lack of standard, commonly accepted student problem-solving techniques. Thus, one objective of the work presented in this paper has been to identify prototypical patterns of student clinical reasoning to create student models that can be used by the tutoring module to generate the various tutoring hints.

2   COMET – COllaborative MEdical Tutor

COMET is designed to provide an experience that emulates that of live human-tutored medical PBL sessions as much as possible while at the same time permitting the students to participate from disparate locations. The system is implemented as a Java client/server combination, which can be used over the Internet or local area networks and supports any number of users. COMET incorporates a multi-modal interface that integrates text and graphics so as to provide a rich communication channel between the students and the system, as well as among students in the group (Fig. 1). COMET can currently support PBL in the domains of Head injury, Stroke and Heart attack. Generating appropriate tutorial actions in COMET requires a model of the students' clinical reasoning for the problem domain. This modeling task is necessarily wrought with uncertainty since we have only a limited number of observations from which to infer each student's level of understanding. Thus we have chosen to use Bayesian networks (BNs) as our modeling technique.

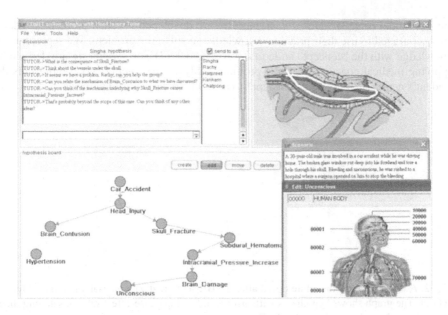

Fig. 1. COMET Student interface. The hypothesis board provides the central shared group workspace. The discussion pane is the place for displaying tutoring hints

3 Clinical Reasoning Model

The following sections describe the structure of the BN domain clinical reasoning model, alternative model structures, how the conditional probabilities are obtained, and how the models are used for individual and collaborative student modeling.

3.1 Domain Clinical Reasoning Model

We investigate issues of generality in clinical reasoning, which will serve as a foundation in developing our domain-general structure. The classic model of clinical reasoning is the hypothetico-deductive model [6], which is incorporated in the PBL process. It is characterized by the generation of multiple competing hypotheses from initial patient cues, followed by the collection of data to confirm or refute each hypothesis. Figure 2 shows a portion of the hypothesis structure created by one PBL group for the problem scenario on the bottom right of Figure 1. It shows a directed acyclic graph representing cause-effect relationships among hypotheses. Since we assume that each student is participating in the process of creating this graph, the graph forms the basis of our student model. The hypothesis graph can be conveniently represented as a BN since BNs are also directed acyclic graphs. In addition, BNs can represent our uncertainty about the state of knowledge of the students.

To come up with hypotheses explaining the case, the clinical reasoning process involves the following iterative 3 steps [2]. (1) *Problem identification* is done by selecting problems from studying the case. This process is similar to "subgoaling" in means-ends problem solving [1]. We represent these problems with the "goal" node in the BN model (Fig. 3). (2) *Problem analyses* are developed for each problem. Students are encouraged to use their previous knowledge to solve the problem. We represent this knowledge with the "concept" node in the BN model. (3) The *hypotheses* are derived by applying medical concepts from the problem analyses. An "apply" node represents the student's action of applying a "concept" to a "goal" to derive a "hypothesis".

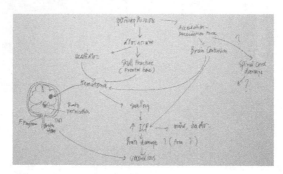

Fig. 2. A photograph of the white board after a PBL session at Thammasat University Medical School. The graph shows hypotheses with arrows indicating cause-effect relations among them. (Note: Some hypotheses are written in Thai)

Although some consistent characteristics of the clinical reasoning process can be identified based on the hypothetico-deductive reasoning model, they are not particularly satisfying for understanding the process of reasoning or useful for communicating it when training future clinicians. For example, how are good hypotheses generated, and what is the nature of a good hypothesis set? We have explored the clinical problem representation called "illness script" proposed by Feltovich and Barrows [7] and incorporated this approach in the design of our system. At its most general level of description, the script proposes that an illness can be characterized by three component parts: enabling conditions, faults and a set of consequences. Enabling conditions are illness features associated with the acquisition of illness (e.g., compromised host factors, hereditary factors). Faults are the major real malfunctions in illness (e.g., direct trauma, invasion of tissue by pathogenic organisms). Consequences are the secondary consequences of faults within the organism (e.g., unconsciousness, brain damage).

Figure 3 shows a portion of the BN domain model built for the head injury scenario of Figure 1. The model contains two types of information: (1) the hypothesis structure based on the differential diagnosis of the case (the right group of nodes); and (2) the application of medical concepts in terms of anatomy and patho-physiology (the left group of nodes) to derive the hypotheses. The figure shows the classification of the hypotheses into the three categories: enabling conditions, faults, and consequences. For each specific scenario, we consulted medical textbooks and experts to obtain the hypotheses, the causal relations among them, the goals, and the medical concepts used to derive the hypotheses. The model for each scenario took about one person-month to build. In Figure 3 (right half), we have seven possible faults associated with the single enabling condition car accident: *Head_Injury*, *Brain_Moving*,

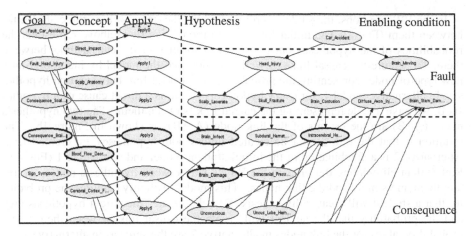

Fig. 3. Part of the Bayesian network student model. The complete network contains 66 nodes

Scalp_Lacerate, *Skull_Fracture*, *Brain_Contusion*, *Diffuse_Axon_Injury*, and *Brain_Stem_Damage*. The remaining hypothesis nodes are consequences of these faults. Each hypothesis node has parent nodes, which have a direct causal impact on it. For example, *Brain_Damage* has parents *Brain_Infection* and *Intracerebral_Hemorrhage*. All hypothesis nodes have two states, indicating whether or not the student knows that the hypothesis is a valid hypothesis for the case.

The application of medical concepts is represented in terms of three kinds of nodes: goals, general medical knowledge, and apply actions. Every hypothesis node (except the root, which represents the scenario itself) has a unique *Apply* node as one of its parents. The *Apply* node represents the application of a medical concept to a goal in order to derive the hypothesis. For example the *Apply3* node indicates that the student is able to use knowledge of the *Blood_Flow_Decrease* medical concept to infer that *Brain_Damage* is a consequence of *Brain_Infection*. Each hypothesis node thus has a conditional probability table specifying the probability of the hypothesis being known conditioned on whether the parent hypotheses are known and whether the student is able to apply the appropriate piece of knowledge to determine the cause-effect relationship. The conditional probability tables for the *Apply* nodes are simple AND gates.

Our BN student model is similar to the student model used by Conati, et al [4]. Their model includes five types of nodes: Context-Rule, Rule-Application, Fact, Goal, and Strategy. The correspondence between their node types and ours is: Context-Rule = Concept, Rule-Application = Apply, Fact = Hypothesis, and Goal = Goal. Strategy nodes, which represent different correct solutions to a problem, are implicitly encoded in our model by the fact that students can enumerate the causal hypothesis structure in any order. Our model contains causal links among hypotheses, which are not present in their model. The reason for this is that in our medical domains a problem solution is represented by the hypotheses and causal links among them, while in their physics domains a problem solution is represented by a sequence of rule applications and the derived facts.

In the PBL sessions, the students create the hypotheses as well as the causal links between them (Fig. 2). The initial BN domain model described above represents the probabilities of the hypotheses but not the probabilities of the causal links between them. To capture the causal links as well, we modified the model by incorporating a new type of node representing the probability of a causal link between two hypotheses. In alternative model 1, for every hypothesis A that is a direct cause of a hypothesis B, we have a node representing the causal link between them. The two hypothesis nodes (A, B) are the parents of the link node (A→B), as shown in Figure 4b. The intuition is that the link cannot be created unless both hypotheses are created first. Alternative 2 is a combination of the initial student model and alternative 1 (Fig. 4c). Rather than eliminating the links in the Bayes net between hypothesis nodes, we retain them and simply add the link nodes. This model explicitly captures the probability that a student will create a hypothesis (B) if he creates the parent hypothesis (A), and the probability that the student will create the causal link between them. The probability tables for the link nodes in alternative 2 are the same as in alternative 1.

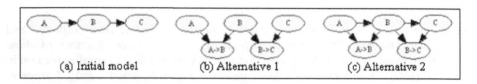

Fig. 4. A simple BN illustrating the hypothesis structure of the initial and alternative domain clinical reasoning models

The conditional probability tables for each network were obtained by learning from data obtained from the transcripts of PBL sessions. A total of 15 groups of third year medical students from Thammasat University Medical School were involved in this study. Each group, consisting of eight students with different backgrounds, was presented with the head injury, stroke and heart attack cases and asked to construct possible hypotheses for the case, under the guidance of a tutor. After the sessions the tape and the results on the whiteboard were analyzed to determine whether or not each goal, concept and hypothesis was mentioned. We used the EM learning algorithm provided by the HUGIN Researcher software to learn the conditional probabilities of each node [10].

3.2 Individual and Collaborative Student Clinical Reasoning Modeling

The domain clinical reasoning model is instantiated for each student prior to group discussion by entering that student's background knowledge as evidence. For example, if a student has a background in anatomy, we would instantiate the *Skull_Anatomy* and *Scalp_Anatomy* nodes. Since all students have *basic* knowledge in anatomy, physiology and pathology before they encounter the PBL tutorial sessions, we make the assumption that once a hypothesis in the domain model is created by one student in the group during discussion, every student knows that hypothesis. So as hypotheses are created, they are instantiated in each student model.

Conflict is an important aspect of group life. Researchers have suggested ways to ameliorate cognitive conflict and increase member productivity in group problem solving, which include combining individual novel ideas (divergent thinking) and narrowing this set to one alternative (convergent thinking) [11]. Following commonly accepted practice in medical PBL [7], we assume that students should and generally do enumerate the possible hypotheses by focusing sequentially on the various causal paths in the domain, linking enabling conditions with faults and consequences. So for each student, we must determine what causal path he is reasoning along, which we do by identifying the path of highest probability in that student's model. This is computed as the joint probability of the nodes along the path, which is a function built into the Hugin software. Suppose we have the following hypotheses entered into the student model: *Car_Accident, Head_Injury, Intracranial_Pressure_Increase, and Unconscious*. The evidence is entered and propagated, and new beliefs are retrieved. Here we have six candidate paths, two of which are:

Path 2: **Unconscious** ← *Brain_Damage* ← **Intracranial_Pressure_Increase** ← *Subdural_Hematoma* ← *Skull_Fracture* ← **Head_Injury** ← **Car_Accident**
Path 4: **Unconscious** ← *Brain_Damage* ← *Intracerebral_Hematoma* ← *Brain_Contusion* ← **Head_Injury** ← **Car_Accident**

The most likely current reasoning path for this student is path 2 since it has the maximum joint probability. Since the students work in a group, it is also necessary to identify a causal path that can be used to focus group discussion, particularly when the discussion seems to be diverging in different directions. Although groups can resolve disagreements in several ways, majorities are important [16], particularly in judgmental tasks that lack demonstrably correct answers (e.g. medical diagnosis). Thus, we would like to identify a path that has much of the attention of much of the group and has at least one member whose attention is focused on that path. This is done as follows. We identify a set of candidate paths by taking the most likely path for each student. This guarantees that each candidate path has at least one student currently focused on it. We then compute the sum of the probabilities of each candidate path over all students and select the path with the highest sum. This gives us the candidate path with the highest average attention over all students.

From our study of PBL sessions [17], we identified and implemented seven tutoring strategies commonly used by experienced human tutors: 1) focus group discussion, 2) promote open discussion, 3) deflect uneducated guessing, 4) avoid jumping critical steps, 5) address incomplete information, 6) refer to experts in the group, and 7) promote collaborative discussion. All strategies except strategy 7 use both the structure and the probabilities of the BN models. Strategies 1, 2, 5 make use of the group reasoning path.

4   Evaluation – Accuracy of the Student Models

In order to determine the accuracy of the model, we compared the probabilities of hypotheses and causal links from the student model with actual student actions considered as a "gold standard", and compared the group path generated by COMET and the path suggested by human tutors.

4.1   Experimental Design

We recruited 15 second-year medical students from Thammasat University Medical School. That is, they had not yet had PBL experience in Head injury, Stroke, or Heart attack. Stratified random sampling was applied to divide the students into 3 groups based on their background knowledge. Ten tutors with at least five years experience in conducting the brain and cardiovascular course were involved in the evaluation of the group path. Students were asked to answer pretest questions to determine their background knowledge. This information was used to instantiate the general student model for each individual student.

Students participated in the problem solving session on head injury, stroke and heart attack scenarios with COMET. Each student was asked to enumerate hypotheses and links using an offline client application. The student actions of creating hypotheses and their links served as a gold standard for comparing with the predicted probabilities from the BN student model. Then groups of 5 students worked collaboratively using an online client application. Ten tutors were asked to identify the reasoning path that the group should follow for each scenario and each group given the partial solutions and the information about the students' background knowledge. This data was used to compare with the group path generated by COMET.

4.2 Results

To determine whether our student models are accurate in predicting individual student actions, we evaluated them by means of receiver operating characteristic (ROC) curve analysis [3]. ROC curves plot sensitivity (true positive ratio) versus 1-specificity (true negative ratio) for a series of thresholds of the posterior probabilities of the nodes in the BN model. The area under the curve (AUC) represents an overall measurement of performance of the student model, with 1.0 a perfect test and 0.5 representing a model with no discriminating capacity. To measure the statistical significance of the difference between two AUCs, we used the between-area correlation and the standard error of the difference in areas [8].

Table 1. ROC curve analysis showing AUC for three student models

Model/Prediction	Head injury	Stoke	Heart attack	All scenarios
Initial/Hypotheses	0.731	0.809	0.843	0.814
Alternative 1/Hypotheses	0.859	0.793	0.917	0.848
Alternative 2/Hypotheses	0.909	0.765	0.868	0.832
Alternative 1/Causal links	0.895	0.814	0.843	0.848
Alternative 2/Causal links	0.897	0.838	0.905	0.899

Table 1 shows the ROC curve analysis of the three alternative models for the Head injury, Stroke, and Heart attack scenarios. For the Head injury scenario, there were no statistically significant differences between the AUCs for alternative 1 and alternative 2, while each of them was more accurate than the initial model in predicting which hypotheses students created. For the Stroke and Heart attack scenarios, there were no statistically significant differences between the AUCs of all three models. Averaging over all scenarios, alternative 1 and alternative 2 were more accurate in predicting which hypotheses students created than the initial model. However, there was no statistically significant difference between the AUCs for the alternative 1 and alternative 2. Alternative 2 was more accurate in predicting which causal links student created than alternative 1.

In order to evaluate the accuracy of our BN student model in predicting the group reasoning path, we compared the group reasoning path generated by COMET to the paths suggested by 10 human tutors for 3 scenarios and 3 groups. This gave us 90 data points for comparison. Total number of reasoning paths containing at least one node that was created for the Head injury, Stroke and Heart attack scenarios was 6, 65, and 125 respectively.

Table 2. Results comparing COMET and human tutor group paths

Scenario	COMET's path	Human tutors' path (% of tutors suggesting the path)		
Head injury	12	12 (85%)	14 (15%)	
	14	14 (70%)	12 (10%)	Others (20%)
Stroke	23	23 (85%)	24 (10%)	Others (5%)
	24	24 (60%)	23 (20%)	Others (20%)
Heart attack	31	31 (90%)	32 (10%)	
	32	32 (70%)	31 (20%)	Others (10%)

The results show that COMET's group paths are in line with the majority consensus of those suggested by the human tutors. For example, in the situation where COMET generated path no. 12, 85% of the tutor also suggested the same path, and 15% suggested path no. 14. To test the statistical significance of the agreement between the system and the human tutors, we used the McNemar test and Kappa statistic, which are commonly used in medicine to determine the degree of agreement between two alternative testing procedures [5]. There were no statistical differences between the human tutors and COMET (McNemar test, $p = 0.774$). The results show a high degree of agreement between the group path generated by COMET and by the human tutors (Kappa index = 0.823).

5 Conclusions and Future Work

We have described a general domain-independent BN clinical reasoning model for medical PBL that integrates hypothesis structure based on differential diagnoses of the patient case and the application of the corresponding medical concepts in the problem solving process. Student background knowledge as well as individual and group reasoning behavior play an important role in modeling individual and collaborative student clinical reasoning. The positive result from the model's evaluation in three different scenarios provides encouraging support for our framework.

Future work will include more extensive evaluation. We are planning a full scale evaluation of COMET's effectiveness in imparting clinical reasoning skills and medical knowledge to students. Specifically, our empirical study will focus on student clinical reasoning gains obtained using COMET versus those obtained from human tutored PBL sessions.

Acknowledgements

We thank Hugin Expert for providing us the use of the Hugin Reseacher software. Thanks to Thammasat University Medical School for their participation in the data collection and system evaluation, and to Dr. Kesorn Jongjarern and Dr. Pornchai Yodvisitsak for their helpful suggestions in designing the student clinical reasoning model.

References

1. Anderson, J. R.: Problem solving and learning. American Psychologist. 48 (1993) 35-44
2. 2. Barrows, H. S.: A taxonomy of problem-based   learning methods. Medical Education. 20 (1986) 481-486
3. Bradley, A. P.: The Use of Area under ROC Curve in the Evaluation of Learning Algorithms. Pattern Recognition. 30 (1995) 1145-1159
4. Conati, C., Gertner, A., VanLehn, K.: Using Bayesian Networks to Manage Uncertainty in Student Modeling, Journal of User Modeling and User-Adapted Interaction. 12 (2002) 371-417
5. Dawson, B., Trapp, R. G.: Basic & Clinical Biostatistics (McGraw-Hill, 2001)
6. Elstein, A. L., Shulman, L. S., Sprafka, S. A.: Medical Problem Solving - An Analysis of Clinical Reasoning (Cambridge: Harvard University Press, 1978)
7. Feltovich, P. J., Barrows, H. S.: Issues of generality in medical problem solving, in H. G. Schmidt and M. L. De Volder, eds., Tutorials in problem-based learning: A new direction in teaching the health professions (The Netherlands, Van Gorcum, 1984) 128-142
8. Hanley, J. A., McNeil, B. J.: A Method of Comparing the Areas Under Receiver Operating Characteristic Curves Derived from the Same Case. Radiology. 148 (1983) 839-843
9. Jameson, A., Baldes, S., and Kleinbauer, T.: Generative Models of Group Members as Support for Group Collaboration. Workshop on User and Group Models for Web-Based Adaptive Collaborative Environments Proceedings of the International Conference on User Modeling. (2003) 1-14
10. Lauritzen, S. L.: The EM-algorithm for graphical association models with missing data, Computational Statistics and Data Analysis. 1 (1995) 191-201
11. Levine J. M., Moreland, R. L.: Collaboration: The social context of theory development. Personality and Social Psychology Review. 8 (2004) 164-172
12. Lock, Z.,Kudenko, D.: Multi-component User Models of Team Members. Workshop on User and Group Models for Web-Based Adaptive Collaborative Environments, in International Conference on User Modeling. (2003) 25-34
13. Martens, A., Bernauer, J., Illmann, T., Seitz, A.: Docs 'n Drugs - The Virtual Polyclinic. An Intelligent Tutoring System for Web-Based and Case-Oriented Training in Medicine. Proceedings of the AMIA Fall Symposium. (2001) 433-437
14. Masthoff, J.: Modeling a group of television viewers. Proceedings of the Workshop Future tv, in Intelligent Tutoring Systems Conference. (2002) 34-42
15. Mitrovic, A.: Experiences in Implementing Constraint-Based Modeling in SQL-Tutor, Proceedings of the 4th International Conference in Intelligent Tutoring Systems. (1998) 414-423
16. Stasser G., Kerr N. L., Davis J. H. : Influence processes and consensus models in decision-making groups, in P. B. Paulus, ed., Psychology of group influence (Hillsdale, Erlbaum, 1989) 279-326
17. Suebnukarn, S., Haddawy, P.: A collaborative intelligent tutoring system for medical problem-based learning. Proceedings of the 9th International Conference on Intelligent User Interfaces. (2004) 14-21

User Modeling in a Distributed E-Learning Architecture[1]

Peter Brusilovsky, Sergey Sosnovsky, and Olena Shcherbinina

School of Information Sciences,
University of Pittsburgh, Pittsburgh PA 15260, USA
{peterb, sas15, ols1}@pitt.edu

Abstract. This paper is focused on user modeling and adaptation in distributed E-Learning systems. We describe here CUMULATE, a generic student modeling server developed for a distributed E-Learning architecture, KnowledgeTree. We also introduce a specific, topic-based knowledge modeling approach which has been implemented as an inference agent in CUMULATE and used in QuizGuide, an adaptive system that helps students select the most relevant self-assessment quizzes. We also discuss our attempts to evaluate this multi-level student modeling.

1 Introduction

A number of researchers working on adaptive E-Learning technologies argue that the way to E-Learning classroom for these technologies goes through a distributed, component-based architecture for adaptive E-Learning [2; 5; 6]. The problem is to develop an architecture that will allow independent teams to develop user-adaptive components that could interact in parallel with the same user while integrating collected information, resulting in better adaptations for the user. At the moment, there are two main competing approaches to user modeling in a distributed, component-based architecture: centralized [1; 7] and decentralized [9] user modeling. Decentralized (or distributed) user modeling had its roots in agent-based architectures, while centralized user modeling had its start in user modeling shells and is currently represented by user modeling servers such as CUMULATE and Personis [8]. In our past projects we have explored both centralized [1] and distributed [3] modeling and we think that the former approach currently provides a more reliable and practical solution. We continue to explore the centralized approach in the context of KnowledgeTree, a distributed architecture for adaptive E-Learning based on reusable intelligent learning activities [2]. This paper focuses on student modeling in the context of the KnowledgeTree architecture. We introduce the student modeling server CUMULATE, which was developed to support centralized student modeling. We provide an example of its support of user modeling in QuizPACK - an adaptive

---

[1] This material is based upon work supported by the National Science Foundation under Grant No. 0310576.

L. Ardissono, P. Brna, and A. Mitrovic (Eds.): UM 2005, LNAI 3538, pp. 387–391, 2005.

hypermedia service for delivering self-assessment quizzes. We also discuss the issue of the evaluation of CUMULATE-like servers and present our attempt to evaluate the performance of CUMULATE in the context of the QuizPACK service.

2   CUMULATE, a User Modeling Server

The KnowledgeTree architecture is based on a centralized approach. This architecture assumes the presence of four kinds of components in the distributed E-Learning system: student portals, activity servers, value-added services and student modeling servers. A *learning portal* supports the course-authoring interface and maintains a runtime interface for the student. The content of the course is formed by interactive reusable learning activities that are delivered by *activity servers*. A *value-added service* is able to "pass through" the "raw" content adding some valuable functionality to it - such as adaptive sequencing, annotation, visualization, or content integration. All components that interact directly with a student are expected to send information about each important student action to the student modeling server. The server processes this information into a student model and provides student information by request to any interactive component that wants to adapt to the student. The architecture allows the presence of multiple servers of the same kind - including portals and student modeling servers, however, it is assumed that each user works with one portal and one student-modeling server in the context of each course. Any server that complies with the set of inter-component communication protocols could be immediately integrated into the architecture. A student-modeling server should comply with two protocols - accepting student events and replying to requests about the student sent by other components. The internal organization of the server, including the organization of the user modeling is not dictated. Space is provided for competition between different server organizations and user modeling approaches.

The CUMULATE server (Centralized User Modeling for User and Learner-AdapTive Environments) was developed as a generic student-modeling server for the KnowledgeTree project. Following earlier approaches [1; 7] CUMULATE represents information about a student on two levels (Fig. 1): the event storage and an inferenced User Model. All student actions that each interactive component is able to trace are sent to CUMULATE, using a standard http-based event-reporting protocol. The structure of this protocol allows an interactive component to report the kind of event (i.e., a specific learning activity or a specific step within more complex activities), the progress (for example, success or failure) and any additional component-specific information). CUMULATE adds a timestamp to each reported event and stores it permanently in the event storage. This is different from traditional student modeling approach in which these events are immediately processed and discarded. The event storage is open to a variety of inference agents that process this data in different ways and convert it into a more familiar form of name-value pairs that altogether form the inferenced UM. Various agents can attempt to infer a multitude of user parameters using different methods. For example, some agents could be focused on inferring the student's knowledge from different aspects, others could store the student's interests, even others could monitor the student's level of motivation. Different agents could attempt to infer the same parameters from the same event storage using different methods. The architecture anticipates the use of internal (i.e., in-server) and external inference agents. The latter kind requests information from event storage and updates inferenced UM using dedicated protocols. Moreover, an application could access event storage directly and process the events in a specific way.

The current architecture could be considered unnecessarily general and flexible, but this was a design decision. We need a student modeling architecture which would allow us to explore a range of different student modeling approaches which cover the same event storage. At the moment, we have implemented several internal inference agents that are used by different activity servers and services within KnowledgeTree. To provide a complete example of CUMULATE user modeling and its use in KnowledgeTree, we will focus the rest of the paper on the specific inference agent that performs the topic-based modeling of student knowledge.

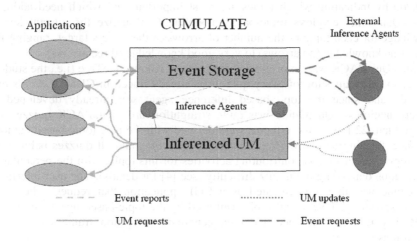

Fig. 1. The structure of the CUMULATE server

3 Topic-Based Knowledge Modeling and Its Implementation

Topic-based knowledge modeling is a simplification of the *concept-based knowledge modeling* used in a number of adaptive systems. The state of student knowledge is represented as a weighted overlay covering a set of coarse-grain elements called topics. Each educational activity can contribute to only one topic (whereas in the concept-based approach, it can contribute to multiple concepts). A typical course-level domain model includes just 40-60 topics (in contrast to the several hundred concepts used in concept-based modeling).

Due to its simplicity, topic-based modeling was the first approach implemented within CUMULATE. Our implementation of topic-based modeling is transparent for course authoring: under each topic, the author identifies several educational activities. Student progress within these activities defines the user's understanding of a topic. CUMULATE provides a form-based authoring interface for topics and activities and a *topic-based inference agent*. The interface supports definitions of topics and their relationships with activities. For each activity associated with a topic (and, if necessary, for each substep within an activity step) the author can specify its contribution to the topic. The agent uses the authored relationships between topics and activities to transform events that were reported during the student's work with the topic-related activities into a student knowledge level for that topic (0 to 1). The agent uses a relatively simple method of knowledge calculation. For all activities belonging to that topic, it calculates the weighted average score of reported results.

The first system to explore topic-based knowledge modeling was QuizGuide - a value-added service that provides personalized access to self-assessment quizzes for the C programming language. The quizzes are generated by an activity server called QuizPACK [4]. The "added value" provided by QuizGuide is adaptive annotations. QuizGuide groups all QuizPACK quizzes into topics and adaptively annotates a link to each topic with a target-arrow icon. This icon helps the student choose the topic to work on by indicating which topics are most important and which need additional work. QuizGuide employs topic-based modeling to visualize the current level of knowledge for each topic as the number of arrows in the topic's target, ranging from little or no knowledge (no arrows) to very good knowledge (three arrows).

Since QuizPACK was an original component of KnowledgeTree (i.e., the student's answer to every question of every quiz were already traced in CUMULATE's event storage), and since the topic-based inference agent was already developed, the implementation of QuizGuide was quite straightforward. QuizPACK quizzes were grouped into 22 topics; these topics were defined with the new topic-based authoring interface, forming unique *C-Programming topic scope*; and all quizzes belonging to each topic were added as contributing activities for this topic, with the percentage of contribution depending upon quiz difficulty (see [4] for details). The user interface of QuizGuide was then implemented as a CGI application that requests the current student knowledge level of all topics (inferred by the topic-based agent) through the CUMULATE query interface and then generates navigation frame with adaptive annotations.

4   The Evaluation of QuizGuide

We have evaluated QuizGuide using the traditional "with or without" approach. Some evaluation details are provided in [4]. Despite the relatively simple user modeling and adaptation techniques used in QuizGuide, the system has achieved a remarkable impact on student learning and performance. Guided by adaptive annotations, the students explored more questions, worked with questions more persistently, and accessed a larger variety of questions. The increase in participation resulted in the increase of their knowledge at the end of the course. However, what can really be evaluated in a "with or without" study of a system driven by a universal user modeling server, which has an inference engine based on authored rules? Are we evaluating the server itself, the topic-based student modeling approach implemented by one of its inference agents, or just the quality of the job done by the author in defining topics and connecting them with activities? The user modeling literature provides no guidance on how to evaluate user modeling servers or approaches. In our opinion, the "proof" of the success of our architecture is its very ability to implement a new student modeling approach and to author the student modeling part of a new adaptive application. The fact that the present application has been successful is, however, an additional argument in favor of topic-based student modeling.

References

1. Brusilovsky P (1994) Student model centered architecture for intelligent learning environment. In Fourth International Conference on User Modeling, Hyannis, MA, 15-19 August 1994, pp. 31-36, also available at http://www2.sis.pitt.edu/~peterb/papers/UM94.html
2. Brusilovsky P (2004) KnowledgeTree: A distributed architecture for adaptive e-learning. In The Thirteenth International World Wide Web Conference, WWW 2004 (Alternate track papers and posters), New York, NY, 17-22 May, 2004, pp. 104-113
3. Brusilovsky P, Ritter S, and Schwarz E (1997) Distributed intelligent tutoring on the Web. In du Boulay B and Mizoguchi R (eds) In AI-ED'97, 8th World Conference on Artificial Intelligence in Education, 18-22 August 1997. IOS, Amsterdam, pp. 482-489
4. Brusilovsky P, Sosnovsky S, and Shcherbinina O (2004) QuizGuide: Increasing the Educational Value of Individualized Self-Assessment Quizzes with Adaptive Navigation Support. In World Conference on E-Learning, E-Learn 2004, Washington, DC, USA, November 1-5, 2004, pp. 1806-1813
5. Carmona C and Conejo R (2004) A learner model in a distributed environment. In De Bra P and Nejdl W (eds) Third International Conference on Adaptive Hypermedia and Adaptive Web-Based Systems (AH'2004), Eindhoven, the Netherlands, August 23-26, 2004. Lecture Notes in Computer Science 3137, Springer-Verlag, Berlin, pp. 353-359
6. Conlan O, Wade V, Gargan M, Hockemeyer C, and Albert D (2002) An architecture for integrating adaptive hypermedia services with open learning environments. In World Conference on Educational Multimedia, Hypermedia and Telecommunications, ED-MEDIA'2002. Denver, CO, June 24-29, 2002, pp. 344-350
7. Kay J (1995) The UM toolkit for cooperative user models. User Modeling and User-Adapted Interaction 4: 149-196
8. Kay J, Kummerfeld B, and Lauder P (2002) Personis: A server for user modeling. In De Bra P, Brusilovsky P and Conejo R (eds) Second International Conference on Adaptive Hypermedia and Adaptive Web-Based Systems (AH'2002), Málaga, Spain, May 29-31, 2002, pp. 201-212
9. Vassileva J, McCalla G, and Greer J (2003) Multi-Agent Multi-User Modeling. User Modeling and User-Adapted Interaction 13: 179-210.

Computer Adaptive Testing: Comparison of a Probabilistic Network Approach with Item Response Theory

Michel C. Desmarais and Xiaoming Pu

École Polytechnique de Montréal, Montréal, QC, Canada
{michel.desmarais, xiaoming.pu}@polymtl.ca

Abstract. Bayesian and probabilistic networks are claimed to offer powerful approaches to inferring an individual's knowledge state from evidence of mastery of concepts or skills. A typical application where such tools can be useful is Computer Adaptive Testing (CAT). Bayesian networks have been proposed as an alternative to the traditional Item Response Theory (IRT), which has been the prevalent CAT approach for the last three decades. We compare the performance of one probabilistic network approach, named POKS, to the IRT two parameter logistic model. Experimental results over a 34 items UNIX test and a 160 items French language test show that both approaches can classify examinees as master or non master effectively and efficiently. Implications of these results for adaptive testing and student modeling are discussed.

Keywords: CAT, IRT, Probabilistic networks, Bayesian networks, adaptive testing, student models, knowledge assessment.

1   Introduction

Computer Adaptive Testing applications, or CAT, are possibly the earliest examples of adaptive interfaces. The principle behind CAT is to adjust the test items presented to the user's knowledge, or, using CAT terminology, to adjust the items characteristics to the examinee's ability level. Akin to the architectures of adaptive systems, CAT systems analyze the behaviour of the user to build a dynamic model of his/her knowledge state and choose the next item that is most appropriate for this state. In the specific context of CAT, the most appropriate items are the ones that will allow the system to determine, with the least number of test items administered, if the examinee is a "master" or a "non-master" with respect to the measured ability.

We compare two approaches to CAT, namely the Item Response Theory framework (IRT), more specifically the two-parameter logistic model, and a probabilistic graphical framework named POKS [1]. The POKS framework is particularly well suited for a comparison with other CAT techniques, because, akin to the IRT framework, it does not require any knowledge engineering effort to build the network. Instead, it uses a small sample of test data to build automatically the links among the items themselves. We review the basis of each approach before describing the experimental procedure and results of their comparison.

L. Ardissono, P. Brna, and A. Mitrovic (Eds.): UM 2005, LNAI 3538, pp. 392–396, 2005.

2   Item Response Theory

The prevalent means of conducting Computer Adaptive Testing (CAT) is based on the Item Response Theory (IRT) (see [2]).

For the current study, we adopted the *two parameter logistic"* model (IRT-2PL) which is one of the common IRT models. In this model, the probability of an examinee of ability level θ to answer item i correctly is: $P(X_i \mid \theta) = \frac{1}{1+e^{-a_i(\theta-b_i)}}$ where X_i represents a correct response to item i (a shorthand for $X_i = 1$), b_i is the item's *difficulty* parameter, and a_i is its *discrimination* parameter. This function defines what is known as the Item Characteristic Curve (ICC). Typically, the difficulty and discrimination parameters are estimated from empirical data by a maximum likelihood approach or by a least square fit.

Estimating an examinee's level of ability, θ, is based on maximizing the likelihood function $P(\mathbf{X_k} \mid \theta) = \prod_{i=1}^{k} P(X_i|\theta)$ where $\mathbf{X_k}$ is the vector of previous response values $X_1, X_2, \ldots, X_i, \ldots, X_k$. See [3] for a review of the different algorithms that are used for this estimation procedure.

3   The POKS Approach

The POKS approach is a graphical probabilistic network, such as Bayesian Networks and a number of other variants [4]. However, it is not a Bayesian Network as it makes stronger independence assumptions: the induction of the graphical structure and the probability updating scheme both assume the local independence of all test items relations. This assumption has the major advantage of allowing the induction of the network from a very small number of data cases. In the current experiment, less than fifty data cases were used to build the two graphs structures. Whether local independence is a reasonable assumption[1] will be assessed empirically with the performance comparison in section 4.

3.1   POKS Network Induction

The POKS technique derives the graph structure from empirical data. For the purpose of comparing IRT and POKS, the structure nodes are limited to representing test items and no knowledge engineering is involved. There are no other types of node, and each node is a test item. This is not a limitation of the POKS approach itself, but a constraint imposed for this study in order to compare POKS on the same footing as IRT.

Each node, X_i, is assigned a probability that represents an examinee's chances of mastery of that item, $P(X_i)$. Contrary to the IRT model, $P(X_i)$ is not a function of θ, the ability level. It is a direct function of the probability of other items from which it is linked with, (see section 3.2).

Network Structure: In accordance with the assumption of local independence, the network construction process consists in comparing items pairwise to look for a relation.

---

[1] Note that the local independence assumption is also an issue for IRT based CAT in general [5].

Let X_a and X_b be two items in the test. Then, to determine if there is a directed link, $X_a \rightarrow X_b$, the three following conditions must hold:

$$P([P(X_b|X_a) \geq p_c] \mid D) > (1 - \alpha_c) \tag{1}$$
$$P([P(\neg X_a|\neg X_b) \geq p_c] \mid D) > (1 - \alpha_c) \tag{2}$$
$$P(X_b|X_a) \neq p(X_b) \tag{3}$$

The first condition (inequality 1) states that the conditional probability of a success for X_b given a success for X_a must be above a minimal value, p_c, and that we can derive such conclusion from a sample distribution, D, with an error rate no greater than α_c. The second condition (inequality 2) is analogous to the first and states that the probability of failure for X_a given a failure for X_b must be greater than p_c, with an error rate of α_c given distribution D. The third condition states that the conditional and non conditional probabilities are *not* independent.

These first two conditions are computed from a Binomial distribution. The third condition (inequality 3) is an independence test and it is verified by a χ^2 distribution test on the 2×2 contingency table of distribution D.

3.2   Item Probability Update

When an item's probability of mastery in the network changes, either through observation or through a change in the probability of a neighboring node, evidence is propagated through the connected items in the graph structure.

When a node is observed, the neighboring nodes' probability are updated through the standard Bayes posterior probability procedure. For propagating further, Giarratano's algorithm is used ([6]), which corresponds to an interpolation scheme. It performs a posterior update of a node proportional to the evidence node's probability change. We refer the reader to [1, 7] for the details.

4   Experimental Evaluation of the Approaches

The performance comparison between POKS and 2PL-IRT rests on the simulation of the adaptive question answering process. The answers given by the examinee during the simulation are based on the actual answers collected in the test data. An examinee is classified as *master* if his/her estimated ability, θ, above a given *cutting score*, θ_c, and *non master* otherwise. The classification by the IRT-2PL and POKS approaches after each item response given is then compared to the actual examinee score in the test data.

The simulations are made on two sets of data: (1) a 34 items test of the knowledge of UNIX shell commands administered to 48 examinee, and (2) a 160 items test of French language administered to 41 examinees. Mean scores for the UNIX and French language tests are respectively 53% and 57%, and standard deviation is about 50% for both.

4.1   Results

The simulation results for the cutting score $\theta_c = 60\%$ are summarized in figure 1. They show the number of correctly classified examinees as a function of the number of items asked.

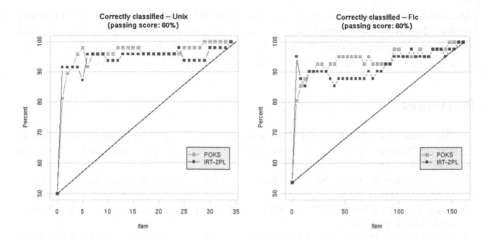

Fig. 1. Results from the Unix (left) and French language (right) tests comprised respectively of 48 and 160 items. The percentage of correctly classified examinees, averaged over 48 simulation cases for the Unix test and 41 for the French language one (Flc), are plotted as a function of the number of item responses. Passing score is 60%

The simulation shows that the POKS approach performs slightly better than the IRT-2PL approach and that the gain is more important for the FLC test than the UNIX one. In general, both POKS and IRT-2PL approaches yield relatively good classification after only a few item responses, especially considering the low number of data cases used for calibration. These results vary slightly from cutting scores ranging from 50% to 70%, with IRT sometimes performing slightly better (see [7] for further details). Overall, both methods have similar performance.

5   Related Work

Vanlehn, Martin and Conati have been amongst the most early and active users of Bayesian Networks (BN) for student assessment. In the latest of a series of three tutors embedding a BN, the Andes tutor [8] incorporates a BN composed of a number of different types of nodes (rules, context-rules, fact, goal nodes). In Hydrive, [9] used a BN for assessing a student's competence at troubleshooting an aircraft hydrolics system.

The work of [10] is among the first to specifically create a CAT with a Bayesian network. In a more recent CAT system, [11] defined a hierarchical BN with three layers: concepts, topics, and subjects. In contrast with the previous approaches, [12] has conducted experiments with a BN that is, in part, derived empirically.

6   Discussion

The comparison of the POKS approach with the IRT-2PL one, indicates that they both can perform correct classification of examinees. It shows that a graph structure can be algorithmically induced from the same data as an IRT model and can yield comparable results. Moreover, the approaches were tested with very few data cases, and yet, their performance is quite valuable. This is an important feature from a practical perspective since it makes them beneficial to a large number of application contexts.

References

1. Desmarais, M. C., Maluf, A., Liu. J: User-expertise modeling with empirically derived probabilistic implication networks, User Modeling and User-Adapted Interaction, vol. 5, no. 3-4, (1995) 283–315
2. van der Linden W. J., Hambleton, R. K., eds.: Handbook of Modern Item Response Theory. Springer-Verlag (1997)
3. Baker, F. B.: Item Response Theory Parameter Estimation Techniques. New York, NY: Marcel Dekker Inc. (1992)
4. Almond, R. G., Mislevy, R. J.: Graphical models and computerized adaptive testing, Applied Psychological Measurement, vol. 23, no. 3, (1999) 223–237
5. Mislevy, R. J., Chang., H: Does adaptive testing violate local independence?, Psychometrika, vol. 65, (2000) 149–156
6. Giarratano J., Riley G.: Expert Systems: Principles and Programming (3rd edition). Boston, MA: PWS-KENT Publishing (1998)
7. Desmarais, M. C., Pu X.: A bayesian inference adaptive testing framework and its comparison with item response theory, tech. rep., Ecole Polytechnique de Montreal, Montreal, Canada (2005)
8. Conati C., Gertner A., VanLehn K.: Using bayesian networks to manage uncertainty in student modeling, User Modeling and User-Adapted Interaction, vol. 12, no. 4, (2002) 371–417
9. Mislevy, R. J., Gitomer D.: The role of probability-based inference in an intelligent tutoring system, User Modeling and User-Adapted Interaction, vol. 42, no. 5, (1995) 253–282
10. Collins, J. A., Greer, J. E., Huang, S. X.: Adaptive assessment using granularity hierarchies and bayesian nets, in Intelligent Tutoring Systems, (Montreal, Canada), (1996) 569–577
11. Millán E., Pérez-de-la-Cruz, J. L.: A bayesian diagnostic algorithm for student modeling and its evaluation, User Modeling and User-Adapted Interaction, vol. 12, no. 2–3, (2002) 281–330
12. Vomlel J.: Bayesian networks in educational testing, International Journal of Uncertainty, Fuzziness and Knowledge Based Systems, vol. 12, no. Supplementary Issue 1, (2004) 83–100

A Framework for Browsing, Manipulating and Maintaining Interoperable Learner Profiles*

Peter Dolog and Michael Schäfer

L3S Research Center, University of Hannover,
Expo Plaza 1, 30539 Hannover, Germany
dolog@l3s.de

Abstract. Learners are assessed by several systems during their life-long learning. Those systems can maintain fragments of information about a learner derived from his learning performance and/or assessment in that particular system. Customization services would perform better if they would be able to exchange as many relevant fragments of information about the learner as possible. This paper presents the conceptualization and implementation of a framework which provides a common base for the exchange of learner profiles between several sources. The exchange representation of learner profiles is based on standards. An API is designed and implemented to create/export and manipulate such learner profiles. The API is implemented for two cases, as a Java API and as web services with synchronized model exchange between multiple sources. Application cases of the API are discussed shortly as well.

1 Introduction

Each user adapted service or application needs a user profile to perform the adaptation accordingly. In the area of education, several approaches have been proposed to collect information about users such as preferences, following clicking behavior to collect likes and dislikes, and questionnaires asking for specific information to assess learner features (e.g. tests, learner assessment dialogs, and preference forms). In addition, several tools have been designed to improve learner models by open active learner modelling. The variety of use cases are supported by such tools like maintaining and comparing the student's own and the system's believes about his knowledge [3], multiple choice questionnaires [2], collaborative peer assessment in discussions [1], and dialogues with interactive topic maps [4].

These systems can be seen as services to improve user or learner models in open environments. Different users may prefer a different style of evaluation and thus may want to choose one or more of them which are the most suitable for them to evaluate their profiles. To benefit from such heterogeneous services, an interoperable learner profile and an infrastructure to support its exchange should be provided. The following questions arise: *how to represent the learner profile, how to access the learner profile,* and *how to provide an extensible API to process heterogeneous profiles.*

---

* This work is partially supported by EU/IST ELENA project IST-2001-37264.

L. Ardissono, P. Brna, and A. Mitrovic (Eds.): UM 2005, LNAI 3538, pp. 397–401, 2005.

The rest of the paper is structured as follows: Section 2 discusses standard based representations of learner profiles, its instantiation, and mappings from internal data models. Section 3 discusses how the models can be accessed by means of a Java API, webs services, querying infrastructure for RDF, and application cases which have been implemented. Section 4 provides a summary and an outline of possible further work.

2   Learner Profile Exchange Model

In order to be able to exchange a learner profile between e-Learning and learner assessment systems, we need to provide explicit information about what is going to be exchanged, which values of the specific subject are considered and how the information is bound to a learner. Learner profile standards and open specifications provide us with a representation for subjects of exchange, e.g. learner performance, portfolio, preferences, learning style, certificates, evaluations, and assessment. Domain ontologies provide us with exchangeable/sharable models of domains. Such ontologies can model either the domain which will be overlaid in the learner profile, learner competencies/skills, or can model stereotype structures.

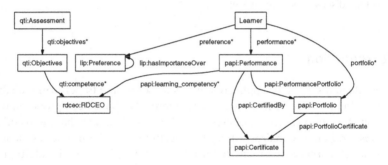

Fig. 1. An excerpt of a conceptual model for learner profile based on standards

Learner Ontology. Figure 1 depicts an excerpt of a learner profile ontology configured from fragments based on three specifications[1]. The conceptual model describes a situation where a learning performance[2] of a student is exchanged as his achieved competency[3,4] records. The competencies have been evaluated by learner assessment (e.g. tests) and were derived from learning objectives of tests[5]. Furthermore, all other educational activities, further materials, and projects created within the activities are reported

---

[1] Refer to http://www.l3s.de/~dolog/learnerrdfbindings/ for an extended model of the learner profile.

[2] IEEE PAPI is being used to model performance and portfolio: http://ltsc.ieee.org/archive/harvested-2003-10/working_groups/wg2.zip.

[3] IMS reusable definition of competency and educational objectives (IMS RDCEO).

[4] Refer to http://www.imsglobal.org/ for all IMS specifications.

[5] IMS questions and test interoperability (IMS QTI).

within the portfolio of the performance. Additional information which is reported under preferences[6] comprises language, device, resource and learning style preferences. The standards and open specifications guarantee wider acceptance between eLearning systems and as such can be seen as good candidates for the learner exchange models.

Instantiation and Mappings from Internal Models. The tools, which use a different internal data model and would like to participate in an exchange of learner profiles, have to provide mappings between their internal data model and the exchange model. Besides that, an evidence about how a learner model was derived should be provided to allow other systems to interpret the model correctly. If we take for example an overlay model of a domain, the sub domain concepts are bound to the learner performance together with time stamps, certificates and resources which contributed to the performance. The sub concepts, referenced as competency hierarchies, are further bound to assessment resources like dialogs used, questionnaires filled in with their results, activities with concept maps performed, and so on. This information allows to trace back the computation of particular learner model fragments and to determine how they contribute to the overall integrated model.

3 Accessing the Learner Profile

Figure 2 depicts several scenarios of how to access and exchange learner profile fragments. The fragments can be accessed programmatically by the use of a Java API, the web service which exports the learner model through the API and acts as a learner model server, and through a query infrastructure for RDF repositories like Edutella [9].

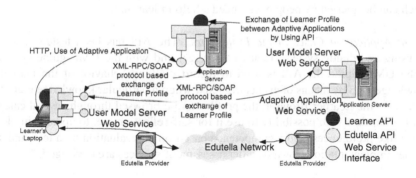

Fig. 2. The use of the API in several scenarios

Access through Java API. We build a Java API which is structured according to the learner profile fragments mentioned above. The API is meant to be used to retrieve, insert, and update the learner profiles stored in the structures described above. The API defines a class and properties for each class from the RDFS for the learner model. The

---

[6] IMS learner information package (IMS LIP).

interface provides access functions for getting, deleting and updating a model of the fragment. It provides further functions to derive additional information or to process more complex manipulations over referenced information types as well. The API is implemented for the RDF representation (instances of the RDFS described above). The API is easily extensible by providing further specializations if additional extensions and interface implementations for local repositories and data models are needed.

Access through API as Web Services. The second implementation is provided through web services where several clients can access one model which is persistent on one server. The server holds the main model, i.e. the data of a learner profile gathered from several sources, and handles all requests from the clients. Each client is uniquely identified at the server and can be used by a browsing or assessment system. Furthermore, a client can be used by other learning systems which want to make use of the learner profiles or which want to contribute to them. The model can be accessed directly by invoking functions of a web service or in a synchronized replicated way; i.e. each client has its own repository which is synchronized with the main server every time a change occurs. The web services framework can be used in a distributed way as well (several servers exchanging learner models between each other).

Retrieval through RDF querying infrastructure. The learner profiles are created in RDF. Therefore, a query infrastructure for RDF data is another access option. Edutella provides a datalog-based language to query RDF data provided in a distributed P2P environment. This option enables to collect various fragments by utilizing for example the algorithm from [5]. Another advantage of the P2P sharing infrastructure used with the learner profiles is that it can facilitate an expert finding based on the provided profile which can be queried by people who need a help in learning.

Recent Application Cases of the Framework. The API has been tested at a simple browsing and dialog system (Learner Browser) and with the UML-guide system [7]. In the UML-Guide the API is used to record clicking behavior of the learner in a knowledge map by means of events triggered when a particular knowledge map item is clicked. In the Learner Browser, the profile can be browsed through several categories of a learner data with possibility to use it for self-reflection; i.e. to update simple categories like preferences, add a competence based on an evaluation by a test, and so on. Further implementations towards other assessment services are envisaged.

4   Conclusions and Further Work

We have described a framework which utilizes standards to make learner profiles interoperable. A user model server similar to the one described in [8] is implemented by making use of the framework. The server is accessible as a web service. A Java API was implemented making use of the framework to allow other systems to plug into the standard based learner modelling component. We have also discussed how to map internal data models of user modelling systems to the standard based descriptions to enable exchange of learner models.

In our further work we would like to further investigate how this API can be used within P2P environments similarly to [10]. We have made first steps towards such an environment in [6, 5] where we discussed how to collect fragments. The API provides us with manipulation functionalities. The combination of both might lead to interesting solutions. Privacy will be further investigated as well.

References

1. Bull, S., Brna, P., Critchley, S., Davie, K., and Holzherr, C.: The missing peer, artificial peers and the enhancement of human-human collaborative student modelling. In *Proc. of Intl. Conference on Artificial Intelligence in Education*, 269–276. IOS Press, 1999.
2. Bull, S. and Nghiem, T.: Helping learners to understand themselves with a learner model open to students, peers and instructors. In Paul Brna and Vania Dimitrova, editors, *Proc. of Workshop on Individual and Group Modelling Methods that Help Learners Understand Themselves, Intl. Conference on Intelligent Tutoring Systems*, 5–13, 2002.
3. Bull, S. and Pain, H.: Did I say what I think I said, and do you agree with me? In *Proceedings World Conference on Artificial Intelligence in Education, AACE*, 501–508, 2002.
4. Dimitrova, V.: Style-olm interactive open learner modelling. *Intl. Journal of Artificial Intelligence in Education*, 13:35–78, 2003.
5. Dolog, P.: Identifying relevant fragments of learner profile on the semantic web. In *Proc. of SWEL'2004 — Intl. Workshop on Semantic Web for eLearning, Intl. Semantic Web Conference 2004*, Hiroshima, Japan, November 2004.
6. Dolog, P. and Nejdl, W.: Challenges and benefits of the semantic web for user modelling. In *Proc. of AH2003 — Workshop on Adaptive Hypermedia and Adaptive Web-Based Systems, WWW2003 Conference, Hypertext'03 Conference, User Modelling Conference 2003*, Budapest, Hungary, Nottingham, UK, Johnstown, PA, USA, 2003.
7. Dolog, P. and Nejdl, W.: Using UML and XMI for generating adaptive navigation sequences in web-based systems. In Perdita Stevens, Jon Whittle, and Grady Booch, editors, *Proc. of UML 2003 — The Unified Modeling Language. Model Languages and Applications. 6th Intl. Conference*, volume 2863 of *LNCS*, 205–219, San Francisco, CA, USA, October 2003. Springer.
8. Fink, J. and Kobsa, A.: User modeling in personalized city tours. *Artificial Intelligence Review*, 18(1):33–74, 2002.
9. Nejdl, W., Wolf, B., Qu, C., Decker, S., Sintek, M., Naeve, A., Nilsson, M., Palmér, M., and Risch, T.: EDUTELLA: a P2P Networking Infrastructure based on RDF. In *In Proc. of 11th World Wide Web Conference*, 604–615, Hawaii, USA, May 2002.
10. Vassileva, J., McCalla, G., and Greer, J.: Multi-agent multi-user modelling in I-Help. *User Modeling and User-Adapted Interaction*, 13(1–2):179–210, 2003.

Towards Efficient Item Calibration
in Adaptive Testing

Eduardo Guzmán and Ricardo Conejo

Departamento de Lenguajes y Ciencias de la Computación,
E.T.S.I. Informática, Universidad de Málaga, Apdo. 4114, Málaga 29080, Spain
{guzman, conejo}@lcc.uma.es

Abstract. Reliable student models are vital for the correct functioning of Intelligent Tutoring Systems. This means that diagnosis tools used to update the student models must be also reliable. Through adaptive testing, student knowledge can be inferred. The tests are based on a psychometric theory, the Item Response Theory. In this theory, each question has a function assigned that is essential for determining student knowledge. These functions must be previously inferred by means of calibration techniques that use non-adaptive student test sessions. The problem is that, in general, calibration algorithms require huge sets of sessions. In this paper, we present an efficient calibration technique that just requires a reduced set of prior sessions.

1 Introduction

The construction of Intelligent Tutoring Systems (ITSs) requires the development of reliable mechanisms to supervise interaction with the students. One of the most common solutions to this end is testing. Generally, test-based diagnosis systems use heuristic solutions to infer student knowledge, but these solutions are in conflict with the aim of obtaining a reliable diagnosis. In contrast, adaptive testing theory guarantees this reliability, since it is based on a well-founded theoretical background.

The advantages of adaptive tests are that they require a smaller number of questions (called in this context *items*) than conventional tests. Each student usually takes different sequences of items, or even different items. Factors such as the items that must be posed to the student and when the test must finished are dynamically determined in relation to a previously established estimation of the student's knowledge.

However, one of the most important shortcomings of adaptive testing is that, in order to be used, items included in this type of tests require a preliminary calibration process. Through calibration, item characteristic functions are determined. These functions are vital to the proper functioning of an adaptive test. Thus, this disadvantage can be considered the most important, since it is essential to get valid and reliable adaptive testing based diagnosis. Calibration requires having available huge sets of test sessions previously done by students. These students were administered non-adaptive tests.

L. Ardissono, P. Brna, and A. Mitrovic (Eds.): UM 2005, LNAI 3538, pp. 402–406, 2005.
© Springer-Verlag Berlin Heidelberg 2005

In previous papers [4], we presented an adaptive testing-based cognitive assessment model. This paper introduces the item calibration technique that has been developed. This technique is more efficient than conventional approaches, and the general requirements have been considerably relaxed. In particular, it reduces the number of prior test sessions needed.

This paper is structured as follows: The next section is dedicated to adaptive testing and Item Response Theory. In section 3 a brief description of the cognitive assessment model is outlined. In section 4, the mechanism used for item calibration is studied. Finally, Section 5 discusses the contributions of this paper and future tasks that we plan to accomplish.

2 Theoretical Background

Generally, in adaptive testing (a.k.a. *Computerized Adaptive Testing*) [10], items are posed one at a time. The final goal of an adaptive test is to estimate quantitatively the level of student knowledge as expressed by means of a numerical value (usually in the real number domain). The response model is the central element of the adaptive testing theory. This model supplies the underlying theoretical background. It is usually based on the *Item Response Theory* (IRT) [5]. IRT is a probabilistic theory that determines: how the student knowledge is inferred, how to calculate the most suitable item that must be posed to each student during the test, and when it must finish. It is based on two principles: a) Student performance in a test can be explained by means of his/her knowledge level. b) The performance of a student with a certain knowledge level answering an item can be probabilistically predicted and modeled by means of functions called *characteristic curves*.

There are hundreds of IRT-based models and different classification criteria of them. One of these criteria deals with how the models update the estimated student knowledge in terms of his/her response. Thereby, IRT-based models can be: (1) *Dichotomous models*: Only two possible scores are considered: correct or incorrect. A characteristic curve is enough to model each item, the *Item Characteristic Curve* (ICC). It expresses the probability that a student with a certain knowledge level has to answer the item correctly. (2) *Polytomous models*: The former family of models does not make any distinction in terms of the answer selected by the student. No partial credit is given. This means information loss. To overcome this problem, in this family of models each possible answer has a characteristic curve called *Trace Line* (TC). It expresses the probability that a student with a certain knowledge level will more than likely select this answer.

Polytomous models usually require a smaller number of items per test than the dichotomous ones. Nonetheless, dichotomous models are most commonly used in adaptive testing environments. The main reason is that the calibration process is harder in polytomous models. Instead of calibrating one curve per item, a set of TCs must be determined per item. This means that the prior set of non-adaptive test sessions is greater. While a test of dichotomous items requires several hundreds of prior test sessions, a test of polytomous items requires several thousands [4].

3 The Cognitive Assessment Model

This model assumes that the declarative knowledge in a certain subject (or course) can be represented by means of a hierarchy of topics (or concepts), forming the curriculum. All these topics are related by means of aggregation relations. Accordingly, this curriculum can be seen as a granularity hierarchy [6]. These topics symbolize knowledge pieces, where leaf nodes represent a unique concept or a set of concepts inseparable from the assessment point of view.

In order to assess the student knowledge state in part of (or in the whole) curriculum, items must be created and linked to the topics they assess. Thus, items are student knowledge evidence providers. The relationship between an item and a topic expresses that the item is used to assess the topic. Thanks to the aggregation relation between topics, if an item provides evidence about the student knowledge in a topic T, it will provide evidence of the knowledge in all preceding topics of T in the curriculum hierarchy. This relation is supported by means of characteristic curves as will be explained in a posterior subsection.

For this cognitive model, an IRT-based model has been developed. It uses a discrete scale to measure the knowledge level, where the number of knowledge levels in which the students can be classified is a configurable parameter. Let K be the number of knowledge levels, student knowledge can be found between 0 (absence of knowledge) and $K-1$ (full knowledge). Accordingly, characteristics curves turn into vectors, i.e. a probability value per knowledge level. This model is also polytomous. Therefore, for each pair item answer-topic assessed, there will be a different TC. Consequently, the number of item TCs is equal to the topics it assesses, multiplied by the number of possible answers. A restriction must be imposed to ensure the maintenance of all probabilistic properties: for each pair item-topic the sum of all the TCs must be equal to one in each knowledge level.

This response model uses a non-parametric approach. This means that, characteristic curves are not constrained by any model. [9] indicates that parametric models are commonly used without checking if they actually are appropriate for calibration input data, and this is unacceptable from a statistical perspective. The goal of calibration is to infer the TCs that represent the real student behavior while taking a test, not to force the TC shape to fit certain model far away from this behavior. In addition, the use of a non-parametric approach facilitates the calibration process, as will be shown in the next section.

4 Item Calibration

Kernel smoothing [7] is a statistical technique very popular thanks to its simplicity. It has been traditionally used to determine non-parametric regression curves. It is based on the principle that given a set of observations X and a function m, the set of observations next to x, should contain information about the value of m in x. Accordingly, to estimate the value of $m(x)$ it is possible to use some kind of local average of the data closest to x [8].

Some psychometricians have previously used kernel smoothing in adaptive testing [7]. In our cognitive assessment model, kernel smoothing is used to calibrate the TCs of our polytomous response model. Accordingly, using kernel smoothing, the TCs will be determined for each pair item-topic. The procedure for calibrating the set of TCs of all items that assess certain topic C has the following steps:

1) *Prior student session compilation*: From all test sessions available, all of them that involved the topic C are collected. The information of these sessions required for calibration is the answer that each student selected per item. Information on any other item not involving topic C is purged.
2) *Score computation*: For each student, his/her score is computed. This is done heuristically, since it is useful just for ordering the students' performance in the test. For instance, one of the ways to do this is by calculating the percentage of items successfully answered.
3) *Score transformation*: The percentage obtained in the former phase is transformed into a temporary knowledge level. It is made by calculating the corresponding quartile in a standard normal distribution. After that, this value is mapped to the discrete scale used to represent the knowledge level.
4) *Session sort*: Student test sessions are ordered in terms of their temporary knowledge level.
5) *Smoothing*: For each item, their TCs are computed using Equation 1. $p(u_i=r_j|\theta_k)$ is the probability value of the TC vector of the answer j of the item i for the knowledge level k.

$$P(u_i = r_j \mid \theta_K) = \sum_{s=1}^{N} w_{sjk} u_{sji} \qquad (1)$$

where N is the number of the prior student sessions. u_{sji} is equal to 1 if the student s selected the answer j of the item i. Its value is zero otherwise. w_{sjk} is a weight computed as follows:

$$w_{sjk} = \frac{F((\theta_k - \theta_s)/h)}{\sum_{a=1}^{N} F((\theta_k - \theta_a)/h)} \qquad (2)$$

where F is the so-called *kernel function*.
6) *Iterative refinement*: This step is optional. Using the calibrated TCs obtained in the previous step, the student real knowledge levels in topic C are computed. These new values can be used as a feedback to recalibrate the TCs. This process should continue until the values of the student knowledge levels and the TC values remain unchanged.

This calibration procedure must be repeated for all the topics of the curriculum. Once all the TCs have been calibrated, any time they will be used (now in adaptive tests), they could be updated with these new test session results. Accordingly, this process could be repeated, automatically or on demand, getting more accurate estimations of the characteristic curves.

Conventional calibration techniques are iterative procedures that require too much time [9]. In contrast, through kernel smoothing, calibration is a non-iterative procedure (even when the refinement step is carried out, it just requires a few iterations). Using this calibration technique, the number of prior student sessions can be reduced, yet reasonable estimations are still obtained[1].

5 Conclusions and Future Work

The main contribution of this paper is a calibration technique that makes feasible the use of adaptive testing with a polytomous response model. This method is based on kernel smoothing. It requires a reduced number of prior student sessions in comparison to the conventional calibration algorithms. This calibration technique has been included in a polytomous response model.

This algorithm just represents the starting point of this research. Exhaustive experiments must be carried out in order to study its behavior and to determine the prerequisites for the minimum requirements of the prior student sessions necessary to obtain reasonable calibration results.

A prototype of the cognitive model and the calibration technique is currently implemented in the SIETTE system (http://www.lcc.uma.es/siette) [1]. It is a web-based system that can be used as a diagnosis tool inside web-based ITSs, or as an independent testing application. It allows teachers to include new items and tests through an elicitation tool.

References

1. Conejo, R.; Guzmán, E.; Millán, E.; Pérez-de-la-Cruz, J. L., Trella, M. and Ríos, A. SIETTE: A web-based tool for adaptive testing. *International Journal of Artificial Intelligence in Education*, 14 (2004). 29-61.
2. Eubank, R. Spline smoothing and nonparametric regression. Deker, New York (1988).
3. Guzmán, E. and Conejo, R. A library of templates for exercise construction in an adaptive assessment system. *Technology, Instruction, Cognition and Learning (TICL)*, 2(1-2). (2004). 21-43.
4. Guzmán, E. and Conejo, R. A Model for Student Knowledge Diagnosis Through Adaptive Testing. *LNCS, 2363. ITS 2004.* Springer Verlag; 2002: 12-21.
5. Lord, F. M. *Applications of item response theory to practical testing problems*. Hillsdale, NJ: Lawrence Erlbaum Associates; 1980.
6. McCalla, G. I. and Greer, J. E. Granularity-Based Reasoning and Belief Revision in Student Models. In: Greer, J. E. and McCalla, G., eds. *Student Modeling: The Key to Individualized Knowledge-Based Instruction*. Springer Verlag; 1994; 125 39-62.
7. Ramsay, J.O. Kernel smoothing approaches to nonparametric item characteristic curve estimation. *Psychometrika* **56**, 611-630 (1991).
8. Simonoff, J.S. Smoothing Methods in Statistics. Springer-Verlag, New York (1996).
9. Stout, W. Nonparametric Item Response Theory: A Maturity and Applicable Measurement Modeling Approach. *Applied Psychological Measurement* **25**, 300-306 (2001).
10. van der Linden, W. J. and Glas, C. A. W. *Computerized Adaptive Testing: Theory and Practice*. Netherlands: Kluwer Academic Publishers; 2000.

---

[1] Experimental results have not been included due to lack of space.

Synergy of Performance-Based Model and Cognitive Trait Model in DP-ITS

Zoran Jeremić[1], Taiyu Lin[2], Kinshuk[2], and Vladan Devedžić[1]

[1] FON – School of Business Administration, University of Belgrade,
Serbia and Montenegro
jeremycod@yahoo.com, devedzic@fon.bg.ac.yu
[2] Advanced Learning Technologies Research Centre, Massey University,
New Zealand
t.lin@massey.ac.nz, kinshuk@ieee.org

Abstract. Information about the student in student model is the basis for virtual learning environments to provide the necessary adaptation. Cognitive Trait Model (CTM) profiles the student based on cognitive traits, such as his/her working memory capacity and inductive reasoning ability. Performance-based adaptation can guide the student to the required concept, whereas cognitive support serves to prevent the student's cognitive overload while still representing sufficient challenges to the student. This paper describes the synergy of a performance-based student model and CTM in an intelligent tutoring system called DP-ITS.

1 Introduction

Information about the student in student model is the basis for virtual learning environments (VLEs) to provide the necessary adaptation. There are many different types of student models such as overlay model [7] and differential model [8], implemented in various VLEs (including adaptive hypermedia systems and intelligent tutoring systems). However, most of the student models in existing VLE are what is called performance-based models [4]. A performance-based model (PBM) profiles the student using his/her domain performance. The adaptive support the VLE can provide is therefore limited to what the PBM supports – the student's domain performance.

Lin, Kinshuk and Patel proposed a different kind of student model called Cognitive Trait Model (CTM) [4]. CTM profiles the student based on his/her cognitive traits, such as working memory capacity and inductive reasoning ability. Due to the nature of cognitive traits, CTM can be persistent and stay valid over a long period of time, is transferable across different domains and courses, and can provide the necessary information for the VLE to provide cognitively adapted support. Furthermore, CTM can be used together with any PBM. The information recorded in CTM is qualitatively different from that in a PBM, hence if the two models are used together the adaptive support a VLE can provide is thereby also different but complementary.

L. Ardissono, P. Brna, and A. Mitrovic (Eds.): UM 2005, LNAI 3538, pp. 407–411, 2005.

This paper describes both performance-based model and CTM and a synergistic combination of them in an intelligent tutoring system called DP-ITS. It starts with a detailed description of DP-ITS and its student model. Then it analyses and discusses the proposed approach, and finally summarizes its benefits and open issues.

2   Student Models in DP-ITS

DP-ITS is an Intelligent Tutoring System (ITS) for teaching design patterns for software engineering [3]. A frequently encountered issue in teaching design patterns is the organization of the learning process. With the help of DP-ITS, it is possible for both tutorial mode and self-paced mode to learn design patterns. DP-ITS provides an intelligent representation of educational material adjusted to the parameters of the students' performance, such as the background knowledge, performance in the current domain, and cognitive capacity.

The structure of DP-ITS follows the design is consisted of Pedagogical Module, Expert Module, Student Model, Domain Model, Coordinator and GUI [1]. *Domain Model* is designed as a network of concepts. A concept corresponds to a single design pattern. Each concept is decomposed in units – elementary pieces of domain knowledge. *Pedagogical Module* provides the knowledge infrastructure necessary to tailor the presentation of the teaching material according to the student model. *Student model* is explained in detail in the next section. *Pedagogical module* uses the *Expert Module* for making decisions in curriculum sequencing and evaluating the *Student Model*. Expert Module deploys Jess (Java Expert System Shell) rule-based inference engine to reason about the student model and the system's pedagogical actions. *Coordinator* controls the functionality of the whole system. HTML-based *GUI* is used on the client side and Tomcat 5.0 Web Server as JSP container on the server side.

The student performance model stores and updates data about the student's domain performance. It is essential for system operations that adapt instructional material to the student's characteristics [1] and comprises both the model of the student and the mechanisms for creating the model.

The student performance model may have any number of characteristics of the student, depending on the system requirements. In DP-ITS, three basic categories of the students' characteristics are used:

1. Personal data – personal characteristics of the students (name, ID, e-mail, etc.).
2. Performance data – information about the student's domain performance (long-term characteristics generally).
3. Teaching history – the knowledge of design patterns and attributes related to the topic in the domain model. These characteristics are related to the corresponding chapters (teaching history), but they are also used to update the overall assessment results.

When registering a new student, the system creates the student's model and populates it with XML-based data with default values. Based on the student's initial interaction with the system, the system classifies the student into one of the following categories: beginner, intermediate, advanced (expert), i.e. it classifies the student according to a predefined stereotype. Learning session then proceeds in compliance with the assigned stereotype until the completion of the first concept, when the test for the concept is conducted. Based on the test results, the Pedagogical Module updates the "actual skill level" attribute in the Student Model. The session then develops according to the value of this attribute.

Apart from the "actual skill level", other attributes of the student model are also taken into account, such as his/her learning style and desirable level of details. The values of the student model attributes are calculated by applying groups of rules and simple functions from the *Pedagogical Module* to the group of parameters which the system gets automatically and updates during each session. At the end of the session, the student model is recorded in an XML document and read in again at the beginning of the next session. At any time during the session, the student is allowed to check his performance, so that reflective learning can take place.

2.1 Cognitive Trait Model

The modelling of individual differences in cognitive processing is one of the areas where the full potential of student modelling has not yet been achieved [6].

CTM profiles the students' cognitive traits, which are innate abilities that are more or less persistent over time and independent of the domain. Working memory capacity and inductive reasoning ability are examples of cognitive traits. CTM could enable the learning environment to provide fine-grained adaptivity that takes each individual student's cognitive abilities and resources into account. Ideally, this approach may also enable predicting individual student's performance in a new task without new parameters, presumably after deriving an estimate of each student's processing parameter from previous modelling of other tasks. The CTM offers the role of a learning-companion that the student can consult and that can interact with different learning environments. Furthermore, due to the persistent nature of cognitive traits, CTM is particularly suitable for life-long learners. The combination of CTM and

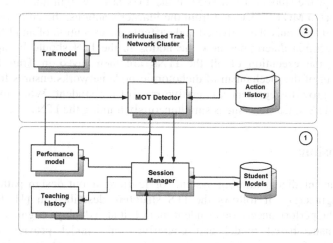

Fig. 1. Student model components: 1-Performance-based student model, 2-cognitive trait model

performance-based model allows DP-ITS to provide not only performance-based support but also support according to the student's cognitive capacity. The combined student model is shown in Figure 1.

Performance model and Teaching history are already described above, the other components are:

1. *Trait Model* – values representing the student's cognitive traits. The values are calculated from the interaction of the *Session Manager*, *MOT Detector*, and *Individualized Trait Network Cluster*.
2. *Session Manager* – manages the operation of all the other components and makes their coordination possible. It also enables reading-in the student model from the corresponding XML document at the beginning of the session writing out the student model to that XML document at the end of the learning session.
3. *Student models database* – The system creates a separate XML document for each student
4. *Action History* – The student's interactions with the system are interpreted as a series of his/her actions performed on learning objects.
5. *MOT Detector* – Various manifestations of traits (MOTs) are defined for each cognitive trait [4]. Each MOT is a piece of an interaction pattern that manifests a student's cognitive capacity. For example, Huai's experiment found that students who prefer linear navigation tend to have higher working memory capacity [2]. Therefore, the MOT of linear navigation can be used to manifest high working memory capacity. The *MOT Detector* encodes the knowledge of a number of MOTs and searches for those MOTs in a series of student's actions stored in the *Action History*. The result of the detection is the forwarded to the *Individualized Trait Network Cluster*.
6. *ITN Cluster* – The *Individualized Trait Network Cluster* in Figure 2 can have more than one individualized trait network (ITN). Each ITN is an instance of dichotomic node network [4] and represents a particular cognitive trait (e.g. working memory capacity) of the student. Each node in the ITN has a weight and corresponds to a MOT. Once a MOT is detected from the learner's actions, the corresponding node is activated, and only the activated node affects the execution of an ITN. The result of the execution determines how the nodes in the ITN should be updated. The results of the execution of all the ITNs are then saved in Trait Model. The deployment of the mechanism of dichotomic node networks ensures for an ITN to gradually grow to represent a cognitive trait of the student. When the student is using DP-ITS to learn, he/she is simultaneously training the ITNs.

3   Conclusions

DP-ITS is an intelligent tutoring system for learning about design patterns used in software engineering. It follows the ITS structure described in [1]. However, in addition to the performance-based student model, it also deploys cognitive trait model [4]. Performance-based model and cognitive trait model provide qualitatively different kinds of support to the students – both are very important in virtual learning environments. Performance-based adaptation guides the student to the required concept, whereas cognitive support serves to prevent the student's cognitive capacity overload while still representing sufficient challenges to the student. Since initial evaluation of this synergistic approach to student modeling is encouraging, future work will include applying it to other ITS in order to gain more experience with deploying it in practical systems.

Acknowledgement

This research is partially supported by Online Learning Systems Ltd (NZ) in conjunction with the New Zealand Foundation for Research, Science & Technology, as well as by the ProLearn Network of Excellence project, funded by the Framework 6 IST (Information Society Technology) program of the European Commission dealing with technology enhanced professional learning.

References

1. Devedžić, V: Knowledge Modeling – State of the Art. Integrated Computer-Aided Engineering Vol. 8 No. 3 (2001) 257-281
2. Huai, H.: Cognitive style and memory capacity: effects of concept mapping as a learning method. Doctoral Thesis, Twente University, The Netherlands (2000)
3. Jeremić, Z., Devedžić, V.: Student Modeling in Design Pattern ITS. In Proc. of the 8th International Conference on Knowledge-Based Intelligent Information and Engineering Systems, Wellington, New Zealand (2004) 299-305
4. Lin, T., Kinshuk, Patel A.: Cognitive Trait Model - A Supplement to Performance Based Student Models. Proc. of International Conference on Computers in Education 2003, Hong Kong (2003) 629-632
5. Lin, T., Kinshuk: Dichotomic Node Network and Cognitive Trait Model. Proceedings of the 4th IEEE International Conference on Advanced Learning Technologies, Joensuu, Finland (2004) 702-704
6. Lovett, M. C., Daily, L. Z., Reder, L. M.: A Source Activation Theory of Working Memory: Cross-task Prediction of Performance in ACT-R. Journal of Cognitive System Research, Vol. 1 (2000) 99-118
7. Mitrovic, A., Ohlsson, S.: Evaluation of a Constraint-Based Tutor for a Database Language. International Journal on Artificial Intelligence in Education, Vol. 10 (1999) 238-256
8. Staff, C.: HyperContext: A Framework for Adaptive and Adaptable Hypertext. PhD Thesis, University of Sussex (2001)

Up and Down the Number-Line: Modelling Collaboration in Contrasting School and Home Environments

Hilary Tunley, Benedict du Boulay, Rosemary Luckin,
Joe Holmberg, and Joshua Underwood

IDEAs Laboratory, Department of Informatics,
School of Science and Technology, University of Sussex, Brighton, BN1 9QJ, UK
B.du-Boulay@sussex.ac.uk

Abstract. This paper is concerned with user modelling issues such as adaptive educational environments, adaptive information retrieval, and support for collaboration. The HomeWork project is examining the use of learner modelling strategies within both school and home environments for young children aged 5 – 7 years. The learning experience within the home context can vary considerably from school especially for very young learners, and this project focuses on the use of modelling which can take into account the informality and potentially contrasting learning styles experienced within the home and school.

1 Introduction: The HomeWork Project

The user modelling problem being explored by the Homework project is how to build a learner model for young children that takes account that they will be working in diverse contexts (home and school), in diverse groups (on their own, in groups at school, with carers and siblings at home), across a range of technologies (PC tablets, interactive whiteboard) and compiling information from a variety of sources (teachers, parents and log files of system usage).

The main aim of the HomeWork project is to to provide adaptive, personalised learning experiences to pupils aged 5 – 7 years of age. The main content material being used by the project is based on the Number Crew, a popular mathematics televisions series developed by Open Mind Productions for Channel 4 Learning. This consists of broadcast quality video from 60 TV programmes. All this material is divided into chunks, each of which is tagged with meta-data according to the schema we have developed as an extension to SCORM. The HomeWork system helps the teacher select the material for a lesson so that activities, such as the interactive games, that are more suitable for children to use individually or in small groups, are deployed to a child's wirelessly connected tablet PC and material that is more suited to whole class activity will be displayed on the class interactive whiteboard. As well as using the system within the classroom, the project is aiming to test the technology within the home by enabling the teacher to also select individual homework to be supplied to each child's tablet PC and taken home. This will enable us to examine the use of the

L. Ardissono, P. Brna, and A. Mitrovic (Eds.): UM 2005, LNAI 3538, pp. 412–416, 2005.

system within a less formal home environment. It should be noted that whilst at the moment we are concentrating on these young learners many aspects of the system would be equally applicable to material for older learners too.

In order to address this need the HomeWork project team are building up a detailed model of each child's needs and abilities (including any special educational needs: SEN) and extending the descriptors provided within SCORM in order to classify the resources in such a manner that they can be optimally mapped to each learner. In other words it is the evolving description of our learners that is driving the way we describe the learning resources.

2 Pedagogical Adaptation, Collaboration and Context Sensitivity

The learner model used for the HomeWork project has been extended from the Broadband Learner Model (BLM) developed earlier [5, 8] and has also been influenced by teachers who attended a design workshop [11]. It was considered important to develop a user model that was not only comprehensive, but also practical and accurately reflected the needs perceptions and interests of practising teachers. For example, the teachers were interested in including categories, such as "concentration", which would directly impact on their teaching and the kinds of resources available to them in the classroom, rather than 'academic' categorisations of learning styles which were of limited practical use. The categories identified by these teachers informed many of the fields used in the HomeWork model.

The specification of the HomeWork learner model and associated meta data schema evidences the emphasis we have placed on two main areas: Context: in particular, the formal and informal learning contexts of classroom and home; and Collaborative learning with which we associate social and affective issues. This emphasis upon collaboration is a logical progression of our previous work. There is a large literature on the benefits of peer collaboration in general [4], in paired reading [13] and in learning through interactive multimedia [10]. In the design of Interactive Learning Environments much attention has been paid to the notion of Scaffolding, a term coined by Wood [16, 17] from the ideas of Vygotsky [14, 15] to account for how a more knowledgeable partner can assist the cognitive development of a less able one, and gradually foster the development of successful independent task performance. Examples of systems using scaffolding techniques can be found in [6, 10, 17]. In some systems scaffolding is provided through support for peer collaboration, in others it is provided through graded interventions by the system. More recently, emphasis has also been placed upon learners' metacognitive skill development (see [1, 9, 16] for example). In addition to attending to the cognitive aspects of learning, we are also concerned with "affective" aspects and recognize the influence of a student's emotional state. Again there is increasing attention to these issues, see [2, 3, 7]. For these reasons we have created a learner model profile which allows collaborative skills and context of use to be monitored.

2.1 Outline of the Learner Model

Selected parts of the learner model are illustrated in the Table 1 below. The fields have two representations, *formal* (for school-based learning) and *informal* (for home-based). To save space only some the informal representations are shown.

Table 1. Selected parts of the Learner Model

Record name	Details	Purpose
SEN. formal	checkbox list for SEN categories: learning difficulties (4 levels); behaviour, emotional & social diffs; speech, language and comms. needs; hearing, visual or multi-sensory impairment; physical difficulties; autistic spectrum disorder; other	ensures that system sends appropriate material to student tablet – e.g. severely deaf student would have no use for voice-over software, a statemented student may have LSA support
SEN. informal	As above but within a home context	Certain SEN altered by environment e.g.a deaf child may have access to a signing parent/sibling
friendships/ collaborators	if entered by user then names (auto updated to IDs by system), system updated entries will be user IDs	allows teacher and/or system to establish (un)successful groupings of workers. +ID = good pairing, -ID = avoid pairing
confidence level formal	3 level system: high, average, low.)	establish whether learner would aid in peer teaching or be prepared to tackle work above their current attainment level
collaborative skills formal	3 level scale (see confidence level) connected to number of positive/negative collaborators in collaborators record	students with high collab. skills would be more likely to be included in larger groups during interactive activities. Those with low levels may require further help
collaborative skills informal	as above but for home context	some children will not have any home-based collaborators (only child/busy parents)
concentration skills formal	3 level scale (as above)	useful for younger learners. those with a low level would require material of a shorter duration than others

2.2 Adaptive Learning Environment: Formal and Informal Education

Whilst most projects of this kind have been focussed exclusively on the school context (see e.g. [12]), the HomeWork model is designed with both the school and less formal home contexts in mind. A number of pedagogical categories were felt to vary between formal and informal environments, especially for very young learners who have far less control of their environments. For example, the confidence of a child with a non-English home language may well be considerably lower within the school context compared to the home where they can discuss their work with a native speaker. Conversely, the collaboration potential would be far lower for a child with no siblings within the home compared to the classroom setting. Such variations require consideration when designing a single user model profile for each child. The question: "How can the profiles for these two contexts be combined into a single learner profile?" is one which is currently under consideration.

2.3 Interaction: Support for Collaborative Learning

The second area of emphasis for the learner model is that of collaboration. Whilst each child can work on his/her own tablet at an individual task there is also considerable scope for collaborative learning. The HomeWork project is developing a number of collaborative tools and games which will allow children to learn through shared tasks. The games are designed to require all parties to work together towards a goal. Children can work in small or larger groups to develop a particular strategy. The players can also be in different locations, from close proximity in neighbouring seats, to different classroom locations, to the extreme instance in which resources can be used over the internet from home settings — particularly useful for children in isolated home circumstances.

3 Summary and Conclusions

The basic fields defined by SCORM do not contain much pedagogical information to inform potential users or to ensure that the most pertinent choices are made for a particular learner and/or lesson. In earlier work we described how we had extended SCORM categories in order to identify mutual pedagogic relationships between resources [5]. If the rich information designed to be modelled in the user profile is to be adequately exploited it is vital to ensure there is optimal mapping between the model and the classification of the resources available to each user. The HomeWork project has therefore expanded the pedagogical areas of SCORM to improve the fit between the user and the resources. The project has mapped between pertinent SCORM fields and the learner model (as well as the lesson planning stage and the underlying system when appropriate).

We have argued that special care needs to be taken to model both context and collaboration so as to maximise the effectiveness of educational resources used by children. We have set out the mapping between the Learner Model (LM) and Lesson Planning (LP) as being used in the development of the HomeWork system. The proposed learner model will go some way towards addressing the balance between formal and informal educational profiling for young learners, in particular taking account of the fact that children often evidence different capabilities and attitudes in home and school settings. By emphasising the specific context and the differing kinds of collaborative learning available in these contrasting settings, enjoyable and successful resources can be made available by the system to provide a good start to the learning experience. The design of the overall architecture of the system has been completed and some parts of the system are about to be evaluated in two school settings. Detailed interactions have already taken place with parents to ascertain their current use of technology (if any) and how they would like to engage with the work brought home by the children.

Acknowledgements. We thank the teachers, parents and children for their help with this study which is funded by an EPSRC/ESRC/DTI PACCIT grant.

References

1. Aleven, V. & Koedinger, K.R. Limitations of Student Control: Do Students Know when they Need Help? In *Intelligent Tutoring Systems (Vol. 1839)* (eds. G. Gauthier, C. Frasson & K. VanLehn) Springer Verlag, Montreal (2000) 292–303

2. Conati, C., & Zhou, X. Modelling students' emotions from cognitive appraisal in educational games. In Cerri, S. A., Gouard`eres, G., & Paraguacu, F. (Eds.), 6th International Conference, ITS 2002, Berlin Heidelberg. Springer-Verlag (2002) 944–954

3. de Rosis, F. Preface: Towards adaptation of interaction to affective factors. User Modeling and User-Adapted Interaction, 11, (2001) 267–278

4. Dillenbourg, P., Baker, M., Blaye, A. & O'Malley, C. The Evolution of Research on Collaborative Learning. I. In *Learning in Humans and Machines*. (eds. P. Reimann & H. Spada). Pergamon, Oxford. (1995) 189–211

5. du Boulay, B. and Luckin. R., Resource reuse in ie-TV. In Judith Mastoff and Rosemary Luckin, editors, *Future TV: adaptive instruction in your living room. Workshop proceedings held in conjunction with Sixth International Conference, ITS2002, Spain, June*, (2002) 19-21

6. Guzdial, M., Kolodner, J., Hmelo, C., Narayanan, H., Carlson, D., Rappin, N., Hubscher, R., Turns, J. & Newstetter, W. Computer support for learning through complex problem solving. *Communications of the ACM*, **39**, 4 (1996) 43–45

7. Lepper, M. R. Motivational considerations in the study of instruction. Cognition and instruction, 5(4), (1988) 289–309

8. Luckin R. and du Boulay. B., Imbedding AIED in ie-TV through broadband user modelling (BbUM). In Johanna D. Moore, Carol Luckhardt Redfield, and W. Lewis Johnson, editors, *Artificial Intelligence in Education: AI-ED in the Wired and Wireless Future*, IOS Press, Amsterdam (2001) 322-333

9. Luckin, R. & Hammerton, LGetting to know me: helping learners understand their own learning needs through metacognitive scaffolding. In *Intelligent Tutoring Systems* (eds. S.A. Cerri, G. Gouarderes & F. Paranguaca) Springer-Verlag, Berlin. (2002) 759–771

10. Luckin, R., Plowman, L., Laurillard, D., Stratfold, M. & Taylor, J. Scaffolding learners' constructions of narrative. In *International Conference of the Learning Sciences*, (eds. A. Bruckman, M. Guzdial, J. Kolodner & A. Ram). AACE, Atlanta (1998) 181–187

11. Luckin, R., Underwood, J., du Boulay, B., Holmberg, J.,and Tunley. H., (2004). The NINF and the teacher: exploring teachers' views of the role of narrative in lesson planning. In Paul Brna, editor, *NILE 2004: proceedings Narrative and Interactive Learning Environments, Edinburgh* (2004) 101-108

12. Soloway, E., & Norris, C. Having a Genuine Impact on Teaching and Learning — Today and Tomorrow. In James C. Lester, Rosa Maria Vicari, and Fabio Paranguacu, editors, *Intelligent Tutoring Systems: Seventh International Conference, ITS2004, Maceio, Alagoas, Brazil, September*, number 3220 in Lecture Notes in Computer Science, Springer (2004) 903

13. Topping, K.J. *The Peer Tutoring Handbook: Promoting Co-Operative Learning*. Croom-Helm, London (1988)

14. Vygotsky, L.S. *Mind in Society: the Development of Higher Psychological Processes* (Translated by M. Cole, V. John-Steiner, S. Scribner & E. Souberman.) Harvard University Press, Cambridge, MA (1978)

15. Vygotsky, L. S. *Thought and Language*. Cambridge, Mass: The MIT Press (1986)

16. Wood, D. & Wood, H.A. Vygotsky, tutoring and learning. *Oxford Review of Education*, **22**, 1 (1996) 5–16

17. Wood, H.A. & Wood, D. Help seeking, learning and contingent tutoring. *Computers and Education*, **33**, 2–3 (1999) 153–169.

Temporal Blurring: A Privacy Model for OMS Users

Rosa A. Alarcón, Luis A. Guerrero, and José A. Pino

Department of Computer Science, Universidad de Chile,
Blanco Encalada 2120, Santiago 6511224, Chile
{ralarcon, luguerre, jpino}@dcc.uchile.cl

Abstract. Stereotypes and clustering are some techniques for creating user models from user behavior. Yet, they possess important risks as users actions could be misinterpreted or users could be associated with undesirable profiles. It could be worst if users' actions, beliefs, and comments are long term stored such as in Organizational Memory Systems (OMS) where users' contributions are available to the whole organization. We propose a privacy model based on four privacy roles that allow users to control the disclosure of their personal data and, when recovered, blurs such data as time passes.

1 Introduction

User modeling addresses the need to improve user/computing system interaction. The system must have certain knowledge about users' preferences, strengths, weaknesses or other aspects relevant to the interaction to achieve this goal [7]. Two techniques for obtaining user information are stereotyping and clustering. Stereotyping captures predefined, default information about groups of people, while clustering techniques dynamically derive clusters of people with similar behavior under certain circumstances. Both techniques let the system predict user behavior, preferences or intentions. Thus, the software can adapt to the user and improve the interaction [8].

A promising area where users' models can help users to find the appropriate information is Organizational Memory (OM). An OM can be seen as the knowledge accrued by an organization and the set of mechanisms to preserve, distribute and reuse it [10]. An OM is immersed in an organizational setting and present important challenges regarding users privacy. An OM records users' actions, opinions, comments, etc. for long periods of time and make such data available to the whole organization. It is quite easy for an organization to derive user models not only from users' behavior but also from their knowledge, explicitly or implicitly stated in an OM. Some of these uses may be legitimate but others may be unethical and undesirable. In addition, people's knowledge, opinion and behavior change with time.

Some approaches have been proposed to support users' privacy ranging from anonymity to disclosure of user identity and are applied according to a privacy policy [6]. However, for OM users it is hard if not impossible to anticipate all future cases where such data could be retrieved and how a privacy policy will be applied.

In addition, OM content is created by collaborative interaction among colleagues. However, group members need information about others' status and actions. This

L. Ardissono, P. Brna, and A. Mitrovic (Eds.): UM 2005, LNAI 3538, pp. 417–422, 2005.

tradeoff between the need of parallel work visibility and privacy is well known [1], but surprisingly, it is neglected in most development proposals. If users have serious concerns about undesirable use of personal information (e.g. ideas, opinions) it is possible they refrain from making honest contributions to the OM, sustain another opinion outside the OM, or try to cover their identity by performing a false behavior. This undesirable situation will lead to the failure of the OM system.

2 Organizational Memory

Organizational memory (OM) refers to the stored information that can be reused for present decisions [10]. It allows capturing, organizing, disseminating and re-using the organization employees' formal and informal knowledge. OM content can be derived from individuals, organizational culture, transformation mechanisms, organizational structure, ecology and external information [10].

To allow users making sense of retrieved information from the OM it is important to present the context where it was created. Then, an OM system must also capture, store and distribute context-dependent knowledge. For instance, if a *lesson* is learned, then the *task* that *caused* the *lesson* and the relationship among both knowledge pieces is stored (context); when the *lesson* is retrieved, the *task* is also available, and vice versa, when the *task* is retrieved, the *lesson* is also available.

3 Privacy Strategies for Single and Groupware Users

OMS require particular privacy strategies due to three main reasons: a) the possibility of obtaining implicit knowledge, since it is unethical to attribute authoring of implicit knowledge; b) knowledge could be interpreted out of context, specially for subjective information such as evaluations; and c) the long-term nature of stored knowledge.

In groupware, privacy contradicts the need of sharing information about others (awareness). Awareness is crucial for workgroups' success because it allows efficient coordination and makes possible users be accountable for their actions and decisions. Bad privacy policies could hinder the interaction. Thus, ad hoc strategies are proposed or privacy is neglected in most research. Some strategies are: forbid access for non-members (secrecy); outgoing data filters, where users choose if an object is public, but they lose control once published [9]; social conventions, where users agree on common policies; social translucence, where actions visibility is based on reciprocity [3], and anonymization based on data distortion, e.g., aggregation, minimizing [9].

In single user systems, privacy is related to protect personal data such as name or credit card number of an identifiable person. Main concerns are the storage, transfer, unsought collection and processing of personal data; and its transfer to places with other privacy laws. Kobsa [6] proposes a reference architecture for pseudonymity in user-adaptive systems and mentions strategies ranging from secrecy to levels of anonymity such as: super-identification (authentication), identification (login), pseudonymity (users adopt a unique, linkable, unlinkable, unobservable or unidentifiable pseudonymous) and full anonymity (user cannot be identified).

3.1 Users' Privacy Roles

Experience with an OM system made us aware of two periods: 1) knowledge creation during intensive periods of collaboration, and 2) created knowledge is retrieved afterwards, with decreasing interest for authorship unless users are trying to find experts. Our aim is to find a strategy to support both collaboration and privacy.

We can identify at least four users' privacy roles or levels of identity disclosure: no privacy, alias-based identification, pseudonymity and anonymity in decreasing order. Table 1 shows the support those generic roles provide for collaboration. We consider meta-roles or users' stereotypes regarding privacy. They can also be applied in conjunction with other users' models (e.g. users' intentions when searching, task stereotypes such as "coordinator"), in a way guaranteeing users' privacy prevails. These roles are not contained in one another and neither can be arranged in a hierarchy, as we can observe from the properties in Table 1. Besides, it is desirable users could choose the kind of privacy role to be applied for certain circumstances.

Table 1. Impact of privacy roles on collaboration

User's Privacy role	Privacy Level	Collaboration Support
1. No privacy	None	Very high
2. Aliases	Low	High
3. Pseudonymity	Medium	Low
4. Anonymity	Very high	Very Low

4 Proposed Privacy Model

Our OM system is composed of a groupware subsystem capturing information while users work (PRIME) [4], and an Information Retrieval subsystem performing know-ledge recovery and context retrieval implementing our privacy policy (OMUSISCO) [5]. PRIME (PRe-meetings Information Management Engine) is a Web-based system supporting a *collaborative* activity: asynchronous meetings preparation.

4.1 Privacy Strategy

If all or most PRIME users choose an anonymous profile, then their collaboration gets less effective; e.g., it would not be possible to know who was responsible for a task, or users could do free riding. However, anonymity is useful in collaborative systems because it allows users to participate in conversations or voting-systems without fear of reprisal [2]. If people use aliases, then it will be possible to identify poor contributors and perhaps motivate them. Of course, users could have more than one alias (otherwise they could be easily identified) and then a problem arises: user accountability and reward would be very difficult to achieve. Finally, users could be supported by pre-defined roles with various restrictions [6] and disclosure levels (e.g. coordinator), so they can have some control for protecting their identity.

Although each approach seems promising, none of them fully answers OM needs. An OM must gather information from users to reuse it in the future, but under this scenario, users could restrain of making sincere contributions because of fear of later stereotyping, misunderstanding and reprisal. Our model applies previous techniques and takes into account the passing of time by means of a progressive forgetting or *authorship blurring* function. This function is a metaphor of the real world: when remembering a conversation held some time ago one typically reminds "someone" said "something" but can not fully recall the author's name perhaps because the focus is on the subject of the conversation and not on the author's identity.

In our approach, users can choose to log into the system or make a contribution with any of the four privacy roles defined: 1) full identification (an organization account), 2) an alias name, 3) a role name and 4) anonymity. A name for each role is assigned to each user: e.g. *john@uchile.cl*, *"Doomsday"*, *"Tester"* and *"Anonymous"* respectively. At the beginning, a first time frame (t_1) for a subset of participants (p_1, p_2, ... , p_k), a *"No privacy"* role is defined by default. Retrieved information related to such time frame and participants will show their full identity. However, users can choose any other role explicitly. For instance, in Fig. 1, during *time frame 1*, a user may choose to vote using his/her anonymous role. OMUSISCO will keep the user's choice: it will show *"Anonymous"* as the contribution author.

This approach makes possible to fully support users' needs for awareness information during an intense collaboration phase. After this phase (suppose it lasted one month), the discussion is closed (no further modifications are possible) and a new time frame is defined (t_2). OMUSISCO will blur authorship for information modified or created during *time frame 1* by replacing full identification with the corresponding alias name. Again, a user can choose another role when making a contribution. For instance, in *time frame 1* a user chooses the role *"No privacy"* explicitly and then creates an *argument* describing a paper written by him/her. Future retrieval of this information will always show the user's full identity (e.g. "john@uchile.cl" in Fig. 1).

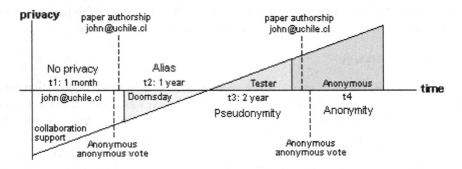

Fig. 1. Our approach progressively applies four privacy *roles* to a *subset* of *participants*

Under this scenario, there is no collaboration as the discussion is finished. Consider staff members retrieving knowledge from discussion of the previous project in this period: they could be interested in the topics and only referentially in the authors.

After a year, a third time frame is created and again, OMUSICO will distort author's full identification and alias name providing only the user role name (e.g. "Tester"). Finally, a fourth period is defined (e.g. after 2 years) where authorship will be blurred and regarded as "Anonymous" unless the author explicitly chooses another role such as in the "paper authorship" and "anonymous vote" events shown in Figure 1.

5 Conclusions

Techniques for retrieving and mining information make possible to discover otherwise unknown information. They help to find out user patterns of behavior, goals and needs, knowledge, so accurate user models can be derived. However, users may be concerned about possible unethical use of such information [6, 7, 8], and refrain to behave sincerely or fake their behavior. This concern may occur in organizational environments, but also includes open settings such as the Web. Poor user models can be derived if users distort their behavior due to perceived lack of privacy.

We grounded our model in an organizational setting such as the OM systems. Our privacy model is based on assumptions about users' privacy needs in such system. Such needs had been identified from the literature as well as from our experience. Our approach changes the system behavior in time, according to the users' privacy roles. The privacy roles encapsulate and describe characteristics of OM users regarding information privacy. Naturally a system implementing our model must guarantee the model itself is applied. We implemented our privacy model as part of the retrieval engine (OMUSISCO) of our OM system called PRIME. PRIME has been developed and initially tested with users at a large organization; the results are encouraging [4]. An OMUSISCO prototype has also been developed but not tested yet.

Acknowledgments

This work was partially supported by grants No. 1030959, and 1040952 from Fondecyt (Chile), and grant N° UCH0109 from MECESUP (Chile).

References

1. Borges, M.R.S., Pino, J.A.: Requirements for Shared Memory in CSCW Applications. Proc. of 10th Workshop on IT and Systems (WITS'00), Brisbane, Australia (2000) 211-216
2. Briggs, R.O., de Vreede, G.: Meetings of the Future: Enhancing Group Collaboration with Group Support Systems. Creativity and Innovation Management, 6(2) (1997) 106-116
3. Erickson, T., Kellogg, W.A.: Social Translucence: An Approach to Designing Systems that Support Social Processes. Transactions on Computer-Human Interaction, 7(1) (2000) 59-83
4. Guerrero, L.A., Pino, J.A.: Preparing Decision Meetings at a Large Organization. Proceedings of DSIage' 02, Cork, Ireland, Oak Tree Press (2002) 85-95

5. Guerrero, L.A., Pino, J.A.: Understanding Organizational Memory. Proceedings of 21st International Conference of the Chilean Computer Science Society, Punta Arenas, Chile, November, IEEE CS Press (2001) 124-132
6. Kobsa, A., Schreck, J.: Privacy through Pseudonymity in User-adaptive Systems. ACM Transactions on Internet Technology, 3(2) (2003) 149-183
7. Kobsa, A.: Supporting User Interfaces for All Through User Modeling. Proc. of the 6th Int. Conf. on Human-Computer Interaction, HCI, Yokohama, Japan (1995) 155-157
8. Schwab, I., Kobsa, A.: Adaptivity through Unobstrusive Learning. KI-3 (2002) 5-9
9. Sohlenkamp, M.: Supporting Group Awareness in Multi-user Environment through Perceptualization, Dissertation, Paderborn. GMD Research Series, No. 6 (1999)
10. Walsh, J.P, Ungson, G.R.: Organizational Memory. Academy of Management Review 16(1) (1991) 57-59

A Framework of Context-Sensitive Visualization for User-Centered Interactive Systems

Eui-Chul Jung and Keiichi Sato

The Institute of Design, Illinois Institute of Technology,
350 North LaSalle Street,
Chicago, Illinois 60610, USA
{jung, sato}@id.iit.edu

Abstract. This research proposes an adaptive mechanism of information visualizing that responds to context changes in knowledge-intensive work. A framework of Context-Sensitive Visualization (CSV) was introduced as a conceptual foundation for developing a middleware with three features to maximize performance of interactive systems. These features provide a mechanism for selecting appropriate content, scope, resolution, format, and timing of information delivery for effective use in changing context. In order to embed context sensitivity into the information mapping and visualization, the concept of the Context-Sensitive Object (CSO) was developed as a basic system structure for implementing the CSV.

Keywords: Context-Sensitive Visualization, Knowledge-Base, Interactive System, Context-Sensitive Object.

1 Introduction

As computing and information systems become ubiquitous and pervasive in our activity space, the way users experience active delivery of functions and information embodied in the systems has become an important issue in interactive system design [1]. The performance of interactive systems is attributed to the quality of information and service delivery that responds to users' needs in changing contexts of use. Knowledge-intensive work involving complex information and decision-making particularly requires effective visual information delivery that provides appropriate selection of content, scopes, delivery timing, representation format, and information granularity. This information visualization mechanism needs to reflect users' needs that vary as context changes. However, the notion of context used in existing information systems is limited to simple states of the system or users, such as user profile, operation history, location and time.

This research introduces a conceptual framework of Context-Sensitive Visualization (CSV) as shown in Fig. 1 by incorporating the internal definition of context proposed in the authors' previous work [6]. This framework provides a structural foundation for developing context-sensitive information visualization systems with a CVS middleware embedded between the domain knowledge-base and the visualization subsystem to maximize the performance of the information system. The CSV adopts

L. Ardissono, P. Brna, and A. Mitrovic (Eds.): UM 2005, LNAI 3538, pp. 423–427, 2005.

the Context-Sensitive Object (CSO) as the foundation, which incorporates users' context models in its data representation.

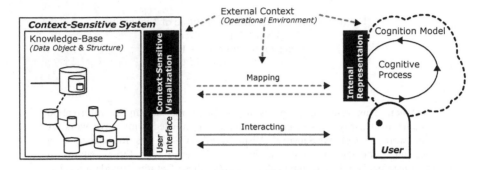

Fig. 1. Conceptual Structure of Context-Sensitive Visualization

2   Definition of Context

Diverse explanations of contexts can be found from different interests such as urban planning, usability analysis, context aware computing, and linguistics. Definitions of context found in these areas cover social, cultural and organizational aspects as well as operational aspects such as information flow, project history, and daily activity patterns. Context-aware computing includes operational environments such as location in its definition of context [2, 3]. In linguistics-based AI, contexts are considered as parameters and dynamic cues across sentences for contextual reasoning [4]. In theses examples, contexts are considered as sources of influences that affect the performance of systems. Such explanations can be categorized as an external definition since it primarily refers to external factors of human cognition. These externally defined contexts are only meaningful to a human or machine agent when they are recognized and associated with the current cognitive state and actions of the agent. Internal definition of context, therefore, considers context as a set of mental models within the human cognition system activated by the recognition of the current situation [5, 6]. For example, a person's selection of transportation to the airport depends on several aspects of context such as mental models of causal relations among possible events, geographic relations of routes and traffic conditions, and cost and convenience.

3   Context-Sensitivity in Interactive Systems

When the information is visualized in coherence with contexts or user's mental models evoked by the situation, the content of the information is effectively transferred to the user. The Context-sensitive Object (CSO) as depicted in Fig. 2 was introduced as the basic structure of the CSV.

The CSO consists of the user object and contextualized knowledge frames with the operations that bridge the knowledge-base and visualization engine. Knowledge-base contains knowledge frames and their meta-frames [8]. The CSO is activated by trigger elements such as goals, tasks, state changes, and actions from external sources. Depending on the goal of an operation, relevant knowledge frames in the domain knowledge-base are selected by the CSO operation for delivery to the user. User object built in the CS Middleware are collections of meta-models and models of contexts. The CSO operation then selects or activates a set of context models based on the selected domain knowledge and the external information. The selected knowledge elements and external information are then mapped on and positioned in the activated context models to develop contextualized knowledge as internal representation in the CSO. The internal knowledge representation and the associated context models are then mapped onto the visual objects and structure by the operation of the visualization engine. Methods for context model representation and the mechanism of the four operations defined in the diagram are critical to develop the CSO. Frames for context models must be generated dynamically for diverse situations based on consistent parametric structures stored in meta-context model. Parameters are detachable variables that store data for contexts, conditions, and states.

The benefits of introducing the CSO are: 1) keeping information mapping consistent with human cognitive models to enhance the effectiveness of the information delivery, and 2) representing contexts explicitly through the visualization process to allow a user's interaction with deeper levels of the visualization mechanism.

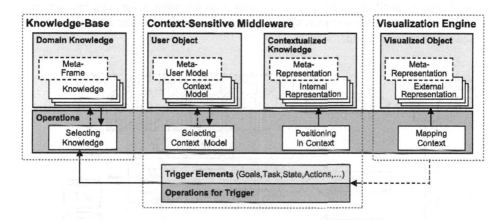

Fig. 2. Basic Structure and Information Flow of Context-Sensitive Object

For implementing the operations, contextual reasoning can be introduced as one of the methods for selecting contexts and positioning domain-knowledge and information in the selected context. Linguistic based AI defines three general reasoning mechanisms: Localized Reasoning, Push & Pop, and Shifting [4]. By controlling contexts as parameters dynamically, these mechanisms can be incorporated into the operations for generating contextualized knowledge. *Localized Reasoning* contains basic mechanisms how systems control meta-frames and meta-user models to answer for triggering elements internally. Calculating the optimized route to destination for user's goal is an example of *localized reasoning*. However, sometimes a user wants to manipulate contexts directly to get more meaningful knowledge by adding and/or removing contextual parameters. *Push & Pop* works here. For instance, if a driver finds the routed road is suddenly not available, a driver must control the state of road (the value of meta-frame) directly to get another route. A context of road availability is *pushed* by the user. Or, a context can be *popped* out in some cases. *Shifting* provides users with new viewpoints of the knowledge by controlling the value of meta-frame and meta-user model for context data. If a user is driving on a busy road, time-based distance representation is the optimal visualization solution. However, an indexical representation for gas station is better for visualization, if the fuel gauge is approaching empty.

4   System Architecture for Context-Sensitive Visualization

The basic system architecture in Fig. 3 was developed to implement a software platform for simulating and evaluating the CSV concept and functional subsystems. The CSV-based system can be effectively implemented for diverse applications for knowledge-intensive work such as business, engineering, education, communication, and medical work where contexts take critical roles. As shown in Fig. 3, it consists of three parts: Visualization Engine, Data-Processing Engine, and DBMS. Visualization engine has the component of stage creator, interaction controller, and manager for visual objects, attributes, and spaces in visual representation. Users can interact with the displayed information objects to make them consistent with their mental models to enhance their performance.

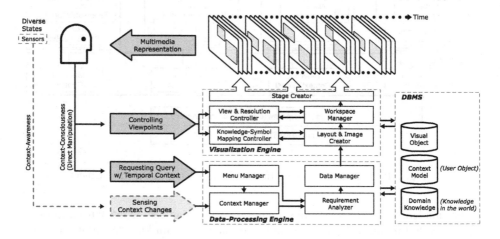

Fig. 3. System Architecture for CVS-based information systems

Data-processing engine is a collection of functional modules such as managers for menu and data, and analyzer for interpreting information. This part is for analyzing the external situations through sensors, actions, and internal contexts like gathered patterns of history to decide the appropriate context models for visualization in the situation. A context manager handles these processes and an interface manager enables a user to control the initial index of context. A data manager works as a gate between DBMS, visualization engine, external DBMS, and requirement analyzer.

DBMS consists of knowledge-base encoded in the CSV, context model, and visual object. It also has temporal DBMS for storing the trigger elements and history of users' action. The CSV middleware provides the control of selecting: 1) knowledge content, resolution, format, and timing for effective information delivery in changing context, 2) interaction methods to control and monitor information for capturing context for understanding information and making better decision by enhancing users' cognitive capacity, and 3) data accumulation methods to record the history of users' interactions for elicitation of their mental models through the evolution of context models.

5 Conclusion and Perspectives

This research introduced a conceptual framework for developing context-sensitive visualization systems. In the course of the framework integration, internal definition of context was explained as a set of mental models and incorporated as the context representation method in CSV. In order to develop the CSV middleware applicable to diverse interactive systems, further studies such as building the knowledge class libraries for context models, and the mapping and visualization logics between data and visual objects with case studies must be conducted.

References

1. Dourish, P.: Where the Action is; The Foundations of Embodied Interaction. MIT Press, Cambridge, MA (2001) 1-23
2. Schmidt, A., Beigl, M., and Gellersen, H. W.: There is more to Context than Location. Proceedings Workshop on Interactive Applications of Mobile Computing (IMC' 98), Rostock, Germany (1998)
3. Benerecetti, M., Bouquet, P., and Ghidini, C.: Contextual Reasoning Distilled, Journal of Theoretical and Experimental Artificial Intelligence, 12(3) (2000) 279-305
4. Kokinov, B.: Dynamics and Automaticity of Context; A Cognitive Modeling Approach. In Lecture Notes in Artificial Intelligent, Springer Verlag (1999)
5. Sato, K.: Context-Sensitive Design; Bridging Viewpoints for Human-Centered Design, Proceedings of the FutureGround 2004 Conference, Design Research Society, Melbourne (2004)
6. Kobsa, A.: Generic User Modeling Systems, User Modeling and User-Adapted Interaction 11 (2001) 49-63
7. Bresillon, P.: Making Context Explicit in Communicating Objects, in Communicating with Smart Objects: Developing Technology for Usable Pervasive Computing Systems, Kogan Page, London (2003)
8. Kashyap, V. and Sheth, A.: Semantic and Schematic Similarities between Database Object: A Context-Based Approach, The VLDB Journal, Springer-Verlag (1996) 5:276-304

GUMO – The General User Model Ontology

Dominik Heckmann, Tim Schwartz, Boris Brandherm, Michael Schmitz,
and Margeritta von Wilamowitz-Moellendorff

Saarland University, Saarbrücken, Germany
{dominik, schwartz, brandherm, schmitz}@cs.uni.sb.de

Abstract. We introduce the general user model ontology GUMO for the uniform interpretation of distributed user models in intelligent semantic web enriched environments. We discuss design decisions, show the relation to the user model markup language USERML and present the integration of ubiquitous applications with the u2m.org user model service.

Keywords: User model ontology, semantic web, ubiquitous user model service, intelligent environments, user model markup language.

1   Motivation and Introduction

A commonly accepted top level ontology for user models could be of great importance for the user modeling research community. This ontology should be represented in a modern semantic web language like OWL and thus via internet be available for all user-adaptive systems at the same time. The major advantage would be the simplification for exchanging user model data between different user-adaptive systems. The current problem of syntactical and structural differences between existing user modeling systems could be overcome with a commonly accepted ontology, specialized for user modeling tasks. We are suggesting a user model ontology rather than a user model*ing* ontology, which would additionally include the inference techniques or knowledge about the research area in general. We are collecting the user's dimensions that are modeled within user-adaptive systems like the *user's heart beat*, the *user's age*, the *user's current position*, the *user's birthplace* or the *user's ability to swim*. Furthermore, the modeling of the user's interests and preferences like *reading poems*, *playing adventure games* or *drinking certain French Bordeaux wines* is analyzed.

1.1   Choosing OWL as Ontology Language for GUMO

Ontologies provide a shared and common understanding of a domain that can be communicated between people and heterogeneous and widely spread application systems, as pointed out in [3]. Since ontologies have been developed and investigated in artificial intelligence to facilitate knowledge sharing and reuse, they should form the central point of interest for the task of exchanging user models. XML is designed to serve for weakly structured data as an interchange format. The user model markup language USERML is defined as an XML application, see [4]. However, XML is purely syntactic and structural in nature. The RDF standard has been proposed as a data model for representing

L. Ardissono, P. Brna, and A. Mitrovic (Eds.): UM 2005, LNAI 3538, pp. 428–432, 2005.

meta data by [8]. Nonetheless, the web ontology language OWL has more facilities for expressing semantics, [10], and it has a greater machine interpretability than XML and RDF. It adds more vocabulary for describing properties and classes. OWL can be used to explicitly represent the meaning of terms in vocabularies and the relationships between those terms. OWL is a revision of the DAML+OIL web ontology language in which we presented the first user model ontology[1]. To summarize, OWL is our choice for the representation of user model terms and their interrelationships.

1.2   GUMO Is Influenced by UserML, SUMO and UbisWorld

The main conceptual idea in USERML's approach of SITUATIONALSTATEMENTS, see [5], is the division of user model dimensions into the three parts: auxiliary, predicate and range as shown below.

$$\text{subject} \; \{ \; UserModelDimension \; \} \; \text{object}$$
$$\Downarrow$$
$$\text{subject} \; \{ \text{auxiliary, predicate, range} \} \; \text{object}$$

If one wants to say *something about the user's interest in football*, one could divide this into the auxiliary=*hasInterest*, the predicate=*football* and the range=*low-medium-high*. If one wants to express something like *knowledge about symphonies*, one could divide this into the auxiliary=*hasKnowledge*, the predicate=*symphonies* and the range=*poor-average-good-excellent*. GUMO is designed according to this USERML approach. Approximately 1000 groups of auxiliaries, predicates and ranges have so far been identified and inserted into the ontology[2]. However, it turned out that actually everything can be a predicate for the auxiliary *has-Interest* or *hasKnowledge*, what leads to a problem if one does not work modularized. The suggested solution is to identify basic user model dimensions on the one hand while leaving the more general world knowledge open for already existing other ontologies on the other hand. Candidates are the general suggested upper merged ontology SUMO, see [9] and the UBISWORLD ontology[3] to model intelligent environments. This insight leads to a modular approach which forms a key feature of GUMO. Nevertheless, since no top level user model ontology has been proposed so far, it is done so in this paper. Which groups of user dimensions can be identified? In [6] and [7] rough classifications for such categories can be found.

2   Defining GUMO Auxiliaries and Predicates

Identified user model auxiliaries are *hasKnowledge, hasInterest, hasBelieve, has-Plan, hasProperty, hasGoal, hasPlan, hasRegularity* and *hasLocation*. This listing is not intended to be complete, but it is a start with which a lot of user facts can be real-

---

[1] First user model ontology in DAML: http://www.daml.org/ontologies/444

[2] GUMO homepage: http://www.gumo.org

[3] UbisWorld homepage: http://www.ubisworld.org

Fig. 1. Some *BasicUserDimensions*: Emotional States, Characteristics and Personality. The complete ontology can be inspected with a foldable tree browser at www.gumo.org

ized. We restrict ourself in this paper to present user model predicates that fit to the auxiliary: *hasProperty*, the so called *BasicUserDimensions*.

The following listing presents the concept *PhysiologicalState* defined as owl:Class. It is defined as a subclass of *BasicUserDimensions*. A class defines a group of individuals that belong together because they share some properties. Classes can be organized in a specialization hierarchy using rdfs:subClassOf.

```
<owl:Class rdf:ID="PhysiologicalState.700016">
  <rdfs:label> Physiological State </rdfs:label>
  <rdfs:subClassOf rdf:resource="#BasicUserDimensions.700002" />
  <gumo:identifier> 700016 </gumo:identifier>
  <gumo:lexicon>state of body or bodily functions</gumo:lexicon>
  <gumo:privacy> high.640033 </gumo:privacy>
  <gumo:website rdf:resource="&GUMO;concept=700016" />
</owl:Class>
```

Every concept has a unique rdf:ID, that can be resolved into a complete URI. Since the handling of these URIs could become very unhandy, a short identification number was introduced, the so called gumo:identifier. The identification number has the advantage of freeing the textual part in the rdf:ID from the need of being semantically unique. Apart from solving the problem of conceptual ambiguity, this number facilitates the work within relational databases, which is important for the implementation. The lexical entry gumo:lexicon is defined as *the state of the body or bodily functions*, while it could also be realized through a link to an external lexicon like WORDNET. The attribute gumo:privacy defines the default privacy status for this class of user dimensions. It can be overridden in the concrete SITUATIONALSTATEMENT. The attribute gumo:website points towards a web site, that has its purpose in presenting this ontology concept, to a human reader. The abbreviation &GUMO; is a shortcut for the complete URL to the GUMO ontology in the semantic web. The next listing defines the dimension *Happiness* as an rdf:Description. The attribute gumo:expiry provides a default value for the average expiry which carries the qualitative time span of how long the statement is expected to be valid. In most cases when user model dimensions are measured, one has a rough idea about the expected expiry. For instance, emotional states hold normally no longer than 15 minutes, however personality traits won't change within months. Since this qualitative time span is dependent from every user model dimension, it should be defined within GUMO.

```
<rdf:Description rdf:ID="Happiness.800616">
  <rdfs:label> Happiness </rdfs:label>
  <rdf:type rdf:resource="#EmotionalState.700014" />
  <rdf:type rdf:resource="#FiveBasicEmotions.700015" />
  <gumo:expiry> 15 minutes </gumo:expiry>
  <gumo:image rdf:resource="http://u2m.org/img/happiness.gif" />
</rdf:Description>
```

Another important point that is shown here is the ability of multiple-inheritance in OWL. In detail, *happiness* is defined as `rdf:type` of the class *EmotionalState* and *FiveBasicEmotions*. Thus OWL allows to construct complex, graph-like hierarchies of user model concepts, which is especially important for ontology integration. Some examples of rough expiry-classifications are:

– physiologicalState.heartbeat - can change within seconds
– mentalState.timePressure - can change within minutes
– characteristics.inventive - can change within months
– personality.introvert - can change within years
– demographics.birthplace - can't normally change at all

The idea behind `gumo:expiry` is that if no new actual value is available on the user model server after a while, one can still work with old values, probably combined with reduced confidence values. The presented new GUMO vocabulary for the user model ontology language consists of `gumo:identifier`, `gumo:expiry`, `gumo:image`, `gumo:privacy`, `gumo:website`, `gumo:image` and `gumo:lexicon`. To support the distributed construction and refinement of GUMO, we developed a specialized online editor to introduce new concepts, to add their definitions and to transform the information automatically into the required semantic web language.

3   UserModelService and Ubiquitous Applications Using GUMO

A user model *service* manages information about users and contributes additional benefit compared to a user model *server*. The `u2m.org` user model service is an application-independent server with a distributed approach for accessing and storing user information, the possibility to exchange and understand data between different applications, as well as adding privacy and transparency to the statements about the user. The key feature is that the semantics for all concepts is mapped to the GUMO ontology. Applications can retrieve or add information to the server by simple HTTP requests, alternatively, by an USERML web service. A basic request looks like:

```
http://www.u2m.org/UbisWorld/UserModelService.php?
subject=Peter&auxiliary=hasProperty&predicate=Happiness
```

The ALARMMANAGER, see [1], is a notification service for instrumented environments that adapts the presentation of announcements to the user's state of arousal and the user's location. Both are retrieved from the GUMO enabled `u2m.org` user model service. The location is derived from a POSITIONINGSERVICE application, see [2]. This service runs on the user's PDA and uses infrared beacons and active RFID tags that are installed in the environment to estimate the location of the user which is then send via WiFi to the user model service.

4   Summary

We presented the general user model ontology GUMO, discussed why we have used the ontology language OWL to define it and showed by integrating ubiquitous user-adaptive applications that the interaction of the ontology with the exchange language UserML and the u2m.org user model service is promising.

Acknowledgements

This research is being supported by the German Ministry of Education and Research (BMB+F) under grant 524-40001-01 IW C03, the project SPECTER; by the German Science Foundation (DFG) in its Collaborative Research Center on Resource-Adaptive Cognitive Processes, SFB 378, Project EM 4, BAIR, and its Transfer Unit on Cognitive Technologies for Real-Life Applications, TFB 53, Project TB 2, RENA. Special thanks go to Vadim Chepegin and Lora Aroyo for fruitful discussions about GUMO.

References

1. Brandherm, B., Schmitz, M.: Presentation of a modular framework for interpretation of sensor data with dynamic Bayesian networks on mobile devices. In: LWA 2004, Lernen Wissensentdeckung Adaptivität, Berlin, Germany (2004) 9–10
2. Brandherm, B., Schwartz, T.: Geo referenced dynamic bayesian networks for user positioning on mobile systems. In: Proceedings of the International Workshop on Location- and Context-Awareness (LoCA), Munich, Germany (2005)
3. Fensel, D.: Ontologies: A Silver Bullet for Knowledge Management and Electronic Commerce. Springer-Verlag Berlin Heidelberg (2001)
4. Heckmann, D., Krüger, A.: A user modeling markup language (UserML) for ubiquitous computing. Lecture Notes in Artificial Intelligence **2702** (2003) 393–397
5. Heckmann, D.: Introducing situational statements as an integrating data structure for user modeling, context-awareness and resource-adaptive computing. In: ABIS2003, Karlsruhe, Germany (2003) 283–286
6. Jameson, A.: Systems That Adapt to Their Users: An Integrative Perspective. Habil, Saarbrücken, Germany (2001)
7. Kobsa, A.: Generic user modeling systems. User Modelling and User-Adapted Interaction Journal **11** (2001) 49–63
8. Ora Lassila, R.R.S.: Resource Description Framework (RDF) Model and Syntax Specification. W3C. (1999) W3C recommendation.
9. Pease, A., Niles, I., Li, J.: The suggested upper merged ontology: A large ontology for the semanticweb and its applications. In: AAAI-2002Workshop on Ontologies and the Semantic Web. Working Notes (2002)
10. McGuinness, D.L., van Harmelen, F.: OWL web ontology language overview. http://www.w3.org/TR/owl-features/ .W3C Recommendation (2003)

Balancing Awareness and Interruption:
Investigation of Notification Deferral Policies

Eric Horvitz, Johnson Apacible, and Muru Subramani

Microsoft Research, One Microsoft Way
Redmond, Washington 98052, USA
{Horvitz, Johnsona, Murus}@microsoft.com

Abstract. We review experiments with bounded deferral, a method aimed at reducing the disruptiveness of incoming messages and alerts in return for bounded delays in receiving information. Bounded deferral provides users with a means for balancing awareness about potentially urgent information with the cost of interruption.

1 Introduction

The increasing dependence on computers for communication has made typical computing environments disruptive places to work. We investigate the promise of a method named *bounded deferral* [3] for providing calmer computing environments. Bounded deferral captures a simple but powerful idea: If users are busy when an alert arrives, they may be willing to wait some prespecified maximum amount of time before being informed about the alert, so as to minimize interruptions in return for a relatively small cost of delayed awareness. With the approach, messages are delivered when the user transitions to a non-busy state, if such a transition occurs before the maximal deferral time. Should the user remain busy, the alert is guaranteed to be delivered at the maximal deferral time. We now review several exploratory studies that probe the potential value of bounded deferral.

2 Studies of Bounded Deferral

We shall now investigate properties of bounded-deferral policies with three studies.

2.1 Analysis of Data from Interruption Workbench Studies

To explore the promise of bounded deferral for reducing the disruptiveness of incoming notifications, we initially examined data that had been collected as part of research with the Interruption Workbench [2]. The two subjects in the study used a tagging tool to label situations captured in a recording of 5 hours of their office activities as either being high, medium, or low cost of interruption states. The video captured the details of work on their computer screens and surrounding office environment. Participant 1, a program manager, spent .20, .61, and .18 of the total time in high, medium, and low cost states respectively, and remained in a busy state for a mean time of 21 seconds before transitioning into a lower cost state. Participant 2, a software developer, spent .29, .48, and .23 of the total time in high, medium, and low cost states, and remained in a high cost state for a mean time of 202 seconds,

L. Ardissono, P. Brna, and A. Mitrovic (Eds.): UM 2005, LNAI 3538, pp. 433–437, 2005.
© Springer-Verlag Berlin Heidelberg 2005

before transitioning into a lower cost state. Assuming that notifications arriving during high costs states come at random times during these periods, we found that Participant 1 would transition into a lower cost state in a mean time of 11 seconds after the arrival of an alert. Participant 2 would transition into a lower cost state at a mean time of 101 seconds after the arrival of an alert. Thus, we found that for these two subjects, allowing a relatively small, bounded deferral on the delivery of messages could significantly minimize disruptions.

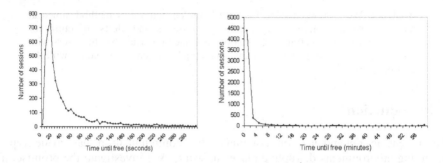

Fig. 1. Left: Distribution of the durations of busy situations for 113 users over three business days. Right: A longer-duration view of the distribution of durations of busy situations

2.2 Analysis of Data from Busy-Context Tool

For the second study, we analyzed data from users who had defined a set of deterministic policies about their availability with a prototype called the Busy Context tool. We had initially fielded the tool within our organization within an application for routing real-time communications based on a user's interruptability. The tool allows users to define when they are busy with rules, and to define available as the complement. Observations include computer activities and conversation near a user's computer.   The policies work in conjunction with an event-sensing system that monitors computer activity and that compiles a time-stamped event stream in a computer log. The log can be uploaded continually to a server for studies of user activity. The conversation detector appeared to perform reliably in tests, discriminating typical noise in an office environment from conversations.

We investigated the busy versus free situations for 113 users for several weeks to months at the time of the study. The users included 42 program managers, 25 software developers, 10 administrators, 7 midlevel managers, 2 senior managers, 4 people in sales and marketing, 19 software testers, and 4 research scientists. The participants granted us access to their busy/free definition settings and to their free and busy states. Both the settings and the states were monitored via a server. We analyzed data collected over three sequential business days between 10am and 4pm when users were active at their desktops. We collected 4,803 busy situations. The graph at the left side of Fig. 1 shows the distribution over durations of the monitored busy sessions for the participants. The mean duration of the busy sessions was found to be 43.12 seconds with a standard deviation of 51.79 seconds. The graph on the right side shows a view of the data zoomed out to one hour. The data shows that a great majority of busy situations transition to free situations within 1 to 2 minutes. The results underscore the potential value of bounded deferral. If users associate being interrupted during a busy state with a significantly higher cost of interruption than being interrupted during a free time, then simple bounded deferral strategies can provide great value. We note that the value provided by bounded deferral is likely to be greater than suggested by the results in Fig. 2 as these represent capture the time until transition from the beginning of busy states to the start of free states. This is an upper bound on the times that messages will have to wait as messages arriving while a user is busy can arrive at any time during the busy context.

2.3 A Case Study of Bounded Deferral for Email

We recruited two participants at our organization for a case study with the use of bounded deferral in email alerting. Participant 1 is a program manager and participant 2 is a software developer lead. The participants agreed to share out their email stores for the study. Both participants had been using the Busy Context system in a prototype for routing phone calls, and had also been using an email triage system, called Priorities, that our team had developed in earlier research [1].[1] Priorities assigns scores to each incoming email based on a classifier learned via supervised or unsupervised learning. At run-time, incoming messages are assigned an urgency score. The approximate classification provided by the tool was sufficient for the purposes of our study, which was focused on the overall experience with using bounded deferral with such a system, rather than on a study of the triaging tool.

The messages for each participant were segmented into low, medium, and high urgency messages via the mappings to these categories that the user had made within the email classification system. We asked users to explore the assignments and to note misclassifications by the automated system for messages received during the work week. Although the classifier was judged to perform well, a small percentage of messages were viewed as misclassifications. Rather than use a cleaned data set, we carried out our analyses with the raw output of the automated triage system so as to get a sense for the experience with extending an existing email triage system with bounded deferral policies. We considered all email messages for the two participants for a business week, from 9am to 5pm. Junk email was removed from consideration.

After collecting the data, we aligned the busy and free states of these users, as collected by the monitoring of the user busy states via the log provided from the Busy Context tool, with the receipt time of the incoming mail and considered the number of total email messages that arrived while the user was in a busy state. Assuming a system that would alert users for all incoming email, we considered how different message deferrals would influence the number of alerts while they were in a busy state. We identified, for each deferral setting, the likelihood that messages would disrupt users, based on the alignment of incoming messages and the user's free and busy states. Fig. 2 shows the likelihood that each user would transition to a free situation if currently busy, starting at the beginning of the busy state. These curves were computed by noting all durations of busy sessions as we did in the prior analysis, but normalizing the total number of sessions to 1.0. As indicated by the graphs, both users transition from being busy to being free within two minutes, with the first participant transitioning to free with a 0.5 probability within approximately 25 seconds and the other to a 0.5 probability of transitioning within 50 seconds.

---

[1] Priorities is the ancestor of Microsoft's Outlook Mobile Manager, an email triaging product.

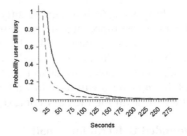

Fig. 2. Probability distribution of the time of transition of participants from busy to free situations (solid curve: participant 1; broken curve: participant 2)

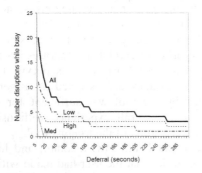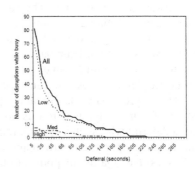

Fig. 3. Number of disruptions for incoming messages when busy as a function of increasing amounts of deferral for participant 1 (left) and participant 2 (right). (Solid curve: all incoming email; Broken curves: email assigned low, medium, and high urgencies by a classifier)

Moving onto an exploration of the value of bounded deferral in the real-context of email, we first explored how often a user would have been alerted with alerts about incoming email during busy times, at different maximal deferrals, for all of their incoming messages. The solid curves in the graphs in Fig. 3 show, for each user, the diminishment of alerts during busy times with increasing deferral times, for all of their incoming email. The broken curves represent the numbers of alerts associated with the arrival of messages assigned high, medium, and low urgency scores. In the all-email condition, a deferral of 4 minutes would lead to a diminishment of alerts during busy times from 20 to 4 alerts for participant 1 and a diminishment of 80 to zero alerts for participant 2. Turning to the curves for the different classes of urgency, for participant 2, a deferral of a little more than 1 minute for email classified as high urgency email would suppress all alerts by important email during busy times with only a small delay in transmission of information to the user. A 3 minute deferral for the user would suppress all medium urgency alerts, and a delay of transmitting low urgency email of 4 minutes would suppress all low-urgency email for a likely tolerable wait to see such alerts. We note that the results are worst-case analyses, as we consider the durations of busy states as starting when the users became busy. Based on the results of our study, we extended the Priorities email triage system with bounded deferral and bounded deferral controls and forecasts. A view of the controls for defining email as low, medium, and high urgency and for setting different deferral policies for the different classes of email is displayed in Fig. 4.

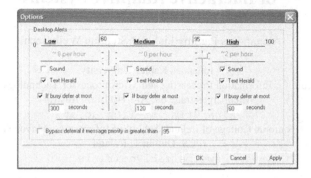

Fig. 4. Controls for a tool for specifying bounded-deferral policies for guiding alerting by the Priorities email triage system. Forecasts of the numbers of interruptions per hour for each class of email are displayed above each message-urgency column

Users can use sliders to define how urgency scores for email provided by the classifier are mapped to three urgency classes. Users can also change the way that alerts are rendered or suppress alerting completely by class. To provide users with feedback about the influence of deferrals and mappings of automatic assignments of urgency to email, the system provides a view of forecasts of the number of alerts that they can expect within each category over a workday. The forecasts are computed by maintaining a log of incoming email and its scores, as well as a log of a user's busy states, and making an assumption that recent history is an indicator of the near future. We shall be studying user experiences with this bounded deferral prototype.

3 Summary

We presented studies of bounded-deferral policies. Bounded deferral and variants provide a framework for designing notification systems that take as inputs assessments about a user's willingness to trade off delays in information delivery for reductions in disruption during times that they consider busy situations. We believe that bounded-deferral policies show promise for quieting the noisy chatter of incoming alerts, while allowing people to stay aware of important information.

References

1. Horvitz, E., Jacobs, A. and Hovel, D. (1999). Attention-Sensitive Alerting. In: Proceedings of the Fifteenth Conference on Uncertainty and Artificial Intelligence, Stockholm, Sweden, July 1999, pp. 305-313. Morgan Kaufmann: San Francisco.
2. Horvitz, E. and Apacible, J. (2003). Learning and Reasoning about Interruption, *Proceedings of ICMI 2003*, pp. 20-27.
3. Horvitz, E., Kadie, C. M., Paek, T., and Hovel, D., (2003). Models of Attention in Computing and Communications: From Principles to Applications, Communications of the ACM 46(3):52-59, March 2003.

A Decomposition Model for the Layered Evaluation of Interactive Adaptive Systems

Alexandros Paramythis[1] and Stephan Weibelzahl[2]

[1] Johannes Kepler University,
Institute for Information Processing and Microprocessor Technology (FIM),
Altenbergerstraße 69, A-4040 Linz, Austria
alpar@fim.uni-linz.ac.at
[2] National College of Ireland, School of Informatics, Mayor St.,
IFCS, Dublin 1, Ireland
sweibelzahl@ncirl.ie

Abstract. A promising approach towards evaluating adaptive systems is to decompose the adaptation process and evaluate the system in a "piece-wise" manner. This paper presents a decomposition model that integrates two previous proposals. The main "stages" identified are: (a) collection of input data, (b) interpretation of the collected data, (c) modeling of the current state of the "world", (d) deciding upon adaptation, and (e) applying adaptation.

1 Introduction

The evaluation of interactive adaptive systems (IAS) is currently receiving considerable attention. This can be attributed, at least in part, to the largely unsolved problems involved in the evaluation of IAS (see, e.g., [2], [4]): There are currently only few empirical studies that evaluate interactive adaptive systems; furthermore, most of the existing studies provide ambiguous results. Although these two claims have been stated repeatedly in the past (e.g., [2]), they are still valid and unresolved.

Recently, there have been attempts at tackling the problem of evaluating IAS by "decomposing" adaptation and evaluating it in a "piece-wise" manner. The premise behind these attempts is that the evaluation of adaptive systems should not treat adaptation as a singular, opaque process; rather, adaptation should be "broken down" into its constituents, and each of these constituents should be evaluated separately where necessary and feasible. The constituents into which adaptation is decomposed are typically termed "layers" and the resulting approach "layered evaluation".

This paper reports on work-in-progress aimed at combining and expanding upon two of the "layered evaluation" frameworks reported in the literature. The process-based framework presented in [9] discerns four layers that refer to the information processing steps within the adaptation process. The framework has a very clear focus on the empirical evaluation of IAS and has been applied in practice to different adaptive learning courses, including several studies with thousands of users [9]. The second framework presented in [7] addresses the issue of formative vs. summative evaluation and, overall, adopts a more "engineering" perspective in the identification of layers, focusing on the different components involved in the adaptation process.

L. Ardissono, P. Brna, and A. Mitrovic (Eds.): UM 2005, LNAI 3538, pp. 438–442, 2005.

2   A New Model for "Decomposing" Adaptation

Our efforts towards a merging or unification of the two alternative propositions centered on the introduction of a model of decomposition, which: has the widest possible applicability on existing and forthcoming IAS; makes few (if any) assumptions about implementation and architectural properties of the system; but, at the same time, offers a concrete enough guide to evaluation activities.

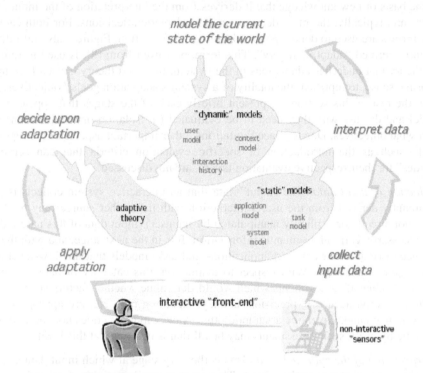

Fig. 1. The proposed adaptation decomposition model

To arrive at the desired decomposition model, we have examined the common properties of existing models and architecture for, adaptation (e.g., [3], [5], [6], [8]). In doing so, we have restricted ourselves to the process-oriented models, so as to allow for the maximum possible degree of flexibility in terms of implementing adaptation (where, in fact, approaches proliferate).

The proposed model is depicted in Figure 1. The main "stages" of adaptation identified are: (a) collection of input data, (b) interpretation of the collected data, (c) modeling of the current state of the "world", (d) deciding upon adaptation, and (e) applying adaptation (i.e., effecting adaptation decisions). It is argued that each of these adaptation stages needs to be evaluated explicitly, although not all stages can be "isolated" and evaluated separately in all systems. Furthermore, the nature of the IAS will necessarily dictate the relevance of each of these stages.

Note that this figure contains several elements, "internal" to the IAS, which are not part of the model itself, and are included solely to facilitate understanding of the model and support discussion. Further, the decomposition model explicitly makes no assumptions regarding specific approaches to intelligence, or decision-making.

The models potentially maintained by the IAS are separated into two broad categories. The first groups together the IAS's "static" models (e.g., the system model, the task model, the application model, etc.), which are used, implicitly or explicitly, when interpreting input data. The second category groups together the IAS's "dynamic" models (e.g., the user model, the context model, etc.), which are updated by the IAS, on the basis of new knowledge that it derives from the interpretation of the input data. These are, typically, the main determinant for adaptation decisions. For both categories, arrows are used to denote potential flows of information. Figure 1 also introduces an entity termed "adaptive theory". This term, borrowed from [8], is used to refer to the theory that underlies adaptations in the system; the word theory is used here in an informal sense, to represent the totality of a system's adaptation goals / objectives.

In the rest of this section we present briefly each of the stages that appear in the model and discuss why they need to be evaluated (in isolation or combination) and with what objectives. Due to space limitations, other important aspects of the reported work, such as the introduction of specific evaluation criteria that can serve as "guides" for their respective evaluation layers, are not discussed.

Collection of input data: The "input" data that an interactive system collects is predominantly derived from the user's interaction with it (another source may be "sensors" not directly or explicitly manipulated by the user). Input data of this nature does not necessarily carry any semantic information. It is in the next stage, and with the assistance of (implicit or explicit) application- and task- models that this low-level data will acquire "meaning". With respect to evaluation, this category of data is subject only to "technical" assessments which would determine whether factors such as reliability, validity, accuracy, precision, latency, sampling rate, etc. are appropriate for the system at hand. Given the assumption that "raw" input data does not carry semantic value by itself, such assessments may be all that is necessary at this level.

Interpretation of the collected data: This is the very stage at which input data acquire "meaning" of relevance to the system. The distinction between this stage and the collection of the input data is intended to identify and conceptually dissociate the two stages, thus making it possible to address them in isolation. The interpretation process may be straightforward in those cases that there exists a direct, one-to-one mapping between the raw input data and their semantically meaningful counterparts. When the interpretation is unambiguous, and independently of whether it employs any of the system's "static" models, it can be assessed objectively and in a user-independent manner. Potential problems arise when: (a) the interpretation makes use of assumptions, or (b) the interpretation requires some level of inference. Assumptions and inferences are quite commonly employed in existing IAS, mainly due to the lack of additional data that can better describe the context of interaction.

Modeling of the current state of the "world": This stage concerns the derivation of new knowledge about the user, the user's group, the interaction context, etc., as well as the subsequent introduction of that knowledge in the "dynamic" models of the IAS. There is a definite overlap between this stage and the interpretation of the input data;

in fact, in several cases, there is no "second-level inference" in adaptive systems, which simply go from interpreting the input data to representing those interpretations in an appropriate model. The main evaluation goal for this stage is validity of the interpretations / inferences. Secondary yet important concerns that also relate to the modeling process include: (a) comprehensiveness of the model; (b) redundancy of the model; (c) precision of the model; and, (d) sensitivity of the modeling process.

Deciding upon adaptation: During this adaptation stage (also referred to as the "efference" stage), the IAS decides upon the necessity of, as well as the required type of, adaptations, given a particular "state" (as expressed in the various models maintained by the system, or directly from input data). We make a very clear distinction between this stage and the next (see "Applying adaptation decisions" below), as a way of facilitating the conceptualisation of the steps that are involved in the derivation and application of adaptation decisions. A "rule of thumb" we propose for separating the two stages is: decisions made at this stage are mainly at the semantic and upper syntactic level of the interaction results; further decisions made while effecting adaptation belong to the lower syntactic, or to the lexical / physical level of interaction. The goal in making this distinction is to foster the separation of the adaptation theory from decisions that represent a typical interaction design task, rather than a particular adaptation artefact. The primary aim of this evaluation step is to determine whether the adaptation decisions made are the optimal (e.g., necessary, appropriate, subjectively accepted by the user) ones, given that the user's properties have been inferred correctly.

Applying adaptation decisions: This stage refers to the actual introduction of adaptations in the user-system interaction, on the basis of the related decisions. Although typically subsumed by adaptation decision making in the literature, this stage may be varied independently of the decision making process, e.g., to account for different adaptation strategies. More importantly, this stage usually "hides" a level of adaptation (i.e., the transformation of possibly high-level adaptation decisions to a "concrete" form experienced by the user), which only too often, and in several cases mistakenly in the authors' opinion, gets evaluated in tandem with the higher-level decision making stage. The evaluation criteria that are applicable at this stage depend very much on the type of adaptation effected. In most cases, traditional evaluation criteria, such as usability, will be highly relevant. The identification of these criteria can only be performed on a case-by-case basis, although the application of some general criteria (e.g., timelines, obtrusiveness, level of user control) may be feasible.

Evaluating adaptation as a whole: The "piece-wise" evaluation of adaptation, as proposed herein, can provide valuable insight into the individual adaptation stages through which an IAS goes. However, what is still missing is the "big picture" – the evaluation of the primary adaptation theory (or theories). To assert whether such high-level theories (or, seen from a different perspective, hypotheses) hold true, one needs metrics that transcend the layered evaluation of adaptation, as this has been discussed so far. Such metrics must adequately capture the application- and adaptation- domains, to be able to more holistically assess the "success of adaptation". Browne, Norman and Riches [1] have proposed that this problem be addressed by: (a) articulating and assessing against the system's objectives, and / or (b) assessing indirectly against the underlying theory. According to these authors, many of the objectives of an adaptive system can be expressed as lists of purposes, which, in turn, can be loosely interpreted as the collection of "reasons" that led to the introduction of adaptation in the system. Metrics and assessment methods can then be devised to measure the extent to which the stated objectives are met.

3 Summary

The postulation of layered evaluation of IAS is that adaptation needs to be decomposed and assessed in layers in order to be evaluated effectively. The decomposition model proposed here takes a process-oriented approach to the decomposition, identifying the logical stages through which adaptation progresses. A brief rationalization of the decomposition and a preliminary set of criteria have also been put forward.

An important point we would like to make about the proposed decomposition is that it is neither the only one feasible, nor, necessarily, the most appropriate one for all types of assessment of IAS one might want to perform. For instance, it would be possible to decompose adaptation on the basis of the software components involved in its implementation. The same is true for the level of granularity be employed.

References

1. Browne, D., Norman, M., Riches, D.: Why Build Adaptive Systems? In: D. Browne, P. Totterdell, & M. Norman (Eds.): *Adaptive User Interfaces,*.London, Academic Press (1990) 15-58
2. Chin, D. N.: Empirical evaluation of user models and user-adapted systems. User Modeling and User-Adapted Interaction (2001) 11(1-2), 181–194
3. de Bra, P., Houben, G.-J., Wu, H.: AHAM: A Dexter-based reference model for adaptive hypermedia. In: Tochtermann, K., Westbomke, J., Wiil, U. K., Leggett, J. (Eds.), *Proceedings of the ACM Conference on Hypertext and Hypermedia* (1999) Darmstadt, 147–156
4. Höök, K.: Steps to take before intelligent user interfaces become real. *Interacting with Computers* (2000) 12(4), 409-426
5. Koch, N., Wirsing, M.: The Munich Reference Model for adaptive hypermedia applications. In de Bra, P., Brusilovsky, P., Conejo, R. (Eds.), *Proceedings of the Second International Conference on Adaptive Hypermedia and Adaptive Web Based Systems*, Málaga, Spain, AH2002 (2002) Berlin, Springer, 213–222
6. Oppermann, R.: Adaptively supported adaptability. *International Journal of Human Computer Studies* (1994) 40(3), 455–472
7. Paramythis, A., Totter, A., Stephanidis, C.: A Modular Approach to the Evaluation of Adaptive User Interfaces. In: S. Weibelzahl, D. Chin and G. Weber (Eds.) *Empirical Evaluation of Adaptive Systems.* Proceedings of workshop held at the Eighth International Conference on User Modeling in Sonthofen, Germany, July 13th (2001) Freiburg, Pedagogical University of Freiburg, 9-24
8. Totterdell, P., Rautenbach, P.: Adaptation as a Problem of Design. In: D. Browne, P. Totterdell, M. Norman (Eds.), *Adaptive User Interfaces* (1990) London, Academic Press, 61-84
9. Weibelzahl, S., Weber, G.: Evaluating the inference mechanism of adaptive learning systems. In: *User Modeling 2003: Proceedings of the Eighth International Conference, UM2003* (2003) Berlin, Springer

User Control over User Adaptation: A Case Study

Xiaoyan Peng and Daniel L. Silver

Acadia University, Jodrey School of Computer Science,
Wolfville, NS, Canada B4P 2R6
danny.silver@acadiau.ca

Abstract. The A theory of user expectation of system interaction is introduced in the context of User Adapted Interfaces. The usability of an intelligent email client that learns to filter spam emails is tested under three variants of adaptation: no user modeling, user modeling with fixed (optimal) spam cut-offs, and user modeling with user adjustable spam cut-offs. The results supported our hypothesis that user control over adaptation is preferred because the user can maintain the system's interaction state within a region of user expectation. This remains true even when performance of the system (accuracy of spam filtering) degrades because of errors in user control (adjustment of spam cut-offs).

1 Introduction

Research into User Adapted Interfaces (UAI) brings together concepts from Human-Computer Interaction (HCI) and User Modeling (UM) to improve the usability and performance of software systems. Controllability is one of the major usability issues for UAI technology. Some researchers advocate maximum user control over all aspects of system adaptation, others suggest that maximum control is not always be the best approach as it can lead to distraction and inefficiency [1]. There has been much discussion among researchers about controllability trade-offs. However, as Jameson [2] argues, there is a deficiency of systematically gathered evidence about what users themselves think about adaptation and controllability.

Our research investigates UAI technology in the context of an intelligent email client. This paper focuses on user control over a learned User Model that is able to predict the priority of incoming e-mail messages. We theorize that as long as the state of system interaction is within the current region of user expectation, the user will be satisfied with adaptation. If the system's interaction falls outside of this region of expectation then user satisfaction will degrade. To prevent dissatisfaction the user must be given control over aspects of adaptation that limit changes in interaction state.

An adaptive intelligent email client is our application of choice for employing UAI because it offers a lot of functionality that can be personalized, example data is readily available and knowledgeable test subjects are easily found [3]. In this study we focus on predicting the priority of incoming email messages based on a learned user model. Consequently, the predicted priorities can be used to filter out low priority and unsolicited "spam" email. There has been some excellent work in this area using Naïve Bayes, Bayesian networks, artificial neural networks, and k-nearest neighbour

L. Ardissono, P. Brna, and A. Mitrovic (Eds.): UM 2005, LNAI 3538, pp. 443–447, 2005.

methods [4]. Most of this research has focused on the performance of the learning algorithms, with little attention given to usability of the system from the user's perspective. The lack of a user's point of view has led to a significant barrier against acceptance of UAI technology. For example, some email filters automatically file spam into a spam folder. This can be problematic as users have varying tolerance for placement of legitimate email into a spam folder [5].

Although UAI has great potential, much research is needed. Perhaps most importantly, UAI can frustrate good HCI design because the interface may be perceived as a moving target that at times does not meet the expectations of the user [6]. The following section presents a theoretical model of the relationship between the expectations of a user and the changing state of a UAI.

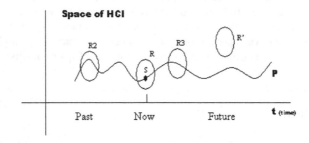

Fig. 1. Adaptation viewed as movement through an HCI state space

2 User Interaction Expectation and Adaptation

Consider a space of HCI states, as shown in Figure 1, where interaction states are topologically organized such that similar states are proximal to each other. System adaptation can be described as a trajectory, P, through the space. Each point along P represents the system's state of interaction with the user at a particular time. A user has a region of interaction expectation, R, that preferably is centered on the systems current state of interaction, s, or at least contains the s. The size of R, |R|, is the number of interaction states within R. If |R| = 1, then no variation from s will be tolerated by the user; this user is very conservative in terms of adaptation. If |R| = n then there are n states within R that will be acceptable to the user; this user is more accepting of adaptation. Ideally, as the system interface adapts, the user shifts her R so as to centre it once again on the new s. This transition is not always in concert. If the system adapts too quickly then the user is left behind at R2. If the system adapts too slowly then the user may assume an interaction state too far in advance of the current s, at R3. In either case the user will not be satisfied with the system and task performance will suffer. The worst case is when the user's expectation region is R', a region of interaction space through which adaptation will never pass; the user is continually dissatisfied. To be successful, a UAI must provide the user with control over adaptation. We advocate that user control should be exercised over the deployment of user models rather than their development. Model deployment requires minimal knowledge of the UM subsystem. In the case of an email client, a user model for setting incoming e-mail priority can be automatically developed using information retrieval and machine learning methods [4]. Control over automatic spam filtering can then be provided by allowing the user to adjust cut-off values that determine when the predicted priority of a message is at the level of legitimate or spam.

We have created an intelligent email client using this approach and developed an intuitive user interface for controlling adaptation. There are two priority cut-off values; one is the suspect cut-off and the other is the spam cut-off. Email with a priority value lower than the spam cut-off will be placed in the Spam folder. Email with a priority value equal to or higher than the suspect cut-off will be filed into the Inbox folder. Email with a priority equal to or higher than the spam cut-off and lower than the suspect cut-off will be put in a Suspect folder. Provided the user model is accurate, the approach will direct the most important legitimate email to the Inbox folder. The Suspect folder can be cleaned up periodically, sorting legitimate and spam email. Notably, it is this process that provides data for improving the user model. Using a simple GUI slider, a new or conservative user can select cut-off values that curtail the UAI's automated classification of legitimate and spam messages (thus reducing risk). A more experienced user can establish cut-offs that give the UAI greater freedom to classify email messages (maintaining risk as the user model improves over time). In this way, adaptation of the systems interaction state can be kept within the user's current region of interaction expectation.

3 Empirical Study

The objective of this experiment is to demonstrate that user control over appropriate aspects a UAI can improve the usability of the application and user satisfaction.

3.1 Materials and Methods

The study scenario is as follows: Each subject is working as a secretary for a professor. She or he must classify the incoming email (initially received in either the Inbox, Suspect or Spam folder) by moving the messages into one of six relevant folders including the Spam folder. Twenty eight subjects were selected from the university campus (ages 18-38). The performance of the email UAI is recorded in terms of false positives (FP - legitimate emails placed in the Spam folder) or false negatives (FN - spam email placed in the Inbox folder) and overall error (FP+FN).

Three variants of the system were tried by each subject and compared as per [2]. Variant N employs a UAI based on "no user model". The subjects had to manually sift through the email messages for legitimate and spam email messages. Variant F develops a user model but uses "fixed cut-off values" to determine the priority required for spam and legitimate emails. The fixed cut-off values are set to optimal values as determined by preliminary trials. No adjustment from these values would make significant improvement in UAI performance. Variant A for "adjustable cut-off values" develops a user model and allows the subjects to adjust the spam and suspect cut-off values as desired. This gives the subjects control over the UAI.

A within-subject experimental design was selected because the subjects were expected to vary considerably in their use of the system and tolerance to adaptation. Each subject was provided the same working environment. Each subject learned the experimental procedure from an instruction file without prompting by a researcher. Each subject used all 3 system variants in one of two possible orders; the first order being N, F and A and the second being N, A, and F. A different subset of emails was used for each variant to prevent subjects from memorizing the content of messages.

The data used in the experiment was collected from a professor at Acadia over a 5 month timeframe in 2003 [4]. A different subset of 200 emails was used for each of the 3 variants of the system. 100 emails from a subset were sent to the email client and the subject was asked to manually classify them into their respective folders. A message was given a priority of 0 if placed in the Spam folder and a priority of 1 otherwise. This acted as training data for developing a user model for predicting message priority. A final 100 emails from the subset were sent to the email client for automatic prioritization and classification.

Each subject was surveyed following their trial of the 3 system variants [2]. The survey asked the subjects for their opinions on 5 questions: (1) Did you find the system easier to user after the user model was developed; (2) Did you prefer being able to adjust the spam and suspect cut-off values; (3) Do you think the cut-off adjustment increased the accuracy of email classification; (4) Would you like to have user modeling on you current email client; and (5) Would you like to have user model with cut-off adjustment on you current email client? The subjects were asked to respond using a five-level scale of agreement as shown in Figure 2 and to explain their reasoning in a comment area. In addition, each subject indicated if they had any significant problems using the system and whether they preferred false positives or false negatives when filtering email. The FP and FN statistics were tracked for each subject and used to determine the performance of the UM on incoming email.

3.2 Results and Discussion

The results from the post-trial surveys show that 92.86% preferred the UAI variant of the system after the user model was developed, with 82.14% preferring the adjustable spam and suspect cut-offs over the fixed cut-offs. 78.57% felt that the cut-off adjustment increased the accuracy of email classifications with more subjects preferring cut-off adjustment on their current email clients (78.57%) than user modeling with fixed cut-offs (71.43%). These statistics indicate that user control contributes to user satisfaction. In contrast, the system variant with adjustable cut-offs had higher mean misclassifications (25.64%) than the fixed cut-off variant (20.04%). The difference between misclassifications caused by variant A and F is significant (p-value = 0.01).

Despite the fact that significantly more misclassifications were made by variant A, 67.9% of the subjects (19/28) preferred variant A over F. Subject 14 was an extreme case of where a user preferred control even though it reduced system performance. He generated 5 misclassifications under variant F and 49 misclassifications under variant A. His comment "this allows me to set up values to better match my profiles" shows a strong desire to remain in control. Other typical responses for those who preferred adjustable cut-offs were: "It helps me to control how the emails will be separated", "It is good to add user's point view to the system", and "I like the feeling of control".

The majority of subjects liked adaptation as long as they felt in control. Of the subjects who liked cut-off adjustment, 95.65% preferred FN over FP meaning they most dislike finding legitimate email messages in the Spam folder. Adjustment of the cut-offs allows the users to err on the side of FN classifications even if this reduces the overall performance of the UAI. Of the subjects who responded "do not know" or "disagree" to cut-off adjustment, 80% are less sensitive to FP (legitimate emails classified as spam). The fixed default cut-off values worked well for that purpose, the subjects recognized this and preferred it.

4   Conclusions and Future Work

This paper has investigated the relationship between user control over a UAI and user satisfaction and system performance. We presented a theoretical model that suggests users will be satisfied with a UAI provided the interaction state of the system is maintained within the current region of user expectation. If the system's interaction falls outside of this region of expectation then user satisfaction will degrade. One approach to preventing this from happening is to give the user control over aspects of adaptation that limit changes in interaction state. Specifically, in the case of the email client, the user controls the cut-off at which emails are considered legitimate or spam. The results of an empirical study using 28 subjects demonstrated that user satisfaction is improved with control over adaptation even if this means reducing system performance (higher misclassification rates). We are currently working on a related problem of automatically classifying emails to one of several category folders.

References

1. Kay, J.: Learner control, Proceedings of User Modeling & User-Adapted Interaction (2001)
2. Jameson A., and Schwarzkopf, E.: Pros and Cons of Controllability: An Empirical Study, Adaptive Hypermedia and Adaptive Web-Based Systems: Proceedings of AH (2002)
3. Crawford, E., Kay, J., and McCreath E.: An Intelligent Interface for Sorting Electronic Mail, IUI'02, San Francisco, California, USA (2002) 13-16
4. Fu, C.: User Modelling for an Adaptive System: an Intelligent Email Client, Master Thesis, Jodrey School of Computer Science, Acadia University, Wolfville, Canada (2003)
5. Crawford, E., Kay, J., and McCreath, E.: Automatic Induction of Rules for Email Classification, Proceedings of 6th Australian Document Computing Symposium (2001)
6. Cranor, L., F.: Designing a Privacy Preference Specification Interface: A Case Study, Proceedings of the Workshop on HCI and Security Systems, CHI2003, Florida (2003)

Towards User Modeling Meta-ontology

Michael Yudelson[1], Tatiana Gavrilova[2], and Peter Brusilovsky[1]

[1] School of Information Sciences, University of Pittsburgh,
Pittsburgh PA 15260, USA
{mvy3, peterb}@pitt.edu
[2] Department of Intelligent Computer Technologies,
St.-Petersburg State Technical University, Polytechnicheskaya St. 29,
195251 St.-Petersburg, Russia
gavr@csa.ru

Abstract. The paper proposes meta-ontology of the user modeling field. Ontology is meant to structure the state-of-the-art in the field and serve as a central reference point and as a tool to index systems, papers and learning media. Such ontology is beneficial for both the user modeling research community and the students as it creates a shared conceptualization of the known approaches to building user models and their implementations.

1 Introduction

User modeling (UM) is a heterogeneous field. The terminology is still not standardized. A lot of terms have multiple synonyms (e.g. behavioral user model, feature-based user model, individual user model). Terms are often fuzzy. There exist a lot of approaches to UM but a common schema that would attempt to classify them has not been proposed yet. Such lack of structure makes it harder to conduct novel research or implement known approaches in the area of UM.

This paper presents our attempt to develop a meta-ontology (a top level classifycation) of UM field. The role of such User Modeling Meta-Ontology (UMMO) is manifold. First, it can serve as a central reference point, just like ACM computing classifycation system [1]. It is an important uniform framework to structure UM field in general. UMMO can help to present in a condensed visual form the current state of the art.

Second, such ontology will serve as a structuring basis for UM resources. It will help to collate a great number of UM approaches, papers, and systems by indexing them with the terms from ontology to be able to compare them and/or relate them to each other. The presence of a well-developed UMMO will help index coherently various information resources such as projects, papers as well as enable semi-automatic indexing.

Third, UMMO may serve as an educational tool. It will help to convey the state-of-the-art in UM field and to eliminate the synonymy problem. Finally, we hope to use UMMO as a basis to develop an adaptive educational hypermedia system for UM. Since modern adaptive hypermedia systems rely on advanced concept indexing, ontology development should be the first step toward such a system.

L. Ardissono, P. Brna, and A. Mitrovic (Eds.): UM 2005, LNAI 3538, pp. 448–452, 2005.
© Springer-Verlag Berlin Heidelberg 2005

2 Known Approaches

Previously there have been several attempts to create some kind of shared conceptualization of user models. In [8] authors define user model as a set of hierarchies of personal and demographic characteristics, domain [in]dependent data, context, and low-level sensor data. Authors of [3] (mainly Peter Dolog) yet have another view of user model externalization. They view user modeling from the point of standards (such as IEEE PAPI, IMS LIP, or ISO). Although presence of standards constrains the flexibility of the user model description, but in return a more general solution is achieved, that can be applied to virtually any domain user models can be used it. The approach of the authors of the Onto-logging project [13] focuses on collaborative conceptualization in developing domain ontologies.

The first two of the mentioned above approaches make an emphasis on decomposing the user model itself. They do not touch upon the methodology surrounding user modeling, let alone classification of such methods and systems that implement them. The approach of the authors of [13] comes closest to our intentions, yet lacks some specification and structure (namely it is not an ontology). We propose an attempt to create a meta-ontology that would help to present a more general view of the user modeling field.

3 Ontology Development Process

Ontology being a useful structuring tool provides an organizing axis to help mentally mark the vision in the information hyper-space of the domain knowledge. **Fig. 1** presents our view on the mainstream state-of-the-art categorization in ontological engineering [15], [8].

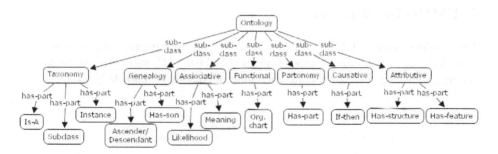

Fig. 1. Ontology classification (mixed ontology)

Creating ontology is a procedure that cannot be fully automated since ontology development is rather creative than formal process. Major works in this field deal with syntax problems, not semantics. Until now, only few effective domain-independent methodological approaches have been reported [12], [15], and [4]. However, in practice each development team usually follows their own set of principles, design criteria, and steps in the ontology development process.

Generalizing our experience in developing different teaching ontologies for e-learning in the field of artificial intelligence and neurolinguistics [4], [6], [7] we propose a four-step algorithm that may be helpful for visual ontology design.

1. *Glossary development* – selecting and verbalizing the essential domain concepts.
2. *Laddering* – defining the main levels of abstraction. It is also important for the next stages of the design to elucidate the type of ontology according to **Fig. 1** classification.
3. *Disintegration/Categorization* –breaking high level concepts into a set of detailed when needed (top-down strategy) and associating similar concepts to generalize meta-concepts (bottom-up strategy.
4. *Refinement* – updating the visual structure by excluding the excessiveness, synonymy, and contradictions.

The main goal of the algorithm above is to create a visually appealing ontology that means that ontology developer should observe conceptual balance ('harmony') and clarity of the ontology. A well-balanced ontological hierarchy equals a strong and comprehensible representation of the domain knowledge. Here are tips on how to achieve 'harmony'. First, sibling concepts should be linked to the parent concept by one type of relationship. Second, the depth of the branches should be more or less equal (±2 nodes). Third, the general outlay should be symmetrical. Fourth, cross-links should be avoided as much as possible.

Ontology clarity can be achieved by optimizing the number of concepts and types of the links between them. Minimizing the number of concepts is the best tip according to Ockham's razor principle. The maximal number of branches and the number of levels should also follow 7±2 rule by Miller. The type of relationship should be clear and obvious if the name of the relationship is omitted.

4 UMMO Development

The current version of UMMO was developed in part by extracting information about user modeling domain from various sources ([2], [10], [11], and [14]) and in part by eliciting knowledge of experts (auto-elicitation of co-authors' knowledge so far).

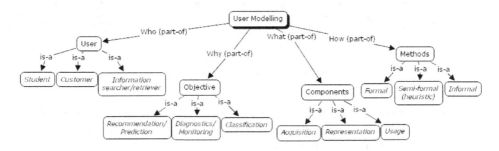

Fig. 2. User Modeling Meta-Ontology upper tier

The process of UMMO development was guided by the aforementioned algorithm. At the glossary development stage performed both semi-automatically (keyword extraction) and manually a set of roughly 150 terms was extracted up to this moment. The laddering, generalization, and refinement stages have gone through 10 extensive iterations. A special attention was paid to generalization, since some of the concepts in the UM field have multiple terms associated with them. E.g. behavioral user model, feature-based user model, and individual user model are all synonyms. Monosemic terms were grouped in clusters, the dominated term was chosen at the authors' discretion.

UMMO is a mixed ontology: the top layer is a partonomy, the lower layers are taxonomies. The most stable upper tier of the ontology is shown in **Fig. 2**. **Fig. 3** shows the top part of the UMMO that contains 37 concepts (only a subset of the full ontology due to space limitation). Along with concepts **Fig. 3** shows 'markup' nodes that depict systems/approaches (10 nodes) and people (12 nodes) that fit the concepts (systems/approaches and people are displayed as rectangles and rounded rectangles respectively).

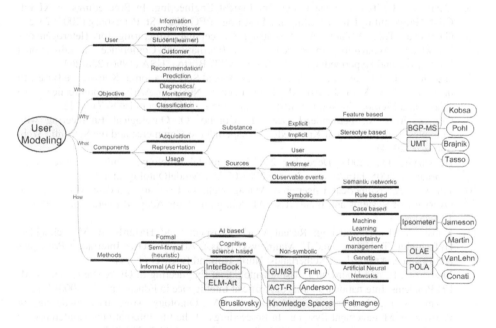

Fig. 3. User Modeling Meta-Ontology (UMMO) upper tier and one of the branches

5 Conclusions

The challenge of such meta-ontology construction is *not* to identify the lower tier concepts that correspond to the individual approaches, but to work out and verbalize the upper tier concepts that would help generalize about UM methodology. UMMO is an attempt to externalize the current approaches, techniques, and tools.

The development of UMMO is a part of wider research aimed at development of user model centered learning portal. The UMMO development is a work in progress. Comments and suggestions would be highly appreciated at www.pitt.edu/~mvy3/ummo_index.htm and/or at http://ummo.blogspot.com.

References

1. ACM Computing Classification System (n.d.). Retrieved November 16, 2004, from http://www.acm.org/class
2. Brusilovsky, P.: Methods and techniques of adaptive hypermedia. In: P. Brusilovsky, A. Kobsa and J. Vassileva (eds.): Adaptive Hypertext and Hypermedia. Dordrecht: Kluwer Academic Publishers (1998) 1-43
3. Dolog, P., Nejdl, W.: Challenges and Benefits of the Semantic Web for User Modelling. In Proc. of AH2003 workshop at 12th World Wide Web Conference, Budapest, Hungary (2003)
4. Fensel, D.: Ontologies: Silver Bullet for Knowledge Management and Electronic Commerce. Springer-Verlag, Berlin (2001)
5. Gavrilova, T.: Teaching via Using Ontological Engineering. In Proceedings of XI Int. Conf. "Powerful ICT for Teaching and Learning" PEG-2003, St. Petersburg (2003) 23-26
6. Gavrilova, T.A., Voinov, A.: Visualized Conceptual Structuring for Heterogeneous Knowledge Acquisition. In Proceedings of International Conference on Educational Multimedia and Hypermedia, EDMEDIA'96, MIT, Boston, USA (1996) 258-264
7. Gavrilova, T., Voinov, A.: Work in Progress: Visual Specification of Knowledge Bases. In del Pobil, A.P., Mira, J., Ali, M. (Eds), Lecture Notes in Artificial Intelligence 1416 "Tasks and Methods in Applied Artificial Intelligence". Springer (1998) 717-726
8. Gómez-Pérez, A., Fernández-López, M., Corcho, O. Ontological Engineering with examples from the areas of Knowledge Management, e-Commerce and the Semantic Web. Springer (2004)
9. Heckmann, D.: (2003. December 22). User model ontology. (Online), retrieved on February 2, 2005. http://www.u2m.org/2003/02/UserModelOntology.daml
10. Jameson, A.: Numerical Uncertainty Management in User and Student Modeling: An Overview of Systems and Issues. User Modeling and User-Adapted Interaction, 5, (1996) 193-251
11. Kobsa, A.: User Modeling: Recent Work, Prospects and Hazards. In M. Schneider-Hufschmidt, T. Kühme, and U. Malinowski (Eds.). Adaptive User Interfaces: Principles and Practice. Amsterdam, Netherlands: North Holland Elsevier (1993)
12. Mizogushi, R. and Bourdeau J.: Using Ontological Engineering to Overcome Common AI-ED Problems. International Journal of Artificial Intelligence in Education, 11, (2000) 1-12
13. Razmerita, L., Angehrn, A., and Maedche, A.: Ontology based user modeling for Knowledge Management Systems. In Proceedings of the 9th International Conference on User Modeling, Pittsburgh, USA, 2003, Springer-Verlag (2003) 213-217
14. Rich, E.: User Modeling via Stereotypes. In M. Maybury & W. Wahlster (Eds.). Readings in Intelligent User Interfaces. Morgan Kaufmann Press, CA: San Francisco (1998) 329-342
15. Tu, S., Eriksson, H., Gennari, J., Shahar, Y. & Musen M.: Ontology-Based Configuration of Problem-Solving Methods and Generation of Knowledge-Acquisition Tools. In Artificial Intelligence in Medicine, N7 (1995) 257-289
16. Uschold, M., Jasper, R.: A Framework for Understanding and Classifying Ontology Applications. In Proceedings of the IJCAI-99 Workshop on Ontologies and Problem-Solving Methods (KRR5), Stockholm, Sweden (1999)

Evaluation of a System for Personalized Summarization of Web Contents*

Alberto Díaz[1], Pablo Gervás[2], and Antonio García[3]

[1] CES Felipe II – Universidad Complutense de Madrid
adiaz@cesfelipesegundo.com
[2] SIP – Universidad Complutense de Madrid
pgervas@sip.ucm.es
[3] Departamento de Comunicación - Universidad Rey Juan Carlos
an.garcia@cct.urjc.es

Abstract. Existing Web personalized information systems typically send to the users the title and the first lines of the chosen items, and links to the full text. This is, in most cases, insufficient for a user to detect if the item is relevant or not. An interesting approach is to replace the first sentences by a personalized summary extracted according to a user profile that represents the information needs of the user. On the other side, it is crucial to measure how much information is lost during the summarization process, and how this information loss may affect the ability of the user to judge the relevance of a given document. The system-oriented evaluation developed in this paper indicates that personalized summaries perform better than generic summaries in terms of identifying documents that satisfy user preferences. We also considered a user-centred qualitative evaluation indicating a high level of user satisfaction with the summarization method described, in consonance with the quantitative results.

1 Introduction

Web content personalization is a technique for reducing information overload through the adaptation of contents to each type of user. A Web personalization system is based on 3 main functionalities: content selection, user model adaptation, and content generation. For these functionalities to be carried out, they must be based on information related to the user that must be reflected in his user model or profile [8].

Content selection refers to the choice of the particular subset of all available documents that will be more relevant for a given user, as represented in his user profile or model. User model adaptation is necessary because user needs change over time as a result of his interaction with information [1]. For this reason the user model must be dynamic to adapt to those interest changes.

Content generation involves generating a new result web document that contains, for each selected document, some extract considered indicative of its content. Existing

---

* This research has been partially funded by the Ministerio de Ciencia y Tecnología (TIC2002-01961).

L. Ardissono, P. Brna, and A. Mitrovic (Eds.): UM 2005, LNAI 3538, pp. 453–462, 2005.

Web personalized information systems typically send to the users the title and the first lines of the chosen items, and links to the full text. This is in most cases insufficient for a user to detect if the item is relevant or not, forcing him to inspect the full text of the document. An interesting approach is to replace the first sentences sent as a sample of a document by a proper summary or extract.

Personalized summarization is understood as a process of summarization that preserves the specific information that is relevant for a given user profile, rather than information that truly summarizes the content of the news item. The potential of summary personalization is high, because a document that would be useless if summarized in a generic manner may be useful if the right sentences are selected that match the user interest.

If automatic summarization is to be used as part of a process of intelligent information access, it is crucial to have some means of measuring how much information is lost during the summarization process, and how that information loss may affect the ability of the user to judge the relevance of a given document with respect to his particular information needs.

In this paper we focus on a system-oriented and user-centred evaluation of the content generation (summarization) process. Section 2 describes previous work. The multi-tier selection process employed for evaluation is described in section 3. Section 4 describes the personalised summarization method. The experimental set up and results are given in section 5. Section 6 outlines the main conclusions.

2 Relevant Previous Work

Automatic summarization is the process through which the relevant information from one or several sources is identified in order to produce a briefer version intended for a particular user - or group of users - or a particular task [6]. This paper considers indicative summaries of single documents, intended to help the user to decide on the relevance of the original document. Summaries can be *generic*, if they gather the main topics of the document and they are addressed to a wide group of readers, or *user adapted*, if the summary is constructed according to the interests of the particular reader that the system is addressing.

Techniques for selection of phrases extract segments of text that contain the most significant information, selected based on linear combination of the weights resulting from the application of a set of heuristics applied to each of the units of extraction. These heuristics may be *position dependent*, if they take into account the position that each segment holds in the document; *linguistic*, if they look for certain patterns of significant expressions; or *statistical*, if they include frequencies of apparition of certain words. The summary results from concatenating the resulting segments of text in the order in which they appear in the original document [4].

There are similar works that use personalized summaries in information retrieval. In this case, the personalization is based on the user query [7, 11]. In particular, in [11] the initial segment of the documents is compared with query oriented summaries using a IR system. The results are shown to the users as title and initial segment or title and automatic summary. The evaluation was performed with 50 TREC queries with 50 documents per query. Measures were taken on precision, recall, speed in the decision process, number of access to the full document and subjective opinion of the user about the received information (initial segment or summary). The results show that the query oriented summaries are significantly more effective that the initial segment for the information retrieval task.

Work on evaluation of item summarization has already shown that indirect evaluation methods of summarization - where summaries are evaluated in terms of their ability to recreate the ranking obtained by the full items when submitted to a given information selection process - provide reasonable means of measuring the amount of information loss involved in summarization. In particular, the selection process used in [7] was keyword-based single-tier over a corpus of 5000 news items and 50 queries from the TREC collection. Generic and personalized summarization heuristics are considered. The results show that the query oriented summaries are better than the first sentences and the generic summaries.

On the other side, existing literature provides different techniques for defining user interests: keywords, stereotypes, semantic networks, neural networks, etc. A particular set of proposals [1, 8] model users by combining long term and short term interests: the short term model represents the most recent user preferences and the long term model represents those expressed over a longer period of time. Various classification algorithms are available for carrying out content selection depending on the particular representation chosen for user models and documents. The feedback techniques needed to achieve a dynamic modeling of the user are based on feedback given by the user with respect to the information elements selected according to his profile. The information obtained in this way can be used to update accordingly the user models in representation had been chosen.

3 Multi-tier Content Selection

The multi-tier content selection process [2] to be employed in this paper involves a domain specific characterization, an automatic categorization algorithm and a set of keywords (long-term model), and a relevance feedback tier (short-term model).

The first tier of selection corresponds to a domain specific given classification (for digital newspapers, the assignment of news items to sections). For the second tier, the user enters a set of keywords - with an associated weight - to characterize his preferences. These keywords are stored, for each user u, as a term weight vector (k_u). For the third tier the user must choose - and assign a weight to them - a subset of the 14 categories in the first level of Yahoo! Spain. This information is stored as a matrix where rows correspond to general categories and columns correspond to users (G_{gu}). These categories are represented as term weight vectors (g) by training from the very brief descriptions of the first and second level of Yahoo! Spain categories entries [5]. In the fourth tier, short-term interests are represented by means of feedback terms obtained from feedback provided by the user over the documents he receives [2]. The term weight vector for each user (t_u) represents the short-term interests of that user, information needs that loose interest to the user over time, so their weight must be progressively decreased.

Documents are downloaded from the web of a daily Spanish newspaper as HTML documents. For each document, title, section, URL and text are extracted, and a term weight vector representation for a document d (d_d) is obtained by application of a stop list, a stemmer, and the *tf · idf* formula for computing actual weights [9].

Each document is assigned the weight associated with the corresponding specific category associated to it in the particular user model, which represents the similarity between a document d, belonging to a specific category c, and a user model u (s^c_{du}). The similarities between a document d and a general category g (s_{dg}), between a document d and the keywords of a user model u (s^k_{du}), and between a document d and a short-term user model u (s^t_{du}) are computed using the cosine formula for similarity within the vector space model [9]:

$$s_{dg} = sim(d_d, g) \qquad s^k_{du} = sim(d_d, k_u) \qquad s^t_{du} = sim(d_d, t_u) \qquad (1)$$

The similarity between a document d and the general categories of a user model is computed using the next formula:

$$s^g_{du} = \sum_{i=1}^{14} G_{iu} s_{dg_i} \left/ \sum_{i=1}^{14} G_{iu} \right. \qquad (2)$$

The results are integrated using a particular combination of reference frameworks. The similarity between a document d and a user model u is computed as:

$$s_{du} = \frac{\delta s^c_{du} + \varepsilon s^g_{du} + \phi s^k_{du} + \gamma s^t_{du}}{\delta + \varepsilon + \phi + \gamma} \qquad (3)$$

where Greek letters δ, ε, ϕ, and γ represent the importance assigned to each of the reference frameworks -specific categories, general categories, keywords, and feedback terms, respectively. To ensure significance, the relevance obtained from each reference framework must be normalized.

4 Applying Long and Short Term User Models to Personalize Summaries

Our system uses three phrase-selection heuristics to build summaries: two to construct generic summaries, and one for personalized summaries. To generate summaries a value is assigned to each phrase of the text being summarized, obtained as a weighted combination of the results of the three heuristics. This value is used to select the most relevant phrases, which will be used to form an extract of the news item later used as summary.

The *position heuristic* assigns the highest value to the first five phrases (1, 0.99, 0.98, 0.95, 0.9) of the text [3]. These provide the weights A_{pd} for each phrase p of a news item d using the position heuristic. These values are independent of the user u being considered.

Each text has a number of thematic words, which are representative of its content[1]. To obtain the M most significant words of each document, documents are indexed to

---

[1] This set of content based keywords for a document should not be confused with the set of keywords specified by a user to define his interests.

provide the weight of each word in each document using the $tf \cdot idf$ method [9]. The *thematic words heuristic* extracts the M non-stoplist most significant words of each text. To obtain the value for each phrase p within the document d using the thematic words heuristics (B_{pd}), the number of thematic words appearing in the phrase is divided by the total number of words in the phrase. This is intended to give more weight to sentences with a higher density of thematic words [10]. The values obtained in this way are also independent of the particular user u being considered. We have chosen M=8.

The *personalization heuristic* boosts those sentences that are more relevant to a particular user model. The user model provides a vector of weighted terms (k_u) corresponding to the chosen keywords of the long-term model and a vector of weighted terms (t_u) corresponding to the feedback keywords of the short-term model. This information is used to calculate the similarity (C_{pdu}) between the user model u and each phrase p of news item d, assigning the final weight to the sentence as:

$$C_{pdu} = \frac{\chi\, sim(p_{pd}, k_u) + \beta\, sim(p_{pd}, t_u)}{\chi + \beta} \tag{4}$$

where p_{pd} is the term weight vector representing the phrase p of news item d, and sim is the cosine formula of the Vector Space Model [9].

The values resulting from each of the three heuristics are combined into a single value (Z_{pdu}) for each phrase p of each news item d for each user u:

$$Z_{pdu} = \frac{\mu A_{pd} + \nu B_{pd} + \sigma C_{pdu}}{\mu + \nu + \sigma} \tag{5}$$

The parameters μ, ν and σ allow relative fine-tuning of the different heuristics, depending on whether position (μ), thematic key words (ν) or similarity to the user model (σ) is considered more desirable. Values of σ determine the degree of personalization of the summaries: if σ is 0, the resulting summaries are generic, and for σ greater than 0 personalization increases proportionally to σ. Again, to ensure significance, the relevance obtained for each framework must be normalized.

The summary is constructed by selecting the top 20% of the ranking of sentences by the value Z_{pdu} and concatenating them according to their original order of appearance in the document.

5   Evaluation

We have performed two kinds of evaluations. System-oriented evaluation is based on the precision and recall metrics obtained through different configurations of the system, and intends to identify which is the best way of carrying the content generation process through the effect in the selection process. User-centred evaluation collects the opinions of the users about the use of summaries instead of the complete news items.

5.1   System-Oriented Evaluation

Experiments are evaluated over data collected for 106 users and the news items corresponding to three weeks – the 14 working days of the period 1st -19th Dec 2003 - of the digital edition of the ABC Spanish newspaper [2]. The set of users includes 18 lecturers, 4 teachers, 77 students and 7 professionals from no education areas. The students come from the fields of computer science, journalism and advertising. The average of news item per day is 78.5.

To carry out the system-oriented evaluation, judgments from the user are required as to which news items are relevant or not for each of the days of the experiment. To obtain these judgments users were requested to check the complete set of news items for each day, stating for each one whether it was considered interesting (positive feedback) or not interesting (negative feedback).

As the evaluation process involved an effort for the users, only 37.4 users per day actually provided judgments. Additionally, some users only perform feedback for less than 10 news items per day. These users have been eliminated for the evaluation in order to obtain more significant results. The final collection contains, on average, 28.6 user per day.

For evaluating summarization, the effect of selection (formula (3) with $\delta=\varepsilon=\phi=\gamma=1$) over the different types of summaries is measured. This involves checking what results are obtained, as compared with user judgments, if instead of selecting news items based on their full text they are selected based on the summaries.

Normalized recall and precision are used as evaluation metrics, given the users binary relevance judgments are compared against the ranking provided by the system [9]. These metrics measure the difference between an ideal ranking, with the relevant documents at the top, and the actual ranking provided by the system. On the other hand, the recall and precision metrics are computed with respect a selected fixed number of documents and they don't use the information about the ranking.

Data are considered statistically significant if they pass the *sign-test*, with paired samples, at a level of significance of 5% ($p \leq 0.05$) [9].

5.1.1 Experiment 1. Personalized Summaries

The generation of personalized summaries (formula (5) with $\mu=\nu=0$ y $\sigma=1$) combines the long-term model (keywords provided by the user) and short-term model (feedback terms obtained from the interaction with the user).

Several evaluation collections have been generated for each user. Each one of them is obtained by summarizing the complete set of original news items according to a particular method for generating personalized summaries of those indicated above (formula (4)). There is a collection for each user of personalized summaries generated using the short term model (Ps(S): $\chi=0,\beta=1$), a different collection for each user generated using the long term model (Ps(L): $\chi=1,\beta=0$) and a third different collection for each user generated using a combination of long term and short term models (Ps(LS): $\chi=1,\beta=1$). In each case, values of normalized recall and precision have been computed. These experiments have been repeated for all users during the 14 days of evaluation. The results for the three types of personalized summaries have been compared only from the second day on, to allow for the fact that on the first day there is no short-term model based on user feedback.

If different summarization methods lead to different degrees of loss of relevant information, the resulting rankings will differ amongst them in a proportional way. The results shown in Table 1 show that the combination of long and short term models for the generation of personalized summaries provides significantly better results than the use of each model separately, in terms of normalized precision (1.6% against long term only, 2.8% against short term only). As an additional result, it is observed that the short term model on its own is better than the long term model in terms of normalized precision (1.2%), though not significantly so. In terms of normalized recall, results are similar: significant improvement of the long term-short term combination over both short and long on their own, and non-significant improvement of short term only over long term.

The use of both heuristics adjusts the summaries better to the preferences of the user, as shown by higher values of precision and recall. The slightly better results for the short term could be due to the fact that the terms introduced by the user in his long term model are in general too specific, whereas those obtained through user feedback are terms that appear in the daily news.

Table 1. Normalized precision (P) and recall (R) for different combinations of long and short-term model for generating personalized summaries

	P	R
Ps(LS)	0.592	0.684
Ps(S)	0.583	0.678
Ps(L)	0.576	0.674

From here on, mentions of personalized summaries (Ps) refer to the personalization obtained by means of a combination of the long and short-term models.

5.1.2 Experiment 2. Heuristic Combination for Summary Generation

Experiment 2 tests whether summaries obtained by using only the personalization heuristic are better in terms of precision (formula (3) with $\delta=\epsilon=\phi=\gamma=1$) with respect to information selected by the user than other summaries (including the first lines of the document) but worse than the complete news item.

The following types of summaries are involved (formula (5) with (4) with $\chi=\beta=1$): Fs (baseline reference), 20% first phrases of the corresponding news item; Gs, using generic heuristics ($\mu = 1$, $\nu = 1$, $\sigma = 0$); Ps, using personalization heuristics ($\mu = 0$, $\nu = 0$, $\sigma = 1$); GPs, using both types of heuristics ($\mu = 1$, $\nu = 1$, $\sigma = 1$).

Several different evaluation collections – consisting each one of summaries obtained from the news items in the original collection by applying a different summarization method – are built for each user. The multi-tier selection process is applied to each one of these collections, using the corresponding user profile as source for user interests. In each case, the values of normalized recall and precision have been computed in experiments that have been repeated over the 14 days for all users.

Table 2. Normalized precision (P) and recall (R) for news item (N), personalized (Ps), generic-personalized (GPs), generic (Gs) and first phrases (Fs) summaries

	N	Ps	GPs	Fs	Gs
P	0.603	0.593	0.584	0.581	0.577
R	0.694	0.686	0.680	0.678	0.675

Personalized summaries (Ps) offer better results (table 2) with respect to normalized precision and recall than generic-personalized summaries (GPs), though the difference is not significant. With respect to baseline summaries (Fs) and generic summaries (Gs) the difference is significant. Generic-personalized summaries (GPs) are better than baseline summaries (Fs), and baseline summaries (Fs) are better then generic summaries (Gs), but the differences involved are not statistically significant. Personalized summaries are worse than full news items (N) under the same criteria.

This suggests that the personalization heuristic generates the summaries better adapted to the user, followed by a combination of all possible heuristics. Baseline summaries using the first lines of each news item are better than those generated by a combination of the position and keyword heuristics. For newspaper articles, the generic heuristic does not improve on simply taking the opening lines.

This technique has been used in similar works with similar results. In [7] the query oriented summaries (title, location, thematic and query heuristics) obtained significant better average precision than generic summaries and first sentences, and the full document improve the adapted summaries but no significantly. In [11] the query oriented summaries show better effectiveness that the initial segment.

5.2 User-Centred Evaluation

The qualitative user-centred evaluation was based on a questionnaire that users completed after using the system. In most questions there were 5 options to indicate the degree of satisfaction: very high, high, medium, low and very low. There were 38 users that completed the final evaluation.

Users indicated that the summaries were of high or very high quality in 83.3% of the cases, with 5.6% of very low. Concerning the coherence and clarity of the summaries, the results were as follows: 81.1% valued them as high or very high, and 5.4% as low or very low. With respect to the ability of the system to avoid redundancies, evaluation was high or very high for 69.4% of the users, against 2.8% of low evaluation. At the same time, adaptation of the summary to the user profile was considered high by 59.5% of the users, and low or very low by 8.1%.

The degree of adaptation of the summaries to the information needs was high or very high in 70.3% of the cases, and low or very low in 10.8%. Regarding the extent to which the summaries reflect the content of the original documents, for 81.1% of the users this extent was high or very high, and it was low or very low for 5.4%. Finally, 89.5% of the users consider that the main ingredients of the news item are represented in the summary. The other 10.5% indicated that at times the summaries were too brief to include them.

Most users consider that the summaries are of high quality, coherent, and clear, and that they reflect the content and the main ingredients of the corresponding document. Most of them also consider, though to a lesser degree, that the summaries contain no redundancies and that they are well adapted to user profile and user needs. This positive evaluation indicates that the method of sentence selection for the construction of summaries is a valid approach for content generation in the face of possible problems of clarity, coherence and redundancy.

Users indicate that they sometimes used the summaries to establish the relevance of a news item. This was said to be often so by 48.6% of the users, sometimes by

29.7% and few by 21.6%. Against these data, 89.2% of the users relied on the heading often, and 10.8% only did in some cases. The section heading was used sometime by 45.9%, often by 29.7%, few by 13.5% and none by 10.8%. The stated relevance was used sometimes by 35.1% of the users, few by 24.3%, none by 21.6% and often by 18.9%. Finally, the full news item was used few times by 51.4% of the users, some times by 29.7% and none by 18.9%. In conclusion, the summary becomes an important element for defining the relevance of a news item.

6 Conclusions

We can conclude that personalized summaries that use a combination of long and short term models are better than other types of summaries in terms of normalized precision and recall. Full news item offer only a slight improvement against personalized summaries, which seems to indicate that the loss of information for the user is very small with this type of summary. Generic summaries perform very closely to summaries obtained by taking the first few lines of the news item. This seems to indicate that the position heuristic is overpowering the thematic word heuristic, which may be corrected by refining the choice of weights. Although a first-sentences approach may provide good results for indicative summarization, it does not do so well in terms of personalized summarization, where it is crucial to retain in the summary those specific fragments of the text that relate to the user profile. This explains why the generic-personalized summaries perform so poorly in spite of being a combination of good techniques: given a fixed limit on summary length, the inclusion of sentences selected by the generic heuristics in most cases pushes out of the final summary information that would have been useful from the point of view of personalization.

The user centred evaluation further sanctions the concept that offering users summaries of the news items helps to decrease information overload on the users. As shown in these results, the possible problems of sentence extraction as a summary construction method do not affect performance in the present context of application. The fact the summaries are said to be employed by users much more often than the full original text or the stated relevance to determine how relevant a news item is to them justifies the content generation method described in this paper.

We can conclude that user adapted summaries are a useful tool to assist users in a personalization system. Notwithstanding, the information in these summaries can not replace the full text document from an information retrieval point of view.

References

1. Billsus, D. & Pazzani. M.J.: User Modeling for Adaptive News Access. User Modeling and User-Adapted Interaction Journal 10(2-3) (2000) 147-180
2. Díaz, A. & Gervás, P.: Adaptive User Modeling for Personalization of Web Contents. Third International Conference on Adaptive Hypermedia and Adaptive Web-Based Systems (AH2004). LNCS 3137. Springer-Verlag (2004) 65-75
3. Edmundson, H.: New methods in automatic abstracting. Journal of the ACM 2(16) (1969) 264–285

4. Kupiec, J., Pedersen, O., Chen, F.: A trainable document summarizer. Research and Development in Information Retrieval (1995) 68–73
5. Labrou, Y. & Finin, T.: Yahoo! As an Ontology: Using Yahoo! Categories to Describe Documents. Proceedings of the 8th International Conference on Information Knowledgement (CIKM-99). ACM Press (2000) 180-187
6. Mani, I. & Maybury, M.: Advances in Automatic Text Summarization. The MIT Press (1999)
7. Maña, M., Buenaga, M., Gómez, J.M.: Using and evaluating user directed summaries to improve information access. Proceedings of the Third European Conference on Research and Advanced Technology for Digital Libraries (ECDL1999). LNCS 1696. Springer-Verlag (1999) 198–214
8. Mizarro, S. & Tasso, C.: Ephemeral and Persistent Personalization in Adaptive Information Access to Scholarly Publications on the Web. Second International Conference on Adaptive Hypermedia and Adaptive Web-Based Systems (AH2002). LNCS 2347. Springer-Verlag (2002) 306-316
9. Salton, G.: Automatic Text Processing: The Transformation, Analysis and Retrieval of Information by Computer. Addison-Wesley Publishing (1989)
10. Teufel, S. & Moens, M.: Sentence extraction as a classification task. Proceedings of ACL/EACL Workshop on Intelligent Scalable Text Summarization. Madrid, Spain (1997) 58–65
11. Tombros, A. & Sanderson, M.: Advantages of query-biased Summaries in IR. Proceedings of the 21st ACM SIGIR Conference (1998) 2-10

Social Navigation Support Through Annotation-Based Group Modeling

Rosta Farzan[2] and Peter Brusilovsky[1,2]

[1] School of Information Sciences and
[2] Intelligent Systems Program
University of Pittsburgh, Pittsburgh PA 15260, USA
peterb@pitt.edu, rosta@cs.pitt.edu

Abstract. Closed corpus AH systems demonstrate what is possible to achieve with adaptive hypermedia technologies. However, they are impractical for dealing with the large volume of open corpus resources. Our Knowledge Sea project explores social navigation support, an approach for providing open corpus personalized guidance that is based on past learners' interaction with the system. The most recent stage of our project focuses on using annotations for social navigation support. We present here Knowledge Sea II, which implements annotation-based social navigation support, and report the results of several classroom studies, which have evaluated this technology.

1 Introduction

Day by day, the amount of information on the Internet grows, which makes the Internet an important resource in learning. However, learners are having a hard time finding what they are looking for and are very often frustrated with the search process. Adaptive navigation support techniques developed in the field of Adaptive Hypermedia [1] could be used to guide learners to the right resources at the right time. However, concept-based navigation support mechanisms used in traditional Adaptive Hypermedia (AH) systems are not suitable for the large volume of open corpus documents [2]. When searching for a mechanism to deal with the large scale of adaptive navigation support needed in open corpus hypermedia, we turned to the ideas of social navigation [5]. We have attempted to develop personalized navigation support techniques that are based on past learners' interactions with the system. We call this *social navigation support* (SNS). Unlike traditional adaptive navigation support, which relies on expert-provided knowledge about each resource, *social navigation support relies on the *collective knowledge* of a large community of learners, casually gathered through many different forms of feedback.

We explored social navigation support in the context of Knowledge Sea, a project that currently focuses on helping students of introductory programming courses find relevant readings among hundreds of online tutorial pages distributed over the Web. In the first stage of our project, we explored the relatively straightforward "footprint" techniques suggested in early papers on social navigation [4; 8]. The idea of the

L. Ardissono, P. Brna, and A. Mitrovic (Eds.): UM 2005, LNAI 3538, pp. 463–472, 2005.

"footprints" is to count how many users are passing through a link or visiting a page, in order to recommend the most popular links and pages. Combining the ideas of social navigation with the ideas of group modeling and adaptive navigation support, we have implemented a "socially adaptive" system, Knowledge Sea II [2]. This system changes the intensity of a cell's background color, to indicate how many users of the current group have visited each tutorial page and each cluster of tutorial pages: the more visits, the more intensive the color (Fig. 1). This kind of SNS helped the learners to clearly recognize the most and the least visited pages and guide their navigational choices appropriately. Our classroom study [2] demonstrated that a footprint-based SNS is able to increase the usage of open corpus resources and that the learners appreciate it immensely. At the same time, a few students pointed out that the number of visits to a page is not always a reliable measure of its relevance to their needs and asked for better relevance indicators.

This paper presents the second stage of our project, which focused on providing a more reliable SNS: predict learner interest in resources through other learners' feedback. Our main challenge was to extract feedback from actions that users are naturally performing while working with the system. To answer this challenge, we explored *annotation-based social navigation support*. We encouraged learners to annotate pages they are reading by writing notes or highlighting parts of the page they found important. These annotations were used as an implicit indicator of page relevance for the current group of learners. The annotation-based SNS was implemented in the newest version of Knowledge Sea II (KSII) and explored in two classroom studies. The results indicate that it is a promising approach for open corpus adaptive navigation support. In the following sections we introduce KSII, describe two consecutive implementations of annotation-based SNS, present the results of the classroom studies, and analyze similar projects.

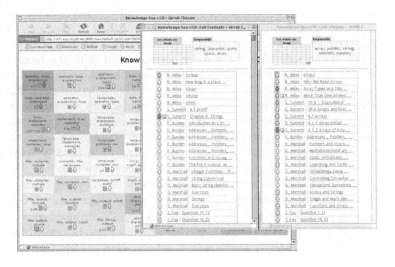

Fig. 1. The map view and two cell views in Knowledge Sea II

2 Annotation-Based Social Navigation Support in Knowledge Sea

The starting point for our work on annotation-based SNS was the first version of Knowledge Sea II system (Fig. 1), which combined the use of a self-organized knowledge map [3] with a simple "footprint" SNS [2]. The first version of KSII provided a simple interface for annotating tutorial pages by adding written notes. To help students navigate back to pages with notes, all such cells and pages were marked with a note icon (Fig. 1). In the first version, all notes were private: students were not able to see note icons or annotation made by others.

As a part of our evaluation of KSII, we asked the students several questions about the system's annotations. The answers showed that about 60% of the students appreciated the ability to annotate and further, were interested in sharing their annotations, seeing annotations made by others, and knowing which pages were annotated (Fig. 4). In addition, we examined the notes that the students created for themselves and discovered that almost all notes could be categorized into three groups: praise, problem, or general (37 praise, 36 problem, 34 general). This data motivated us to proceed with expanding the role of annotations in KSII and exploring the use of annotation as a source of a more reliable SNS, which we called annotation-based SNS. The current version of annotation-based SNS was developed in two phases, which were evaluated during the spring and fall semesters of 2004. The remaining part of this section presents the new features for annotation-based SNS which were introduced during these phases. The following section focuses on assessing the value of these features.

2.1 Phase 1: Public and Private Notes

The second version of KSII offered students the ability to make their annotations public and to choose one of three types of annotations (praise, problem, or general note). To make the presence of public annotations visible on the navigation level, we augmented the links inside the cell content window, and the links between tutorial pages with a small sticky note icon inside a yellow square. The color of the square represented the density of public annotations and the color of the sticky note represented the density of the personal annotations. Therefore, students could more easily make their navigation decisions, based on annotation information in addition to the traffic information, which had been provided in the first version of the system.

We expected two effects from the new annotation interface. We expected that the presence of public annotation would affect the students' navigational behavior, i.e., students would be more likely to visit pages with annotations. We also hoped that students would categorize the annotations by type, to express themselves more clearly. The main objective of the Spring 2004 classroom study was to assess these hypotheses.

2.2 Phase 2: Stronger Annotation-Based Navigation Support

In the second stage, we introduced several new features, motivated by the results of the Spring 2004 evaluation. From the *authoring side*, we attempted to encourage students to annotate by simplifying the annotation interface. To do this, we added highlighting (hypothesizing that highlighting would be easier for the students to use than writing notes). Fig. 2 presents the final version of annotation interface (available on the right side of each tutorial page). To highlight, a student can easily select part of the text inside the tutorial page and click on highlight button. Likewise, they can deselect the text. To write notes, students need to specify the following: type of the note (praise, problem, or general), visibility of the note (public versus private note), and anonymous versus signed. We added the option to sign notes in this phase in order to motivate students to share feedback with their classmates. As Fig. 2 shows, students can view any previously written notes they are the authors of but only the public notes written by others.

From the *usage side*, we tried to offer stronger navigation support by visualizing annotation *temperature* and by using the annotation *type,* which had been provided by the student author. Every link in a cell content or a tutorial window is augmented with one or two icons inside a small square. As in the previous phase, the background color of the square gives information about the density of group annotations. The icon inside the square now indicates the type of personal annotation (if present). A thumbs-up icon indicates that the current student has written a positive annotation or has highlighted part of the page. A question mark shows that the current student has written a problem-type annotation, while a sticky note indicates the existence of a general note. In addition, a thermometer icon shows the "temperature" of the annotations of the students in the current group. The temperature is warmer when more students have associated positive annotations with the page and colder when more students have associated problem-type annotations with the page. Fig. 3 presents part of the cell content window with annotation-based social navigation support. Labels explain the icons in the picture below.

We hypothesized that the usage of annotation ability and typed notes will be higher since the benefit of it is clearer. We expected to see stronger correlation between annotated pages and students' navigation behavior. We also expected that usage of the system will increase since it is easier for students to find relevant information.

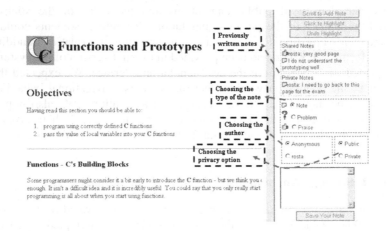

Fig. 2. Tutorial page with the annotation frame

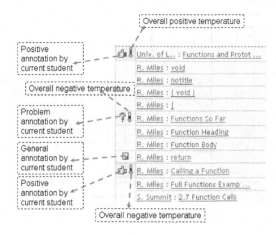

Fig. 3. Cell content window with annotation-based social navigation support

3   Evaluation

We assessed the effectiveness of the system and evaluated our hypotheses through a three-semester user study. The study was done in an introductory C programming course taught every semester at the School of Information Sciences, University of Pittsburgh. During the study, students' interaction with the system was logged. In addition, each student's opinion about the system and its features was solicited through a non-mandatory questionnaire presented at the end of each semester. Analyzing students' logs, we evaluated the effect of annotation on students' navigation and overall usage of the system. The questionnaire provided data on the students' opinion about the annotation ability of the system, their interest in visiting pages annotated by others, and their interest in sharing annotations with others. The rest of this section describes the evaluation of the system in detail. The three versions of KSII compared in this section (Fall 2003, Spring 2004, Fall 2004) differed only in the annotation authoring and its use for navigation support, as explained in section 2.

3.1   Students' Attitude Toward Annotations

As shown in Fig. 4, about 60% of students appreciated the ability to annotate and very few gave negative ratings to it, within the first two semesters. This positive attitude further increased after we expanded both the authoring and usage aspects of annotations. For the most recent version, evaluated in the Fall 2004 semester, 90% of the students found the ability to annotate to be a positive asset and none gave any negative feedback. We also asked students for their opinion of annotation-based navigation support (usage of public annotation to guide navigation). About 70% of the students rated annotation-based navigation support in a positive way. The graph shows that the enhancement of annotation abilities increased positive attitude toward annotation.

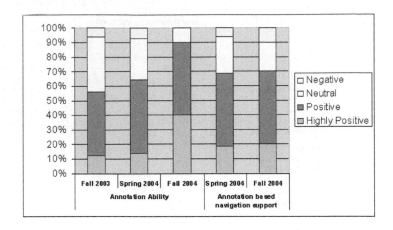

Fig. 4. Student's opinions about the annotation feature of the system

3.2 Effect of Annotation on Usage of the System

Fig. 5 presents the usage of three versions of KSII over three semesters. Note that it is only in the third version of KSII, which balanced an extended annotation interface with a more comprehensive annotation-based navigation support, we were able to achieve a visible increase of all usage parameters. However, even the first simple version of annotation-based navigational support (showing only the density of public annotations) caused a very solid increase in the percentage of students actively using the system.

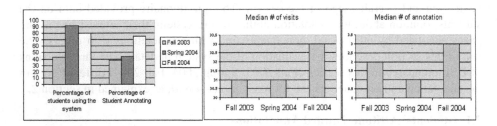

Fig. 5. Overall usage of KS system over the 3 semesters of users study

3.3 Effect of Annotations on Students' Navigational Behavior

To analyze the effectiveness of annotation-based navigation support, we compared navigation behavior of students related to presence of annotation. We looked at documents with public annotations over the last two semesters and analyzed the percentage of activity on each document before and after public annotation existed. We also looked at documents with public and private annotations to investigate the effect of annotation on revisiting a document by the author of the annotation.

Annotated Pages Versus Useful Pages: The first thing we have attempted to evaluate is a correlation between page quality for the given group and presence of annotation. To argue that guiding students to annotated pages is meaningful, we need to show that pages that get annotated are attractive and useful for the group. One way to evaluate the quality of a page is by the frequency of its access. Table 1 shows that page access probability (the number of visits divided by the possible number of documents to be visited) is significantly larger for annotated pages. This is a two-way correlation. From one side, most-visited pages get annotated. From the other side, the presence of annotation encourages student to visit pages.

Table 1. Effect of annotation in visiting a page

	Average visit		p-value	
	Spring 2004	Fall 2004	Spring 2004	Fall 2004
Annotated	4.87	5.38	0.00001	0.00001
Not Annotated	0.025	0.033		

Another (and probably more reliable) indicator of page quality is average page-reading time. Table 2 compares time spent reading (TSR) for pages with and without annotation. For comparison, we looked at the median TSR over all the pages, by category, for all students. The median was chosen, in order to give less significance to extreme TSRs. The data shows that students spend significantly more time reading pages with annotations than those without annotations. Thus, annotation-based navigation support does indeed guide students to important pages.

Table 2. Effect of annotation on Time Spent Reading (TSR in second) a page

	Median TSR		p-value	
	Spring 2004	Fall 2004	Spring 2004	Fall 2004
Annotated	363	177	0.00001	0.00001
Not Annotated	28	27		

The Effect of Annotation on Group Navigation Behavior: Once we established that guiding students to annotated pages is meaningful, the next question is to ask whether or not the annotation-based navigation support succeeded in guiding students to these pages. To answer it, we computed the normalized access rate before and after the presence of public annotation. To normalize, we divided the number of page-visits by the number of possible days to access a page. Namely, the number of visits before annotation is divided by the number of days from the first day of using the system until the date of first public annotation and activity after annotation is divided by the number of days after the first public annotation until the last day of using the system. Fig. 6 shows that in spring and fall of 2004, in most cases, more than 50% of the visits to a page were done after public annotation existed. The difference is statistically significant (p-value= 0.00001).

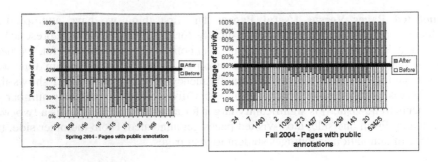

Fig. 6. Effect of presence of public annotation on student visits

Effect of Personal Annotation on Personal Navigational Behavior: In the analysis of effectiveness of annotation, we looked at the effect of annotation on revisiting a page by the author of the annotation. We compared the probability of visiting a page that had been annotated by the student herself in the past with the probability of visiting a page that had not yet been annotated by this student. As shown in Table 3, in both semesters, students were more likely to revisit a page that they had already annotated. The difference in both cases is statistically significant. The students annotate pages that they want to revisit, so showing previously annotated pages is useful for navigational support.

Table 3. Chance of self-revisit on annotated and not annotated pages

	Without annotation	**With annotation**	**p-value**
Spring 2004	17%	48%	0.01
Fall 2004	18%	47%	0.03

Effect of Thermometer on Group Navigation Behavior: While the presence of both public and private annotations significantly influenced navigational behavior, we were not able to demonstrate the influence of the temperature icon on navigation behavior. The frequency of visits to pages with a positive temperature was not very different from pages with neutral or even negative temperatures. After more careful analysis of students' annotations we discovered that the difference between types of annotation was not very clear to the students. First, many obviously positive annotations were typed by students as being merely "general" notes. Table 4 shows that more than 50% of "general" annotations were really "praise." Secondly, "problem" annotations were used not to indicate a bad page (as we assumed), but to report problems with the page to the teacher. In effect, the thermometer icon was useful to indicate pages with public annotations. However, the students could not rely on the "temperature" to show the quality of the information.

Table 4. Usage of type of annotations

	Total Number of Annotations	Praise	General	Typed as General but is really Praise
Spring 2004	41	16	25	17
Fall 2004	51	24	21	11

4 Previous Work

Several e-learning systems have been developed using the idea of social navigation. Most relevant to our project are CoFIND [6] and Educo [7]. CoFIND is a self-organized learning environment that organizes online resources through the counting of votes cast by learners. Learners can associate different types of qualities (such as "simple", "good for beginners") with each resource to help with the organization of the resources. Although CoFIND has been pretty successful among its users, it relies heavily on explicit feedback. Providing explicit feedback can interfere with the students' learning process and can increase students' extraneous cognitive load. Educo is a collaborative learning environment that supports social navigation in direct and indirect ways. Direct social navigation is supported through real-time discussion via chat rooms. Indirect social navigation is supported by annotating resources according to the number of visits. Although direct social navigation is interesting, what is more interesting and important to us is indirect social navigation. Indirect social navigation is well suited for online settings since people access the resource on an individual basis at discrete, disjointed times and locations. Direct social navigation can offer very little help to those who are not able to participate in real time discussions. It is hard to respond to discussions when people are online at different times and it is more difficult to associate topics in the discussion with specific content within the resources. The discussion could be totally irrelevant to the associated resource. In terms of indirect support of social navigation, Educo relies on simple implicit feedback from students: the number of visits. Although Educo also enables learners to annotate documents, this information is not used for navigation support.

5 Conclusion

Social navigation is a promising approach for providing navigation support inside a community of online learners. However, the challenges of collecting feedback from learners make reliable social navigation support difficult. Our results show that annotation-based social navigation support is more attractive for learners. Yet, the learners have to be motivated to annotate the tutorial pages. As a future direction of this work, we are planning to provide bridges from students' annotation to course material by letting student bookmark pages as related to specific lectures or assignments. We believe this will give more motivation and clearer navigational support to students who are authoring annotations and those who are later influenced by them.

References

1. Brusilovsky P (1996) Methods and techniques of adaptive hypermedia. User Modeling and User-Adapted Interaction 6: 87-129
2. Brusilovsky P, Chavan G, and Farzan R (2004) Social adaptive navigation support for open corpus electronic textbooks. In De Bra P and Nejdl W (eds) Third International Conference on Adaptive Hypermedia and Adaptive Web-Based Systems (AH'2004), Eindhoven, the Netherlands, August 23-26, 2004, pp. 24-33
3. Brusilovsky P and Rizzo R (2002) Using maps and landmarks for navigation between closed and open corpus hyperspace in Web-based education. New Rev Hypermedia & Multimedia 9: 59-82
4. Dieberger A (1997) Supporting social navigation on the World Wide Web. Int J Human-Comp Interact 46: 805-825
5. Dieberger A, Dourish P, Höök K, Resnick P, and Wexelblat A (2000) Social navigation: Techniques for building more usable systems. interactions 7: 36-45
6. Dron J, Boyne C, and Mitchell R (2001) Footpaths in the stuff swamp. In Fowler W and Hasebrook J (eds) WebNet'2001, World Conference of the WWW and Internet, Orlando, FL, October 23-27, 2001, pp. 323-328
7. Kurhila J, Miettinen M, Nokelainen P, and Tirri H (2002) EDUCO - A collaborative learning environment based on social navigation. In De Bra P, Brusilovsky P and Conejo R (eds) Second International Conference on Adaptive Hypermedia and Adaptive Web-Based Systems (AH'2002), Málaga, Spain, May 29-31, 2002, pp. 242-252
8. Wexelblat A and Mayes P (1999) Footprints: History-rich tools for information foraging. In ACM Conference on Human-Computer Interaction (CHI'99), Pittsburgh, PA, pp. 270-277

Discovering Stages in Web Navigation[*]

V. Hollink, M. van Someren, and S. ten Hagen

Faculty of Science, University of Amsterdam,
Amsterdam, The Netherlands
{vhollink, maarten, stephanh}@science.uva.nl

Abstract. Users of web sites often do not know exactly what they are looking for or what the site has to offer. During navigation they use the information found so far to formulate their information needs and refine their search. In these cases users need to pass through a series of pages before they can use the information that will eventually answer their question. Recommender systems aimed at leading users to target pages directly do not provide optimal assistance to these users. In this paper we propose a method to automatically divide web navigation into a number of stages. A recommender can use these stages to recommend pages which do not only match the topic of a user's search, but also the current stage of the navigation process. As these recommendations are more tailored toward the user's current situation, they can provide better assistance than recommendations made by traditional recommender systems.

1 Introduction

In recent years web sites have evolved from small electronic leaflets to continually changing highly complex information systems. This development has urged the need to provide users of web sites with navigation assistance to prevent them from drowning in the available information. Recommender systems provide such assistance by selecting a limited number of pages which they believe to be interesting for the user. Many recommender systems, including [7, 9, 4], form groups of pages with similar topics in such a way that users who are interested in some of the pages from a group have a high probability of also being interested in the other pages from that group. These systems represent user interests as clusters of pages. When a user visits a page, other pages from the cluster of the currently visited page are recommended. In this situation recommendations act as shortcuts, which allow the user to reach his goal without passing through a series of less interesting pages.

However, users do not always know exactly what they are looking for or what the site has to offer, especially when they are visiting the site for the first time. Sometimes users search the site to find a solution to a problem, without knowing which solutions are available. In these cases pages and links include

---

[*] This research is supported as ToKen2000 project by the Netherlands Organization for Scientific Research (NWO) under project number 634.000.006.

L. Ardissono, P. Brna, and A. Mitrovic (Eds.): UM 2005, LNAI 3538, pp. 473–482, 2005.

navigation information. They do not provide an answer to the user's question but rather help to articulate the question or tell her where to look further. In this case the order in which pages are viewed is relevant: the users first need to get information about the available solutions before they can benefit from pages describing specific solutions. In general the navigation stage in which a page is viewed is important in all cases where users can not fully understand the page that will eventually answer their question without passing through a series of pages. We argue that a model of user interest should not only contain clusters of pages with interesting topics, but also prescribe in which stage of the navigation each page is relevant. Recommender systems can use such a model to select pages that match both the stage and the topic of the user's search.

The need for a richer model of user preferences is supported by the work in [1]. This study shows that web users vary substantially in the extent to which they know what information they are searching for. Users who have only a rough idea of what they are looking for, can benefit more from a recommender that guides them step by step through the available information than from a recommender aimed at presenting the target information immediately.

One commonly used type of order sensitive models are Markov chains (e.g. [6]). Markov chains make predictions about the next step of a user using the observed frequencies of sequences of pages in a log file. Since Markov chains do not generalize over individual sequences, the models tend to be very large and the predictions inaccurate for infrequently visited pages.

In [8] web user behavior is represented as a hidden Markov model. In theory, the states contain pages with similar topics as well as similar stages, but in practice, inspection of the states reveals that the states primarily categorize the pages per topic. Another disadvantage of this method is that the stage and topic assignments are optimized simultaneously, which is very time consuming.

The method presented in this paper automatically discovers relevant navigation stages without depending on a topic clustering. The algorithm initially assigns every page of a site to a stage on the basis of the parts of the user sessions in which the page occurs. Then bootstrapping is applied to improve the initial assignments. Section 2 describes the stage discovery algorithm. In Section 3 we evaluate the algorithm on log data collected in a user experiment. In Section 4 artificial data is used to examine the conditions that the algorithm requires. Section 5 demonstrates the value of the stage model obtained in Section 3 and discusses how this model can improve web page recommendation. The last section contains conclusions and presents our plans for the future.

2   The Stage Discovery Algorithm

In this section we present an algorithm that takes a log file of a web site and divides the navigation into a number of stages assigning each page to a stage.

2.1   Initialization

To determine in which parts of the sessions the pages occurs most, we normalize the positions of the pages in each session to a scale of 0 to 1. The position of a page at the kth place in a session with m pages is called position $(k-1)/(m-1)$. We define the *average relative position* (ARP) of a page as the average over all of its positions in all sessions.

We make an initial classification by dividing the ARP range into as many parts as the number of stages we want to find (n). We assume that within one stage people have no preference for viewing the pages in one order over viewing them in another order. If this assumption is correct, the distribution of the ARPs of all pages from one stage follows the normal distribution. The Expectation Maximization (EM) algorithm [2] is used to fit a mixture of n one-dimensional Gaussians to the ARP values. In the resulting mixture each Gaussian corresponds to a stage. The Gaussian with the smallest mean corresponds to the first stage, the Gaussian with the second smallest mean to the second stage etc. For each Gaussian we compute in which part of the ARP range the Gaussian has the highest probability of all Gaussians. The boundaries of these regions determine the stage boundaries.

We assign the pages to stages on the basis of their ARPs. The assignment of pages with ARP values close to the boundaries of the stages is insecure. Therefore, for each stage we increase its lower boundary and decrease its upper boundary until only 70% of the stage's original ARP range remains. Pages with ARPs within these parts are assigned to the corresponding stages. Pages with ARP values outside the stage boundaries are assigned to a stage in the bootstrapping phase.

The number of stages that should be distinguished is determined using EM as well. Mixtures with various numbers of components are fitted to the ARP data. The average log-likelihood of the ARP values given a mixture gives information about how well the mixture fits the ARPs. Another measure that can be used to estimate the number of stages is the number of irregular transitions in the log data (transitions to a stage other than the current stage or the stage directly following the current stage). We define the *Fitness* of a model as a linear combination of its average log-likelihood and its number of irregular transitions.

2.2   Bootstrapping

In the previous section the pages were assigned to stages on the basis of the parts of the sessions in which they occurred most. Here we improve this classification by looking at the context in which the pages occur in the individual sessions.

In our model stages are strictly ordered, so that most navigation steps occur within one stage or from a page from one stage to a page from the next stage. As a consequence, a page which occurs in the sessions mostly between two pages from stage s has a high probability of belonging to stage s. We use this idea to correct misclassifications. For each page p and each stage s we count the number of times p occurs between two pages of stage s. We define the *evidence of misclassification* of p as the difference between the number of times p occurs in its current stage and the maximum number of times p occurs in some other stage. The pages with the highest evidence of misclassification are reassigned to the stage in which they occur most. With this new classifications for each page the evidence of misclassification is recomputed and again the stages of the pages with the highest evidence are changed. This process is continued until no more stage changes are made or until a maximum number of cycles is reached.

3   Discovering Stages in Experimental Data

We evaluate the presented methods on web log data of the SeniorGezond site[1]. The SeniorGezond site is a Dutch site developed by the Netherlands Organization for Applied Scientific Research (TNO) in cooperation with domain specialists from the Geriatric Network and the Leiden University Medical Center. It contains information for elderly people about the prevention of falling accidents. The developers of the site categorized the pages into descriptions of problems, descriptions of solutions and descriptions of specific products or services. A navigation menu helps the users to find descriptions of their problems and guide them to the appropriate solutions and the matching products and services.

To acquire log data a user experiment was performed. We removed the menu and all links from the SeniorGezond pages and added to each page a complete list of links to all pages of the site, so that each page could be reached from each other page. Thirty subjects were asked to play the role of an elderly person in a problematic situation who visited the site to find a solution to his of her problem. We recorded the clicks of the subjects during 10 search assignments. For each assignment of each subject we listed the pages that were viewed consecutively during the performance of the assignment. This resulted in 244 lists of pages or *sessions* with a total of 90 different pages.

We analyzed the behavior of the subjects by looking at the log files. Figure 1 shows the distribution of the ARPs of the pages of each of the three page types. The figure clearly shows that the problem pages are visited mostly in the beginning of the sessions, the solution pages in the middle and the product pages in the end. This indicates that the page types coincide with navigation stages. The navigation stages can be seen even more clearly from the transition matrix in Table 1. This matrix shows for each page type how many times someone went from a page of this type to a page of each other type. From the matrix it is clear that by far most transitions occur within stages or go from one stage to the next stage. From these results, we conclude that the three page types of the SeniorGezond site form three navigation stages: the problem pages form the first stage, the solutions the second stage and the products the third stage.

We applied the stage discovery algorithm to the data from the SeniorGezond experiment. To determine the number of stages we fitted models with one up to eight Gaussians and determined the fitness of these models. With appropriate combinations of the average log-likelihood and the number of irregular

---

[1] http://www.SeniorGezond.nl/

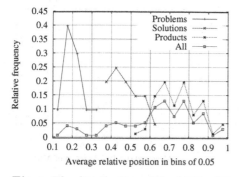

Fig. 1. The distribution of the ARPs of the pages in the log data of the SeniorGezond experiment

Table 1. Relative frequency in percentages of transitions between the page types of the SeniorGezond site

From type	To type			
	Problem	Solution	Product	Stop
Start	75.4	20.1	4.5	0
Problem	42.2	47.3	5.5	5.0
Solution	4.8	62.5	25.0	7.6
Product	3.7	9.3	65.9	21.1

Table 2. Accuracy of the stage discovery algorithm on the pages of the SeniorGezond site

Operations	Accuracy
Initialization	0.84
Initialization and bootstrapping	0.99

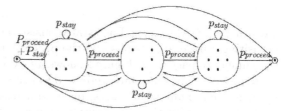

Fig. 2. A simulation model with three content states. States are represented by circles, pages in the states by dots. All unlabeled arrows have probability $p_{jump}/2$

transitions, the algorithm correctly inferred that the navigation contained three stages. Then the model with three stages was used to assign each page to a stage. Table 2 shows the part of the SeniorGezond pages that was classified correctly, the accuracy. The initialization already led to an accuracy of 84%. Bootstrapping added another 15%. In the end only one page was assigned to an incorrect stage. These results lead to the conclusion that the stage discovery algorithm provides an adequate way to model the navigation stages of the SeniorGezond site.

4   Discovering Stages in Artificial Data

In order to determine the sensitivity of the algorithm to the characteristics of the data we generated data sets with various specifications. For this purpose, the behavior of users was simulated with a finite state automaton. The automaton consisted of an ordered set of states and a transition function. The states in the automaton corresponded to navigation stages. The transition probabilities were the probabilities of going from a page in one stage to a page in another stage. For all stages the probability of staying in the same stage was p_{stay}, the probability of going to the next stage was $p_{proceed}$ and the probability of going to

Table 3. Part of the runs in which the correct number of stages was found with (a) various numbers of training sessions and (b) various numbers of stages

No sessions	Accuracy	No stages	Accuracy
244	0.24	1	0.96
500	0.40	2	1.00
1000	0.68	3	0.72
1500	0.96	4	0.12
2000	1.00	5	0.00

(a)   (b)

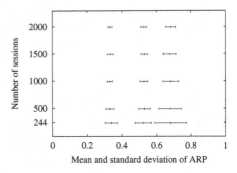

Fig. 3. The average mean and standard deviations of the ARPs of the pages from three stages and various amounts of training sessions

any other stage was p_{jump}. Each state consisted of a set of pages. The probability of visiting a page p in stage s was the probability of going to stage s divided by the number of pages in s. Figure 2 shows an example of an automaton with three content states. The automata were used to generate sets of user sessions (log files) with the same number of stages, pages and sessions as the SeniorGezond data. Furthermore we set the probability of going to a random stage (p_{jump}) and the average length of a session equal to the values found in the SeniorGezond data.

To determine under which conditions the right number of stages can be found we used the simulation model to generate log files with various numbers of training sessions and various numbers of stages. We had the stage discovery algorithm choose between models with one up to six stages. We repeated each experiment 25 times and evaluated in how many cases the algorithm was able to find the correct number of stages. The part of the log files for which the correct number of stages was found is given in Table 3. Table 3(a) shows that the estimation of the number of stages becomes much more accurate if more training sessions are available. From Fig. 3 we can see why: when more data is available each page is visited more often so that the deviations of the ARPs of the pages in the various stages are smaller. This results in larger 'gaps' between the ARPs of the pages from different stages which makes the stages more easily separable. As visible in Table 3(b), the higher the number of stages, the more difficult it is to find the correct number of stages. When there are more stages, the means of the ARPs of the pages of the stages lie closer together, while the variance does not change. This increases the overlap between the stages making the individual stages harder to distinguish.

We tested the effects of a number of properties of the generated log data on the stage assignment accuracy. We generated sets of 50 log files and fitted models with the correct number of Gaussians to each log file. All presented accuracies are averages over the 50 log files. First, we varied the number of sessions per log file. Figure 4(a) shows the accuracy after initialization (initial) and after

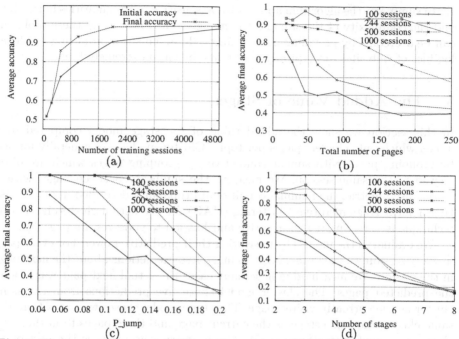

Fig. 4. The average accuracy with various settings for (a) the number of training sessions (b) the number of pages (c) P_{jump} (d) the number of stages

initialization followed by bootstrapping (final). Both the initial and the final accuracy are higher when more training data is available. The effect on the final accuracy is stronger, because bootstrapping benefits from more data as well as a better initialization.

We varied the total number of pages while keeping the ratio between the numbers of pages in the three stages fixed. The results are presented in Fig. 4(b). If there are more pages, the available data per page is less, which results in a decrease in initial precision. When there are many pages the final accuracy suffers from the lower initial accuracy. At the same time more pages also mean that there is more data available for the bootstrapping phase. If there are more pages in a stage, the probability is higher that a misclassified page occurs between two correctly classified pages, so that the misclassification is fixed. These two opposite effects mean that the lines in Fig. 4(b) start out almost flat.

We made the behavior of the simulated users less predictable by increasing the probability of making irregular stage transitions (p_{jump}). Figure 4(c) shows the results of varying the value of p_{jump}, while keeping the ratio between p_{stay} and $p_{proceed}$ constant. The accuracy dropped when the percentage irregular transitions exceeded a certain minimum, but more data allowed for more irregularity.

The number of stages was varied by adding more stages with 20 pages between the first and the last stage. From Fig. 4(d) we can see that there is a maximum number of stages that can be learned with a certain amount of training data. More stages can be learned if more training sessions are available.

In summary, the algorithm appears to be sensitive to irregularities in the data and the complexity of the site and the navigation. However, all these problems can be overcome by providing more training data. This is a promising result, as log files of web sites are typically very noisy but also extremely large.

5   The Added Value of Stages

In this section we show the added value of the stage model compared to a model which only clusters pages per topic. Cluster models are generally formed by grouping pages with similar content or by grouping pages which are often viewed in the same session. We measure the similarity between pages with a usage based metric, the minimal conditional probability described in [5]. We use Hierarchical Agglomerative Clustering (HAC) for the actual clustering, as this technique is very simple and intuitive and has led to good results (e.g. [3]).

We evaluated the models by measuring their predictive power. For every page in every session we used the models to make five predictions about the next page in the session. We measured in how many cases the actual next page was among the predicted pages. The cluster model chose five predictions from the same cluster as the currently visited page. The stage model chose two pages from the same cluster and same stage as the current page and three pages from the same cluster and next stage (See Fig. 5). The prediction accuracy is the part of all cases in which a correct prediction was made. We used a 10 fold cross validation to split the sessions for forming the clusters from the sessions that were used during evaluation. Each prediction was made 100 times. All presented figures are macro averages over the 100 runs of the 10 folds.

Figure 6 shows the prediction accuracy of the cluster model (HAC) and the stage model (HAC with stages) for all possible numbers of topic clusters. The figure clearly shows that the stage information makes a large improvement in

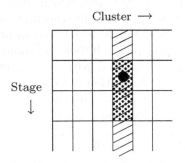

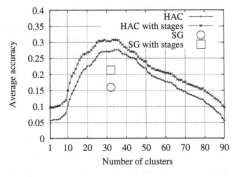

Fig. 5. Part of the pages that might be predicted from a cluster model (hatched) and from a cluster model extended with navigation stages (dotted). The large bullet indicates the current page

Fig. 6. The average prediction accuracy of the clusters formed with HAC and the SeniorGezond clusters (SG) with and without the use of navigation stages with varying numbers of clusters

the accuracy. The accuracy increased about 0.04, which is an improvement of 10 to 70%. In two situations the stage model has an advantage over the cluster model. First, when the cluster of the current page contains more than five pages, the stage information is used to refine the set of predictions. Second, when the cluster contains too few pages or even no pages at all, the stage model yields pages that are at least from the right stage, while the cluster model has to make predictions at random.

The original SeniorGezond site contained a hand crafted hierarchical navigation menu. We extracted a set of clusters from this menu and evaluated the resulting model. The prediction accuracy is shown in Fig. 6. The addition of stage information to the SeniorGezond clusters made an equally large improvement as the addition to the HAC clusters. In the figure the performance of the SeniorGezond clusters might seem pretty dramatic, but we have to bear in mind that these clusters are optimized for use in a navigation menu rather than for prediction. However, inspection of the HAC clusters might yield some useful suggestions for improvement of the SeniorGezond menu.

From these experiments we conclude that using both topic and stage information leads to a more accurate model of user behavior than using topic information alone. The stage model can be applied in a straightforward manner in a recommender to make recommendations which match both the topic and the stage of a search process. As these recommendations are more tailored toward the user's current situation they can potentially provide better assistance than recommendations based only on the topic of the user's search.

6   Conclusion

Interests of web users are typically represented as sets of interesting pages which do not include the order in which the pages should be viewed. We argue that in some cases this is suboptimal. We present a richer model in which each page belongs to a navigation stage and we give an algorithm to learn the parameters for this model from log files. An experiment with the Dutch SeniorGezond site showed that the three page types of this site were used during different navigation stages. The presented algorithm was able to discover the stages in the SeniorGezond data and assign 99% of the pages of the SeniorGezond site to the correct stage. Simulation experiments showed that the algorithm is able to discover stages even in noisy data as long as enough log data is provided.

Results of an experiment in an offline setting showed that incorporating stage information in a model of web navigation improves the prediction accuracy of the model. This suggests that recommender systems can benefit from the use of navigation stages. In case not all pages with a relevant topic can be recommended, the stages of the pages can narrow down the set of possible recommendations. At the same time navigation stages can be used to find more reasonably good recommendations, in case not enough pages with a relevant topic can be found.

Navigation stages are clear from the SeniorGezond data, but we do not know whether the navigation on other sites contains similar patterns. We expect that users who enter a site with a vague question, will navigate from pages which give an overview of the available options to pages with more specific content. In these cases navigation is likely to contain stages, but more research is needed to determine the exact conditions under which a stage model should be used.

Like most recommenders (e.g. [4, 6, 8, 5]) the presented algorithm uses log information to learn about the users' interests. If the navigation of the previous users was not optimal, this can easily lead to incorrect conclusions and suboptimal recommendings. An alternative approach is asking users to provide explicit feedback about the visited pages (e.g. [9]), but the feedback can be very sparse and not representative of the whole user population. In future research it might be useful to look at combinations of log information and explicit feedback.

We demonstrated the working of the stage discovery algorithm on experimental and artificial data. We are currently investigating how well our methods work on log files from online web sites. As these log files are typically much larger, but less complete, clean and uniform than experimental files, we will run the algorithm only on the sessions which seem to follow a meaningful pattern. This extension will boost the algorithm's robustness to noise and at the same time make it efficient enough to be used on very large data sets.

References

1. Choo, C.: Working the web: an empirical model of web use. Proceedings of the 33rd Hawaii International Conference on System Sciences (HICSS), Maui, Hawaii (2000)
2. Dempster, A., Laird, N., Rubin, D.: Maximum likelihood from incomplete data via the EM algorithm. Journal of the Royal Statistical Society **39** (1977) 1–38
3. Dubes, R., Jain, A.: Algorithms for clustering data. Prentice Hall (1988)
4. Mobasher, B., Dai, H., Luo, T., Nakagawa, M.: Discovery and evaluation of aggregate usage profiles for web personalization. Data mining and knowledge discovery **6** (2002) 61–82
5. Perkowitz, M., Etzioni, O.: Towards adaptive web sites: Conceptual framework and case study. Artificial Intelligence **118** (2000) 245–275
6. Sarukkai, R.: Link prediction and path analysis using Markov chains. Proceedings of the Ninth International World Wide Web Conference, Amsterdam, The Netherlands (2000)
7. Schwab, I., Pohl, W.: Learning user profiles from positive examples. Proceedings of the ACAI'99 Workshop on Machine Learning in User Modeling, Chania, Greece (1999)
8. Ypma, A., Heskes, T.: Categorization of web pages and user clustering with mixtures of hidden Markov models. Proceedings of the International Workshop on Web Knowledge Discovery and Data Mining (WEBKDD), Edmonton, Canada (2002)
9. Zhu, T., Greiner, R., Häubl, G.: Learning a model of a web user's interests. Proceedings of the Ninth International Conference on User Modeling (UM), Johnstown, PA, USA, (2003)

The Impact of Link Suggestions on User Navigation and User Perception

Ion Juvina[1] and Eelco Herder[2]

[1] Institute of Information and Computing Sciences, Utrecht University,
Padualaan 14, De Uithof, 3584 CH Utrecht, The Netherlands
ion@cs.uu.nl
[2] Department of Computer Science, University of Twente,
P.O. Box 217, 7500 AE Enschede, The Netherlands
herder@cs.utwente.nl

Abstract. The study reported in this paper explores the effects of providing web users with link suggestions that are relevant to their tasks. Results indicate that link suggestions were positively received. Furthermore, users perceived sites with link suggestions as more usable and themselves as less disoriented. The average task execution time was significantly lower than in the control condition and users appeared to navigate in a more structured manner. Unexpectedly, men took more advantage from link suggestions than women.

1 Introduction

For many people, the web has become a major source of information. More and more people primarily use the web for private matters such as planning their holidays, deciding between products and many other activities.

In contrast to most desktop applications, web sites generally are designed for a general audience with varying goals [14]. As it is hard to satisfy all categories of users with one design, adaptive hypermedia systems try to better support the users by personalizing content or link structure. Traditional techniques in the latter category involve link hiding, sorting, annotation, direct guidance and hypertext map adaptation [2]. When trying to find information related to a task, users have to rely on proximal cues such as the link anchor text to decide what their next action will be [10]. If the proximal cues are not clear enough, or if the users do not have sufficient insight on the structure of the site, they may become disoriented, i.e. they don't know their current position in a web site, how they came to that point or where to go next [4]. Various studies have been carried out to infer user goals from their actions [e.g. 3]. Given these goals, the utility of the various navigation options on a web page can be estimated [7][12] and communicated to the user by means of link relevancy indicators, or *link suggestions*.

While user-adaptive systems appear to be a good idea, it still is an open issue how the benefits from adaptations can be evaluated [17]. We conducted a user study in which participants were asked to carry out several predefined everyday tasks. In one

L. Ardissono, P. Brna, and A. Mitrovic (Eds.): UM 2005, LNAI 3538, pp. 483–492, 2005.

condition, the participants were provided with predefined link suggestions. Various indicators of user's behavior and perception were measured. We found evidence that link suggestions based on the user's goals have a positive impact: they cause the users to navigate in a more structured way, which makes them less vulnerable to disorientation [4].

The remainder of this paper is structured as follows. In the next section we present our research questions. We continue with the setup of the experiment. After presenting the results, we conclude with a short discussion.

2   Individual Differences, Disorientation and Navigation Styles

There is a vast amount of literature on individual differences in web navigation. In a previous study we found *spatial ability* and *domain expertise* to be the most important determinants of user performance in web tasks [6]. It has been shown that there are differences in favor of men with regard to spatial ability [15], web searching behavior, and learning performance [13]. Women are more likely to use a rote way-finding strategy – attending to instructions on how to get from place to place – whereas men are more likely to report to use an orientation strategy – maintaining a sense of their own position in relation to environmental reference points [15]. For this reason, we expect women to benefit from navigation support that supports the rote way-finding strategy, more so than men, thus compensating for the so-called 'gender gap' in web use.

As mentioned in the introduction, disorientation is a major issue in web navigation that is mainly caused by the non-linearity of web sites; on each page, users have to decide between alternative options, which includes following links or backtracking to pages visited earlier. Although the problem has been given the label 'disorientation', it is hard to measure or to quantify. Ahuja and Webster [1] developed a questionnaire that is shown to indicate a user's perceived disorientation. Various attempts have been made to relate patterns in user navigation, most importantly patterns related to page revisits, to success measures and disorientation [5][8][16]. In a previous study [4] we found a weak navigation style that was associated with perceived disorientation.

Based on these previous findings, we formulated the following hypotheses to guide the study:

1. Link suggestions will generally be well received.
2. Link suggestions improve perceived usability and reduce disorientation, as experienced by the users.
3. Link suggestions will influence the way users navigate; the differences can be interpreted as an argument in favor of providing support.
4. Women will benefit more from link suggestions than men.

3   Experimental Setup

In order to check for differences caused by link suggestions to users perceptions and navigation behavior an experimental approach was employed, which is described in this section.

3.1 Web Navigation Tasks

First matter of concern for the experimental setup was triggering realistic web navigation behavior. Five web navigation tasks were created based on the collection of cases presented in [9], following suggestions from [7]. An example task is presented in figure 1.

Participants were instructed to start each task at a specified website's home page. They were allowed to use other websites than the indicated ones; the only restriction was to start at the specified websites.

This summer you will spend a long weekend in London with your girl/boy friend. Both of you would like to visit the top attractions and some museums. But, most importantly, you want to visit one of the great musicals in West End.

Given Facts:
- You already have plane tickets to Heathrow Airport
- You still have to book a hotel, preferably near the West End theatre district
- You have sufficient money to spend during the weekend

To do:
Go to http://www.visitlondon.com and find answers to the following questions:
- Find a small hotel in the West End district
- How do you get from Heathrow Airport to the city center?
- In what theatre does the Lion King play?
- Find a restaurant in Covent Garden that offers pre-theatre menus.

Fig. 1. An example web navigation task

3.2 Experimental Manipulation

Various strategies for generating link suggestions can be thought of. The simplest case is when the content providers indicate the most important sections of the content from their point of view. As users may have different goals for visiting a site, it might be a better idea to provide link suggestions that match the current context of use. In this experiment we provided users with suggestions that are relevant to their tasks.

Suggestions were generated based on simulations of a cognitive model similar in principle to CoLiDeS, a cognitive model of web navigation presented in [7]. CoLiDeS uses Latent Semantic Analysis (LSA) to calculate the semantic similarity between goal description and the available links on the current webpage. The link most similar in description to the task goal is selected to be clicked on. User behavior was simulated in advance based on the task descriptions. Semantic similarities

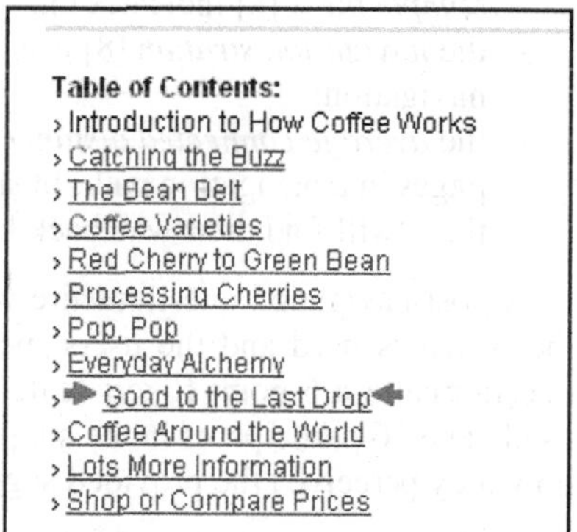

Table of Contents:
- Introduction to How Coffee Works
- Catching the Buzz
- The Bean Belt
- Coffee Varieties
- Red Cherry to Green Bean
- Processing Cherries
- Pop, Pop
- Everyday Alchemy
- ➡ Good to the Last Drop ⬅
- Coffee Around the World
- Lots More Information
- Shop or Compare Prices

Fig. 2. Example of link suggestion: the two red arrows point at (suggest) the link text "Good to the last drop"

between these task descriptions and the texts of the links leading to task solutions were calculated with LSA.

For each task, one or more successful paths were generated. In the *navigation support condition*, links on these paths were highlighted to the participants – see figure 2. In the control condition, participants executed the same tasks without any support. The link suggestions were generated on the fly using the Scone framework for development and evaluation of web enhancements [18].

Participants in the support condition were instructed that suggestions were automatically generated by a cognitive robot, they were meant to help participants in doing their tasks, and they could be followed or not. Participants got suggestions only when they arrived at specific pages.

3.3 Participants

Thirty-two participants, mainly students of various studies at Utrecht University, were recruited with advertisements. To qualify for participating, a minimum level of English language skills and Internet experience was required. The participants were randomly assigned to one of the two conditions – sixteen participants in each condition.

3.4 Measures of User Navigation and User Perceptions

Several measures on navigation complexity and patterns of page revisits were calculated. For matters of brevity we limit ourselves to describing the most relevant measures in the context of this study and refer to [4][5] for a more complete overview. The meaning of these measures is described below and illustrated in figure 3.

- *back button usage* is the percentage of back button clicks among the navigation actions;
- *the relative amount of home page visits* is the number of visits to the web pages that the participants used to start the different tasks, divided by the total number of page visits;
- *compactness* [8] indicates that users follow a 'shallow' search strategy;
- the *navigation stratum* [8] is a measure designed to capture the linearity of user navigation;
- the *average connected distance* indicates the average distance between any two pages in a navigation path. In short, it indicates how confident users are that they 'will find their way back later' [4].

A post-navigation questionnaire was used to measure user opinions on usability of the websites used and the users' perceived disorientation [1]. For each item of the questionnaire a 5-point Likert scale from 'strongly disagree' to 'strongly agree' was used. The 16 participants in the support condition were given four additional items on how they perceived the provided suggestions:

- The suggestions given by the robot were helpful
- I felt the suggestions were intrusive / annoying
- I believed I could trust the suggestions given by the robot
- I felt being manipulated by the given suggestions

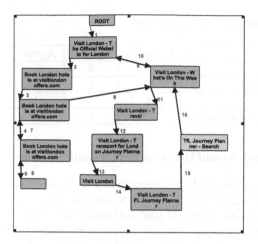

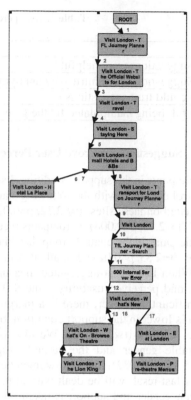

Fig. 3. Two visualizations of user navigation paths with highly different values for compactness and stratum. On the left a path with high compactness (0.80) and low stratum (0.38). On the right, a path with low compactness (0.45) and high stratum (0.86). As expected, the back button usage in the left picture is lower (12%) than in the right picture (16%). Due to the small size of this example, no difference in average connected distance can be observed

The variable *gender* was added as an independent variable in the analysis phase to check whether it interacts with the fixed factor (support). The duration of each session was 55 minutes, of which 40 minutes were spent on carrying out the navigation tasks.

4   Results

In this section we present the results of the study described above. We start with the participants' opinions on link suggestions. Then we describe the impact of link suggestions on user perceptions and task execution time. We continue with the influence of link suggestions on user navigation behavior. We conclude with a brief look at gender differences.

4.1   Link Suggestions Are Positively Received

Table 1 shows the number of participants expressing their agreement or disagreement with each of the four questionnaire items concerning the way suggestions are perceived. It can be observed that most participants (13) do not perceive suggestions as intrusive, annoying or manipulative. A relatively high number of participants (11) trusted link suggestions; but there is no clear evidence that the suggestions are perceived as useful.

Table 1. User perception of link suggestions

	Disagree	Neutral	Agree
Suggestions were helpful	5	4	7
Suggestions were intrusive / annoying	13	1	2
I could trust suggestions	4	1	11
I felt being manipulated by the given suggestions	12	1	3

4.2   Suggestions Improve User Perceptions and Decrease Task Execution Time

Participants in the support condition disagreed to a larger extent than participants in the control condition with the following statements: 'It was difficult to find the information I needed on these sites' (t=-2.72, p=0.01), and 'Labels of links and categories confused me' (t=-2.83, p=0.008). Participants receiving suggestions agreed to a larger extent than participants in the control group that 'the websites can be used without previous experience' (t=2.33, p=0.027). For all other items, differences were not significant.

When looking at aggregated measures of user perceptions – perceived disorientation and perceived usability – the differences between conditions appear to be non-significant. However, there is a marginally significant result: the level of disorientation is lower in the support condition, but this difference is significant only at an alpha level of 0.10 (two tailed). We also observed a significant interaction between the variable gender and the variable support in relation to perceived disorientation (F=5.12, p=0.032); men and women benefit to different extents from link suggestions. This last result will be dealt with at the end of this section. When the interaction between gender and support is taken into consideration, the effect of support becomes significant (F=9.43, p=0.005). Therefore, it is now clear that there is a significant effect of providing suggestions on perceived disorientation, but only for men.

When the two conditions are compared based on the average task execution time, a significant difference is revealed – see table 2. On average, participants in the control condition spent 558 seconds per task. In the support condition, the average time spent per task is 391 seconds (t = 5.99; p<0.01). The spread of task execution times in the support condition is almost twice as low as in the control condition. This difference in variance between the two groups is a natural consequence of our manipulation; the aim of link suggestions is to prevent users from spending time on unsuccessful trials.

Table 2. Task execution times per condition

	N	Mean	Std. Dev.
Control	16	558,22	99,93
Support	16	390,98	50,05

4.3   User Navigation Is Better Structured

The results presented in the previous subsections indicate that participants did believe that the link suggestions could be trusted and that they were considered slightly helpful.

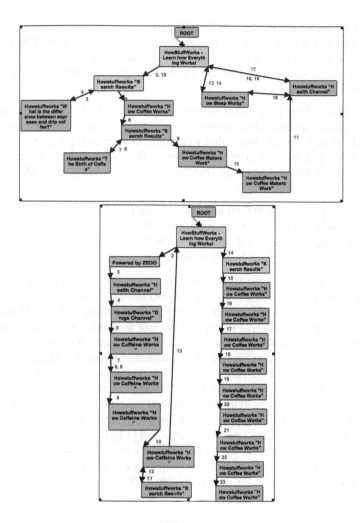

Fig. 4. In the first picture the navigation path of a participant working on a task without link suggestions is displayed. The randomness of page revisits and the amount of visits is clearly visible. In the second picture the navigation path of a participant working on the same task, but with link suggestions, is displayed

We now turn to the question whether the link suggestions actually changed the participants' approach to solving the tasks at hand.

As explained in section 3.4, we extracted a number of measures from the navigation paths that captured patterns of page revisits, page view times and navigation complexity [4][5]. An independent-samples t-test was carried out to find significant differences in means between the two conditions. The result showed that participants in the support condition:

- used the back button less (t=-2.24, p=0.03);
- the navigation paths had a lower compactness (t=-3.02, p=0.005) and a higher stratum (t=3.42, p=0.002), i.e. the paths were more linear;
- the average connected distance in the navigation path was higher (t=2.26, p=0.031)

We also carried out principal component analysis on the twenty-two measures with equamax rotation to find linear combinations of the measures that indicate navigation patterns. Four factors were found that were quite similar to the four factors found in a previous study [5]. We will concentrate here on the fourth factor, of which the means differed significantly between the two conditions (t=-4.01, p=0.000). This factor correlates with (p<0.05):

- high compactness (r=0.896) and low stratum (r=-0.861)
- many visits to the site's home page (r=0.496),
- short average connected distance (r=-0.388)
- frequent use of the back button (r=0.361)

Apparently, the link suggestions caused the participants to navigate in a more linear manner and reduced the number of visits to the site's home pages. There are two possible explanations for this effect: either the participants simply followed the suggested links, without bothering to explore the site structure [8] – a negative effect, or the participants got stuck less often – getting stuck usually results in returning to the site's home page to start another trial [11] – which is a positive effect.

Analysis of the navigation path visualizations led us to the firm belief that the latter is the case – see figure 4. In three of the five tasks the participants that were not provided with link suggestions typically appeared to randomly return to pages visited before and eventually return to the site's home page for another trial – effects that are frequently reported to be caused by disorientation [11][16].

There is no significant interaction between the variables gender and support with respect to any of the navigation measures considered. In other words, navigation patterns are basically the same for men receiving link suggestions as for women receiving link suggestions.

4.4 Winners Win Even More – Gender Differences

In general, when all participants from both conditions were pooled together, no differences between men and women were found in this study, at least with respect to the variables we have considered here - i.e. navigation measures and user perceptions.

However, although in the control condition women and men declare about the same level of disorientation, in the support condition men declare a much lower level of disorientation than women. Women do not seem to benefit from being provided with navigation support, their perceived disorientation levels are about the same in the 2 conditions. In the support condition, men and women also differ with respect to perceived usability. Men receiving navigation support perceive the websites more usable than men not receiving support (t = -2.66, p=0.029). The difference is not significant for women.

Therefore, there seems to be a gender gap indeed, but in this study we were able to find it only with respect to how much the two genders are able to benefit from being provided with navigation support and how they perceived the usability of the systems they used when such support was offered.

5 Discussion and Conclusion

In this study we explored the impact of providing link suggestions on user navigation behavior and on user perceptions. In general, highlighting links that are relevant to the task at hand is a well-received navigation support. Link suggestions make navigation path more linear, more structured and less redundant – a style that is associated with low degrees of perceived disorientation. Users provided with link suggestions were expected to perceive websites as more usable and themselves as less disoriented, but this expectation was confirmed only for men. Women seem to profit from suggestions only objectively – their navigation path becomes more structured, but not subjectively – their perceptions do not improve when receiving link suggestions. A possible explanation for this effect is that men use the link suggestions *in addition to* the available orientation clues.

There are a number of limitations to this study. First, we have not yet evaluated the impact of link suggestions on task performance. So far we only know that link suggestions make users' navigation more structured, reduce task execution time and improve user perceptions, but we don't know whether they actually help users. However, the lack of task performance results is not that important, as the impact of link suggestions on task performance varies per usage context and the way link suggestions are generated. Second, the number of female participants exceeded more than twice the number of male participants (22 female, 10 male) due to the way participants were recruited.

In our study we explicitly attempted to let users carry out real-life tasks. This aim is obviously violated by the fact that the participants were given predefined tasks – or scenarios – in a laboratory setting. Although we have the impression that the impact of the artificial context is quite low, it is an open question what the effect of link suggestions will be in real-life situations in which users work on multiple tasks simultaneously. Nevertheless, before being able to observe the effects 'in the wild' it is necessary to first study them in more controlled settings.

In conclusion, link suggestions relevant to users' tasks have in general a positive impact on users. However, due to individual differences between users, the effects might not be the same for all users. Moreover, these differences might lead to other – possibly counter-intuitive – effects than anticipated. More research and user studies on the effects of personalization techniques are needed to find out what techniques are best suitable for various personalization goals.

Acknowledgements

The second author's work is carried out in the context of the PALS project, which is sponsored by the Dutch innovative Research Program IOP-MMI.

References

1. Ahuja, J.S. and Webster, J. Perceived disorientation: an examination of a new measure to assess web design effectiveness. *Interacting with Computers, 14(1)*, 2001, 15-29.
2. Brusilovsky, P. Adaptive Hypermedia. *User Modeling and User-Adapted Interaction 11*, 2001, 87-110.
3. Chi, E.H., Rosien, A., Supattanasiri, G., Williams, A., Royer, C., Chow, C., Robles, E., Dalal, B., Chen, J. and Cousins, S. The Bloodhound Project: Automatic Discovery of Web Usability Issues using the InfoScent Simulator. *Proc. CHI 2003*, 2003.
4. Herder, E. and Iuvina, J. Discovery of Individual User Navigation Patterns. *Proc. Workshop on Individual Differences in Adaptive Hypermedia, held at AH2004.* 2004, 40-49.
5. Herder, E. and Van Dijk, E.M.A.G. Site Structure and User Navigation: Models, Measures and Methods. *Adaptable and Adaptive Hypermedia Systems. ISBN 1-59140-536-X*, 2004, 19-34.
6. Juvina, I., & van Oostendorp, H. Individual differences and behavioral aspects involved in modeling web navigation. *Proc.User Interfaces for All*, 2004.
7. Kitajima, M., Blackmon, M.H., & Polson, P.G. A Comprehension-based Model of Web Navigation and Its Application to Web Usability Analysis. *People and Computers XIV*, Springer: 2000, 357-373.
8. McEneaney, J.E. Graphic and numerical methods to assess navigation in hypertext. *Intl. Journal of Human-Computer Studies, 55*, 2001, 761-786.
9. Morrison, J. B., Pirolli, P., and Card, S. K A taxonomic analysis of what World Wide Web activities significantly impact people's decisions and actions, *UIR Technical report UIR-R-2000-17*, 2000.
10. Olston, C. & Chi, E.H. ScentTrails: Integrating Browsing and Searching on the Web. *ACM Trans. On Computer-Human Interaction 10 (3)*, 2003, 177-197.
11. Otter, M. and Johnson, H. Lost in hyperspace: metrics and mental models. *Interacting with Computers, 13(1)*, 2000, 1-40.
12. Pirolli, P., & Fu, W.-T. SNIF-ACT: A Model of Information Foraging on the World Wide Web. *Proc. User Modeling 2003*, 2003.
13. Roy, M., & Chi, M.T.H. Gender Differences in Patterns of Searching the Web. *Journal of Educational Computing Research 29*, 2003, 335-348.
14. Shneiderman, B.: Designing Information-Abundant Websites: Issues and Recommendations. *International Journal of Human-Computer Studies 47 (1)*. Academic Press, 1997.
15. Sjolinder, M., Individual differences in spatial cognition and hypermedia navigation, *Towards a Framework for Design and Evaluation of Navigation in Electronic Spaces.* 1998, Swedish Institute of Computer Science.
16. Smith, P.A. Towards a practical measure of hypertext usability. *Interacting with Computers, 8(4)*, 1997, 365-381.
17. Weibelzahl, S., Lippitsch, S. & Weber, G. Advantages, opportunities, and limits of empirical evaluations: Evaluating adaptive systems. *Künstliche Intelligenz 3 (02)*, 2002, 17-20.
18. Weinreich, H., Buchmann, V. & Lamersdorf, W. Scone: Ein Framework zur evaluativen Realisierung von Erweiterungen des Webs. *Proceedings KiVS 2003*, 31-42.

Modeling Emotions from Non-verbal Behaviour in an Affective Tutoring System

Samuel Alexander

Institute of Information and Mathematical Sciences,
Massey University, Private Bag 102 904, NSMC, New Zealand
S.T.Alexander@massey.ac.nz

Abstract. Emotions are an important issue in user modeling. This paper presents a proposal for an Affective Tutoring System (ATS) that can recognise emotions through automated facial expression and gesture analysis, and show emotions through an animated agent. The domain of the system will be addition for 8 to 9 year olds. An observational study of human tutors has been conducted as a basis for developing the tutoring strategies of the ATS.

1 Introduction

An increasingly prominent issue in the field of user modeling is the role that the affective state of users should play in the adaptation of systems. Many researchers now feel strongly that human-computer interactions could be significantly enhanced if computers could adapt according to the emotions of users (e.g. [10], [8]).

This paper proposes an interface that will enable a computer to model the affective state of users according to their non-verbal behaviour. In particular, an Affective Tutoring System (ATS) for addition is being developed based on an existing New Zealand Numeracy Project exercise.

2 Related Work

This research falls within the field of affective computing [10], which broadly defined concerns artificial systems that are able to recognise or exhibit emotions.

Modeling the affective state of a user is fundamentally concerned with the first of these traits – the ability to *recognise* the emotions of a user. However, it is not an easy task to find examples of systems that adapt to recognised affect or non-verbal behaviour. Some of the more recent work in affective modeling is by Lisetti et al. [3], who propose a multimodal interface for tele-health that will provide health-care providers with affective state information about their patients. As far as tutoring systems are concerned, Kort et al. [2] propose to build a Learning Companion that will initially use eye-gaze as an input of affective state. Litman and Forbes [4] propose an Intelligent Tutoring System that adapts to the emotions revealed by the acoustic and prosodic elements of student speech.

L. Ardissono, P. Brna, and A. Mitrovic (Eds.): UM 2005, LNAI 3538, pp. 493–495, 2005.
© Springer-Verlag Berlin Heidelberg 2005

Many groups (e.g. [6]) are certainly working towards systems that can model the affective state of users, but most are still at the stage of recognising affect with an acceptable accuracy. The author of this paper is currently unaware of any ATSs that have actually been implemented.

3 Proposal: An ATS for Addition

The overall aim of this research is to develop an ATS that can recognise and adapt to the affective state of students. The content of this particular system will help 8 to 9 year old students understand the concept of part-whole addition [7]. The tutoring system will feature an animated pedagogical agent that is able to both recognise and display emotions in the manner of a real human tutor. Animated agents carry a persona effect that has been shown to increase learner motivation, although its overall benefits remain unclear [5].

The affective state of the student will be modeled based upon input from automated facial expression and gesture analysis systems that are currently being developed in-house [1]. These systems identify expressions in images taken in real time by a web-cam mounted on the student's monitor. This means that the ATS will be able to "see" the expressions of students, and thus to adapt accordingly through the animated agent.

Armed with a student model that encompasses both the affective and cognitive state of the student, the ATS will base its adaptations on the tutoring strategies of human tutors. The system's animated agent will adapt in two ways:

- by presenting the most appropriate material, and
- by empathising with the student, and providing verbal and non-verbal encouragement.

Therefore the agent will be potentially beneficial in at least two ways:

- if the tutoring material most appropriate to the student's affective state is presented, then this should facilitate learning, and
- if the agent is believably sincere in its empathy, then this could amplify the motivational benefits of the persona effect.

4 An Observational Study of Human Tutors

A model of affective state would be of little use to an ATS without accompanying strategies to use it. Therefore, to fill a gap in the psychology and education literature, it was decided to conduct an observational study of how human tutors adapt to affect.

Three professional tutors were videoed while tutoring participants one-on-one at a local primary school in Auckland. There were nine participants in all; each participant was an 8 or 9 year old student at the local school. Each participant was tutored for about 20 minutes, which generated about 3 hours worth of videos.

The domain that was chosen for the observational study was the concept of part-whole addition [7]. The study used an existing exercise developed by the New Zealand Numeracy Project.

To analyse the videos, a coding scheme was developed expanding on previous work by Person and Graesser [9]. Preliminary results from the coding include a matrix of the frequency of particular tutor responses to student behaviours and emotions. This information can be used to calculate the probability of human tutor responses to particular student behaviours and expressions; these probabilities can be used as a basis for tutoring strategies in the ATS.

5 Future Work

Future work will commence with a more thorough analysis of the tutoring strategies in the human tutoring videos, especially focussing on how a tutor's response may be influenced by the indefinitely preceding dialogue between tutor and student.

Then the ATS itself will be developed; the tutoring system will be based on exactly the same New Zealand Numeracy Project exercise that was used in the observational study of human tutors. The tutoring system will feature an animated pedagogical agent that is able to both recognise and show emotion like a human tutor. The system will maintain a model of the affective state of the user through the use of automated facial expression and gesture analysis systems.

References

1. Fan, C., Johnson, M., Messom, C., & Sarrafzadeh, A.: Machine Vision for an Intelligent Tutor. Proceedings of the International Conference on Computational Intelligence, Robotics and Autonomous Systems, Singapore (2003)
2. Kort, B., Reilly, R., Picard, R.W.: An Affective Model of Interplay Between Emotions and Learning: Reengineering Educational Pedagogy - Building a Learning Companion. IEEE International Conference on Advanced Learning Technologies (2001) 43-48
3. Lisetti, C.L., Nasoz, F., Lerouge, C., Ozyer, O., Alvarez, K.: Developing Multimodal Intelligent Affective Interfaces for Tele-Home Health Care. International Journal of Human-Computer Studies (2003) 59 (1-2) 245-255.
4. Litman, D., Forbes, K.: Recognizing Emotions from Student Speech in Tutoring Dialogues. In Proceedings of the IEEE Automatic Speech Recognition and Understanding Workshop (ASRU), St. Thomas, Virgin Islands (2003)
5. van Mulken, S., André, E., & Muller, J.: The persona effect: How substantial is it? Proceedings of Human Computer Interaction, Berlin, Germany (1998)
6. Nasoz, F., Lisetti, C.L., Alvarez, K., Finelstein, N.: Emotional Recognition from Physiological Signals for User Modeling of Affect. In Proceedings of the 3rd Workshop on Affective and Attitude User Modeling, Pittsburgh (2003)
7. New Zealand Ministry of Education: Book 1, The Number Framework. Numeracy Professional Development Projects. Ministry of Education, Wellington (2003)
8. Pantic, M., Rothkrantz, L.J.M.: Toward an affect-sensitive multimodal human-computer interaction. Proceedings of the IEEE (2003) 91(9) 1370-1390
9. Person, N.K., Graesser, A.C., & The Tutoring Research Group: Fourteen facts about human tutoring: Food for thought for ITS developers. AI-ED 2003 Workshop Proceedings on Tutorial Dialogue Systems: With a View Toward the Classroom, Sydney, Australia (2003)
10. Picard, R.W.: Affective Computing. Cambridge, Mass., MIT Press (1997)

Ubiquitous User Modeling in Recommender Systems

Shlomo Berkovsky

Computer Science Department, University of Haifa, Israel
slavax@cs.haifa.ac.il

Abstract. The existing personalization services usually base on proprietary and partial user models. This work attempts at evolving inference-based mediation mechanism that will facilitate integrating user models coming from different sources, such as repositories of other service providers and user's personal devices. This will allow obtaining more information about the users and providing more accurate personalization. The efficiency of the above approach will be demonstrated using the techniques from Recommender Systems domain.

1 Better Personalization with Ubiquitous User Modeling

Nowadays, the quantity of the available information rapidly grows and exceeds our limited processing capabilities. This is regarded in the literature as the 'Information Overload' problem [5]. As a result, there is a pressing need for intelligent systems that provide services according to user's personal needs and interests, and deliver tailored information in a way that will be most appropriate and valuable to the user. The state-of-the-art personalization techniques basically overcome the Information Overload by filtering the irrelevant information reaching the user.

An essential input for every personalization technique is the model of the user [1] that is either collected by the service providers (through accumulating the information on user's preferences and interests), or imported into the system from user's personal devices (e.g., PDA, mobile phone, or personal media). For example, user's reading preferences might be stored by *Amazon* and *BarnesAndNoble* websites, and also by user's reading device. Thus, in the rest of this paper the term 'data source' refers to the repositories of service providers, and of users' devices.

Typically, the models stored by the repositories of service providers are proprietary and partial, as they fit a specific application and are limited to its domain. Since the level of personalization a system presents depends on the detailing of the input user models, different systems would improve the provided services by sharing the models stored in their repositories. However, due to the commercial competition service providers neither cooperate, nor share the data stored in their repositories.

A natural way of resolving this issue might be replicating the interactions between users and service providers also at the user side and directly accessing the models stored by users' personal devices. Hence, part of the user model and other personalization information will be obtained from the collaborating users, and combined locally by the service provider that needs it. In addition to resolving the problem of non-cooperative service providers, direct interaction between different data sources in user modeling will partially resolve privacy concerns [4].

L. Ardissono, P. Brna, and A. Mitrovic (Eds.): UM 2005, LNAI 3538, pp. 496–498, 2005.
© Springer-Verlag Berlin Heidelberg 2005

In this work we aim at developing an abstract mediation mechanism that will allow upgrading the existing personalization systems by integrating user models from different data sources (both users and service providers). This will facilitate obtaining more information about users and providing more accurate personalization services.

2 Integration of User Models

The principal architecture of the evolving ubiquitous user modeling platform is represented in Figure *1*. The core of the platform is the mediating mechanism that facilitates user modeling data sharing by translation and integration of user models. As each service provider stores partial user model according to its own format and representation, mediating mechanism is responsible for the following tasks:

1. Mapping from specific services to a generic representation and vice versa.
2. Providing standard language/interface for user modeling data exchange.
3. Maintaining user modeling semantic knowledge facilitating ad-hoc mapping.

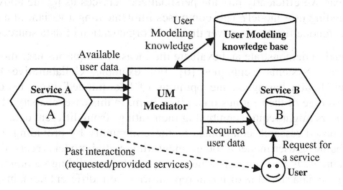

Fig. 1. Principal architecture of ubiquitous user modeling platform

We propose to cluster the data sources storing user models from similar domains in order to improve the integration task and minimize the communication overhead tied with it. Note that the structure of the clusters is highly dynamic, as they comprise user's devices (providing partial user models), whose availability is unstable.

When different data sources share a model related to the same domain (e.g., models from *Amazon* and *BarnesAndNoble*), the integration of partial user models is performed using the mediator's domain knowledge. It should support identifying semantic relations between different concepts in the domain. For example, it should integrate partial models from systems using different ontologies to model user's preferences in the same domain. Thus, the mediator should be capable of resolving conflicts and ambiguities, and facilitate obtaining accurate and expressive user model.

Another issue that should be tackled by the mediator is integrating partial models from different domains. For example, consider the repositories of books and DVDs stores. Although the domains are not identical, user's interest in a particular genre of books can be inferred from the DVDs model. This requires identifying the relationships between the domains, e.g., when building a model for books domain, data from DVDs model is of some value, while data from cars domain probably gives no benefit. Knowing relationships between the domains, we plan to develop inferring mechanism from domain-specific representations to a generic user model and vice versa.

3 Major Issues and Demonstration in Recommender Systems

Evolving ubiquitous user modeling mechanism over a dynamic set of heterogeneous data sources raises three major research questions:

1. How can we evolve an organization of user modeling services and data sources using on semantic relationships and similarities between them? This requires expanding the ideas proposed in [2], inferring relationships between data sources and different domains, and defining explicit similarity metrics.
2. How can we build an accurate user model over the above distributed organization? This comprises developing a stable (to dynamic environments) protocol for combining partial user models obtained from different data sources.
3. How can we efficiently provide personalized services using the above technique for building user model? This comprises implementing a variant of a personalization technique functioning over the above organization of data sources.

We intend to demonstrate and evaluate the ideas of ubiquitous user modeling using Recommender Systems techniques [6]. For example, Collaborative Filtering [3] builds a prediction basing on the opinions of 'like-minded' users by computing a weighted average of their ratings on a given item. In this case, sparsity of information about the users might require combining their ratings from different data sources.

The proposed research contributes to the community by providing a novel technique for building user model through integrating partial models received from multiple data sources. It also suggests a novel approach for building recommendations by integrating the data stored in different repositories from different domains.

References

1. J.Fink, A.Kobsa, *"A Review and Analysis of Commercial User Modeling Servers for Personalization on the World Wide Web"*, in UMUAI, vol. 10 (2-3), pp.209-249, 2000.
2. D.Heckmann, *"Ubiquitous User Modeling for Situated Interaction"*, in proceedings of the 8th International Conference on User Modeling, Germany, 2001.
3. J.L.Herlocker, J.A.Konstan, A.Borchers, J.Riedl, *"An Algorithmic Framework for Performing Collaborative Filtering"*, in proceedings of the 22nd ACM SIGIR Conference, CA, 1999.
4. A.Kobsa, *"Tailoring Privacy to Users' Needs"*, in proceedings of the 8th International Conference on User Modeling, Germany, 2001.
5. P.Maes, *"Agents that Reduce Work and Information Overload"*, in Communication of the ACM, vol. 37 (7), pp. 31-40, 1994.
6. P.Resnick, H.R.Varian, *"Recommender Systems"*, in Communications of the ACM, vol. 40(3), pp. 56-58, 1997.

User Modelling to Support User Customization

Andrea Bunt

Department of Computer Science, University of British Columbia, 2366 Mail Mall,
Vancouver, B.C., V6T 1Z4, Canada
bunt@cs.ubc.ca

Abstract. The following describes ongoing doctoral research on creating a mixed-initiative framework to help users customize complex interfaces. The framework relies on a rich user model to provide customization suggestions with the goal of improving user performance while maintaining a high level of user satisfaction.

1 Research Problem

As the functionality offered by common software packages continues to grow, it is becoming desirable to provide users with a way to cope with the increasing complexity of their graphical user interfaces. Some researchers suggest placing users in control of managing this complexity by making the interface *adaptable*, i.e., giving users the power to customize the application to suit their needs. Others advocate making the interface *adaptive*, i.e., able to model the individual user's interests, preferences and usage characteristics to allow the interface to tailor itself (e.g., see [9] for a discussion). Both approaches have benefits and drawbacks. With adaptive interfaces, users do not have to invest the effort to customize, but the interfaces can suffer from some users feeling a lack of control over the process, a lack of transparency, and a lack of predictability [3]. As for the adaptable approach, users are in full control, but not all users are willing to customize (e.g., [6]) and some are not able to do so effectively (e.g., [1]).

The goal of this Ph.D. work is to investigate a *mixed-initiative* [4] solution that lies between the adaptive and adaptable extremes. Users will be provided with a customization facility that gives them control over the interface, but system-initiated adaptive support will be employed to help them take full advantage of this facility. Such adaptive support will be guided by a user model that can gauge when to provide adaptive suggestions and how to tailor the support to the user's work patterns, ability, and preferences.

2 User Modelling Contributions

While mixed-initiative paradigms have been investigated in other forms of human-computer interaction (e.g., [4]), there have been few attempts to apply the approach to the adaptation of interface elements. Exceptions ([2] and [8]) differ from this work in two main ways: 1) they focus on a different customization context (the creation of macros and short-cuts) and 2) their user models

L. Ardissono, P. Brna, and A. Mitrovic (Eds.): UM 2005, LNAI 3538, pp. 499–501, 2005.

consist primarily of frequency counts. This work explores the role of a more comprehensive user model that includes two main sources of information. The first pertains to the performance implications of customization decisions, assessed using a novel application of a simplified form of cognitive modelling known as GOMS analysis. The model will also consider relevant user preferences in order to maintain a high degree of user satisfaction. Other related work (e.g., [5]) focuses on increasing users' understanding of available functionality, a different (but complementary) approach to helping users cope with interface complexity.

Our work aims to contribute the field of user modelling by 1) identifying the factors that a user model in such environments should incorporate, 2) creating a user-modelling framework that performs the assessment, and 3) demonstrating how to apply such a user model to generate adaptive support that helps users manage interface complexity.

3   Current Progress and Work to Be Completed

The mixed-initiative framework (see fig. 1) is being built on top of McGrenere et al.'s customization facility for Microsoft Word [7], which allows users to maintain two versions of the Word interface: the Full Interface and a Personal Interface (a feature-reduced interface with only those features that the user has chosen to add). At the start of this Ph.D. work, we conducted a proof-of-concept simulation experiment using this two-interface model and information about actual user customization strategies to demonstrate that adaptive support does have the potential to help users customize more effectively [1].

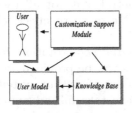

Fig. 1. Architecture

The Customization Support Module (CSM) uses information from the User Model to decide when and how to provide the user with customization suggestions, consisting of features that the user should add or remove from his/her Personal Interface. Using information found in the User Model, the CSM weighs the costs and benefits of set of customizations suggestions. The User Model assesses the potential performance implications of having a Personal Interface customized according to these suggestions, in addition to how they align with user-specific preferences. For example, some users prefer to maintain a feature-reduced interface [7], possibly even at the cost of performance if the potential performance penalty is minimal (a hypothesis to be investigated as part of this work).

The work completed to date has concentrated on the framework necessary for the CSM to compute the optimal Personal Interface given performance implications alone. Currently, the CSM performs a greedy search through the space of potential Personal Interfaces. At each step in the algorithm, the CSM asks the User Model to compute a performance estimate for a potential Personal Interface. This involves computing the time it would take for the user to invoke all features according to their expected usages (described below) given that potential Personal Interface. This computation is based on GOMS analysis (whose methods reside in the Knowledge Base) and requires the User Model to have information on the following factors:

- **Expected Usage Frequencies:** the number of times the user is expected to invoke each feature.
- **Expertise:** the user's familiarity with each feature. As discussed in [1], there is reason to believe that the lower the expertise, the more likely the user is to be affected by interface complexity.
- **Switching Overhead:** the amount of time it would take the user to switch to the Full Interface to invoke a feature not present in the Personal Interface.

Plans for immediate future work involve ways for the User Model to assess the above factors. We would like to assess expertise based on observed usage frequencies, initial self-reports, and usage patterns. Unfortunately, MSWord exposes very few user interface actions, thus the model is dealing with a very low bandwidth environment. To estimate expected usages, we plan to investigate plan recognition, machine learning, and directly asking the user. Sensitivity analysis has revealed that the model is fairly sensitive to the Switching Overhead, thus we plan to conduct some user testing to inform the model's assessment of this factor. Longer-term goals include eliciting and incorporating user preferences, extending the CSM to make decisions based on both performance and preferences, and developing effective and low-cost ways to present users with customization suggestions both when they initiate customization and while they perform their primary task. Finally, we will evaluate our solution, ideally against purely adaptive and adaptable alternatives.

References

1. Bunt, A., Conati, C., McGrenere, J.: What role can adaptive support play in an adaptable system? In *Proc. of IUI'04*, pages 117–124, 2004.
2. Debevc, M., Meyer, B., Donlagic, D., Svecko, R.: Design and evaluation of an adaptive icon toolbar. *User Modeling and User-Adapted Interaction*, 6(1):1–21, 1996.
3. Hook, K.: Steps to take before intelligent user interfaces become real. *Interacting with Computers*, 12:409–426, 2000.
4. Horvitz, E.: Principles of mixed-initiative user interfaces. In *Proc. of CHI'99*, pages 159–166, 1999.
5. Linton, F., Schaefer, H.: Recommender systems for learning: Building user and expert model through long-term observation of application use. *User Modeling and User-Adapted Interaction*, 10:181–207, 2000.
6. Mackay, W.E.: Triggers and barriers to customizing software. In *Proc. of CHI'91*, pages 153–160, 1991.
7. McGrenere, J., Baecker, R.M., Booth, K.S.: An evaluation of a multiple interface design solution for bloated software. In *Proc. of CHI 2002*, pages 163–170, 2002.
8. Oppermann, R.: Adaptively supported adaptability. *International Journal of Human-Computer Studies*, 40:455–472, 1994.
9. Shneiderman, B., Maes, P.: Direct manipulation vs. interface agents. *interactions*, 4(6):42–61, 1997.

ETAPP: A Collaboration Framework That Copes with Uncertainty Regarding Team Members*

Christian Guttmann

School of Computer Science and Software Engineering,
Monash University, Clayton, VICTORIA 3800, Australia
xtg@csse.monash.edu.au

1 Introduction

The organized nature of human collaboration is often used as a metaphor for computational theories of collaboration. Knowledge of collaborators' capabilities and reliability of decision making processes are important factors in collaborative activities. In this thesis, we investigate these factors in the context of an important collaborative activity – the assignment of team members to tasks.

Many collaboration theories assume that agents have correct and complete knowledge of the capabilities of team members as well as team members that make decisions in a reliable manner. Making decisions in a reliable manner means that decisions are made to optimize utility according to the criteria of a task (rather than an agent's own criteria). In the assignment of agents to activities, team performance is optimized by assigning optimal agents (whose capabilities are known) to activities.

Consider a simplified scenario where a doctor refers patients to specialists. Assume the doctor knows the specialists' capabilities and makes decisions to optimize the treatment of patients. Based on these assumptions, the doctor would refer patients to optimal specialists in order to obtain optimal treatment. However, we argue that such referrals are not optimal when a doctor is not fully aware of the capabilities of specialists and/or makes decisions according to the doctor's own criteria. Consider some examples in support of our argument.

- **Limited reasoning capabilities** of decision makers. A doctor can not take into account all specialists when making a referral, because a doctor can only remember and assess the capabilities of a limited number of specialists.
- **Variable performance** of specialists. A doctor can make a wrong recommendation based on the overall performance of a specialist, because a specific performance is due to factors that are not known to the doctor (e.g., a specialist has a bad day).
- **Decision making** in an unreliable manner. A doctor can make bad referrals, because the doctor is lazy, meaning that the doctor does not deliberate about which specialist could be optimal, thus selecting an arbitrary specialist.

---

* This research was supported in part by Linkage Grant LP0347470 from the Australian Research Council, and by an endowment from Hewlett Packard. I would like to thank my supervisor Ingrid Zukerman, and also Michael Georgeff for his advise on this paper.

L. Ardissono, P. Brna, and A. Mitrovic (Eds.): UM 2005, LNAI 3538, pp. 502–505, 2005.

The assumptions of correct and complete knowledge of collaborators' capabilities and reliability of decision makers simplify the problem of agent collaboration. Relaxing these assumptions raises several issues.

- How should agent performance be modelled? How do the limited reasoning capabilities of agents influence model accuracy? How do model accuracy and variable agent performance influence collaborative activities?
- What constitutes decisions that are made in an unreliable manner? How does the unreliability of decision makers influence collaborative activities?
- A team may decide to make group decisions to cope with agents that have incomplete knowledge and agents that make decisions in an unreliable manner. Which kind of group decision procedures improve the quality of collaborative activities? What are the transaction costs involved to arrive at a group decision? What are the tradeoffs between transaction costs and team performance? How many reliable team members are required for robust performance?

These questions are addressed as part of the research in this thesis. Our *research goal* is to analyze collaborative multi-agent behaviour, determine the factors that influence team performance, make predictions of the outcome of team performance, and offer guidelines for efficient collaboration. To this end, we have designed a framework according to a view of agent collaboration which focuses on modelling agents and coping with decisions that are made in an unreliable manner.

Apart from medical referral scenarios, our approach can be applied to a number of examples. For example, making allocations in peer-to-peer networks, where a group of peers is selected based on their bandwidth to establish a transmission routing between two remote peers. Single peers have incomplete knowledge of the current bandwidth of peers in the network, because peers may have insufficient capabilities to monitor every peer, and peers may have insufficient memory to store information of all peers in a network. Additionally, single peers can make decisions that do not optimize the overall performance of a network, instead they make decisions that saves their own bandwidth.

2   Related Research

The development of our framework involved research on a number of topics – agent modelling/tracking/monitoring, decision making, distributed control, and social choice. Our research project is different to other research projects in terms of the research goal, which defines assumptions and agent features considered by an approach. For example, according to Suryadi and Gmytrasiewicz [4] agents do not communicate, thus relying on observations to model other agents. This framework contrasts with research where agent models are derived only from communication [1, 5]. In each project, agents use models of different agent features. For example, expertise is used in student support environments [5], and availability is important in agenda scheduling [1].

3   ETAPP: A Framework of Agent Collaboration

We define a framework called *ETAPP (Environment-Task-Agents-Policy-Protocol)*, that offers an approach to cope with large numbers of collaborating individuals [2, 3, 6]. This framework expresses the collaboration of a team of agents in terms of five operating parameters: Environment, Task, Agents, Policy and Protocol. Briefly, the *Task* given to a group is to be performed in the *Environment*, and the *Policy* and *Protocol* are procedures agreed upon by all the agents in a group, but performed autonomously (this is similar to abiding by certain rules in order to belong to a society). Central to the ETAPP framework is the idea that the team members do not know the real capabilities of the agents in a team. Hence, individual agents employ models of collaborators' capabilities in order to estimate the value of contributions of team members to a task. We also examine agents that make decisions in an unreliable manner, meaning that agents can make decisions that do not optimize utility according to the criteria of a task (but according to an agent's own criteria). The *Agents* component describes a group of agents where each agent stores these models and uses mechanisms to reason about them.

4   Current Contributions and Thesis Schedule

Our specific contributions to research in agent collaboration include the following.

- **A collaboration framework** which offers novel contributions.
  - A probabilistic representation of agent performance in terms of the evaluation criteria of a task (such as time or quality).
  - Cost functions that measure the extent to which communication, computation and memory is used in each collaboration.
  - Voting policies that aggregate decisions of individual agents.
- **Insights, predictions and guidelines**. Based on empirical studies, we found that
  - Several reasoning limitations influence the performance of a team and the transaction costs of a collaboration, e.g., memory and the ability to learn are the most influential factors of team performance and transaction costs [2].
  - Appropriate policies should be used to cope with selfish, conservative, lazy, and corrupt agents, e.g., if agents make decisions in a reliable manner, group decision policies should be simple to improve the performance of the team [3].
  - Variability of individual agent performance influences team performance, e.g., the more variable the agent performance the worse the team performance [6].

We propose the following extensions to our research.

- **Investigate models of team performance** as an extension of our current implementation, where we consider models of only one agent.
- **Decentralize the evaluation of performance**. This means that each agent uses a different function to evaluate observed performance, as opposed to our current approach where one evaluation function is used by all agents.
- **Compare central with distributed decision making procedures**, specifically decisions made by a leader, or decisions derived from voting and auctioning.
- **Provide guidelines** on balancing transaction costs against task performance.

References

1. Leonardo Garrido, Katia Sycara, and Ramon Brena. Quantifying the Utility of Building Agents Models: An Experimental Study. In *Proceedings of the Agents-00/ECML-00 Workshop on Learning Agents*, Barcelona, Spain, 2000.
2. Christian Guttmann and Ingrid Zukerman. Towards Models of Incomplete and Uncertain Knowledge of Collaborators' Internal Resources. In Jörg Denzinger, Gabriela Lindemann, Ingo J. Timm, and Rainer Unland, editors, *Second German Conference on MultiAgent system TEchnologieS (MATES) 2004*, LNAI 3187, 58–72, Erfurt, Germany, 2004. Springer.
3. Christian Guttmann and Ingrid Zukerman. Voting policies that Cope with Unreliable Agents. In *Proceedings of the Fourth International Joint Conference on Autonomous Agents and Multiagent Systems*, Utrecht, The Netherlands, 2005.
4. Dicky Suryadi and Piotr J. Gmytrasiewicz. Learning Models of Other Agents Using Influence Diagrams. In *Proceedings of the Seventh International Conference on User Modeling*, 223–232, Banff, Canada, 1999.
5. Julita Vassileva, Gordon McCalla, and Jim Greer. Multi-Agent Multi-User Modeling in I-Help. *User Modeling and User-Adapted Interaction*, 13(1-2):179–210, 2003.
6. Ingrid Zukerman and Christian Guttmann. Modeling Agents that Exhibit Variable Performance in a Collaborative Setting. In *Proceedings of the Tenth International Conference on User Modeling*, Edinburgh, Scotland, 2005.

Towards Explicit Physical Object Referencing

Michael Kruppa[1,2,3]

[1] International Post-Graduate College Language Technologies and Cognitive
Systems, Saarland University, Saarbrücken, Germany
[2] DFKI GmbH, Saarbrücken, Germany
[3] University of Sydney, Australia
mkruppa@cs.uni-sb.de

Abstract. The main goal of the work presented in this paper is to
determine an optimal strategy for virtual characters performing judicious
combinations of speech, gesture and motion in order to disambiguate
references to objects in the physical environment. The work is located in
the research area of mobile computing and deals with the combination
of mobile and stationary devices.

Introduction – The Migrating Character Concept

In the research areas of mobile-, ubiquitous- and pervasive computing, computer
technology becomes merged with the physical world. The main benefit of this development is, among the fact that the technology becomes accessible almost everywhere, the possibility to build applications which incorporate the physical environment around the user and hence offer location sensitive services. The basis
for these applications is formed by a combination of sensory data and knowledge
about the physical world. In addition, efficient methods allowing for explicit references to physical objects will be a key element within reasonable solutions for
mobile applications. Since virtual characters have proven to successfully disambiguate references in virtual 3D worlds (see [1] and [2]), these characters seem
to promise similar results when performing references in the physical world. The
Migrating Character Concept described in this paper allows virtual characters to
dislocate themselves in physical space. Furthermore, the Migrating Characters are
capable of performing many different types of references, depending on the available technology. A character may for example exist on a mobile device, referring
to physical objects by performing gestures on photos or abstract object representations on the screen, or it may also appear on a wall (using a projector) or on a
stationary screen right next to the referred object. Based on a user model representing both the user's actual context and preferences and an ontology representing the world knowledge, a set of rules determine an optimal referencing solution
in an arbitrary situation. The Migrating Character Concept is based on three major elements: mobility, reactivity and adaptivity.

Character Locomotion – Mobility: Character locomotion is the key element
of the Migrating Character concept. It allows virtual characters to move throughout the physical world and also to assist users by means of deictic gestures.
I classify character locomotion into two categories: active and passive. The active

L. Ardissono, P. Brna, and A. Mitrovic (Eds.): UM 2005, LNAI 3538, pp. 506–508, 2005.

locomotion category subsumes all methods allowing the character to dislocate itself, regardless of the users movements (e.g. a virtual character "jumping" from one device to another or dislocating itself by means of a steerable projector), whereas passive character locomotion depends on the user's movements (e.g. a character on a mobile device, carried by the user).

Physical Context – Reactivity: The first step towards performing a reference to a physical object is sensing the object's presence close to the user. Secondly, information about the object itself is necessary (e.g. *What is it?; How big is it?; Which objects are next to it?*). Depending on the position, size, proximity and similarity of physical objects, different strategies need to be chosen in order to disambiguate references. The objects could be equipped with active senders, emitting all the necessary information in a narrow range. However, it is also possible to determine the users position and orientation, and store the information on physical objects in a database. Organizing this "world knowledge" in an hierarchical structure like an ontology will allow a system to determine relative position information (e.g. *User is in room x; User is close to object y; User can see object z*).

Personal Context – Adaptivity: When deciding on a specific reference strategy, the interaction history between the character and the user is of utmost importance. Keeping track of former references will allow the character to refer to previously mentioned objects more easily (e.g. *The red box we just saw on the other side of the room*). In addition, personal preferences may also influence the reference strategy decision. For example, a user might prefer to reduce the number of references, where the character utilizes a public audio system, to a minimum in public situations.

Finding a Reference Strategy: To determine an appropriate reference strategy, a number of steps need to be taken, depicted in the following graph:

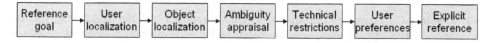

After a reference goal has been identified, the reference planning mechanism starts by locating the user and the physical object to be referenced. Based on a "world knowledge ontology", the next step is to identify possible ambiguities caused by similar objects close to each other. Based on these possible reference ambiguities, a list of reference methods is calculated, ordered by the presumed usefulness in resolving these ambiguities (e.g. sometimes a spoken reference will be sufficient, sometimes a combination of character movement, gesture and speech may be necessary and in some cases it may even be inevitable to ask the user to move to another physical location prior to performing a reference to a specific object). In a next step, only those reference methods remain on the list, which are technically feasible at the location where the reference occurs. Since the main goal is to disambiguate references, the user preferences may only be applied if several reference strategies have been identified, guaranteeing for an explicit physical object reference.

Actual State of Affairs and Open Questions

Within the scope of two prototype implementations, several different methods for physical object references by means of virtual characters have been realized and evaluated. While in the first project (PEACH, see [3]) a virtual character is used on a Personal Digital Assistant (PDA) to guide users through the physical space of a museum, the second project (VRI, see [4]) implemented a virtual character capable of moving along arbitrary walls by utilizing a steerable projector and a spatial audio system. In the PEACH prototype, the character performs references to physical objects by a combination of gestures and speech related to photos/videos of physical objects shown on the screen of the PDA. In addition, the character may "jump" from the PDA onto large, stationary screens in order to refer to virtual objects shown on those screens. In contrast, the character in the VRI project is capable of positioning itself right next to a physical object and is hence capable of giving very precise references.

The technology for physical character mobility is well established, however a rule based system capable of determining an optimal reference strategy, still needs to be realized. These rules will be based on the work described in [1] and [2], but will add the technical restriction dimension and personal user preferences. In order for these rules to work, I will adopt the location technology used in PEACH and VRI and I will add a "world knowledge base" using UbisWorld (an online Ontology for ubiquitous computing applications[1], see [5]). Based on this ontology and a user model (including the user's physical location- and orientation, the history of previous references and the modality preferences of the user), it will be possible to let a virtual character effectively perform references to physical objects in arbitrary situations.

References

1. Lester, J.C., Towns, S.G., Callaway, C.B., Voerman, J.L., FitzGerald, P.J.: Deictic and emotive communication in animated pedagogical agents. Embodied conversational agents (2000) 123–154
2. Towns, S.G., Vorman, J.L., Callaway, C.B., Lester, J.C.: Coherent gestures, locomotion, and speech in life-like pedagogical agents. In: Proceedings of the international conference on Intelligent User Interfaces (IUI). (1997)
3. Kruppa, M., Krüger, A., Rocchi, C., Stock, O., Zancanaro, M.: Seamless personalized TV-like presentations on mobile and stationary devices in a museum. In: Proceedings of the International Conference on Hypermedia and Interactivity in Museums (ICHIM). (2003)
4. Kruppa, M., Spassova, M., Schmitz, M.: The Virtual Room Inhabitant. In: Proceedings of the 2nd IUI workshop on Multi-User and Ubiquitous User Interfaces (MU3I). (2005)
5. Heckmann, D.: Integrating privacy aspects into ubiquitous computing: A basic user interface for personalization. In: AIMS03 Workshop, in conjunction with UbiComp2003. (2003)

---

[1] http://www.u2m.org

Adaptive User Interfaces for In-vehicle Devices

Talia Lavie

Department of Industrial Engineering and Management,
Ben Gurion University of the Negev Beer Sheva 84105, Israel
tlavie@bgu.ac.il

Abstract. Adaptive user interfaces (AUIs) have become the focus of various scientific disciplines and are studied extensively over the last decade. The studies exploring the field investigate a broad range of adaptation methods in different types of applications. Although some progress was made in the study of AUIs, many issues need additional exploring. The objective of this research is to extend previous research on AUI and to examine different levels of adaptivity in AUIs, rather than viewing adaptivity as an all or none process. This research will attempt to identify the levels of adaptivity appropriate for different users, tasks and situations when using AUIs. In particular, the research will assess the effects of different levels of adaptivity on the performance of routine and infrequent tasks. A series of experiments will be conducted to develop and evaluate a model specifying the factors that influence the user's interaction with the AUI. Four different levels of adaptivity will be used, ranging from totally manual to fully adaptive with two intermediate levels. The AUI will be examined in the context of in-vehicle systems. The results of the research are expected to facilitate a better understanding of AUIs, clarify uncertainties and specify the situations in which adaptivity should be beneficial. Finally, the results of this research will assist in-vehicle system designers, by providing guiding principles for designing more usable AUIs.

1 Introduction

The literature on AUI is very diverse, focusing on narrow domains in a wide range of applications, investigating a broad range of adaptation methods, classes and interfaces. Because of this diversity, there is no consensus regarding the characteristics, behavior and essential components of adaptive systems [9]. Also, few empirical studies examined the situations in which adaptation is valuable [3]. Most of the few empirical studies of adaptivity compared systems with adaptivity to the same systems without it. In a number of cases AUIs were examined as comprising of different levels of adaptivity. [4], for example, identified four stages (initiative, proposal, decision and execution) in which either the user or the system control or perform the stage. A term that is often used in relation to this allocation of control is mixed-initiative interaction. This term has been used in various ways. [1], for example, refers to a flexible interaction strategy, where the user or the system contributes to the task to best suite the situation. At any time, the system or the user may control the interaction, while the other works to assist as necessary or vice versa. Although research in this field is in its infancy, some researchers have proposed

L. Ardissono, P. Brna, and A. Mitrovic (Eds.): UM 2005, LNAI 3538, pp. 509–511, 2005.

taxonomies (i.e. [1]) and some systems have been developed according to this type of interaction (i.e. [2] AIDE; [5] Lookout). In many cases the levels of adaptivity refer to different levels of control the user has over the system. In the non-adaptive case the user makes all the changes in the system to suit his or her needs. [8] refers to these systems as adaptable systems. On the other hand, in the fully adaptive case, the system adjusts automatically according to a user model it generated (adaptivity). According to [7], adaptability and adaptivity may coexist in the same system. Intermediate forms of adaptivity include, for example, user-controlled adaptivity in which the user makes the selection and performs the selected adaptation, and user-initiated adaptivity in which the user initiates the adaptation.

The research presented here proposes a different view of levels of adaptivity, which refers to the process itself and not to the level of automation that adapts to the user. In this case, in the non-adaptive condition the users performs all tasks according to their preferences, while in the fully adaptive condition, the system performs the tasks for the users according to their requirements or preferences. This research attempts to implement this view on adaptive systems. Another aspect this research deals with relates to the frequency at which the tasks occur. In particular, adaptive systems should be more beneficial to the user when performing frequent and routine tasks. On the other hand, when infrequent tasks arise, the adaptive system will most likely cease to provide benefits, and it may even become a burden on the user. Previous research has raised the value of task frequency in the context of adaptable systems [3] and of routine vs. failure modes in the context of automation [6].

2 Research Contribution

To date no clear guidelines exist for dealing with the conditions in which AUIs may be most beneficial, and only few studies have examined the subject empirically. This research will delineate the level of adaptivity appropriate for different users, tasks and situations when using AUIs. Additionally, the research will examine more closely the added value of AUIs according to different task frequencies, and see whether intermediate levels of adaptivity may provide a partial solution. The research will generate a model consisting of the factors influencing the user's interaction with AUIs, specifying the situations and the level of adaptivity in which adaptation is most suitable. The AUI will be examined in the context of in-vehicle systems and therefore may also provide designers of such systems with guiding principles for designing more usable systems.

3 Planned Research Description

This research will generate a model by conducting a series of experiments that will examine the influence of different variables such as task type (i.e., routine vs. infrequent tasks), user characteristics (i.e., age, experience with automated systems) and situational factors (i.e., conditions in which the tasks are performed) on the interaction with an adaptive system. The experiments will simulate a driving task while using an adaptive in-vehicle system. For this purpose, a driving simulator was developed and integrated with a simulation of a telematic system. Each experiment will examine the influence of different variables on objective performance measures and subjective evaluations, using four levels of adaptivity. A first experiment was already conducted and examined the influence of using four levels of adaptivity when performing routine and uncommon tasks. The following example will demonstrate the levels of adaptivity. In one of the routine tasks, the participants received text messages they had to respond to by sending back the message: "I'm driving". In the manual condition the participants respond by typing their response manually, using a virtual keyboard. In the User Selection (US) condition the system presents the participants with a number of optional responses they usually type and the participants select their preferred response. In the User Approval (UA) condition, the system presents the participants with the response they use most frequently and the participants send that response. In the highly adaptive condition, the system automatically sends the participants' usual response. In the uncommon tasks the participants were not able to respond as usual and therefore were required to respond manually. The results showed that intermediate levels of adaptivity (US and UA) provided similar benefits as a highly adaptive system when frequent tasks needed to be performed. When infrequent tasks were performed, the performance decrements with the intermediate levels of adaptivity were clearly smaller than with the high level of adaptivity. Future experiments will examine additional variables, such as the frequency ratio of task occurrences, the difficulty level of the tasks, and the age of the user.

References

1. Allen, J. F.: Mixed Initiative Interaction. In Hearst, M. A.: Mixed-Initiative Interaction. Trends and Controversies, September/October (1999)
2. Amant, R. St., Cohen, P.R.: Interaction with a Mixed-Initiative System for Exploratory Data Analysis. Knowledge-based systems, Vol. 10(5) (1999)
3. Bunt, A., Conati, C., McGrenere, J.: What Role Can Adaptive Support Play in an Adaptable System? IUI 04, January (2004) 13-16
4. Dieterich, H., Malinowski, U., Kuhme, T., Schneider-Hufschmidt, M.: State of the Art in Adaptive User Interfaces. In Schneider-Hufschmidt, M., Kuhme, T., Malinowski, U. (eds.) Adaptive User Interfaces Principles and Practice. Elsevier Science Publishers B.V. (1993) 13 – 48
5. Horvitz, E.: Principle of Mixed-Initiative User Interfaces. Proc ACM SIGCHI Conf. Human Factors in Computing Systems. ACM Press (1999), 159-166
6. Kaber, D.B., Omal, E., Endsley, M.R.: Level of Automation Effects on Telerobot Performance and Human Operator Situation Awareness and Subjective Workload. In Scerbo, M.W., Mouloua, M. (eds.): Automation Technology and Human Performance: Current Research and Trends. Mahwah, N.J. Lawrence Erlbaum (1999)
7. Kobsa, A., Koeneman, J., Wolfgang, P.: Personalized Hypermedia Presentation Techniques for Improving Online Customer Relationships. The knowledge engineering review, Cambridge University Press, Vol. 6:2, (2001) 111-155
8. Oppermann, R.: Adaptively Supported Adaptability. International Journal of Human-Computer Studies, Vol. 40 (1994) 455-472
9. Stephanidis, C., Karagiannidis, C., Koumpis, A.: Decision making in intelligent user interfaces. Proceedings of ACM IUI 97 (1997) 195 - 202

Agent-Based Ubiquitous User Modeling

Andreas Lorenz

Fraunhofer Institute for Applied Information Technology Schloss Birlinghoven,
53754 Sankt Augustin, Germany
Andreas.Lorenz@fit.fraunhofer.de

Abstract. The main objective of the thesis is to define and implement a framework for agent-based distributed user-modeling. This paper introduces the approach for applying agent technology and illustrates the research issues in distributing the knowledge about the user among active entities, and distributed user-model acquisition and application methods.

1 Problem Description

In the vision of ubiquitous computing the technology becomes invisible to the user and will be embedded in the objects of our daily life. The user will be surrounded with capabilities for gaining information everywhere with many different information devices, which have direct contact to each other for offering common services. For future application development in ubiquitous computing, we expect centralized design-approaches to be confronted with uncountable clients on heterogeneous devices with different properties, such as personal or wearable devices of the users, embedded technology in displays or printers, and everyday-objects like keys or coffee-machines. Beside the complexity of techniques to fulfill the basic requirements of adaptive systems [1], passing all data from clients to servers for analyzing and centralized decision finding will put both the networks and servers out of business.

To give access to a centralized *User Modeling Service*, the user model exchange language *UserML* [2] supports the communication between different user adaptive systems, which base their decisions on the state of the same central user model. It enables small devices even with limited memory and computing power to have access to both a meaningful and consistent user model. Like for central *User-Model Servers* [3] as application-external knowledge-bases, we think this will not be applicable mainly for two reasons: First, devices of mobile users will not have permanent access to a specific server but will continually connect to neighboring devices in an ad-hoc manner; and second, to make a local decision the system will not need all-embracing knowledge about the user collected from every other component. In our vision, each local component might detect a section of the global state, but the network of components must piece together these partial states for *distributed representation of knowledge about the user*. To become true, this vision requires several pre-conditions to be fulfilled:

L. Ardissono, P. Brna, and A. Mitrovic (Eds.): UM 2005, LNAI 3538, pp. 512–514, 2005.

1. The network of distributed components needs to be self-adapting, especially regarding available communication partners and technology.
2. The information needs to migrate between different hosts and platforms without being central-controlled.
3. The communication infrastructure and technical details need to be hidden from the user modeling components, and their developers.
4. Typical non-functional requirements for building distributed applications, like scalability, openness, heterogeneity, fault-tolerance, and resource sharing.

2 Proposed Solution: Agent-Based Distributed User Modeling

To be able to fulfill the requirements of ubiquitous computing, we propose to have a network of small active entities on the client side, building ad-hoc networks and deliver requested information on demand. On each level of the system-design, we therefore propose to have *distributed active entities receiving data from and delivering information to other entities.* For *distributed user modeling* approaches this implies that monolithic user modeling is replaced by distributed user model fragments [4]. As active entities, software-agents have their own thread of control making them appear like "active objects with initiative" [5] localizing not only code and state but their invocation as well. In other words, when and how an agent acts is determined by the agent [6]. In *agent-based user modeling* approaches (such as the I-Help system [7]), the internal knowledge-base of *personal agents* usually are or refer to a user model to represent the user or user characteristics.

To ensure encapsulated inter-package communication inside and broadcasting to a specific category, we based on our previous work [8, 9] to categorize the agents virtually in four categories of *sensoring, modeling, controlling* and *actuating agents*, although system developers are able to integrate their own packages For each category, networks of highly specialized software-agents process small tasks like delivering one information snippet or deciding to display data on a particular device. Each category is distributed over different devices, e.g. among others the light sensor of a PDA, the infrared sensor of an automatic door and the GPS-sensor of the car are part of the sensor-package regardless to their physical location and environment. In turn, each device potentially hosts agents of several categories, e.g. one and the same PDA independently hosts controlling agents for content-selection and actuators for video-streaming or adjustment of the display-brightness as well.

The basic underlying cooperation-approach between the agents is *cooperation by information-exchange.* For knowledge-exchange and command-delivery, the agents share local message-boards on their hosting devices managed by specific information-brokering agents: For local agents, the broker provides access to a message-board whereas the information flow between devices is based on message-sending between the brokers. By creating unique interfaces for all local components, the brokers release a potentially high number of local agents from discovering and accessing the communication-infrastructure in the current environment.

For the agent-specification we decided to model all agents in a *state-based* manner, except the controlling-agents. Incoming messages trigger transitions in state-based agent-modeling, which sufficiently describes the agent's behavior and allows reacting both to their environment and to messages received from neighboring components. Since state-based agent-modeling is not useful for knowledge-based agents, a rule-based approach based on the common "IF condition THEN action" metaphor for controlling agents will be more appropriate to determine their behavior. In this approach, incoming messages trigger the interpretation of the rule's conditions and fire all rules with fulfilled pre-conditions.

3   Current State of Work and Future Work Plan

Currently, our main objective is to provide a well-defined conceptual basis, in particular specifying the architecture and agents, communication and information-exchange, and cooperation-techniques and conflict-management [10], e.g. if many agents are potentially able to process the same information or agents receive ambiguous answers to a request. The realization phase has already been launched starting with and the specified communication-protocols for check-in/check-out, subscribe-inform and question-reply mechanisms. In the next steps, we will finish the work on the specification, continue to implement the framework and focus on the implementation of the specified agents.

References

1. Brusilovsky, P.: Methods and techniques of adaptive hypermedia. UMUAI 6(2-3):87-129 (1996)
2. Heckmann, D., Krüger, A.: A User Modelling Markup Language (UserML) for Ubiquitous Computing. In: Brusilowsky, P., Corbett, A., de Rosis, F., (eds.): 9th international conference on user modeling. Springer (2003) 403–407
3. Fink, J., Kobsa, A.: A review and analysis of commercial user modeling servers for personalization on the world wide web. UMUAI 10(2-3):209–249 (2000)
4. Vassileva, J.: Distributed User Modelling for Universal Information Access. In: Stephanidis, C. (ed.): Universal Access in HCI, Lawrence Erlbaum:, N.J. (2001) 122-126.
5. Odell, J.: Objects and agents compared. Journal of Object Technology 1(1):41–53 (2002)
6. Jennings, N.R., Wooldridge, M.J.: Agent Technology. Springer (1998)
7. Vassileva J., McCalla G., Greer J.: Multi-Agent Multi-User Modeling, UMUAI 13(1):1-31 (2003)
8. Zimmermann, A., Lorenz, A., Specht, M.: User modeling in adaptive audio-augmented museum environments. In: Brusilowsky, P., Corbett, A., de Rosis, F., (eds.): 9th international conference on user modeling. Springer (2003) 403–407
9. Lorenz, A.:Towards a new role of agent technology in user modelling. Workshop on Adaptivity and User Modeling in Interactive Systems (2003)
10. Tessier, C., Chaudron, L., Müller, H.-J.: Conflicting Agents: Conflict management in multi-agent systems. Kluwer Academic Publishers (2000)

Using Qualitative Modelling Approach to Model Motivational Characteristics of Learners

Jutima Methaneethorn[1]

The SCRE Centre, University of Glasgow, Glasgow, UK, G3 6NH
jutima@scre.ac.uk

Abstract. Recent research points to the notion that motivation is a crucial factor when creating Intelligent Learning Environments (ILEs). Yet the research in motivation in tutoring systems has not fully considered relationships between features of ILEs and components of learners' motivational structure. This paper proposes to use a qualitative modelling approach to model motivational characteristics of learners while interacting with an ILE within the context of educational game and narrative.

1 Introduction

Learners' motivation is now regarded as a crucial aspect in developing an intelligent learning environment. The work by del Soldato & du Boulay [1] was foundational in that it dealt with motivational aspects of Intelligent Tutoring Systems (ITSs), in particular by including a motivational module which can perform motivational state modelling and motivational planning. de Vicente & Pain [2] also dealt explicitly with motivation in ITSs. They detailed an interesting approach to the detection of motivation and the outcome of their study was a set of 85 inferred motivational rules. However, the above research has not focused on how an ILE impacts on the learner's motivation.

In section 2, we present the aim of our research. Next, we describe a qualitative modelling approach to modelling the motivation of learners. We then end with our future steps and the setting of the work with an educational game.

2 Modelling the Motivational Characteristics for an ILE

Since there are no explicit models of how learners are motivated while using an ILE this initiates the aim of our research: to create a predictive model of motivation for an ILE in a particular context. We believe that such a model will be potentially of great benefit when creating tutoring systems that take into account the motivational aspects of the learners.

---

[1] The author is under the supervision of Prof. Paul Brna. Many thanks to him for his advice.

L. Ardissono, P. Brna, and A. Mitrovic (Eds.): UM 2005, LNAI 3538, pp. 515–517, 2005.

Given that the motivational structure of any intelligent instruction is likely to change from context to context, it is necessary to select one context - preferably one which strongly features the factors in which we are interested. Thus, we choose to narrow down our attention to a narrative-based educational game since the association between motivation, game and narrative seems to be strong [3-4]. Hence, our main research questions are: given a specific context for an ILE, can we determine a motivational structure for learners during their interaction? Can we make progress in determining the way this might change during the interaction?

We chose to investigate the relationship between the ILE features (the basic elements that make up an ILE), and a learner's motivational characteristics (motivational variables of the learners which can be placed into two categories: trait (permanent characteristics) and state (transient characteristics) (adopted from de Vicente & Pain's motivation model [2])) because we believe that there is a strong relationship between them.

3 Qualitative Modelling and Motivation

The motivation for applying the qualitative modelling approach to our research stem from our view of motivation as a dynamic and complex system which is difficult to inspect. The qualitative approach can be used to deal with such a system [5]. From the literature, one technique used for modelling learner's affective states is based on Bayesian approach; for example, Conati & Zhou [6] use Dynamic Decision Networks (DDN) to model emotional states of the user during interactions with a computer-based educational game, aiming to help students learn number factorization. We consider that using the Bayesian approach can produce a numerical probabilistic model but it cannot easily provide information about the dynamics of the learners' motivation. Thus we are interested in giving a cognitive account of what is going on when learners are motivated, so we can seek to manipulate that in a sound ethical and pedagogical manner. From our point of view, there are methodological advantages in developing an explicit qualitative model before a quantitative one.

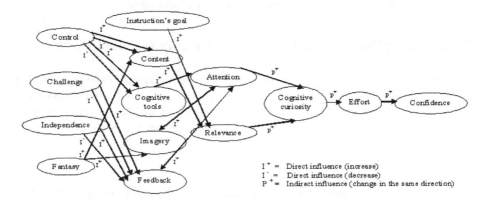

Fig. 1. Causal model showing the relationship between learner's motivation and ILE features

When creating a qualitative model, some main characteristics are needed to be identified such as the model structure, the behaviour, etc [7]. A major focus of our research is a causal model of which the current version is shown in Figure 1.

4 The Future Steps

The research presented in this paper is ongoing, with future work including not only the development of the prototype, but also validation for the plausibility of the model.

We are applying this model with the particular type of game, role-playing games (RPG) which are computer games in which the human players assume the characteristics of some person or creature type. The domain knowledge that we are working on is the concept of Entity Relationship Modelling (ERM). A story line for our prototype is already created. Currently, we are looking for the engine which can be used with the model to predict the learners' motivation.

As part of the model validation, we plan to deploy our system with a group of students to estimate values of their motivation. The methodology used for capturing these values must take into account the problems of interrupting participants while they are working with the system as this might make it difficult to keep on track with what they are doing. Hence, we need to specify points at which we can easily interrupt the processes and use questions about the variables of interest to get some data for verifying our model in terms of the total model and the separate components.

References

1. del Soldato, T., du Boulay, B.: Implementation of Motivational Tactics in Tutoring Systems. International Journal of Artificial Intelligence in Education. 6 (1995) 337-378.
2. de Vicente, A., Pain, H.: Informing the Detection of the Students' Motivational State: An Empirical Study. In: Cerri, S.A., Gouarderes, G., Paraguacu, F. (eds.). Lecture Notes in Computer Science, Vol. 2363. Springer-Verlag, Berlin Heidelberg (2002) 933-943.
3. Malone, T.W., Lepper, M.R.: Making Learning Fun: A Taxonomy of Iintrinsic Motivations for Learning. In: Farr, M.J., (ed.). Cognitive and Affective Process Analyses. Hillsdale New Jersey (1987) 223-253.
4. Luckin, R., Plowman, L., Laurillard, D., Stratfold, M.,Taylor, J., Corben, S.: Narrative Evolution: Learning from Students' Talk about Species Variation. International Journal of Artificial Intelligence in Education. 12 (2001) 100-123.
5. Brown, J.S., de Kleer, J.: A Framework for a Qualitative Physics. In Proceedings of the Sixth Annual Conference of the Cognitive Science Society. Laurence Erlbaum Associates (1984) 11-18.
6. Conati, C., Zhou, X.: Modeling Students' Emotions from Cognitive Appraisal in Educational Games. In: Cerri, S.A., Gouarderes, G., Paraguacu, F. (eds.). Lecture Notes in Computer Science, Vol. 2363. Springer-Verlag, Berlin Heidelberg (2002) 944-954.
7. Bredeweg, B., Winkels, R.: Qualitative Models in Interactive Learning Environments: An Introduction. Interactive Learning Environments. 5(1-2) (1998) 1-18.

Improving Explicit Profile Acquisition by Means of Adaptive Natural Language Dialog

Rosmary Stegmann

Technische Universität München, Insitut für Informatik, Boltzmannstr. 3,
85748 Garching b. München, Germany
stegmann@in.tum.de

Abstract. As opposed to implicit user profiling, there are only few explicit approaches, which furthermore suffer from problems that prevent them from being truly viable in practice. In this paper we present an approach to explicit user profiling by means of an adaptive natural language dialog. The dialog adapts to interests the user has mentioned and captures new, not predefined user information, which is stored in a semantically structured explicit user profile.

1 The Problem

User profile acquisition is typically divided into implicit and explicit methods. A lot of research has been done on implicit profiling methods, such as observing the user's behavior and transactions. Implicit profiles often lack of accuracy and reliability, however, and in general cannot be made transparent to the user for corrections.

Comparably fewer approaches exist for explicit user profiling, where users enter information directly into the system, e.g. by filling in questionnaires or rating products. Although these methods in general lead to more reliable profiles, the problem is that users can become overstrained by filling in large forms or rating hundreds of items.

Alternative explicit profiling methods are needed. This view is supported by many authors, who emphasize the need for structured user data that spans various topics (e.g. lifestyle, interests, taste) and that can be shared by different applications [1]. New explicit profiling approaches should also not overstrain the user, but still create adequate and personalized profiles, which can be seen and modified by the user.

2 Aim of the Thesis and Main Contributions

The PhD thesis described in this paper suggests a new method for explicit profile acquisition, which can also be combined with implicit methods. We have developed an approach which flexibly captures the nature of an individual more adequately than standardized questionnaires or profiles with a static structure. We do not only collect individual information about a user, but also assign him to a group of similar users. The profiling approach can be used by various systems offering personalization ser-

L. Ardissono, P. Brna, and A. Mitrovic (Eds.): UM 2005, LNAI 3538, pp. 518–520, 2005.
© Springer-Verlag Berlin Heidelberg 2005

vices (e.g. recommender systems). Our dialog can terminate after a few adaptively selected questions, whereas a questionnaire is mostly evaluated *after* the completion. So, the effort to fill in a questionnaire is at least equal to or higher as the dialog effort. Two aspects might furthermore help to increase acceptance, trust, and cooperation of the user. First, the information is presented to him in a structured and modifiable way. Secondly, many customers (especially inexperienced ones) perceive natural language dialog as more user-friendly than questionnaires or command-driven interaction.

3 Adaptive Natural Language Dialog for Acquiring User Interests

Our approach is to acquire explicit profile information by means of an adaptive natural language dialog. We focus on *personal interests*, which are a subset of user information and have a rich semantic structure that can be refined step by step during the dialog. Interests are entered by the user as short phrases such as "spannende Bücher lesen (reading exciting books)". These may, for example, contain an object of interest ("books"), an activity related to it ("reading"), and may be enriched with additional information, such as an object property ("exciting"), frequency, location, rating, etc.

These interests are acquired during an adaptive dialog, in which the system reacts to what the user has mentioned and asks refining questions about it. The dialog is controlled by using a sociological group model. Each user group in this model has attributes, which describe the interests of their members and which are compared with the profile of a new user. Most important, however, is not to assign the user to a group, but to collect as many individual data about him as possible. The user input is analyzed linguistically to extract attribute values, which characterize an interest, such as objects, activities, ratings, etc. A statistical hypothesis is made about the best matching group(s) at the current state of the dialog. Next, a refining question is selected to extend the information already known about the user. For this purpose, the system uses a set of question frames, which contain variables. If certain conditions are met by the user input and by the matching group, a special question frame is selected and its variables are instantiated on the basis of user input and group attributes.

If the user likes "reading", for example, and one group is characterized by an interest in reading novels, whereas another group prefers reading newspapers, the dialog will ask a refining question with respect to the favorite items or objects the user prefers to read (e.g. "What do you read?"). So the dialog is conducted adaptively to what the user has mentioned (activity "reading") but also according to the group attributes.

As soon as the user can be assigned to one group clearly, the dialog terminates. We have integrated two configurable thresholds which override this default strategy. They are used to restrict or extend the dialog duration according to the needs of different applications. For details on the dialog concept see [4].

A related approach is LifestyleFinder [3], which also assigns users to groups by asking questions, but with two differences: After having identified a matching group, LifestyleFinder merely assigns the group profile to the user, whereas we store individual information. Secondly, LifestyleFinder only offers a small predefined set of answers, from which the user can select, whereas we allow free-text answers.

Our system constructs an individual user profile according to a profile model, which defines valid data structures. For the construction we use the semantic-lexical ontology GermaNet, a natural language processing resource for German [2]. Each profile we create is a subgraph of GermaNet enriched with complex, individual interest nodes.

A profile is constructed and updated by first analyzing a user interest linguistically. From the extracted attribute-value pairs (object, activity, property, etc.) a complex interest node is built. Attribute values of this node are searched in GermaNet according to a specific algorithm. If one can be found, the user interest is inserted, together with its GermaNet path, into the profile graph. If none can be found, further information about this interest can be acquired during the dialog. A crucial aspect is that GermaNet helps us to insert new, not predefined information dynamically during the dialog. The profile construction and linguistic analysis of user answers is described in detail in [5].

4   State of Implementation and Future Work

At the moment we are realizing a prototype implementation in Java. Until now we have implemented the profile construction by means of GermaNet and the linguistic analysis of the user input. The user profiles are represented in XML. Next, we will combine these components into an integrated system. We will also refine and implement the dialog strategy. Finally, we plan to evaluate the system in a Wizard-of-Oz experiment with test users, where the generation of final natural language questions is accomplished by a human assistant according to a defined algorithm. The quality of the created profiles will be evaluated by means of a set of criteria yet to be defined.

References

1. Ghani, R., Fano, A.: Building Recommender Systems using a Knowledge Base of Product Semantics. In: Workshop on Recommendation and Personalization in ECommerce at the 2nd Int. Conf. on Adaptive Hypermedia and Adaptive Web-based Systems. Malaga (2002)
2. Hamp, B., Feldweg, H.: GermaNet - A Lexical-Semantic Net for German. In: Proceedings of the ACL Workshop Automatic Information Extraction and Building of Lexical Semantic Resources for NLP Applications. Madrid (1997)
3. Krulwich, B.: Lifestyle Finder – Intelligent User Profiling Using Large-Scale Demographic Data. AI Magazine (1997), 18(2), 37 – 45
4. Stegmann, R., Koch, M., Wörndl, W.: Acquisition of Customer Profiles by Means of Adaptive Text-Based Natural Language Dialog. In: Proc. of the Ann. Workshop of the SIG Adaptivity and User Modeling in Interactive Systems of the GI (ABIS04). Berlin (2004)
5. Stegmann R., Wörndl W.: Using GermaNet to Generate Individual Customer Profiles. In: Proc. of the Workshop Anwendungen des GermaNet II at GLDV 2005. Bonn (2005)

Modelling User Ability in Computer Games

David Storey

School of Information Technology, University of Sydney
dstorey@it.usyd.edu.au

Abstract. User Modelling in computer games is an area that holds much research potential which can lead to practical benefits for computer game players. Our research is looking into the problem of concretely defining what makes a player 'good' at both games in general, specific game genres and individual games. We shall then devise a way of measuring ability to produce numerical rankings. These rankings, after being put through comprehensive evaluation by players, have many potential uses including more in-depth comparison methods, opponent matching and coaching applications.

1 Modelling the Player

1.1 What to Look at?

The first issue to tackle is to determine what we should be trying to measure. The factors we will be examining are those that relate to the players personal ability such as their reflexes. An entire industry has arisen that pits top-ranked players against each other. Of those the World Cyber Games Championship [1] and the Cyberathlete Professional Gamers League [2] hold tournaments that bring the best of the world together to compete.

However although there is much discussion between players about why the champions of these tournaments win, their training routines and how hand-eye coordination, reflexes, short and long term strategies, opponent anticipation/prediction and adaptability influence their chances of victory nobody has sat down and detailed what effect each of these has or how they are influenced by practice.

Thus our first goal is to crystallise the vast amount of rumour and theory out there into a strong set of criteria that defines a player's performance. Whilst it would be nice if these criteria covered gaming in general we will initially be looking at the First Person Shooter genre.

1.2 How to Measure Ability?

This is the second issue we will tackle. Once we have identified what to look for and created a list of criteria and the theory behind them the problem is then how do we turn information available from the game into numeric ranks?

L. Ardissono, P. Brna, and A. Mitrovic (Eds.): UM 2005, LNAI 3538, pp. 521–523, 2005.

The information available from any specific game varies, many reveal nothing at all however some do provide modification packages that allow people with some programming experience to hook into and extract data from the game. We have used such a modification package to generate a series of events which we believe are important such as player movement, weapons fire and damage being applied.

Now that we have these events they still need to be processed with some sort of algorithm in order to generate our rank. The algorithms must take into account both major and minor influences for the different criteria so that they can differentiate between players of similar skill levels.

1.3 Evaluating the Ranks Generated

Generating ranks using some algorithm is a good start however they need to be put through comprehensive evaluations by players of all skill levels to ensure that the numbers generated do in fact accurately reflect the player's ability.

To do this we will carry out several test sessions and have the players comment on the theory behind the ranks and how they feel the ranks they were given match their ability. We will also players to comment on each others ranks as often an individual will be a little biased when evaluating their own ranks as opposed to evaluating somebody else.

From these sessions' improvements to the supporting theory, tweaks to our algorithms and refinement of which minor factors we include will be made. The test sessions will also provide feedback on other issues such as the interface used to present the data, ease and understanding of what went into generating their ranks and how responsive the system is.

2 Preliminary Work – Quake 3

We have already made some progress with our research using the First Person Shooter Quake 3 developed by ID Software [3] and released in 1998. In short Quake 3 puts the player up against one or more opponents within set combat arenas. The players shoot each other in an effort to kill their opponents without being killed themselves and have at their disposal several weapons with which to do this. A round of battle ends when one person has reached a specific number of kills (called 'frags' in the game) or when a time limit is reached.

So far we have used some well known Quake tactics [4] to devise a set of 10 criteria that cover a players motor skills (reflexes), awareness, game knowledge and short term planning ability. Utilising a modification that runs on any Quake 3 server we are able to access what happened in a gaming session in an event-by-event form which can be processed by our analysis application.

This application allows users to see what ranks they are given for the 4 criteria implemented so far and also to examine what supporting events were involved. As yet no testing has been carried out to determine how accurate our algorithms are nor is there any ability to process multiple sessions to view a performance history.

3 Potential Uses

Being able to measure a user's ability at a deeper level then just basic win/loss statistics allows us to improve several services normally used within games. Having these criteria and their ranks allows us to compare people at a deeper level and in a variety of different ways beyond the current win/loss based approaches.

We can also use it to improve match-making services which automatically try and provide opponents of a similar skill level which should make for a more enjoyable game as both sides are evenly matched. Coaching also holds some potential, where the system provides suggestions that can improve a player's performance or which highlights weaknesses both in general and within a specific round. Such a coaching system may also be used in tutorials that teach players how to play the game - explaining game mechanics and time-saving shortcuts as the user learns to play rather then being forced to follow a scripted tutorial or spend time (re)reading the manual.

4 Conclusion

User modelling in games is an area which holds much potential. Our research will look at how to measure a player's ability and turn what happens within a game into a numerical rank. This rank will then be evaluated to ensure the theory and algorithms behind it are accurate and then we can examine the various applications of the research.

Acknowledgements. Many thanks to my supervisors Judy Kay and Irena Koprinska and to my family for their unwavering support.

References

1. World Cyber Games Championship. [cited; Available from: http://www.worldcybergames. com/
2. Cyberathlete Professional League (CPL).[cited; Available from: http://www.thecpl.com/ league/
3. ID Software - Quake 3. 1998 [cited; Available from: http://www.idsoftware.com/games/ quake/quake3-gold/
4. Kan, M. Quake Tactics for Dummies. 2001 [cited; Available from: http://www.kan.org/ michael/Quake/tactics.htm

Constraint-Sensitive Privacy Management for Personalized Web-Based Systems[1]

Yang Wang

Donald Bren School of Information and Computer Sciences,
University of California, Irvine, U.S.A
yangwang@ics.uci.edu

Abstract. This research aims at reconciling web personalization with privacy constraints imposed by legal restrictions and by users' privacy preferences. We propose a software product line architecture approach, where our privacy-enabling user modeling architecture can dynamically select personalization methods that satisfy current privacy constraints to provide personalization services. A feasibility study is being carried out with the support of an existing user modeling server and a software architecture based development environment.

1 Introduction

The benefits of web-based personalization for both online customers and vendors have been challenged and counteracted by privacy concerns [1]. When privacy laws and regulations are in effect, they restrict not only the personal data that can be collected and manipulated by the personalized websites, but also the *methods* [2] that can be used to process the data. For instance, the German Teleservices Data Protection Act [3] that mandates personal data to be erased immediately after each session except for very limited purposes would preclude the employment of certain machine learning methods where the learning takes place over several sessions. On the other hand, though, alternate personalization methods can often provide the same or similar personalization services with possibly fewer privacy impacts but possibly also lesser quality [4]. In our example, a personalized website could use incremental machine learning (that discards all raw data after the end of a session) to provide personalization to web visitors from Germany[2], while it can use possibly better one-time machine learning with the data stored across several sessions to provide personalization to web visitors from the U.S. who are not subject to this constraint.

From a personalization point of view, we ask the research question: how can personalized web-based systems maximize the personalization benefits, while

---

[1] This research has been supported through NSF grant IIS 0308277. I would like to thank Alfred Kobsa, André van der Hoek and Eric Dashofy for their help in preparing this paper.
[2] This is not yet a complete solution though since the German Teleservices Data Protection Act also mandates that profiling requires the use of pseudonymous or the consent of the user.

L. Ardissono, P. Brna, and A. Mitrovic (Eds.): UM 2005, LNAI 3538, pp. 524–526, 2005.

respecting the privacy constraints that are currently applicable (such as privacy laws and regulations, and the user's privacy preferences)? [3]

2 Proposed Approach

Because of the high cost of personalization [5], we suggest to address this issue early in the design of a User Modeling Server (UMS) [6]. We propose a software architecture that can dynamically select methods to provide personalization services. To incarnate this idea, we choose the Software Product Line (SPL) approach from software architecture research. SPLs have been successfully introduced in industrial software development for improving productivity, software quality and time-to-market [7]. Product-line software development exploits commonalities between related products via a shared repository of carefully selected software artifacts, from which a particular product can be generated using built-in variability mechanisms [8]. The idea to treat software as a product line brings a new way of supporting "any-time" software variability (i.e. at design, invocation and run time) [9].

We conceive our UMS as an extensible SPL architecture where each of the different personalization methods is embedded in an individual component and new methods (components) can be easily plugged into the architecture. The software architecture can dynamically filter all components that violate the current privacy constraints and then, optionally, elect one or more of the remaining components to provide the personalization service based on their anticipated quality of service. Thereafter the SPL can instantiate a separate run-time system instance of the remaining or the selected components to serve the current user. In order to prevent the situation that too many run-time system instances degrade the overall performance of the UMS, the system can merge instances that have the same system configurations.

3 Feasibility Study

We are conducting a feasibility study which utilizes an existing LDAP-based UMS [10] and ArchStudio 3.0, a software architecture based development environment. The UMS is expressed in xADL 2.0 [11], the underlying XML-based architectural description language for ArchStudio 3.0 that supports architecture-level configuration management (such as versioning, diff and merge operations). Different personalization methods are treated as variant components guarded by Boolean expressions with privacy constraints in the architecture. If the Boolean expression of a variant component can be fully resolved to be TRUE or FALSE, the component is included or excluded in the architecture, and a new run-time system is instantiated for the current user that is consistent with the currently prevailing privacy constraints. If such a runtime system already exists, the user session will be assigned to this session instead.

We are currently developing a prototype system that we intend to evaluate against privacy laws from several countries and privacy attitudes that were solicited

---

[3] While there is no unanimous measure of personalization benefits, we utilize the anticipated quality of personalization methods being used as a quantitative indicator of these benefits.

from Internet users. This will help us verify whether these privacy constraints can indeed be expressed in our system and whether it is able to cater to the users in the expected manner. It will also give us an indication of the performance and scalability of our approach.

4 Conclusions

Enabling personalized websites to operate in a privacy-aware manner (both with respect to legal and user requirements) will allow users to utilize personalization services with less privacy concern. Our approach allows personalized websites to address the combinatorial complexity of privacy constraints in a systematic and flexible manner, building on state-of-the-art industry practice for managing software variants at runtime. We aim at exploring the feasibility of this approach using an existing user modeling server and empirically established privacy constraints.

References

1. Teltzrow, M. and A. Kobsa, *Impacts of User Privacy Preferences on Personalized Systems: a Comparative Study*, in C.M. Karat et al, ed.: *Designing Personalized User Experiences for eCommerce*, 2004, Dordrecht, Netherlands: Kluwer
2. Kobsa, A., J. Koenemann and W. Pohl, *Personalized Hypermedia Presentation Techniques for Improving Online Customer Relationships*. The Knowledge Engineering Review, 2001. **16**(2): p. 111-155
3. DE-TS, *German Teleservices Data Protection Act*. 1997.
4. Kobsa, A. *A Component Architecture for Dynamically Managing Privacy in Personalized Web-based Systems*. in R. Dingledine, ed.: *Privacy Enhancing Technologies: Third Intern'l Workshop*. 2003. Dresden, Germany: Springer. 177-188
5. Jupiter, *Beyond the Personalization Myth*. 2003. http://www.jupiterresearch.com/bin/item.pl/research:vision/79/id=94553,keywords1=personalization/
6. Kobsa, A., *Generic User Modeling Systems*. User Modeling and User-Adapted Interaction, 2001. **11**(1-2): p. 49-63.
7. Bosch, J., *Design and Use of Software Architectures: Adopting and Evolving a Product-Line Approach*. 2000, New York: Addison-Wesley
8. Paul Clements, Linda M. Northrop, *Software Product Lines: Practices and Patterns*. 2002, New York, New York: Addison-Wesley
9. Hoek, A.v.d., *Design-Time Product Line Architectures for Any-Time Variability*. Science of Computer Programming, **53**(30): p. 285-304
10. Fink, J., *User Modeling Servers: Requirements, Design, and Evaluation*. 2004, IOS Press, Netherlands (Infix)
11. Dashofy, E. M., A. van der Hoek, and R. N. Taylor. *A Highly-Extensible, XML-Based Architecture Description Language*. In *Proceedings of the Working IEEE/IFIP Conf. on Software Architecture*. 2001. Amsterdam, Netherlands.103-112

Modularized User Modeling in Conversational Recommender Systems

Pontus Wärnestål

Department of Computer Science, Linköping University, Sweden
ponjo@ida.liu.se

1 Introduction

My research interest lies in investigating user-adaptive interaction in a conversational setting for recommender systems, with particular focus on *modularized* user model components and the use of a *dialogue partner* (DP) in such systems.

Research on recommender systems have focused mostly on the back-end algorithms they employ, whereas front-end interaction issues have not been as thoroughly studied [2], and most recommender systems rely on the graphical point-and-click metaphor. The area of conversational recommender systems explores another interaction metaphor; that of natural language (NL) interaction in a dialogue (e.g. with spoken interaction [8, 5]). Other recommender system approaches acknowledge the benefits of NL and/or dialogue-based interaction in their systems, but employ graphical user interfaces since their primary focus lies elsewhere (e.g. [1, 6]). Underlying motivations for the conversational approach are that the initializing and updating of the user preference model can be carried out efficiently and enjoyably using natural language, that an on-going dialogue supports evolving user queries and continuous updating of user preference data, and that NL facilitates rich feedback in a way that is natural to end-users.

A related metaphor—however often lacking proper conversational interaction— is the *virtual assistant* approach, which takes the form of an animated character (e.g. the Microsoft Office assistant, and the SitePal guides) that provides help with a software application or web site. Such virtual partners display a number of different interaction strategies and varying adaptive functionality.

User-adaptive functionality based on user models has long been proposed in order to meet individual needs and make interaction more usable and efficient [4]. In order to make full use of and to better understand conversational DP interaction with user-adaptive recommenders, research addressing the following issues seems to be needed: (a) how to design and implement conversational virtual assistants, (b) how to endow such assistants with appropriate NL dialogue capabilities to effectively render them as DPs, and (c) how to adapt DPs to individual users.

2 Research Problems

Implementation details may vary, but essentially a generic NL dialogue system architecture can be described as consisting of the following phases (in order): (a) interpretation, (b) dialogue management, (c) domain reasoning, and (d) generation.

L. Ardissono, P. Brna, and A. Mitrovic (Eds.): UM 2005, LNAI 3538, pp. 527–529, 2005.

Different forms of adaptivity are prominent in these phases. In each phase there is thus a potential for modeling user attributes and/or preferences. For example, individual users have their own way of expressing queries and their vocabulary preferences. This is clearly an adaptive functionality of the interpretation phase, and is facilitated by a personalized lexicon and grammar. Moving to the dialogue management phase, it is considered necessary to include adaptation if the dialogue is to be viewed as cooperative [7]. One important example of adaptation of the dialogue is the DP's strategy and initiative, such as whether the DP should be more pro-active or more reactive. When considering domain reasoning—and connection to the system back-end—there are yet other types of user data that require modeling (e.g. item ratings for collaborative filtering systems, or user needs and interests for knowledge-based recommender engines, etc.). Finally, Zukerman and Litman [10] conclude that user models are required in order to enable systems to generate appropriate and relevant responses in dialogue systems. The generation phase is concerned with generating responses that fit a specific user (e.g. content planning, surface generation, and modality considerations and feedback).

User-adaptive system performance depends on how the user model is (1) initialized, (2) updated, and (3) put to use in order to achieve adaptive functionality. These three aspects need to be addressed for each phase's user model. The aspects and phases define a two-dimensional problem space of modularized user modeling components that frames this research.

My work is aimed at investigating what kind of modeling is carried out at the different points of this problem space; and finding out how different phenomena and problems are handled in each phase. Contributions for developers include a theoretical framework and corresponding tool linking what needs to be modeled, and how, with the desired adaptive functionality of the system.

3   Previous and Current Work

So far, I have developed a conversational movie recommender system [5], which implements an empirically based recommendation dialogue strategy described in [9]. The system supports initialization and continuous updating of a user's movie preferences, and gives personalized recommendations and explanations through NL dialogue. In terms of the architecture outlined above this work thus focuses on the domain reasoning phase, and forms the base on which I will continue to develop and investigate user modeling for the remaining phases.

Using an existing phase-based dialogue system architecture [3], I have started to work on a user modeling component framework that functions as pluggable modularized intercepting filters for each of the standard dialogue system phases as outlined above. The filters are configurable and will contain formalisms and mechanisms for initializing, updating, and putting the different models to use.

4   Contributions

Concrete contributions of this work will include:

- a theory for explaining and designing DP recommender systems with modularized and transparent adaptivity according to the problem space described in section 2,
- a tool that implements the theory, and that provides developers with configurable and transparent user modeling components that generate desired adaptive functionality for their end-users, and
- an application built with the tool for end-user evaluation of the approach.

Acknowledgments. This work is supervised by Arne Jönsson and Lars Degerstedt, and supported by GSLT (Sweden) and Santa Anna IT Research.

References

1. Robin D. Burke, Kristian J. Hammond, and Benjamin C. Young. The FindMe Approach to Assisted Browsing. *IEEE Expert*, 12(4):32–40, 1997.
2. Giuseppe Carenini, Jocelyn Smith, and David Poole. Towards more conversational and collaborative recommender systems. In *Proceedings of the International Conference of Intelligent User Interfaces*, pages 12–18, Miami, Florida, USA, 2003.
3. Lars Degerstedt and Pontus Johansson. Evolutionary Development of Phase-Based Dialogue Systems. In *Proceedings of the 8th Scandinavian Conference on Artificial Intelligence*, pages 59–67, Bergen, Norway, 2003.
4. Gerhard Fischer. User modeling in human-computer interaction. *User Modeling and User-Adapted Interaction*, 11:65–86, 2001.
5. Pontus Johansson. Design and development of recommender dialogue systems. Licentiate Thesis 1079, Linköping Studies in Science and Technology, Linköping University, April 2004.
6. Lorraine McGinty and Barry Smyth. Deep dialogue vs casual conversation in recommender systems. In F. Ricci and B Smyth, editors, *Personalization in eCommerce at the Second International Conference on Adaptive Hypermedia and Web-Based Systems (AH-02)*, pages 80–89, Malaga, Spain, 2002.
7. Katarina Morik. Discourse models, dialog memories, and user models. *Computational Linguistics*, 14:95–97, 1988.
8. Cynthia Thompson, Mehmet Göker, and Pat Langley. A personalized system for conversational recommendations. *Journal of Artificial Intelligence Research*, 21:393–428, 2004.
9. Pontus Wärnestål. Modeling a dialogue strategy for personalized movie recommendations. In *Beyond Personalization'05 Workshop*, pages 77–82, San Diego, CA, USA, January 2005.
10. Ingrid Zukerman and Diane Litman. Natural language processing and user modeling: Synergies and limitations. *User Modeling and User-Adapted Interaction*, 11:129–158, 2001.

Author Index

Lecture Notes in Artificial Intelligence (LNAI)

Vol. 3366: I. Rahwan, P. Moraitis, C. Reed (Eds.), Argumentation in Multi-Agent Systems. XII, 263 pages. 2005.

Vol. 3359: G. Grieser, Y. Tanaka (Eds.), Intuitive Human Interfaces for Organizing and Accessing Intellectual Assets. XIV, 257 pages. 2005.

Vol. 3346: R.H. Bordini, M. Dastani, J. Dix, A.E.F. Seghrouchni (Eds.), Programming Multi-Agent Systems. XIV, 249 pages. 2005.

Vol. 3345: Y. Cai (Ed.), Ambient Intelligence for Scientific Discovery. XII, 311 pages. 2005.

Vol. 3343: C. Freksa, M. Knauff, B. Krieg-Brückner, B. Nebel, T. Barkowsky (Eds.), Spatial Cognition IV. XIII, 519 pages. 2005.

Vol. 3339: G.I. Webb, X. Yu (Eds.), AI 2004: Advances in Artificial Intelligence. XXII, 1272 pages. 2004.

Vol. 3336: D. Karagiannis, U. Reimer (Eds.), Practical Aspects of Knowledge Management. X, 523 pages. 2004.

Vol. 3327: Y. Shi, W. Xu, Z. Chen (Eds.), Data Mining and Knowledge Management. XIII, 263 pages. 2005.

Vol. 3315: C. Lemaître, C.A. Reyes, J.A. González (Eds.), Advances in Artificial Intelligence – IBERAMIA 2004. XX, 987 pages. 2004.

Vol. 3303: J.A. López, E. Benfenati, W. Dubitzky (Eds.), Knowledge Exploration in Life Science Informatics. X, 249 pages. 2004.

Vol. 3301: G. Kern-Isberner, W. Rödder, F. Kulmann (Eds.), Conditionals, Information, and Inference. XII, 219 pages. 2005.

Vol. 3276: D. Nardi, M. Riedmiller, C. Sammut, J. Santos-Victor (Eds.), RoboCup 2004: Robot Soccer World Cup VIII. XVIII, 678 pages. 2005.

Vol. 3275: P. Perner (Ed.), Advances in Data Mining. VIII, 173 pages. 2004.

Vol. 3265: R.E. Frederking, K.B. Taylor (Eds.), Machine Translation: From Real Users to Research. XI, 392 pages. 2004.

Vol. 3264: G. Paliouras, Y. Sakakibara (Eds.), Grammatical Inference: Algorithms and Applications. XI, 291 pages. 2004.

Vol. 3259: J. Dix, J. Leite (Eds.), Computational Logic in Multi-Agent Systems. XII, 251 pages. 2004.

Vol. 3257: E. Motta, N.R. Shadbolt, A. Stutt, N. Gibbins (Eds.), Engineering Knowledge in the Age of the Semantic Web. XVII, 517 pages. 2004.

Vol. 3249: B. Buchberger, J.A. Campbell (Eds.), Artificial Intelligence and Symbolic Computation. X, 285 pages. 2004.

Vol. 3248: K.-Y. Su, J. Tsujii, J.-H. Lee, O.Y. Kwong (Eds.), Natural Language Processing – IJCNLP 2004. XVIII, 817 pages. 2005.

Vol. 3245: E. Suzuki, S. Arikawa (Eds.), Discovery Science. XIV, 430 pages. 2004.

Vol. 3244: S. Ben-David, J. Case, A. Maruoka (Eds.), Algorithmic Learning Theory. XIV, 505 pages. 2004.

Vol. 3238: S. Biundo, T. Frühwirth, G. Palm (Eds.), KI 2004: Advances in Artificial Intelligence. XI, 467 pages. 2004.

Vol. 3230: J.L. Vicedo, P. Martínez-Barco, R. Muñoz, M. Saiz Noeda (Eds.), Advances in Natural Language Processing. XII, 488 pages. 2004.

Vol. 3229: J.J. Alferes, J. Leite (Eds.), Logics in Artificial Intelligence. XIV, 744 pages. 2004.

Vol. 3228: M.G. Hinchey, J.L. Rash, W.F. Truszkowski, C.A. Rouff (Eds.), Formal Approaches to Agent-Based Systems. VIII, 290 pages. 2004.

Vol. 3215: M.G.. Negoita, R.J. Howlett, L.C. Jain (Eds.), Knowledge-Based Intelligent Information and Engineering Systems, Part III. LVII, 906 pages. 2004.

Vol. 3214: M.G.. Negoita, R.J. Howlett, L.C. Jain (Eds.), Knowledge-Based Intelligent Information and Engineering Systems, Part II. LVIII, 1302 pages. 2004.

Vol. 3213: M.G.. Negoita, R.J. Howlett, L.C. Jain (Eds.), Knowledge-Based Intelligent Information and Engineering Systems, Part I. LVIII, 1280 pages. 2004.

Vol. 3209: B. Berendt, A. Hotho, D. Mladenic, M. van Someren, M. Spiliopoulou, G. Stumme (Eds.), Web Mining: From Web to Semantic Web. IX, 201 pages. 2004.

Vol. 3206: P. Sojka, I. Kopecek, K. Pala (Eds.), Text, Speech and Dialogue. XIII, 667 pages. 2004.

Vol. 3202: J.-F. Boulicaut, F. Esposito, F. Giannotti, D. Pedreschi (Eds.), Knowledge Discovery in Databases: PKDD 2004. XIX, 560 pages. 2004.

Vol. 3201: J.-F. Boulicaut, F. Esposito, F. Giannotti, D. Pedreschi (Eds.), Machine Learning: ECML 2004. XVIII, 580 pages. 2004.

Vol. 3194: R. Camacho, R. King, A. Srinivasan (Eds.), Inductive Logic Programming. XI, 361 pages. 2004.

Vol. 3192: C. Bussler, D. Fensel (Eds.), Artificial Intelligence: Methodology, Systems, and Applications. XIII, 522 pages. 2004.

Vol. 3191: M. Klusch, S. Ossowski, V. Kashyap, R. Unland (Eds.), Cooperative Information Agents VIII. XI, 303 pages. 2004.

Vol. 3187: G. Lindemann, J. Denzinger, I.J. Timm, R. Unland (Eds.), Multiagent System Technologies. XIII, 341 pages. 2004.

Vol. 3176: O. Bousquet, U. von Luxburg, G. Rätsch (Eds.), Advanced Lectures on Machine Learning. IX, 241 pages. 2004.

Vol. 3171: A.L.C. Bazzan, S. Labidi (Eds.), Advances in Artificial Intelligence – SBIA 2004. XVII, 548 pages. 2004.

Vol. 3159: U. Visser, Intelligent Information Integration for the Semantic Web. XIV, 150 pages. 2004.

Vol. 3157: C. Zhang, H. W. Guesgen, W.K. Yeap (Eds.), PRICAI 2004: Trends in Artificial Intelligence. XX, 1023 pages. 2004.

Vol. 3155: P. Funk, P.A. González Calero (Eds.), Advances in Case-Based Reasoning. XIII, 822 pages. 2004.

Vol. 3139: F. Iida, R. Pfeifer, L. Steels, Y. Kuniyoshi (Eds.), Embodied Artificial Intelligence. IX, 331 pages. 2004.

Vol. 3131: V. Torra, Y. Narukawa (Eds.), Modeling Decisions for Artificial Intelligence. XI, 327 pages. 2004.

Vol. 3127: K.E. Wolff, H.D. Pfeiffer, H.S. Delugach (Eds.), Conceptual Structures at Work. XI, 403 pages. 2004.

Printed in the United States
By Bookmasters

Printed in the United States
By Bookmasters